THE LYRICS

VOLUME 1

第一卷

Paul McCartney

THE LYRICS

1956 TO THE PRESENT

保罗·麦卡特尼

歌抒人生

A-K

[英] 保罗·麦卡特尼 著

[爱尔兰] 保罗·马尔登 编

杨海崧 译

中信出版集团 | 北京

图书在版编目（CIP）数据

保罗·麦卡特尼：歌抒人生 / (英) 保罗·麦卡特
尼著;(爱尔兰) 保罗·马尔登编;杨海崧译 . -- 北京:
中信出版社 , 2023.9
书名原文：The Lyrics: 1956 to the Present
ISBN 978-7-5217-5637-1

Ⅰ . ①保… Ⅱ . ①保… ②保… ③杨… Ⅲ . ①保罗·
麦卡特尼 – 自传 Ⅳ . ① K825.615.76

中国国家版本馆 CIP 数据核字 (2023) 第 068707 号

保罗·麦卡特尼：歌抒人生

著　　者：[英] 保罗·麦卡特尼
编　　者：[爱尔兰] 保罗·马尔登
译　　者：杨海崧
出版发行：中信出版集团股份有限公司
　　　　　（北京市朝阳区东三环北路 27 号嘉铭中心 邮编 100020 ）
承 印 者：北京利丰雅高长城印刷有限公司

开　　本：889mm×1194mm　1/16　　　印　张：57　　　字　　数：400 千字
版　　次：2023 年 9 月第 1 版　　　　印　　次：2023 年 9 月第 1 次印刷
京权图字：01-2023-2955
书　　号：ISBN 978-7-5217-5637-1
定　　价：498.00 元

献给我的妻子南希，以及我的妈妈玛丽和爸爸吉姆忠实于自己。

——威廉·莎士比亚,《哈姆雷特》,第一幕,第三场

To thine own self be true.

—WILLIAM SHAKESPEARE, *HAMLET*, ACT I, SCENE 3

第一卷
Volume 1

第二卷
Volume 2

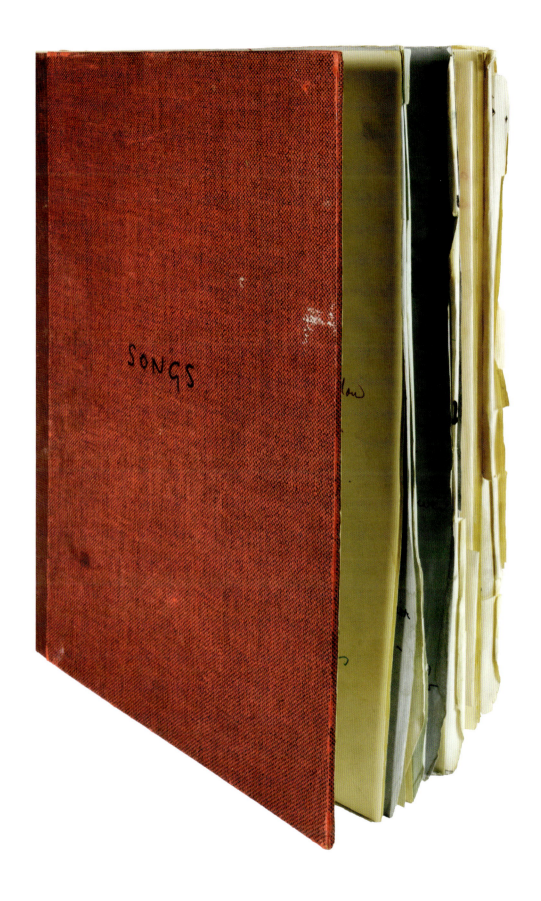

前 言

　　已经数不清有多少次，我被问到写自传的事情，但时机一直不成熟。通常，我都在养家或者巡演，对于需要长期集中注意力的事情，这向来不是理想状态。不过，无论是在家里还是在路上，总有一件事情是我能做的，那就是写新歌。有些人到了一定的年纪，就喜欢凭借日记去回忆过去的日常事情，不过我没有这样的笔记本。我拥有的是我的歌曲——数以百计的歌曲——这些歌曲起到的作用和日记差不多。这些歌贯穿了我的一生，因为当我在利物浦我们家的小房子里得到第一把吉他时，尽管才十四岁，我的本能却是开始写歌。从那以后，我从未停止。

　　学习歌曲写作有一个完整的过程，但对不同的人来说是不一样的。对我来说，第一件事就是模仿别人，比如巴迪·霍利和小理查德，还有猫王[1]（虽然我后来听说，他的歌甚至都不是自己写的），这意味着要记住他们的歌，学习早期摇滚乐的标准曲目。然后，十几岁的时候，我开始尝试自己写歌。我从最简单的想法开始，然后看看会出来什么。

　　这本书里最早写的歌词是《我失去了我的小女孩》（I Lost My Little Girl）。我是在母亲去世后不久写的。她当时只有四十七岁，我十四岁。早在 1956 年，我写这首歌的时候，一个音乐方向出现了：你可以听到下行的和弦序列，而旋律或人声在上升。我已经在玩一些音乐上的小东西了，非常简单的东西，这些东西让我着迷，尽管我不知道它们是什么。令人惊讶的是，约翰·列侬，在他咪咪姑妈的家里，做着类似的事情。所以，当我们第一次走到一起，向对方展示自己的作品时，很快双双意识到，我们都对歌曲

1　巴迪·霍利（Buddy Holly，1936—1959）、小理查德（Little Richard，1932—2020）、猫王（Elvis Presley，1935—1977），均为美国摇滚乐先驱。（本书脚注均为译者注）

创作着迷，并且通过合作，我们可以走得更远。

在我们早期的尝试中，你能看出来我们还是孩子，那时候的我们并未真正有意识地创作歌曲。但是成立披头士后，我们意识到我们突然有了一些热情的观众。所以，一开始我们是为这些观众（主要是心目中的年轻女孩）写歌的。早期的歌曲，像《谢谢你姑娘》（Thank You Girl）、《我对你的》（From Me to You），或者《爱我吧》（Love Me Do）都是针对歌迷的，虽然很多创作都基于我们个人的故事。我们知道这些歌可能成为热门歌曲，并且我们可以一直写这样的歌。但我们渐渐成熟，渐渐意识到可以把歌曲创作带到另一个方向，到达另一个水平，这意味着要为自己写歌。

当然，我们必须在自己感兴趣的歌曲和面向歌迷的歌曲之间保持微妙的平衡。而随着越来越多的尝试，我们也越来越清晰地意识到，我们的创作可以不受任何束缚，这意味着更具创造性的方向。我们可以进入一个超现实主义世界，那里的故事不是完全线性的，那里的歌曲不一定要有意义。我一直是刘易斯·卡罗尔的超级粉丝，在学校时就读过他的书，所以，当我开始越来越喜欢文字游戏时，卡罗尔是一个重要的灵感来源，歌词逐渐演变成一些更出人意料的东西，比如《麦当娜夫人》（Lady Madonna）或《便士巷》（Penny Lane）。尝试渐渐变成了惊人的启示：我们可以充满诗意而不失去与歌迷的联系，或者你甚至可以说，情况恰恰与预期的相反——当我们变得更具实验性，更加倾向于意识流，我们实际上赢得了更多的歌迷。

随着时间的推移，我开始把每首歌看作一片新的拼图。它会照亮我生命中某个时刻里最重要的东西，尽管表面上来看，意义并不总是很明显。歌迷或读者，甚至评论家，那些真心希望更了解我生活的人应该读读我的歌词，这可能比任何一本关于披头士的书都能揭示更多。然而，直到我的妻弟、朋友兼顾问约翰·伊斯曼（John Eastman），以及我的出版商罗伯特·威尔（Robert Weil），最初在 2015 年鼓励我写这本书之时，我仍然觉得，如果不那么草草了事的话，翻阅上百首歌词（有些还是我十几岁时写的）有点太花时间。这是我负担不起的奢侈时间。我总是把所有创造力投入音乐，要说担心，也是创作完成之后，才会担心它内在的意义。但当保罗·马尔登和我开始讨论所有这些歌曲的起源和影响时，我意识到，深入研究这些歌词，可能是一场有意义，并且有启发性的探索。

首先，我知道保罗是一个善于倾听的人。他不是寻找八卦或秘密，希望挖掘我和约翰或洋子之间的一些所谓恩怨的传记作家；他也不是狂热歌迷一般希望把每句话变成某种神圣文本的作家。立即吸引我的是，马尔登是一位诗人。和我一样，他喜欢文字，并能理解文字的诗性——歌词本身如何成为自身的音乐形式，并且在与旋律搭配时变得更加神奇。

我们的谈话进行了五年，有一些在伦敦，不过大多数是在纽约。我每次进城都会想方设法见他。那是一段很长的时间，我们聊得越多，越能意识到我们有很多共同点。我十分认同保罗，不仅因为他是一位诗人，而且因为我们继承了共同的爱尔兰传统，我们的家族在遥远的过去曾有古老的联系，更别提保罗也玩摇滚乐并自己写歌了。

我从没想过我会分析这些歌词，其中许多要回溯到 1960 年代和 1970 年代，许多是我多年来没有想起过的，还有许多是我几十年没有在音乐会上表演过的。但有了保罗作为我的传声筒，这成了一个挑战，一次非常愉快的挑战：重温这些歌曲，并将它们拆解开来，发现我未意识到的规律。

写歌是一种独特的体验，与我知道的任何事情都不同。你必须有恰当的心情，并且从清醒的头脑开始。你必须相信你最初的感觉，因为在一开始，你并不知道自己要去哪里。与保罗的谈话差不多也是这样。每次见面之前，我们唯一知道的是我们要讨论哪些歌曲；其他一切都可以自由支配。不可避免地，沉睡已久的记忆被唤醒，新的意义和形态突然出现。

我能想到的最合适的比喻就是一本一直放在满是灰尘的阁楼上的旧照片簿。有人把它拿下来，突然间，你面对的是一页又一页的回忆。有些老照片看起来很清晰且熟悉，有些则稍显模糊。面对歌词时，我发现，回忆这些歌曲的创作过程是一种挑战：我是如何架构它们的；什么样的事件可能启发了这些歌曲——去看一部电影、和一个我以为是朋友的人吵架，以及我当时的感受。

考虑到记忆的工作方式，年轻时最久远的歌曲往往是最容易记住的。比如说，我可以轻松回想起我二十几岁住在温波尔街时，与简·阿舍[1]的母亲的对话，她是我非常尊敬的一位女士；然而仅仅十年或十五年前的演出记忆却更难找回。但是和保罗谈话的价值在于，一句过去的歌词会引向另一句，直到突然间，不知道从何而来的记忆洪流将我淹没。

写歌就像走进森林。一开始你只看到灌木丛，但随着你深入森林，你开始欣赏你以前可能没有注意到的东西。你开始向两边看，上下看，注意到各种起初并不明显的东西。而一旦你探索了这些东西，就会想走出森林。这是多年来形成的一种模式：一次又一次地走同一条路是一种倾向，那很容易；不过如果你不停地重复自己，最终可能会认识到，你没有取得任何进步。

一个家具制造商，一个真正的工匠，可能会有不同的看法。他满足于一次又一次地制作同一把椅子，但是如果他被迫制作不一样的椅子呢？他必须考虑它们会有什么样的腿，座垫要如何构成，以及它们能承受多少重量。他的家具开始有了某种风格，但是他制作的两把椅子不可能完全一样。我的歌也是这样。

我很多歌曲最初的灵感来自我在利物浦和其他地方认识的人。读者也许会惊讶于我如此频繁地提到父母。当我刚开始这个计划时，吉姆（Jim McCartney）和玛丽·麦卡特尼（Mary McCartney）肯定不是我最先想到的人。但是，开始思考职业生涯每一个阶段所写的歌曲时，我不禁意识到，即使没有主观意识，他们也是我歌曲创作中很多灵感的来源。

我很幸运，因为我在利物浦的直系亲属都是普通的工人阶级。他们不信教，但他

1　简·阿舍（Jane Asher，1946—），英国女演员，保罗·麦卡特尼在 1963 年至 1968 年间的女友。

们是善良的人，潜移默化地向我展示了一种良好的世界观。在学校和教堂里，我们被赋予更为正式的宗教信仰——你可能会说是耶稣的版本，但我自己的善恶观，某种精神，家庭早已赋予我。父母的信仰对我产生了很大影响，所以我在成长过程中自然而然地认为，正确的事情是宽容和善良。家里从来没有人告诉我们，你不应该这样做，你不应该那样做。长大时，我们认为整个世界是以几乎同样的方式运转的，所以当我成熟到能够把自己的想法和感受融入歌曲时，就从这样的精神根基中汲取了灵感。

我妈妈去世时，我才十四岁。因为她去世得很早，你可能会认为她对我的歌曲没有太大的影响。但我越回头想，就越感激她对我成为词曲作者的影响。现在回忆起她时，我意识到今天，9 月 29 日，是她的生日，所以——说到精神——她肯定在这里；那个确保我们好好吃饭，并且把耳朵后面洗干净的母亲，似乎从未离开过。

想起她时，我想起的是她的口音。利物浦地区的各种口音可以有很大的差别，从有点温柔的，到相当强硬和富于侵略性的，但她的口音更轻快。因为她的祖先是爱尔兰人，同时受到爱尔兰和威尔士的影响。就像她的口音一样，她非常温柔，我从来没有听过她叫喊。她从来不需要这么做，我和弟弟迈克（Mike McCartney）始终知道，她想把最好的给孩子们。

尽管妈妈不会演奏乐器，但她很喜欢音乐。我还记得她做饭时在厨房吹口哨。也许是收音机里的东西，也许是她知道的曲子。我当时觉得，"她开心真是太好了。"而这种感觉，我一直带到了今天。

在战后的那些年里，我们会看到她穿着护士服出门和回家。无论在家里还是在外面，她似乎随时准备好投入护理工作。如果我们出了什么事，譬如生病了或是在院子里擦伤，她就在那里，好像随时待命。有时候她会决定给我们灌肠，即使我们是小孩子，这也有点太过分了。但总的来说，她很有爱心，并且说话温和。

我理所当然地觉得，我天生会与女性产生很多共鸣，但有一天，我想明白了自己所谓的"天生"，当时一个女孩拦住我问："你有没有意识到你有多少歌是关于女人的？"我没有真正想过这些，只能回答："是的，嗯，我真的爱女人，并且尊重女人。"但是我开始思考时，发现我对于女性的感觉可能都来自妈妈——事实上，我一直记得她温柔快乐的样子。在最基本的层面上，以无法解释的方式，她体现了你也许在我的歌曲中发现的人性。

我的母亲一直喜欢音乐，而我的父亲确实懂音乐。我想在另一个时代，他也许会成为音乐家，但他在利物浦为一家从美国、埃及、印度、南美洲，乃至全世界进口棉花的公司做推销员。作为一名业余钢琴家，他在一个叫吉姆·麦克爵士乐队（Jim Mac's Jazz Band）的小乐队中演奏。这是 1920 年代，利物浦的摩登时代[1]，所以在乐队里演奏对他那个年纪的年轻人来说一定很刺激。当然，那时还没有我；不过当我还是个孩子时，会听到他在家里弹钢琴。他会坐在钢琴前弹奏老曲子，一般是美国标准曲目，像

1　摩登时代（the Flapper Era）即爵士时代，指一战后至经济大萧条前青年狂欢的文化时期。彼时年轻人决定放弃令人窒息的道德准则，沉溺于更加自我专注、享乐主义的生活方式。"Flapper"一词则指 1920 年代不受传统拘束的时髦女郎，深化了部分年轻人在该年代的自我定位，宣告了女性与传统女性角色的分道扬镳，强调华丽装饰的风格。

保罗·惠特曼[1]和他的管弦乐队创作的《芝加哥》(Chicago),或者《天堂的阶梯》(Stairway to Paradise)。有一首歌对我来说是一种真正的教育,那是一首我仍然可以哼唱的小调,叫作《跌倒》(Stumbling),后来有人告诉我,这是一首1922年的美国狐步舞曲。《跌倒》中的切分音让我着迷。我会躺在地毯上,头枕在手上,听着爸爸演奏。家里的每个人都听着他演奏他最喜欢的乐曲,但对我来说这是一种音乐教育,聆听所有这些节奏、旋律以及和声的样本。

他确保接力棒能传下去。有一天,他把我和弟弟叫到一边,向我们展示和声的含义。"如果你在那里唱那个音符,他在这里唱那个音符,"他指示我们,"两个音符的混合就叫作'和声'。"有时候,当我们在收音机里听到一首歌时,他会说:"你能听到那里低低的噪声吗?"我们会说:"可以。"然后他会回答:"嗯,那是贝斯。"

虽然爸爸的观众通常只有我们四个人,不过每年的新年夜都会有唱歌和聚会。大家庭——我们这个年龄的孩子、大一点的孩子、年轻的父母和年长的父母——会聚到一起,我们会从这几代人那里习得一种非常开放、充满活力的人生观。地毯会被卷起,爸爸会坐在钢琴前;女士们会坐在靠墙的椅子上唱歌,有时会跳舞;而那些总是津津乐道最新笑话的男士,则会站在旁边喝几品脱啤酒。这真是太棒了,我从小就认为每个人都有这样一个充满爱的家庭——可爱的,总是相互支持的。长大后,我震惊地发现,这不是真的:许多人都有灾难性的童年,约翰·列侬就是其中之一。

我们第一次见面时,我并不知道约翰经历了太多的个人悲剧。他的父亲在他三岁时便消失了,很久以后才出现,当时约翰已经出名了,他发现父亲在当地的酒吧洗盘子。约翰不被允许和母亲住在一起,所以家里人把他送到咪咪姑妈和乔治叔叔那里住,他们认为这样对他更好,也许是这样,但谁真的知道呢?约翰童年的大部分时间都与咪咪和乔治住在一起,但是在他大概十四岁时,乔治去世了。我不认识他的叔叔,但我记得几年后约翰对我说:"我觉得我是我父辈的厄运。"我得安抚他并回应说:"不,你父亲离开你,或者乔治叔叔去世了都不是你的错,这与你无关。"我试着用这种方法带给他我从家里得到的那种安慰。

父亲的影响远不止音乐,他为我带来了对文字的热爱,这在我上学时第一次显现。作为一个孩子,很难不注意到他改造文字的方式,或者他有多喜欢玩填字游戏。说些傻话是非常利物浦的,但他更进一步,要花一点力气才跟得上他的玩笑和双关语的微妙之处。他会告诉我们,"疼痛是优雅的(exquisite)",但他实则是在开玩笑说疼痛很折磨人(excruciating),因为你不会期望疼痛是优雅的(我觉得当面听上去更妙)。他受教育程度不高;因为家里没有钱,他很早就离开了学校,十四岁时就被迫马上去工作,但是离开学校并没有打消他对文字的热爱。作为一个男孩,我没有意识到我吸收了父亲对词语和短句的热爱,但是我相信,这对我来说是一切的开始。音乐家要应付的只有十二个音符,而在一首歌里,你通常只用到它们中的大约一半。但是伴随着文字的

---

1   保罗·惠特曼(Paul Whiteman,1890—1967),美国古典音乐家。在1920年代因演奏他改编自流行音乐和古典轻音乐的"交响爵士乐"而名噪一时。

选择是无限的，于是我明白，就像我爸爸一样，我可以和它们一起演奏。这就好像我可以把它们抛到空中，然后看看当它们全部落下时，语言是如何变为魔法的。

我很容易回忆起父亲，不过也有很多其他人帮助我塑造了我写歌的方式。回忆过往，我会几次提到艾伦·杜邦德（Alan Durband），我在利物浦学院男子高中的老师。和其他人一样，他激发了我对阅读的热爱并为我打开眼界，使我进入一个由书籍构成的幻想世界。首先，我会在学校里学习一些关于某位作家或诗人的知识；然后，我会去书店补充我不知道的东西。我开始买平装书——通常是小说，不过也有诗集，譬如狄兰·托马斯的《在牛奶森林下》（Under Milk Wood），只是为了看看它是什么，以及托马斯是如何处理文字的。我还买了一些剧本，比如田纳西·威廉斯的《卡米诺实》（Camino Real）和奥斯卡·王尔德的《莎乐美》（Salome）。

顺理成章地，我开始去看在利物浦演出的戏剧。我只能买得起剧场里最便宜的座位。我通常很喜欢这些戏剧，像亨利克·易卜生的《赫达·加布勒》（Hedda Gabler），不过我也喜欢在幕间休息时偷听别人的对话，听那些楼梯间的闲聊。我只是站在那里，静静地听着。这是值得的，因为我会收集意见、批评、措辞，以及诸如此类的东西。我吸收的一切都将对自己的写作产生影响。

这大约是我遇见约翰·列侬的同一时间，现在大家很清楚，我们对彼此有着巨大的影响。读者也许会在我对约翰的回忆中察觉到决斗的情绪，那是因为我和他的关系很复杂。有时它充满了巨大的爱和钦佩；但有时候不是，特别是披头士解散的时候。不过，一开始，这段关系不过是一个年轻的利物浦小伙子仰慕着另一个比他大一岁半的小伙子。

很难不佩服约翰的机智和智慧。但是当我开始将他看作一个生动、具体的普通人时，显然，争吵开始出现。不过我们之间从来没有任何暴力行为，即使有一部电影里约翰的角色殴打过我的角色，但事实是，他从来没有打过我。和许多友谊一样，我们之间也有争执和争吵，但并不多。不过，有的时候，我确实认为约翰是个十足的白痴。虽然我更年轻，我也会试图向他解释为什么他会显得愚蠢，以及为什么他所做的事情如此不像他。我记得他对我说过："你知道，保罗，我担心人们在我死后会怎么想我。"这样的想法让我震惊，我会回答："等等，等一下。人们会认为你很伟大，你已经创作了足够多的作品来证明这一点。"我经常觉得我是他的牧师，并且不得不说："我的孩子，你很伟大。别担心那个。"

我的安慰似乎让他感觉好些，但在我们的歌曲创作中，我有时不得不变得强硬。当他建议一句歌词时，有时我不得不告诉他这句歌词来自其他地方，比如《西区故事》（West Side Story）。我就是那个不得不说"不，那个以前有人做过"的人。有时，我会拿一首他写的歌，建议他用另一种方式塑造它。值得赞扬的是，他会接受我的建议；就像如果他告诉我，我也会这么做，"哦，不，我们不能那样写"——我们会改变歌词。这就是我们合作的伟大之处：我们以各种特别的方式尊重彼此的意见。

在披头士开始分裂的时候，琳达·伊斯曼（Linda Eastman）走进了我的生活——不仅作为我的妻子，同时也是我的缪斯女神。那个时候，没有人对我的词曲创作有更大的影响。她能理解，并且明白我想做什么；仅仅这个事实就已经让我感到安慰，所以她也会频繁地出现在回忆录中。如果我写一首歌并唱给她听，她可能会鼓励我，但我一直知道，她会给我一个直截了当的意见。在这个层面上，她对我助益良多。她对音乐的热爱和我对音乐的热爱很好地结合在了一起，我们可以毫无负担地向对方提出建议，如果她对一两首歌有想法，我可以接受，然后改进。那个时候，我真的需要这样的人，因为披头士刚刚解散。

琳达在其他方面也有极大的帮助，或许《歌抒人生》的读者会对此心怀感念。披头士刚刚成立时，我们一直关注新闻剪报之类的东西。当伴随着乐队而来的事情开始变得疯狂之后，我爸爸继续从报纸上收集文章，他为我们所做的事情感到骄傲。不过，正是琳达帮助我认识到我们所保存的东西的重要性。在那之前，我们一直认为写出来的歌词是短暂的。我们把它们草草记下来，以便创作和录制这首歌。在那个时候，我们的注意力似乎都集中在音乐上，这是你看不到的东西。之后我们只是把歌词页扔掉，想到那些最终被扔进阿比路录音棚（Abbey Road Studios）废纸篓里的东西就觉得很有趣。不过，琳达曾是摄影师，她有制作美丽的图片的技巧，这也是她追求的艺术，她进入的是一个实物手工的世界。她开始捡起我们留在录音棚里的手写歌词，然后帮我把它们贴到一本剪贴簿子里。她把它们看作我的回忆和历史的一部分。

有人告诉我，我的存档文件现在有超过一百万件物品，这展示了一个人的生命中，会有多少物品进进出出。我时不时地坐在这些东西旁边——这些东西我已经很久没见过了，比如我的旧课本，或者原始的《佩珀军士》[1] 套装。对我来说，这是一次去往记忆小巷的旅行，但在编写这本书的过程中，我想确保我们用我过去的物品和图片来描绘回忆录，以便读者能够沉浸在歌曲创作的那段时期。这一切都是为了让人们了解，当时发生了什么。

书中的插图有些相当直截了当，但有些相当狂野，它们会以不可预测的方式打动读者。通过分析歌词，有人可能会认为某首歌来自我的妈妈或爸爸，或是受到玛哈里希[2] 的启发，或者来自我与我非常尊敬的女王的会面。不过歌曲创作，以及人们看待歌曲的方式，往往来自纯粹的偶然，完全的意外。谁会猜到"辛劳一日的夜"（A Hard Day's Night）[3] 这个颠倒的措辞来自林戈曾经的口误？或者《可爱的丽塔》（Lovely Rita）的灵感来自波特兰广场中国大使馆对面一位真实的女交警？或者飓风鲍勃和发生在长岛的大停电让我写了《印花布的天空》（Calico Skies）？或者《现在就做》（Do It Now）的灵感来自在利物浦时我父亲命令我和我弟弟在家附近捡马粪？

生活告诉我，这个社会崇拜名人。六十年来，我不得不面对成为名人的问题，这

1　全称为《佩珀军士孤独之心俱乐部乐队》（Sgt. Pepper's Lonely Hearts Club Band）。
2　指玛哈里希·玛赫西·优济（Maharishi Mahesh Yogi, 1911—2008），印度冥想和精神导师。
3　"A Hard Day's Night"歌曲的同名电影国内通译名为《一夜狂欢》，但其歌词内容主述辛劳一天后的夜，故本书中歌曲名及专辑名译为《辛劳一日的夜》，电影译为《一夜狂欢》。

是我在利物浦刚刚起步时无法想象的事情。即使到了我这个年纪，记者和摄影师仍然想抢到什么新闻或揭露一些负面的事情，比如我突然和披头士的伙伴林戈翻脸，或者与洋子——一个现在已经八十多岁的女人——之间的战斗。不难理解为什么有些名人会选择遁世，比如葛丽泰·嘉宝或我的朋友鲍勃·迪伦。我也同情那些被名声压垮的歌手——这名单太长了。

虽然我真的希望能带妻子南希（Nancy Shevell）出去吃饭，且不会在咀嚼意大利面时被人拦下五六次，或者被不停拍照，但我也很感激父母相信我和我的弟弟，爱我们，并为我们提供了一个基石，使我能够处理我经历过的那些坎坷时刻。用五年的时间浏览我的一百五十多首歌曲，帮助我把很多事情放到了放大镜下，尤其是吉姆和玛丽·麦卡特尼言传身教地告诉我"人性本善"——而我吸收了这一理念，并传递给了孩子们。当然，世界上也有一些坏人，但大多数人都有一颗善良的心。

我仍然可以勾勒出父亲带着我和弟弟在利物浦一个公共汽车站排队等车的画面。他戴着他的软毡帽，一种当时男人们像穿制服一样戴着的帽子。他会确保我们面对女性时脱下学生帽致意。"早上好。"我们会说。这是一个如此甜蜜、老派的姿态，多年来一直伴随着我。我还记得，爸爸总是和我们谈论宽容。"宽容"和"节制"是他最喜欢的两个词。

这一切的发生是一个谜。人们在街上拦住我，他们会变得非常激动。他们说，"你的音乐改变了我的生活"，我知道他们的意思——披头士给他们的生命带来了非常重要的东西。但这仍然是个谜，而我不介意成为一个谜。关于这个无所不在的谜，有一件小事我会永远记住。我们开着一辆面包车向北行驶，只有我们四个披头士和巡演助理。天气非常寒冷，有一场大暴风雪，伸手不见五指——这显然不是开车的良好状态。我们能做的就是跟着前面汽车的尾灯走。雪大到我们认不出路来。有一次，我们的车失控从路堤上滑了出去。我们抬头看着路，浑身发抖，但没什么大碍，我们想："我们到底怎么才能到那里？"这是个谜。但我们中的一个人说（我不记得是谁）："会有事情发生。"

有些人可能会觉得这种观点——"会有事情发生"——简单或平庸，但我认为这是一种伟大的哲学。最近，我把这个故事告诉一个朋友，一个做生意的大人物，他被这句话迷住了，并一再重复跟我说："会有事情发生。"这句话的意思是，无论你多么绝望，无论一切看起来多么糟糕，总会有事情发生。我觉得这种态度很有帮助，这是一种值得坚持的处世哲学。

保罗·麦卡特尼

萨塞克斯郡，英格兰

2020 年秋

致读者

保罗·麦卡特尼和保罗·马尔登之间的对话，构成了回忆录《保罗·麦卡特尼：歌抒人生》的基础，对话开始于 2015 年 8 月 5 日，星期三下午的纽约。从 2015 年夏天到 2020 年 8 月 19 日星期三的最后一次谈话，两人在二十四次谈话中总共聊了大约五十个小时。最后一次谈话是在世界上大部分地区因新冠肺炎疫情进入封锁状态后通过视频进行的。

尽管保罗·麦卡特尼于 MPL 公司的制作团队在 2015 年通过一系列初步研究促成了这本图书计划的启动，不过直到 2019 年夏天，我们才正式开始进行这项工作。工作非常多，其中包括帮助保罗·马尔登进行详细的研究，并转录将收入这本书的一百五十四首歌曲的相关对话。团队的各个成员也开始深入研究 MPL 的档案，去搜寻图片和物品，来为对谈添加注解。

关键的挑战之一是歌词的标准化。我们基本上以专辑中印刷的歌词册为准，但由于歌词格式偶尔在不同发行版本之间有所不同，我们设定了一些基本规则：歌名首字母大写，尽量减少重复，合理减少标点符号，并且默认为英式英语拼写。对于有些找不到标准发行版本的歌曲，我们搜索了 MPL 的档案，尽管在很多情况下，我们找到的是工作文件，而不是最终文本。而最终，我们认为《保罗·麦卡特尼：歌抒人生》首次呈现出了这一百五十四首歌曲权威版本的歌词。

正如读者可能想象的那样，从 1956 年年末保罗写完第一首歌到现在，许多细节和名字发生了变化。比如，披头士在 1962 年与乔治·马丁[1] 一起录音时，并不是在阿比路

---

1   乔治·马丁（George Martin，1926—2016），披头士乐队的制作人。

录音棚的二号棚；彼时，那个录音棚名叫百代录音棚（EMI Recording Studios）。为了保持这本书的一致性，保罗要求我们将所有在此地的录音记录为出自阿比路录音棚。其他录音棚也采取了类似的方法，如 AIR 录音棚和哥伦比亚录音棚（Columbia）。1990 年代初，AIR 录音棚在伦敦的地址发生了变化，我们对其进行了标准化，而 CBS 录音棚有时也被称为哥伦比亚，但是在这里，我们以母带标签为准进行记录。我们列出了一首歌进行大部分录音的录音棚，但没有包括所有叠录录音棚的细节。

我们也设计了标准化元数据，为每首歌记录了它在英国和美国的首次发行信息，按时间顺序列出。我们将歌曲的附带信息限制在这两个国家。制作一份全世界各种版本的完整列表似乎是一项真正的西西弗斯式尝试；这需要新的一册书，而且在这样一本重点是保罗歌词的书里并不合适。

用以描绘保罗回忆的绝大多数照片和纪念品都来自 MPL 档案。正如他在前言中所指出的，这个档案馆包含了超过一百万件物品，所有这些物品都被数字化和关键词化。当我们开始研究这个项目时，保罗要求我们收录能找到的相关语境最有趣和最有活力的物品，以便将歌曲创作的那个时间点生活化。在少数情况下，当我们没有合适的物品时，会从第三方获得许可，对此，我们十分感激（在本书末尾可以找到致谢名单）。在 MPL 档案中深入挖掘的一个显著优势是，我们收录在本书的图片，有大半是从未被公众看到过的，我们甚至发现了一首披头士乐队未发表的歌曲《告诉我他是谁》（Tell Me Who He Is）。

话说回来，《保罗·麦卡特尼：歌抒人生》是一次大范围的合作。我们真诚地希望你享受阅读过程，就像我们享受将它们整理起来出版一样。

MPL 团队

导 言

    大概在 2016 年年底，我接到一个陌生号码的电话，但那个声音立刻让人感到熟悉。彼时新当选的总统唐纳德·特朗普相当"实事求是"地介绍了自己，并不失时机地切入正题：我愿意来华盛顿担任他的"诗歌领袖"吗？

    保罗·麦卡特尼爵士的模仿能力原来如此出色，这并不令人惊讶。像几乎所有伟大的创作者一样，他向大师们学习，其中包括一系列令人印象深刻的文学大师：狄更斯、莎士比亚、罗伯特·路易斯·史蒂文森、刘易斯·卡罗尔 —— 这些名字很自然地在他的嘴里滚动。而所有学徒训练都以讽刺和模仿为特点。

    了解李尔王，以及 —— 同样重要的 —— 爱德华·李尔[1]是如何影响了保罗，对于理解他的成就至关重要。保罗出生于 1942 年，是第一批直接受益于 1944 年《教育法案》的英国公民，该法案为历史上的弱势群体提供了更多的机会。保罗的父母都来自有爱尔兰血统的移民家庭，与英格兰有着古已有之的复杂关系，又对利物浦庞大的爱尔兰社区有一种归属感。不过，更重要的是，他们是自信并相对乐观的全新战后一代。

    正如保罗·麦卡特尼所证明的那样，父母一直希望他和弟弟迈克能有"伟大的成就"，于是鼓励孩子们去最好的学校读书。他的父亲，一名棉花销售员，有"很强的语言能力"，而他的母亲是一名护士，这一事实确保了保罗是"班上唯一可以正确拼写'痰'的人"。

    对年轻的麦卡特尼影响最大的是高中英语老师艾伦·杜邦德，他曾就读于剑桥唐宁学院，是精通"书面文字"的资深学者 F. R. 利维斯（F. R. Leavis）的学生。保罗的文

---

[1]   爱德华·李尔（Edward Lear，1812—1888），英国博物学家、画家、诗人，被誉为英国"胡话诗"第一人。

本分析能力 —— 无论是对自己的作品还是对其他作品 —— 也许可以直接追溯到杜邦德的影响。我确信，在另一种生活中，保罗·麦卡特尼也许会是一名中学教师或大学教师，顶着和拖把头[1]一样轻盈的学士帽。

拥有如此稳固的英语文学基础只是保罗成功的一部分原因，他同样沉浸在流行歌曲的传统中 —— 不仅是小理查德和查克·贝里，还有布里尔大厦和锡盘巷的词曲作者们[2]。这赋予了他非常广泛的音乐词汇。他最早的英雄包括弗雷德·阿斯泰尔[3]、霍吉·卡迈克尔[4]、格什温兄弟[5]及科尔·波特[6]。尽管保罗后来会与卡尔海因兹·斯托克豪森[7]和约翰·凯奇[8]这样的前卫作曲家深入交流，但对他产生直接影响的是埃弗利兄弟[9]，尤其是巴迪·霍利。他评论说："猫王不是创作者或主音吉他手，他只是一位歌手；杜安·艾迪[10]是一位吉他手但不是歌手。而巴迪身兼以上所有。"他指的是巴迪·霍利自己写歌、唱歌，并且弹吉他。

在自己的歌曲创作伙伴约翰·列侬身上，保罗最初发现的是约翰同样惊人的声音模仿（ventriloquism）能力。无论他们的作品多么具有开创性，披头士都是在不断地与同时代的人对话，无论是与相关的艺术家，譬如摩城唱片音乐家[11]、沙滩男孩[12]，或者鲍勃·迪伦，还是更早时期的歌手和词曲作家。即使是现在，保罗也会模仿小理查德或是弗雷德·阿斯泰尔，以他们的状态发声，以此让自己浸入创作状态。他甚至偶尔会模仿约翰·列侬；他承认有一天，列侬的名字会与他的名字协调地写在一起，就像吉尔伯特与沙利文[13]，罗杰斯与哈默斯坦[14]。他承认列侬和麦卡特尼的互动"简直是奇迹"，并描述了他们如何"用两把吉他写歌"。"好玩的是我是左撇子，而他是右撇子，就好像我在照镜子，他也在照镜子一样。"

保罗·麦卡特尼最初在约翰·列侬身上发现的另一份礼物是，他不仅愿意即兴创作，而且愿意改进。在一起的时候，他们总是在"寻找一些之前从未真正在流行歌曲里出

1　拖把头（Mop Tops），披头士乐队的发型，披头士出名后，这种发型在年轻人中风靡一时。
2　布里尔大厦（Brill Building）位于美国纽约时代广场附近，锡盘巷（Tin Pan Alley）位于美国纽约西 28 街，两地都有很多音乐出版公司在那里办公，因此几乎成为音乐产业的代名词。
3　弗雷德·阿斯泰尔（Fred Astaire，1899—1987），美国电影演员、舞蹈家、舞台剧演员、编舞、歌手、制片人。
4　霍吉·卡迈克尔（Hoagy Carmichael，1899—1981），美国作曲家。他是 1930 年代锡盘巷最成功的词曲作者之一，也是大众传媒时代第一批利用电视、电子麦克风和录音等新兴通信技术的创作歌手之一。
5　指乔治·格什温（George Gershwin）和艾拉·格什温（Ira Gershwin）兄弟，二人曾共同创作多首经典爵士歌曲。
6　科尔·波特（Cole Porter，1891—1964），美国音乐家，其许多作品都成为百老汇经典。
7　卡尔海因兹·斯托克豪森（Karlheinz Stockhausen，1928—2007），德国前卫作曲家、音乐学家，在二战后严肃音乐创作领域有着巨大的影响。
8　约翰·凯奇（John Cage，1912—1992），美国先锋派古典音乐作曲家，勋伯格的学生，电子音乐的先驱之一。
9　埃弗利兄弟（The Everly Brothers），由哥哥唐·埃弗利和弟弟菲利普·埃弗利组成的二重唱民谣组合。
10　杜安·艾迪（Duane Eddy，1938— ），美国电吉他演奏家，其演奏方法影响了许多吉他手。
11　摩城唱片（Motown Records）1959 年成立于美国底特律，签约的歌手主要是黑人音乐家。
12　沙滩男孩（The Beach Boys），1960 年代美国加州迷幻摇滚乐队。
13　指英国歌舞剧词曲合作者吉尔伯特（William S. Gilbert）与沙利文（Arthur Sullivan）。
14　指美国歌舞剧词曲合作者罗杰斯（Richard Charles Rodgers）与哈默斯坦（Oscar Hammerstein Ⅱ）。

现过的主题"。他们用胡说八道和童谣延续着永远的学生时代的约定，为略显古怪的韵脚附上拜伦式的缠绵，无论是"Edison/medicine"（爱迪生／医学），还是"Valerie/gallery"（瓦莱丽／旁听席）。他们很幸运地找到了能同他们步调一致的制作人乔治·马丁——实际上，有时候马丁是设定步调的那个人。马丁对弦乐编曲的建议，以及对罗伯特·穆格[1]和其新式合成器的开创性抱持的开放态度，使得披头士乐队得以长期发挥自己的创造性。

广播的影响在披头士的声音场景中长期存在，却时常被忽视。保罗将《佩珀军士》描述为"一个大型广播节目"。和披头士的其他成员一样，他从小就喜欢疯狂的广播喜剧，比如《傻瓜秀》(*The Goon Show*)，该剧从 1951 年一直持续到 1960 年，由彼得·塞勒斯（Peter Sellers）、斯派克·米利根（Spike Milligan）和哈里·塞科比（Harry Secombe）主演。其他广播明星包括利物浦喜剧演员肯·多德（Ken Dodd），他经常被认为是最后一位杂耍剧院喜剧演员。广播潜移默化地影响了保罗对"那些缺失的部分"的迷恋，以及如何借助精心挑选的词语渲染场景。而广播剧震撼性的冲击力——包括狄兰·托马斯 1954 年的杰作《在牛奶森林下》——无论怎样夸大都不为过。正是 1966 年播出的阿尔弗雷德·贾里[2]的《愚比龟》(*Ubu Cocu*)广播剧版本，向保罗介绍了"荒诞玄学"一词，描述了当时科学的一个特别领域。一些舞台剧的角色同样施加了不小影响，无论出自肖恩·奥凯西[3]的《朱诺和孔雀》(*Juno and the Paycock*)，还是尤金·奥尼尔的《长夜漫漫路迢迢》(*Long Day's Journey Into Night*)。我们也可以认为，保罗·麦卡特尼是一位迷你剧作家，他有能力从原本可能仅仅是一个缩略草图的地方渲染出一个完整的角色。

保罗长期以来一直感兴趣的另外两个领域属于视觉艺术范畴。其一是绘画，他既是名副其实的画家，完成了数百幅油画作品，也是（就修辞角度来说）形象的呈现者。第二是电影，他展示所有变动不居，一路走来，都在坚持"我的镜头环顾四周，搜寻生活中的线索"。

理解《埃莉诺·里格比》(*Eleanor Rigby*) 的一个方式，是把这首歌想象成分镜剧本，这是保罗·麦卡特尼最著名的歌曲之一。在这里，我将像艾伦·杜邦德或 F. R. 利维斯会做的那样，试着解释它的某些形态。像利维斯一样，杜邦德也许会抵制将这首歌从历史背景中分离出来的举动。另一位伟大的剑桥评论家，I. A. 理查德（I. A. Richards）会坚持认为这首诗（或歌）是一个自我独立的艺术作品，但利维斯和杜邦德会倾向于考虑语境。

以主角的名字为例。这首歌发行于 1966 年，当时英国最著名的埃莉诺是埃莉诺·布隆（Eleanor Bron），1964 年至 1965 年大受欢迎的电视喜剧《与其说是一个节目，不如说是一种生活方式》(*Not So Much a Programme, More a Way of Life*) 中的明星，她也曾出演

---

1   罗伯特·穆格（Robert Moog, 1934—2005），合成器的发明者。
2   阿尔弗雷德·贾里（Alfred Jarry, 1873—1907），法国荒诞派戏剧作家。
3   肖恩·奥凯西（Sean O'Casey, 1880—1964），爱尔兰编剧。

1965 年披头士的电影《救命!》(*Help!*)。第一批听到这首歌的英国观众，对埃莉诺·里格比的想象很可能受到这位美丽得惊人的布隆女士的强烈影响。"里格比"是维京人的名字，意思是"山脊农场"或"山脊村庄"，这会将这首歌定位在英国北部的某个地方。身为苏格兰人，麦肯齐神父（Father McKenzie），这首诗的另一个主要人物，也呼应了英国北部的场景设定。

《埃莉诺·里格比》的一部分冲击力来自它电影式的结构，在第一段和第二段主歌中介绍两个主要角色，然后在第三段主歌中把两者结合在一起。这是阿尔弗雷德·希区柯克在 1960 年的电影《惊魂记》(*Psycho*) 的淋浴场景中使用的手法的一种变体：片中，导演展示了血水流下排水沟的画面，然后切入清澈的水打着旋排入同一个排水沟的镜头。同时，乔治·马丁编曲的双弦乐四重奏的疯狂演奏，让人联想起伯纳德·赫尔曼[1] "锐利的"电影配乐，令《惊魂记》中的淋浴场景和这首歌产生了关联。所以，对那些第一次听到《埃莉诺·里格比》的人来说，叠加在埃莉诺·布隆形象上的是《惊魂记》中干尸母亲的形象。《埃莉诺·里格比》的部分冲击力来自这个几乎看不见的孤独和死亡的潜台词。

十四岁时母亲的去世——这个他"从未克服"的事情——对保罗·麦卡特尼的伤害被写进了歌曲里。从《我失去了我的小女孩》到类似《尽管一再警告》(*Despite Repeated Warnings*) 这样的作品，保罗将一系列令人惊讶的话题作为创作题材——从他与简·阿舍、琳达·伊斯曼及南希·谢维尔的关系，气候变化和种族不平等，到家庭宠物狗和家庭汽车。《保罗·麦卡特尼：歌抒人生》的读者会有一种感觉，他们是在一位诗人面前，对这位诗人来说"伦敦的书店几乎和吉他店一样好"。当保罗提醒我们"披头士之所以成为如此伟大的乐队，是因为没有两首歌是相似的"时，我们确实清楚地记得，在他和羽翼乐队（Wings）一起，以及作为单飞艺术家的漫长的职业生涯中，他一直"厌恶无聊"。六十年来，他始终展示着我们认为一流艺术家特有的那种不安分。不仅如此，保罗·麦卡特尼的非凡之处还在于，他是极少数的不仅未受到时代影响，而且其作品实质上定义了那个时代的人之一。他活生生地证明了同为抒情诗人的威廉·华兹华斯的精辟格言："每一位伟大而有独创性的作家，与其伟大和独创性相称，都必须自己创造出让人津津乐道的品位。"

关于这本巨著，还有一些只言片语。本书基于 2015 年 8 月至 2020 年 8 月，五年期间的二十四次单独会面。在 2015 年初，罗伯特·威尔和约翰·伊斯曼把我介绍给了保罗·麦卡特尼。这些会面大多发生在纽约，每次都涉及两三个小时细致的对话。这一过程有点让人想起列侬-麦卡特尼这对搭档"两三个小时的写歌环节"的合作特点，

1　伯纳德·赫尔曼（Bernard Herrmann，1911—1975），美国作曲家、电影配乐大师。

尽管喝的是绿茶，而不是布鲁克·邦德或者 PG Tips[1]。小吃有带鹰嘴豆泥的百吉饼、奶酪和泡菜，偶尔还有马麦酱。我们在一起的时间普遍很快乐，有时甚至是喧闹的。我们相处得这么好的一部分原因是共同的文化和经验范围，考虑到我们出生时间相隔不过九年。我们的生日也只相差两天，我们的名字都叫保罗是出于同样的原因：圣彼得和圣保罗的殉道日是 6 月 29 日。

无论保罗·麦卡特尼多么擅长让人放松，无论他内心多么安详，他永远是 20 世纪的偶像，这是无法回避的事实。因此，如果没有其他原因，我确实偶尔允许自己有追星逐月的片刻。每一次保罗·麦卡特尼登上舞台的时候，都是追星时刻。他的现场表演仍然会迸发巨大的能量，以至令人觉得他会燃烧起来。不过，在我们合作的过程中，他经常拿起吉他演示一个和弦排列，并为我这个唯一的观众演奏他的某首歌的几个小节，这是一种特别的乐趣。

尽管有这些来来回回的事情，我们还是设法在每次见面时讨论六到八首歌曲。我们的对话被同步录在两台设备上，进行专业转录处理。然后，我将保罗对歌词的讲解编辑成几近无缝连接的叙述，避开了我自己的问题和评论，有时会为了行文逻辑而重新排序。文本随后由可敬的罗伯特·威尔逐行编辑；同样可敬的伊西·宾厄姆（Issy Bingham）和史蒂夫·伊瑟尔（Steve Ithell）偶尔会补充一些事实信息，他们俩都来自 MPL。

保罗·麦卡特尼歌词标志性的深刻和隽永源于两种看似不可调和的力量，我将这两种力量描述为歌曲的"物理性"和"化学性"。决定"物理性"的是歌曲的结构规划，以及我前文提到的制作过程。据估计，1960 年至 1962 年期间，披头士在德国演出了近三百场。"诗人"（poet）一词在希腊语中是"制作者"（maker）的意思，从词源来讲，它显然根植于对歌曲结构的全然了解。苏格兰对诗人或吟游诗人的一个称呼是"诗匠"，这并非偶然。

"化学性"反映在诗人的另一个称谓——"吟游诗人"（troubadour）中。"吟游诗人"一词与法语单词"遇见 / 发现"（trouver）有关。保罗经常以"我遇到了这些和弦"之类的话，来描述一首歌如何不可思议地诞生。正是两种元素的神奇结合——音符与"奇遇"——引起了化学反应。

保罗经常提到他没有灵感时自我激发的方式。他始终认为"声音模仿"在创作中极有价值，就像他说的，"唱小理查德的歌得全身心投入，你不能真的去思考它"。他记得父亲"喜欢填字游戏"，承认自己"继承了对单词和填字游戏的热爱"。他用"迷恋"一词来表述他对歌曲中文字游戏的态度——如果歌曲中的字谜有谜底的话，这也是答案。这让人想起 W. B. 叶芝的坚持："对困难的迷恋 / 已经使我的血管干涸。"[2] 和叶芝一

1　布鲁克·邦德（Brooke Bond）和 PG Tips 均为英国红茶品牌。
2　原句为 "The fascination of what's difficult / Has dried the sap out of my veins"。

样,保罗也坚信面具(mask)理念,或说人格面具(persona)理念的适用性[1],提醒我们"出现在我歌曲中的角色,都始于自我的想象",并且这"一切都和虚构有关"。

　　保罗也有几分喜爱法国哲学家罗兰·巴特描述的"作者之死",即阅读行为必然涉及一定程度的写作,甚至重写文本。对保罗来说,这一理念体现在,他相信世界各地的数百万歌迷都会唱出自己版本的"麦卡特尼歌曲"。一首歌只有在被听到和被传唱时,才成为它最真实的样子。而保罗·麦卡特尼最伟大的品质则是他有目共睹的谦逊。他与睿智的作家唐纳德·巴塞尔姆[2]颇有共识。巴塞尔姆在一篇题为《不知道》(Not-Knowing)的文章中,将作家归类为"一个在开始一项任务时,不知道该做什么的人"。《歌抒人生》磅礴的情感和坚实的思想见证了保罗·麦卡特尼的坦诚与无私——不言自明,他恰恰展示了巴塞尔姆所说的"作品自我创作的方式"。

保罗·马尔登

沙伦斯普林斯,纽约

2020 年 10 月

1　"人格面具"(persona)一词是希腊文"mask"的譬喻,本意指演员在剧中扮演某个特殊角色而戴的面具。人格面具是荣格的精神分析理论之一,是个人适应或应对世界所采用方式的体系。叶芝的"面具理论"与荣格的"人格面具"概念相仿,他认为"面具"即"反自我",用以隐藏内在的自我,以达到公众期待。
2　唐纳德·巴塞尔姆(Donald Barthelme,1931—1989),美国后现代主义小说家。

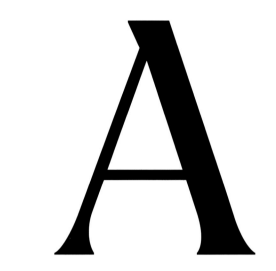

All My Loving

我所有的爱

作　者	WRITERS	保罗·麦卡特尼和约翰·列侬　Paul McCartney and John Lennon
艺术家	ARTIST	披头士乐队　The Beatles
录　音	RECORDED	伦敦阿比路录音棚　Abbey Road Studios, London
发　行	RELEASED	《和披头士一起》，1963 年　*With The Beatles*, 1963
		《遇见披头士！》，1964 年　*Meet The Beatles!*, 1964

Close your eyes and I'll kiss you
Tomorrow I'll miss you
Remember I'll always be true
And then while I'm away
I'll write home every day
And I'll send all my loving to you

I'll pretend that I'm kissing
The lips I am missing
And hope that my dreams will come true
And then while I'm away
I'll write home every day
And I'll send all my loving to you

All my loving, I will send to you
All my loving, darling, I'll be true

Close your eyes and I'll kiss you
Tomorrow I'll miss you
Remember I'll always be true
And then while I'm away
I'll write home every day
And I'll send all my loving to you

All my loving, I will send to you
All my loving, darling, I'll be true
All my loving, all my loving
All my loving, I will send to you

我们参加过一次联合巡演，大概有五六个其他乐队，因为一支乐队撑不起票房。即使在纽约，一场演出也会囊括巴迪·霍利、杰瑞·李·刘易斯、小理查德、胖子多米诺[1]、埃弗利兄弟——全在同一张演出名单上！

我在英国某处的一辆巡演大巴上，无所事事，于是开始思忖这些词："闭上你的眼睛……"这时候我已经和简·阿舍结识，而且在追求她，但我不记得写这些词时，心中是否有具体所指。可能这首歌更像对我们当时生活的写照——离开家人和朋友去巡演，体验新的冒险。这是为数不多的我先写出歌词的歌曲之一。这种情况真的很罕见，毕竟我通常都带着乐器。总而言之，我开始在大巴上写歌词。那时我们参加的是"莫斯帝国"巡演（Moss Empires circuit）。莫斯帝国公司在全国拥有许多场地，而那些场地就是巡演的站点，都是些 20 世纪初的华丽大型音乐厅——不过现在大多数都变成了宾果游戏厅——后台特别舒适，宽敞而空旷。我记得我们和罗伊·奥比森[2]一起巡演，到达场地时，各种各样的乐队、巡演工作人员和舞台工作人员四处奔忙。在喧嚣中，我走到一架钢琴前，不知怎么就找到了和弦。那时候，它是一首纯正的乡村音乐，一首情歌。

创作的时候，你以一种风格构思歌曲（因为你不能用上千种风格来构想事物），就会有一种相应的聆听方式。如果写出了一首好歌，你会意识到它具有某种灵活性；歌曲可以是灵活的。然后，当披头士乐队的其他成员进入录音棚时，这种灵活性就会发挥作用。

录制《我所有的爱》时，让我印象深刻的是约翰的吉他部分；他把和弦演奏成三连音。那是他在最后一刻冒出的主意，它改变了整首歌，歌曲因此有了某种活力。这首歌显然是关于某人离开去旅行的，而约翰强劲的节奏恰好呼应了飞驰的旅行感。它听上去就像是高速公路上辘辘滚动的车轮，信不信由你，1950 年代末，高速公路才真正在英国出现。不过，我们录音时经常是这样的。我们中的一个会施展一个小魔术，让歌曲成为它需要的样子。

这是一首书信体歌曲，与《爱我吧》的 B 面歌曲《另外，我爱你》（P.S. I Love You）风格相同，承袭了譬如胖子沃勒[3]的《我要坐下来给自己写一封信》（I'm Gonna Sit Right Down and Write Myself a Letter），或者帕特·布恩[4] 1956 年的热门歌曲《我会回家》（I'll Be Home）等书信体歌曲的部分传统。所以，《我所有的爱》是一首有"谱系"的歌。

在披头士的故事里，也可以为《我所有的爱》绘制某种谱系图。这张专辑录制于1963 年夏天，并最终出现在我们同年晚些时候发行的第二张专辑《和披头士一起》里，或者说英国版的《和披头士一起》里。对美国乐迷来说，这首歌收录于 1964 年初发行的《遇见披头士！》。从披头士的职业生涯刚起步，直到《救命！》时期，美国版的专辑都会和英国版不一样。国会唱片公司（Capitol Records）通常从这里那里东拼西凑几首

1　胖子多米诺（Fats Domino，1928—2017），美国摇滚乐先驱之一，被猫王称为"真正的摇滚之王"。
2　罗伊·奥比森（Roy Orbison，1936—1988），美国流行乐歌星，他将乡村流行音乐元素与摇摆乐结合，开辟了一支全新的音乐派系。
3　胖子沃勒（Fats Waller，1904—1943），美国爵士乐大师，首次将管风琴引入爵士乐。
4　帕特·布恩（Pat Boone，1934—），美国歌手、演员，以全然与猫王相反的温柔且富有朝气的形象，获得极强的号召力。

歌，再加进一两首单曲，就成了美国版专辑。不过，《和披头士一起》和《遇见披头士！》最了不起的地方是，两者的封面是罗伯特·弗里曼[1]拍摄的同一张照片。

罗伯特曾与一些非常酷的爵士乐音乐家合作，比如约翰·柯川和迪兹·吉莱斯皮[2]。我们给他看了一些心爱的集体照——那是我们的朋友阿斯特丽德·科尔什赫[3]在汉堡拍摄的——要求他延续那种风格，如果你看了阿斯特丽德给我们拍的照片，绝对能辨识出其中的亲缘关系。人们问过我很多关于这个封面的问题，得知它如此迅速地完成时，往往十分惊讶。这张照片的阴影效果看起来像是出自有专业灯光的工作室，但实际上，它是在英格兰西海岸古老的海滨小镇，滨海韦斯顿的一个酒店走廊里拍摄的。我们在那里的奥登剧院进行了一系列演出，然后罗伯特来到我们的酒店，花了一个小时拍摄封面照。他摆好一排椅子，尝试了几种不同的安排——有时让约翰坐在前排，有时是我或乔治（George Harrison）。但这一切都是用自然光迅速完成的。那张照片现在已经成为我们的标志性照片，所以我们很高兴它出现在两个版本的封面上。

这些专辑发行时，正逢披头士狂热（Beatlemania）如日中天。华盛顿特区的一位年轻女士联系了当地电台，让他们播放《我想牵你的手》（I Want to Hold Your Hand）。我想，当时他们得从英国弄一张碟，但最终他们还是播放了这首歌，甚至让那位女士在电台上介绍了这张唱片。那是一切的开端，几周后，这首歌登上了冠军宝座。我们一直说，在拥有榜首唱片之前，我们不想去美国——现在我们有了。这一切促成了我们的首次美国之旅。

我们起飞时，伦敦机场出现了疯狂的场面，有一千多名歌迷和媒体向我们挥手致意，祝我们一切顺利；约翰的妻子辛西娅（Cynthia Lennon）把尖叫声误认为飞机的声音。我们到达肯尼迪机场时，场面更为疯狂。机场刚刚以肯尼迪之名重新命名，我们的巡演只是在他遇刺的几个月之后——《和披头士一起》就在他遇刺的同一天在英国发行；并且，尽管不应该由我来说，但有些评论指出，在为总统吊唁之后，这个国家，特别是青少年，一直在寻找一些全新、积极、有趣的东西以安放心灵。这或许是披头士狂热在美国迅速蔓延的原因之一。不过当时，我想我们并没有意识到这一点。

我们的美国厂牌国会唱片进行了一次宣传活动，以确保人们知道我们要来，他们也确实达到了目的。在纽约，我们遇到了五千名尖叫的歌迷和一百多个试图阻止他们的警察。有一段我们刚下飞机后召开记者招待会的录像，你可以看到这一切有多失控。

《遇见披头士！》发行两周后，我们上了《艾德·沙利文秀》[4]。艾德·沙利文对我们来说是一位真正的绅士，他总是穿着剪裁精致的西装。那个时候，美国只有三个主要频道，他的节目定义了人们谈论的话题。上了这个节目，你才算是征服了美国。我们听说我们的一些偶像都在这个节目中表演过，比如巴迪·霍利和蟋蟀乐队（Buddy Holly and The Crickets），还有一个关于猫王的故事，猫王在表演完《猎犬》（Hound Dog）后重

1　罗伯特·弗里曼（Robert Freeman，1937—2019），美国摄影师、导演。
2　约翰·柯川（John Coltrane，1926—1967）、迪兹·吉莱斯皮（Dizzy Gillespie，1917—1933），均为美国爵士乐大师。
3　阿斯特丽德·科尔什赫（Astrid Kirchherr，1938— ），德国摄影师，艺术家。
4　《艾德·沙利文秀》（Ed Sullivan Show），艾德·沙利文在1948年至1971年间主持的一档美国音乐现场表演类电视节目。

新上台，但他只能展示腰部以上的部分。

在披头士的故事里，我们的首次出镜已经有点像是某种神话了。就在节目播出前，我们收到了猫王的电报，他祝愿我们顺利。我原本在学校里表现挺好，然后猫王出现了，学校立刻被我抛在脑后；而现在，他在祝我们好运。观众的声音也仍然在我的耳边回响。这场演出提供了七百张演播室门票，但收到了大约五万份申请；节目播出时，有七千三百万人观看。它成了一个文化标志。多年来，很多人特意告诉我，他们看了这个节目，譬如布鲁斯·斯普林斯汀[1]、汤姆·佩蒂[2]、克里希·海德[3]、比利·乔尔[4]——他们全都看过。据说当天的犯罪率也下降了，连强盗都在看节目；不过这可能不是真的。我们就以这样一个绝妙的方式被引入美国。在我们的第二首歌《直到有你》（Till There Was You）中，他们切入了我们每个人的镜头，并把我们的名字打在屏幕上。轮到约翰时，他们补充道："对不起姑娘们，他结婚了。"——在此之前，这一直是个保守得不太好的秘密。

不过，第二天的一些媒体报道有点刻薄。《纽约先驱论坛报》（The New York Herald Tribune）——我可以补充一句，这份报纸已经不在了——写道，披头士乐队是"百分之七十五的知名度，百分之二十的发型，以及百分之五轻快的哀歌"。但随后，"拖把头"成了一种新的潮流，十几岁的男孩开始蓄这种发型。那时的审美是刘海不应该长到眉毛附近。但一切都变了，你甚至可以买到披头士的假发。

《艾德·沙利文秀》可以把我们引回正题。《我所有的爱》的现场表现一直很好，所以，在艾德·沙利文向观众们介绍"这几位来自利物浦的年轻人"后，《我所有的爱》成为美国看到披头士在电视直播中现场演出的第一首歌曲。大约一个月后，我们的歌闯入了公告牌排行榜前五名。

《我所有的爱》大概是一个注解，展示了那些时日我们的发展有多迅捷——这首歌见证了我们在六个多月的时间里，从莫斯帝国巡演到征服美国。而几个月后，我二十二岁了。

在披头士的故事里，我们的首次出镜已经有点像是某种神话了。就在节目播出前，我们收到了猫王的电报，他祝愿我们顺利。我原本在学校里表现挺好，然后猫王出现了，学校立刻被我抛在脑后；而现在，他在祝我们好运。

1　布鲁斯·斯普林斯汀（Bruce Springsteen，1949—），美国摇滚乐明星。
2　汤姆·佩蒂（Tom Petty，1950—2017），美国摇滚乐明星。
3　克里希·海德（Chrissie Hynde，1951—），美国摇滚乐明星，伪装者乐队主唱。
4　比利·乔尔（Billy Joel，1949—），美国流行歌手。

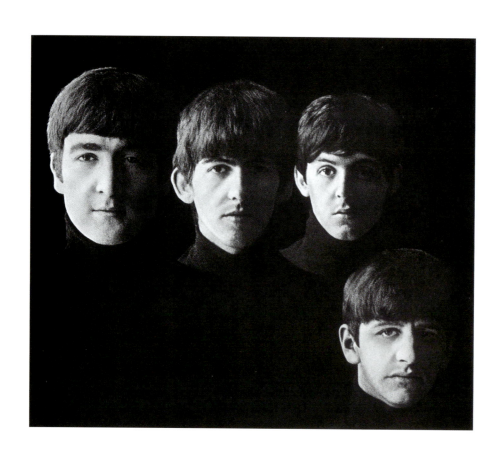

左图：罗伯特·弗里曼拍摄的照片，被用于 1963 年《和披头士一起》，以及 1964 年《遇见披头士！》的封面。

右图：布莱恩·爱泼斯坦[1]的经纪公司 NEMS（NEMS Enterprises Ltd.）公布的披头士 1963 年夏天巡演行程。"NEMS"之名来自爱泼斯坦在利物浦的家族企业北区音乐商店（North End Music Stores），保罗的父亲吉姆在那里给他买了钢琴。

下图：罗伯特·弗里曼，保罗拍摄，迈阿密，1964 年 2 月。

1　布莱恩·爱泼斯坦（Brian Epstein，1934—1967），披头士乐队经纪人。

NEMS ENTERPRISES LTD

DIRECTORS: B. AND C. J. EPSTEIN

PRESS OFFICE : 13, MONMOUTH STREET, LONDON W.C.2.　　TELEPHONE COVent Gdn 2332

ENGAGEMENT LIST FOR THE BEATLES : MONDAY 10 JUNE to SUNDAY 1 SEPTEMBER 1963

Monday 10 June	: Pavilion, BATH
Wednesday 12 June	: Grafton Ballroom, LIVERPOOL (Charity function in aid of N. S. P. C. C.)
Thursday 13 June	: Offerton Palace Club and Southern Sporting Club, MANCHESTER
Friday 14 June	: Tower Ballroom, NEW BRIGHTON
Saturday 15 June	: City Hall, SALISBURY
Sunday 16 June	: Odeon, ROMFORD
Wednesday 19 June	: Recording 'EASY BEAT' (BBC, LONDON) for broadcast Sunday 23 June.
Friday 21 June	: Odeon, GUILDFORD
Saturday 22 June	: Town Hall, ABERGAVENNY
Sunday 23 June	: Filming 'THANK YOUR LUCKY STARS' (ABC TV, BIRMINGHAM) for screening on Saturday 29 June (special all-Merseyside edition)
Monday 24 June	: Recording 'SATURDAY CLUB' (BBC, LONDON) for broadcast Saturday 29 June.
Tuesday 25 June	: Astoria, MIDDLESBROUGH
Wednesday 26 June	: Majestic, NEWCASTLE
Friday 28 June	: Queens Hall, LEEDS
Sunday 30 June	: Regal, YARMOUTH
Wednesday 3 July	: 'THE BEAT SHOW' (BBC, MANCHESTER)
Saturday 6 July	: Memorial Hall, NORTHWICH
Sunday 7 July	: ABC BLACKPOOL
Monday 8 July to Saturday 13 July	: Week at Winter Gardens, MARGATE
Sunday 14 July	: Princess, TORQUAY
Friday 19 July	: Ritz Ballroom, RHYL
Saturday 20 July	: Ritz Ballroom, RHYL
Sunday 21 July	: Queens, BLACKPOOL
Monday 22 July to Saturday 27 July	: Week at Odeon, WESTON-SUPER-MARE
Sunday 28 July	: Regal, YARMOUTH
Wednesday 31 July	: Imperial Ballroom, NELSON
Friday 2 August	: Grafton Ballroom, LIVERPOOL
Saturday 3 August	: Cavern Club, LIVERPOOL
Sunday 4 August	: Queens, BLACKPOOL
Monday 5 August	: Urmston Show, URMSTON
Tuesday 6 August	: Springfield Hall, JERSEY
Wednesday 7 August	: Springfield Hall, JERSEY
Thursday 8 August	: Springfield Hall, JERSEY
Friday 9 August	: Springfield Hall, JERSEY
Saturday 10 August	: Springfield Hall, JERSEY
Sunday 11 August	: Queens, BLACKPOOL
Monday 12 August to Saturday 17 August	: Week at Odeon, LLANDUDNO
Sunday 18 August	: Filming 'BIG NIGHT OUT' (ABC TV, MANCHESTER) for for screening on Saturday 24 August
Monday 19 August to Saturday 24 August	: Week at Gaumont, BOURNEMOUTH
Sunday 25 August	: Queens, BLACKPOOL
Monday 26 August to Saturday 31 August	: Week at Odeon, SOUTHPORT
Sunday 1 September	: Regal, YARMOUTH

With Compliments from

Tony Barrow

Press & Public Relations Officer

Nems Enterprises Ltd.
Service House (1st Floor),
13 Monmouth Street,
LONDON, W.C.2.

Telephone: COVent Garden 2332

And I Love Her
并且我爱她

作 者 WRITERS	保罗·麦卡特尼和约翰·列侬 Paul McCartney and John Lennon
艺术家 ARTIST	披头士乐队 The Beatles
录 音 RECORDED	伦敦阿比路录音棚 Abbey Road Studios, London
发 行 RELEASED	《辛劳一日的夜》，1964 年 *A Hard Day's Night*, 1964

I give her all my love
That's all I do
And if you saw my love
You'd love her too
I love her

She gives me everything
And tenderly
The kiss my lover brings
She brings to me
And I love her

A love like ours
Could never die
As long as I
Have you near me

Bright are the stars that shine
Dark is the sky
I know this love of mine
Will never die
And I love her

抛开《红楼春怨》[1]中的温波尔街，说说温波尔街的阿舍家。准确地说是 57 号。一提到伦敦，许多人或许就会想到这个地方。它地处马里波恩村，有点像《欢乐满人间》（*Mary Poppins*）中的场景——爱德华时代的联排别墅，有着相当丰富的文学背景：伊丽莎白·巴瑞特在那里遇到了罗伯特·勃朗宁[2]；弗吉尼亚·伍尔夫把那里描绘为"最有威严的伦敦街道"；《卖花女》[3]中的亨利·希金斯据说就住在那里。也正是在我女朋友简·阿舍的家里，我写了这首歌。

披头士乐队真正步上正轨时，大约在 1963 年，我们从利物浦搬到伦敦。部分原因是我们的音乐"业务"在这里，但它同时也是一个充满冒险的新世界。这座城市仍然遍布战争时期的轰炸遗迹，正在进行大规模重建。当时我住在温波尔街，在建的邮政局大楼离阿舍家大约十分钟路程。有一段时间，那是城里最高的建筑，我可以透过阁楼卧室的窗户看见它的崛起。伦敦有一种真正的复兴感，并且任何事情都会发生；这是一个令人兴奋的地方。

我和简住在一起的部分原因是我不喜欢布莱恩·爱泼斯坦为我们在梅费尔安排的地方。他温文尔雅、品位高雅，但那个地方没有灵魂，即使我出身贫寒——特别是与奢华的梅费尔区相比——可我们家有灵魂，我叔叔和姨妈家都有灵魂。那是一套简陋的公寓，没什么家具。我当时才二十一岁，从没想过买些画挂在墙上；我只是因为墙上什么都没有而生气。

简和我第一次见面是在 1963 年春天，当时，她来到皇家阿尔伯特音乐厅为《广播时报》（*Radio Times*）采访披头士。我记得，我们都被她的红发惊艳了，因为我们之前只在黑白照片上见过她。不久后，我和她开始约会，到那年年底，阿舍夫妇想必是听到我抱怨梅费尔，向我提出了邀请："那么，你想住在这儿吗？"这一举动有着悠久的传统——为饥饿的艺术家提供一间阁楼房间。于是，我在楼上有了一个小房间，就在简

上图：简·阿舍在家中，伦敦温波尔街，1963 年。

下图：从温波尔街望见的英国电信塔大楼（之前的邮政局大楼），由保罗抓拍，伦敦，1964 年。

1　《红楼春怨》（*The Barretts of Wimpole Street*），1934 年上映的美国电影，片名又译《温波尔街的巴雷特一家》。

2　英国女诗人伊丽莎白·巴瑞特（Elizabeth Barrett，1806—1861）与诗人罗伯特·勃朗宁（Robert Browning，1812—1889）在见面前通过诗歌神交已久，他们的相遇及相爱是世界文学史上的爱情佳话之一。

3　《卖花女》（*Pygmalion*），英国电影，由安东尼·阿斯奎斯和莱斯利·霍华德导演，1938 年上映。亨利·希金斯是片中男主角的名字。

的哥哥彼得的房间旁边。这个时候简大约十七八岁，彼得稍大一些，大约十九岁或是二十岁。虽然严格来说我只是房客，但我经常和他们一家一起吃饭，而且我记得一切都非常愉快。

住在那里让我大开眼界，因为除了在电视上，我从没见过这个阶层的人。我不认识像那样的人。布莱恩·爱泼斯坦是有点上流阶层，但不是这种上流阶层；某种意义上，这是一个娱乐圈的家庭。简的母亲玛格丽特带她去试镜，简也拍过一些广告什么的。〔《别把你女儿推上舞台，沃辛顿太太》（Don't Put Your Daughter on the Stage, Mrs. Worthington），一首诺埃尔·考沃德[1]的老歌。〕因为简的成功——她从 1950 年代就开始演戏和拍电影了——我想彼得和妹妹克莱尔可能也去试镜了。

所以，这个家庭对艺术、文化和社会都了如指掌，而我从来不认识什么了解试镜，或者有经纪人的人。住在那个房子里真是太好了：大量书籍、墙上挂着艺术品、许多有趣的对话，而且玛格丽特是位音乐老师。这至少是个家，自从我从利物浦来到这里，自从我妈妈六七年前去世后，我始终怀念这种氛围。

对八卦专栏来说，简和我就是他们眼中的"新闻"。有一天晚上，我们在一家剧院（我喜欢文学和戏剧，当然，作为一名演员，她也喜欢，这也许可以很好地解释为什么我一开始会被她吸引），幕间休息时，灯光亮了起来。我们决定不去吧台了，所以就坐在那里。尽管已经开过一些大型演唱会，但我真的不习惯名声带来的个人负担，所以我们只是在座位上聊天。突然有十个狗仔记者蹦蹦跳跳地过来，那些相机咔嚓、咔嚓、咔嚓，像《甜蜜的生活》（La Dolce Vita）里一样；然后，就在一瞬间，他们又都蹦蹦跳跳地离开了。他们就像启斯东警察[2]。但是，天哪，我们被惊呆了。剧院可能向他们通风报信，想为这出戏做点宣传。

但正是因为简是我的女朋友，我想在那里告诉她我爱她，这就是这首歌最初的灵感来源；这就是它的内容。在这么多年之后再听它，我确实觉得，这是一段漂亮的旋律。它从升 F 小调开始，没有跟随 E 大调的根音和弦，然后慢慢地转回去。我写完后，几乎立刻感到自豪，我想："这是一个好东西。"

它真的触动了我，所以我想，它可能也会触动其他人。我把它带到了录音棚，乐队的制作人乔治·马丁听到了它。我们准备录这首歌时，马丁说："我想这首歌最好有一个前奏。"我发誓，就在那时那刻，乔治·哈里森说："这个怎么样？"然后他弹了前奏的连复段，很有吸引力；没有它，这首歌什么都不是。我们非常迅速地工作，并且想法自发地出现。

另一件值得回忆的事情是，乔治·马丁受到启发，在歌曲独奏中加入了和弦转调，他知道这个变调在音乐性上会非常令人满意；我们把和弦进行改成从 G 小调开始，而不是升 F 小调——所以，升高了半度。我想，马丁受过的古典音乐教育告诉他，这将是一个非常有趣的改变。而且确实是这样。类似这样的帮助使得披头士的作品比其他

1　诺埃尔·考沃德（Noël Coward，1899—1973），英国演员、歌手、导演。
2　启斯东是无声电影时代美国一家电影制作公司，以制作滑稽喜剧为主。在启斯东公司的镜头里，警察往往是被嘲笑的对象。"启斯东警察"（Keystone Cops）后来成为美国社会生活中"愚蠢、无能"的代名词。

上图：在《一夜狂欢》电影中所穿的夹克，1964 年。

右图：和简·阿舍在剧院。

歌曲作者的作品更好。就这首歌而言，两位乔治——乔治·哈里森的前奏和乔治·马丁在独奏中编排的变调——赋予它更多音乐性的能量。我们曾对人们说："我们比一般熊[1]更具音乐性。"然后，当然，这首歌现在是 F 大调，或者也可以说是 D 小调——最终以明亮的 D 和弦收尾，一个可爱的、令人愉快的决定。所以，我非常自豪。当时，为简写了这首歌，能录制这首歌，让我心满意足。

许多年之后，我们已经在圣约翰森林别墅居住很久，我去温波尔街看医生时遇见了她。我从马里波恩走到街上，经过那栋房子，想，"哇，那里有美好的回忆"，然后我沿着街道走远，到了医生那里，刚刚按下铃，突然感觉到身后有人。我转过身来，那是简。我说："天哪，我刚刚正是在想你和那个房子。"

那是我最后一次见到她，但记忆不会消逝。

1　一般熊（the average bear），源自动画片《瑜伽熊》中瑜伽熊的口头禅"我比一般熊更聪明"。

Another Day
又一天

作　者　WRITERS	保罗·麦卡特尼和琳达·麦卡特尼　Paul McCartney and Linda McCartney	
艺术家　ARTIST	保罗·麦卡特尼　Paul McCartney	
录　音　RECORDED	纽约 CBS 录音棚　CBS Studios, New York	
发　行　RELEASED	单曲，1971 年　Single, 1971	

Every day she takes a morning bath she
　　wets her hair
Wraps a towel around her as she's
　　heading for the bedroom chair
It's just another day

Slipping into stockings, stepping into shoes
Dipping in the pocket of her raincoat
It's just another day

At the office where the papers grow she
　　takes a break
Drinks another coffee and she finds it
　　hard to stay awake
It's just another day

It's just another day
It's just another day

So sad, so sad
Sometimes she feels so sad
Alone in apartment she'd dwell
Till the man of her dreams comes
　　to break the spell
Ah stay, don't stand her up
And he comes and he stays but he
　　leaves the next day
So sad
Sometimes she feels so sad

As she posts another letter to The Sound of Five
People gather round her and she finds it
　　hard to stay alive
It's just another day

It's just another day
It's just another day

So sad, so sad
Sometimes she feels so sad
Alone in apartment she'd dwell
Till the man of her dreams comes
　　to break the spell
Ah stay, don't stand her up
And he comes and he stays but he
　　leaves the next day
So sad
Sometimes she feels so sad

Every day she takes a morning bath she
　　wets her hair
Wraps a towel around her as she's
　　heading for the bedroom chair
It's just another day

Slipping into stockings, stepping into shoes
Dipping in the pocket of her raincoat
It's just another day

It's just another day
It's just another day

想象一下《埃莉诺·里格比》遇见希区柯克的《后窗》。因为，尽管我很不愿意承认，这首歌确实有偷窥的因素。像许多作者一样，我确实有点喜欢窥视；如果有一扇亮着的窗户，里面有人，我会看着他们。我承认这不太好，但这是非常自然的事情。

或许有些奇怪吧，我对这个主题感兴趣，可能是因为我有一张辨识度很高的脸，我自己也经常被别人盯着看，这种情况在我坐地铁时经常发生（有机会的话，我通常选择坐地铁）。你不觉得人们在看你，但过了一会儿，你意识到他们确实在盯着你看。当然，我也在看着他们。所以我对两方面都有体验。

礼貌起见，或说出于不成文的规则，你对此不发表意见。但你确实能识别出不同的性格类型。有些人会直接过来对你说："嘿，你好吗，哥们儿？"你会击个掌什么的。还有一些人根本不说话。我交谈的对象是那些不说什么的人。比如，我在健身房的垫子上，周围有很多人，有个家伙拿着杠铃锻炼，他的锻炼吸引了我。我说："哦，这太神奇了。"于是我们开始交谈。他说："我记得你有几匹马。"然后他开始谈论马。这种交谈可能涉及任何东西，甚至可能是"雨衣的构成"什么的。听到这些故事总是很有趣，它们有时会以迂回的方式成为歌词。

人们确实会注意到我，我也意识到了这一点，而这条不成文的规则意味着，你们不会谈论任何显而易见的事情，而且当然不会拍照或者要求签名。如果他们这样做，我通常会告诉他们，我正在享受一段私人时间，几乎每个人都能明白言下之意。

我提到了《埃莉诺·里格比》。这两首歌拥有相同的主题——试图捕捉角色的日常生活；不过《又一天》的语言更正式，没有那么印象派。埃莉诺·里格比"生活在梦中"，这表现在"Wearing the face that she keeps in a jar by the door"[1] 这样的歌词里；而这首歌的主人公在办公室工作，歌词几乎像一张清单，仿佛是她一天的行程表。我在这首歌中窥视的人，正是遇见我之前独自在纽约生活的琳达；不过，《五音》（*The Sound of Five*）是一个英国的广播节目，人们会给节目组写信倾诉自己的问题。这首歌的故事横跨大洋。但我更愿意认为我是歌中她到来的"梦中人"。所以，我和菲尔·雷蒙（Phil Ramone）在纽约录制这首歌再合适不过了。菲尔是一位伟大的制作人，他制作了很多令我钦佩的唱片。他曾经与保罗·西蒙[2]和比利·乔尔合作。

那是在披头士解散后，我正试图用新的表演曲目确立自己单飞艺术家的身份。如果我希望表演曲目不输给披头士，那我必须要有金曲。每两首歌中，就要有一首成为金曲。因此，这首歌是一次慎重的、有意创作金曲的尝试，而菲尔在其中助益良多。我们知道，一首金曲将巩固我们的关系，并引导我们继续合作〔后来我们确实一起做了专辑《拉姆》（*RAM*）〕，也能够证明我们俩都很不错——作为制作人的他和作为唱作人的我。乐队解散后，发行我的第一首个人作品对我来说是个重大时刻，令人兴奋，尽管有一丝悲伤。同时，我觉得我需要证明自己，而这种挑战永远让人激动。《又一天》

1　"戴起她放在门口罐子里的面具"，出自《埃莉诺·里格比》（Eleanor Rigby）。
2　保罗·西蒙（Paul Simon，1941— ），美国民谣／流行歌手。

在英国单曲榜上排名第二，在美国公告牌百强单曲榜上位列第五。所以，它干得确实不错。

当然，在这个时间段，约翰和我之间仍然有些矛盾，这有时会渗入我们的创作中。约翰在他自己的一首歌《你如何入睡？》（How Do You Sleep?）中嘲笑了这首歌。

右图：伦敦地铁贝克鲁线，1969 年。

> 你所做的事情只是昨天
> 自从你离开你就成了另一天[1]

这是他的刻薄的表现之一。

1　原句为 "The only thing you done was yesterday / And since you've gone you're just another day"。

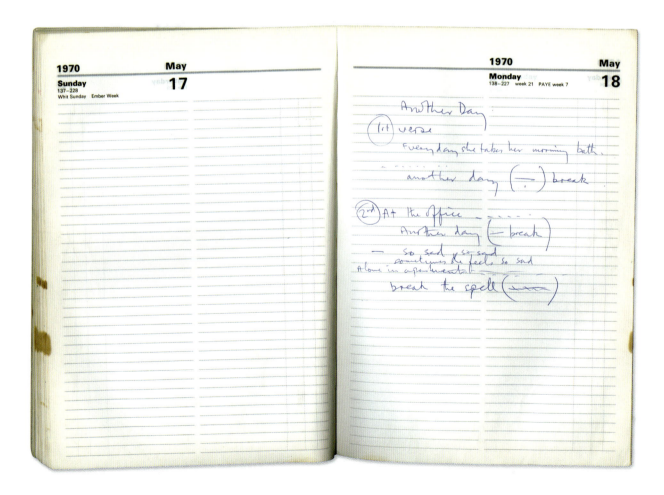

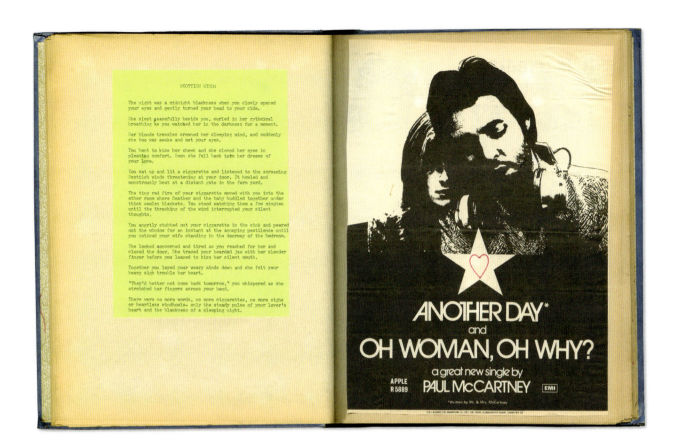

上图：麦卡特尼家庭剪贴簿，
1970 年代早期。

左图：伦敦摄政公园，1968 年。

礼貌起见，或说出于不成文的规则，你对此不发表意见。
但你确实能识别出不同的性格类型。
有些人会直接过来对你说："嘿，你好吗，哥们儿?"
你会击个掌什么的。
还有一些人根本不说话。
我交谈的对象是那些不说什么的人。

Arrow Through Me
穿过我的箭

作 者 WRITER   保罗·麦卡特尼 Paul McCartney

艺术家 ARTIST   羽翼乐队 Wings

录 音 RECORDED 伦敦阿比路录音棚、苏格兰拉那坎精神录音棚 Abbey Road Studios, London and Spirit of Ranachan Studio, Scotland

发 行 RELEASED 《回到蛋中》，1979 年 *Back to the Egg*, 1979

          美国单曲，1979 年 US single, 1979

Ooh baby, you couldn't have done
A worse thing to me
If you'd have taken an arrow
And run it right through me

Ooh baby, a bird in the hand
Is worth two flying
But when it came to love
I knew you'd be lying

It could have been a finer fling
Would have been a major attraction
With no other thing
Offering a note of distraction
Come on, get up
Get under way
And bring your love

Ooh baby, you wouldn't have found
A more down hero
If you'd have started at nothing
And counted to zero

Ooh baby, you couldn't have done
A worse thing to me
If you'd have taken an arrow
And run it right through me

It could have been a finer fling
Flying in a righter direction
With no other thing
Featuring but love and affection
Come on, get up
Get under way
And bring your love

Ooh baby, you wouldn't have found
A more down hero
If you'd have started at nothing
And counted to zero

1971 年组建的羽翼乐队，从很多方面来说是一个试验，看看在披头士之后能否再走乐队生涯，看看乐队的成功能否延续。羽翼也是一个答案。我问自己："我现在就要结束吗？"披头士乐队那么神奇且包罗万象，那么成功，现在，我是否应该停下来找些其他的事情做？但我想："不。我那么热爱音乐，所以无论其他事情是什么，总归都将是音乐。"实际上，有一天晚上，我在电视上看见约翰尼·卡什[1]，他有一支乐队，而在我的认知里，他从来没有过乐队。我觉得"那看起来挺有意思"，而约翰尼看上去也很享受。那时我和琳达在一起：我们在一起已经差不多三年了，女儿玛丽一岁出头，我们是一个比较新的家庭。我对她说："你想过组一支乐队吗？"对我们来说，这就好像一次有趣的全新冒险。然后她说："好啊。"

乐队的名字，羽翼，源于彼时另一个女儿斯特拉（Stella McCartney）的出生。分娩过程很艰难，斯特拉不得不进入恒温箱接受重症监护。我待在医院里，在她们恢复期间，就睡在琳达病房隔壁房间的一张行军床上。在那种情形之下，你的大脑会超负荷运转。我想着天使，因为我们刚刚渡过这次家庭危机，然后一位长着巨大羽翼的天使的幻象出现在我眼前。羽翼真的令我着迷。但乐队名只会是单纯的"羽翼"，而不像披头士那样以单词"The"特指。[2]

在披头士之后，我的问题是，谁将会和他们一样出色？我想，"在乐队一途，披头士已经做到极致，但我们可以成为另一种东西。"我知道，如果要继续这个计划，我就要坚持到底。而在披头士的初创阶段，在斯特劳德的礼堂里，有人向我们扔硬币时，作为披头士的一员，我有了足够的勇气。

我不得不再次承受同样的压力。最难的是和琳达一起做，她完全是个门外汉，但

上图：早期设计的羽翼乐队标志。于 1972 年的羽翼乐队欧洲巡演上第一次使用。

1　　约翰尼·卡什（Johnny Cash，1932—2003），美国乡村乐创作歌手，被认为是美国音乐史上最具影响力的音乐家之一。
2　　指羽翼乐队名为 Wings，披头士乐队名为 The Beatles。

是我想："好吧，乔治加入乐队时，他也是个门外汉，我也一样，约翰也是，林戈也是一样。"我向她演示了一点键盘技巧，然后她自己学习并上了几节课。事实证明，虽然琳达成了键盘手，但她的强项不一定是键盘。她似乎更长于精神鼓励。她是一位很好的啦啦队长，她会鼓舞观众，让观众拍手并一起合唱。

在那个年代，乐队中的女性不是很多，所以她可以说是女性乐手的先驱。回过头听这些录音，你会听出她是个很棒的歌手，特别是和声方面。她会一边拍手，一边唱和声。这可不是轻易能做到的——这就是人们会使用磁带和背景音轨的原因。组建一支新乐队总是有很多乐趣，但是也有很多艰难的工作要做；你不得不建构自己。追随披头士之路，对我来说最困难的事情之一是不辜负那些期望。这对她来说更加困难。

我从 1971 年前后开始为羽翼乐队写歌，当时我们刚成立，而我也试着避开披头士的风格。我有很多方向可以走，那是我不会和披头士一起走的方向，比如引入我和琳达在牙买加接触的雷鬼乐元素。我想做一些疯狂的东西，而羽翼乐队也让我有了更多的自由度。《穿过我的箭》是一首情歌，其中提到丘比特的箭，但这是一支恶毒的箭。灵感或许源于我曾经看过一幅丘比特的插图，我想："丘比特拉开了弓，但我要换掉这支箭。它不是爱之箭，它将是相反的东西。"

这首歌里的人物受到了伤害。他受到了欺骗。而这本可以成为一段很好的关系，本可以很美好。就目前看来，你不会"found a more down hero"（找到一个更沮丧的英雄），因为在那个时候，没人比我更沮丧。所以，带着你的爱，把它聚合在一起。

我一直喜欢这首歌。里面有一个好听的管乐连复段，很有节奏感。相比写一篇完美而"准确"的歌词，有时候你写得更像是一种感觉。有时候，感觉比歌词更重要。《穿过我的箭》更多关乎感觉，与律动。

在那个年代，乐队中的女性不是很多，
所以她可以说是女性乐手的先驱。
回过头听这些录音，
你会听出她是个很棒的歌手，特别是和声方面。

ARROW THROUGH ME

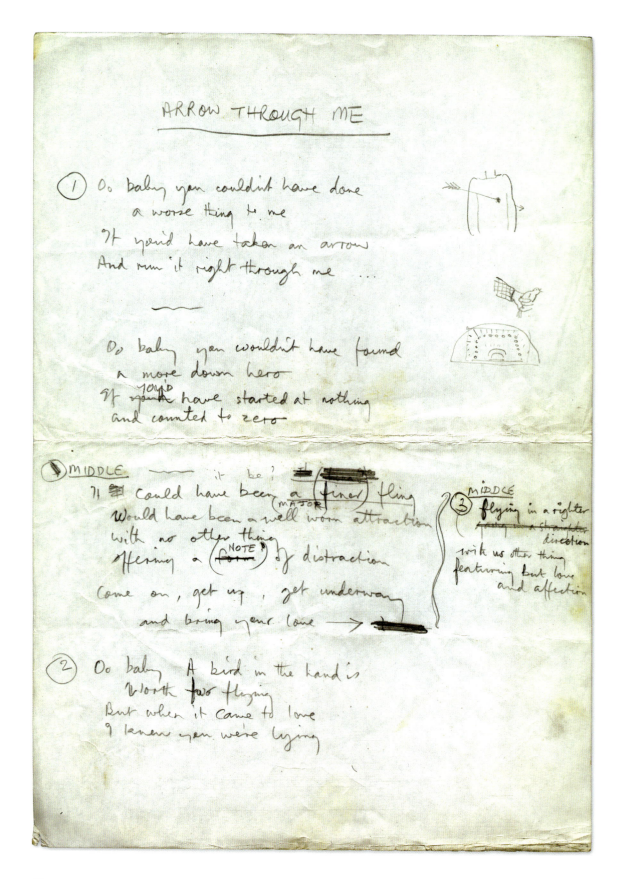

① Oo baby you couldn't have done
a worse thing to me
If you'd have taken an arrow
And run it right through me ...

Oo baby you wouldn't have found
a more down hero
If you'd have started at nothing
and counted to zero

①MIDDLE ~~~~ it be?
It could have been a (finer) fling
(MAJOR)
Would have been a well worn attraction
with no other thing
offering a (NOTE) of distraction

Come on, get up, get underway
and bring your love →

③ MIDDLE
flying in a righter
a straighter
direction
with no other thing
featuring but love
and affection

② Oo baby A bird in the hand is
Worth two flying
But when it came to love
I knew you were lying

和玛丽、斯特拉及琳达在羽翼乐
队欧洲巡演的大巴顶层。瑞典，
1972 年。

Average Person
普通的人

作　者 WRITER	保罗·麦卡特尼	Paul McCartney
艺术家 ARTIST	保罗·麦卡特尼	Paul McCartney
录　音 RECORDED	蒙特塞拉特岛 AIR 录音棚、伦敦 AIR 录音棚　AIR Montserrat and AIR Studios, London
发　行 RELEASED	《和平管乐》，1983 年　*Pipes of Peace*, 1983

Look at the Average Person
Speak to the man in the street
Can you imagine the first one you'd meet?

Well I'm talking to a former engine driver
Trying to find out what he used to do
Tells me that he always kept his engine
Spit and polished up as good as new
But he said his only great ambition
Was to work with lions in a zoo
Oh to work with lions in a zoo

Yes dear, you heard right
Told me his ambition was to work with
  lions every night

Look at the Average Person
Speak to the man on the beat
Can you imagine the first one you'd meet?

Well I met a woman working as a waitress
I asked exactly what it was she did
Said she worked the summer crowd at seasides
Wintertime she ran away and hid
Once she had a Hollywood audition
But the part was given to a kid
Yes the part was given to a kid

Yes sir, you heard right
Hollywood ambition made a starlet
  grow up overnight

Well I bumped into a man who'd been a boxer
Asked him what had been his greatest night
He looked into the corners of his memory
Searching for a picture of the fight
But he said he always had a feeling
That he lacked a little extra height
Could have used a little extra height

Yes mate, you heard right
He always had a feeling that he might have
  lacked a little height

Look at the Average Person
Speak to the man in the queue
Can you imagine the first one is you?

Look at the Average Person

　　《明星猜猜看》(*What's My Line?*)是一个综艺节目,在这个节目中,一个四人小组必须通过一系列"是与不是"的问题猜出神秘嘉宾的职业。节目特别好玩,并且很流行。英国版开播于1950年代早期,我们经常在家里播放这个节目,所以它长久地留在我的记忆中,并且,我得说,它是这首歌核心的一部分。

　　你走过街道,所有人看上去都很普通,但他们中的一位也许是牧师,而另一位也许是罪犯、水管工或面包师。我感兴趣的是,人们都有隐藏的一面及野心。我想,创作者会被这样的人吸引。比起纯粹辉煌的人,辉煌但身具小小的致命弱点的人无疑更有趣。这些人在某种程度上都有污点,都想成为其他人。

　　我想我对这类故事的兴趣,部分源自成长于紧密团结的工人阶级社区的背景。我们总是和家人在一起,而且邻居总是互相帮助。爸爸经常让我和弟弟迈克挨家挨户地敲门,为斯皮克园艺协会的新成员拉票,他是那个协会的秘书。咚咚咚,"你愿意加入园艺俱乐部吗?""滚开。"于是,我们必须得知道,谁家的门可以敲,而谁家要避开。你会听到他们的生活,他们的烦恼;记得吗,那是战后时期,我们遭遇了轰炸,实行定量配给制度。而那让你意识到,我们所有人都有自己的故事、自己的焦虑。《普通的人》多少有点辛酸,会引起人们的共鸣。

　　这也让故事变得更加有趣。我知道这个例子可能算不上"普通的人",但是,如果哈姆雷特的父亲是自然死亡,而他刚刚继承王位,我们还会对他感兴趣吗?也许不会。正因为他怀疑父亲被谋杀,从而陷入痛苦的境地,所以这出戏才如此丰满。正是他的内心世界和心理挣扎,使他成为如此引人注目的角色。

　　这首歌的另一个灵感来自我小时候在电视上看到的一个无聊的老式歌舞杂耍表演[1]节目,关于一个窗户清洁工的身份。我的爸爸生活在杂耍剧院的时代,全家都有点乐

上图:披头士与玛琳·黛德丽,伦敦,1963年。

1　歌舞杂耍表演(music hall),英国1850年代至1960年代流行的一种娱乐形式,包括音乐、舞蹈和喜剧演出,因往往在杂耍剧院上演而得名。

在其中；我们会看节目，并且在钢琴上弹唱所有那些歌。我的米妮阿姨和金阿姨经常唱一首叫作《面包和蝴蝶》（Bread and Butterflies）的杂耍表演老歌。我爸爸后来在棉花交易所工作，不过他在 1920 年代时是一名灯光师，在利物浦一个叫皇家剧院的地方操作老式的舞台灯光。所以，我想，或许很多音乐就是这样悄悄渗入我们的记忆。每晚，我爸爸都会听到 1920 年代和 1930 年代的杂耍剧院歌曲，所有那些艺术家都在巡演，他们会来利物浦的剧院演出，然后去曼彻斯特的音乐厅，诸如此类。爸爸说了一个关于他如何在灯光下喷洒石灰的故事——在杂耍剧院里，那相当于今天聚光灯的作用。

所以，因为我的爸爸，那些老派的杂耍剧院音乐典故有时会出现在我的作品中。我知道诺埃尔·考沃德的音乐也是因为我的爸爸，诺埃尔显然非常有名。他的歌曲很合我的创作口味。有一次，他和披头士都在罗马，我们的经纪人布莱恩·爱泼斯坦（他是同性恋，并且非常善于用自己的方式交际）认识一些诺埃尔身边的人。我们住在同一家酒店，但我们是那种摇滚乐孩子，所以，被问及是否想去见他时，其他人都有点犹豫，但是我说："我要去。"通常，我是那个说"不，我们不能"的人，但这一次，我的反应是："我们不能怠慢他，他是诺埃尔·考沃德。"

于是，我和布莱恩下楼到他的酒店房间去见他，他说："你好，亲爱的孩子。"他非常诺埃尔·考沃德。他的姿态，他的举止——完全是你想象中他该有的样子。

不过有时候，和这种名人见面也会有点古怪。我们和玛琳·黛德丽[1]的会面就很古怪，她是个巨星。我们在威尔士王子剧院同场表演——1963 年的皇家汇演（Royal Variety Performance），在那场演出中，约翰开了一个关于时髦人士晃动他们珠宝的玩笑。我记得她唱了《莉莉·玛琳》（Lilli Marleen）和《花儿都到哪里去了？》（Where Have All the Flowers Gone?）。这正是披头士狂热变得真正疯狂的时候，有人从她的化妆间出来邀请我们去问声好："你们愿意见见黛德丽小姐吗？"于是我们回答："噢，好啊！"听说她一直以自己的双腿为傲，但那会儿她已经老了，也许六十多了，而我们都正是二十出头的年纪，所以那就好像是看着你的阿姨或者祖母的腿。我不太确定我们想这么做。但一进她的房间，我们中的一个说："噢该死的，你的腿多美啊！"我想，总得有人这么说，但是这一切有点尴尬。

在黛德丽的《莉莉·玛琳》这样的歌中，你可以感受到一对相爱的恋人被战争分开时的挣扎。渴望和心碎让这首歌如此凄美。我想，正是这样的悲怆感吸引了我，并让人们与埃莉诺·里格比或麦肯齐神父这样的角色产生了共鸣。所以那也是为什么，在《普通的人》里，我们遇见了梦想在动物园里和狮子一起工作的前汽车司机，在好莱坞试镜的女招待，总是觉得自己身高不够的拳击手。有着普通烦恼的普通的人。

1　玛琳·黛德丽（Marlene Dietrich，1901—1992），德裔美籍演员、歌手。

THE AVERAGE PERSON

Look at the average person
Speak to the man in the (street)
on the site (beat)
Can you imagine the first one
you'd meet –

ENGINE DRIVER

(1) Talking to a former engine driver
Trying to find out what he used to do . . .
Tells me that he always kept his engine
(spanking)
Spit and polished (up as) good as new
But he said his only great ambition
LIONS
was to work with (pythons) in a zoo
LIONS
oh to work with pythons in a zoo

yes dear – you heard right
He told me his ambition was to
every night
work with pythons in a zoo once a night.

Look at the average person
Speak to the man in the street
You can imagine the first one you'd meet

(2) WAITRESS.

Met a woman working as a waitress
Asked ~~her just~~ exactly what it was she did
Said she ~~(served)~~ (worked) the summer crowd at seaside's
Wintertime she ran away and hid
~~S~~ Once she had a Hollywood ~~audition~~ (ambition)'
But the part was given to a kid,
Yeah the part was given to a kid.

Yes sir, you heard right
Hollywood ambition made a starlet
grow up overnight

_____

(HORUS
(3) _____ BOXER.

Bumped into a man who'd been a boxer
Asked him what ~~his greatest night~~ (had been his greatest night)

(he) looked into the corners of his memory
Searching ~~for the old familiar cause~~ (for the) BEFORE 1 OF ~~dreams~~ TITE – (fight)
~~(long forgotten)~~
~~But he had a little known ambition~~
~~he always had a small ambition~~
~~just to gain a little extra height~~
~~Yes, indeed, you heard right~~
THEN ~~But~~ he says he always had a feeling
That he ~~might~~ MIGHT have lacked a little height
~~thought he might have lacked a little height~~
(could have used a little ~~extra~~ height)

Yes mate, you heard right

Always had a feeling that he
~~might~~ have lacked a little height —
~~Yes~~ — ~~sir~~ — — —
Told me his ambition

was to never have another fight.

B

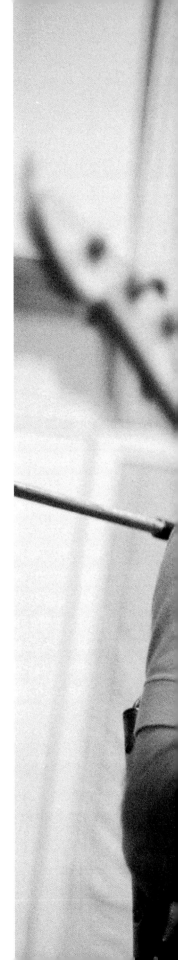

Back in the U.S.S.R.

回到苏联

作　者	WRITERS	保罗·麦卡特尼和约翰·列侬　Paul McCartney and John Lennon
艺术家	ARTIST	披头士乐队　The Beatles
录　音	RECORDED	伦敦阿比路录音棚　Abbey Road Studios, London
发　行	RELEASED	《披头士》，1968 年　*The Beatles*, 1968

Flew in from Miami Beach BOAC
Didn't get to bed last night
On the way the paper bag was on my knee
Man I had a dreadful flight

I'm back in the U.S.S.R.
You don't know how lucky you are, boy
Back in the U.S.S.R.

Been away so long I hardly knew the place
Gee it's good to be back home
Leave it till tomorrow to unpack my case
Honey disconnect the phone

I'm back in the U.S.S.R.
You don't know how lucky you are, boy
Back in the U.S.
Back in the U.S.
Back in the U.S.S.R.

Well the Ukraine girls really knock me out
They leave the West behind
And Moscow girls make me sing and shout
That Georgia's always on my mind

Oh show me round your snow-peaked
　　mountains way down south
Take me to your daddy's farm
Let me hear your balalaikas ringing out
Come and keep your comrade warm

I'm back in the U.S.S.R.
You don't know how lucky you are, boy
Back in the U.S.S.R.

　　显而易见，1966 年，沙滩男孩发行的《宠物之声》（Pet Sounds）专辑，向我们展开了严肃的竞争。在那之前，他们一直是一支相当不错的冲浪乐队，有一些很棒的作品，在嘟喔普音乐[1]的传统中进行了创新。我们在他们的作品中偷取过一些小灵感，和声就是一个很好的例子。当然，他们也从我们这里偷了一些。每个人都从其他人那里获取一些灵感。对整个行业来说，这就是一个循环。

　　无论如何，这首歌的苏联"主人公"[2]毫无疑问受到了沙滩男孩，以及查克·贝里的歌曲《回到美国》（Back in the U.S.A）的影响。他受到沙滩男孩的影响十分合乎情理，毕竟，他从迈阿密搭乘飞机，一直在听《加州女孩》[3]——所以我们在桥段提及"Ukraine girls really knock me out"（乌克兰女孩真的让我神魂颠倒），背景中有一段明目张胆模仿沙滩男孩的合唱。

　　还有一些对雷·查尔斯曲目《佐治亚在我心中》（Georgia on My Mind）的幽默引用，但指的是苏联时期的格鲁吉亚，而不是美国的佐治亚州。这首歌的有趣之处是，这个角色在某种程度上更喜欢苏联，而不是美国。进入苏联领土后，还要经历几个小时的飞行，在这一阶段，仿佛这首歌在自我创作。"Show me round your snow-peaked mountains way down south"（给我看看你往南延伸的雪峰山脉）这句歌词有一点顽皮的学生色彩，更别提"Come and keep your comrade warm"（来留下你同志般的温暖）了。

　　但苏联人说"你不知道你生活在苏联有多么幸运"这个想法，在某些方面被弱化了。比如"disconnect the phone"（挂断电话），电话窃听可能是许多人对苏联的第一印象；考虑到苏联当时的集体化制度，"your daddy's farm"（你爸爸的农场）也意味复杂，"爸爸"也许是指斯大林，或者彼时当权的勃列日涅夫。

　　披头士乐队在苏联被禁了，当然，这通常会让我们在那里更受欢迎。2003 年，我最终在红场唱响《回到苏联》，那是一个值得回味的时刻。

1　嘟喔普音乐（Doo-wop），流行于 1940 年代的一种音乐风格，由一人担任领唱，其他人以密集和声做伴唱。
2　"主人公"（protagonist）一词此处有双关含义，亦指"拥护者"。
3　《加州女孩》（California Girls），沙滩男孩乐队的一首歌曲，其中有句歌词为"And the Southern girls with the way they talk, they knock me out"。

上图："回到世界"巡演，莫斯科红场，
2003 年 5 月 24 日。

左图：保罗在歌词里提到的巴拉莱卡琴。

Flew in from Miami Beach B O A C
Didn't get to bed last night
On the way the paper bag was on my knee
Man I had a dreadful flight
I'm back in the U S S R
You don't know how lucky you are boy
Back in the U S S R .

Been away so long I hardly knew the place
Gee it's good to be back home.
Leave it till tomorrow to unpack my case
Honey disconnect the phone
I'm back in the U S S R ------

Well the Ukraine girls really knock me out
They leave the west behind
& Moscow girls make me sing & shout
that Georgia's always on my...... mind.

Show me round ~~the~~ your snow peaked mountains
                              way down South
Take me to your daddy's farm
Let me hear ^{see} your balalaika working out

Band on the Run

逃亡乐队

作 者	WRITERS	保罗·麦卡特尼和琳达·麦卡特尼　Paul McCartney and Linda McCartney
艺术家	ARTIST	保罗·麦卡特尼和羽翼乐队　Paul McCartney and Wings
录 音	RECORDED	拉各斯百代录音棚、伦敦 AIR 录音棚　EMI Studios, Lagos and AIR Studios, London
发 行	RELEASED	《逃亡乐队》，1973 年　*Band on the Run*, 1973
		单曲，1974 年　Single, 1974

Stuck inside these four walls
Sent inside forever
Never seeing no one nice again
Like you, mama, you, mama, you

If I ever get out of here
Thought of giving it all away
To a registered charity
All I need is a pint a day
If I ever get out of here
If we ever get out of here

Well the rain exploded with a mighty crash
As we fell into the sun
And the first one said to the second one there
I hope you're having fun

Band on the run
Band on the run
And the jailer man and Sailor Sam
Were searching everyone
For the band on the run
Band on the run
For the band on the run
Band on the run

Well the undertaker drew a heavy sigh
Seeing no one else had come
And a bell was ringing in the village square
For the rabbits on the run

Band on the run
Band on the run
And the jailer man and Sailor Sam
Were searching everyone
For the band on the run
Band on the run

The band on the run
The band on the run
The band on the run
The band on the run

Well the night was falling as the desert world
Began to settle down
In the town they're searching for us everywhere
But we never will be found

Band on the run
Band on the run
And the county judge who held a grudge
Will search for evermore
For the band on the run
The band on the run
Band on the run
The band on the run

　　这首歌标题中的"band"一词主要指逃离监狱的一群人，一帮亡命之徒。它的某些方面让我想起《虎豹小霸王》[1]。葬仪师敲了钟，因为他很生气没有多少顾客。水手山姆是玛丽·图特尔[2]创作的连环漫画《宝贝熊鲁伯特》中的角色，他不知怎么地，和这首歌很相称。

　　这首歌凑巧在尼日利亚拉各斯的百代录音棚录制。拉各斯听起来不错，充满异国情调。它和我想象得不太一样。我没有想象过霍乱、抢劫、准备不足的工作室，或者我的孩子因为赤身裸体而被禁止进入酒店游泳池之类的事情。你排除了所有糟糕的东西，记住了所有很酷的东西。

　　阿比奥拉酋长（Chief Abiola）："嗨，你好麦卡。"（他叫我麦卡。）"麦卡，为什么你没有四个老婆？"

　　"一个已经够麻烦了，酋长。"

　　重点是，这是一首叙述性的歌曲，关于自由的歌曲。那个时候，我们中的很多人从文明的束缚中解脱，那是关于摇滚乐最伟大的事情之一：它允许你打破规则。一条经常被打破的规则是，一段音乐必须非常复杂才能成为好音乐。

　　我不时提到这个，它也确实值得回味：披头士成立时，我们几乎不怎么懂音乐，只知道几个和弦；但我们在进步——披头士解散时，我们已经变成一台相当复杂的机器。而羽翼的情况是，我们去找学生组织问："我们能做场演出吗？"因为我们知道他们能提供一个演出厅，而且有观众群体。我们的门票卖五十便士。我们只有十一首歌，所以不得不重复其中的一些曲目。有些演出一定很糟糕，因为我们确实不知道自己在做什么。

上图：于拉各斯录制《逃亡乐队》期间，和费拉·库蒂[3]在一起，1973年。

1　《虎豹小霸王》（Butch Cassidy and the Sundance Kid），美国电影，由乔治·罗伊·希尔导演，1969年上映。
2　玛丽·图特尔（Mary Tourtel，1874—1948），英国艺术家，创作了在英国家喻户晓的《宝贝熊鲁伯特》（Rupert Bear）。
3　费拉·库蒂（Fela Kuti，1938—1997），尼日利亚音乐家，开启了非洲节拍音乐风格。

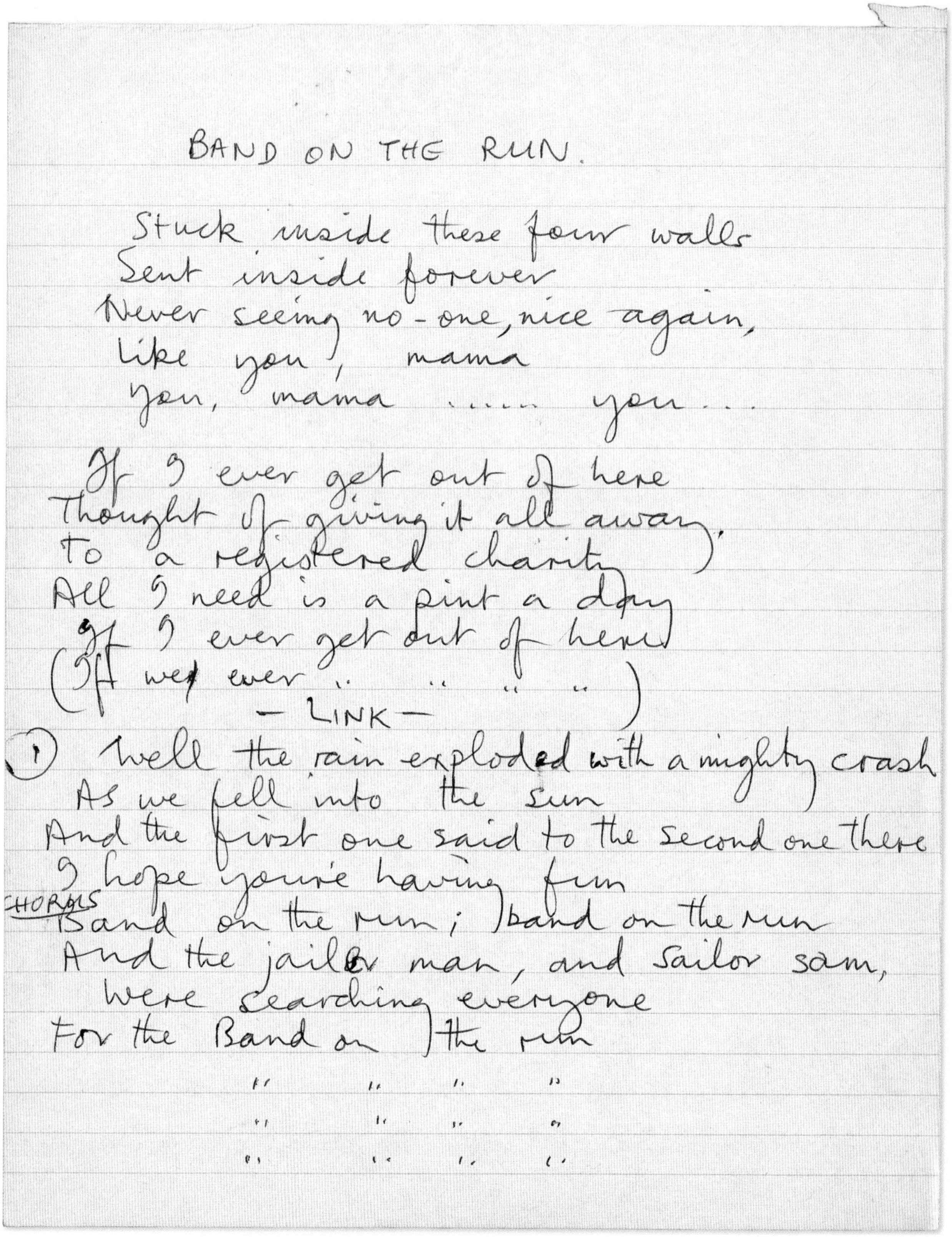

BAND ON THE RUN.

Stuck inside these four walls
Sent inside forever
Never seeing no-one, nice again,
Like you, mama
You, mama ...... you ...

If I ever get out of here
Thought of giving it all away,
To a registered charity)
All I need is a pint a day
If I ever get out of here
(If we ever .. .. " ")

— LINK —

① well the rain exploded with a mighty crash
As we fell into the sun
And the first one said to the second one there
I hope you're having fun

CHORUS
Band on the run;) band on the run
And the jailer man, and sailor sam,
Were searching everyone
For the Band on) the run
          "   "   "   "
          "   "   "   "
          "   "   "   "

40

② well, the undertaker drew a heavy sigh
Seeing noone else had come
And a bell was ringing in the village square
For the rabbits on the run,
CHORUS   Band on the run

    and the "jailer" man etc...

③   well the night was falling
As the desert world began to settle down
In the town they're searching for us everywhere
But we never will be found
CHORUS Band on the run
    "   "   "   "

And the county judge, who held a grudge
Will search forever more,
    For the   BAND ON THE RUN

41

Birthday
生 日

作　者　WRITERS　　保罗·麦卡特尼和约翰·列侬　Paul McCartney and John Lennon
艺术家　ARTIST　　　披头士乐队　The Beatles
录　音　RECORDED　伦敦阿比路录音棚　Abbey Road Studios, London
发　行　RELEASED　《披头士》，1968 年　*The Beatles*, 1968

You say it's your birthday
It's my birthday too, yeah
They say it's your birthday
We're gonna have a good time
I'm glad it's your birthday
Happy birthday to you

Yes we're goin' to a party, party
Yes we're goin' to a party, party
Yes we're goin' to a party, party

I would like you to dance
(Birthday) Take a cha-cha-cha-chance
(Birthday) I would like you to dance
(Birthday) Dance

You say it's your birthday
It's my birthday too, yeah
They say it's your birthday
We're gonna have a good time
I'm glad it's your birthday
Happy birthday to you

"MACH SCHAU[1]! MACH SCHAU!" 1960 年，披头士乐队第一次来到汉堡时，靠玉米片和牛奶过活，试图吸引更多歌迷，有人告诉我们要以德语大喊"看一看"。表演一直是披头士的重要组成部分，我也将继续做下去。我们试图把人们吸引到汉堡的英德拉俱乐部（Indra Club），但需要学习一些技巧来达成目的。比如说，我们经常唱一首叫《在街上跳舞》（Dance in the Street）的歌，以吸引人们进来。约翰不拿吉他，站在那里拍手，就像是"在街上跳舞"。一点小表演，不过确实能吸引人。

《生日》是那些为现场表演而写的歌曲之一，目的就是表演。有些歌曲，比如《佩珀军士》里面的歌词"We'd like to take you home with us"[2]，在演出结束时效果非常好。《生日》仍然很受观众欢迎，因为总会有人过生日。我的一些歌曲有着自己进入这个世界的方法。

有一天晚上，这首歌自阿比路来到这个世界。我们差不多住在二号录音棚，当时还有几个朋友在那里。我记得乔治·哈里森的妻子帕蒂·博伊德（Pattie Boyd）在场，我很确定埃里克·克莱普顿也在。录音棚里通常没有访客，不过这次有点特别，那天可能是某个人的生日。

我们决定当场编些东西。我们经常用一段连复段开始一次即兴，对我们来说，最精彩、最经典的连复段是小理查德的《露西尔》（Lucille），罗伊·奥比森以它的连复段改编成《漂亮女人》（Pretty Woman）。我们也这样处理了《生日》，全部都是很基本的连复段。

我重点关注的两句歌词是"would like you to dance / Take a cha-cha-cha-chance"（我想请你跳个舞 / 碰碰运运运气）。我记得那时另一支非常突出的乐队，谁人乐队的《我的时代》（My Generation）中有一句十分精彩，以我们常形容为结巴或口吃的方式处理"消逝"（fade away）这个词。但是，当你在英国电视直播上发出"f-f-f"这种声音时，它就是会引起人们的注意。我对那一句记忆犹新。这种"口吃"——我们姑且这么说吧——是《生日》里"cha-cha-cha"的灵感来源，就像大卫·鲍伊的《变化》（Change）中"cha-cha-cha"受到了《生日》的影响。作为一名歌曲作者，就是拿起接力棒，握一会儿，然后把它传下去。

---

1 德语，意为"看一看"。
2 "我们想带你一起回家"，出自《佩珀军士孤独之心俱乐部乐队》（Sgt. Pepper's Lonely Hearts Club Band）。

RIFF

THEY SAY ITS YOUR BIRTHDAY
WELL ITS MY BIRTHDAY TOO YEAH
THEY SAY ITS YOUR BIRTHDAY
WE'RE GOING TO HAVE A GOOD TIME
IM GLAD ITS YOUR BIRTHDAY
HAPPY BIRTHDAY TO YOU

DRUMS

E 8 - - - - - -

I WOULD LIKE YOU TO DANCE
TAKE A CHA CHA CHA CHANCE
I WOULD LIKE YOU TO DANCE

SOLO

STAGGERS

THEY SAY ITS YOUR BIRTHDAY
WELL ITS MY BIRTHDAY TOO YEAH
THEY SAY ITS YOUR BIRTHDAY
WERE GOING TO HAVE A GOOD TIME
IM GLAD ITS YOUR BIRTHDAY
HAPPY BIRTHDAY TO YOU.

上图：和斯图尔特·萨克利夫（Stuart Sutcliffe）、约翰·列侬、乔治·哈里森同台。汉堡前十俱乐部（Top Ten Club），1961年。

右图：披头士乐队，汉堡，1960年代初。

Blackbird

黑 鸟

作 者	WRITERS	保罗·麦卡特尼和约翰·列侬　Paul McCartney and John Lennon
艺术家	ARTIST	披头士乐队　The Beatles
录 音	RECORDED	伦敦阿比路录音棚　Abbey Road Studios, London
发 行	RELEASED	《披头士》，1968 年　*The Beatles*, 1968

Blackbird singing in the dead of night
Take these broken wings and learn to fly
All your life, you were only waiting
For this moment to arise

Blackbird singing in the dead of night
Take these sunken eyes and learn to see
All your life, you were only waiting
For this moment to be free

Blackbird fly
Blackbird fly
Into the light
Of a dark black night

Blackbird singing in the dead of night
Take these broken wings and learn to fly
All your life, you were only waiting
For this moment to arise
You were only waiting
For this moment to arise
You were only waiting
For this moment to arise

　　诗人阿德里安·米切尔（Adrian Mitchell）是我的一位好友，在他的帮助下，我写过一本名为《黑鸟歌唱》（*Blackbird Singing*）的小诗集，由鲍勃·威尔编辑。我当时正在做一些阅读活动来宣传那本书，我问阿德里安："你在朗诵时会做些什么？你只是读你的诗吗？"他回答："呃，如果你能想到任何关于诗的趣闻，都是很好的开场白。然后你就可以开始念诗了。"

　　《黑鸟》是我计划朗诵的作品之一，我恰好记得关于它的两个故事。一个与音乐有关，当歌词进行到"Blackbird singing in the dead of night"（黑鸟在深夜里歌唱）时，不多的吉他部分是这首歌非常重要的部分。这是乔治·哈里森和我小时候会弹的那种派对娱乐曲目，约翰·塞巴斯蒂安·巴赫的鲁特琴作品片段。指弹风格则是切特·阿特金斯[1]令我们钦慕之处，特别是在名叫《有轨电车》（Trambone）的作品中。不过雷莫四人组[2]的科林·曼利（Colin Manley）也这么弹，他们几乎同时和披头士在利物浦出道。

　　另一个相关的故事是，"黑鸟"是称呼黑人女孩的俚语。我很清楚利物浦曾经是一个奴隶港口，并且有英国的第一个加勒比社区。所以我们遇见过很多黑人，尤其在音乐界。我马上想到的是伍德宾勋爵（Lord Woodbine），一位卡里普索[3]歌手和宣传者，在利物浦经营几处娱乐场所，包括新卡巴莱艺术家俱乐部（New Cabaret Artists' Club），他曾在那里举办银色甲壳虫[4]的演出。还有德里和老头乐队[5]的德里，这个乐队为我们在

1　切特·阿特金斯（Chet Atkins, 1924—2001），美国乡村乐歌手、吉他大师。
2　雷莫四人组（The Remo Four），活跃于 1950 年代至 1960 年代的摇滚乐队，成立于利物浦。
3　卡里普索（calypso），流行于加勒比地区的民歌风格。
4　披头士早年曾用名 The Silver Beetles。
5　德里和老头乐队（Derry and The Seniors），活跃于 1950 年代至 1960 年代的摇滚乐队，成立于利物浦。

上图：披头士乐队录音期间，
伦敦阿比路录音棚，1968 年。

---

1 1957 年，美国阿肯色州小石城
   学校委员会在白人的中心中学
   录取了九名黑人学生，引发围
   绕公立学校中种族隔离政策的
   对抗事件。后来在美国总统艾
   森豪威尔的介入下，九名黑人
   学生最终得以入学。该事件被
   称为"小石城事件"，这九名
   学生后被称为"小石城九人"
   （Little Rock Nine）。

汉堡铺平了道路。

1968 年，写《黑鸟》的时候，美国种族矛盾的尖锐程度堪称可怖。前一年，1967
年，是特别糟糕的一年，但是 1968 年更糟。这首歌是在马丁·路德·金遇刺几周后写的。
那对破损的翅膀，以及凹陷的眼睛，还有普遍渴望自由的意象恰逢其时。

阿德里安·米切尔关于诗歌朗诵中开场白的重要性的建议，让我开始在演出中更
多地讲述歌曲背后的故事。看到了月球的背面，便得以找到进入星际云层的角度——
或许就歌曲而言，观众也会高兴获得这样的信息。

Black bird singing
in the dead of night
Take these broken wings
and learn to fly
All your life
you were only waiting for
this moment to arise
Black bird singing
in the dead of night
Take these sunken eyes
and learn to see
All your life

Paul McCartney

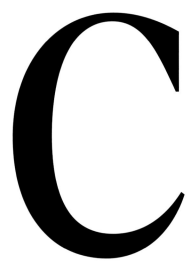

C

Café on the Left Bank

左岸咖啡馆

作　者 WRITER	保罗·麦卡特尼　Paul McCartney	
艺术家 ARTIST	羽翼乐队　Wings	
录　音 RECORDED	维京群岛费尔卡罗号　*Fair Carol*, Virgin Islands	
发　行 RELEASED	《伦敦城》，1978 年　*London Town*, 1978	

Café on the Left Bank
Ordinary wine
Touching all the girls with your eyes

Tiny crowd of Frenchmen
Round a TV shop
Watching Charles de Gaulle make a speech

Dancing after midnight
Sprawling to the car
Continental breakfast in the bar

English-speaking people
Drinking German beer
Talking far too loud for their ears

Café on the Left Bank
Ordinary wine
Touching all the girls with your eyes

Dancing after midnight
Crawling to the car
Cocktail waitress waiting in the bar

English-speaking people
Drinking German beer
Talking way too loud for their ears

Café on the Left Bank

廉价葡萄酒是我们在那些日子里唯一知道的红酒。我不能理解人们为什么喜欢红酒；每一次品尝，感觉都很糟糕。1961 年，约翰和我搭车去巴黎时，我们去了一家左岸的咖啡馆，女招待比我们年长——那时候约翰刚到二十一岁，而我将近二十。她为我们倒了两杯廉价葡萄酒，我们注意到她的腋毛，不由得为之震惊："哦我的天，看那个，她有腋毛！"法国人会这样，但英国人——或者，就像我们后来了解的，美国女孩——死也不会留着腋毛，除非是个真正的垮掉派。这段记忆如此清晰，所以，我设置这个场景时，它就出现在我的脑海里。

我其实是"廉价"——或者说"普通"——的拥趸，我希望它能在很多方面定义我，以及我创作的大部分歌曲。不要误解我，我喜欢特别的人和事物，不过如果人们可以既伟大又普通，那对我来说就很特别。我在利物浦的家人——我的父母，所有的阿姨和叔叔——他们既伟大又普通，而我认为这两种品质的混合很容易被忽略，这个事实使得它更加特别。很多人对我的利物浦家人不屑一顾，但要说起来，实际上他们比玛姬·撒切尔夫人[1] 这样的人聪明多了。他们的人生态度并不像我后来遇到的许多人那样保守。比如说，他们总是围着酒吧钢琴唱歌。所以你可以选择见多识广但很保守，也可以成为没见过什么世面但心平气和的人。我试着成为两者的混合体，我对那样的普通非常珍视。

上图：费尔卡罗号游艇，维京群岛，1977 年。

1　玛姬·撒切尔夫人（Maggie Thatcher，1925—2013），政治家，1979 年至 1990 年间担任英国第 49 任首相。

　　我记得有一次我透过商店的橱窗看电视 —— 那时候还是黑白电视（对年轻的一代来说，没有色彩的电视很难想象）—— 而人们围成一圈，看着戴高乐戴着他的法军平顶帽。现在已经很少能看到那种场景了，实际上，现在根本看不到了。它曾经是，现在也是，一幅非常引人注目的图像。

　　在美属维京群岛的一艘游艇上，用移动录音棚录制这首歌的情景记忆犹新。录音棚有二十四个音轨 —— 别忘了，《佩珀军士》只是录在四轨上 —— 所以这是仅次于阿比路的最佳选择。羽翼乐队的经典阵容都在，丹尼·莱恩（Denny Laine）和吉米·麦克洛赫（Jimmy McCulloch）弹吉他，乔·英格利希（Joe English）打鼓，琳达担任键盘手和主唱，我担任贝斯手和主唱。这首歌是我制作的。这有点像在一家左岸咖啡馆，既当客人，又当服务员。

上图：在费尔卡罗号游艇上，和丹尼·莱恩一起录音，维京群岛，1977 年。

右图：在费尔卡罗号和乔·英格利希、丹尼·莱恩、吉米·麦克洛赫及琳达一起录音，维京群岛，1977 年。

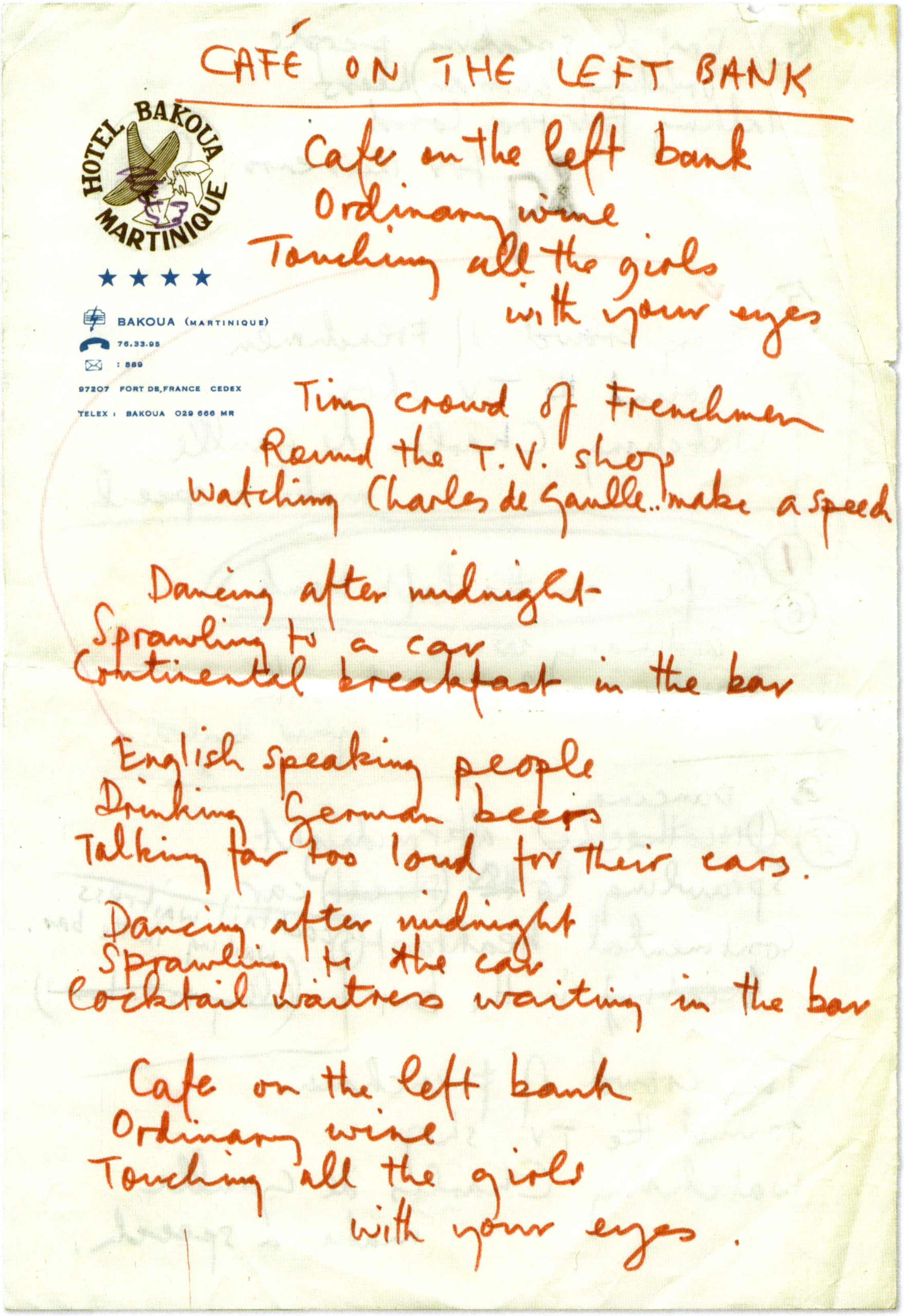

CAFÉ ON THE LEFT BANK

HOTEL BAKOUA MARTINIQUE

★ ★ ★ ★

BAKOUA (MARTINIQUE)
76.33.95
: 889
97207 FORT DE FRANCE CEDEX
TELEX : BAKOUA 029 666 MR

Cafe on the left bank
Ordinary wine
Touching all the girls
with your eyes

Tiny crowd of Frenchmen
Round the T.V. shop
Watching Charles de Gaulle.. make a speech

Dancing after midnight-
Sprawling to a car
Continental breakfast in the bar

English speaking people
Drinking German beers
Talking far too loud for their ears.

Dancing after midnight
Sprawling to the car
Cocktail waitress waiting in the bar

Cafe on the left bank
Ordinary wine
Touching all the girls
with your eyes.

④ English speaking people
Drinking (German) beers
Talking far too loud
                    for their ears

b q

② Tiny crowd of Frenchmen
Round the T.V. shop
Watching Charles de gaulle
                    make a speech.

① Cafe on the left bank
⑥ Ordinary wine
Touching all the girls with
                    your eyes

③ Dancing
⑤ (Discotheque) after midnight
Sprawling to the (Street) car
Continental breakfast ⑤ cocktail waitress
(feeding) in the bar   waiting in the bar.
                    (calling to the bar)

Tiny crowd of Frenchmen
round the T.V. shop
watching Charles de gaulle
                    make a speech.

57

Calico Skies

印花布的天空

作　者　WRITER　　　保罗·麦卡特尼　Paul McCartney
艺术家　ARTIST　　　保罗·麦卡特尼　Paul McCartney
录　音　RECORDED　　萨塞克斯郡猪山磨坊　Hog Hill Mill, Sussex
发　行　RELEASED　　《火焰派》，1997 年　*Flaming Pie*, 1997

It was written that I would love you
From the moment I opened my eyes
And the morning when I first saw you
Gave me life under calico skies
I will hold you for as long as you like
I'll hold you for the rest of my life

Always looking for ways to love you
Never failing to fight at your side
While the angels of love protect us
From the innermost secrets we hide
I'll hold you for as long as you like
I'll hold you for the rest of my life

Long live all of us crazy soldiers
Who were born under calico skies
May we never be called to handle
All the weapons of war we despise
I'll hold you for as long as you like
I'll hold you for the rest of my life
I'll hold you for as long as you like
I'll love you for the rest of my
For the rest of my life

如果琳达被问及什么是属于她的符号，她通常会说"禁止停车"。我向来不怎么关注占星术，我想那是因为在 1960 年代，关于星座的没完没了的讨论太多了。不管怎么说，我是双子座。

双子座出生在一年的中间。一年有"一切即将开始"，和"一切已经结束"，而你恰好出生在这中间。据说，这会影响你的性格。我无疑有那种对立统一的性格倾向，但我想每个人都有：乌木和象牙；你好和再见；你说是，我说不。我经常做那种二分法的游戏。我是真正的双子座。

这首歌的开场语——"It was written"（上面写着 / 命中注定）——指的是一个人的命运确实"被写在"星星上。"印花布的天空"？谁知道那会是什么样。我可能在某个地方听到过这种话，不过我觉得那是我发明的。我知道印花布是来自加尔各答一种棉制品，怀着"这首歌让印花布流行起来"这样的想法也很不错。

今天，我在回顾一些与专辑《火焰派》发行有关的笔记，这首歌也在其中，它让我想起了这首歌是怎么来的。他们终于开始给飓风起男孩的名字了，一场被命名为"鲍勃"的强大飓风导致了长岛停电，一切都中断了。那是一个好机会，世界关闭时，你就可以去创作。不管怎样，我一直在寻求这样的情境。如果我在家里写歌，我会尽量避免活动，这通常意味着躲进壁橱、衣柜，或者浴室，某个我可以成为洞穴隐士的地方。所以，停电时，突然间，你不必在这里或那里隐藏自己，你可以去地下室，完全与歌曲融为一休。

如果你在写一首歌，你要让它押韵；总比那种枯燥无聊的歌要好。所以，我有了一个想法，并且知道自己要找和"眼睛"押韵的词后，我会开始通过潜在的选择来尝试。我觉得我爸爸在用类似的方式解决纵横填字游戏，在脑海中反复思考一些词的可能性。所以，写歌时，我只是提前想好，我知道会有一个韵脚，而我试着让它成为一个很好的，好到能够推进情节的韵脚。在这首歌里，"天空"这个词出现了，所以我想，应该着眼于"多云的天空""暗蓝色的天空""深蓝色的天空"，或者甚至"印花布的天空"。你要根据那个词的语境来定。

"While the angels of love protect us / From the innermost secrets we hide"（当爱的天使保护着我们 / 远离我们内心隐藏的秘密）。每个人的内心都有很多东西，但是爱、尊重和正直的观念保护我们免受内心深处那些糟糕秘密的影响。你可能对某人的想法不好，但除非他们真的激怒了你，否则你不会说出来，而那是爱的天使在保护你。我想这种情况一直在发生。这也可以称为你的良心。我的意思是说，我喜欢有两个人在我的头脑里这个主意。好吧，至少两个。

"Long live all of us crazy soldiers"（所有我们疯狂的士兵万岁）。有一些我们不喜欢的政客、元首、首相，等等，他们满口谎言，而我一生都在以自己的方式和他们对抗。对我来说，这段歌词所表现出的抗议就像是皮特·西格[1]、鲍勃·迪伦《我们将会胜利》（We Shall Overcome）。我把它放进了一首浪漫歌曲里，作为第三段主歌的开始，它有点

1　皮特·西格（Pete Seeger，1919—2014），美国民谣歌手。

警钟的意思，因为在此之前，歌词更加倾向于个人化，而没有真正涉及政治或社会。但这段歌词把我们带进了一个疯狂士兵的帮派——我们一帮兄弟。我很高兴能够加入。

你在学生时代有那么多的争吵和讨论，以我们为例，披头士成了我的同学、伙伴。我们会坐下来喝一杯，然后天南地北地闲聊，而且，鉴于我们的年纪，我们会讨论如果宣战并被征召的话，我们会怎么做。我们会战斗吗？我想，这是我这一代的很多人必须考虑的问题。披头士的好事之一是，我们组建乐队的那一刻，英国停止了征兵，那在美国被叫作"选拔"。

事实上，我们所有人都可能会去。林戈符合服兵役的条件，接下来，我和约翰，以及乔治，也都会符合。我们中没人有那种可以让人逃避兵役的臭名昭著的幸运骨刺。我们总是说，结束征兵就像上帝以摩西的方式，为我们劈开了海洋，我们只是走过去。事实上，我们真的很幸运。

所以问题是，我们会战斗吗？我的观点是我不会，除非境况像敦刻尔克或希特勒入侵那样危急，在那种情况下，我会觉得自己必须去战斗。除此之外，我选择和平，而这种想法在我们这一代人中非常普遍。事实上，我们认为，如果能够说服这些政客，我们就有可能实现和平。

到头来，你似乎无法说服他们，但你必须继续努力。我很高兴丘吉尔能够站出来反对希特勒，当时他的许多同僚（包括内维尔·张伯伦）声称，"不，我们要'我们这个时代的和平'[1]。"张伯伦并不孤单。很多人认为他们应该让步，因为在战争开始前，他们非常错误地觉得，希特勒基本上是无害的。

这就像某些政客对新冠病毒所做的公开声明。

1　1938 年，英国首相内维尔·张伯伦与法国总理达拉第为避免战争爆发，牺牲捷克斯洛伐克的利益，与希特勒、墨索里尼签署《慕尼黑协定》，将苏台德区割让给纳粹德国。张伯伦回到伦敦后，宣称带回"我们这个时代的和平"（Peace for Our Time）。

上图：多云的天空，琳达拍摄。

右图：东汉普顿，1991 年。

Can't Buy Me Love
买不到我的爱

作　者	WRITERS	保罗·麦卡特尼和约翰·列侬　Paul McCartney and John Lennon
艺术家	ARTIST	披头士乐队　The Beatles
录　音	RECORDED	巴黎马可尼之路录音棚、伦敦阿比路录音棚　Pathé Marconi, Paris and Abbey Road Studios, London
发　行	RELEASED	单曲，1964 年　Single, 1964
		《辛劳一日的夜》，1964 年　*A Hard Day's Night*, 1964

Can't buy me love, love
Can't buy me love

I'll buy you a diamond ring, my friend
If it makes you feel alright
I'll get you anything, my friend
If it makes you feel alright
'Cause I don't care too much for money
Money can't buy me love

I'll give you all I've got to give
If you say you love me too
I may not have a lot to give
But what I've got I'll give to you
I don't care too much for money
Money can't buy me love

Can't buy me love
Everybody tells me so
Can't buy me love
No, no, no, no

Say you don't need no diamond rings
And I'll be satisfied
Tell me that you want the kind of things
That money just can't buy
I don't care too much for money
Money can't buy me love

Can't buy me love
Everybody tells me so
Can't buy me love
No, no, no, no

Say you don't need no diamond rings
And I'll be satisfied
Tell me that you want the kind of things
That money just can't buy
I don't care too much for money
Money can't buy me love

Can't buy me love, love
Can't buy me love

从很早的时候起，我们就把自己想成"列侬和麦卡特尼"。因为我们听说过吉尔伯特和沙利文、罗杰斯和哈默斯坦。列侬和麦卡特尼听起来很不错。我们有两个人，正好可以套进这个模式。我们在学校练习本上把名字写在一起。《爱我吧》和《909后的一个》（One After 909）都来自那个时期，那恐怕要回到遥远的1957年。大约十年或者十五年前，我找到了那本练习本，把它放在书架上。那以后，它好像又丢失了，我不知道它在哪儿，但我想它总会在某个地方出现。这是列侬和麦卡特尼的第一份手稿。

　　无论如何，买到唱片后，除了看唱片名，我们还会查看下面标注的人名。莱伯和斯托勒[1]、戈芬和金[2]。对我们来说，这都是些神奇的名字，特别是这些美国名字——虽然罗杰斯和哈默斯坦没那么神奇，他们已经有点儿过时了。这是我们的时代，而这些名字代表着我们时代的一位位创作者。我们搬到伦敦后，约翰和我开始结识专业的作曲人，譬如米奇·穆瑞（Mitch Murray）和彼得·卡兰德（Peter Callander）。他们在我们出版商的办公室工作，只制作金曲——也可以说是炮制。米奇写一些《你怎么做到的?》（How Do You Do It?）这样的歌，乔治·马丁为我们录了这首歌，它差点成为披头士的第一首单曲。所以，约翰和我看着这些所谓的专业作曲人，觉得："好吧，我们也能做。一旦做出金曲，我们就有钱了。这也许买不到爱情，但可以为我们买辆车。"

　　不光是钱的事儿，这同样是种乐趣——从帽子里抓出一首歌，然后和我们的乐队一起演奏，而乐队恰好需要歌曲。所以我们有点像加足马力的机器。我们会问唱片公司："你需要多少首，老板?"国会唱片的沃伊尔·吉尔摩（Voyle Gilmore）和艾伦·利文斯顿（Alan Livingston）来找我们，这两位西装革履的加州绅士说："好吧，我们希望每年有四首单曲和一张专辑。"我们觉得那一点儿都没问题。

　　所以，布莱恩·爱泼斯坦，我们说话温和、举止优雅的经纪人，会用轻柔但完美的上流社会口音（丝毫没有他在利物浦成长的痕迹）提醒我们："你们下周有时间，可以写下一张专辑。"而我们会说："太好了，没问题。"我们每天写一首歌。我们会在我家或约翰家见面。一般是两把吉他，两个便签本，两支铅笔。很多其他的东西是在路上写的——这个地方，那个地方，每个地方——但是做一张专辑，你确实需要一周左右的时间来安排。

　　制作过程中总是会有好的想法出现，因为我们会想，"写一首听起来像那样的歌如何"，或者"我们应该写一首听起来像这样的歌"。我们发现了一个需要填补的坑，这和其他东西一样可以启发我们。我们在创作唱片，并且它们很成功，这个事实对我们很有帮助。这就好像你是一名运动员，你赢得了比赛，于是你可以说："噢是的，我觉得我也可以试试那个。"

　　这首歌是在巴黎乔治五世酒店的一架钢琴上写成的。几年前，约翰和我搭车去巴黎，在一些咖啡馆附近逛了逛。而这次是完全不同的旅行。酒店靠近香榭丽舍大街，我们的套房大得足以放下一架钢琴。我们在奥林匹亚剧院有为期三周的演出。那时候演出很短，但我们每天要演两场。现在做演出时，我们要在三个小时内表演大约四十首歌；而那个时候可能还不到十首，所以加上和观众聊几句的时间，演出大约只有半

1　指杰瑞·莱伯（Jerry Leiber）和迈克·斯托勒（Mike Stoller），两人合作创作了很多早期摇滚乐的畅销金曲。
2　指杰拉德·戈芬（Gerald Goffin）和卡罗尔·金（Carole King），两人合作创作了很多摇滚乐和流行乐的畅销金曲。

个小时。我们的表演曲目有《我对你的》、《她爱你》(She Loves You)、《这个男孩》(This Boy)，以及《我想牵你的手》，其他的则是《超越贝多芬》(Roll Over Beethoven)和《扭摆和尖叫》(Twist and Shout)这种翻唱歌曲，用《高个子莎莉》(Long Tall Sally)来结尾。我们在汉堡的日子——那时经常整夜整夜地表演——可以说是对这种长期驻场表演的良好演练。

但似乎四十多场演出还不够似的，布莱恩也安排了其他事情，比如写歌和录音。于是我们在巴黎时，重新录制了《我想牵你的手》和《她爱你》的德语版本：来自 Die Beatles 的 "Komm, gib mir deine Hand" 和 "Sie liebt dich"——乔治·马丁为此去了马可尼之路录音棚，与此同时，我们也录下了《买不到我的爱》的基础音轨。

这是首十二小节的布鲁斯，副歌是披头士风格的摇摆感——使用了几个小和弦。一般来说，小和弦会用在一首歌的主歌部分，而大和弦会为副歌段带来提振，制造一种明亮的感觉。在这首歌里，我们反其道而行之。《买不到我的爱》要表达的是，所有这些物质财富都很好，但金钱买不到你真正需要的东西。具有讽刺意味的是，来巴黎之前，我们去过佛罗里达，在那里，金钱当然可以买来许多你想要的东西，除了爱。但我认为前提是成立的：金钱买不来快乐的家庭或值得信赖的朋友。同年晚些时候，艾拉·菲兹杰拉德[1]也录了这首歌，这真是一种荣幸。

这首单曲还不错，在英国和美国同时登上了榜首。然后，有趣的是，它在英国被《一个没有爱的世界》(A World Without Love)踢下了榜首位置，那是我为简·阿舍的哥哥彼得写的歌。他和朋友签约了百代，把那首歌作为他们的首张单曲，以彼得和戈登(Peter and Gordon)的名义发行。我很确定，《一个没有爱的世界》在美国也是第一名。那是我十六岁时在利物浦的家里写的歌。我觉得以披头士的标准，它还不够精彩，不过它对彼得和戈登的职业生涯来说，确实是首好歌。那首歌的第一句歌词是"请锁住我"，而当我演奏它的时候，约翰会回应道："噢，好的。"然后我们开玩笑说，那就是歌曲的结束了。

可能有不少人会把《买不到我的爱》和电影《一夜狂欢》联系在一起。它出现在我们最终决定逃离录音棚去找点乐子的场景中，有点像是音乐宣传视频。这首歌实际上是专门作为电影配乐写的，而影片使用了许多简短的原声片段——虽然阿伦·欧文(Alun Owen)编写的剧本相当丰富——这样我们就不用练习长台词了。《一夜狂欢》在某种程度上赋予我们每个人一种公众形象：约翰是个聪明、尖刻的人；乔治是沉默的人；林戈是风趣的人；我是刻板的可爱人物。在世人眼中，我们被奇怪地简化为几个速写人格，并且我觉得，直到今天，仍有许多人认为我们就是那部电影描画的样子。这种观点可能会对我们有相当大的限制，但我们学会了忽略它。

不过，有一件重要的事情并没有改变：我的外套尺寸。在 1964 年，我穿着一套天鹅绒镶边燕尾服外套去参加《一夜狂欢》的首映。在 2016 年，披头士的巡演电影《一周八天》(Eight Days a Week)首映时，还是在伦敦——也许要感谢我做了四十年素食主义者——我穿着同样的外套。

---

1 艾拉·菲兹杰拉德(Ella Fitzgerald，1917—1996)，20 世纪最重要的爵士乐歌手之一，被誉为"爵士乐第一夫人"。

左图：早期披头士的演出歌单。

右图：利物浦学院男子高中的课本。

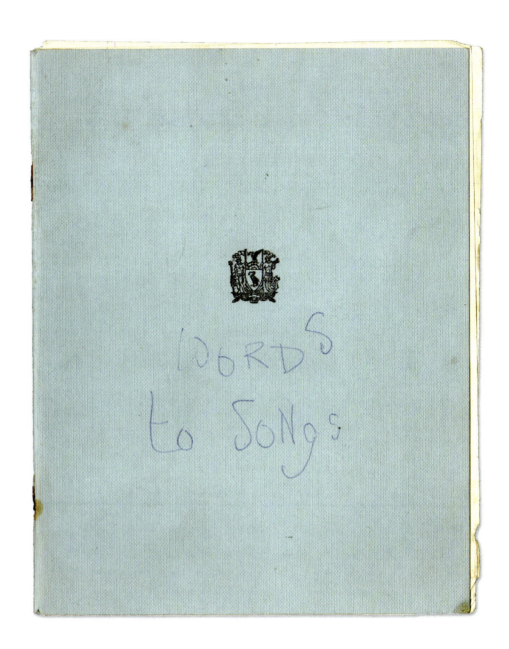

顶图：和列侬在市民中心的后台，
巴尔的摩，1964 年。

上图：布莱恩·爱泼斯坦，保罗
拍摄，1964 年。

上图：和斯图尔特·萨克利夫、乔
治·哈里森及约翰·列侬在一起，
汉堡前十俱乐部，1961 年。

右图：约翰·列侬，巴黎，1961 年。

下图：《一个没有爱的世界》
单曲碟，1964 年发行。

右图：与林戈·斯塔尔于《一周
八天》首映式上，保罗身着 1964
年《一夜狂欢》首映时穿过的外
套，伦敦，2016 年 9 月 15 日。

Carry That Weight
承担重负

作　者	WRITERS	保罗·麦卡特尼和约翰·列侬　Paul McCartney and John Lennon
艺术家	ARTIST	披头士乐队　The Beatles
录　音	RECORDED	伦敦阿比路录音棚　Abbey Road Studios, London
发　行	RELEASED	《阿比路》，1969 年　*Abbey Road*, 1969

Boy, you're gonna carry that weight
Carry that weight a long time
Boy, you're gonna carry that weight
Carry that weight a long time

I never give you my pillow
I only send you my invitations
And in the middle of the celebrations
I break down

Boy, you're gonna carry that weight
Carry that weight a long time
Boy, you're gonna carry that weight
Carry that weight a long time

　　1960 年代中后期，有一阵子我们服用 LSD[1]，彻夜不眠，希望药效慢慢消失，然后发现其实并不会。一次糟糕的幻觉之旅可能会留给你沉重的感觉，而不是享受正常的明亮朝气。你知道，我们一开始是抽大麻，我们觉得这似乎没什么大不了的。但一旦你开始尝试一些更"硬"的东西，事情就不是这么轻松了，可能会很抑郁。

　　那时我们还要面对苹果唱片那些可怕的业务问题。商务会议简直会摧毁灵魂。我们坐在办公室里——在一个你不想去的地方，和你不想见的人待在一起。琳达给艾伦·克莱因[2]拍过一张很棒的照片，照片里他拿着一把"麦克斯韦的银锤"似的锤了。这很有象征意义。这就是为什么我们会在《你从来不给我你的钱》（You Never Give Me Your Money）这首歌的中间，以及在唱到"I never give you my pillow / I only send you my invitations"（我不会让你倚靠 / 我只是向你发出邀请）这句歌词时挤眉弄眼。

　　这段时期我的压力极大，甚至开始将这一切归咎于我们背负原罪。我妈妈为我做了天主教的洗礼，但我们不是在天主教的环境中长大的，所以我并没有在日常生活中接受原罪这一观念。想到你生来就是个失败者，真的很让人沮丧。

　　承担重负的概念也许受到了乐队[3]的歌曲《重量》（The Weight）的影响，这首歌出自 1968 年 7 月的专辑《来自大粉的音乐》（Music From Big Pink）。我在《嘿，裘德》（Hey Jude）宣传片淡出部分引用了这首歌完全是个巧合。

　　我们主要还是因为鲍勃·迪伦才知道了乐队。我们非常喜欢迪伦，尤其喜欢他是位诗人这一事实，而他也确实善于表达。我们也喜欢他的演唱风格，以至约翰开始像他一样唱歌——听听《你要把你的爱藏起来》（You've Got to Hide Your Love Away）。

1　麦角酸二乙基酰胺，是一种人工合成致幻剂。
2　艾伦·克莱因（Allen Klein，1931—2009），滚石乐队经纪人。在披头士乐队后期接手管理披头士的商业事务。
3　乐队（The Band），加拿大乐队，最初作为鲍勃·迪伦的伴奏乐队出现，1967 年出版了第一张专辑。

Boy, you're going to carry that weight
carry that weight a long time
Boy you're gonna carry that weight
carry that weight a long time.

I never give you my pillow
I only send you my invitations
And in the middle of the celebrations
I break down,

Boy you're gonna carry that weight
carry that weight a long time.

Repeat.....

Check My Machine
检查我的机器

作 者	WRITER	保罗·麦卡特尼　Paul McCartney
艺术家	ARTIST	保罗·麦卡特尼　Paul McCartney
录 音	RECORDED	萨塞克斯郡低闸农场　Lower Gate Farm, Sussex
发 行	RELEASED	《瀑布》B 面单曲，1980 年　B-side of 'Waterfalls' single, 1980

Hi George
Morning Terry
Sticks and stones may break my bones
But names will never hurt me

Check
My machine
Check
My machine
Check
My machine
Check
My machine

I want you to check
My machine

Check
My machine

有一段时间，我独自在录音棚工作——我的"疯狂教授"时期——大约在 1970 年代末。我会做一张唱片，准备发行时，我办公室里的某个人会意识到他们需要歌词，于是试着猜想我会说些什么。我可能并没有检查他们那番猜想的成果。我觉得更有可能是这样的情况——我们都听了录音，心想，"在结尾的地方，我要说点儿有意思的东西。"

拟声演唱[1]是一种伟大而古老的传统，我一直喜欢聆听胖子沃勒或者路易斯·阿姆斯特朗的唱片，听他们用这种技法演唱。所有拟声演唱者中最伟大的是艾拉·菲兹杰拉德。拟声演唱者在无意义的词语中找到节奏的方式极有启发性，而你看得出他们乐在其中。

关于这首歌，我很清楚我会给人声上加很多混响，也知道歌词的内容对任何人来说都无关紧要——我随便编的。一个响亮而清晰的想法是"检查我的机器"，这就是我想表达的全部意思。

我考虑了几种机器。电脑是其中一个。他们说电脑会大大加快录音的速度，不过在启动和运行电脑的时间里，披头士可能已经录完两首歌了。

效率更高和速度更快的承诺是不真实的。依靠一支铅笔、一张纸和一把吉他速度更快，并且效率更高。一些最好的想法已经写在一张纸上，或者一张餐巾上，或者任何在你手头的东西上。但显然，从那时起，电脑和科技取得了长足的进步。在那个时代，电话答录机都是个大东西；我几乎不敢相信电话答录机和复印机现在已经是过去式了。

上图：《麦卡特尼 II》录音期间，萨塞克斯郡，1979 年。

1　拟声演唱（Scatting），演唱者在与乐队的即兴交流中，以没有词义的拟声词唱出各种复杂多变的节奏型，是一种高度炫技性的演唱方式。

在家里，萨塞克斯郡，1980 年。

依靠一支铅笔、一张纸和一把吉他速度更快，
并且效率更高。
一些最好的想法已经写在一张纸上，
或者一张餐巾上，
或者任何在你手头的东西上。

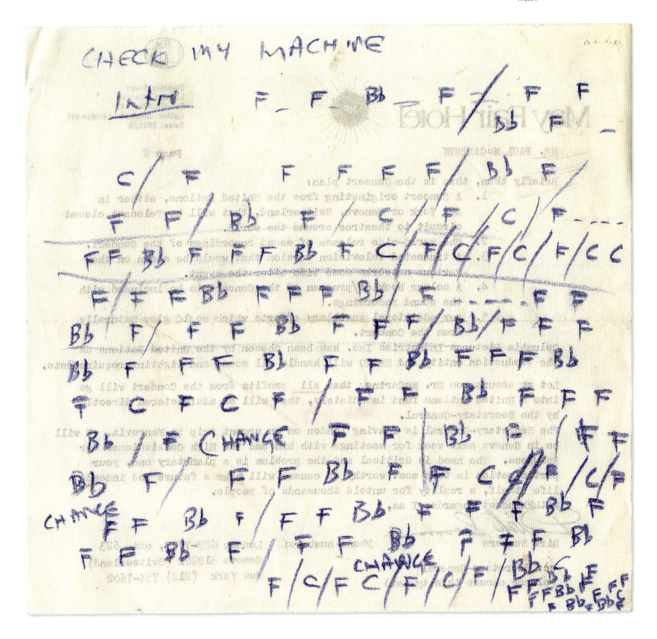

保罗手写的《检查我的机器》和弦。

Come and Get It

过来拿吧

作　者　WRITER　　　保罗·麦卡特尼　Paul McCartney
艺术家　ARTIST　　　坏手指　Badfinger
录　音　RECORDED　　伦敦阿比路录音棚　Abbey Road Studios, London
发　行　RELEASED　　单曲，1969 年　Single, 1969

《神奇的基督徒音乐》，1970 年　*Magic Christian Music*, 1970

If you want it, here it is, come and get it
Make your mind up fast
If you want it, anytime, I can give it
But you'd better hurry 'cause it may not last

Did I hear you say that there must be a catch?
Will you walk away from a fool and his money?

If you want it, here it is, come and get it
But you'd better hurry 'cause it's goin' fast

If you want it, here it is, come and get it
Make your mind up fast
If you want it, anytime, I can give it
But you'd better hurry 'cause it may not last

Did I hear you say that there must be a catch?
Will you walk away from a fool and his money,
　sonny?

If you want it, here it is, come and get it
But you'd better hurry 'cause it's goin' fast
You'd better hurry 'cause it's goin' fast
Fool and his money, sonny

If you want it, here it is, come and get it
But you'd better hurry 'cause it's goin' fast
You'd better hurry 'cause it's goin' fast
You'd better hurry 'cause it's goin' fast

1960 年代行将结束时我仍在伦敦，在披头士乐队计划的间隙，有时间制作其他音乐家的项目。比如说，我们创立自己的厂牌苹果音乐时，签下了玛丽·霍普金（Mary Hopkin），她当时已经在一个叫作《机会来敲门》（*Opportunity Knocks*）的电视才艺秀里成名。我们还签了坏手指——几个英格兰和威尔士小伙子组成的乐队，我们的巡演经理迈尔·伊文思（Mal Evans）看过他们的演出后，向我们推荐了这支乐队。我想，那时他们似乎依旧用着"常春藤乐队"（The Iveys）这个名字，但和另一支同名乐队混淆了，所以改名为坏手指，这一灵感来自"坏手指布吉"（Bad Finger Boogie），它曾经是《在我朋友们的一点帮助下》（With a Little Help from My Friends）的暂定名。

　　那时我考虑着如何栽培他们——我需要能让他们大获成功的作品。有一天晚上，我躺在床上迟迟没有入睡，试图寻找灵感。这首歌开始在我的脑海里盘旋，然后我想："噢，这可以的，这歌不错。"琳达和我刚刚结婚，我不希望吵醒她或者女儿希瑟（Heather McCartney），于是我轻声起床下楼——楼下有个房间放着一台小型磁带录音机。为了避免弄出太大的噪声，我关上所有的门，然后写了这首歌。从根本上说，它就是为坏手指所写的歌。相当直接的摇滚乐，非常直接。

　　它有点像《爱我吧》——动机十分类似。但我还是想写一首金曲，所以不想要过于复杂的东西。当你为听众创作时——就像莎士比亚，或是狄更斯，他的作品在报刊连载，公之于众——首先需要吸引听众。而有意思的是，我很清楚自己希望这首歌听起来是什么样子。

　　我当晚写了这首歌；第二天我们要为《阿比路》专辑录音，我知道大家都会准时到场，于是特意提前半小时赶到录音棚。我对录音师菲尔·麦克唐纳（Phil McDonald）说："瞧，我有这么一首歌。我会去打鼓，弹点钢琴，在上面加点贝斯，然后我来唱，我们可以花十五分钟做完这个。"他很有兴趣，所以我确实如我所言，就这么做了。我弹了段钢琴，加了些鼓点，所有的都是一遍过。随后其他人到了，我们开始录制披头士的专辑。但是那时，我已经有了这首歌的样带，可能问了一句："你们介意我快速做个混音吗？"但事实是它仿佛已经自己完成了混音，这是《过来拿吧》很棒的地方——它已经如此完整，我只是跳进去，在十五分钟或者二十分钟内，就这样录制了一张唱片。

　　后来，我对坏手指说："你们要这么演绎这首歌。"而他们说："呃……我们还是希望用自己的方式处理。"我表示了反对："不，我不希望你们这样做。我希望你们忠实地照着这版做，因为这是一首标准金曲。你们要按照这种方式演绎。"他们对此有些犹豫，但最终他们的录音和我的样带确实非常相似。你可以在披头士的专辑《选集 3》（*Anthology 3*）和《阿比路》五十周年重制版里听到我的版本。

　　我能理解他们不想亦步亦趋地复制我的作品，也理解他们希望把自己的东西加进来，但是我怕给他们那样的自由会把事情搞砸。简单来说，我告诉他们："这是一个完成品，你们只要做一个翻版，它就是你们的了，而我不会把我的作品拿出来。但你们需要自己复制。"

　　这首歌很成功；我想，在一些国家，它帮助坏手指拿到了冠军单曲；收录它的专辑也是一张大热专辑。我还记得他们在苹果音乐又做了一两张专辑。他们的主唱名叫

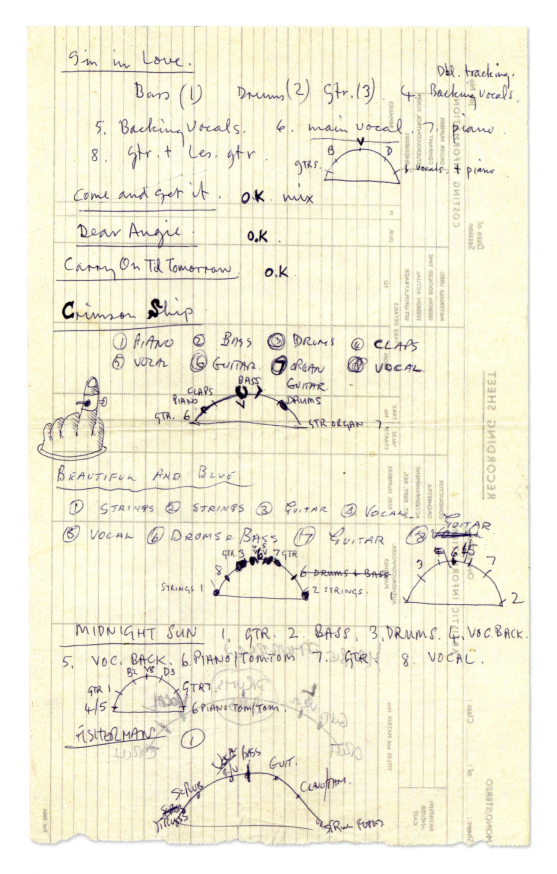

Sin in Love.

Bass (1)   Drums (2)   Gtr. (3)   4. Backing Vocals.   Dbl. tracking.

5. Backing Vocals.   6. main vocal.   7. piano.

8. Gtr. + Les. gtr.

gtrs.   B   V   D   8. vocals + piano

Come and get it.   O.K. mix

Dear Angie.   O.K.

Carry On Til Tomorrow   O.K.

Crimson Ship

① PIANO   ② BASS   ③ DRUMS   ④ CLAPS
⑤ VOCAL   ⑥ GUITAR   ⑦ ORGAN   ⑧ VOCAL

CLAPS   BASS   GUITAR
PIANO   DRUMS
GTR. 6   STR. ORGAN 7

BEAUTIFUL AND BLUE

① STRINGS   ② STRINGS   ③ GUITAR   ④ VOCAL
⑤ VOCAL   ⑥ DRUMS & BASS   ⑦ GUITAR   ⑧ GUITAR

GTR. 3 6 7 GTR
8   6 DRUMS + BASS
STRINGS 1   2 STRINGS.

GUITAR
6 4 5
3   7
2

MIDNIGHT SUN   1. GTR.   2. BASS.   3. DRUMS.   4. VOC. BACK.

5. VOC. BACK.   6. PIANO / TOM TOM   7. GTR   8. VOCAL.

B2 V8 D3
GTR 1   GTR 7
4/5   6 PIANO TOM/TOM.

FISHERMAN   ①

BASS   GUIT.
SCRUB   CLAV/TAM.
STRINGS   DRUM FUZZ

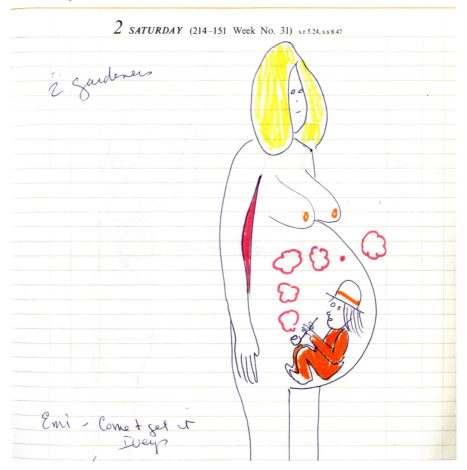

皮特·汉姆（Pete Ham），是一个了不起的家伙，也是一个优秀的创作人。他和队友汤姆·伊文思（Tom Evans）合写了《没有你》（Without You），这首歌成了哈里·尼尔森（Harry Nilsson）的金曲。上帝啊，这是一首那么动情的歌，听到时我就在想："难以置信，皮特，那真是太棒了。我的天，你是怎么做到的?"然而，让人伤心的是，不久之后，他就自杀了。

事情的结局如此悲伤。他写出了获得巨大成功的金曲，给了尼尔森；或者也许这只是坏手指专辑中的一首歌，而尼尔森注意到了，说："这会是一首伟大的单曲。"我不太清楚其中有怎样的故事。这也是一种悲伤的讽刺，我为皮特·汉姆写了这首歌，而他说："呃……"然后他写了另一首歌，把它给了其他人，而那个人有了金曲。但事情已成定局。

Coming Up
即将来临

作　者　WRITER	保罗 · 麦卡特尼　Paul McCartney	
艺术家　ARTIST	保罗 · 麦卡特尼　Paul McCartney	
录　音　RECORDED	苏格兰拉那坎精神录音棚　Spirit of Ranachan Studio, Scotland	
发　行　RELEASED	单曲，1980 年　Single, 1980	
	《麦卡特尼 II》，1980 年　*McCartney II*, 1980	

You want a love to last forever
One that will never fade away
I want to help you with your problem
Stick around, I say

Coming up
Coming up, yeah
Coming up like a flower
Coming up, I say

You want a friend you can rely on
One who will never fade away
And if you're searching for an answer
Stick around, I say

It's coming up
It's coming up
It's coming up like a flower
It's coming up, yeah

You want some peace and understanding
So everybody can be free
I know that we can get together
We can make it, stick with me

It's coming up
It's coming up
It's coming up like a flower
It's coming up for you and me

Coming up
Coming up

It's coming up
It's coming up, I say
It's coming up like a flower
It's coming up, I feel it in my bones

You want a better kind of future
One that everyone can share
You're not alone, we all could use it
Stick around we're nearly there

It's coming up
It's coming up everywhere
It's coming up like a flower
It's coming up for all to share
It's coming up, yeah
It's coming up, anyway
It's coming up like a flower
Coming up

这是一首非常积极的歌曲。事情会变好。这反映了我非常积极的态度。这首歌始于一种对录音的渴望，想在录音棚里找点乐子。我总是把独自在录音棚里工作比作化学教授的实验室。你可以随便摆弄点什么。

于是，我去了我在苏格兰的录音棚录鼓的音轨——我一般都从鼓开始。我有时会使用鼓机，但是我喜欢用真鼓重录一遍，我很享受打鼓。然后我编进去一些贝斯。我只是在做一些实验性的东西。我在胡闹和实验。把磁带的速度放慢，或者加快。

这首歌最初是羽翼乐队临近解散时在格拉斯哥的现场演奏的。我发行的则是更具实验性的录音室版，它开启了我个人独奏生涯。我们拍了一部相当好的录影带，由基思·麦克米兰（Keith McMillan）导演，里面我假装自己是所有乐器的演奏者。而事实是，我曾经确实如此。

"即将来临"这个短语通常出现在电影片花中，在你身边的剧院"即将上映"。当然，使用像"来临"（coming）这样的词时，你的潜意识里会有某种性暗示。因此，这类词很适合用来玩一些文字游戏。这不等于我在直言"哇，我要做有伤风化的事情了"，但是我确实喜欢它可以在多种层面上来解读这一事实。

我很高兴《即将来临》在美国成为冠军单曲。第一名总是不错的，因为你没法更高了。如果一首歌没有成为冠军单曲，我也不会烦恼，但那个排名是人们喜欢这首歌的标志。

约翰曾在某个场合表示《即将来临》是"一首不错的作品"。他一直有点懒懒散散，无所事事，这首歌在某种程度上让他从惰性中惊醒。我很高兴得知这首歌引起了他的共鸣。披头士解散后，我们起初没有联系，但有很多事情需要讨论。因为事关生意，我们的关系有时会有点紧张，有时甚至会在电话里侮辱对方。但渐渐地，我们就过去了，如果我在纽约，我会打电话问："你想喝杯茶吗？"

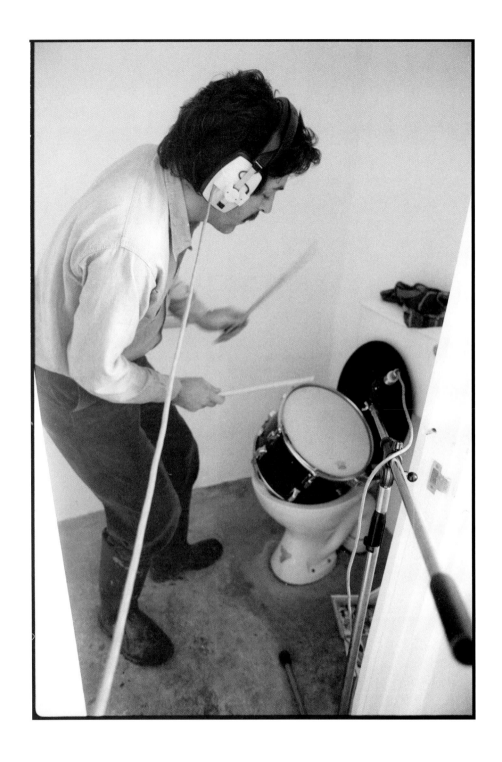

左图：为了得到"沼泽混响"，在卫生间录鼓。苏格兰拉那坎精神录音棚，1979 年。

86—87 页：生活空间，苏格兰拉那坎精神录音棚。

这首歌始于一种对录音的渴望，想在录音棚里找点乐子。
我总是把独自在录音棚里工作比作化学教授的实验室。
你可以随便摆弄点什么。

COMING UP

1   2   3   4   Sax RIFF

1   2   3   4   RIFF

(1) You want a love   to last forever
One that will never   fade away
I wanna help you with your problems.
Stick around I say

CHORUS   Coming Up.

1 2

(2)   You want a friend   you can rely on
One who will never fade away
+ if your searching for an answer
stick around I say

CHORUS   Coming up .   like a flower   Hey!!
HARMONY

1   2   3   4   (SOLO)   Long (1 2 3 4)

(3) You want some peace + understanding
So everybody   can be free
I know that   we can get together
We can make it stick   with   me

CHORUS   Coming up   like a flower
for you + me

1   2   3   4   1 2 /(SOLO)   short (1 2 3 4)

(4) You want a better... kind of future
One that everyone can share
I know if we can get together
well hear — music everywhere

CHORUS   Coming Up   BREAK B/D.

1   2   3   4   Hand Claps   Coming up ANYWAY.

1   2   3   4

CHORUS   Coming Up — I say —
like a flower

Feel it in my bones ————   yea yea yea yea

Salex Oxford Limited.

Confidante

知 己

作 者	WRITER	保罗·麦卡特尼　Paul McCartney
艺术家	ARTIST	保罗·麦卡特尼　Paul McCartney
录 音	RECORDED	萨塞克斯郡猪山磨坊　Hog Hill Mill, Sussex
发 行	RELEASED	《埃及站》，2018 年　*Egypt Station*, 2018

You used to be my confidante
My underneath the staircase friend
But I fell out of love with you
And brought our romance to an end

I played with you throughout the day
And told you every secret thought
Unlike my other so-called friends
You stood beside me as I fought

In your reflected glory I
Could dream of shining far-off lands
Where serpents turn to bits of string
And played like kittens in my hand

In our imaginary world
Where butterflies wear army boots
And stomp around the forest chanting
Long lost anthems
Long lost anthems

You used to be my confidante
My underneath the staircase friend
But I fell out of love with you
And brought our romance to an end

I played with you throughout the day
And told you every secret thought
Unlike my other so-called friends
You stood beside me as I fought
You stood beside me as I fought

You used to be my confidante

那把吉他就架在客厅一角靠窗的座椅上，在萨塞克斯郡的某个村庄。我突然意识到自己有一阵子没弹这把琴了，我看了看它，心想："天哪，这样真不好，我应该和你一块儿演奏一番的，你一定很孤独。"

我有点儿内疚，所以走过去开始拨弄这把琴，流泻出的旋律就成了这首歌——我直接与吉他对话，讲述一直以来它对我的帮助。我们常说，当你拿着吉他坐下来写歌的时候，你就是在告诉它你的秘密，然后它就变成了一首给全世界听的歌。但在那一刻，你独自一人时，吉他就是你的知己，你轻轻抱着它。吉他看起来也像是女人。你们之间有许多特殊的情感。而你走到钢琴前时，就好像你在把钢琴推开；这是完全不同的行为。

"My underneath the staircase friend"（我在楼梯下的朋友）是指利物浦的一栋政府出租房，我们后来搬到了那儿——我想是福特林路的那栋，它现在是受国民信托[1]保护的建筑；也很有可能是我们之前在斯皮克地区的那栋房子。楼梯下面有个三角形的橱柜，就像哈利·波特小时候生活的地方。这通常是放置家庭电话的地方，但如果你想找个藏身之处，那也是个好去处——我就是这么干的。我现在仍会这么干，我总是在寻找我的藏身之处。言归正传，我回顾往昔，开始思考："将吉他引为知己这种事是什么时候开始的？"那要追溯到我站在楼梯下面，抱着一件乐器，向它倾诉我的烦扰，而这渐渐成为我延续半生的传统。我只是喜欢这样的想法：有了这把吉他，我就可以告诉他们，我是多么感激有一位知己能和我一起远行。这就是我对吉他的感觉。

我以"You used to be my confidante"（你曾是我的知己）开头，这番陈情却走向"But I fell out of love with you / And brought our romance to an end"（但是我不再爱你 / 我们的浪漫走到了尽头）。我喜欢的是你写一句歌词，而它向不同的人暗示了不同的东西。我并不是在考虑结束与这首歌的陈情对象——吉他的关系，但我喜欢使用那些可以有多重解释的言语，让人们自己的想法得以映射其中。所以，对很多听众来说，这句歌词很自然地反映了一段关系的结束。

当时我想："噢，人们会认为在影射披头士的解散。关于我的吉他站在我身边，我的乐队伙伴却没有。"大概在我的内心深处，我认为确实如此，某种程度上，当时我就是这么想的。

"Serpents turn to bits of string"（大蛇变成一小段细绳）是指 1968 年，我们和玛哈里希一起在瑞诗凯诗冥想时发生的事情。每天晚上，人们都会见面交谈，玛哈里希会回答问题，有一件事令我记忆犹新。大家总是说："冥想吧。别担心，一切都没关系。"而有一个人说："玛哈里希，我来自纽约，我必须告诉你，我害怕蛇。"这个可怜的家伙对蛇有恐惧症。他说："我正在冥想，在冥思中看见这条蛇冲我游来。我真的很害怕，但我记得你说过的话：看看它，并且冥想。然后，蛇变成了一小段绳子。"我一直觉得这是一个了不起的故事，对它印象深刻。

1　国民信托，全称为"美丽国家名胜古迹信托"（National Trust for Places of Historic Interest or Natural Beauty），是专注于保护当地文化遗产与自然风光的慈善机构。

CONFIDANTE

Intro.

1. You used to be my confidante
My underneath the staircase friend
But I fell out of love with you
And brought our romance to an end

(CH.) I played with you throughout the day
And told you every secret thought
Unlike my other so called friends
You stood beside me as I fought

2. In your reflected glory I
Could dream of shining far off lands
Where serpents turn to bits of string
And play like kittens in my hand

(CH.) In our imaginary world
The butterflies wear (Army) boots
And stamp around the forest chanting
long lost Anthems ...

(Instrumental)

[Instrumental]

Repeat 1. You used to be my confidante
My underneath the staircase friend
But I fell out of love with you
And brought our romance to an end

Repeat
(CH) I played with you throughout the day
I told you every secret thought
Unlike my other so called friends
You stood beside me as I fought

"Butterflies wearing army boots"（蝴蝶穿着军靴）则完全是自由发挥。我在想象的世界中信马由缰，这里有蝴蝶，而我觉得可以听凭这些蝴蝶被想象力塑造成任何形象——我喜欢它们穿着巨大而笨重的军靴的想法。一旦穿上这双靴子，它们就会在森林里跺脚，唱着久违的颂歌。我把它们想象成朋克——像朋克蝴蝶，唱着朋克歌曲四处游行。这一切都是从一把吉他开始的。

虽然不想承认，但如今我有太多的吉他。实在太多了。我时常想到这件事：当你还是个孩子时，你有一把吉他，它是你最珍贵的吉他，而第一把不可避免地是原声吉他；获得一点成功后，你可能会弄一把电吉他；当你更加成功时，另一把稍微有点不同的电吉他可能会引起你的兴趣。从那时起，你要么再买一把吉他，因为它很可爱，你喜欢它；或者一旦当你真正广受赞誉，人们开始送吉他给你。总会有一把新的琴很可爱，令你无法说不。有人会送你一把有这个或那个优点的吉他——一把非常好的 Alvarez，或者 Taylor[1]——多年来，公司和个人送给我不少吉他。最近，我得到了猫王的伟大吉他手斯科蒂·摩尔（Scotty Moore）弹过的吉他。那一把有着特别的意义。

不过，在所有这些吉他中，我最喜欢的电吉他是我的 Epiphone Casino。我走进伦敦查令十字街的一家吉他店，对店员说："你能不能给我选一把有回授效果的吉他，因为我喜欢吉米·亨德里克斯那种音色。"我是吉米的崇拜者。我很幸运地在他早期伦敦的一次演出中见过他，就好像天空被炸裂一般。他是个很好的人，很和善。现在我们经常在现场表演中向吉米致敬，即兴演奏《狐狸精》（Foxy Lady）。言归正传，吉他店的店员说："这把可能是回授效果最好的，它的琴身是空心的，会比实心吉他制造更大的音量。"于是我把它带到了录音棚，这把琴附有比格斯比牌（Bigsby）的颤音摇把，你可以用它制造并控制回授效果，完美极了。它着实是一把非常棒的吉他，非常性感。于是，它成了我最喜欢的电吉他，《平装书作家》（Paperback Writer）的前奏连复段和乔治的歌曲《税务员》（Taxman）的独奏都是用它弹的，这些年来，我用它演奏了许多作品。我今天还在弹它。那把 Epiphone Casino 已经是我一生的伴侣。

虽然不想承认，但如今我有太多的吉他。
实在太多了。
当你还是个孩子时，你有一把吉他，它是你最珍贵的吉他。

---

1   Alvarez、Taylor，及下文的 Epiphone 均为著名吉他品牌，Casino 则为 Epiphone 经典琴型。

我最喜欢的电吉他是我的 Epiphone Casino。
我走进伦敦查令十字街的一家吉他店，对店员说：
"你能不能给我选一把有回授效果的吉他，
因为我喜欢吉米·亨德里克斯那种音色。"
我是吉米的崇拜者。
我很幸运地在他早期伦敦的一次演出中见过他，
就好像天空被炸裂一般。

Cook of the House

家里的厨师

作　者	WRITERS	琳达·麦卡特尼和保罗·麦卡特尼　Linda McCartney and Paul McCartney
艺术家	ARTIST	羽翼乐队　Wings
录　音	RECORDED	伦敦阿比路录音棚　Abbey Road Studios, London
发　行	RELEASED	《以音速》，1976 年　*At the Speed of Sound*, 1976
		《愚蠢的情歌》B 面单曲，1976 年　B-side of 'Silly Love Songs' single, 1976

Ground rice, sugar, vinegar, Seco salt
Macaroni too
Cook of the house
I'm the cook of the house

No matter where I serve my guests
They seem to like the kitchen best
'Cause I'm the cook of the house
Cook of the house

The salad's in the bowl
The rice is on the stove
Green beans in the colander
And where the rest is heaven only knows

Cinnamon, garlic, salt, pepper
Cornbread, curry powder, coffee too
Cook of the house
I'm the cook of the house

No matter where I serve my guests
They seem to like the kitchen best
'Cause I'm the cook of the house
Cook of the house

And the rest is heaven only knows

Cinnamon, garlic, salt, pepper
Cornbread, curry powder, coffee too
Cook of the house (that's the cook of the house)
I'm the cook of the house (she's the cook
  of the house)

No matter where I serve my guests
They seem to like the kitchen best
'Cause I'm the cook of the house (that's
  cook of the house)

Cook of the house (she's the cook of the house)
Cook of the house (that's the cook of the house)
I'm the cook of the house
Take it, fellow

"No matter where I serve my guests / They seem to like the kitchen best"（不管我在哪里招待客人，他们似乎都最喜欢厨房）是我们租住的房屋中厨房里的一个标记；我记得似乎是在澳大利亚，也许是在我们的儿子詹姆斯（James McCartney）出生前，羽翼乐队世界巡演期间。所以应该是琳达、希瑟、玛丽、斯特拉和我都住在一起。

那是琳达记得的一件趣事——这基本上是琳达的歌，我帮了点忙。在这个时候，羽翼乐队的每个成员都会有一首歌收录在专辑中，而这是《以音速》里她的歌。有时，一首歌的内容就是你环顾四周，说出你看见的所有东西的名字。在这首歌中，她选择了各种香料——肉桂、大蒜、咖喱粉，因为作为一个家庭，我们花了很多时间在厨房里协作干活儿。琳达是一个很棒的厨师，而且喜欢给家人和朋友做饭，她的歌是《家里的厨师》，这再合适不过了。

孩子们还小的时候，我们经常玩一个游戏：蒙上他们的眼睛，给他们一些东西，让他们靠嗅觉猜出那是什么。咖啡和茶很容易，肉桂很容易，然后你会慢慢加大难度：面粉有点难，盐也不简单。这是我们自娱自乐的方式。那时还没有电子游戏，那时几乎消遣什么都没有。

无论如何，这首歌是一种简单但经典的摇滚乐之声，简单来说就是三和弦，而第四个和弦出现在副歌和主歌的转折处。从 1950 年代到现在，这种模式出现在无数歌曲中。并不是每个人都倾向于在降 E 调用煎培根的声音为这首歌开场。这就是它的特别之处。另外，我在《家里的厨师》中弹奏的贝斯曾经属于比尔·布莱克（Bill Black），猫王的贝斯手，这一传承带来了复古感。我现在有两把乐器曾经属于猫王乐队的成员！

左图：琳达在做饭，伦敦，1977 年。

右图：琳达、希瑟、斯特拉，以及宠物狗"幸运"在厨房，苏格兰，1970 年代中期。

2 weeks. x rays/12

Goldilock's Xray Lungs
Suzie Home tomorrow
Mumps 12:30
Dog Next Week
Monkey - Heart
1995/

Mouse. 200
Teddy - 300
Badger - 4.00 = nose Box
Leg

COOK of The House

ground rice, Sugar, Vinegar, Sage (saco)
Salt macaroni too
The Cook of The House
" , ,

no mater were I serve my guests
They seem to like my Kitchen Best
The Cook of the House
" ,

The Salads in the Bowl, The rice is in the stove, green Beans in the Colender
and where the rest is Heaven only Knows
Cinnamon, garlic, Salt pepper corn bread
curry powder coffee too
Cook of The house
I'm the COOK of The house

no matter where I serve my guests
They seem to like my Kitchen Best
Oh - macaroni too
COOK of The house
no mater where I serve my guests - cook of The house

Country Dreamer

乡村梦想家

作　者	WRITERS	保罗·麦卡特尼和琳达·麦卡特尼　Paul McCartney and Linda McCartney
艺术家	ARTIST	保罗·麦卡特尼和羽翼乐队　Paul McCartney and Wings
录　音	RECORDED	伦敦阿比路录音棚　Abbey Road Studios, London
发　行	RELEASED	《海伦之轮》B 面单曲，1973 年　B-side of 'Helen Wheels' single, 1973

I'd like to walk in a field with you
Take my hat and my boots off too
I'd like to lie in a field with you
Would you like to do it too, May?
Would you like to do it too?

I'd like to stand in a stream with you
Roll my trousers up and not feel blue
I'd like to wash in a stream with you
Would you like to do it too?

You and I, country dreamer
When there's nothing else to do
Me oh my, country dreamer
Make a country dream come true

I'd like to climb up a hill with you
Stand on top and admire the view
I'd like to roll down a hill with you
Would you like to do it too, May?
Would you like to do it too?

You and I, country dreamer
When there's nothing else to do
Me oh my, country dreamer
Make a country dream come true

I'd like to climb up a hill with you
Take my hat and my boots off too
I'd like to lie in a field with you
Would you like to do it too, May?
Would you like to do it too?

Would you like to do it too?

如果要用一个词来概述我和琳达的哲学观：简单。我们热爱自由，热爱自然，热爱生活中所有美好的事物。时至今日，我仍对大自然怀有很深厚的感情，我觉得我是其中的一部分。人类、动物、生物，我们都在这个星球上，我不吃动物，是因为想让它们有机会，就像我有机会一样。我有机会抚养孩子，我能做爱，为什么它们不行呢？主要归咎于我们剥夺了它们的生命，相比作为传统食肉动物，我是素食主义者的时间更长。

《乡村梦想家》的第一段歌词是在向艾弗·卡特勒（Ivor Cutler）致敬，他是杰出的苏格兰诗人和词曲作者，曾自称为"倾斜的音乐哲学家"。和我一样，他也喜欢超现实主义。我在收音机里听过他，可能是在约翰·皮尔[1]的著名节目中（尽管皮尔也有可能是通过披头士乐队遇到了他）。但不管怎样，我打电话给艾弗说："你想共进晚餐吗？"我们的友谊就是这样开始的。艾弗在我们的电影《魔幻之旅》（*Magical Mystery Tour*）中饰演巴斯特·布拉德维塞尔（Buster Bloodvessel），他写了一首叫作《我要去田野》（I'm Going in a Field）的可爱短歌。直到今天我都还很喜欢：

> 我要去田野
> 我要去田野
> 我要去田野去躺下
> 我要躺在青草旁
> 我要躺在青草旁
> 我要躺在青青的青草旁[2]

所以，我的歌从"I'd like to walk in a field with you / Take my hat and my boots off too"（我想和你在田野里散步 / 脱下我的帽子和靴子）开始。这正是我们会在夏天的苏格兰做的事情，我喜欢他穿戴着帽子和靴子的想法。苏格兰经常下雨，到处会泥泞不堪，或者我们会在农场，所以你会经常穿着雨靴。不是那种非常漂亮的靴子。但你会来到一条小溪旁，脱掉它们，踏进水中。

"Would you like to do it too, May?"（你是否也愿意这样，梅？）我叫她"梅"，我意识到，这也可以理解为"你想对我做吗"，所以它也有某种情色的成分。但我总是这么做——加入一些有点厚颜的东西。这是允许的，就像琳达说的那样。这是她的一句名言："这是允许的。"

梅成了一个乡村梦想家："You and I, country dreamer / When there's nothing else to do"（你和我，乡村梦想家 / 当无事可做时）。这其实都是非常简单的事情，我确实很喜欢这么做。"I'd like to climb up a hill with you / Stand on top and admire the view / I'd like to roll down a hill with you"（我想和你爬上山丘 / 站在山顶上欣赏风景 / 我想和你滚下山坡），就像杰克和吉尔[3]。这是所有孩子都喜欢做的事。这是你在山丘上应该做的事情。当年纪渐长，我们就不常这样做了。或许是因为我们知道之后会疼。

---

1   约翰·皮尔（John Peel，1939—2004），英国广播公司电台资深音乐主持人。
2   原句为"I'm going in a field / I'm going in a field / I'm going in a field to lie down / I'll lie beside the grass / I'll lie beside the grass / I'll lie beside the green grass"。
3   英国童谣《杰克和吉尔》（Jack and Jill）的主人公。

COUNTRY DREAMER

1) I'd like to walk through a field with you
Take my hat & my boots off too
I'd like to lie in a field with you
Would you like to do it to, ——,
would you like to do it too,

2) I'd like to stand in a stream with you
Roll my trousers up & not feel blue
I'd like to wash in a stream with you
Would you like to do it to me,
.. .. TOO,

CHORUS
me oh my COUNTRY DREAMER
When theres nothing else to do
You & I COUNTRY DREAMER
Make a country dream come true.

3.) I'd like to climb up a hill with you
Stand on top & admire the view
I'd like to roll down a hill with you

On the farm. Scotland, 1970

在农场，苏格兰，1970 年。

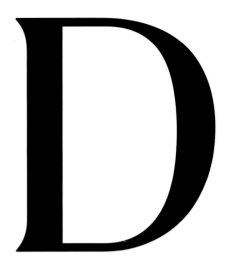

D

A Day in the Life
生命中的一天

作 者	WRITERS	约翰·列侬和保罗·麦卡特尼　John Lennon and Paul McCartney
艺术家	ARTIST	披头士乐队　The Beatles
录 音	RECORDED	伦敦阿比路录音棚　Abbey Road Studios, London
发 行	RELEASED	《佩珀军士孤独之心俱乐部乐队》，1967 年　*Sgt. Pepper's Lonely Hearts Club Band*, 1967

I read the news today, oh boy
About a lucky man who made the grade
And though the news was rather sad
Well I just had to laugh
I saw the photograph

He blew his mind out in a car
He didn't notice that the lights had changed
A crowd of people stood and stared
They'd seen his face before
Nobody was really sure if he was from
the House of Lords

I saw a film today, oh boy
The English army had just won the war
A crowd of people turned away
But I just had to look
Having read the book

I'd love to turn you on

Woke up, fell out of bed
Dragged a comb across my head
Found my way downstairs and drank a cup
And looking up, I noticed I was late

Found my coat and grabbed my hat
Made the bus in seconds flat
Found my way upstairs and had a smoke
And somebody spoke and I went into a dream

I read the news today, oh boy
Four thousand holes in Blackburn, Lancashire
And though the holes were rather small
They had to count them all
Now they know how many holes it takes to fill
the Albert Hall

I'd love to turn you on

怎么强调广播对披头士的影响都不为过。事实上，你可以把《佩珀军士》当成一个大型广播节目。比如，我们使用音效来扩展我们的创作能力和范围。百代是一家包罗万象的老式唱片公司，录音棚所在的大楼里有一个声音档案馆。如果我想在歌曲《黑鸟》里加入黑鸟的叫声，只需在目录中找到并预定，就会有人从档案馆把它拿到录音棚来。于是，我们开始通过这个档案馆瞎玩，而这让我们的创作非常自由。

小时候，我极为好奇的事情之一是，广播中的主持人是如何出场的。就以了不起的利物浦喜剧演员肯·多德作比吧。他上台后会说"呃"，然后演播室里的观众会"哇哦"然后大笑。我心里激动坏了。他做了什么？他脱掉裤子了吗？他做鬼脸吗？他在摆弄他标志性的痒痒耙吗？他做了什么？我真的很喜欢那种神秘感。于是我对其他人说："报幕'独一无二的比利·希尔斯（Billy Shears）'演唱《在我朋友们的一点帮助下》时，我们用档案馆里观众的笑声做素材吧。"我们会像肯·多德那样来使用这种效果。我们真的很喜欢激发想象力。

你的想象力是强大的力量。在电视和电影里，一切已经确定，你可以看到一个名叫亨利埃塔·吉布斯（Henrietta Gibbs）的角色的长相；在广播中，你能创造自己的亨利埃塔·吉布斯。那是《佩珀军士》最了不起的地方。他们想把它拍成电影，但没有成功，因为每个人都已在心中描绘了它。

《佩珀军士》吸收的另一重要养分在《生命中的一天》里非常突出，那时我听了很多前卫的东西。斯托克豪森、卢西亚诺·贝里奥[1]、约翰·凯奇——你知道，凯奇的无声作品《4分33秒》。那些先锋音乐令我着迷，我希望《生命中的一天》中也能有非同寻常的器乐段落。于是我跟乔治·马丁谈了谈，他负责安排管弦乐队。正如舞蹈指导莫斯·康宁汉[2]会说"用一根绳子把他们拉过舞台"，我在这里的指示是，管弦乐队的每个人从乐器的最低音开始，在一定的小节内演奏到最高音。

我们开始录音时，乔治·马丁不得不先行为他们安排演奏计划。人们通常认为科班出身的音乐家不喜欢即兴演奏，不过我发现，有趣的是，管弦乐队自行分为几个小组。弦乐组像绵羊："如果你往上走，我就上去。我不会被落在后面。"小号和管乐组则很容易接受无拘无束、自由即兴的想法，也许是因为他们在管弦乐队中经常被忽视。他们乐于尝试任何事。

我们自己也下定决心全力以赴，想办法把所有这些元素融入所谓的"流行"音乐中。我们喜欢这个主意：我们在尝试延伸传统，而非止于延续。

---

1 卢西亚诺·贝里奥（Luciano Berio，1925—2003），意大利前卫音乐家。
2 莫斯·康宁汉（Merce Cunningham，1919—2009），美国舞蹈家、现代舞编舞大师，他创造了"机遇"编舞法，树立了"纯舞蹈"风格。

于是我跟乔治·马丁谈了谈，他负责安排管弦乐队。
正如舞蹈指导莫斯·康宁汉会说"用一根绳子把他们拉过舞台"，
我在这里的指示是，
管弦乐队的每个人从乐器的最低音开始，
在一定的小节内演奏到最高音。

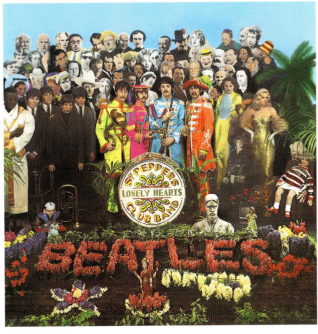

上图：指挥管弦乐团，伦敦阿比路录音棚一号棚，1967 年 2 月。

右图：《佩珀军士孤独之心俱乐部乐队》专辑封面，卡尔海因兹·斯托克豪森是最后一排左数第五位，1967 年。

Dear Friend
亲爱的朋友

作 者	WRITERS	保罗·麦卡特尼和琳达·麦卡特尼 Paul McCartney and Linda McCartney
艺术家	ARTIST	保罗·麦卡特尼和羽翼乐队 Paul McCartney and Wings
录 音	RECORDED	伦敦阿比路录音棚 Abbey Road Studios, London
发 行	RELEASED	《狂野生活》，1971 年 *Wild Life*, 1971

Dear friend, what's the time?
Is this really the borderline?
Does it really mean so much to you?
Are you afraid, or is it true?

Dear friend, throw the wine
I'm in love with a friend of mine
Really truly, young and newly wed
Are you a fool, or is it true?

Are you afraid, or is it true?

我经常想起约翰，很遗憾，我们有时会公开地激烈争吵。这首歌写于 1971 年初，那时他在《滚石》杂志上说《麦卡特尼》这张专辑是"垃圾"。那段时期真的很难熬。我为我们友谊的破裂而难过，这首歌有点像是在倾诉："Dear friend, what's the time? / Is this really the borderline?"（亲爱的朋友，什么时候了？/ 这真的是底线吗？）我们分手了吗？这是否就是"各走各路"？

1969 年底，约翰兴奋地告诉我们，一切都结束了。当时，我们几个人在苹果公司的会议室里。乔治应该是去探亲了，林戈和我出席了会议，约翰拒绝了每一个建议。我觉得我们应该再去演一些小演出，但约翰的回答是"不"。最后，约翰说："哦，我一直想告诉你们，我要离开披头士了。"我们都感到震惊。此前，乐队的关系已经变得很紧张，但那一刻，我们坐在那里，问："什么？为什么？为什么？为什么？"这就像是离婚，他前一年刚和辛西娅离婚。我还记得那时他说："哦，这太令人兴奋了。"这就是约翰的风格，我小时候第一次见到他时，曾经很欣赏他这种逆反行为。从最好的方面来说，他确实有点疯。虽然我们都明白他的意思，对那些被留在另一边的人来说，这并不那么令人兴奋。

关于约翰和披头士的分手，我一直对媒体保持沉默。我真的没有抱怨太多，但约翰在采访中有过不少指责。他指责我宣布披头士的解散是为了宣传《麦卡特尼》这张专辑，但我只是诚实地回答了苹果媒体部的提问。我不想借由采访来宣传唱片，苹果公司的彼得·布朗（Peter Brown）问过这样的问题："你是否计划与披头士乐队合作推出新专辑或单曲？"我的回答是"不"。我觉得撒谎毫无意义。

约翰会说这样的话——"那是垃圾。披头士是垃圾"，还有"我不相信披头士，我不相信耶稣，我不相信上帝"。他抛出的这些挖苦的话语十分伤人，而我是挖苦的对象，我确实被刺伤了。但我不得不阅读所有他吐露给媒体的责难，一边气恼地觉得"滚蛋吧，你这个该死的白痴"，一边又忍不住揣测："你为什么那么说？你是在生我的气，还是在嫉妒什么？"五十年之后再回想，我仍然不知道他当时的感受。他经历了很多。他父亲失踪了，然后他失去了父亲般的叔叔乔治，接着是他的母亲、斯图尔特·萨克利夫、布莱恩·爱泼斯坦——另一位父亲般的人；现在，他失去了他的乐队。但是约翰把所有这些情绪投入名为"列侬"的狂欢中。那就是他。那就是他的魅力所在。

我尝试过。以询问"必须如此伤人吗"的方式，这首歌也是某种我对他的回答。我想这是一句很好的歌词："Are you afraid, or is it true?"（你感到恐惧吗，或者这都是事实？）意思是，"为什么要这样争吵？是因为你恐惧什么吗？你害怕分开吗？你害怕我做事不需要你吗？你害怕你的行为带来的后果吗？"而"or is it true"是在问，所有这些伤人的指控都是真的吗？这首歌就是在这种情绪下创作出来的。它本可以是"搞什么鬼，哥们儿"，而那个时候我不确定我们是否能摆脱这些。

我们三个人——乔治、林戈和我——是否想过在没有约翰的情况下继续披头士的生涯？不，我认为不行。披头士就是这样的团体，这样一个四人组。我们曾开玩笑说要成立一个叫"披头三人组"的乐队，但我们并没有当真。这不过是个玩笑。

在我们各奔东西之前，我们确实一起做了一些零碎的片段。约翰、洋子和我做了《约翰和洋子的歌谣》（The Ballad of John and Yoko）。他邀请我参与，是因为他知道这是制作唱片的好方式。"我们要去阿比路录音棚。谁住在附近？保罗。谁可以在这张唱片里打鼓？保罗。谁可以弹贝斯？保罗。如果我客气地请求帮助，谁会应允？保罗。"他丝毫不羞于开口。他大概这么问了："哦，我有首歌要录音。你能过来吗？"我也许回答说："可以，为什么不呢？"

还有很多悬而未决的事情需要处理。那些商务问题横亘在我们之间。你想必记得，我起诉了他。我在利物浦的法庭上起诉了我一生的朋友。但最后，我认为与他和洋子一起录制那张唱片，促成了我们之后的一些友好的见面和交谈。

我觉得这首歌，《亲爱的朋友》，也对和解有所助益。我想他听到了。我想我的唱片发行时他就会听，但他从来没有直接回应我。那不是他的方式。我们是哥们儿，不同于男孩和女孩相处的方式。在那些日子里，你们彼此不会表达太多的情感。

我很高兴最后几年我们相处得很好，在他被刺杀之前，我和他相处得很愉快。毫无疑问，如果他在我们关系不好时遇害，那对我来说会是世界上最糟糕的事情。我会想："哦，我本应该，我本应该，我本应该……"我将会背负巨大的内疚感。但幸运的是，我们最后的会面十分友好。我们讨论了如何烤面包。

下左：《约翰和洋子的歌谣》单曲碟。琳达拍摄的封面照片，1969 年 4 月 30 日。

下右：约翰·列侬，琳达拍摄。圣莫妮卡，1974 年。

对页：和约翰·伊斯曼、约翰·列侬、小野洋子、艾伦·克莱因、林戈·斯塔尔、莫琳·斯塔基（Maureen Starkey）及彼得·霍华德（Peter Howard）在一起，苹果办公室，1969 年。

16 TUESDAY   (259–106 Week No. 38)

Eq Davis   call agent
       Call Davis
Mary's Rice Cereal

12:00 Mrs. Meyer

THE·END

Justin + Twiggy's dinner

17 WEDNESDAY   (260–105 Week No. 38)   Ember Day

Alex   Barbara
Print-   agents
           slides

1:00 Lew Grade
      lunch – a-la-deal deli
            by Kathy

3:00 Meeting – Capital EMI agreement

我们三个人 —— 乔治、林戈和我 —— 是否想过在没有约翰的情况下继续披头士的生涯？不，我认为不行。

披头士就是这样的团体，这样一个四人组。我们曾开玩笑说要成立一个叫"披头三人组"的乐队，但我们并没有当真。

Despite Repeated Warnings
尽管一再警告

作　者　WRITERS　　　保罗·麦卡特尼　Paul McCartney

艺术家　ARTIST　　　　保罗·麦卡特尼　Paul McCartney

录　音　RECORDED　　洛杉矶汉森录音棚、萨塞克斯郡猪山磨坊、伦敦阿比路录音棚

　　　　　　　　　　　Henson Studios, Los Angeles；Hog Hill Mill, Sussex and Abbey Road Studios, London

发　行　RELEASED　　《埃及站》，2018 年　*Egypt Station,* 2018

Despite repeated warnings
Of dangers up ahead
The captain won't be listening
To what's been said

He feels that there's a good chance
That we have been misled
And so the captain's planning
To steam ahead

What can we do?
What can we do?
What can we do to stop this foolish plan going
　　through?
What can we do?
What can we do?
This man is bound to lose his ship and his crew

Despite repeated warnings
From those who ought to know
Well he's got his own agenda
And so he'll go

Those who shout the loudest
May not always be the smartest
But they have their proudest moments
Right before they fall

Red sky in the morning
Doesn't ever seem to faze him
But a sailor's warning signal
Should concern us all

How can we stop him?
Grab the keys and lock him up
If we can do it
We can save the day

The engineer lives with
His wife and daughter Janet
But he misses them so

Although he's working with
The best crew on the planet
They never want him to go

He had a premonition
He senses something's wrong
And by his own admission
He knew it all along

The captain's crazy
But he doesn't let them know it
He'll take us with him
If we don't do something soon to slow it

How can we stop him?
Grab the keys and lock him up
If we can do it
We can save the day

Below decks the engineer cries
The captain's gonna leave us when
    the temperatures rise
The needle's going up
The engine's gonna blow
And we're gonna be left down below
Down below

Yes we can do it
Yeah we can do it now

If life would work out
The way you plan it
That'd be so fine
For the wife and Janet
Sometimes you might
Have to battle through it
But that's the way you learn
How you've got to do it

Yes we can do it, whoa whoa

Despite repeated warnings
Of dangers up ahead
Well the captain wasn't listening
To what was said

So we went to the captain
And we told him to turn around
But he laughs in our faces
Says that we are mistaken

So we gather around him
Now the ropes that have bound him
Prove that he should have listened
To the will of the people
It's the will of the people
It's the will of the people

美国前总统特朗普认为气候危机是一场骗局——是中国人制造的骗局。可悲的是，他不是唯一无视这种生存威胁的人。我记得在日本的报纸上读到一篇文章说，"尽管一再警告，但没有人对此采取任何行动。"这足以成为我的创作动机。

气候危机并不新鲜。事实上，少年时期在利物浦时，我看过一档很早的黑白电视节目，一档少儿节目，类似《蓝彼得》（Blue Peter）——这是一个有时会涉及时事的专题节目。三位在我看来非常年迈的科学家，在节目中谈论世界的未来和我们必须做的事情。他们称之为"未来蓝图"。当时我才十几岁，对此印象深刻。我想："这是个好主意，现在就开始努力吧。"

我总是写一些我感兴趣的歌曲。主题不必很重要；它可以只是一首感伤的情歌，也可以是一首悲伤的歌。而有时，它承载着我想向人们说的话，包含着我认为值得传递的信息。说来有些矛盾，那些并非人们必须掌握的信息，但我知道有些人能领会其间意义，因此值得这么做。

我们开始在洛杉矶的汉森录音棚录制《尽管一再警告》时，这首歌在我的脑海中已经有些歌剧色彩。这些歌词仿似化作舞台上的场景，就像在吉尔伯特和沙利文的歌剧里，船员们穿着条纹衬衫，疯狂的船长戴着一顶花哨的、黄金装饰的帽子。

《尽管一再警告》是一首史诗般的歌曲，在节奏和曲调上，它都进行了一系列变化。它有点像《逃亡乐队》和《阿比路》B面歌曲的混合。我真的很喜欢这种挑战：把歌曲糅在一起，让它们开始新的旅程。我一直很想看到这首歌上演。在我的脑海中，它在一个教堂大厅被搬上舞台，由一个学生团体伴唱副歌，"What can we do? / What can we do? / What can we do? /…this foolish plan"（我们能做什么？ / 我们能做什么？ / 我们能做什么？ /……这个愚蠢的计划）。很像《如何处置醉水手》（What can we do with the drunken sailor?），曲调变得和那首歌非常相似。

汉森录音棚，2017 年。

我把我的演出团队称为"地球上最好的团队"，在演出中，我会对观众说，"让我们为地球上最好的团队欢呼"，于是，他们也悄悄出现在歌曲中。

就大局而言，我们面临的政治局势似乎相当不稳定。尤其在美国，这个国家由吹牛者掌权。他喊得最响亮，但未必最聪明。我觉得有些人相信自己的执念，那些执念在他们心中就是事实。我时常困惑："一个人怎么能不为自己的话负责呢？"但是，两天后，媒体会带来他说的其他话，我们以为他永远无法蒙混过关的那些言论，在信息的洪流中销声匿迹，很难再引起人们的注意。

就好像报纸上对你进行了不实报道，你给他们打电话说："这完全是捏造的，我没有这么做。"他们会回复："好吧，我们会改正的。"他们把那个故事刊发在头版，如果你要寻找更正的话，它在第 29 页——当然是在底部："哦，有人告诉我们那不是真的。"不幸的是，人们记得首次刊载的内容，他们永远看不到更正。

但我是那种心怀希望的人，因此，我们发起"周一素食"[1] 运动，以提醒人们，你的生活方式只要进行小小的改变，就可以对环境产生积极的影响。当然，如果你不仅在周一食素，我们会非常高兴；每周有一天不吃肉，真的能带来改变。像格丽塔·桑伯格[2] 这样的人产生的影响是很鼓舞人心的。在一年的时间里，她从独自一人在校外抗议气候危机，发展到吸引成千上万的人听她演讲。气候危机已经引起她那一代人的极大关注。所以，也许那些反复的警告开始生效了。

像格丽塔·桑伯格这样的人产生的影响是很鼓舞人心的。
在一年的时间里，她从独自一人在校外抗议气候危机，
发展到吸引成千上万的人听她演讲。
气候危机已经引起她那一代人的极大关注。
所以，也许那些反复的警告开始生效了。

1　"周一素食"（Meat Free Monday），号召素食的全球性运动。
2　格丽塔·桑伯格（Greta Thunberg），又名气候少女。2003 年出生于瑞典斯德哥尔摩。宣传环保和抗议气候变暖的青年代表之一。

The engineer lives with
His wife and daughter Janet
But he misses them so

    Although he's working with
The 'best' crew on the planet
    They never want him to go

He had a premonition
He senses something wrong
And by his own admission
He knew it all along

The captain's going crazy
But he doesn't know it
He'll take us with him
If we don't do something
Soon to slow it

How can we stop him
Grab the keys & lock him up

If life would work out
The way you plan it
That'd be just fine
For the wife and Janet
Sometimes you might
Have to battle through it
    that's the way you learn
How you're got to do it.

Yes you can do it whoa . . .

DESPITE
End Section.

So we went to the captain
And we told him to turn round
But he laughs in our faces
Says that we are mistaken

So we gather around him
Now the ropes that have bound him
Prove that he should have listened
To The will of the people
To the will of the people
It's the will of the people

Distractions
心烦意乱

作　者　WRITER　　保罗·麦卡特尼　Paul McCartney
艺术家　ARTIST　　保罗·麦卡特尼　Paul McCartney
录　音　RECORDED　萨塞克斯郡猪山磨坊　Hog Hill Mill, Sussex
发　行　RELEASED　《泥土中的花朵》，1989 年　*Flowers in the Dirt*, 1989

What is this thing in life
That persuades me to spend
Time away from you?
If you can answer this
You can have the moon

This is the place to be
Any way you can see
There's a lovely view
Why are there always
So many other things to do?

Distractions
Like butterflies are buzzing
Round my head
When I'm alone
I think of you
And the life we'd lead if we could only be free
From these distractions

The postman's at the door
While the telephone rings
On the kitchen wall
Pretend we're not at home
And they'll disappear

I want to be with you
Tell me what I can do
Nothing is too small
Away from all this jazz
We could do anything at all

Distractions
Like butterflies are buzzing
Round my head
When I'm alone
I think of you
And the things we'd do if we could only be through
With these distractions

I'll find a peaceful place
Far away from the noise
Of a busy day
Where we can spend our nights
Counting shooting stars

Distractions
Like butterflies are buzzing
Round my head
When I'm alone
I think of you
And the things we'd do if we could only be through
With these distractions
Like butterflies they're buzzing
Round my head
When I'm alone
I think of you
And the life we'd lead if we could only be free
From these distractions

有时，写完一首歌后，我会意识到它缺乏一点激情。我用古他创作了《心烦意乱》，觉得它需要好好编曲，才能成为流行曲目。我在王子[1]1987年的专辑《时代的标志》（Sign o' the Times）里听过一段编曲，发现编曲者名叫克莱尔·菲舍尔（Clare Fischer），唯一的信息只有这个名字。我猜为王子的作品施展魔法的，是一位很有才华的女人。

说到披头士，我们一开始只是一支非常简单的四人摇滚乐队，为其他音乐家做编曲是我们从未探索过的世界。学会一首新歌时，我们只会互相示范如何演奏：在这里演弹 G 和弦，然后转到 C 和弦，在 C 和弦上继续。我们过去常常把自己简单地描述为"伴舞乐队"。事实上，我写了几封信给记者之类的人说，"我们是一支半专业的摇滚伴奏乐队"，试图自我推荐。在阿比路录音棚制作专辑之前，我们甚至从未想过，除了我们用的这些，还有其他乐器。

1960 年代中期，在约翰的歌《你要把你的爱藏起来》中，我们第一次引入了其他乐器。乔治·马丁建议我们加入一段长笛独奏，于是我们想，"好吧，我们试试。"乔治向来善于挑选音乐家。他对那个圈子很熟悉，所以我们总能请到顶尖的家伙，通常是古典音乐家或爵士乐音乐家，他们来参加录音赚点外快。那是我们第一次被连哄带骗地有了加入其他乐器的想法。随后，当然是同一张专辑《救命！》中我的歌《昨天》（Yesterday），乔治搞了弦乐四重奏为我的原声吉他伴奏。这是第一次披头士的歌曲里只有我们其中一人；在那之前，一直是整个乐队。所以，看到了这一切如何完成时，我们开始放开眼界，天空才是极限。

言归正传，在我的妻子琳达的帮助下——她很擅长寻人，我和克莱尔·菲舍尔在洛杉矶安排了一次会面，打算聊聊合作的可能性。我想象中的克莱尔是一位前途无限的年轻女士，但原来，这是个男人，一个相貌普通的中年绅士。人不可貌相！我和他商量着，或许可以在歌里加点管乐四重奏什么的。我告诉他，在我的孩提时代，我父亲就曾经尝试演奏黑管，他总是在楼上的房间里弄出尖锐短促的声响——如果你不会吹黑管的话，它们就会发出可怕的噪声。部分源于我父亲曾与这种乐器结缘（并在家人的劝阻下最终放弃），我一直很喜欢黑管丰富的木质音色。所以，我们在编曲时用了黑管，让它更接近某种本尼·古德曼的感觉，而不是——比如说——西德尼·贝谢[2]。

这首歌的意思比我其他的一些歌更直截了当。我喜欢这样的想法：在生活中，我们常常无法专注于我们真正要做的事情。这首歌说的是，生活就是你在做其他事情的路上所发生的事情；它变动不居。一如既往，我的表达使用了浪漫的措辞："What is this thing in life / That persuades me to spend / Time away from you?"（生活中有什么 / 可以让我花费 / 时间离你而去？）但我认为这很真实，不仅在情感一途，对无数的事情来说

1　王子（Prince，1958—2016），美国流行音乐传奇人物，开创了"明尼阿波利斯之声"这一音乐风格。
2　本尼·古德曼（Benny Goodman，1909—1986）、西德尼·贝谢（Sidney Bechet，1897—1959），均为美国爵士乐音乐家。

莫里斯·里帕斯（Morris Repass）、哈米
什·斯图尔特（Hamish Stuart）、琳达、
保罗、克莱尔·菲舍尔，以及阿尼·弗拉格
（Arne Frager）。洛杉矶，1988 年。

同样如此。即使你像我一样时常冥想，其他东西也会挤进你的头脑里。若是还能抽出
时间唱诵箴言，你已经很幸运了。你的脑海里满是蝴蝶在打转："噢，这是个好主意，
我会那么做的。"平静下来，静心默诵箴言是很困难的事情。我想这就是冥想的价值
所在。我的思维如此活跃，尝试将所有那些挡在你道路上、试图阻碍你的小事拒之门外，
是件好事。否则，就像 T. S. 艾略特所写的，你最终会"由于分心而神色木然"[1]。

1　出自美国诗人、文学评论家 T. S. 艾略特名篇《四个四重奏》，原句为"Distracted from distraction by distraction"。此句
　　采用裘小龙译本（《四个四重奏：艾略特诗选》，译林出版社，2017 年）。

DISTRACTIONS.

(1) What is this thing in life
That persuades me to spend
Time away from you
If you can answer this (Amin7 – maj)
you can have the moon.

(2) This is the place to be
Any way you can see
There's a lovely view
Why are there always so many other things to do?

(CHORUS) Distractions
Like butterflies are bugging
round my head
When I'm alone I think of you
And the life we'd lead if we could only be free
from these distractions

(BASS BIT)

(5) I'll find a peaceful place far away from
The noise of a busy day
where we can spend our nights
Counting shooting stars
If you CAN TRUST

(6) AND IF YOU TRUST IN ME
YOU'LL BE ABLE TO SEE
THERE'S ANOTHER WAY.
WHY IS there always someone
with something else to say......
" Distractions ." .

Do It Now

现在就做

作　者　WRITER　　　保罗·麦卡特尼　Paul McCartney

艺术家　ARTIST　　　保罗·麦卡特尼　Paul McCartney

录　音　RECORDED　洛杉矶汉森录音棚、萨塞克斯郡猪山磨坊、伦敦阿比路录音棚

Henson Studios, Los Angeles; Hog Hill Mill, Sussex and Abbey Road Studios, London

发　行　RELEASED　《埃及站》，2018 年　*Egypt Station*, 2018

Got the time, the inclination
I have answered your invitation
I'll be leaving in the morning
Watch me go

I don't know where the wind is blowing
Got directions to where I'm going
Nothing's certain
That's the only thing I know

Do it now, do it now
While the vision is clear
Do it now
While the feeling is here

If you leave it too late
It could all disappear
Do it now
While your vision is clear

I don't regret the steps I'm taking
The decision that I'm making
Is the right one, or I'm never
Going to know

Got the time, the inclination
　(It's not too late)
I have answered your invitation
　(You've still got time)
I'll be leaving in the morning
　(Follow the beat of your heart)
Watch me go

So do it now, do it now
While your vision is clear
Do it now
While the feeling is here

If you leave it too late
It could all disappear
So do it now
While your vision is clear

　　如果我弟弟迈克或我在做作业或家务活时拖拖拉拉，或者如果爸爸想让我们去街上捡马粪——现在很难想象，但我小时候，街上还有马——他会递给我们一个桶和一把铲子，然后说："去捡吧。"

　　他是对的，这是一件非常明智的事情。他在花园里施用马粪当作肥料，让花朵长得很好。他喜欢园艺，种过大丽花、金鱼草，以及薰衣草之类的花卉。但捡屎这种事，对两个小孩来说非常尴尬。我们会说："爸爸，别；真丢脸！"如果我们想拖延时间或是以"我明天就做"敷衍，他会说："不，现在就做。D-I-N：现在就做。"我的孩子们都知道这句话，我告诉过他们，我爸爸这么说过："不要拖延。D-I-N。"要知道，我一直认为"D-I-N"是唱片厂牌的完美名字。嘈杂。噪声。

　　"Do it now, do it now / While the vision is clear / Do it now / While the feeling is here"（现在就做，现在就做 / 当愿景清晰可见 / 现在就做 / 当感觉就在这里），这是我爸爸传递给我们的信息，当我们还是孩子时，这话是真理，今天同样如此。我想它准确地说明了这一点：你摆脱了犹豫和怀疑，就会勇往直前，这样，第二天就不必去想，"这样做对吗？"你已经打出你的牌，你已经在纸面诉尽衷肠，不管你喜不喜欢，它就在那里了。我完全赞成那种工作方式。我们刚开始写歌的时候，可没有"推迟到明天"这种奢侈的选项。一旦约翰和我（或者我自己）开始创作，我们别无他路，必须完成它，这是一项很好的准则。有想法的时候就去做，这种观念意义重大。

　　在其他创造性的工作中也是如此。我在 1990 年代画了很多画，几乎总是一口气画完，这意味着在画架前花上三四个小时，因为我发现回头再画毫无乐趣——那就像一个需要解决的问题："我当时的心情如何？我当时的愿景是什么？是什么样的感觉让我走到了这一步？"而当你一步到位，你已经解决了足够多的问题，并且回答了足够多的问题。你瞧，这是你的画，或者这是你的歌。如果愿意的话，你也可以稍后再处理它，但你不必回头想："哦，我对这个东西是怎么设想来着？""当愿景清晰可见，现在就做"是一个好建议。

和父亲吉姆及弟弟迈克在一起。
利物浦，1960 年代早期。

一位英国画家朋友在看我的画时对我说："嗯，这种绘画风格叫作直接画法（alla prima），字面意思是'第一遍'。"用于绘画时，我想它的意思是"一次性的"。你不会没完没了地在上面涂抹，很多伟大的画家会那样做，但那样会让我失去乐趣，我是为了乐趣而画，为了快乐而画。我读过一些关于画家生活的书，其中很多人的生活显然比较无趣，他们快把自己逼疯了。我最近读了威廉·德·库宁[1]的传记，至少有一幅画，他耗费了一整年去创作。当然，成果很棒，但伴随着无穷无尽的问题。他喝醉了，他疯了，他离开了他的女人，他过着疯狂的生活，只为把这幅画画好。我对这种做事方式不感兴趣，我总能听到父亲的声音，也许不再是大喊大叫，而是在我耳边低语："现在就做吧。"

1　威廉·德·库宁（Willem de Kooning，1904—1997），荷兰抽象表现主义画家。

DO IT NOW

Piano intro

V.1) GOT THE TIME — THE INCLINATION
I HAVE ANSWERED YOUR INVITATION
I'LL BE LEAVING IN THE MORNING
WATCH ME GO

V2) DON'T KNOW WHERE — THE WIND IS BLOWING
GOT DIRECTIONS TO WHERE I'M GOING
NOTHING'S CERTAIN
THAT'S THE ONLY THING I KNOW

CH. DO IT NOW, DO IT NOW
WHILE THE VISION IS CLEAR
DO IT NOW WHILE
THE FEELING'S STILL HERE

IF YOU LEAVE IT TOO LATE
IT COULD ALL DISAPPEAR
(SO) DO IT NOW
WHILE YOUR VISION IS CLEAR

V1) GOT THE TIME — THE INCLINATION
I HAVE ANSWERED YOUR INVITATION
I'LL BE LEAVING IN THE MORNING
WATCH ME GO
V2) DON'T KNOW WHERE etc. ↑

CH. DO IT NOW (SO) DO IT NOW
WHILE YOUR VISION IS CLEAR
DO IT NOW WHILE THE FEELING IS HERE
IF YA LEAVE IT TOO LATE
IS COULD ALL DISAPPEAR
(SO) DO IT NOW WHILE YOUR VISION IS CLEAR

左图：保罗画作《双生怪胎》，1990 年。

下图：保罗画作《埃及站》，1988 年。

右图：东汉普顿，1990 年。

Dress Me Up as a Robber

把我打扮成强盗

作 者 WRITER	保罗·麦卡特尼　Paul McCartney
艺术家 ARTIST	保罗·麦卡特尼　Paul McCartney
录 音 RECORDED	蒙特塞拉特岛 AIR 录音棚、伦敦 AIR 录音棚　AIR Montserrat and AIR Studios, London
发 行 RELEASED	《拔河比赛》，1982 年　*Tug of War*, 1982
	《带走它》B 面单曲，1982 年　B-side of 'Take It Away' single, 1982

You can dress me up as a robber
But I won't be in disguise
Only love is a robber
And he lives within your eyes

You can dress me up as a sailor
But I'll never run to sea
As long as your love is available to me
What do I do with a sea of blue?

Dressing me up
It doesn't make a difference
What you want to do
Whichever way you look at it
I'm still in love with you
We go on forever
I may never make a change

Dressing me up
And if I don't convince you
You needn't look too far
To see that I'm not lying
I love you the way you are
What's the point of changing
When I'm happy as I am?

You can dress me up as a soldier
But I wouldn't know what for
I was the one that told you he loved you
Don't wanna go to another war
No no no

不可否认，我真的很喜欢跳舞。如果聚会上响起欢快的音乐，我会跳舞。我和妻子南希热衷于此。演出结束后，当乐队和工作人员聚在一起喝一杯时，我们总是率先来到舞池。某些歌曲会让你闻之起舞，而你也有一些曲目始料不及地成为跳舞音乐。

约翰和我写的一些歌，比如《我看见她站在那里》（I Saw Her Standing There），能让每个人都站起来，《扭摆和尖叫》也真的让他们开心。跳舞一直是一项重要的社交活动。在网络聊天兴起之前，这就是认识伴侣的方式。我记得有一次和南希、林戈及他的妻子芭芭拉（Barbara Bach）去跳舞，我们坐在那里想："我们为什么在这里？"你知道，我们已经有了伴侣。

尝试创作时，你通常会寻找一个标签来开始。我想，这首歌写于 1980 年的夏天，可能在苏格兰。出丁某种原因，我当时想着，"你可以把我打扮成强盗，但这不会改变我对你的感觉"，这就是这首歌最初的创作核心。"You can dress me up as a soldier / But I wouldn't know what for / I was the one that told you he loved you / Don't wanna go to another war"（你可以把我打扮成士兵 / 但我不知为何而战 / 是我向你揭开了他的爱意 / 我不想参加另一场战争），其中有些反战意味。

与参战士兵有关的歌曲可谓历史悠久。你可以在歌曲中看到时代趋向，我想我们很多人都有朋友去了越南，或者试图避免去越南。它关于我们这一代，我们的同龄人；和我们同龄的美国人要去越南这个事实激发了我们的反战情绪。

从 1960 年代起，反战一直是一件大事。就我而言，加入反战行列始于在伦敦遇到伯特兰·罗素[1]，那时他已经九十多岁了。我想那是在 1964 年前后，他住在切尔西的某个地方（也许是福拉德街），一个朋友的朋友说："你应该去见见他。"我在电视上见过罗素，觉得他是个有趣的演说家；我也读过他的一些作品，他的尊严和强悍的表达能力给我留下了深刻的印象。所以我叩响了他家的门，出来应门的是一个美国学生，他的助手什么的，我说："哦，嗨。我能见见罗素先生吗？"我只是去碰碰运气，我们以前经常这么做。这是 1960 年代，记得吗，自由的 1960 年代 —— 那时不需要预约或事先征求许可，就可以打电话给别人。所以，即使到了今天，我也会想："好吧，如果他在，是个不错的开端；如果他想见我，而且能抽出五分钟，那就太好了；如果他愿意花更多的时间，棒极了。"

总之，我进去见了伯特兰·罗素，我们聊了聊。那个时候，他正把精力集中在他一年前创立的伯特兰·罗素和平基金会上，同时在为反对越南战争而奔走。他是第一个告诉我越南发生了什么的人，他解释说这是一场由既得利益集团支持的帝国主义战争。那时候，我们没有人真的了解这些。你要知道，这仍在战争的早期阶段，在抗议活动真正开始之前。

我记得我回到录音棚，告诉约翰这件事，他同样不知道越南正在发生战争。但我认为，这是一个开始：我们更清楚地意识到人们卷入了什么样的战争，政治开始成为乐队成员、我们的朋友和往来者经常讨论的话题。因此，刚刚起步的和平运动的某些

1　伯特兰·罗素（Bertrand Russell，1872—1970），英国哲学家、数学家、历史学家、文学家，分析哲学的主要创始人。

瞬间，送来了这首歌中的士兵之类的歌词。

在乔治·马丁位于蒙特塞拉特岛的 AIR 录音棚录制这首歌时，我们请来戴夫·马塔克斯（Dave Mattacks）打鼓。他是个很有趣的英国鼓手。第一次听到他演奏时，我还以为这是齐柏林飞艇[1]的约翰·博汉姆。我很钦佩博汉姆，也是他的朋友，但当我问起时，被告知："不，这是戴夫·马塔克斯。"这是一个很大的惊喜，因为博汉姆看起来有点像歌中这个角色。他就像一个了不起的大个儿农夫，打起鼓来极度生猛，一直希望自己的鼓点听起来像"该死的大炮"。戴夫则是一个瘦小的家伙，更像一个小学老师，你不会想到这么巨大的鼓声是由他发出来的。我们一起工作了一段时间，他非常优秀。他也是个有趣的家伙，会说一些关于鼓手的笑话："你怎么知道一个鼓手到门口了？敲门的速度越来越快。"他还会分享当时鼓手们给一些鼓点连复段取的名字，比如，有一些加花被称为"el-e-phant，el-e-phant，duck bill plat-y-pus"。

《把我打扮成强盗》是一首适合跳舞的歌，但它也是一首伪装的情歌，戴着面具的情歌。我觉得这首歌应该用在威尼斯人的假面舞会上。随着 2020 年的事态发展，假面舞会可能会卷土重来——它现在大概已经在各地上演，而不仅仅是在威尼斯。

---

1   齐柏林飞艇（Led Zeppelin），英国摇滚乐队，1968 年组建于伦敦，约翰·博汉姆（John Bonham）为乐队鼓手。

DRESS ME UP

~~(DRESSING UP)~~

Intro riff....

① Well you can dress me up as a robber
But I wont be in disguise,
(EVEN) Only love is a robber
And he lives within your eyes   ooh ..... ee oo....

        ("harmonies   ")

② Well you can dress me up as a sailor
But I'll never run to sea
As long as your love is available to me
What do I do with a sea of blue   oo - ee oo...

        ("harmonies ")

③ (Instrumental)

~~(CHORUS)~~ Dressing me up A difference   DO WHAT YOU WANT TO DO
CHORUS ~~It doesn't make much difference~~   ~~off~~ (IF WE)
~~Whichever way you look at it~~   MAYBE go on for ever
~~I'm still in love with you~~   WANT TO NEVER (I COULD)
Intro riff....   ~~BUT~~   ~~All~~ make   A change.

STOP rythm
    CLAPS (fast music wheel.)

CHORUS (YOU'RE JUST)

④ Well you can dress me up as a soldier
But I wouldn't know what for
I was the one that told you
he loved you
DONT ~~~~ ~~WANNA~~ go ~~TO~~ another war?

    Intro riff.

        END.

→ ("Dressing me up)"
If I ~~DONT~~ convince you
you need'nt look too far
to see that I'm not lying

    I love you as you are
and what's the point of changing
when (if) I'm happy as I am

Drive My Car

开我的车

作　者　WRITERS　　　保罗·麦卡特尼和约翰·列侬　Paul McCartney and John Lennon
艺术家　ARTIST　　　　披头士乐队　The Beatles
录　音　RECORDED　　伦敦阿比路录音棚　Abbey Road Studios, London
发　行　RELEASED　　《橡胶灵魂》，1965 年　*Rubber Soul*, 1965

Asked a girl what she wanted to be
She said, baby, can't you see?
I wanna be famous, a star of the screen
But you can do something in between

Baby you can drive my car
Yes I'm gonna be a star
Baby you can drive my car
And maybe I'll love you

I told that girl that my prospects were good
And she said, baby, it's understood
Working for peanuts is all very fine
But I can show you a better time

Baby you can drive my car
Yes I'm gonna be a star
Baby you can drive my car
And maybe I'll love you
Beep beep, beep beep, yeah

Baby you can drive my car
Yes I'm gonna be a star
Baby you can drive my car
And maybe I'll love you

I told that girl I could start right away
And she said, listen babe, I've got something to say
I got no car and it's breaking my heart
But I've found a driver and that's a start

Baby you can drive my car
Yes I'm gonna be a star
Baby you can drive my car
And maybe I'll love you

Beep beep, beep beep, yeah
Beep beep, beep beep, yeah

约翰和我最接近空谈的创作是一首叫《金戒指》的歌。我带了一个版本到约翰在韦布里奇的住处，当我们进行到"你可以给我买金戒指 / 给我买所有这类东西"那段歌词时就停滞了。我们一遍又一遍地唱，根本进行不下去，因为它实在是太糟糕了。

部分问题在于，《买不到我的爱》里已经有了钻戒，"金戒指"毫无新意，并且让人感觉乏味。我们无法进行下去，于是丢下这首歌，去喝了杯茶。回来后，我们开始把那个女人想象成洛杉矶女孩——情况有了一些改善，她需要一个司机。从某种意义上说，这有点像《挪威木屋》(Norwegian Wood)[1]这首歌，你有了一组角色，然后在你意识到之前，你已经有了一个故事。你会烧掉别人的房子，因为她有很多挪威木柴；那我们就烧了它吧，而且我们要在浴缸里睡觉。一旦你开始创造叙事方式和故事，它会变得有趣得多，更容易指引你前进。然后，我们尝试把采访一个司机的过程戏剧化。我们熬过了那些"歌曲显得枯燥"的时刻，完成了这首歌。它成了灵感成功落地的一员。它的成功需要扔掉"金戒指"，奔向"Baby you can drive my car"（宝贝，你可以开我的车）。

我知道有一种理论认为，如果没有里奥·芬达[2]的吉他，摇滚乐不可能存在；但果没有亨利·福特[3]的话，摇滚乐可能也不会存在。我想的是汽车与后座上发生的事情之间的关系。我们知道人们在汽车出现之前也做爱，但汽车为情爱带来了一种全新的体验。想想查克·贝里那句"riding along in my automobile"[4]。查克是美国伟大的诗人之一。

"Beep beep, beep beep, yeah"（哔哔，哔哔，耶）。你发动了。加点无意义的歌词进去总会有很好的效果，这首歌很适合"哔哔，哔哔，耶"。我们用了密集的和声演唱，所以它听起来有点儿像汽车喇叭。

整个主歌段只有两个和弦。有时候你甚至不需要两个，一个就行了。我最喜欢的只用一个和弦的例子是《她离开了家》(She's Leaving Home)，在那首歌里，我与和弦的变化作斗争。它是这样进行的："她"——E 和弦，我想是的；停留在 E——"正在离开"，变了？没有。"家"，变了？没有。它在 E 和弦上待了很长时间。我为此感到自豪，因为我的本能是随着每一句新歌词的出现而改变和弦。《开我的车》的主歌也是如此。两个和弦已经足够——也许一个和弦就够了。

1　通常译为《挪威的森林》，但实为误译。
2　里奥·芬达（Leo Fender），吉他品牌 Fender 的创立者。
3　亨利·福特（Henry Ford），福特汽车公司的建立者。
4　"坐在我的车里"，出自《没有特别的地方要去》(No Particular Place to Go)。

右图：歌词，1965 年。

我知道有一种理论认为，
如果没有里奥·芬达的吉他，摇滚乐不可能存在；
但如果没有亨利·福特的话，摇滚乐可能也不会存在。
我想的是汽车与后座上发生的事情之间的关系。
我们知道人们在汽车出现之前也做爱，
但汽车为情爱带来了一种全新的体验。

Asked a girl, what she wanted to be
She said, now baby, can't you see?
I wanna be famous, a star on the screen,
but you can do something in between

You can buy me golden rings
get me all the kind of things
oo, if can buy me rings,
then baby I'll love you.

137

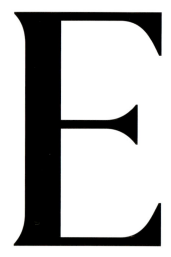

E

Eat at Home

在家里吃饭

作　者　WRITERS　　保罗·麦卡特尼和琳达·麦卡特尼　Paul McCartney and Linda McCartney
艺术家　ARTIST　　保罗和琳达·麦卡特尼　Paul and Linda McCartney
录　音　RECORDED　纽约 CBS 录音棚　CBS Studios, New York
发　行　RELEASED　《拉姆》，1971 年　*RAM*, 1971

Come on, little lady
Lady, let's eat at home
Come on, little lady
Lady, let's eat at home
Eat at home, eat at home

Come on, little lady
Lady, let's eat in bed
Come on, little lady
Lady, let's eat in bed
Eat in bed, eat in bed

Bring the love that you feel for me
Into line with the love I see
And in the morning you'll bring to me
Love

Come on, little lady
Lady, now don't do that
Come on, little lady
Lady, now don't do that
Do that, do that

Come on, little lady
Lady, let's eat at home
Come on, little lady
Lady, let's eat at home
Eat at home, eat at home

Bring the love that you feel for me
Into line with the love I see
And in the morning you'll bring to me
Love

Come on, little lady
Lady, now don't do that
Come on, little lady
Lady, now don't do that
Do that, do that

琳达出色的厨艺最终启发她发明了自己的菜谱。没有人为全素的家常菜写过简单易懂的菜谱。我们俩都喜欢在床上吃东西。还有一些其他的事情我们也很喜欢做，不过那要改天再说了。

这与 1969 年约翰和洋子在阿姆斯特丹一家酒店房间里进行的"床上和平运动"完全不同。起初，他和我在歌曲主题上总是相互呼应。但这首歌描画的世界肯定要安静得多，没有世界媒体的报道。

要记得，琳达和我刚刚结婚，有个孩子，我们拼命地想逃避喧嚣，只想找时间和家人在一起。我们在苏格兰的农场完全与世隔绝，那是我几年前买下的，而琳达真的爱上了这个地方。我们在那里自娱自乐。我们画了很多画，写了很多东西。我们互相启发。琳达拍了很多照片，我认为苏格兰帮助她找到了工作的新方向，远离音乐家的角色，捕捉大自然和家庭生活的每一天。

这是一种田园诗般的生活，远离城市、商业和媒体。在某些方面，这种生活堪称乏味；我喜欢的是它的简单，这里的事物都是小尺度的。我画的画很小，我只买小块的画布。我从没想过我可以做视觉艺术，我一直觉得那是适合"他们"的；如果没有遇到琳达，我也绝不会想到要去骑马，那也是适合"他们"的。骑马不是我的菜。但是在苏格兰，我们真的发现了自我；这里的生活给了我们极大的自由去尝试新事物，只为我们自己。

除了骑马消遣外，农场还有很多工作要做。事实上，我学会了用剪子剪羊毛 —— 现在这种工作已经很少见了，小时候在利物浦时，我也从没想过自己最终会做这种事情。我一天能剪十四到二十只羊，我的农场经理邓肯能剪一百只。仅仅把羊放倒就已经很难了。一张我要把羊翻过来的照片最终成了专辑《拉姆》的封面，这首歌就出现在那张专辑里。那是琳达拍摄的一次剪羊毛的记录的一部分。琳达为羊群中的每只羊都单独拍了照片。

从音乐性上来说，《在家里吃饭》很大程度上要归功于对巴迪·霍利的模仿，在披头士乐队成长并开始创作自己的歌曲时，他对我们有着巨大的影响。我比较喜欢的一处是，在短语"eat in be-e-e-e-d"中引入羊叫声，改进了巴迪·霍利对口吃的模仿。我为此感到骄傲！

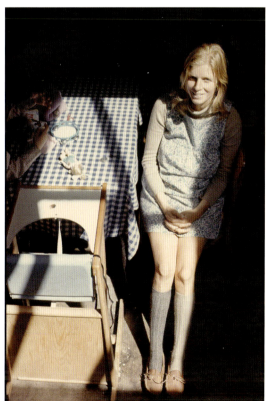

EAT AT HOME

Comeon little **lady**

Lady let's eat at home

Eat at home eat at home

Come on little **lady**

Lady let's eat in bed

Eat in bed eat in bed

Bring the love that you feel for me

Into line with the love I see

And in the morning you'll bring to me love

Come on little **lady**

lady now don't do that

~~Don't~~ do that ~~Don't~~ do that   *INSTRUMENTAL*

Come on little **lady**

lady let's eat at home

eat at home, eat at home

LADY LET'S EAT AT HOME.

① Come on little lady
lady let's eat at home
come on little lady
lady let's eat at home
eat at home
eat at home .

② Come on little lady
lady let's eat in bed.

middle   Bring the love that you feel for me
        Into line with the love I see
And every morning you bring   to   me
love ....

③ Come on little lady
lady now don't do that
... do that ..do that-..

④ .. lady let's eat at home...

145

Ebony and Ivory

乌木与象牙

作　者　WRITER　　　保罗·麦卡特尼　Paul McCartney

艺术家　ARTIST　　　保罗·麦卡特尼及嘉宾主唱史蒂维·旺德　Paul McCartney, with additional vocals by Stevie Wonder

录　音　RECORDED　蒙特塞拉特岛 AIR 录音棚　AIR Montserrat

发　行　RELEASED　单曲，1982 年　Single, 1982

《拔河比赛》，1982 年　*Tug of War*, 1982

Ebony and Ivory
Live together in perfect harmony
Side by side on my piano keyboard
Oh lord, why don't we?

We all know
That people are the same wherever you go
There is good and bad in everyone
When we learn to live
We learn to give each other
What we need to survive
Together alive

Ebony and Ivory
Live together in perfect harmony
Side by side on my piano keyboard
Oh lord, why don't we?

Ebony, Ivory
Living in perfect harmony
Ebony, Ivory

We all know
That people are the same wherever you go
There is good and bad in everyone
We learn to live
When we learn to give each other
What we need to survive
Together alive

Ebony and Ivory
Live together in perfect harmony
Side by side on my piano keyboard
Oh lord, why don't we?
Side by side on my piano keyboard
Oh lord, why don't we?

Ebony, Ivory
Living in perfect harmony
Ebony, Ivory
Living in perfect harmony

黑键和白键一起生活在钢琴键盘上，黑人和白人却并不总能和谐相处。这是斯派克·米利根的一项观察结论。

　　斯派克·米利根是英国爱尔兰喜剧演员，曾在英国广播公司 1950 年代的一个广播系列《傻瓜秀》中担任撰稿和主演。在我们的成长过程中，这个节目对披头士产生过很大的影响，彼得·塞勒斯也在节目里获得了事业上的巨大突破，乔治·马丁也和他们共事过一段时间。话说回来，斯派克住在萨塞克斯郡离我很近的地方，我们都喜欢大笑，这是爱尔兰人的特点。我想爱尔兰人的这种风趣传统延伸到了利物浦。他举办聚会时会要求你带些东西来，不一定要带酒，也可以是一首诗。所以我给他带去了一首诗。他的住所外挂着一块匾额，上面写着"由盲人建筑师设计"，他家的那条路被称为哑女巷——我不是开玩笑的——大概意指不会说话的女人。我写了一首关于哑女巷的诗带给他，在晚饭前读了一遍。

　　这首诗是这样开始的：

> 哑女巷的
> 诗人的声音
> 将被听见
> 穿过糖分蒸发的甘蔗的山谷，
> 并且酣睡在最狂野的
> 黑夜里的鼻孔
> 将会抽搐以获得
> 芬芳的领悟。[1]

　　《乌木与象牙》是针对种族分歧而创作的，种族问题当时在英国引发了很多冲突。1980 年，我在苏格兰的小工作室里写了一个样带，然后给史蒂维·旺德[2]打电话，问他是否愿意参与。史蒂维和我认识很久了。我们第一次见面是 1966 年，当时他在伦敦梅费尔的圣詹姆斯苏格兰俱乐部演出。那时候他只有十五岁。言归正传，我们一直有合作的想法，我说："对了，我有一首特别想做的歌。"于是，我们去了蒙特塞拉特岛为专辑录音。乔治·马丁的录音棚就在那儿，史蒂维本来也应该出现的，但他没有。我们打了很多通电话，史蒂维就是这样。"我们到了。你什么时候出来？"回答总是"这周五"。

　　然后周末就过去了，我周一给他打电话。"哦，我周三到那儿。""哦，好的。"这样的情况发生了很多次。他很有主见，觉得自己准备好后才会出现。但他出现时，感觉非常好，简直让人神魂颠倒，因为他是那样一位音乐大神——他就是音乐。你的演奏必须非常精确，因为他会听出任何错误。他问我们要不要用鼓机，我说不用，于是他坐上了鼓凳。他是一位伟大的鼓手，风格鲜明，在唱片里演奏的就是他。整首歌只

1　原句为："The voice of the poet / Of Dumbwoman's Lane / Can be heard across / Valleys of sugar-burned cane, / And nostrils that sleep / Through the wildest of nights / Will be twitching to gain / Aromatic insights"。
2　史蒂维·旺德（Stevie Wonder, 1950— ），美国流行乐巨星，黑人音乐的重要代表。

左图和下图：与史蒂维·旺德于录制《拔河比赛》期间。蒙特塞拉特岛 AIR 录音棚，1981 年。

右图：《乌木与象牙》摄影作品。

有我和史蒂维。

　　我们拍摄录影带时，同样的事情又发生了。团队和录影棚技术人员、摄影师，以及所有人预约好了时间，史蒂维本该在周一早上或某个时间出现，但他没有。与他沟通是一种挑战，因为事情会是这样的："旺德先生现在在演播室。对不起，你是谁？""我是保罗·麦卡特尼。我们彼此认识；我们一起工作过。""哦，好吧，他在工作，他不能被打扰。"所以一次又一次之后，他最终出现时，我们拍视频的时间已经晚了大约一个星期。所以，没错，和他一起工作很棒，但总出现迟到或缺席之类的状况。我必须说，我不习惯这种事。

　　我从未想过《乌木与象牙》能解决世界的问题，但我认为它的初衷是美好的。当然，有人取笑它。一些人认为这首歌过于多愁善感，或过于简单，也许吧。艾迪·墨菲[1]在《周六夜现场》编了一个关于这首歌的滑稽剧。这是很容易被嘲笑的东西。

　　我在现场演过一两次这首歌。巴拉克·奥巴马当选总统几年后，我获得格什温奖时，在白宫和史蒂维一起演过。真是荣幸。出席的都是一些了不起的人。埃尔维斯·科斯特洛[2]唱了《便士巷》，史蒂维唱了《我们可以解决》（We Can Work It Out），并且和我演了《乌木与象牙》——这是我们第一次一起现场演奏这首歌。

1　艾迪·墨菲（Eddie Murphy，1961—），美国喜剧演员。
2　埃尔维斯·科斯特洛（Elvis Costello，1954—），英国摇滚歌手，其创作以多元化的音乐及大胆的歌词著称。

To SPIKE, MAN,

THE POET OF DUMBWOMANS LANE.

The voice of the poet
of Dumbwoman's Lane,
Can be heard across
Vallies of sugar - burned cane
And nostrils that sleep
Through the wildest of nights
Will be twitching
To gain aromatic insights.

—

The wife of the farmer
of Poppinghole Lane
Can be seen from the
Cab of the Robertsbridge train.
And passengers comments
Will frequently turn
To the wages the wife
of a farmer can earn.

The poet of Dumbwoman's Lane
Sallies forth,
He is hoping for no-one to see.

—

with love Paul (YESTERDAY'S
MAN.

150

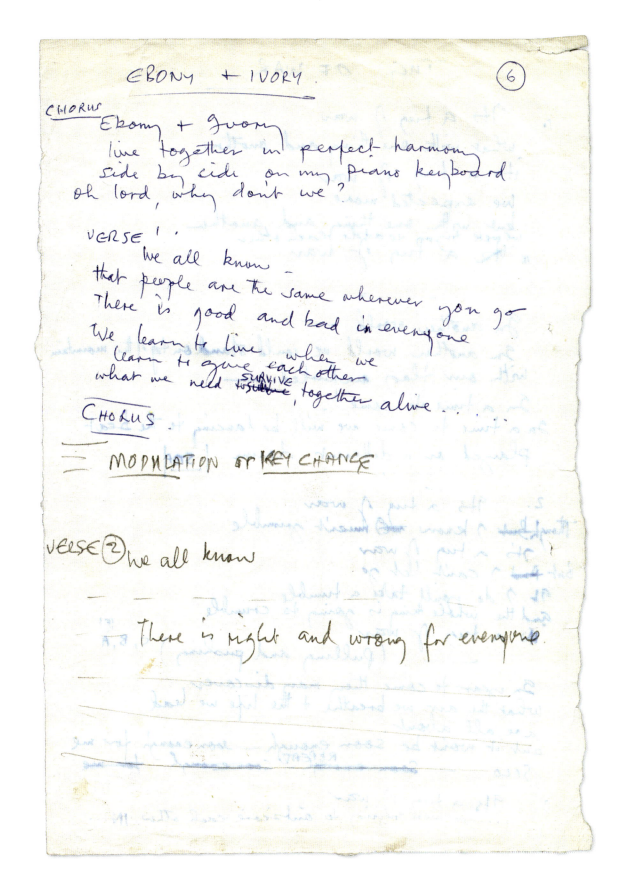

EBONY + IVORY.   ⑥

CHORUS
        Ebony + Ivory
        live together in perfect harmony
        side by side on my piano keyboard
Oh lord, why don't we?

    VERSE¹.
            we all know
        that people are the same wherever you go
        There is good and bad in everyone
        We learn to live   when we
           learn to give each other
        what we need to survive, together alive......

    CHORUS.

=   MODULATION or KEY CHANGE

VERSE② we all know

        There is right and wrong for everyone

Eight Days a Week
一周八天

作　者 **WRITERS**	保罗·麦卡特尼和约翰·列侬	Paul McCartney and John Lennon
艺术家 **ARTIST**	披头士乐队	The Beatles
录　音 **RECORDED**	伦敦阿比路录音	Abbey Road Studios, London
发　行 **RELEASED**	《待售的披头士》，1964 年	*Beatles for Sale*, 1964
	美国单曲，1965 年	US single, 1965
	《披头士 VI》，1965 年	*Beatles VI*, 1965

Ooh I need your love, babe
Guess you know it's true
Hope you need my love, babe
Just like I need you

Hold me, love me
Hold me, love me
I ain't got nothin' but love, babe
Eight days a week

Love you every day, girl
Always on my mind
One thing I can say, girl
Love you all the time

Hold me, love me
Hold me, love me
I ain't got nothin' but love, girl
Eight days a week

Eight days a week
I love you
Eight days a week
Is not enough to show I care

Ooh I need your love, babe
Guess you know it's true
Hope you need my love, babe
Just like I need you

Hold me, love me
Hold me, love me
I ain't got nothin' but love, babe
Eight days a week

Eight days a week
I love you
Eight days a week
Is not enough to show I care

Love you every day, girl
Always on my mind
One thing I can say, girl
Love you all the time

Hold me, love me
Hold me, love me
I ain't got nothin' but love, babe
Eight days a week
Eight days a week
Eight days a week

问题是我们都喜欢开快车，我自己就被抓了太多次。我曾被警察吊销驾照，禁止驾驶　年。如果我想去某个地方，就得坐公共汽车或者火车，有时候还得雇个司机。当我的驾照被恢复时，我们挣的钱已经足够雇用长期司机了。

我经常去韦布里奇的约翰家，有一天我在路上和司机聊天，即将到达目的地时，话题恰巧是他最近在做什么。他说："噢，我一周工作八天。"我跑进约翰家说："有歌名了。"

我和约翰的一大优势在于，我们都善于抓住那些一闪即逝的灵感；以及，我们拥有彼此。如果他被一句歌词困住了，我可以完成它；如果我被困在什么地方，他也会提个建议。我们可以互相建议一条走出迷宫的路，这是一件非常方便的事情。我们互相启发。所以，我想到歌名时，他很高兴我们有了一个起点。我的意思是，大概当时我俩都不觉得这会是一首很棒的歌，但这是一个很酷的想法。

然后，要记住它——这就是诀窍。为了记住它，我们必须写一些难忘的东西。你知道，如果我们写的东西过于机巧，或者太这个、太那个，我们可能会记不住它。我时常在晚上回到家喝一杯的时候，发现自己已经完全忘记方才的创作。"哦，该死，"我会想，"好吧，他会记得的。但如果他也喝了一杯，我们都忘了呢？"

但到了早上，我睡醒时就唱了起来。它就在那里，像雏菊一样清新。我们有了《一周八天》的歌词，而现在，我在脑海中强化了它们，到我们录音时，约翰和我用木吉他弹这首歌给乔治、林戈、乔治·马丁，以及录音师听。他们之前谁也没听过，只有约翰和我知道这首歌的走向，但在二十分钟之内，大家就都学会了。

上图：与约翰·列侬于《准备出发！》(*Ready Steady Go!*) 拍摄期间，伦敦，1964 年。

与林戈·斯塔尔于《谢谢你的幸运星》[1]
排练期间。伦敦，1964 年。

1　《谢谢你的幸运星》(*Thank Your
　　Lucky Stars*)，1961—1966 年播出
　　的英国音乐类真人秀电视节目。

然后记住它 —— 这就是诀窍。
为了记住它，我们必须写一些难忘的东西。
你知道，如果我们写的东西过于机巧，
或者太这个、太那个，
我们可能会记不住它。
我时常在晚上回到家喝一杯的时候，
发现自己已经完全忘记方才的创作。

Eleanor Rigby

埃莉诺 · 里格比

作　者 **WRITERS**	保罗 · 麦卡特尼和约翰 · 列侬	Paul McCartney and John Lennon
艺术家 **ARTIST**	披头士乐队　The Beatles	
录　音 **RECORDED**	伦敦阿比路录音棚　Abbey Road Studios, London	
发　行 **RELEASED**	《左轮手枪》，1966 年　*Revolver*, 1966	
	《埃莉诺 · 里格比》/《黄色潜水艇》双 A 面单曲，1966 年　'Eleanor Rigby' / 'Yellow Submarine' double A-side single, 1966	

Ah look at all the lonely people
Ah look at all the lonely people

Eleanor Rigby
Picks up the rice in the church where a wedding
　has been
Lives in a dream
Waits at the window
Wearing the face that she keeps in a jar by the door
Who is it for?

All the lonely people
Where do they all come from?
All the lonely people
Where do they all belong?

Father McKenzie
Writing the words of a sermon that no
　one will hear
No one comes near
Look at him working
Darning his socks in the night when
　there's nobody there
What does he care?

All the lonely people
Where do they all come from?
All the lonely people
Where do they all belong?

Ah look at all the lonely people
Ah look at all the lonely people

Eleanor Rigby
Died in the church and was buried
　along with her name
Nobody came
Father McKenzie
Wiping the dirt from his hands as
　he walks from the grave
No one was saved

All the lonely people
　(Ah look at all the lonely people)
Where do they all come from?
All the lonely people
　(Ah look at all the lonely people)
Where do they all belong?

Me - those were
the days - shorts.
Behind me is
the "Local."

　　我妈妈最喜欢的面霜是妮维雅，我一直到今天都很喜欢它。那就是我描述埃莉诺放在"门口罐子里"的面具时想到的面霜。女人使用面霜的频率一直让我有些惊讶。

　　我在成长过程中认识了很多老太太，部分是通过所谓的"一先令工作周"，当时，童子军每做一次家务可以得到一先令。打扫棚子或修剪草坪的报酬都是一先令。我想写一首歌来总结这些事情。埃莉诺·里格比的原型是一位我相处得很好的老太太。我甚至不知道我是怎么认识"埃莉诺·里格比"的，但我会去她家转转，而且不只是一次两次。我发现她一个人住，所以会去她家和她闲聊，考虑到那时我是个年轻的利物浦人，这其实有点疯狂。后来，我会主动去帮她买东西。她给我一张单子，我把东西带回来，我们坐在她的厨房里。我仍然清楚地记得厨房，是因为她有一台小小的水晶收音机。这不是品牌名称，里面实际上真的有颗水晶。水晶收音机在 1920 年代及 1930 年代相当流行。所以我时常去看她，光听听她的故事就已经丰富了我的灵魂，也启发了我日后创作的歌曲。

　　这个角色起初有一个完全不同的名字。或许是戴茜·霍金斯（Daisy Hawkins）。我知道"霍金斯"很好听，但它感觉不对。杰克·霍金斯（Jack Hawkins）曾在《宾虚》[1]中饰演昆特斯·阿里乌斯，我最喜欢的书之一《金银岛》中也有一个霍金斯，吉姆·霍

---

[1] 《宾虚》（Ben-Hur），美国史诗电影，由威廉·惠勒导演，1959 年上映。昆特斯·阿里乌斯（Quintus Arrius）为剧中主角宾虚的养父。

金斯[1]。但感觉确实不大对。不过，这是跟历史有关的问题。即使你在那里，显然我就在那里，有时也很难确定。

沃尔顿的圣彼得教堂墓地里，一块墓碑上写着"埃莉诺·里格比"，这大概是这样一个故事。约翰和我确实曾在那儿游荡，没完没了地谈论着我们的未来。我不记得在那里看到过坟墓，但我想我可能下意识地记住了它。

圣彼得教堂在我如今谈论的这些回忆中，扮演着非常重要的角色。回到 1957 年的夏天，我的一位校友伊万·沃恩（Ivan Vaughan）和我一起去了在教堂举办的沃尔顿乡村市集，他把我介绍给他的朋友约翰，后者的乐队"采石人"（The Quarry Men）在那里演出。

那时我刚满十五岁，约翰十六岁，伊万知道我俩都对摇滚乐着迷，于是带我过来介绍我们认识。顺理成章地——典型的青春期男孩的故作姿态什么的——最后我卖弄了一下，用吉他弹奏了埃迪·科克伦[2]的《二十次飞行摇滚》（Twenty Flight Rock），大概还演奏了吉恩·文森特[3]的《波普·卢拉》（Be-Bop-a-Lula）和一些小理查德的歌曲。

大约一个星期后，我骑着自行车出去时碰见了皮特·肖顿（Pete Shotton），他是采石人的搓衣板乐手，那在噪音爵士[4]风格的乐队中是非常重要的乐器。他和我聊了起来，他告诉我约翰认为我应该加入他们。这是一个非常约翰的做法——让别人问我，这样，如果我拒绝，他也不会丢面子。约翰通常很警惕，不过这相当好地平衡了我们的性格。他可以非常刻薄和诙谐，但是深交后，他实际上可爱而温暖。我则相反：相当随和友好，但在需要的时候，我会很强硬。

1　吉姆·霍金斯（Jim Hawkins）为罗伯特·路易斯·史蒂文森的长篇小说《金银岛》（*Treasure Island*）的主人公。
2　埃迪·科克伦（Eddie Cochran，1938—1960），美国摇滚乐先驱之一。
3　吉恩·文森特（Gene Vincent，1935—1971），美国摇滚乐先驱之一。
4　噪音爵士（Skiffle），一种用简陋乐器演奏的音乐风格，1920 年代在美国首次流行，在 1950 年代中期由英国音乐家复兴。

保罗与伊万·沃恩及乔治·哈里森。
利物浦，1950 年代初。

Ah, look at all the lonely people

Eleanor Rigby, picks up the rice
  in the church where a wedding
      has been
  lives in a dream.
Waits at the window, wearing the face
  that she keeps in a jar by the door
              who is it for?
All the lonely. - - - - - - etc.

Father McKenzie, writing the words of a
sermon that no one will hear
          no-one comes near.
look at him working, darning his
    socks in the night when there's
nobody there   what does he care?
All the lonely people . . . . .

Ah look at all the lonely people

Paul McCartney

我说我会考虑一下，然后一周后，我就答应了。从那以后，约翰和我开始经常混在一起。我的学校放假，而约翰即将就读艺术学院，就在我学校的隔壁。我教他如何给吉他调音，他用的是班卓琴的调音法——我想那是他邻居之前为他调的——我们自学了如何弹查克·贝里等人的歌。再后来，当我鼓起分享的勇气时，我给他弹奏《我失去了我的小女孩》，而他也开始给我看他写的歌。那就是一切的开始。

我和家人、朋友回到利物浦时，会进行这种"旅行"。我会开车游览旧地，指出我们在福特林路的老家之类的地方，有时我也开车经过圣彼得教堂。从老家开车只有五到十分钟的路程。我经常停下来想，是什么机缘让披头士走到了一起。我们四个人都住在英格兰北部的这个城市里，但互不相识。然后，很偶然地，我们认识了对方。我们一起演奏的时候，听起来很不错，而且，我们都有一种年轻的冲劲，想把音乐做好。

直到今天，这件事的发生对我来说仍然是个谜。如果我和伊万没有去参加那个市集，约翰和我还会以其他方式见面吗？我其实中途离开了一会儿，去试着勾搭一个女孩。我曾经在薯条店、公共汽车上，等等这类地方见过约翰——尽管他看上去很酷，但我们会聊天吗？我不知道。不过，我碰巧有一个认识约翰的校友，又碰巧和乔治一起坐公共汽车去上学。所有这些小小的巧合，得以让披头士出现，这确实让人觉得有点神奇。这是一个关于当生活为你提供这些机会时，你要说"是"的精彩一课。你永远不知道这些会把你引向何方。

仿佛所有这些疯狂的巧合还不够似的，市集上的某个人正好有一台便携式磁带机——一台老式根德牌磁带机。于是就有了采石人那天表演的录音（老实说质量很差），你可以在网上听到。还有几张乐队在卡车后座上的照片。所以，事实证明，这是我的生命中相当关键的一天，它仍会携着这些过往的幽灵不时这样出现。

我一直认为这样的事情是幸福的意外。就像某人在阿比路倒放磁带机时，我们四个恰巧听到了我们的歌，停下脚步说："噢！那是什么？"然后我们会在一首歌中使用这种效果，比如《我只是睡着了》（I'm Only Sleeping）中倒放的吉他独奏。最近也发生过类似的事情，在《埃及站》的歌曲《恺撒摇滚》（Caesar Rock）中。不知怎的，这首歌鼓的部分在电脑上被意外地拖到了歌曲的开头，我们回放时，它就在那最初的几秒钟里，并且不合拍。但与此同时，它确实合适。

所以，我的生活充满了这些快乐的意外。回到"埃莉诺·里格比"这个名字的由来，回忆将我带到了布里斯托，简·阿舍在那里的老维克剧院表演。我四处转悠，等着演出结束，看到一个写着"里格比"的商店招牌，而我想："就是它！"这真的是那么偶然。回到伦敦后，我在阿舍夫人位于温波尔街57号的地下室的音乐室里写了这首歌，当时我就住在那里。

差不多在同一时间，我又开始上钢琴课了。我小时候上过课，但基本上只是练习音阶，更像是家庭作业。我喜欢音乐，但我讨厌音乐练习的家庭作业。我印象里，自己大概尝试过三次钢琴课。第一次是我小时候，父母把我送到当地认识的某个人那里。然后，十六岁的时候，我想："也许是时候试着学习正确的演奏方式了。"那时我正在写自己的歌，对音乐越来越认真，但仍然是同样的音阶。"啊！离开这里！"再然后，在我二十岁出头的时候，简的妈妈玛格丽特和她工作的市政厅音乐学院的人给我安排了课程。我甚至在钢琴上为老师演奏了《埃莉诺·里格比》，不过那时我没写出歌词。当时，我只是在拼凑的 E 小调上随口唱着"Ola Na Tungee"。我不记得老师对此有什么看法，他们只想听我演奏更多的音阶，于是课程就这样结束了。

当我开始认真写这首歌的歌词时，"埃莉诺"总是其中的一部分，我想是因为我们曾经和埃莉诺·布隆在电影《救命！》中合作——我们在彼得·库克（Peter Cook）位于希腊街的机构俱乐部（The Establishment）认识了她。我想约翰可能和她短暂地约会过，而且我非常喜欢这个名字。一开始，牧师是"麦卡特尼神父"，因为它的音节数很合适。那时我把这首歌拿给约翰听，我记得我给他弹了一遍，他说："太棒了，麦卡特尼神父。"他很喜欢这首歌。但我感觉不太舒服，因为那好像在说我爸爸——我的爸爸麦卡特尼——于是我拿出电话簿，把"麦卡特尼"变成了"麦肯齐"。

写这首歌时，我们有意以孤独为主题，希望能让听众产生共鸣。开场是"Eleanor Rigby / Picks up the rice in the church where a wedding has been / Lives in a dream"（埃莉诺·里格比 / 在举行婚礼的教堂里捡起米粒 / 在梦中的生活）。在婚礼后捡米粒有点奇怪。这是否意味着她是个清洁工，没有被邀请参加婚礼的人，只是远远地观看庆祝活动？

保罗与乔治·马丁、乔治·哈里森及约翰·列侬。伦敦阿比路录音棚，约 1968 年。

上图：和乔治·哈里森、约翰·列侬及丹尼斯·里特尔（Dennis Littler）在金阿姨和哈里叔叔家。利物浦，1958 年。

左图：埃莉诺·布隆于拍摄电影《救命！》期间，巴哈马群岛，1965 年。

她为什么要这么做？我想写得比"她事后打扫卫生"更心酸，所以它更多是关于一个孤独的人。一个人无法拥有自己的婚礼，只有梦想中的婚礼。

艾伦·金斯堡[1]告诉我，这是一首了不起的诗，所以我要和艾伦并列了。他一点也不懒散。这首歌的另一个早期崇拜者是威廉·S. 巴勒斯[2]，当然，他也登上了《佩珀军士》的封面，我们的相识缘于作家巴里·迈尔斯（Barry Miles）和因迪卡书店，他实际上看到了这首歌的成型过程，当时我时不时使用我们在蒙塔古广场林戈公寓地下室建立的人声录音棚。这个录音棚的计划是录制诗歌——几年后，我们在苹果的子公司，实验性的 Zapple 厂牌更正式地进行了这项工作。那阵子，我用磁带循环做了很多实验，使用的是布伦尔牌（Brenell）开盘带——我现在还有——而且，我们开始在歌曲中加入更多的实验元素。《埃莉诺·里格比》最终收录在《左轮手枪》专辑中，这是我们第一次录制无法在舞台上重现的歌曲——像这首歌和《明日永不知晓》（Tomorrow Never Knows）。那会儿，巴勒斯和我混在一起，他有几次向我借开盘带来做他的拼贴。听到《埃莉诺·里格比》的最终版时，他说他对我在三段主歌中的故事叙述印象很深刻。对我来说，它也确实是歌词上的一种突破——一首更严肃的歌。

乔治·马丁在《昨天》中让我尝试了弦乐四重奏。起初，我反对这个主意，但它的效果很好，我爱上了它。所以，我写《埃莉诺·里格比》的时候，就想到了弦乐元素。我把这首歌带给乔治时告诉他，我想要一系列 E 小调断奏作为伴奏。实际上，整首歌其实只有两个和弦：C 和 Em 和弦。在乔治的版本中，他把我关于断奏的想法和他自己从伯纳德·赫尔曼那里获得的灵感整合在一起，伯纳德为电影《惊魂记》创作了配乐。乔治想把那种戏剧性带到编曲中。并且，当然，埃莉诺·里格比，一位陷入困境的老年人，和《惊魂记》中的干尸母亲之间，也有着某种疯狂的联系。

1　艾伦·金斯堡（Allen Ginsberg，1926—1997），美国垮掉派诗人。
2　威廉·S. 巴勒斯（William S. Burroughs，1914—1997），美国垮掉派作家。

The End

结 局

作　者 WRITERS	保罗·麦卡特尼和约翰·列侬　Paul McCartney and John Lennon	
艺术家 ARTIST	披头士乐队　The Beatles	
录　音 RECORDED	伦敦阿比路录音棚　Abbey Road Studios, London	
发　行 RELEASED	《阿比路》，1969 年　*Abbey Road*, 1969	

Oh yeah, alright
Are you gonna be in my dreams tonight?

And in the end the love you take
Is equal to the love you make

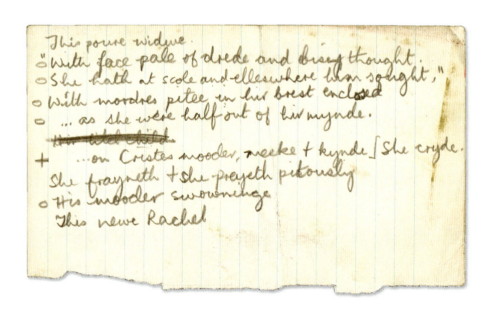

约翰不像我这样对文学感兴趣，尽管他非常喜欢刘易斯·卡罗尔，尤其喜欢温斯顿·丘吉尔。他咪咪姑妈的客厅里放着很多丘吉尔的书。一个不错的教育基础。

就我而言，作为诗歌形式之一的对句一直吸引着我。仔细想想，它一直是英语诗歌的主力军——乔叟、蒲柏、威尔弗雷德·欧文[1]，我特别着迷于莎士比亚用对句结束一场戏或整部戏的方式。举个例子，看看《麦克白》（*Macbeth*），你会发现一些令人兴奋的对句，比如：

> *接受你该得到的欢呼：*
> *黑夜无论怎样悠长，白天总会到来。*

或者

> *我走了，一切都结束了；铃声邀请我。*
> *不要听，邓肯；因为这是丧钟*
> *召唤着你到天堂或者去到地狱。*

这是莎士比亚说话的方式，"就是这样，哥们儿"，以及"结局"，同样是我们的说话方式。

> *最终你所得到的爱*
> *和你付出的爱相等*

这是能让你思考很久的对句之一。也许和善业有关，就像那句谚语：一切皆因果。

我常常思考，如果没有加入一支占据了我全部生活的乐队，我会怎么样呢。我也想知道，我曾打算选择的 A-Level 英国文学之路将会把我领向何处。

左图：摘抄乔叟《坎特伯雷故事集》中《女修道院长的故事》的文本。来自保罗的英文课本。

1　威尔弗雷德·欧文（Wilfred Owen，1893—1918），英国诗人。其诗作力求鲜活地描绘战争的可怖、血腥与悲惨，对世人的战争观影响深远。

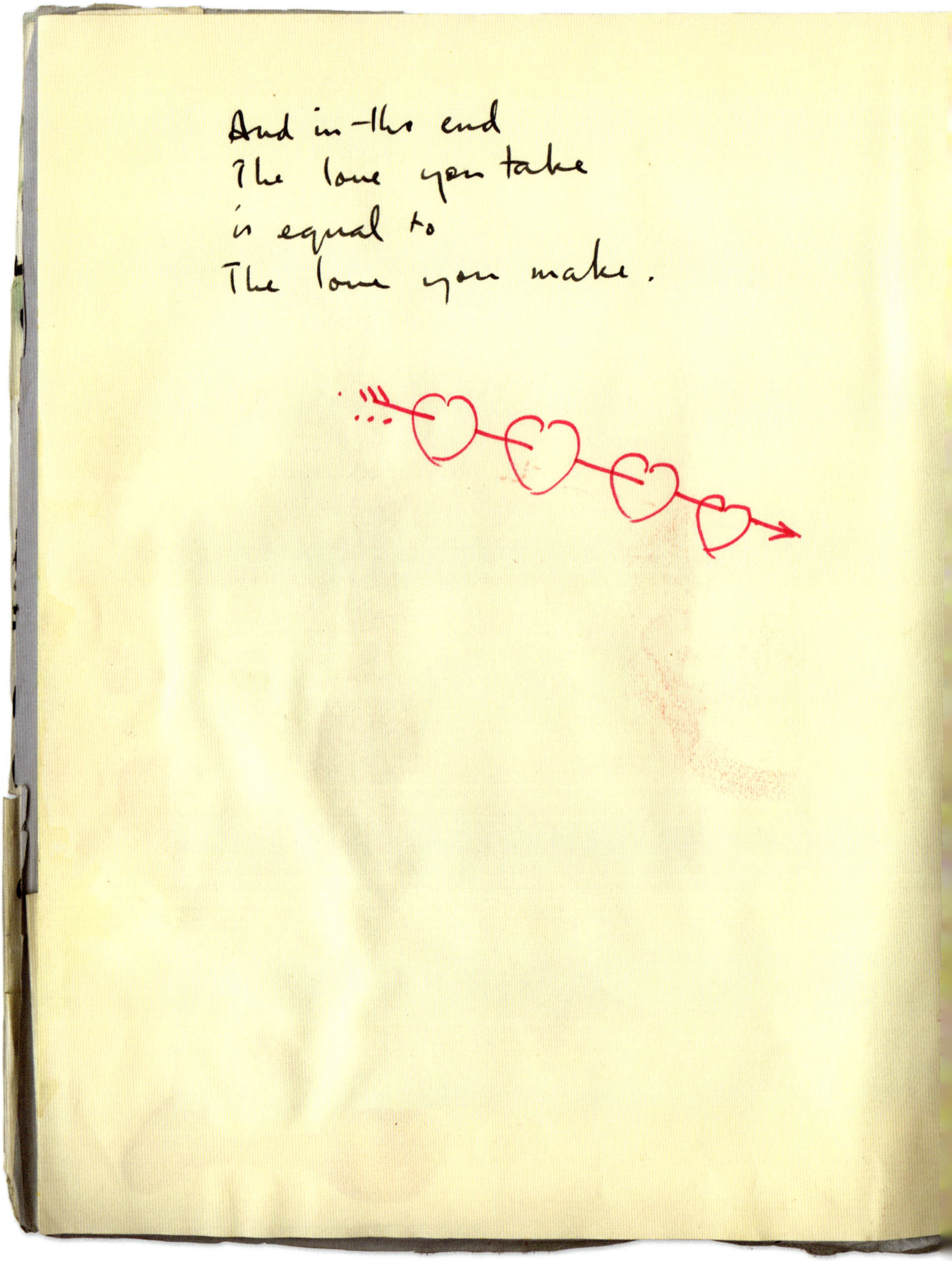

And in the end
The love you take
is equal to
The love you make.

verse Every night I just want to go out
get out of my head.
Every day I don't want to get up
get out of my bed,
Every night I want to play out
Every day I want to do . . . . . .
But tonight I just want to stay in.
And be with you - and be with you.

<u>Chorus</u>
Every day I lean on a lampost
I'm wasting my time
Every night I lay on a pillow
Resting my mind.
Every morning brings a new day.
Every night that day is through.
But tonight I just want to stay in
and be with you . . . . and be with you.
<u>Chorus.</u>

167

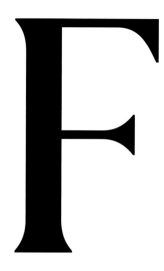

Fixing a Hole

补一个洞

作　者　WRITERS　　保罗·麦卡特尼和约翰·列侬　Paul McCartney and John Lennon

艺术家　ARTIST　　披头士乐队　The Beatles

录　音　RECORDED　伦敦摄政王之声录音棚、伦敦阿比路录音棚　Regent Sound Studio, London and Abbey Road Studios, London

发　行　RELEASED　《佩珀军士孤独之心俱乐部乐队》，1967 年　Sgt. Pepper's Lonely Hearts Club Band, 1967

I'm fixing a hole where the rain gets in
And stops my mind from wandering
Where it will go

I'm filling the cracks that ran through the door
And kept my mind from wandering
Where it will go

And it really doesn't matter if I'm wrong I'm right
Where I belong I'm right
Where I belong
See the people standing there
Who disagree and never win
And wonder why they don't get in my door

I'm painting the room in a colourful way
And when my mind is wandering
There I will go

And it really doesn't matter if I'm wrong I'm right
Where I belong I'm right
Where I belong
Silly people run around
They worry me and never ask me
Why they don't get past my door

I'm taking the time for a number of things
That weren't important yesterday
And I still go

I'm fixing a hole where the rain gets in
And stops my mind from wandering
Where it will go
Where it will go

写一首歌，就像我要用吉他或钢琴填满一个黑洞。以"有缺口需要填满"的想法作为灵感的基础，不亚于天降灵感。不管怎样，这都是个奇迹。我坐着，一片空白，这个洞里什么也没有。也许我开始变戏法，在三个小时后，我会把一只兔子从一个看起来像洞，但实际上是顶帽子的地方拎出来。又或者，在录音结束时，这里不再有黑洞，取而代之的是一片彩色的风景。

关于彩色风景，我是乐队中最后一个使用 LSD 的。约翰和乔治都曾鼓动我，这样，我就和他们保持同一水准了。我很不情愿，因为我实际上是非常古板的，并且我听说，使用 LSD 后，你将永远回不到以前的样子。我不确定我想要那样，也不觉得那是个好主意，所以我很抗拒。但最后我还是妥协了。

我很幸运，LSD 没有让我把事情搞砸。但它依旧有可怕的部分。真正可怕的是，你想清醒时，它的效果并不会结束。你会说："好了，足够了，派对结束了。"而它会说："不，还没有。"所以你不得不带着幻觉入睡。

大约在那个时期，我闭上眼睛时，那里不是一片空白，而是有一点蓝色的洞，就好像有什么东西需要修补。我总是感觉，如果我能走上去仔细看看，就会有答案。现在，我可以没完没了地讨论宾·克罗斯比[1]的歌曲《请》中的文字游戏："Oh, Please / Lend your little ear to my pleas"[2]，也许对"And it really doesn't matter if I'm wrong I'm right / Where I belong"（无论我是对是错真的无所谓 / 我归属的地方）中的文字游戏有所影响。事实上，这首歌最重要的灵感来源甚至不是我前面提到的关于一个洞的形而上学的概念，而是这种绝对的物理现象——我服用迷幻药之后首先出现的东西。我偶尔还是会看到它，并且我很清楚它是什么。我确切地知道它的样子。

有些人认为《补一个洞》是关于海洛因的，这很可能是因为他们将之想象为针孔。写这首歌的时候，我在伦敦基本上一个人住，并且很享受我的新房子。因此，整个"修正居所"的世界开始以一种字面意义上的方式冲击我。

---

1 宾·克罗斯比（Bing Crosby，1903—1977），美国流行歌手。
2 双关意为"哦请把你的小耳朵借我用来辩解"/"请你倾听我的请求"。

左图：《佩珀军士孤独之心俱乐部乐队》的新闻发布会上，这是琳达拍摄的第一张保罗的照片。伦敦，1967 年 5 月 19 日。

右图：和希瑟及玛萨（Martha）在一起。苏格兰，1960 年代后期。

写一首歌，就像我要用吉他或钢琴填满一个黑洞。
以"有缺口需要填满"的想法作为灵感的基础，
不亚于天降灵感。

The Fool on the Hill
山上的愚者

作 者	WRITERS	保罗·麦卡特尼和约翰·列侬　Paul McCartney and John Lennon
艺术家	ARTIST	披头士乐队　The Beatles
录 音	RECORDED	伦敦阿比路录音棚　Abbey Road Studios, London
发 行	RELEASED	《魔幻之旅》，1967 年　*Magical Mystery Tour*, 1967

Day after day
Alone on a hill
The man with the foolish grin
Is keeping perfectly still
But nobody wants to know him
They can see that he's just a fool
And he never gives an answer

But the fool on the hill
Sees the sun going down
And the eyes in his head
See the world spinning round

Well on the way
Head in a cloud
The man of a thousand voices
Talking perfectly loud
But nobody ever hears him
Or the sound he appears to make
And he never seems to notice

But the fool on the hill
Sees the sun going down
And the eyes in his head
See the world spinning round

And nobody seems to like him
They can tell what he wants to do
And he never shows his feelings

But the fool on the hill
Sees the sun going down
And the eyes in his head
See the world spinning round

Round, round, round, round, round

He never listens to them
He knows that they're the fools
They don't like him

The fool on the hill
Sees the sun going down
And the eyes in his head
See the world spinning round

Round, round, round, round, round

一些人认为，玛哈里希·玛赫西·优济是披头士乐队的精神导师。我觉得这样说也很公平。这首歌写于我们沉迷于玛哈里希期间，它当然会涉及那段经历。

我记得我刚开始写这首歌是在威勒尔半岛的赫斯沃尔，我爸爸当时住在那里。他家里有一架钢琴，因为他自己也是个音乐家。也许部分因为他是一个音乐家，并且有自己的爵士乐队，所以他非常欣赏我们的成功。他为我感到骄傲，儿子得到承认使他很高兴。我们走进一家餐馆或者酒吧坐下来时，他会看着周围所有的人。他会注意到认出我的某个人，然后他就会说："他们抓到你了，他们抓到你了。"

奇怪的是，正是因为人们"抓到"了我们，所以我们再也不能保持自我，这使得披头士对玛哈里希所提供的可能性保持了开放态度。我们需要重新回到自我。回到原点。1967年，乔治·哈里森把我们介绍给了玛哈里希，乔治已经去看过他在伦敦公园巷希尔顿酒店里的演讲。不久之后，我们都去了威尔士的班戈和他一起学习。然后，在1968年初，我们去了印度的瑞诗凯诗。我们本计划在那里待久一点，但林戈和他的妻子莫琳十天后离开了；简·阿舍和我在五周后离开；又过了两周，乔治和约翰两对夫妻也离开了。不过，玛哈里希为我们所有人都留下了印记。

我知道有些人认为我把玛哈里希描述为"愚者"是一种毁谤。事实并非如此。比如说，我经常在玩塔罗牌时拿到"愚者"牌。也许是因为我倾向于尝试看到事物积极的一面，或者留意新的想法和冒险。在这首歌中，我只是简单地描述了玛哈里希是如何被那么多人接受的——作为"咯咯笑的精神导师"。那不是我自己的看法。人们在识别讽刺方面的障碍总是很吸引我。

上图：吉姆·麦克爵士乐队（爸爸吉姆是从鼓往右数第三位）。约1920年代。

总而言之，我认为《山上的愚者》是一幅赞美的肖像，并且，它表现出了玛哈里希在一派喧嚣中保持全然平静的能力。他有着让人钦佩的自我克制，并且不太关心大众的观点。他因其信仰而容易招致嘲笑，但是他的信仰很可能是对的。我想，他在某种程度上也许和《李尔王》中那个说真话的傻瓜类似。

和玛哈里希·玛赫西·优济在一起，威尔士，1967 年。

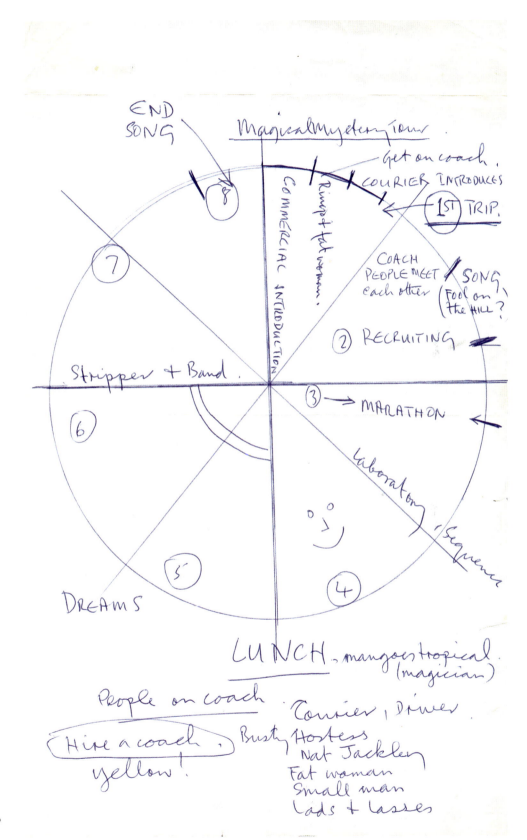

保罗为电影《魔幻之旅》
所做的笔记。

For No One
不为任何人

作 者 WRITERS　　　　保罗·麦卡特尼和约翰·列侬　Paul McCartney and John Lennon
艺术家 ARTIST　　　　披头士乐队　The Beatles
录 音 RECORDED　　　伦敦阿比路录音棚　Abbey Road Studios, London
发 行 RELEASED　　　《左轮手枪》，1966 年　Revolver, 1966

Your day breaks
Your mind aches
You find that all her words of kindness linger on
When she no longer needs you

She wakes up
She makes up
She takes her time and doesn't feel
　　she has to hurry
She no longer needs you

And in her eyes you see nothing
No sign of love behind the tears cried for no one
A love that should have lasted years

You want her
You need her
And yet you don't believe her when
　　she says her love is dead
You think she needs you

And in her eyes you see nothing
No sign of love behind the tears cried for no one
A love that should have lasted years

You stay home
She goes out
She says that long ago she knew someone
　　but now he's gone
She doesn't need him

Your day breaks
Your mind aches
There will be times when all the things
　　she said will fill your head
You won't forget her

And in her eyes you see nothing
No sign of love behind the tears cried for no one
A love that should have lasted years

这是一首关于拒绝的歌。分手，或者说一段不成功的关系的结束，一直以来都是歌曲中一个值得探索的丰富领域。我有过几次这样的经历——我猜很多人都有——这是一种我能理解的情感，把它放进一首歌里似乎是个好想法，因为可能很多人也能理解它。在这首歌里，我说的是两个已经分手的人，但是很明显，和任何作者一样，这一切都来自你自己的经历，你不可避免地在谈论自己。

有两段短歌词："She wakes up / She makes up"（她醒来 / 她化妆）。接着，在两段短歌词之后，你看到的是长歌词："She takes her time and doesn't feel she has to hurry / She no longer needs you"（她不紧不慢不觉得她需要赶时间 / 她已不再需要你），然后是"And in her eyes you see nothing / No sign of love ..."（从她的眼中你一无所获 /……没有爱的痕迹）。和某人分手是一个可怕的时刻，你看着他们——这个你曾经爱过的人，或者你曾经以为你爱过的人——过去的那种感觉一点都不存在了。就好像感觉也被关掉了，这种经历并不好受。

在当时，你认为任何一段恋情都可能，或者应该，或者将会，永远地持续下去，除非是那种"陡然开始，迅速结束"的露水情缘。但是当你和某人约会，当你和女朋友在一起很长一段时间后，那就完全不同了。简·阿舍和我在一起大约有五年了，所以内心深处，我希望能娶她，但随着时间的临近，我想，我也意识到我们不合适。没法准确地说清楚，但在简和我刚分手后不久，琳达出现时，我觉得："哦，我不知道，也许更应该这样。"然后当琳达和我开始互相了解对方后，我感觉："这更像我，我和她更契合。"我和简之间有些不太契合的小细节。我爱她的很多方面，我也会永远倾慕她的很多东西。她是个很棒的女人，但是拼图上的一些小地方合不上。

上图：《不为任何人》创作于拍摄电影《救命！》期间，在奥地利的阿尔卑斯山，1965 年 3 月。

179

可以说有这些歌曲是我的幸运，它们的出现确实出人意料。与其说是我写的，还不如说是它们自己到来的。你会听到很多作曲家这么说。今天早上我在冥想，我认为冥想的要点就是尝试停止胡思乱想，因为你的大脑是如此活跃，一个词会暗示另一个词，而另一个词会引发一连串思考，然后你必须努力将思绪拉回最初的问题上。你总是在思考，即使在睡觉的时候，大脑总是在运转。当你要写作时，这是非常方便的，因为你只是融入那种运转，并把它作为一首歌的开始。通常到来的是你的第一段主歌，它确立了某种押韵的模式，某种节奏的模式，通常你的第二段主歌会遵循这种模式。它可能会有相同的旋律，因为你又回到了主歌中。"Your day breaks"既可以是"你的一天开始了"，也可以是"你的一天结束了"；而"She makes up"也有几种含义：化妆，以及争吵之后的和解[1]。

我认为这是英语的优点之一 —— 你可以用多种方式来理解事物。我总是很怜惜试图学习这种语言的人，有那么多模棱两可的词意，但对一个词曲作者来说，这是一件幸运的事情。你在写作，而它就出现在你的脑海里，你只用抓住你喜欢的片段。你抓住的是什么？这是一种神奇的东西，有时它比你认为的更有意义，但是宇宙希望你写下这些词，因为它们会向某些人解释某些事情。从你自己开始。

1　refrain 既有"副歌；迭句"之意，又有"克制；避免"之意。

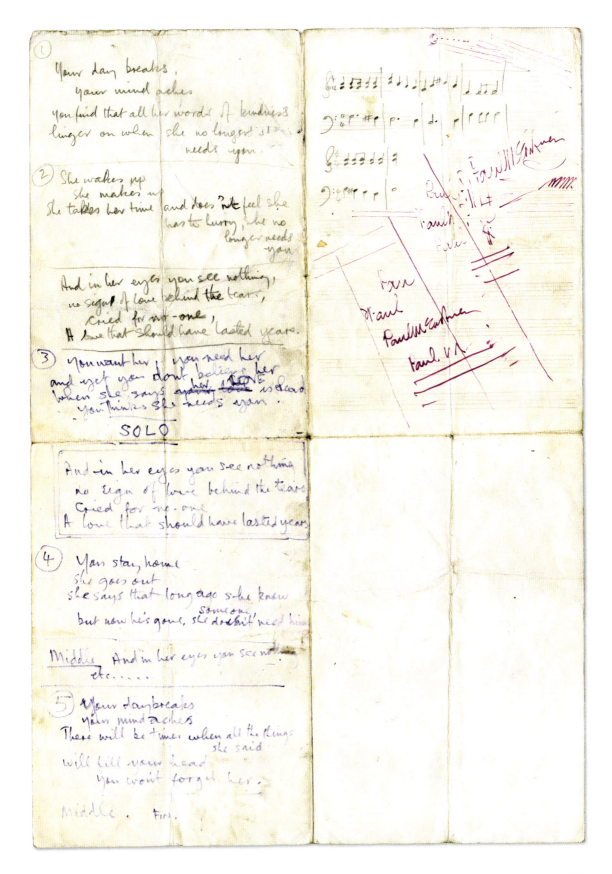

182

From Me to You

我对你的

作　者 WRITERS	约翰·列侬和保罗·麦卡特尼	John Lennon and Paul McCartney
艺术家 ARTIST	披头士乐队	The Beatles
录　音 RECORDED	伦敦阿比路录音棚	Abbey Road Studios, London
发　行 RELEASED	单曲，1963 年	Single, 1963

If there's anything that you want
If there's anything I can do
Just call on me and I'll send it along
With love from me to you

I've got everything that you want
Like a heart that's oh so true
Just call on me and I'll send it along
With love from me to you

I got arms that long to hold you
And keep you by my side
I got lips that long to kiss you
And keep you satisfied

If there's anything that you want
If there's anything I can do
Just call on me and I'll send it along
With love from me to you

From me
To you
Just call on me and I'll send it along
With love from me to you

I got arms that long to hold you
And keep you by my side
I got lips that long to kiss you
And keep you satisfied

If there's anything that you want
If there's anything I can do
Just call on me and I'll send it along
With love from me to you
To you
To you
To you

披头士开始录制唱片时，约翰和我还住在家里，我们忽然想到，我们应该试着和歌迷接触。我们只是想获得更多的喜爱；人们喜欢我们，并竭力向我们展示这一点（比如给我们写信），仍然让我们陶醉。披头士早期的歌曲之一，《谢谢你姑娘》，就总结了我们为与歌迷打成一片所做的努力。而后来成立伪装者乐队（The Pretenders）的克里希·海德，在俄亥俄州的阿克伦听到了这首歌。

我们所有早期作品的歌名中都有人称代词。第一首单曲《爱我吧》，第二首单曲《请让我快乐》（Please Please Me），下一首《我对你的》——我们设法将前两曲融入了这首歌！然后是《她爱你》和《我想牵你的手》。这些歌全都非常个人化，所以我们可以触及任何一个听这首歌的人。

《爱我吧》是非常个人的恳求："Love, love me do / You know I love you"[1]。而《请让我快乐》是我们在英国的第一首榜首歌曲。在那之后，就有了这首歌，《我对你的》。我们使尽浑身解数：开场是一段朗朗上口的合唱，你甚至不需要知道歌词也可以跟着唱；我们在歌中突出了约翰的口琴——之前在《爱我吧》中，现在是《我对你的》；寄信的概念在摇滚乐中一直很好用，想想《求你了邮差先生》（Please Mr. Postman），以及《退回寄信人》（Return to Sender）。

写这首歌时，我们正和罗伊·奥比森一起巡演。我们都在同一辆巡演大巴上，它会中途停靠，好让大家去喝杯茶、吃一顿，而约翰和我会去喝杯茶，然后回到大巴上写点东西。这对我来说是一个特别的场景，在二十一岁的时候，在大巴车的过道上走来走去，大巴车尾部坐着罗伊·奥比森，他穿着黑色衣服、戴着墨镜、弹着吉他，正在写《漂亮女人》。我们间有一种同志情谊，我们互相激励，这永远是一件美好的事情。他为我们弹奏音乐，我们应和："这是首好歌，罗伊，太棒了。"然后，我们会说："那么听听这首。"接着为他弹奏《我对你的》。事实证明，那是一个历史性的时刻。

我们总是有基本和弦。如果在 C 调里，那就是 C、Am、F 和 G；就是这些和弦，你甚至不用多加一个；你不需要这样做，因为你可以用太多的排列组合来写很多首歌，只要改变顺序，它们听起来都很不一样。这是无穷无尽的惊喜。但在这首歌中，进行到桥段时——"I got arms that long to hold you"（我的手臂渴望拥抱你），和弦脱离了 C、Am、F、G 的序列，转到了 Gm。写完这句后，我记得我当时在想："现在我们有突破了。"

1　"爱，爱我吧 / 你知道我爱你"，出自《爱我吧》（Love Me Do）。

披头士、罗伊·奥比森、杰瑞和领跑者乐队[1]在
巡演路上。英国，1963 年。

1　杰瑞和领跑者乐队（Gerry and the Pacemakers），
　　英国乐队，1960 年代初期成立于利物浦。

THE NORTH'S OWN ENTERTAINMENTS PAPER

MERSEY BEAT

FRANK HESSY
LIMITED
62 STANLEY STREET,
(Corner of Whitechapel)
LIVERPOOL 1

FOR ALL MUSICAL
INSTRUMENTS OUR
EASY TERMS ARE
"EASIER"

Vol. 2. No. 45.　　　　　APRIL 11—25, 1963　　　　　Price THREEPENCE

THE BEATLES STORY

PUBLISHED FOR THE FIRST TIME - SEE PAGE SEVEN

THE BEATLES: GEORGE HARRISON, JOHN LENNON, RINGO STARR, PAUL McCARTNEY.　　　(Photo: Peter Kaye)

INSIDE: LEE CURTIS ★ GERRY AND THE PACEMAKERS
ONLOOKER ★ DANCE DATE ★ MERSEY ROUNDABOUT
★ WIN THE BEATLES L.P. COMPETITION ★

ANFIELD
 4500.

Dear Paul,
          Just a few lines
to wish you a happy and
prosperous twenty first birthday
however I do hope you will
accept this small hand-knitted
poodle as a tiny mascot for
yourself, and if the group like
it I will make each of them
one if they wish, I would
very much like to have made
a beetle but was unable
to, so I thought this the
next best thing.

歌迷来信，1963 年。

188

I sincerely hope you had a wonderful time tonight your 21st birthday. Hoping you will let me know if you received same O.K and if you liked it, I hope so very much

I Remain

Yours sincerely

Marjorie

x x x x x x x x x

x x x x x x x x

x x x x x.

(21).

G

Get Back

回到过去

作 者 WRITERS	保罗·麦卡特尼和约翰·列侬 Paul McCartney and John Lennon	
艺术家 ARTIST	披头士乐队 The Beatles	
录 音 RECORDED	伦敦苹果录音棚 Apple Studio, London	
发 行 RELEASED	单曲，1969 年 Single, 1969	
	《顺其自然》，1970 年 *Let It Be*, 1970	

Jo Jo was a man who thought he was a loner
But he knew it couldn't last
Jo Jo left his home in Tucson, Arizona
For some California grass

Get back
Get back
Get back to where you once belonged
Get back
Get back
Get back to where you once belonged
Get back, Jo Jo

Go home

Get back
Get back
Get back to where you once belonged
Get back
Get back
Get back to where you once belonged
Get back, Jo

Sweet Loretta Martin thought she was a woman
But she was another man
All the girls around her say she's got it coming
But she gets it while she can

Get back
Get back
Get back to where you once belonged
Get back
Get back
Get back to where you once belonged
Get back, Loretta

Get back
Get back
Get back to where you once belonged
Get back
Get back
Get back to where you once belonged

Get back, Loretta
Your mommy's waiting for you
Wearing her high-heel shoes
And a low-neck sweater
Get back home, Loretta

Get back
Get back
Get back to where you once belonged

关于披头士的情况是，我们是一支非常优秀的小乐队。我们四个人都知道如何互相配合，如何演奏，那才是我们真正擅长的。想到我们的解散几乎是不可避免，让这一切更让人伤心。

所以《回到过去》中有一种渴望。你应该回到根源，披头士应该回到我们在利物浦的样子。而这些根源体现在这首歌的风格上，那就是直接的摇滚乐。因为乐队解散时，在我看来，这无疑是我们该做的事情——"回到我们曾经属于的地方"，重新成为一个小乐队。我们应该只是演奏，偶尔做点小演出。

其他人对此嗤之以鼻。可以理解，因为在那个时候，这不是一个切实可行的解决办法。约翰刚刚遇到洋子，他显然需要逃到一个新地方，而我说的是我们应该逃到一个老地方。重振过去的披头士并无可能。建议我们不要忘记我们是谁，以及我们曾经从哪里来，都已经太迟了。如果我当时的梦想真的是回到我们曾经属于的地方，约翰的梦想则是超越我们曾经属于的地方，去一个我们还不属于的地方。

我提到过 1969 年 9 月，我们在一次会议上讨论未来的计划，约翰说："哦，我不会这么做。我要离开了。再见。"接下来，他咯咯地笑着说这感觉真的很刺激，就像告诉某人你要和对方离婚，然后大笑。很显然，在那个时候，这十分伤人。这是一个致命的打击。你被打翻在地，而他咯咯地笑着告诉你，把你打晕的感觉有多好。

这花了一段时间，但我想我最终还是接受了现实。这是我从年轻时直到现在最好的伙伴，我和他合作完成了 20 世纪的一些最好的作品（他谦虚的说法）。如果他爱上了这个女人，那和我有什么关系？我不仅不得不让他放手去做，而且不得不佩服他做了这件事。这就是我最终到达的境地：我别无选择，只能冷静面对。

194—195 页：披头士和小野洋子。伦敦特威肯哈姆录音棚（Twickenham），1969 年。

193

Getting Closer

越来越近

作　者　WRITER　　　保罗·麦卡特尼　Paul McCartney

艺术家　ARTIST　　　羽翼乐队　Wings

录　音　RECORDED　　伦敦阿比路录音棚　Abbey Road Studios, London

发　行　RELEASED　　《回到蛋中》，1979 年　*Back to the Egg,* 1979

　　　　　　　　　　单曲，1979 年　Single, 1979

Say you don't love him
My salamander
Why do you need him
Oh no don't answer
Oh no

I'm getting closer
I'm getting closer to your heart

Keeping ahead of the rain on the road
Watching my windscreen wipers
Radio playing me a danceable ode
Cattle beware of snipers

When will you see me
My salamander
Now don't try to tell me
Oh no don't answer
Oh no

I'm getting closer
I'm getting closer to your heart

Hitting the chisel and making a joint
Gluing my fingers together
Radio play me a song with a point
Sailor beware of weather

I'm getting closer
My salamander
Well when will we be there
Oh no don't answer
Oh no

I'm getting closer
I'm getting closer to your heart

Closer, closer

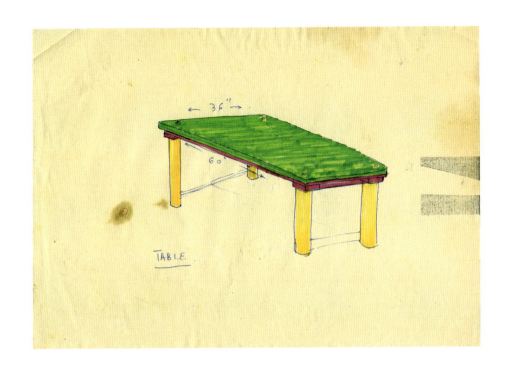

　　林普恩城堡是一座宏伟的老建筑，坐落在英国东南部的肯特郡。它的主人是相当挑剔的一对——哈里（Harry Margary）和德尔德雷·玛格丽（Deirdre Margary）。他们非常时髦。我们会写歌、录音，然后他们会邀请我晚上去喝一杯，而我会应邀，并在回家前喝一点威士忌。我记得在那里写了这首歌，尽管我们最终是在阿比路完成并录制了它。

　　我们在林普恩城堡录了一大堆东西。我也不知道为什么，或许是因为它离我们住的地方很近，就在去南海岸福克斯顿的路上。我们开着一辆移动录音车去了那里，大概还进去录了专辑《回到蛋中》，所以，有这么一些略微古怪的事情发生，就会得到一些古怪的歌曲。我现在比起那时候目标更明确了，当时我可能抽了太多大麻。

　　羽翼乐队的特点之一就是它"无须有意义"的自由。有时候我只是喜欢这些词，根本不在乎是否有意义。"Say you don't love him"（说你不爱他）不是真实的经历，也不是我被抛弃或戴绿帽子什么的，这是一种让我进入歌曲的方法；"I'm getting closer to your heart"（我越来越靠近你的心），我开车去你那儿，也快到达了；"Keeping ahead of the rain on the road / Watching my windscreen wipers / Radio playing me a danceable ode"（在路上赶在大雨之前 / 看着我的汽车雨刷 / 电台里放着一曲跳舞音乐）；"Hitting the chisel and making a joint"（敲打凿子卷一根叶子）……你知道你的听众会被这些小细节逗乐，因为手卷叶子在那个时候还是有点地下的。

　　有时候你就是喜欢一个词，非要想法子把它放进歌里。我记得琳达给我讲过一个故事，说她小时候和我一样是个自然爱好者，她会在石头下面寻找蜥蜴或蝾螈，她会

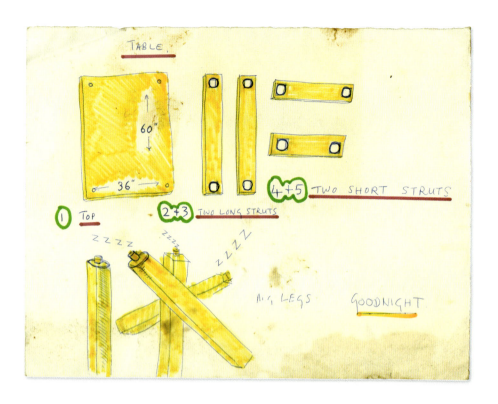

称之为 "salamander"（沙罗曼蛇）。我喜欢在她的世界里它是 "沙罗曼蛇" 的想法 —— 更具异国情调。沙罗曼蛇有一种神话色彩，在火中出生，这就是沙罗曼蛇进入这首歌的方式。

这样的歌可能会被认为像是一幅拼贴画。我把我看到或者听到的东西放在一起，在我们把它们记录下来之前，那些东西已经存在好久了。我好像记得某个沿路的标牌："当心牛"，而且标牌上可能有弹孔，因为有人用它来练习打靶，所以我想，"Cattle beware … Gluing my fingers together / Radio play me a song with a point"（担心……的牛。将我的手指粘在一起／电台里放着一首主题歌曲）。你知道，不是每件事都需要有意义。写歌就像是某种建筑工作，所以按照我通常的做法就是，把它组装起来并把它带到某个地方。

我在学校的爱好之一是木工，这并非偶然。我们住在苏格兰时，我只用胶水就做了一张桌子，没有钉子。起初是些很基本的工作；我画了设计图纸，买了木头。当孩子们玩耍或者准备睡觉时，我就坐在厨房的桌子旁，敲敲凿凿，做这些小榫头。我完成了每一个部件，桌腿或拐角之类的，最终我有了一大堆零部件。有一天我想："我要尝试把这些用胶水粘在一起。"我用我的 Evo-Stik 牌木工胶水，把所有的东西都粘在了一起，除了最后一块有点合不上，其他的都用上了。那一块是下面的横档，所以我把它倒过来把所有东西都装在一起。桌子仍然能站起来。

右图：羽翼乐队。肯特郡林普恩城堡，1978 年。

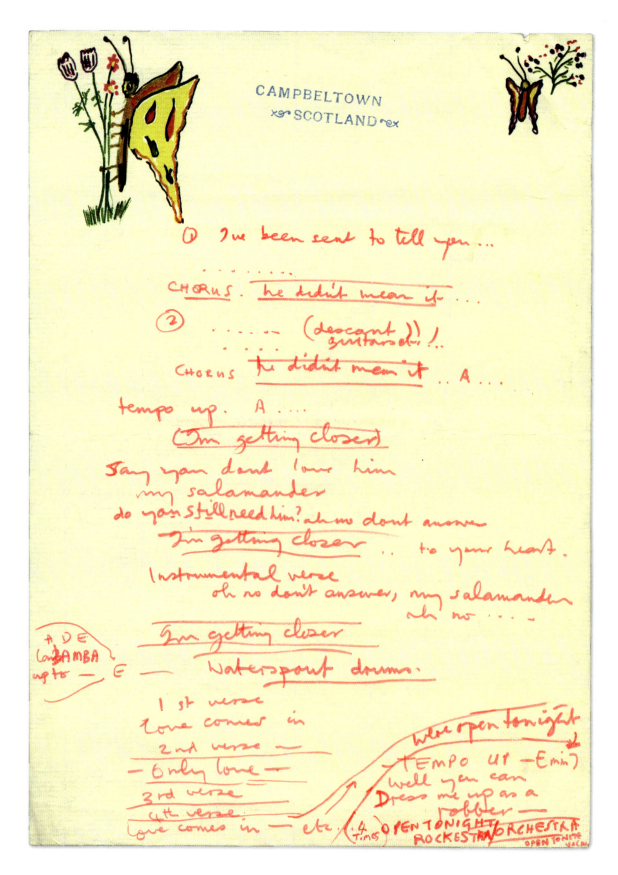

CAMPBELTOWN
SCOTLAND

① I've been sent to tell you...

. . . .

CHORUS. he didn't mean it ...

② . . . . . (descant)
guitars etc.)!..

. . . .

CHORUS he didn't mean it .. A ...

tempo up. A ....

(I'm getting closer)

Say you don't love him
my salamander
do you still need him? oh no don't answer
I'm getting closer .. to your heart.

Instrumental verse
oh no don't answer, my salamander
oh no ... –

I'm getting closer

Waterspout drums.

A D E
conga BAMBA
up to — E —

1st verse
love comes in
2nd verse —
— Only love —
3rd verse
4th verse
love comes in — etc. (4 times)

we're open tonight
TEMPO UP — Emin)
well you can
Dress me up as a
robber —
OPEN TONIGHT
ROCKESTRA ORCHESTRA
OPEN TONITE vocal

GETTING CLOSER

① I'M GETTING CLOSER
~~TRAMPLE THE RUSHES~~

MY SALAMANDER
WHEN WILL WE BE THERE
AH NO   DON'T ANSWER   OH NO

I'm getting closer .... to your heart

② DO ~~THEY~~ THEY TAKE PRISONERS
MY ~~SALAMANDER~~ ? SALAMANDER
WHEN WILL THEY ~~~~ FREE ME ?
~~AH~~ NO   DON'T ANSWER   OH NO

I'm getting closer ... to your heart.

③ CRASH THROUGH THE MOUNTAINS
TEAR THEM ASUNDER
HOW WILL IT BE THERE ?
WHY DO WE WONDER ?   OH — OH

I'm getting closer .... to your heart

Ghosts of the Past Left Behind

过去留下的幽灵

作　者 WRITERS	保罗·麦卡特尼和卡尔·戴维斯　Paul McCartney and Carl Davis	
艺术家 ARTIST	利物浦皇家爱乐乐团　Royal Liverpool Philharmonic Orchestra	
录　音 RECORDED	利物浦天主教堂　Liverpool Cathedral	
发　行 RELEASED	《保罗·麦卡特尼的利物浦清唱剧》，1991 年　*Paul McCartney's Liverpool Oratorio*, 1991	

BOYS
Ghosts of the past left behind

MEN'S CHORUS (GHOSTS)
You're sleeping
Amongst us
We're in your dream

NURSE
You're dreaming
Try to rest, my child

MEN'S CHORUS (GHOSTS)
You called us
We heard you
And we are here

NURSE
To save your child
You must be still

MEN'S CHORUS (GHOSTS)
We're ready
To listen
To what you ask

NURSE
Go to sleep

WOMEN'S CHORUS (GHOSTS)
You're crossing
The water
The tide is strong

MARY DEE
No

WOMEN'S CHORUS (GHOSTS)
Your child is
Drawn to us
Into our throng

SHANTY
No

FULL CHORUS (GHOSTS)
This child is
Most welcome
Soon one of us

MARY DEE
No I tell you
You'll never get through
I'll never let you
No one is stealing this child
I'm not afraid of
Ghosts that the past left behind

SHANTY
Let her recover
Then let me love her
Until we run out of time
And in the future
I will promise to be the man
She had in mind

NURSE
Be still
Be calm
Your child is safe

1991 年，我们在利物浦天主教堂表演了利物浦清唱剧，那是欧洲最大的教堂之一。感觉苦乐参半，因为也是在利物浦天主教堂，还是孩子的我没有通过唱诗班的试唱。

奇怪的是，已经过去快四十年了，我仍然能感到那种刺痛。我想每个人都能回忆起童年的挫折带来的失望感，那种失望感从未完全消失。当时的情况是，如果成为唱诗班成员，你就可以得到免费的书籍作为奖品，我的父母希望我获得那份奖品，但我没有通过试唱。考官也许更喜欢别的男孩。谁知道他想要什么样的唱诗班成员呢？反正不幸的是，我没有达到他的期望。

尽管没有通过唱诗班的选拔，我仍然一直喜欢大天主堂，基督教堂，任何神圣空间一类的建筑结构，所以每次遇到这类教堂，我都会进去。利物浦天主教堂由吉尔伯特·斯科特爵士（Sir Giles Gilbert Scott）设计，他还设计了标志性的红色电话亭，他设计了巴特西和班克塞德的发电站，后者就是现在的泰特现代美术馆。纽约也有几座教堂，像圣帕特里克教堂或者圣托马斯教堂，我路过时是必定会进去的。考虑到它们坐落在一个非常繁忙的城市的中心地带，仍具有这种安静的威严，真有点意思。

我对古典音乐向来不太感兴趣，尽管我在 1960 年代确实有一些收藏。我有一个叔叔，叫杰克·奥利（Jack Ollie），他到伦敦来和我们住了一阵子。他是利物浦工人阶级，但是他有文艺的一面。我收藏了大量黑胶唱片，当我去录音棚或者其他什么地方工作时，他会和他的妻子在我们家里翻阅所有的唱片。他喜欢里姆斯基·科萨科夫[1]的《天方夜谭组曲》（Scheherazade），他称之为"Sherazio"。"我喜欢那个 Sherazio，保罗。""对，

1　里姆斯基·科萨科夫（Rimsky Korsakov，1844—1908），俄罗斯作曲家。

那个不错。"

几十年后，当我应邀为利物浦皇家爱乐乐团的一百五十周年纪念日写些东西时，我想："好啊，太棒了！"就像我一直做的那样。我和卡尔·戴维斯合作编曲。他曾为《法国中尉的女人》（The French Lieutenant's Woman）和《丑闻》（Scandal）等电影谱写过配乐，而他的音乐生涯始于为大卫·弗罗斯特（David Frost）出演的电视讽刺剧《就在那一周》（That Was the Week That Was）创作音乐，这部电视剧的编剧数量惊人，如约翰·克莱斯（John Cleese）、彼得·库克、丹尼斯·波特（Dennis Potter）——他们都处于职业生涯的开端。言归正传，我得开车去卡尔在巴恩斯的家，在泰晤士河畔里士满附近，然后我们在他的钢琴前待上三小时。我们合作的时候，一连几周就是这样。

我喜欢开车去别人家商量创作的事情——去卡尔·戴维斯家里做这个项目，或者1960年代时去约翰·列侬家，甚至去乔治·马丁家。我发现去卡尔家工作真的很温馨。对于这种耗时漫长的项目，我喜欢去在我看来相对中立的空间。我要工作，所以我要离开家——"再见，亲爱的，我一会儿就回来。"我现在仍然这样，我的录音棚离我的住所有二十分钟的路程。人们会说："保罗，你为什么不做个家庭录音棚呢？"我会回答："我试过，那很糟糕，因为你永远不会离开录音棚。你没有生活了。"将"办公室"和家分开真是太好了。

有时候，如果我提前到了卡尔家，我会去当地的酒吧。有一天，我在酒吧和一个爱尔兰人聊天，我只喝了半杯啤酒之类的东西（你不想喝得酩酊大醉），然后话题就来了。他问："你是做什么的？你在做什么？"我回答说："啊，我在为利物浦爱乐乐团写一首古典乐曲。"他说："天哪，你不觉得这事令人生畏吗？"

实话告诉你吧，我从没觉得这是件令人生畏的事。我说："不，我不觉得；我玩

卡尔·戴维斯与保罗。
利物浦，1991 年。

得很开心。"不过那种事经常发生在我身上。我做一件事，一边体味，一边享受，这时会有人问我，"你知道怎么做吗？"我想，"哦，不，我忘记这一点了。你必须知道如何做然后才能做吗？"

总之，在卡尔家，我会给他一个主意，或者给他唱段旋律或者选个调，然后我们顺其自然地创作、编曲。这对我来说是一个极好的练习，因为当我有想法时，他会把它们写下来。卡尔比我大几岁，我想他当时应该是五十多岁，他的背景和我的完全不同。他在纽约长大，大学学习作曲，知道许多我从未接触过的音乐理论，这是一种非常有趣的经历。他会在钢琴上放上大量五线谱稿纸，然后说："哦，等等，等等，等等。我来记下来。等等……"他会把乐谱写下来，并且为了确保没出错，我会让他重弹一遍。然后我会说："太好了。好吧，继续。"

我发现，利物浦皇家爱乐乐团的男声合唱团是一帮利物浦人，休息的时候你会和他们说话，你会说，"你是做什么的？"他们会说"我是水管工。我做水管的小生意，但是我喜欢唱歌"，或者"我是个妇科医生"，等等。我喜欢合唱团，因为他们几乎总是由来自不同行业的人组成的，对音乐的热爱让他们走到了一起。他们变成了一个行业：合唱团。我觉得这很有吸引力。

独唱者非常特别。我又一次有些不知所措，于是我说："我们能请到某某吗？我们能请卡纳娃[1]来唱女高音吗？"她当时是世界上最伟大的歌剧明星之一，我们还是请到了她，于是我们有了绝佳的演员阵容。孩子们也很棒，有一个男孩独唱的部分，我们找到了一个很合适的男孩，他从伦敦飞了过来。

我觉得这一切都很令人兴奋，一点也不艰巨。我唯一一次想到"这太吓人了"，是在广播里谈起它的时候，对方说的话出人意料。那是一个相当时髦的英国广播公司四台的节目，有一位时髦的女士，一位令人愉快的中年女士，她说："呃，一部'清唱剧'？"我解释道："是的，我问卡尔，这像交响乐还是协奏曲？我们在写什么？你管它叫什么？卡尔回答，它的形式是'清唱剧'。于是我说，太好了！这个词很好。我们就叫它《利物浦清唱剧》。"

旋即她问："那么，为什么是卡尔·戴维斯呢？"我回答："他非常优秀，不是吗？""是的，"她应道，"但是还有许多其他指挥家比他更优秀。"所以，突然的一击，我产生了畏难情绪。

评论家们比起实际创作要更吓人。你知道，他们只是把铅笔削尖，然后把我从他们的名单上划掉。不过后来，我收到了当时工党领袖尼尔·金诺克（Neil Kinnock）的一封信，他写道："别担心，保罗，他们总是那么说。他们肯定会说这不好，但这他妈的很好，我很喜欢。"

1　卡纳娃（Kiri Te Kanawa，1944—），新西兰女高音歌唱家。

左图:《利物浦清唱剧》的演出,
利物浦天主教堂,1991 年 6 月。

上图: 和卡纳娃、杰瑞·海德利
(Jerry Hadley)、卡尔·戴维斯、
萨利·伯吉斯(Sally Burgess)
及维拉德·怀特爵士(Sir Willard
White)一起。

右图: 卡纳娃、保罗与卡尔·戴
维斯。

L'pool Oratorio:

mov. 1. [War]

mov. 2. [SCHOOL.]

mov. 3. [CRYPT.]

mov. 4 [Father]

mov. 5. [Wedding.]

mov 6. [WORK.]

mov. 7. [CRISES.]

mov. 8 [Peace.]

She sleeps the GHOSTS ⊛
re-appear. The nurse is
comforting...
The GHOSTS
are ready to
take the
child as it
crosses into "their throng."
SHE cries "NO!"...
HE too, and promises to be
the man she had in mind.

The nurse says the child is safe.

and SHE sings a song of HOPE
and FAITH. Save the child!
                WE MUST
HE joins in. All join them.
They are together ...

209

Girls' School

女子学校

作　者 WRITERS	保罗·麦卡特尼　Paul McCartney
艺术家 ARTIST	羽翼乐队　Wings
录　音 RECORDED	伦敦阿比路录音棚　Abbey Road Studios, London
发　行 RELEASED	《琴泰岬》/《女子学校》双 A 面单曲，1977 年　'Mull of Kintyre' / 'Girls' School' double A-side single, 1977

Sleepyhead kid sister
Lying on the floor
Eighteen years and younger, boy
Well she knows what she's waiting for

Yuki's a cool school mistress
She's an Oriental princess
She shows films in the classroom, boy
They put the paper on the windows

Ah what can the sisters do?
Ah girls' school

Head nurse is Sister Scala
Now she's a Spanish doll
She runs a full-body outcall massage parlour
From the teachers' hall

Ah what can the sisters do?

Ah girls' school
Well now Roxanne's a woman trainer
She puts the kids to bed
She gives them pills in a paper cup
And she knocks them on the head

Ah what can the sisters do?
Ah girls' school

She shows the films in the classroom, boy
Where they put the paper on the windows yeah

Ah what can the sisters do?
Ah girls' school

　　有时候，当你回首往事时，某些歌词的背景颇有帮助。披头士的性事初体验要感谢我们待在汉堡，在绳索街度过的那段时期。我们是和专业舞者混在一起的专业音乐家。所以，我们只是娱乐产业的从业人员，因为所谓的社会原因而聚在了一起。

　　但美国就像是到了另一个星球。我们过去后，许多姑娘投怀送抱。作为青少年，我们很难有机会和女孩亲热，所以这是全新的、完全不同的世界。

　　说到这，性解放是我们对父母那代人的反抗的一部分，那一代也许有点过于保守。在这方面，我们这一代确实改变了很多，而披头士可能比其他人经历得更多。不过我很高兴我的生活中有那么一点出格的部分，其中一些已经渗入了歌词。当然，在写这首歌的时候，情况稳定多了，我有了家庭，也开始专注于其他事情。但是，正如每一次革命，有些人会比其他人走得更远。性解放并没有在 1960 年代停止，在整个 1970 年代仍然有一种想推动或打破性界限的氛围。自由恋爱、"你只需要爱"时期的后遗症就是，有时事情会变得有点肮脏，色情变得相当普遍。另一方面，也有一些言不由衷的、度假明信片式的东西，比如《某某也疯狂》系列电影[1]和《本尼·希尔秀》[2]。所以，所有这些元素都融入了这首歌。

　　如果你是一支摇滚乐队的成员，你总会试图写一些能在现场演出的歌曲。我想这首歌源于一个叫《女子学校》的色情电影的广告，广告里甚至可能说了这样的话（我试着回忆四十年前的事），"看由纪和某某的嬉戏来让你开心"。于是我想："好吧，我要把这所学校想象成一首歌。这是一所女子学校，像乌龙女校那样。"我小时候，

1　《某某也疯狂》系列电影（*Carry On* films），指 1950 年代至 1970 年代杰拉德·托马斯导演的一系列恶搞电影。
2　《本尼·希尔秀》（*The Benny Hill Show*），1955 年至 1968 年英国播出的真人喜剧电视节目。

有一部漫画和一系列电影以这个全女子学校为背景；现在，它将是某种成人版的新乌龙女校。我开始想象所有角色，以及她们都在做什么，这一切都有点情色意味。

于是："Sleepyhead kid sister / Lying on the floor / Eighteen years and younger, boy / Well she knows what she's waiting for"（瞌睡虫妹妹 / 躺在地板上 / 十八岁或更小，天 / 她知道自己在等待什么）。MeToo 运动[1] 确实是她所期待的，但是那个时候没人知道这个。"She's an Oriental princess / She shows films in the classroom, boy / They put paper on the windows"（她是一位东方公主 / 她在课堂教室里放电影，天 / 他们把纸糊在窗户上）和 "Head nurse is Sister Scala"（护士长是斯卡拉修女）——这些可能来自电影，或者我可能在广告中看到过这些。这首歌是一系列小品组成的。在我的很多歌词中，我都这么做了。如果你仔细想想，这种小品真的是我的拿手好戏。

1980 年代出现的许多吉他乐队——华丽金属乐队——都运用了这种危险性的歌词。但对我们来说，这其实只是对当时发生的事情的一次反映。

我不知道我是如何想到预约上门全身按摩这个点子的。通常，人们只是按摩，但一些按摩院提供所谓的"快乐结局"。我以前常常在舞台上小小搞怪一下，我有一个听起来像是按摩音乐的键盘，我会在调音时演奏它，找点乐子，让大家放松一下，我会说："是时候给你按摩了。请面朝下躺下。你想要油还是奶？"

还有一些我在演出中讲过的按摩故事，我有一些非常狂野的按摩体验，我说"狂野"指的是有趣的狂野，而不是性方面的。有一次在日本，一个女孩进来说，"请躺在地板上"，于是我躺在地板上，她开始给我按摩。我渐渐放松下来，但她突然开始唱歌："Yesterday, all my troubles seemed so far away."[2] 我心想："哦，妈的，这也太尴尬了。我能逃出去吗？"谢天谢地，她不知道桥段怎么唱。

还有一次在新奥尔良，全然不同的体验，按摩师是一个很胖的大个子，他说："坐在桌子上就行。"你显然会遵从他的指示，我照做后他说，"现在想象你的腿是空的。"我觉得未尝不可，他接着说，"想象你的脖子是长的，并且是青铜做的。"我对这事儿有些困惑了。随后他问："你感觉怎么样？"我说："我感觉像一只铜颈长颈鹿。"事后看来，这是一首很棒的歌名。

这首歌是一系列小品组成的。
在我的很多歌词中，我都这么做了。
如果你仔细想想，这种小品真的是我的拿手好戏。

1　电影演员艾丽莎·米兰诺（Alyssa Milano）等人在 2017 年 10 月针对美国电影制作人哈维·韦恩斯坦（Harvey Weinstein）性侵多名女星的丑闻而发起的运动，呼吁所有曾遭受性侵犯的女性挺身而出说出自己的经历。
2　"昨天，我所有的烦恼似乎都很遥远。"出自《昨天》（Yesterday）。

右上图：披头士狂热。纽约，1964 年 8 月 28 日。

右下图：披头士在迈阿密着陆时聚集欢迎的人群。保罗拍摄。1964 年 2 月。

MULL OF KINTYRE

WINGS DOUBLE A

GIRLS SCHOOL

214

GIRLS SCHOOL:

(1) Sloxanne the woman trainer
Puts the kids to bed
She gives them thrills in a paper cup
And she knocks them on the head

(2) Yuki is the cool school mistress
— (she's an) oriental princess
She shows fillums films in the classroom
Happputt paper over the windows windless! ✓
Ah oo   what can the sisters sister do?
— ah oo —   girls school

(3) Head nurse is Sister Scala
She's a Spanish doll
She runs a full body out call
massage parlour from the teachers hall
(C) Sleepy heads the kid sister
lyingouton the floor
18 years and younger
dreaming a night with the boys
Knows what she's waiting for

GTR. TUNING. E A♭ E B E E

Give Ireland Back to the Irish

把爱尔兰还给爱尔兰人

作 者 WRITERS 保罗·麦卡特尼和琳达·麦卡特尼 Paul McCartney and Linda McCartney
艺术家 ARTIST 保罗·麦卡特尼和羽翼乐队 Paul McCartney and Wings
录 音 RECORDED 伦敦阿比路录音棚 Abbey Road Studios, London
发 行 RELEASED 单曲，1972 年 Single, 1972

Give Ireland back to the Irish
Don't make them have to take it away
Give Ireland back to the Irish
Make Ireland Irish today

Great Britain, you are tremendous
And nobody knows like me
But really what are you doing
In the land across the sea?

Tell me how would you like it
If on your way to work
You were stopped by Irish soldiers?
Would you lie down, do nothing?
Would you give in or go berserk?

Give Ireland back to the Irish
Don't make them have to take it away
Give Ireland back to the Irish
Make Ireland Irish today

Great Britain and all the people
Say that people must be free
And meanwhile back in Ireland
There's a man who looks like me

And he dreams of God and country
And he's feeling really bad
And he's sitting in a prison
Say should he lie down, do nothing?
Should he give in or go mad?

Give Ireland back to the Irish
Don't make them have to take it away
Give Ireland back to the Irish
Make Ireland Irish today

BANNED EVERYWHERE

New McCartney single

　　我母亲的父亲，欧文·莫汉（Owen Mohan），来自莫纳汉郡的图利纳马拉。后来他搬到了利物浦，成了一名煤矿工人。那是个天主教家庭。我不是很清楚祖父是在爱尔兰的哪里出生的，但我知道他的家族是新教徒。在母亲的坚持下，我和弟弟接受了罗马天主教的洗礼，但我们是在无宗教的环境中长大的。所以，我们的家庭代表了爱尔兰政治和宗教分歧的缩影。

　　1972 年 1 月 30 日，英国士兵在德里市的一次和平抗议中开火，任何在大不列颠生活的人都会记得。二十八名手无寸铁的平民中枪，十四人因伤重死亡。这个令人震惊的事件被称为血腥星期天。碰巧，那天我在纽约，前一天我见到了约翰。在那次见面中，我们多少达成了共识，停止互相攻击。

　　看到一场完全和平的游行活动走向灾难的影像片段，让我深感不安。看起来，我们的士兵们似乎在无差别地向着无辜的人群开火。掩饰的声音很快出现，声称抗议者不是无辜的，而是携带着步枪。但在我看来，这是一场合理的示威游行，在近代史上，这种游行时常出现在黑人社区。所以，意识到我们的士兵们犯下如此恐怖的罪行时，我无比震惊，因为此前，我始终认为我们的士兵是伟大的。然后，我想象自己在成长过程中，利物浦街道上的爱尔兰士兵对我说我不能去这里或不能去那里 ——"Tell me how would you like it / If on your way to work / You were stopped by Irish soldiers?"（告诉我你怎么会喜欢这些 / 如果你在上班的路上 / 被爱尔兰士兵阻挡？）全副武装的士兵阻止我上街，这念头太荒谬了，我不是那种抗议歌手，但我觉得自己必须对此说点什么。

我们录制了唱片，我把它寄给了百代。我立刻接到了百代总裁约瑟夫·洛克伍德爵士（Sir Joseph Lockwood）的电话，我和他一直相处得不错；他非常聪明、迷人，我很喜欢他。他说我们不能发行这张唱片，因为爱尔兰局势微妙。我告诉他这件事对我影响很深，我觉得我必须对此作出回应。他让我重新考虑一下。于是，我想了几天，然后打电话回去说我必须发行它。他说这张唱片会被英国广播公司禁播，这对我没有任何好处。我告诉他我不在乎。这在我的历史上，在我的国家的历史上，是一次非常重要的事件，我要表明某种立场。于是我们发行了它，而约瑟夫爵士是对的。它被禁播了。但它在爱尔兰和西班牙都排名第一，尽管在美国不是。

亨利·麦卡洛（Henry McCullough）当时是羽翼乐队的一员，他受到了一些抨击，因为他是来自北爱尔兰的男孩。亨利是新教徒，所以有些人对他参与这首歌感到有点不安。这在当时真的挺糟糕。还有一些人认为这首歌是为爱尔兰共和军所作的战斗口号。这当然不是为此而写的。不管是好是坏，这一刻我有一种感觉，艺术可以，也应该对某些境况作出反应。不幸的是，这种境况还没有完全解决——也许永远不会解决。

他说这张唱片会被英国广播公司禁播，
这对我没有任何好处。我告诉他我不在乎。
这在我的历史上，在我的国家的历史上，
是一次非常重要的事件，我要表明某种立场。
于是我们发行了它，而约瑟夫爵士是对的。它被禁播了。
但它在爱尔兰和西班牙都排名第一，尽管在美国不是。

218

黑胶厂标设计样板，1972 年。

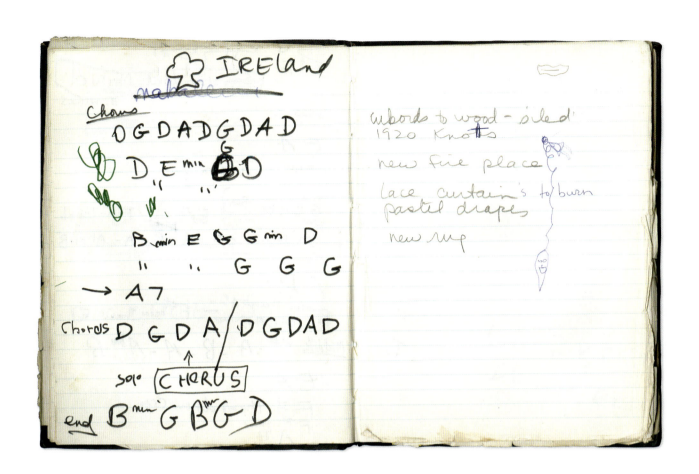

☘ IRELAND

~~make it~~

Chorus

D G D A D G D A D

D E min G G D

B min E G G min D

G G G

→ A7

Chorus D G D A / D G D A D

solo CHORUS

end B min G B min G D

cuboards to wood - oiled
1920 Knotts

new fire place

Lace curtain's to burn
pastel drapes

new rug

上图：琳达为《把爱尔兰还给爱尔兰人》手写的和弦，约 1972 年。

左图：保罗与亨利·麦卡洛，羽翼乐队英国巡演，1973 年。

Golden Earth Girl

金色大地的女孩

作　者　WRITER	保罗·麦卡特尼	Paul McCartney
艺术家　ARTIST	保罗·麦卡特尼	Paul McCartney
录　音　RECORDED	萨塞克斯郡猪山磨坊	Hog Hill Mill, Sussex
发　行　RELEASED	《离开地面》，1993 年	*Off the Ground*, 1993

Golden earth girl, female animal
Sings to the wind, resting at sunset
In a mossy nest
Sensing moonlight in the air
Moonlight in the air

Good clear water, friend of wilderness
Sees in the pool her own reflection
In another world
Someone over there is counting

Fish in a sunbeam
In eggshell seas
Fish in a sunbeam
Eggshell finish

Nature's lover climbs the primrose hill
Smiles at the sky, watching the sunset
From a mossy nest
As she falls asleep she's counting

Fish in a sunbeam
In eggshell seas
Fish in a sunbeam
Eggshell finish

　　虽然这首歌主要是献给琳达的颂歌，它发行时我俩已经结婚二十四年，而她真的是一个"金色大地的女孩"，不过这首歌同时也是对约翰和洋子的小小致意。洋子经常说"看那朵云"这样的话，或者用一些与大自然有关的词。我一直很喜欢她作品里的这种特质，后来约翰用他那种超现实的事物置换方式学到了这一点。

　　我在洋子1960年代中期到伦敦的时候就认识她了。事实上，约翰遇见她之前，我就认识她了。我记得她到我家说："我们正在为约翰·凯奇的生日收集手稿。你有手稿吗？"我说："我们没有那种手稿，我们就是在纸上写一些词，一堆写着歌词的纸。"她说："好啊，那太好了。"我告诉她我自己真的没有这样的东西，但约翰可能有，于是我把她引向了他。但我不确定她是否留意到了那个邀请，因为接下来我就听说，她在我和一些朋友的帮助下在一个小画廊里举办了一个展览。那地方叫因迪卡画廊，位于伦敦梅森小院他们书店的地下室。约翰去看了展览，我想他就是那时和洋子相遇的，大概是1966年底。他爬上梯子，想看她在天花板上写了什么，走近看，上面写着："是。"于是他想，"那是一个征兆；就是这个"，然后他们疯狂地相爱了。

　　他俩在一起后，所有披头士乐队录音的事情，她也会出现。我认为这是从《白色专辑》[1]录音开始的——所以，大约是在1968年的春末。一开始，除了约翰，我们所有人都觉得这很烦人，但我们还是默许了，并且带着她一起工作。事实上，我最后意识到，瞧，如果约翰爱她，我们就得由他去，我们得支持这段关系。这基本上就是我的感觉。

上图：琳达与两只宠物狗"幸运""午夜"在一起。苏格兰，1975年。

1　即同名专辑《披头士》。因为封面为纯白色，因此一般也被称为《白色专辑》。

然后，一两年后，披头士解散了，那是一段糟糕的时期，一个真正的低谷，每个人都在攻击其他人。我觉得约翰和洋子特别擅长攻击，在采访中说些事情，或者对你发表一番评论。他们会说一些不太愉快的事情，回首往事，我觉得："为什么？你很生气，所以才说那些不愉快的话吗？"

随着时间的推移，情况逐渐缓和，我和约翰的关系也有所改善，我经常在纽约和他见面，或者和他通电话。1975 年，他和洋子生了一个儿子，肖恩（Sean），我们有了更多的共同点，时常谈论为人父母的问题。一切都很好，直到他被杀害。当然，从那时起，我真的很同情洋子。我失去了朋友，而她失去了丈夫和孩子的父亲。

在他的歌词中，约翰会间接提到洋子和大自然，比如在歌曲《朱莉亚》中使用"海洋的孩子"[1]，我明白，这是她的名字翻译成英语的含义，我在这首歌里为琳达使用了类似的意象——"Good clear water, friend of wilderness"（清澈的水，荒野的朋友）。有趣的是，约翰为《白色专辑》写了一首歌，叫作《自然之子》（Child of Nature），那首歌最终没有出现在唱片中，他把这首歌改写成了《嫉妒的家伙》（Jealous Guy）。正如我所说的，琳达真的帮助我找到了自己的另一面。如果有人配得上"自然之子"的称号，那就是她。

> 金色大地的女孩，雌性动物
> 迎风而唱，在落日下休息
> 在长满苔藓的巢穴里

在他的歌词中，约翰会间接提到洋子和大自然，
比如在歌曲《朱莉亚》中使用"海洋的孩子"，
我明白，这是她的名字翻译成英语的含义，
我在这首歌里为琳达使用了类似的意象 ——
"清澈的水，荒野的朋友"。

1　所指歌词为 "Julia, Julia, oceanchild, calls me"，出自《朱莉亚》（Julia）。这是披头士唯一由约翰·列侬独立弹奏并演唱的歌曲。

Golden Slumbers

金色梦乡

作　者	WRITERS	保罗·麦卡特尼和约翰·列侬　Paul McCartney and John Lennon
艺术家	ARTIST	披头士乐队　The Beatles
录　音	RECORDED	伦敦阿比路录音棚　Abbey Road Studios, London
发　行	RELEASED	《阿比路》，1969 年　*Abbey Road*, 1969

Once there was a way to get back homeward
Once there was a way to get back home
Sleep, pretty darling, do not cry
And I will sing a lullaby

Golden slumbers fill your eyes
Smiles awake you when you rise
Sleep, pretty darling, do not cry
And I will sing a lullaby

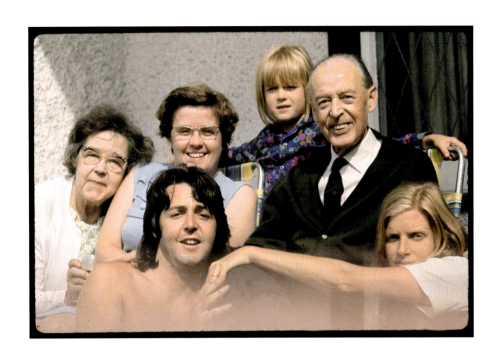

很少有人知道，《金色梦乡》是根据伊丽莎白时代剧作家托马斯·德克尔（Thomas Dekker）的一首诗改编的维多利亚时代老歌。我在利物浦时碰巧在一堆钢琴曲谱里发现了这些词。我父亲再婚了，娶了一个有女儿的女人，我的继妹露丝或者她的母亲会弹一点钢琴。那时，我也总是会看一下钢琴凳里面，因为很多人会将他们的乐谱留在那里。我就是这么发现了《金色梦乡》。

原曲是在唱片广泛传播之前创作的，那时人们不得不自己制造娱乐节目。你可以想象一个维多利亚时代的客厅，漂亮的年轻女孩站着唱歌，而英俊的年轻男人为她伴奏；或者有时候正好相反。这一传统让很多家庭都拥有一架钢琴，以及大量非常成功的乐谱，比如欧文·柏林[1]的《亚历山大拉格泰姆乐队》（Alexander's Ragtime Band），销量达数百万。很长一段时间以来，人们听到新歌的方式是通过家庭钢琴旁边的乐谱。

我爸爸吉姆是我们家的钢琴家，有趣的是，他从哈里·爱泼斯坦在埃弗顿的北区音乐商店——也称为 NEMS——买了我们的立式钢琴。哈里的儿子长大后成了布莱恩，披头士乐队的经纪人。那架立式钢琴就放在我们福特林路的前厅里，我在那里写下了

上图：和金阿姨、米妮阿姨、安吉拉（Angela）、希瑟、爸爸吉姆及琳达在一起。赫斯沃尔，1968 年。

1　欧文·柏林（Irving Berlin，1888—1989），美国作曲家。

《当我六十四岁时》（When I'm Sixty-Four）之类的歌曲。不过，爸爸不会教我钢琴，他想让我去上课。他觉得自己不够好，而且因为父母对我们有所期望，他想让我学习"真正的东西"。我时不时地上几节课，但最终还是自学成才，就像他一样。我发现课程太过拘谨和枯燥，编歌比练习音阶有趣得多。

据我所知，爸爸只写过一首歌，叫作《和艾洛伊丝一起逛公园》（Walking in the Park with Eloise）。1970年代，我们和羽翼乐队在纳什维尔录制了这首歌（好放给他听），然后我们以"乡村火腿乐队"（The Country Hams）为名，把它作为单曲发行了。我有几个朋友，比如像切特·阿特金斯和弗洛伊德·克莱默（Floyd Cramer）在其中演奏。后来，我和爸爸谈起此事："爸爸，你知道你写的那首歌吗？"他说："儿子，我一首歌都没写过。"于是我说："但是，你写了。你知道，《和艾洛伊丝一起逛公园》？"而他回答："不，不是我写的。是我改编的。"

音乐在我们家是件大事。而爸爸在棉花交易所的朋友弗雷迪·里默（Freddie Rimmer）是他家的钢琴家。所以，周围总有人会弹钢琴，这是一件美妙的事情，因为这意味着人们会经常唱歌，就像在音乐剧中一样。第一次世界大战后唱片问世，当时我爸爸还年轻，这改变了人们听音乐的方式。但麦卡特尼家的聚会，或者新年夜"do"（利物浦的"聚会"的意思），形式一如既往。那时美酒不停，琴声不断。每个人都会聚集在钢琴周围，孩子们会在房子周围跑来跑去。

我小时候，那向来是一件非常美妙的事情，因为钢琴会弹出所有人都知道的老歌，尤其是阿姨们；阿姨们唱着歌，还知道所有的段落。所有人都站在一个房间里，喝得酩酊大醉，唱着这些歌，这种友情是很特别的，有点像詹姆斯·乔伊斯的《死人》（The Dead）里的那种。在我成长的过程中，我一直认为麦卡特尼一家很普通，但现在我意识到，有这样一个家庭是多么幸运，那里的人都很体面、善良和友好。不富裕；没有人有钱，但那几乎是一种优势，因为他们什么都得自己做。

我很喜欢那张乐谱上《金色梦乡》的歌词，于是玩笑式地为它们编了一段旋律。我们可以慷慨地称之为采样，当然也可以说这是偷窃。但是因为我不会读乐谱，不知道原本是什么旋律，所以我就唱了自己的。或许由于我在伦敦一直感到沮丧，想退回家庭和利物浦的慰藉中，再加上披头士乐队在南方的烦恼，我大概在想："回到家，重新拥有那种舒适的感觉不是很好吗？"所以，或许有一些这样的背景故事。我不排除这种可能性。

我写这首歌的时候，已经很久没有回到利物浦的家了。现在我在我父亲的住所，那也不太能称得上家，因为那是我有了点钱时给他买的房子——在赫斯沃尔靠近迪伊河附近，一个有五间卧室、模仿都铎风格的公寓。不过仍然在利物浦，而那是"家乡"。所以我加了一句，"Once there was a way to get back homeward / Once there was a way to get back home"（曾经有一条通往家乡的道路 / 曾经有一条回家的路）。这首歌很有感情，我想这正是那些歌词最初吸引我的地方——安抚一个婴儿，或者为孩子们讲睡前故事这种概念。

爸爸吉姆和玛萨，赫斯沃尔，
1971年。

"Sleep, pretty darling, do not cry / And I will sing a lullaby"（睡吧，可爱的宝贝，不要哭泣／我会为你唱一首催眠曲），这些歌词——或者类似的情感——都是父母在孩子成长过程中可能会对他们说的安慰的话。我喜欢写歌以及喜欢写这样的歌词的原因之一是，当你在看电影或者听收音机什么的时候，会有人突然唱起这首歌。我爱那种神经被触动的感觉。最近有一部电影——一部叫作《唱歌》（*Sing*）的动画片——用《金色梦乡》来做开场曲，它非常有力量，当故事结束，一切都解决了时，这首歌又出现了。

人们时常会问我是否介意他们把我的歌做成不同的版本，或者我是否担心原本的含义会被破坏。我会说："不，远非如此。我喜欢听别人对我的歌曲的另一种诠释。"如果有人对某首歌想得够多，想翻唱它，这是一种敬意。最棒的是下一代人现在知道《金色梦乡》了——如果他们看儿童动画片的话。

更让我高兴的是，我知道我爸爸听到了这首歌。我当时并不知道他会在七年后去世，不过，他活着时知道了他对我的生活产生了多大的影响。

④

Golden slumbers fill your eyes
Smiles awake you when you rise
Sleep pretty darling do not cry
and I will sing a lullaby,

Boy, you're going to carry that weight
carry that weight a long time
Boy you're gonna carry that weight
carry that weight a long time.

I never give you my pillow
I only send you my invitations
And in the middle of the celebrations
I break down,

Boy you're gonna carry that weight
carry that weight a long time.

Repeat ....

Apple Corps Ltd., 3 Savile Row, London, W.1. 01-734 8232. Cables Apcore London, W.1. Director, N. S. Aspinall.

Apple

You never give me your money.

Out of college ....
One sweet dream.
The sun king,
Mean mister mustard.
Her majesty.
Polythene Pam,
She came in through the bathroom window.
Once there was a way ......
Golden Slumbers, ...
Carry that weight.

I never give you my pillow ..
Carry that weight.

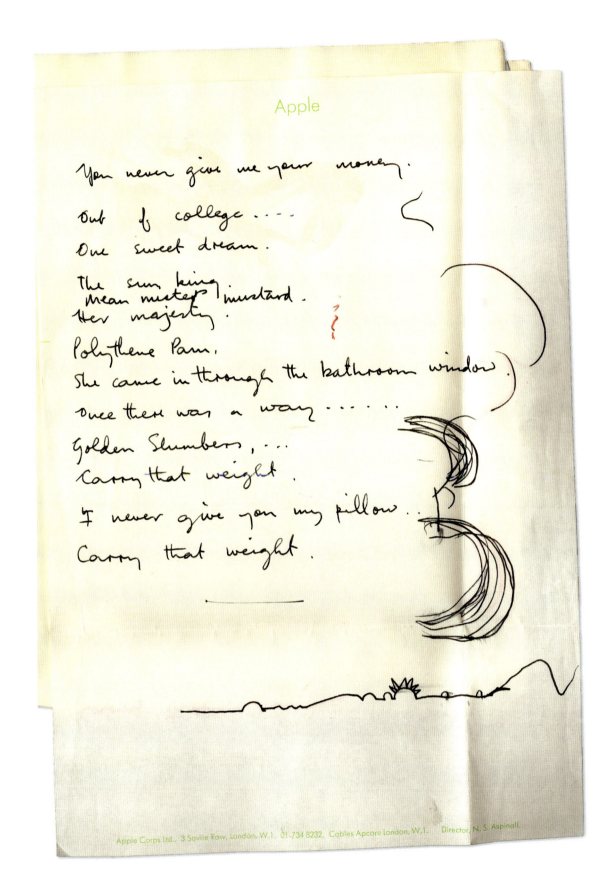

231

Good Day Sunshine
阳光美好的一天

作　者　WRITERS　　保罗·麦卡特尼和约翰·列侬　Paul McCartney and John Lennon
艺术家　ARTIST　　披头士乐队　The Beatles
录　音　RECORDED　伦敦阿比路录音棚　Abbey Road Studios, London
发　行　RELEASED　《左轮手枪》，1966 年　Revolver, 1966

Good day sunshine
Good day sunshine
Good day sunshine

I need to laugh, and when the sun is out
I've got something I can laugh about
I feel good in a special way
I'm in love and it's a sunny day

Good day sunshine
Good day sunshine
Good day sunshine

We take a walk, the sun is shining down
Burns my feet as they touch the ground

Good day sunshine
Good day sunshine
Good day sunshine

Then we'd lie beneath a shady tree
I love her and she's loving me
She feels good, she knows she's looking fine
I'm so proud to know that she is mine

Good day sunshine
Good day sunshine
Good day sunshine

一个美好的夏日。我又一次去了韦布里奇的约翰家。我开着漂亮的带弹射座椅的深蓝色阿斯顿马丁,从伦敦家中出发。我喜欢开车,一小时的车程是思考问题的好时间;如果你有一点儿想法,正好可以在路上充实一下。

我常常带着完全成形的想法来到约翰家。有时如果约翰起晚了,我就得等他;他是个懒惰的浑蛋,而我是个非常热情的年轻人。遇到要等他的情况,我就会坐在旁边的一个小游泳池边上。那是用我们写歌的钱买的。我们过去常拿它开玩笑。一旦我们意识到我们所做的事情的货币价值,就会开玩笑说:"让我们写一个游泳池吧。"

那个时候有大量关于夏天的歌曲。爱之匙乐队[1] 的《白日梦》(Daydream)和《城里的夏天》(Summer in the City),奇想乐队[2] 的《明媚的午后》(Sunny Afternoon)——我想所有这些都是在同一年,1966 年发行的。我们想写些阳光明媚的东西。约翰和我都是在杂耍剧院的传统还很活跃的时候长大的,所以它一直在我们的脑海里。有很多关于太阳的歌,它们让你高兴:《太阳戴上了帽子》(The Sun Has Got His Hat On)或者《在街上有阳光的那一边》(On the Sunny Side of the Street)。

上图:在约翰·列侬家的花园里拍摄的双重曝光胶片影像,韦布里奇。

1　爱之匙乐队(The Lovin' Spoonful),1960 年代美国加州嬉皮乐队。
2　奇想乐队(The Kinks),英国迷幻乐队,1963 年成立于伦敦。

是时候写我们自己的歌了。既然已经有了爱和太阳，我们还想做什么？"We take a walk, the sun is shining down / Burns my feet as they touch the ground"（我们去散步，阳光普照 / 灼热得几乎烫伤我的双脚）——那是夏天的美好回忆。"Then we'd lie beneath a shady tree / I love her and she's loving me"（然后我们躺在树荫下 / 我爱她而她也爱我）。这真是一首非常快乐的歌。

我曾和那些对拍数感到困惑的古典音乐作曲家谈过，但我们从未规定拍数。我们只是说，"它是这样的……"古典音乐家不能说"它是这样的"，因为他们只关注正式的标记——他们必须知道是 3/4 拍还是 5/4 拍或者其他什么——这绝对是所有音乐团体的传统。当然，我们都上过钢琴课，但没人喜欢。很多年后，我和以此而闻名的 ELO 乐队[1]的杰夫·林恩（Jeff Lynne）谈论过这类事情，他说："好吧，我们只是瞎编的，不是吗？"如果乔治·哈里森写道，"太阳出现了，嘀—嘀—嘀—嘀"，那么我们所有人都不得不记住那个。

值得一提的是，当时没有乐谱可看。这是相当棘手的，不过我们的方法就是听一首歌，然后学着演奏，那就是我们投入的地方。如果有人只是在读音符——"一二三,一二三四"，我总觉得他们没有那么喜欢。这只是一份工作。

值得一提的是，当时没有乐谱可看。
这是相当棘手的，不过我们的方法就是听一首歌，
然后学着演奏，那就是我们投入的地方。
如果有人只是在读音符——"一二三,一二三四"，
我总觉得他们没有那么喜欢。
这只是一份工作。

1　ELO 乐队（Electric Light Orchestra），英国乐队，1970 年成立于伯明翰。

INTRO. (then) GOOD DAY SUNSHINE .
(BREAKS ETC.)

① I NEED TO LAUGH , AND WHEN THE SUN IS OUT
I'VE GOT SOMETHING I CAN LAUGH ABOUT

② I FEEL GOOD IN A SPECIAL WAY
I'M IN LOVE AND IT'S A SUNNY DAY

CHORUS GOOD DAY SUNSHINE , ...

③ WE TAKE A WALK , THE SUN IS SHINING DOWN
BURNS MY FEET AS THEY TOUCH THE GROUND
BREAK — B CHORD.
VERSE IN B. SOLO (Guitar.)

GOOD DAY SUNSHINE (BREAKS ETC..)

④ THEN WE LIE BENEATH A SHADY TREE,
I LOVE HER , AND SHE'S LOVING ME

SHE FEELS GOOD, SHE'S KNOWS SHE'S LOOKING
FINE.

I'M SO PROUD TO KNOW THAT SHE IS MINE.

GOOD DAY SUNSHINE . (FORTE
FORTAS
FORTISSIMOS)

repeat-end

Length. 2.10

Goodbye

再 见

作 者 WRITERS 保罗·麦卡特尼和约翰·列侬 Paul McCartney and John Lennon

艺术家 ARTIST 玛丽·霍普金 Mary Hopkin

录 音 RECORDED 伦敦摩根录音棚 Morgan Studios, London

发 行 RELEASED 单曲，1969 年 Single, 1969

Please don't wake me up too late
Tomorrow comes and I will not be late
Late today when it becomes tomorrow
I will leave to go away

Goodbye
Goodbye
Goodbye, goodbye
My love, goodbye

Songs that lingered on my lips
Excite me now and linger on my mind
Leave your flowers at my door
I'll leave them for the one who waits behind

Goodbye
Goodbye
Goodbye, goodbye
My love, goodbye

Far away my lover sings a lonely song
And calls me to his side
When a song of lonely love invites me on
I must go to his side

Goodbye
Goodbye
Goodbye, goodbye
My love, goodbye

在所有人中，是特维吉[1]首先提到："你在电视上看过这个女孩吗？"当时她和她的经纪人贾斯汀·德·维伦纽夫（Justin de Villeneuve）一起来共进晚餐。她说的是一个叫玛丽·霍普金的年轻威尔士歌手。我回答"没有"，然后她说，"那你下周得看看她"。我看了，然后我想："哇，多优美的嗓音。"

玛丽·霍普金参加了一个名为《机会来敲门》的比赛 —— 这是《美国偶像》之类节目的雏形 —— 她赢得了比赛。在节目中看到她之后，我想："好吧，我有一些想法，我可以写点什么让她来唱，还可以制作录音。"

因此，玛丽和我通了几次电话 —— 我也不得不和她的父母通话，因为她才十八岁，我不想让他们认为我在干坏事 —— 她和她妈妈同意来伦敦见个面。我提议在披头士的苹果唱片公司为她制作，还觉得能找到几首能成功的歌曲。

我从一首别人写的俄罗斯老歌的版本开始：《那些日子》（Those Were the Days）。我认识的一位编曲人帮我安排好了：订了一间录音棚，并帮助玛丽学会这首歌。在录音开始前学会一首歌是很重要的，因为这样你不用看词就可以唱，演唱时就可以更投入。玛丽在这方面很在行，她学习得很快。我只是给了她一个小样带什么的，她从中学会这首歌，然后我们就进棚录音。我把所有东西都放在一起，真的是把所有事都放在了一起。走进录音棚里，听听正在录制的声音，鼓励玛丽好好唱，这对她来说很容易，然后做混音。

《那些日子》是她最成功的一首歌，这是一首我知道会成为金曲的歌。事实上，

上图：玛丽·霍普金，专辑《明信片》的未收录照片。

1 特维吉（Twiggy，1949—），英国模特。

这是一个大热金曲，在几个国家都排名第一。然后，我想，接下来如何沿袭它呢——"好吧，我用同样奇怪的调调来写点东西吧。"

即使是在今天，五十多年之后，让我仍然对这首歌词感兴趣的地方——我觉得在此之前或者之后我都没有这样写过——是一遍又一遍地使用同一个词，每一行都是。"Please don't wake me until late / Tomorrow comes and I will not be late / Late today when it becomes tomorrow"（请不要太迟叫醒我 / 明天来到时我不会太迟 / 今天已经迟了而明天来临时）。我通常会避免这么做，试着找到另一个词而不是重复，但我认为，重复有时候是有效的。"Leave your flowers at my door / I'll leave them for the one who waits behind"（把你的花朵留在我的门边 / 我将把它们留给后面等待的人）。"Lonely"一词在第三段主歌的用法是一样的。

《再见》是那种"我要走了，但我很快就会回来"的传统风格，你小时候会经常听到这类歌。它们电台里被点播，送给那些将驻扎在巴林或圣诞岛或者某个地方的士兵。而且利物浦有加入商船舰队[1]的传统。"你是做什么的？"你问别人，他们会说，"我加入了商船舰队"，然后他们就会出海。又或者有人移民到加拿大和澳大利亚，他们会想念家乡。我总是会被这种情况影响，我会把自己想象成一个远离家乡听着这首歌的人。我想象自己是家里的一员，想着："天哪，他们思念着所有叔叔阿姨以及在家里的所有乐趣。"这很悲伤。

有趣的是，几年后我和家人坐在一艘船上，从苏格兰最北端驶向设得兰群岛。这是我们能找到的唯一的船。我们本该乘渡船，但错过了，所以叫了这艘小渔船来载我们。那是一片相当有意思的海域，环绕着一片叫作愤怒角的陆地。那天我们感受到了大海的愤怒，我吐了。但当我们来到奥克尼群岛，在悬崖边看到成群的海雀时，感觉非常愉快。我从没见过海雀。船长被称为乔治船长（Captain George）。他大概算是挪威人，他的前几代血统有点混杂，有些苏格兰血统，也有些挪威血统。他告诉我《再见》是他这辈子最喜欢的歌。我能理解，因为他总是去钓鱼，所以他明白那种"别担心，我会回来的"的情绪。

我很高兴为玛丽制作，但她想成为一名简单纯粹的民谣歌手。我说："好吧，那很好，你去当一名民谣歌手吧，我可以推荐各种优秀制作人跟你合作。"——她最终与大卫·鲍伊的制作人托尼·维斯康蒂（Tony Visconti）合作并结婚了——"但我自己不会那么投入其中。"所以，我和她一起做了一张专辑，不过不是民谣；这是我们都喜欢的歌，但不是她想要的风格。

特维吉跟我提起她是对的。这两首歌——《那些日子》和《再见》——做得很好，专辑《明信片》（Post Card）也做得很好，而在那之后，玛丽确实回到了她的民谣根源。

1　商船舰队（Merchant Navy），二战期间英国将普通商船改造成可以进行海战的舰队，以对付德国对大西洋的海上封锁。

From Apple

Please don't wake me up too late,
Tomorrow comes
And I will not be late.
Late today when it becomes tomorrow
I will leave & go away
Goodbye . . . .
    Songs that lingered on my lips
Exite me now
And linger on my mind
Leave your flowers at my door
I leave them for the one who waits behind,
Goodbye . . . .
    Far away my lover sings
A ~~lonely~~ lonely song
and calls me to his side
where the sound of heavy drums
    invites me on,
    I must be by his side.. ..
        Goodbye------

Apple Corps Ltd 3 Savile Row London WI Gerrard 2772/3993 Telex Apcore London

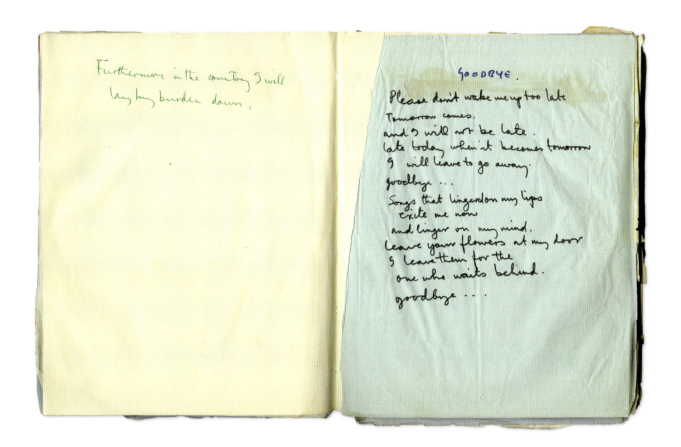

Furthermore in the country I will
lay my burden down,

GOODBYE.

Please don't wake me up too late
Tomorrow comes,
and I will not be late.
Late today when it becomes tomorrow
I will leave to go away.
goodbye ...
Songs that linger on my lips
excite me now
and linger on my mind.
Leave your flowers at my door
I leave them for the
one who waits behind.
goodbye ...

右图：保罗的《再见》原始黑胶
样盘。

Got to Get You Into My Life
让你进入我的生活

作 者	WRITERS	保罗·麦卡特尼和约翰·列侬　Paul McCartney and John Lennon
艺术家	ARTIST	披头士乐队　The Beatles
录 音	RECORDED	伦敦阿比路录音　Abbey Road Studios, London
发 行	RELEASED	《左轮手枪》，1966 年　*Revolver*, 1966

I was alone, I took a ride
I didn't know what I would find there
Another road where maybe I
Could see another kind of mind there

Ooh then I suddenly see you
Ooh did I tell you I need you
Every single day of my life?

You didn't run, you didn't lie
You knew I wanted just to hold you
And had you gone, you knew in time
We'd meet again, for I had told you

Ooh you were meant to be near me
Ooh and I want you to hear me
Say we'll be together every day

Got to get you into my life

What can I do, what can I be?
When I'm with you I want to stay there
If I am true, I'll never leave
And if I do, I know the way there

Ooh then I suddenly see you
Ooh did I tell you I need you
Every single day of my life?

Got to get you into my life

说到我们引入生活的东西 —— 接触大麻之前，我们一直在喝酒。在美国时我们接触了那玩意儿，它震撼了我们小小的心灵。

我以前也提到过这个，确切的情况是，当时我们一起在一间旅馆套房里，大概是1964 年夏天，在纽约，鲍勃·迪伦带着他的巡演助理出现了，那人比巡演助理更亲密一些 —— 还是助手、朋友、伙伴。他刚刚发行了《鲍勃·迪伦的另一面》（*Another Side of Bob Dylan*）。我们只是喝酒，像往常一样，开个小派对。我们点了客房服务部的饮品 —— 那时候我们爱喝苏格兰威士忌、可乐以及红酒 —— 鲍勃消失在后面的房间里。我们以为他去上厕所了，但是林戈从里屋出来，看上去有点奇怪。他说："我刚和鲍勃在一起，他有些大麻。"或者之类的随便什么名字。我们问："哦，什么感觉？"他说："呃，天花板在移动，感觉它在下降。"

林戈说完后，我们其他三个人都跳进了迪伦所在的房间，他让我们在烟斗上抽了一口。所以从那时起，它就成了我们才能的一部分。

有些东西进入我们的生活，而我觉得用"让你进入我的生活"来写一首歌会是一个好主意，只有我知道我说的是大麻。录制这张唱片时，它只是，"I was alone, I took a ride / I didn't know what I would find there"（我独自一人，坐上一辆车 / 我不知道会在那里发现什么）。那时候非常快乐。几年后，随着那些毒品事件的发生，这个场景变得更加黑暗，但一开始那是一种相当阳光花园式的体验。

《让你进入我的生活》这首歌出自《左轮手枪》，我们在编曲中尝试不同的乐器，做得很开心。这张唱片的前面部分有《埃莉诺·里格比》，配乐只是小提琴、中提琴和大提琴；《爱你》（Love You To）里有乔治演奏的西塔琴；而在这首歌里，我们有铜管乐组。我听过很多美国节奏布鲁斯和灵魂乐唱片，那些唱片里有吹管组 —— 乔·特克斯、威尔逊·皮克特、山姆和戴夫，[1] 等等，这足以让我觉得："我要试试这个。"这就是经常发生在我身上的事情。我会在收音机里听到某些东西然后想，"哦，哇，我要做我自己的版本。"所以我们带了一些吹管乐手 —— 大概有小号和萨克斯 —— 进入阿比路二号录音棚，我向他们解释了我想要什么，他们马上就做到了。

克里夫·本内特和反叛煽动者乐队 [2] 做过这首歌的另一个版本。通常情况下我们会写一首歌，和披头士乐队一起录制，然后再决定它是否适合做一首单曲。如果我们接着写了一首我们认为更好的歌，新写的那首歌就会成为单曲，而这首歌可能会成为 B 面歌曲，或者专辑曲目。有时人们会说，"嘿，你有什么歌吗，伙计？"他们的制作人和经理可能会说，"这是一首披头士的好歌，他们没有放出来。你应该把这首歌作为单曲发行。"

克里夫·本内特是我们认识的人。我们几年前在汉堡见过他。我们钦佩他；他

1　乔·特克斯（Joe Tex，1933—1982）、威尔逊·皮克特（Wilson Pickett，1941—2006），均为美国音乐家；山姆和戴夫（Sam&Dave），美国节奏布鲁斯二人组合，活跃于 1961 年至 1981 年期间。
2　克里夫·本内特和反叛煽动者乐队（Cliff Bennett & The Rebel Rousers），1960 年代英国乐队。

钦佩我们。他是最早注意到弗雷迪和梦想家乐队[1]翻唱的《如果你要欺骗某人》（If You Gotta Make a Fool of Somebody）这首歌的人，他说，"哇，这是我听到的第一首 3/4 拍的摇滚歌曲。"他很敏锐地注意到了这样的事。他是一个好歌手，后来成了我们的朋友，他想翻唱《让你进入我的生活》，所以我为他制作了它。

与另一位艺术家合作录制我的歌曲非常有趣，因为这会让我对它的声音提出问题。他的版本应该和我们的完全一样，还是应该改变一下？有些歌曲比其他歌曲有更多的缓和空间，问题在于是否要在这样一首歌中加入即兴成分。如果你开演唱会的目的是取悦别人，那最好还是远离这首歌。有人可能会说"我们应该速度更快"或者"我们应该速度更慢"，而有一两次这真的奏效了。

我最近读到，鲍勃·迪伦认为他表演他的歌时尽量和唱片上的声音差不多，但我不认同。我们最近去听了他的一场音乐会，有时很难认出那些歌。《纽约时报》援引他的话说，他不会即兴创作。我读到那篇文章时笑得前仰后合。我觉得这是我在一段时间里读过的最有趣的东西。他是个好人，但你不知道他是不是在开玩笑。

---

1   弗雷迪和梦想家乐队（Freddie & the Dreamers），1960 年代英国乐队。

左图和右图：披头士在洛杉矶和拉斯维加斯，1964 年。

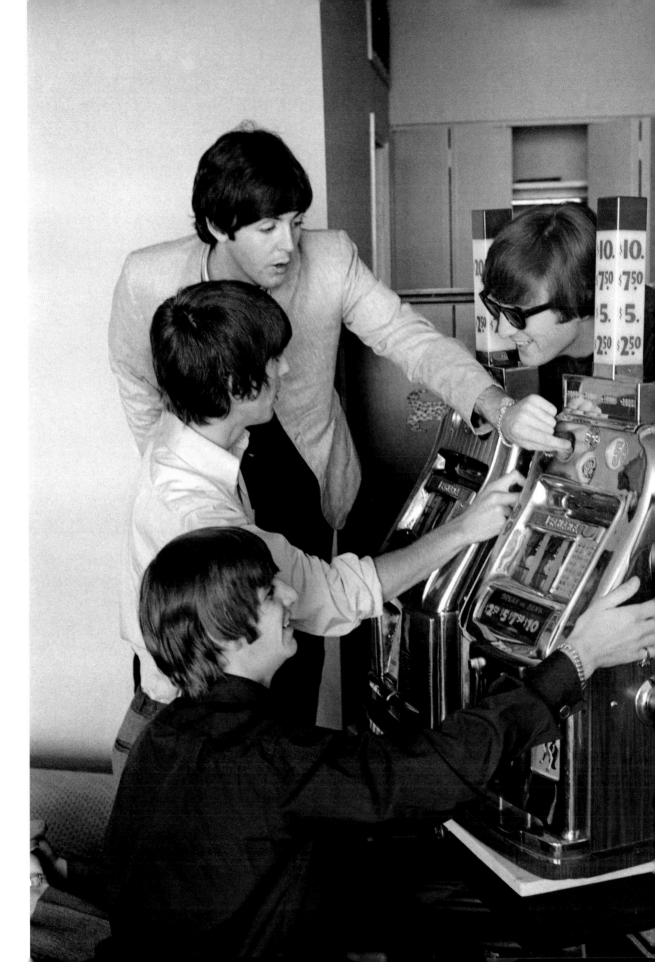

Great Day

好日子

作　者 WRITER	保罗·麦卡特尼　Paul McCartney
艺术家 ARTIST	保罗·麦卡特尼　Paul McCartney
录　音 RECORDED	萨塞克斯郡猪山磨坊　Hog Hill Mill, Sussex
发　行 RELEASED	《火焰派》，1997 年　*Flaming Pie*, 1997

When you're wide awake
Say it for goodness sake
It's gonna be a great day
While you're standing there
Get up and grab a chair
It's gonna be a great day

And it won't be long (oh no it won't be long)
It won't be long (no no it won't be long)
It won't be long (oh no it won't be long)
It won't be long, oh

Ooh oh yeah
Gonna be a great day

And it won't be long (oh no it won't be long)
It won't be long (no no it won't be long)
It won't be long (oh no it won't be long)
It won't be long, ooh yeah

When you're wide awake
Say it for goodness sake
It's gonna be a great day
While you're standing there
Get up and grab a chair
It's gonna be a great day

披头士解散后，我经常独坐很长时间。有时孩子们玩耍时，我坐在厨房里。他们也许在画画，也许在零零碎碎地做作业。

我就是在这种情况下，弹出了这组和弦，感觉还挺不错，我喜欢这首歌的理念：情况即将改善，地平线上出现了一道亮光。我显然没有"会好的"的证据，但我愿意相信。它有助于鼓舞我的精神，推动我前进，希望它也能帮助其他人前进。

歌曲的优势之一是，如果你真的幸运的话，它们能触动人们。我经常意识到也许有很多人不开心，或者只是焦虑，需要一些好运。所以，如果我能成为慰藉他人的声音，那在我看来是非常重要的事。我觉得我小时候听的很多音乐，甚至是我爸爸那一代人的音乐，都很让人振奋。一首歌可以让你感觉更好。令人振奋的音乐是非常有价值的，所以我喜欢这种创作理念，我想这也是我做很多事情的出发点。但这首歌其实非常简单，几乎就像一首童谣："When you're wide awake / Say it for goodness sake / It's gonna be a great day"（当你完全醒来 / 务必请告诉自己 / 这会是一个好日子）。

有人指出这首歌词非常接近披头士的歌曲《这不会太长》（It Won't Be Long），我记得有一次和约翰讨论创作时，就出现了类似的情况。我不记得那句歌词是什么了，我们就假设它来自迪伦的某首歌吧，当时我几乎是偷来放在了我的歌里，而约翰说："噢，不是，这不是剽窃。这是引用。"这让我感觉好多了。

这是《火焰派》专辑的最后一首歌。它被加在最后，有点像我的歌《女王陛下》（Her Majesty）出现在《阿比路》的结尾。我认为这很好，当你有了一大堆显然经过深思熟虑的歌曲时，用一些随性的东西来结尾。它提醒我们并不是每件事都是深思熟虑的，而且它可以让你在夜晚剩下的时间里有一个好心情。

要理解歌词是如何产生的，你必须了解作者的不同人生阶段。今天，我可能会写完全不同的东西，但当你有小孩的时候，就像这时的我，你会经常写一些像《女王陛下》

上图：与斯特拉和玛丽在一起。
苏格兰，1977 年。

247

或《嗨迪多》（Hey Diddle）之类的小曲。

你不会总是坐在那里，试图让事情很有意义。我以前写这些小曲只是为了逗孩子们开心；事实上，我仍然在为孩子们写。也许这意味着我还没有完全长大，我有一首歌叫作《弹性之歌》（The Bouncy Song），还有一首，我承认，叫作《在屋子里跑》（Running Around the Room），这是另一首家庭经典。还有一首大概是这样的："鱼儿，鱼儿，鱼儿在大海里游泳"（Fishes, fishes, fishes swimming in the sea）。有相当多我在孩子们成长时期创作的歌曲——我没有发行过。所以，我想这就是那种传统，这是一首含义很多的小曲。

约翰和我过去常常用三个小时左右的时间来写歌。并不是说我们规定了严格的时间限制；只不过到了三个小时，我们已经受够了，我们也学会了到时候再打磨它。那两三个小时是一种自然周期。这就是为什么大多数课程或研讨会以及大多数录音场次都持续两到三个小时，在那之后，你的大脑就会有点游离了。

这种时间周期延续到了我们的家庭生活中。如果我知道琳达在楼下做什么事情——拍照或者烹饪课——我就会躲起来试着写点什么，部分想法是给她一个惊喜，在这两个小时结束时给她一个小礼物，对她说："猜猜我在做什么！"

即使现在，我仍然会消失在小房间里。这是为了找到一个可以思考的安静空间，创造一个让人幻想的私人空间。不过，你不想让任何人参与那个过程。所以，如果隔壁房间里有人听得见，洗碗时似听非听地注意到了我的动静，当我再次出现时对我说"听起来不错"，我会想："你不应该听到的。但没关系，现在已经完成了。"

右图：写下的歌词，1970 年代初。

左图：亚利桑那，1995 年。

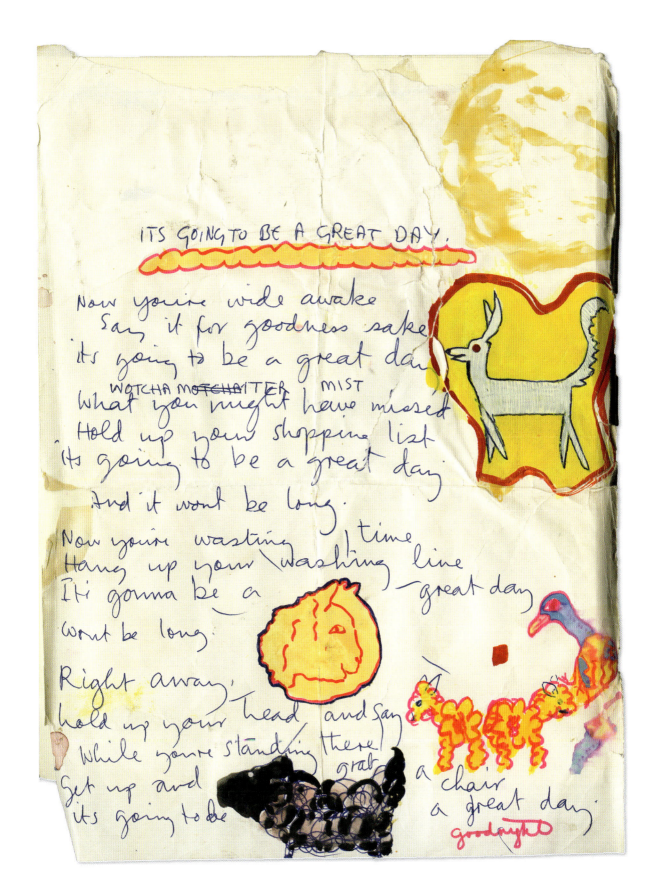

ITS GOING TO BE A GREAT DAY.

Now you're wide awake
Say it for goodness sake
Its going to be a great day
WOTCHA ~~MOTCHATTER~~ MIST
What you might have missed
Hold up your shopping list
Its going to be a great day.

And it won't be long.

Now you're wasting time
Hang up your washing line
It's gonna be a —— great day
won't be long.

Right away,
hold up your head and say
While you're standing there
Get up and grab a chair
its going to be a great day.
goodnight

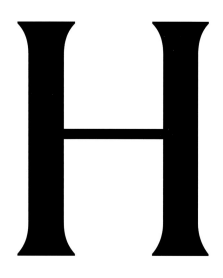

H

A Hard Day's Night
辛劳一日的夜

作 者 **WRITERS** 　保罗·麦卡特尼和约翰·列侬　John Lennon and Paul McCartney

艺术家 **ARTIST** 　披头士乐队　The Beatles

录 音 **RECORDED** 　伦敦苹果录音　Abbey Road Studios, London

发 行 **RELEASED** 　《辛劳一日的夜》，1964 年　*A Hard Day's Night*, 1964

　　　　　　　　　　单曲，1964 年　Single, 1964

It's been a hard day's night
And I've been working like a dog
It's been a hard day's night
I should be sleeping like a log
But when I get home to you
I find the things that you do
Will make me feel alright

You know I work all day
To get you money to buy you things
And it's worth it just to hear you say
You're gonna give me everything
So why on earth should I moan
'Cause when I get you alone
You know I feel okay

When I'm home
Everything seems to be right
When I'm home
Feeling you holding me tight, tight, yeah

It's been a hard day's night
And I've been working like a dog
It's been a hard day's night
I should be sleeping like a log
But when I get home to you
I find the things that you do
Will make me feel alright

So why on earth should I moan
'Cause when I get you alone
You know I feel okay

When I'm home
Everything seems to be right
When I'm home
Feeling you holding me tight, tight, yeah

It's been a hard day's night
And I've been working like a dog
It's been a hard day's night
I should be sleeping like a log
But when I get home to you
I find the things that you do
Will make me feel alright
You know I feel alright
You know I feel alright

当然，这首歌的背景故事部分关乎尤金·奥尼尔的剧作《长夜漫漫路迢迢》（*Long Day's Journey into Night*）。当时，那部剧在伦敦上映，所以，我们多少都知道那句短语。林戈了不起的地方是他会发明这种病句。他会说一些有点不对劲，但是很天才的话。我认为我们和其他很多人的区别在于，我们不仅听到了这些不寻常的短语，而且关注它们。有一天林戈说："天哪，这是辛劳一日的夜"，我们的反应是："什么？辛劳一日的夜？太棒了。"

这个歌名无疑是对我们疯狂生活的注解。我得说，这主要是约翰对事情的评论。但我们全都疲惫不堪，所以这句话非常适合我们当时的生活状态。

我们还是年轻小伙子。我们那时二十二三岁，却已经闻名世界。过了一阵子，我们有点厌倦了。太多的尖叫，太多的签名，太缺乏隐私，这很累人。但早期我们刚开始成名时，我们不由自主地对此万分兴奋。我们一直希望人们向我们索要签名。我练习过，我们都练习过。我今天的签名几乎是一样的，只是现在是"保罗"而不是"JP"。我所有的学校练习本现在看

起来都像是我的签名本。

所以，你知道，你一直都在期待这一切的发生。买一把好吉他，能够给你爸爸买一栋房子，诸如此类的东西。我们就是那样，穿着我们带衣领扣的小衬衫，打着小领带，还有我们漂亮的小领带夹，三纽扣外套。所有人都抽烟，乐富门牌（Rothmans）、彼得史蒂文森牌（Peter Stuyvesant），或者林戈抽的云雀牌（Lark）——你知道，他一直是那种"世故先生"。不管怎么说，年轻、富有，以及出名是非常令人兴奋的。

这首歌开头的和弦做了许多改动。我仍然不知道是什么和弦。如果你让我弹，我弹不了；我得想想办法才能弄出来。我想可能有两个和弦，一个 G 和一个 F。这首歌基本上是约翰写的，我可能贡献了桥段——"When I'm home / Everything seems to be right"（当我回到家 / 一切看起来都正常）。我要唱那一段，可能意味着是我写了它。一般来说，我会唱比较高的部分。

到那时候，我们的录音已经变得更加复杂，更加实验化，所以我们使用了一些小伎俩。比如，乔治·哈里森要弹的独奏有点太快了，所以乔治·马丁会放慢速度，以半速录制。我们总是把乔治·马丁称为玻璃窗后面的成年人，我们是录音间里的孩子。他帮我们编曲，还能弹钢琴，我们从他那里学到了很多技巧。

我不认为我们试图通过歌词暗示什么，我想当时我们只是年轻人。彼得·塞勒斯有一个很不错的版本[1]，很棒地利用了双关语"Feeling you holding me tight"（感受到你紧紧的拥抱）。

---

[1] 1965 年，英国喜剧演员彼得·塞勒斯在致敬披头士的综艺节目《列侬和麦卡特尼的音乐》（*The Music of Lennon and McCartney*）中，模仿劳伦斯·奥利弗演的《理查三世》中理查德一角，背诵了《辛劳一日的夜》的歌词。

后页：《一夜狂欢》的电影剧本。

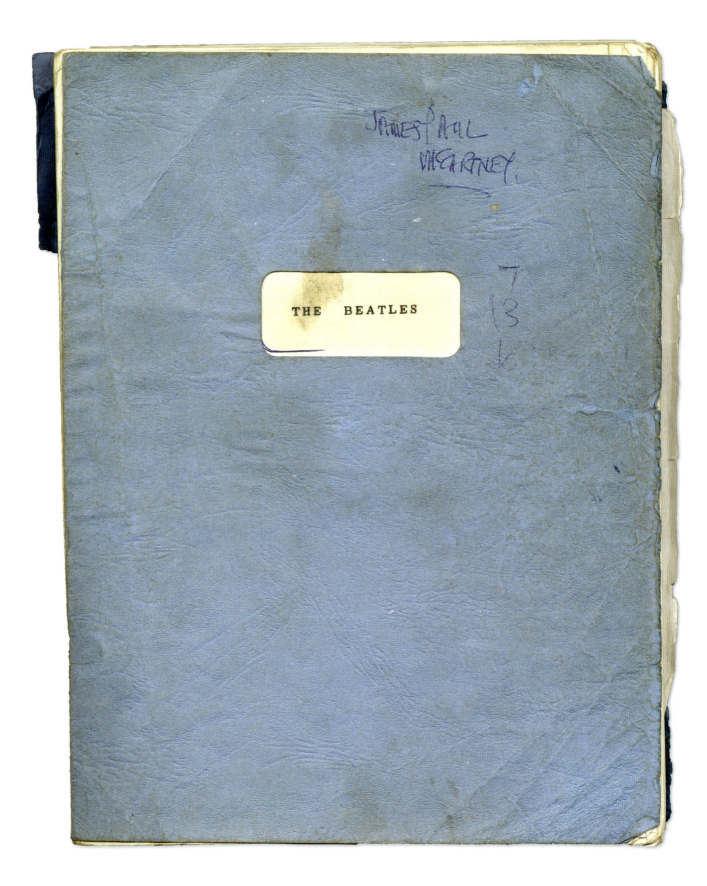

JEBENS
WEL 535

下图：在卡斯巴咖啡俱乐部的杯托垫上练习签名，采石人乐队早期在此地演出。

右图：《一夜狂欢》首映式上的歌迷。伦敦帕维侬剧院，1964年7月6日。

Helen Wheels

海伦之轮

作　者 WRITERS	保罗·麦卡特尼和琳达·麦卡特尼　Paul McCartney and Linda McCartney
艺术家 ARTIST	保罗·麦卡特尼和羽翼乐队　Paul McCartney and Wings
录　音 RECORDED	拉各斯百代录音　EMI Studios, Lagos
发　行 RELEASED	单曲，1973 年　Single, 1973
	《逃亡乐队》美国版，1973 年　*Band on the Run* US release, 1973

Said farewell to my last hotel
It never was much kind of abode
Glasgow town never brought me down
When I was heading out on the road
Carlisle city never looked so pretty
And the Kendal freeway's fast
Slow down driver, want to stay alive
I want to make this journey last

Helen, hell on wheels
Ain't nobody else gonna know the way she feels
Helen, hell on wheels
And they never gonna take her away

M6 south down to Liverpool
Where they play the West Coast sound
Sailor Sam, he came from Birmingham
But he never will be found
Doing fine when a London sign
Greets me like a long lost friend
Mister Motor, won't you check her out
She's got to take me back again

Helen, hell on wheels
Ain't nobody else gonna know the way she feels
Helen, hell on wheels
And they never gonna take her away

Got no time for a rum and lime
I wanna get my right foot down
Shake some dust off of this old bus
I gotta get her out of town
Spend the day upon the motorway
Where the carburettors blast
Slow down driver, wanna stay alive
I want to make this journey last

Helen, hell on wheels
Ain't nobody else gonna know the way she feels
Helen, hell on wheels
And they never gonna take her away

　　"海伦之轮"是我的路虎车的名字。我在苏格兰买下了她,她只是辆小路虎。我需要有车帮我在崎岖的乡间穿行,四轮驱动让她很适合上下陡峭的山丘。

　　我一直想写一首公路歌曲,但我们知道的所有公路歌曲都是美国的——《放轻松》(Take It Easy)、《亚拉巴马甜蜜的家》(Sweet Home Alabama),尤其是《66 号公路》(Route 66),纳特·金·科尔[1]和查克·贝里的两个版本我都喜欢。那时候羽翼乐队演出很多。事实上,在前一年,我们乘坐敞篷双层巴士完成了欧洲巡演。在 1973 年的夏天,我为接下来的《逃亡乐队》专辑写歌的时候,羽翼乐队已经游遍整个英国,那也许也对这首歌产生了影响。

　　十年前,我的妻子南希和我发现,《66 号公路》这首歌有意思的地方是,这首歌中的地名实际上是按照正确的顺序排列的。我们把这首歌当作一张马马虎虎的地图。

　　构思一首英国公路歌曲的想法有一点幽默的成分。因为美国有三千英里的跨度,公路旅行有一定的自由度,而你吐口痰就几乎可以横穿英国,所以你需要一个更长的旅程。幸运的是,从苏格兰到伦敦有八九个小时的路程,而我多次往返两地。

　　从伦敦到利物浦需要四个小时,我们有时会在利物浦停下来歇一下。再过四五个小时到格拉斯哥,然后左转。从苏格兰开始,南下穿过坎布里亚总是很有意思,尤其是在白天。肯德尔在湖区,但"肯德尔高速公路"真的就是一个笑话,因为肯德尔完全是一个瓶颈路段,任何一个经过的人都可以证明。

　　我们以前有一个巡演助理,名叫迈尔,他说他喜欢任何旅程中还剩两百英里的那一刻。"M6 south down to Liverpool / Where they play the West Coast sound"（M6 公路往南到利物浦 / 他们在那里演奏西海岸音乐）这句歌词是为了逗趣地提及沙滩男孩和披头士的互动。"Sailor Sam"（水手山姆）代表了另一种互动的形式。一开始我写"水手山姆"只是想为伯明翰押韵，然后我想："等一下，水手山姆就在《逃亡乐队》里。"他出现在这里，就像在电影中客串一样。然后我说水手山姆"never will be found"（永远不会被发现），结束他的故事，就坐实了《逃亡乐队》的交互重叠。互文性，就像时髦圈子里所说的那样。这些歌在相互交谈。

对话是跨大西洋的。"Spend a day upon the motorway / Where the carburettors blast / Slow down driver, wanna stay alive / I want to make this journey last"（在高速路上度过了一天 / 化油器在那里轰鸣 / 慢一点司机，我还想活下去 / 我想要这段旅程延续）。化油器间接来自查克·贝里，他开创了你所谓的汽车"情色"，特别是在《没有特别的地方要去》中。我想我要说的是，对有些人来说，"化油器"不是他们希望在一首歌中看到的词。尽管这是个好词，不是吗？化-油-器。我不是特别懂机械，所以它可能是我唯一听说过的引擎部件！而且英语单词"汽车"也在这个词里面。

无论如何，写一首英国公路歌曲的想法是有挑战性的，但也值得。我认为这首歌经久不衰。事实上，"海伦之轮"也还在，她还在跑。有些事物，就是为经久耐用而制造的。

左图：《逃亡乐队》录音。尼日利亚拉各斯，1973 年。

右图：坐在"海伦之轮"里，女儿玛丽拍摄。萨塞克斯郡的家中，2020 年。

HELEN WHEELS.

① Said farewell to my last hotel
It never was much kind of abode,
Glasgow town never brought me down
When I was heading out on the road,
Carlisle city never ~~seemed~~ looked so pretty
And the Kendal freeway's fast.
Slow down driver, want to stay
                              alive

I want to make this journey last

CHORUS.   Helen — ~~Helen~~ hell on Wheels
Aint nobody else gonna know the
way she feels
    .   Helen — hell on Wheels
And they never gonna take her away
② M 6   South down to Liverpool
where they play the west coast sound
Sailor Sam ᵘᵈ came from Birmingham
But he never will be found.
Doing fine when a London sign
greets me like a long lost friend,
Mr. motor wont you check her
out, she's got to take me back
                            again.

262

CHORUS
Helen Wheels
and they never gonna take her away...
③ Got no time for a rum + lime
g wanna get my right foot down
Shake some dust off of this
old bus
g Gotta get her out of town
Spend the day upon the motorway
Where the carburettors blast
Slow down driver, wanna stay
alive,
g want to make this journey
last

Chorus HELEN —

263

Helter Skelter

手忙脚乱

作　者　WRITERS　　　保罗·麦卡特尼和约翰·列侬　Paul McCartney and John Lennon

艺术家　ARTIST　　　　披头士乐队　The Beatles

录　音　RECORDED　　伦敦阿比路录音　Abbey Road Studios, London

发　行　RELEASED　　《披头士》，1968 年　*The Beatles*, 1968

When I get to the bottom I go back to the top
of the slide
Where I stop and I turn and I go for a ride
Til I get to the bottom and I see you again
Yeah, yeah, yeah

Do you, don't you want me to love you?
I'm coming down fast but I'm miles above you
Tell me, tell me, tell me, come on, tell me the
answer
Well you may be a lover but you ain't no dancer

Helter Skelter
Helter Skelter
Helter Skelter

Will you, won't you want me to make you?
I'm coming down fast but don't let me break you
Tell me, tell me, tell me the answer
You may be a lover but you ain't no dancer
Look out

Helter Skelter
Helter Skelter
Helter Skelter
Look out, 'cause here she comes

When I get to the bottom I go back to the top
of the slide
And I stop and I turn and I go for a ride
And I get to the bottom and I see you again
Yeah, yeah, yeah

Well do you, don't you want me to make you?
I'm coming down fast but don't let me break you
Tell me, tell me, tell me your answer
You may be a lover but you ain't no dancer
Look out

Helter Skelter
Helter Skelter
Helter Skelter

Look out
Helter Skelter
She's coming down fast
Yes she is

皮特·汤森[1]曾经在音乐媒体上谈论谁人乐队刚刚录下的最吵闹、最肮脏、最摇滚的音乐。我喜欢这个描述,所以我来到录音棚对大家说:"让我们看看我们能有多大声、多刺耳,我们试着把音量调到最大。"

在美国,很多人仍然不知道"Helter Skelter"是什么意思。他们认为这是过山车。它实际上是游乐场的另一个固定装置——圆锥形的,外部有一个滑梯。我们小时候经常玩这个。你爬到滑梯上,你会拿一块垫子——比如门垫那样的——坐在上面滑下来,然后你会再次爬上去。我把它当作生命的象征。前一分钟你还在上面,下一分钟你就撞到了地面。原本你还兴高采烈,突然就会感到痛苦。这就是生活的本质。主歌部分是根据《爱丽丝梦游仙境》中素甲鱼(Mock Turtle)的歌改编的:

> "你能走快一点吗?"鳕鱼对蜗牛说,
> "我们后面有一只海豚,它踩着我的尾巴。你瞧龙虾和海龟们都多么急切地前进!
> 他们在石滩上等待——你来参加舞会吗?
> 你愿意,你愿意,你愿意,你愿意,你愿意,你愿意参加舞会吗?
> 你愿意,你愿意,你愿意,你愿意,你愿意,你不想参加舞会吗?"

约翰和我都崇拜刘易斯·卡罗尔,我们经常引用他的话。像"She's coming down fast"(她下来得很快)这样的歌词多少涉及性,也许还涉及毒品。有点黑暗。

但是一年后,当查尔斯·曼森[2]劫持了这首歌,事情就真的变得黑暗了。他认为披头士是天启四骑士,他把歌词都解读成这些东西,各种各样的秘密含义。显然,他在《手忙脚乱》里读到了地狱。在莎朗·塔特谋杀案[3]之后,我有好几年没唱这首歌了。一切都太扭曲了。

我们依旧喜欢用的失真效果,源自与阿比路才华横溢的录音师一起研究出的声音失真技巧。《手忙脚乱》的录制过程是无穷无尽的、忍耐力的考验,甚至录音结束时,林戈大喊说手指上磨出了水泡。就是这样的录音过程,几乎可以说到了地狱般的程度,所以也许曼森确实从中发现了一些地狱的东西。这首歌有时被认为是重金属音乐的开端。我不知道是不是这样,但摇滚乐之前的音乐,温柔浪漫的舞曲音乐,确实被踢在了一边。我们用这首歌把它踢到了一边。

多年来我一直在寻找皮特·汤森所说的谁人乐队的那首歌,我甚至问过皮特,但他不记得了。也许是《我能看见好几英里》(I Can See for Miles)。最吵闹、最肮脏、最摇滚的东西?我从来没有听到谁人乐队做过什么像我想象中那样吵闹、肮脏的歌曲。

1　皮特·汤森(Pete Townshend,1945—),谁人乐队吉他手。
2　查尔斯·曼森(Charles Manson,1934—2017),美国邪教组织"曼森家族"的领导人,连环杀手。
3　莎朗·塔特(Sharon Tate)是好莱坞1960年代著名女演员,电影大师罗曼·波兰斯基的妻子,1969年8月遭曼森家族成员残忍杀害。

HELTER SKELTER.

DO YOU DONT YOU WANT ME TO LOVE YOU
I'M COMING DOWN FAST BUT I'M MILES ABOVE YOU
    COME ON TELL ME
TELL ME TELL ME TELL ME THE ANSWER
WELL YOU MAY BE A LOVER BUT YOU AINT NO DANCER

LOOK OUT   HELTER SKELTER   HELTER SKELTER
        "   "   YEAH

WHEN I GET TO THE BOTTOM I GO BACK TO THE TOP OF THE
AND I STOP AND I TURN AND I GIVE YOU A THRILL   HILL
        TILL I SEE YOU AGAIN

DO YOU DONT YOU WANT ME TO MAKE IT
I'M LOVING YOU BABY AND I CANT FAKE IT
TELL ME TELL ME TELL ME THE ANSWER
YOU MAY BE A LOVER BUT YOU AINT NO DANCER
LOOK OUT HELTER SKELTER   + +

迈尔·伊文思抄录的歌词，
保罗做了注解，1968 年。

HELTER SKELTER

DO YOU DON'T YOU WANT ME TO LOVE YOU

I'M COMING DOWN FAST BUT I'M MILES ABOVE YOU

TELL ME TELL ME THE ANSWER

YOU MAY BE A LOVER BUT YOU AINT NO DANCER

LOOK OUT   HELTER SKELTER — REPEAT

WHEN I GET TO THE BOTTOM, I GO BACK TO THE TOP
                                    OF THE HILL (RIDE)
AND I STOP AND I TURN AND I GIVE YOU A
                                    THRILL —

TILL I SEE YOU AGAIN.

1st VERSE
CHORUS
2nd VERSE
CHORUS
MIDDLE
SOLO
CHORUS
MIDDLE

Her Majesty
女王陛下

作　者　WRITERS　　　保罗·麦卡特尼和约翰·列侬　Paul McCartney and John Lennon
艺术家　ARTIST　　　　披头士乐队　The Beatles
录　音　RECORDED　　伦敦阿比路录音棚　Abbey Road Studios, London
发　行　RELEASED　　《阿比路》，1969 年　*Abbey Road*, 1969

Her majesty's a pretty nice girl
But she doesn't have a lot to say
Her majesty's a pretty nice girl
But she changes from day to day

I wanna tell her that I love her a lot
But I gotta get a belly full of wine
Her majesty's a pretty nice girl
Someday I'm gonna make her mine
Oh yeah someday I'm gonna make her mine

你闲坐着，弹着木吉他消遣，突然有了一个小动机，而有时它足以最终成为一首"大"歌。《女王陛下》真的只是一个小片段，我不知道该拿它怎么办。歌曲有些玩笑意味，只把女王看作一个可爱的姑娘，不在意她将成为英国有史以来在位时间最长的君主，或者她是国家的女王的事实。这多少有些放肆。"Her majesty's a pretty nice girl / But she doesn't have a lot to say"（女王陛下是一位可爱的姑娘 / 但是她的话不多）——这似乎是真的。她说话不多——只在一年一度的女王圣诞演讲和议会开幕式发言。

不管这首歌有多么微不足道，我都喜欢，所以我把它带到了录音室。它后来应该放在了《阿比路》第二面，当时我们不知道该把它收在哪里。它成为专辑的收尾曲纯属偶然，而我们觉得："嗯，实际上，这是一个好想法。"这会是一个快三十岁的年轻人对于君主制的一种不错的反思，一种有些不敬的审视。

实际上，这些年来我有幸见到女王几次。我认为她受欢迎的部分原因，至少对我这一代人来说，在于她是一个相当有魅力的年轻女孩。1953 年她加冕的时候我才十岁，她才二十七岁左右。所以，以男孩子的方式，我们相当喜欢她。她长得很漂亮，像好莱坞的电影明星。

后来，成为披头士后，我们在某个活动中见过她；我想应该是 1963 年在伦敦帕拉丁剧院的皇家献映礼上。他们叮嘱，如果她停下来，你可以和她说话，但如果她没有停下，不要试图阻止她的脚步。你应该叫她"女士"。"你好，女士。"于是她停下来问："你们下一次演出在哪里？"我回答："斯劳市，女士。"她说："哦，那离我们不远。"她开了一个小玩笑。斯劳在温莎城堡附近。

上图："环保之夜"上的保罗、琳达及女王陛下。伦敦皇家阿尔伯特音乐厅，1982 年 12 月 13 日。

后来，她来为 LIPA —— 利物浦表演艺术学院剪彩，这是帮助我从前就读的文法学校建立的表演艺术院校。她非常亲切地剪断了彩带。所以，我现在见到她时，她会问我："你在利物浦的学校怎么样？"我会回答："运行得相当不错，女士。"

我觉得她很棒。我非常钦慕她。她很理性，很聪明。不像你在历史上读到的一些君主，她相当直率。她也很幽默。伦敦奥运会开幕式上的那一系列邦德创意太棒了。丹尼尔·克雷格[1]在皇宫接上她，他们上了一辆车，然后上了一架直升机，然后，在奥运会现场，你看到穿着同一套衣服的人背着降落伞冲了出来。这很有趣。她喜欢演艺圈。

我认为她是维系国家团结的黏合剂。英联邦不再是帝国，而是聚在一起的人们，他们都喜欢她。我非常高兴她成为在位时间最长的英国君主。她是一个优秀的榜样，坚守岗位，理智。有很多挑战，但她都挺过来了。

我曾经为女王表演过这首歌。我不知道该怎么跟你说，但是她没说什么。

1　丹尼尔·克雷格（Daniel Craig，1968— ），英国演员，从 2006 年开始主演了一系列《007》电影，是第六任詹姆斯·邦德扮演者。

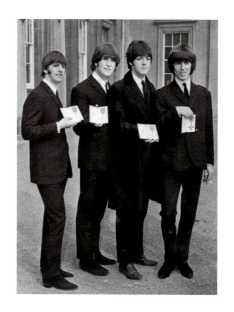

远左图：保罗画作《女王听到一个笑话》（ *The Queen Getting a Joke* ），1991 年。

左图：披头士和他们的皇家勋章，白金汉宫，1965 年 10 月 26 日。

右图：被女王授予荣誉勋爵封号，白金汉宫，2018 年 5 月 4 日。

Here, There and Everywhere
无处不在

作　者	WRITERS	保罗 · 麦卡特尼和约翰 · 列侬　Paul McCartney and John Lennon
艺术家	ARTIST	披头士乐队　The Beatles
录　音	RECORDED	伦敦阿比路录音棚　Abbey Road Studios, London
发　行	RELEASED	《左轮手枪》，1966 年　*Revolver*, 1966

To lead a better life
I need my love to be here

Here, making each day of the year
Changing my life with a wave of her hand
Nobody can deny that there's something there

There, running my hands through her hair
Both of us thinking how good it can be
Someone is speaking, but she doesn't know
　　he's there

I want her everywhere
And if she's beside me I know I need never care
But to love her is to need her

Everywhere, knowing that love is to share
Each one believing that love never dies
Watching her eyes and hoping I'm always there

I want her everywhere
And if she's beside me I know I need never care
But to love her is to need her

Everywhere, knowing that love is to share
Each one believing that love never dies
Watching her eyes and hoping I'm always there

I will be there and everywhere
Here, there and everywhere

想一想《万事皆空》(Anything Goes)。科尔·波特的这首歌里有一个似乎和整首歌毫无关系的序曲："时过境迁 / 我们经常把钟倒转 / 自从清教徒受到惊吓 / 当他们在普利茅斯登陆时……"[1]

创作《无处不在》的歌词时，我们试图模仿一些我们最喜欢的老歌的开场，这些歌都有一个完全杂乱无章的序曲。这就是 "To lead a better life / I need my love to be here"（为了过上更好的生活 / 我需要我的爱在这里）这句歌词背后的含义。

我最喜欢这首歌的一点是，我们以为自己是在荒野的小路上散步，然后突然就到达了我们出发的地方。我们并不是绕了一圈；比那更神奇，我们走到了道路的另一个起点。你可以看到你的来处，你显然不在那里。你在一个新的地方，虽然它有同样的风景。我一直喜欢这个把戏。

不过，就循环性而言，很难否认《无处不在》受到了沙滩男孩《宠物之声》中的《只有上帝知道》(God Only Knows)的直接影响。真正有趣的是《只有上帝知道》的灵感源于布莱恩·威尔逊[2]反复聆听我们《橡胶灵魂》中的歌曲。

我最喜欢的歌词是 "Changing my life with a wave of her hand"（用她的一挥手改变我的人生）。我现在看那句歌词，尝试回忆它的由来。那是什么意思？我在想女王在皇家马车上挥手吗？或者只是小事情的力量。几乎什么都不做的力量。她挥挥手改变了我的生活。它能唤起许多东西。

所以，现在唱这首歌时，我回过头来看它，会觉得"这个还不错"。事实上，如果非要说的话，我会说《无处不在》是我所有作品中我最喜欢的。

1　原句为："Times have changed / And we've often rewound the clock / Since the Puritans got the shock / When they landed on Plymouth Rock . . ."
2　布莱恩·威尔逊（Brian Wilson，1942　），沙滩男孩乐队主唱。

HERE, THERE, and EVERYWHERE.

To lead a better life, I need my love to be ~~here~~ HERE

Here,
    making each day of the year
Changing my life with a wave of her hand,
Nobody can deny that there's something there

there
    Running my hands through her hair,
Both of us thinking how good it can be
                                know he's there
Someone is speaking, but she ~~doesn't seem to care~~

       want
I ~~need~~ her everywhere

AND IF
[as long as] She's beside me, I know I need

But   never care
~~Foot~~ love her is to need her everywhere

Knowing that love is to share.
~~Each~~ one believing that love never dies
Watching her eyes and (hoping She's always
                                    here [NEAR]
         hoping I'm always there) [THERE]

    ETC.

BEATLE PLANS FOR NINETEEN SIXTY-SIX

During early April the Beatles wrote and rehearsed no less than sixteen new songs. The rest of the month and part of May were spent in their London recording studio putting them on tape ready to be made into a new single record and new L.P. album. The album - as yet untitled - is not likely to be issued before August. The single "PAPERBACK WRITER" + "RAIN" - will be in the shops on Friday June 10. To hear it before this date you should send a request on a postcard to at least one of the Radio request programmes or Radio Stations as they are issued with a copy in advance.

"PAPERBACK WRITER" has Paul singing the main verses and John and George joining him on the chorus segments.

"RAIN" is a very simple song featuring John with Paul and George joining in on falsetto chorus parts.

The Beatles will play a short series of concerts in Germany during the final week of June. The schedule is as follows:

June 24 - Munich - Circus Kroner)
June 25 - ESSEN - Grughalle)- two performances each date
June 26 - HAMBURG - Ersst Merk Halle)

Appearing with the Beatles on each of these dates in Germany will be Cliff Bennett & The Rebel Rousers.

On June 27 the Beatles will fly direct from Hamburg to Tokyo for further concert dates in Japan and then on to the Phillippines for two concerts in Manila. The dates are as follows:

June 30)
July 1) -- Budo Kan Theatre Tokyo -- one performance on each date
July 2)

July 4)--- National Football Stadium Manila - two performances

In the middle of August the Beatles will depart from London for a slightly extended repeat of last year's concert tour of America and Canada. The tour will open on Friday August 12 at the International Amphitheatre in Chicago. Then the rest of the schedule reads like this

```
August 13 : Detroit Olympic Stadium Michigan
August 14 : Louisville Fairground Stadium
August 15 : Washington Stadium
August 16 : Philadelphia Stadium
August 17 : Toronto Maple Leaf Gardens
August 18 : Boston Fenway Park
August 19 : Memphis Coliseum
August 20 : Cincinatti Crosley Field
August 21 : St. Louis Busch Stadium
August 23 : New York Shea Stadium
August 25 : Seattle Municipal Stadium
August 28 : Los Angeles Dodge Stadium
August 29 : San Fransisco
```

The above details are included so that if you have a pen-pal living in a country mentioned you can send them on. The club is unable to give information of where tickets may be obtained for overseas performances.

For flight details please ring the fan club at COVent Garden 2332 nearer the time of the tours.

It is unlikely that the Beatles' third film will go into production until the group returns from America. To date The Beatles and their producer Walter Shenson have not chosen a script.

Towards the end of the year Brian Epstein has confirmed that the Beatles will definately undertake a British concert tour, but dates and cities will not be announced until much nearer the time.

Here Today
今天在这里

作 者 WRITER	保罗·麦卡特尼	Paul McCartney
艺术家 ARTIST	保罗·麦卡特尼	Paul McCartney
录 音 RECORDED	伦敦 AIR 录音棚	AIR Studios, London
发 行 RELEASED	《拔河比赛》，1982 年	*Tug of War*, 1982

And if I said
I really knew you well
What would your answer be?
If you were here today
Here today

Well knowing you
You'd probably laugh and say
That we were worlds apart
If you were here today
Here today

But as for me
I still remember how it was before
And I am holding back the tears no more
I love you

What about the time we met?
Well I suppose that you could say that
We were playing hard to get
Didn't understand a thing
But we could always sing

What about the night we cried?
Because there wasn't any reason left
To keep it all inside
Never understood a word
But you were always there with a smile

And if I say
I really loved you
And was glad you came along
Then you were here today
For you were in my song
Here today

上图：拍摄《阿比路》专辑封面照时的约翰与保罗。伦敦阿比路录音棚，1969 年 8 月 8 日。

一首给约翰的情歌，就在他死后不久写的。我想起了我们间的关系，以及我们一起做的无数件事情，从待在彼此家的前厅或卧室，到一起在街上漫步或搭便车长途旅行——这和披头士没有任何关系。我在萨塞克斯郡的录音棚里想着这些事情。在被改造成录音棚之前，它只是一个小房子，楼上有一个小房间，光秃秃的木地板和光秃秃的墙壁，我随身带着吉他，所以我就坐在那里写了这首歌。

一如既往，它始于用吉他弹出了一些美妙的东西，在这首歌里是一个优美的和弦。我只是找到了那个和弦，由此向前推进；那就像是个码头，我把船推出去，完成这段旅程，这首歌。

有一句歌词不大是我的本意——"Well knowing you / You'd probably laugh and say / That we were worlds apart"（非常了解你 / 你也许会笑着说 / 我们有天壤之别）。我展示的是约翰更愤世嫉俗的一面，但我不认为我们真的有那么大的差距。

"But you were always there with a smile"（但你总是微笑着在那里）——这正是约翰。如果你和他争论，气氛有点紧张，他会拉下眼镜说，"这就是我"，然后再把眼镜推上去，仿佛他的眼镜是完全不同的身份的一部分。

"What about the night we cried?"（那么那个我们哭泣的夜晚呢？）那是在基韦斯特，我们第一次美国巡演时，飓风来袭，我们取消了在杰克逊维尔的演出，被迫在基韦斯特汽车旅馆的小房间里待了好几天。我们喝得酩酊大醉，哭着说我们是多么爱对方。昨天我和一个人聊天，他告诉我如果他哭了，他父亲会说："男孩不哭。你不能那么做。"我爸爸不是那样的，但那是一种态度：男人不哭。我想现在大家都知道，哭泣是一件好事，我要说："如果上帝不想让我们哭泣，他就不会给我们泪水。"

我最近在某处听到一个问题："为什么男人们不能对彼此说'我爱你'？"我觉得现在已经不像 1950 年代或 1960 年代那样了，但确实，在我们长大的时候，如果一个男人要对另一个男人说这句话，他一定是个同性恋，所以这种装腔作势的态度滋生了一点愤世嫉俗。如果你说些令人不快的话，就得有人拿它开玩笑，以减轻房间里的尴尬。但是在"If you were here today"（如果你今天在这里）以及"I am holding back the tears no more"（我不再强忍泪水）这样的歌词中有一种渴望，因为写这首歌时，我情绪非常激动。我只是坐在那个空荡荡的房间里，想着约翰，意识到我失去了他。这是一个巨大的损失，所以用一首歌和他交谈是某种慰藉。不知怎么地，我又和他在一起了。"And if I say / I really loved you"（如果我说 / 我真的爱你）——就是这样，我已经说过了。那是我永远不会当面对他说的话。

在演唱会上演唱这首歌总会情绪激荡。只有我和一把吉他。一般演出时，《黑鸟》之后接着就是《今天在这里》，我和这些听众一起被困在一个巨大的场地中间，而且许多人在哭泣。它总是非常感伤、怀旧、情绪化的时刻。

左图：披头士录音期间的约翰·列侬。伦敦阿比路录音棚，1968 年。

上图：伦敦莱斯特广场地铁站，1980 年 12 月 9 日。

279

And its always the same hard luck story.
~~If our Mother was here....~~

Mother: Now, now, thats enough. Are you
seeing Abie tonight?
Norma: Yes, he's picking me up at half
seven.
Mother: I don't know where he gets the
money from, what with the car, and all
these little presents.
Norma: His dad's a wholesale.
Mother: A wholesale what?
Norma: He never told me, he's not a one
for talking.
[Enter Tony] (Exit Mother laughing) car, Tony
Did you see Abies ~~~~

Tony: How could I, I've only been down
the hall? You'd think it was 10 days camel
ride.
Norma: There's no need to be sarcastic,
sonny!
Tony: Just because you're patronising every
~~~~ that crawls into the county, it
doesn't mean that you..... you little ~~~~ What
Norma: ~~~~ the Hell!
Oh, lor if he heard that — 9'll "Come in
Abraham".
Abraham: Is anybody home?

Tony: No, we've gone out for the night...

Abie: ~~~~ Ho, Ho. Enter left
unwanted Abraham, Ho.
Norma: [gushing] He's only joking, aren't
you Tony [
Tony: ~~~~ yes, and a bunch of toast.
Abie: Well Norma, are you ready?
Norma: Coming. (Exit)
Tony: ~~~~ Did you see that mother ~~~~?
(Enter Mother)
Mother: No dear, what happened?
Tony: Oh nothing startling, its just the way
she tags that poor cunt along. He's ~~~~
a mug not to see through her. It doesn't
take much to see what she's after. I should
have thought it was as plain as the nose
on his face.
Mother: I thought she rather liked him.
Tony: Liked him? She likes him like Abie
likes bacon.
[Knock, Knock] [Enter Mrs. Penn]

What is it this time, Penn?
Penn: I wondered if your ma had such
a thing as a cup of sugar, I ~~~~ seem to
have left it off me list.
Mother: Tony, see if you can find some.
Here, take Mrs. Penn's cup. [Tony exit]

Penn: Thanks, luv; [slight pause.] ...and how's

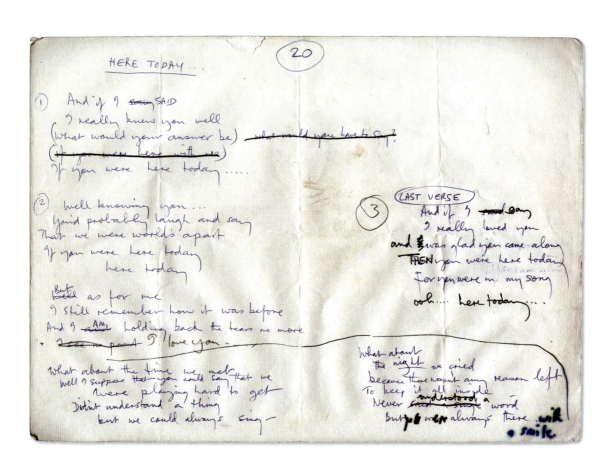

HERE TODAY...   20

① And if 9 ~~said~~ SAID
I really knew you well
(What would your answer be) ~~what would you have to say?~~
~~(if you were here with me)~~
If you were here today......

② Well knowing you...
You'd probably laugh and say
That we were worlds apart
If you were here today
         here today)

But
~~hold~~ as for me
9 still remember how it was before
And 9 ~~am~~ AM holding back the tears no more
~~I see in past~~ I love you.

What about the time we met
Well 9 suppose ~~that~~ you could say that we
      were playing hard to get
Didn't understand a thing
      but we could always sing —

③ LAST VERSE
And if 9 ~~said say~~
I really loved you
and 9 was glad you came along
~~THEN~~ you were here today
For you were in my song
ooh.... here today...

What about
the night we cried
because there wasn't any reason left
To keep it all inside
Never ~~such a smile~~ understood a word
but ~~you~~ were always there with
a smile

左图上：和约翰·列侬合写的故事，1950 年代末。

上图：和乔治·哈里森、约翰·列侬及斯图尔特·萨克利夫在一起，汉堡英德拉俱乐部，1960 年。

右图：保罗与约翰·列侬。伦敦三叉戟录音棚，1968 年。

Hey Jude

嘿，裘德

作 者	WRITERS	保罗·麦卡特尼和约翰·列侬　Paul McCartney and John Lennon
艺术家	ARTIST	披头士乐队　The Beatles
录 音	RECORDED	伦敦三叉戟录音棚　Trident Studios, London
发 行	RELEASED	单曲，1968 年　Single, 1968
		《嘿，裘德》，1970 年　*Hey Jude*, 1970

Hey Jude, don't make it bad
Take a sad song and make it better
Remember to let her into your heart
Then you can start to make it better

Hey Jude, don't be afraid
You were made to go out and get her
The minute you let her under your skin
Then you begin to make it better

And anytime you feel the pain
Hey Jude, refrain
Don't carry the world upon your shoulder
For well you know that it's a fool
Who plays it cool
By making his world a little colder

Hey Jude, don't let me down
You have found her, now go and get her
Remember to let her into your heart
Then you can start to make it better

So let it out and let it in
Hey Jude, begin
You're waiting for someone to perform with
And don't you know that it's just you
Hey Jude, you'll do
The movement you need is on your shoulder

Hey Jude, don't make it bad
Take a sad song and make it better
Remember to let her under your skin
Then you begin to make it better
Better, better, better, better, better

Hey Jude

我第一次为约翰和洋子演奏这首歌是在我的音乐室里，弹着我们所说的"魔法钢琴"。我面向一个方向，他们站在我身后，几乎靠在我的肩膀上。所以当我唱到"The movement you need is on your shoulder"（下一步如何已由你肩负）时，我立刻转身对约翰说："别担心，我会改一下。"他看着我说："你不用改，你知道的。这是最好的一句歌词。"于是这句我本来打算扔掉的歌词留了下来。这是一个关于我们如何合作的好例子。当我现在想起《嘿，裘德》时，他的样子是那么坚定地印在其中，我经常想起约翰，这已经成为这首歌中打动我的那个点。

这是一个微妙的时刻，当然，因为我甚至不确定他当时是否知道这首歌是写给他的儿子朱利安（Julian Lennon）的。这首歌始于有一天我去看朱利安和他的母亲辛西娅。当时约翰已经离开辛西娅了，我作为朋友去肯伍德打个招呼，看看他们过得怎么样。人们都说我喜欢辛西娅，人们以后也还会那么说，但那根本不是事实。我一直在想那对朱尔斯（Jules）——我这么称呼朱利安——会有多么困难，他的父亲离开了他，他的父母正经历离婚。这一开始就是一首鼓励的歌。

一首歌通常以某种脉络开始——在这首歌里，是我担心生活中的某件事，具体的事情，比如离婚——但后来它开始演变为自己的造物。最初的歌名是《嘿，朱尔斯》，但很快就改成了《嘿，裘德》，因为我不想要那么具体。我意识到没人会知道这到底是关于什么的，所以不妨让它开放一点。具有讽刺意味的是，有一段时间，约翰认为这是关于他，以及我允许他和洋子在一起的事情："You have found her, now go and get her"（你找到了她,快去得到她吧）。我不认识任何叫裘德的人,这是我喜欢的一个名字,我想部分源于《俄克拉何马》[1]中那首哀怨的歌《可怜的裘德死了》（Pore Jud Is Daid）！

接下来我开始添加各种元素。当我写下"You were made to go out and get her"（你生来就注定与她在一起）时，场景中出现了另一个角色，一个女人。于是现在它可能是一首关于分手或一些浪漫的不幸的歌。到了这个阶段，这首歌已经不再是关于朱利安的了，它现在可能关乎这个新女人的恋情。我喜欢我的歌曲里有一个普通男人或者普通女人的元素。

歌曲中加入的另一个元素是迭句。《嘿，裘德》本不该这么长，但我们在结尾的即兴表演中玩得很开心，使得它变成了一首颂歌，管弦乐越来越壮大的部分原因是时间允许。

录音时，录音棚里发生了一件有趣的事。我以为大家都准备好了，就开始演奏，但林戈去了厕所。然后，录音进行中，我感觉到他踮着脚尖回到我身后，他及时回到他的鼓边开始敲击前奏，没有错失一拍。所以甚至我们还在录音时，我就在想，"就是它了，你可以再多加一些东西进去。"我们玩得很开心，甚至在歌曲当中留下了一句咒骂，当时我在钢琴部分犯了个错误。你必须仔细聆听才能听到，但它就在那里。

我们混完音后，米克·贾格尔[2]在托特纳姆法院路的维苏威俱乐部听到了一段早期

1　《俄克拉何马》（*Oklahoma*），美国百老汇音乐剧，1943 年首演。
2　米克·贾格尔（Mick Jagger，1943—），滚石乐队主唱。

的醋酸酯试听唱片。我到那里的时候递给 DJ 一份拷贝，并让他在晚上的某个时候偷偷把它放上去，看看会怎么样。放完之后，米克过来说："真特别！就像两首歌！"

　　《嘿，裘德》也是我们新苹果唱片公司的第一首单曲，我相信它会成为我们最热门的单曲。这首歌对一个标准的 7 英寸单曲来说太长了，所以工程师们不得不对音量做一些录音室的小戏法，以把它塞进唱片的一面，结果它几乎登顶所有排行榜。创立这个厂牌很有趣。苹果商标的灵感来自我买的一幅勒内·马格里特[1]的画，我们在唱片标签的 A 面放上了一个绿色的史密斯奶奶牌苹果，在 B 面放上切了一半的苹果。有些人认为 B 面有些暗示意味，甚至可能是色情的，但它只是"苹果公司"的视觉双关语。

　　这首歌从此成为我们现场演出的一大亮点，这个迭句也有了自己的生命。当人们问我为什么我还要巡演时，我告诉他们，是因为有这样的共同时刻：如果没有几万个，可能也会有几千个歌迷，同声齐唱，这是很快乐的。歌词简单到任何人都能跟着唱！

　　所以，《嘿，裘德》一开始是我对朱利安的担心，后来演变成了这种庆祝的时刻。我也欢迎人们对我的歌有自己的诠释。当歌词引起一些困惑时，我总是很高兴。当人们听错了歌词，这表明他们已经"掌握了它们"，正如他们所说。我让这首歌自由。现在它是你的了。现在你可以用你的意愿来改造它。就好像你把这首歌扛在了自己的肩膀上。

1　勒内·马格里特（René Magritte，1898—1967），比利时超现实主义画家。

上图：保罗拍摄的辛西娅·列侬。
伦敦，1964 年 2 月。

右图：和朱利安·列侬在一起。
韦布里奇，1968 年。

284

Hey Jude don't make it bad,
take a sad song and make it better.
Remember to let her into your heart.
then you can start to make it better.

Hey Jude don't be afraid
You were made to go out and get her,
the minute you let her under your skin
Then you'll begin to make it better.

And any time you feel the pain
hey Jude refrain don't carry the world upon
                              your shoulders
For well you know that's it, a fool who plays it cool
by making his (life world) a little colder.

Hey Jude don't let me down.
She had found you now make it better
Remember to let her into your heart,
then you can start to make it better.

So let it out and let it in, hey Jude begin
You waiting for someone to perform with
& don't you know that it's just you

286

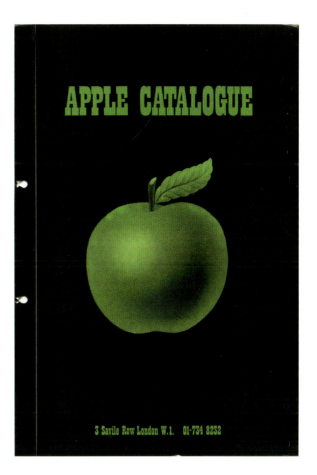

上图左：和玛莎站在马格里特的画旁，那幅画启发了苹果的商标。伦敦，1968 年。

上图右：苹果公司唱片目录，1968 年。

右图：《嘿，裘德》的醋酸酯试听单曲碟，1968 年。

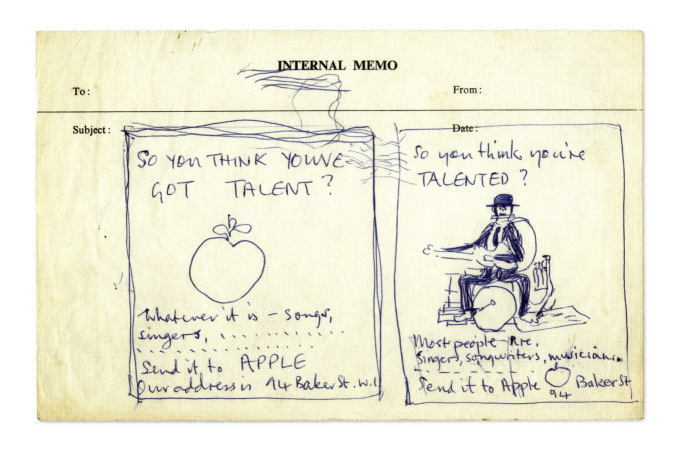

左图：《披头士》专辑录音期间的
林戈·斯塔尔。伦敦阿比路录音棚，
1968 年。

上图和右图：苹果公司宣传海报
的草稿及成稿，1969 年。

在家中坐在魔法钢琴边，
女儿玛丽拍摄。伦敦，2018 年。

Hi, Hi, Hi

嗨，嗨，嗨

作　者	WRITERS	保罗·麦卡特尼和琳达·麦卡特尼　Paul McCartney and Linda McCartney
艺术家	ARTIST	保罗·麦卡特尼和羽翼乐队　Paul McCartney and Wings
录　音	RECORDED	伦敦阿比路录音棚　Abbey Road Studios, London
发　行	RELEASED	《嗨，嗨，嗨》/《新月》双 A 面单曲，1972 年　'Hi, Hi, Hi' / 'C Moon' double A-side single, 1972

Well when I met you at the station
You were standing with a bootleg in your hand
I took you back to my little place for a taste
Of a multicoloured band

We're gonna get hi, hi, hi
The night is young
I'll put you in my pocket, little mama
Gonna rock it and we've only just begun

We're gonna get hi, hi, hi
With the music on
Won't say bye-bye, bye-bye, bye-bye, bye-bye
Til the night is gone
I'm gonna do it to you, gonna do ya, sweet banana
You've never been done
We're going to get hi, hi, hi
In the midday sun

Well well take off your face
Recover from the trip you've been on
I want you to lie on the bed
Getting ready for my polygon
I'm gonna do it to you, gonna do ya, sweet banana
You've never been done
Yes so like a rabbit, gonna grab it
Gonna do it til the night is done

We're gonna get hi, hi, hi
With the music on
Won't say bye-bye, bye-bye, bye-bye, bye-bye
Til the night has gone
I'm gonna do it to you, gonna do ya, sweet banana
You've never been done

We're gonna get hi, hi, hi
We're going to get hi, hi, hi
We're going to get hi, hi, hi
In the midday sun

Hi, hi, hi
Hi, hi, hi
Hi, hi, hi
In the midday sun

荒诞派剧作家阿尔弗雷德·贾里在我的几首歌曲中扮演了重要角色，包括《麦克斯韦的银锤》。他是个与众不同的人，他的作品非常有趣。我第一次见到他大概是创作《佩珀军士》那阵子，在他的戏剧《愚比龟》的广播节目中，这是更为人所知的《乌布王》（Ubu Roi）的续集。《愚比龟》中的一个主要人物叫阿喀拉斯（Achras），他是"多面体"（polyhedra）的饲养员。这就是这首歌中"polygon"（多边体）这个词的灵感来源。《嗨，嗨，嗨》因为性暗示而被我们的朋友英国广播公司禁播。我想他们以为我唱的是"人体枪"（body gun），而不是"多边体"。我不确定这是否更具暗示意味，还是相反。

在此之前，"I met you at the station"（我在车站遇见你）这句歌词在布鲁斯音乐传统中已经很广为人知了：

是的，火车离开车站时
后面有两盏灯亮着
哇，蓝光是我的宝贝
红光是我的心 [1]

它出自罗伯特·约翰逊 [2] 的歌曲《徒劳的爱》（Love in Vain），1969 年，也就是《嗨，嗨，嗨》发行的三年前，滚石乐队翻唱过这首歌。

"bootleg"（私录唱片）[3] 的来源可以追溯到一个来自俄克拉何马州诺曼市的家伙，他到访了我们在苏格兰的农场。有一天，这个家伙带着一张装在布袋——粗麻布袋——里的黑胶唱片出现了，他宣称这是一张私录唱片。这也许就是我在歌曲开头所想的。

然后就是"going to get hi, hi, hi"（将会嗨，嗨，嗨）。我得承认这可能有点鲁莽放肆，英国广播公司显然也这么认为。这恰巧是个大家都在很嗨的感觉中飞高的时刻，每个人都在抽大麻，我们甚至因为在苏格兰的农场里种植大麻而被捕。当然，它也可能指代一种合法的药物，比如酒精。

让摇滚乐保持活力的特点之一是，它对于可能违禁或者通常被认为是违禁的行为，抱有极大的兴趣。

---

1 原句为"Yeah, when the train left the station / It had two lights on behind / Whoa, the blue light was my baby / And the red light was my mind"。
2 罗伯特·约翰逊（Robert Johnson，1911—1938），美国布鲁斯音乐家。
3 指未经版权方授权，由歌迷在音乐会现场私自录下的音乐录音。

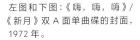

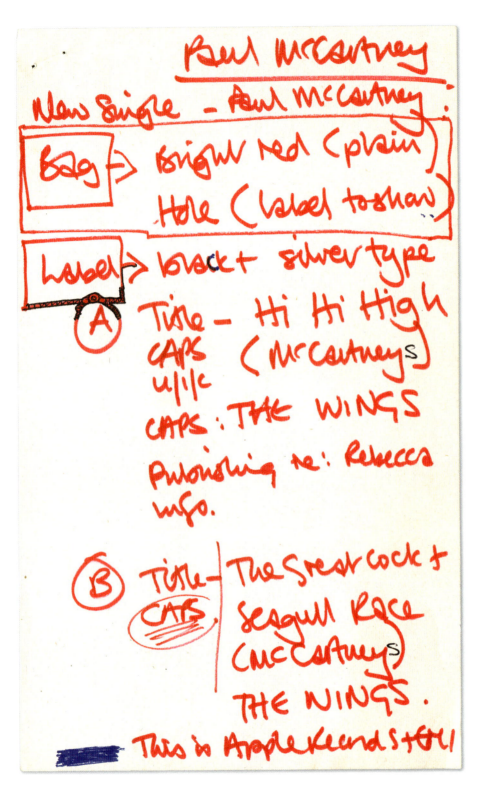

Paul McCartney

New Single — Paul McCartney

Bag → Bright Red (plain)
Hole (label to show)

Label → black + silver type

Ⓐ Title — Hi Hi High
CAPS (McCartneys)
u/l/c
CAPS: THE WINGS

Publishing re: Rebecca
info.

Ⓑ Title — The Great Cock +
CAPS. Seagull Race
(McCartneys)
THE WINGS.

This is Apple Records Still

《嗨，嗨，嗨》单曲碟设计笔记，原本计
划收录《了不起的大公鸡和海鸥的赛跑》
（The Great Cock and Seagull Race）作
为 B 面歌曲，1972 年。

Well —
when I met you at the station
You were standing with a bootleg in your
                                        hand

Drove you back to my little place
For a taste of a multicolour band
were gonna get high high high
   The night is young
Put you in my pocket little mama
gonna rock it and we're only just begun

CHORUS

Were gonna get high high high
   with the music on
we won't say bye bye bye bye —
   till the night has gone
I'm gonna do it to you, gonna do you
   sweet banana
like youve never been done
   gonna get high, high, high,
in the midday sun.

Well-Take off your face, recover from the trip
                              youve been on
   I want you to lie on the bed, getting ready
for my polygon.
I'm gonna do it to you, gonna do you sweet banana
like youve never been done
    + like a rabbit gonna grab it, gonna hit
                         it till the night is done

297

Honey Pie

甜心派

作　者	**WRITERS**	保罗·麦卡特尼和约翰·列侬　Paul McCartney and John Lennon
艺术家	**ARTIST**	披头士乐队　The Beatles
录　音	**RECORDED**	伦敦三叉戟录音棚　Trident Studios, London
发　行	**RELEASED**	《披头士》，1968 年　*The Beatles*, 1968

She was a working girl
North of England way
Now she's hit the big time in the USA
And if she could only hear me
This is what I'd say

Honey Pie, you are making me crazy
I'm in love but I'm lazy
So won't you please come home?

Oh Honey Pie, my position is tragic
Come and show me the magic
Of your Hollywood song

You became a legend of the silver screen
And now the thought of meeting you
Makes me weak in the knee

Oh Honey Pie, you are driving me frantic
Sail across the Atlantic
To be where you belong
Honey Pie, come back to me

Will the wind that blew
Her boat across the sea
Kindly send her sailing back to me?

Now Honey Pie, you are making me crazy
I'm in love but I'm lazy
So won't you please come home?
Come, come back to me, Honey Pie

Honey Pie
Honey Pie

"不会唱歌。不会表演。秃顶。会跳点舞。"[1] 我一直喜欢弗雷德·阿斯泰尔在试镜时得到的评语。弗雷德给了我一点灵感，有的时候，当我唱歌的时候，我会假扮成他去发出那种"小小的"声音。它帮助我到达一个非常特别的境地。有时候我会成为胖子沃勒，这也可以帮助我到达某个境地。

写《甜心派》的时候，我肯定想到了弗雷德和一整个银幕世界。我不仅爱上了弗雷德，还爱上了我童年时听过的那些美丽的歌手。比如说，我仍然记得站在福特林路的厨房里听纳特·金·科尔的《当我坠入爱河》（When I Fall in Love）。当时我正伸手去拿一个棕酱瓶，心想："天哪，这太好听了。"

如果必须选择一个人，我会很高兴被认为是纳特·金·科尔或者胖子沃勒或者弗雷德的附体。我不拒绝通灵。我肯定梦到了《昨天》，所以我确定我还和其他许多歌曲通过灵。

《甜心派》，话说回来，是对 1930 年代甚至 1920 年代，摩登时代和好莱坞（你成为银幕上的传奇）的追溯。音效的使用，一如既往地非常有趣。录音师们使用了大量的均衡器技术来调整频率，让它有一种把扩音器扩大了三倍的感觉。

有时候，人们会认为到了 1960 年代末，把重心放在录音棚工作上已经开始造成损失，使得披头士乐队远离了现场表演。实际上正好相反。现场演出使我们远离了录音。在录音棚时，我们是四位艺术家加上乔治·马丁，以及一位录音师。实际上是六位艺术家，大家在创造一些东西，勤奋且仔细，有很多乐趣和艺术上的自由。出去巡演时情况正好相反。我们被塞进一辆汽车或者一个酒店房间，或者在电梯里窒息，或是被困在所有人都在尖叫的人群中。

从现场演出到把重心放在录音棚里这一转变的催化剂，来自我们在旧金山烛台公园的亲身经历，当时我们所有人都厌倦透了。我通常是那个持乐观观点的人，会说"别担心，伙计们，会过去的，我们可以解决"之类的话，但最后，我同意了另外三个人的意见，而且和他们一样生气。我们被困在一辆钢板运肉车里，像货车车厢里的牛一样四处滑动，就这样被带离了烛台公园。那是最后一根稻草。我们受够了。

1　据《芝加哥论坛报》报道，弗雷德·阿斯泰尔第一次去电影公司试镜时，评估者写下了这句评语："Can't sing. Can't act. Balding. Can dance a little."

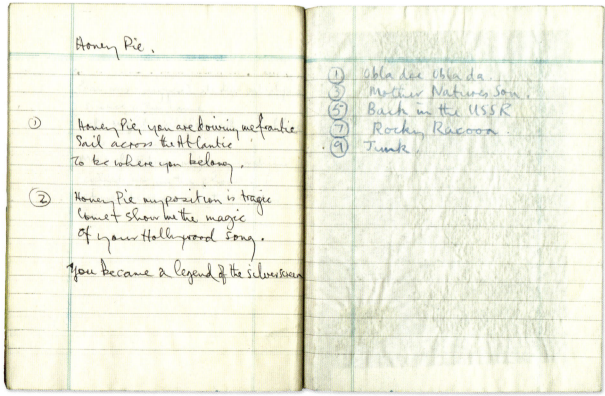

Honey Pie.

① Honey Pie, you are doiwing me frantic
Sail across the Atlantic
To be where you belong.

② Honey Pie my position is tragic
Come + show me the magic
Of your Hollywood song.

You became a legend of the silver screen

① Obla dee Obla da.
③ Mother Natures Son.
⑤ Back in the USSR
⑦ Rocky Racoon.
⑨ Junk.

左图：录制《披头士》期间，保罗与乔治·马丁、林戈·斯塔尔、约翰·列侬及乔治·哈里森。伦敦三叉戟录音棚，1968 年。

右图：录制《披头士》期间，乔治·马丁与保罗。伦敦阿比路录音棚，1968 年。

Hope of Deliverance

解脱的希望

作 者 WRITER	保罗·麦卡特尼	Paul McCartney
艺术家 ARTIST	保罗·麦卡特尼	Paul McCartney
录 音 RECORDED	萨塞克斯郡猪山磨坊	Hog Hill Mill, Sussex
发 行 RELEASED	英国单曲，1992 年	UK single, 1992
	美国单曲，1993 年	US single, 1993
	《离开地面》，1993 年	*Off the Ground*, 1993

I will always be hoping, hoping
You will always be holding, holding
My heart in your hand
I will understand

I will understand someday, one day
You will understand always, always
From now until then

When it will be right, I don't know
What it will be like, I don't know
We live in hope of deliverance
From the darkness that surrounds us

Hope of deliverance
Hope of deliverance
Hope of deliverance
From the darkness that surrounds us

And I wouldn't mind knowing, knowing
That you wouldn't mind going, going
Along with my plan

When it will be right, I don't know
What it will be like, I don't know
We live in hope of deliverance
From the darkness that surrounds us

Hope of deliverance
Hope of deliverance
Hope of deliverance
From the darkness that surrounds us

Hope of deliverance
Hope of deliverance
I will understand

特定的宇宙主题可以追溯到几个世纪以前。在《圣经》或犹太律法中，你可以读到这些相当原始但非常深刻的概念。其中之一是关于如何走出黑暗。

这不仅对我们是真实存在的，对动物也是一样，它们活在回头只能看见自己肩膀的生活中。我认为这是一种宇宙的感觉，我们都想从某种东西中解脱出来，从黑暗中，这对一首歌来说是一个非常值得写的主题。你注定会感觉到世界上所有的问题，所以让我来帮助你，我也很愿意这样做。那是最核心的故事线。

"Deliverance"（解脱）对我来说，是一个宗教词汇，一个你在教堂里听到的圣经词汇，我很高兴把它用在世俗的语境中，也就是说，一首情歌的语境中。我们希望从所有包围我们的黑暗中解脱。

我在家里的阁楼上写了这首歌，来让自己找到某种祥和和安宁。有一个通向活板门的小梯子，一旦你关上它，其他人就够不着你了。我带了一把马丁十二弦吉他，琴颈上有一个变调夹，用来改变音色。这样听起来更为透亮，让我想起了圣诞节和教堂。也许就是这个把我引向了希望和解脱这个概念。

上图：《解脱的希望》音乐录影带拍摄中，保罗与罗比·麦金托什（Robbie McIntosh），1992 年。

303

有很多关于云、黑暗、光、电筒、蜡烛，以及火的意象。一切都很原始。"We live in hope of deliverance / From the darkness that surrounds us"（我们活在解脱的希望中 / 摆脱包围我们的黑暗）——那可以是任何东西。对于一个在海上的水手，它在字面意义上指夜晚的黑暗和看到灯塔的希望；但对于生活在陆地（特别是美国）的人，它可能是政治动荡，因为现在存在着两极分化，我们正在寻找走出黑暗的方法。浪漫一点的话，这可能意味着你和你的伴侣相处不好，你需要解脱。你一直以一种方式思考，而突然，你需要改变。这种改变可能只需要在你在大脑中做一次小小的切换。

我和我的乐队巡演时，我们经常在调音时唱这首歌。通常情况下，我们不打鼓，当它是一首原声歌曲，除了键盘手维克斯·维金斯（Wix Wickens），所有人原声演奏——鼓手阿布·拉伯里尔（Abe Laboriel）会弹木吉他，跟我唱和声。我们真的非常喜欢演这首歌，但这不足以让它进入演出主歌单。不管怎么样，都还没有。

上图：《解脱的希望》音乐录影带中的保罗与琳达，1992 年。

右图：《离开地面》的专辑笔记，1992 年。

ALBUM IMAGES -

__Ground.__ (Vid. (We can all fly!)
Still. feet.

__Looking.__ — Still. 4 illustrations. cat, rabbit, monkey.
(Chrissie?)

Vid. holding animals (approaching cam.)

__Hope.__ Vid. religions (Sally army / cosmic)
(Spiritual)

__Mistress.__ Vid. hologram game operated by humans.....

hologram
illustrates
words of
song

Still. 50's/60's
flat with couple.

__(_ O it al .__ Vid. French caves/
locations mentioned in words)

__Bikes.__ Icon pic. Vid. wild ones movie.

__Get Out.__ Vid. illustrates words.

__Golden__ Still. fish in a sunbeam
(or vid.)

__Peace.__ neighbourhood barbacue
(veggie of course)

__Cmon People__ ancient minstrels / tibetan monks.

__Winedark.__ Style. Vie ZZ top legs continuation
of opening girl (babies?)

__Long Leather__ illustration of story? Lichtenstein style.

House of Wax

蜡像馆

作　者　WRITER　　保罗·麦卡特尼　Paul McCartney
艺术家　ARTIST　　保罗·麦卡特尼　Paul McCartney
录　音　RECORDED　伦敦阿比路录音棚　Abbey Road Studios, London
发　行　RELEASED　《记忆将满》，2007 年　*Memory Almost Full*, 2007
　　　　　　　　　《消逝的现在》B 面单曲，2007 年　B-side of 'Ever Present Past' single, 2007

Lightning hits the house of wax
Poets spill out on the street
To set alight the incomplete
Remainders of the future

Hidden in the yard
Hidden in the yard

Thunder drowns the trumpets' blast
Poets scatter through the night
But they can only dream of flight
Away from their confusion

Hidden in the yard
Underneath the wall
Buried deep below a thousand layers
Lay the answer to it all

Lightning hits the house of wax
Women scream and run around
To dance upon the battleground
Like wild demented horses

Hidden in the yard
Underneath the wall
Buried deep below a thousand layers
Lay the answer to it all

我与阿德里安·米切尔共同创作《黑鸟歌唱》时，我们进行了一次小型巡演。我说："不如我们搞一些复兴 1960 年代的事情，我们可以演奏一些背景音乐，然后你朗诵一首诗？"他喜欢这个主意，所以我们就做了。

阿德里安是我的头号诗人，因为我太了解他了，所以会问他关于诗歌的各种事情。大约在那个时候，我想我正在尝试写一些更倾向于诗歌的东西。我一直在努力延伸自己，努力突破自己的界限，自我学习，不要被老一套的东西困住。如果我只是写了一些非常直截了当的东西，比如"真甜蜜，哦宝贝"，那么最好不要马上再写一个那样的。我有一种诗意的心态。

"Lightning hits the house of wax"（闪电击中蜡像馆）——我记得我对阿德里安说过这句话，而且很为它自豪。"蜡像馆"有多种解释。它既可以是杜莎夫人蜡像馆，也可以是他们制作唱片的地方——蜡做成唱片，就像"给圆盘打蜡"。我想最著名的蜡像馆就是 1953 年那部同名恐怖电影中的那个，由文森特·普莱斯（Vincent Price）主演，令人毛骨悚然。我脑海里没有一个具体的蜡像馆，我无法想象我是从可怕的普莱斯杀人犯那里受到的启发——这不是我的菜——但我喜欢蜡像馆的想法。

现在，当我拉开距离读它时，我发现第一段主歌非常激烈。我不确定我是不是有意这么做的——"哇，着火了！"你跳上思想的列车，事情就在你不知不觉中发生了。诗人们即将"To set alight the incomplete / Remainders of the future"（点燃不完整的 / 未来的残留）。我想这只是"阐明事物"的一种说法。

"Hidden in the yard / Underneath the wall / Buried deep below a thousand layers / Lay the answer to it all"（在院子里隐藏 / 在围墙下面 / 深埋在千层之下 / 安放着一切的答案）。我只是放大了女性的形象，尖叫着，跑来跑去，"Like wild demented horses"（就像狂野的疯马）。这首歌本身就很有戏剧性。我有一个小小的想法："未来的残留"仿佛埋

上图：加州，帕皮和哈丽特的先锋城宫殿。2016 年 10 月 13 日。

在院子里的某个地方，就像一个隐藏的宝藏。意思是我们不知道这些不完整的残留的答案，我们不知道会发生什么。我的意思是，现在我们正处于新冠病毒的危机之中，我们真的不知道会发生什么，但是我看到孩子们很自觉地戴着口罩，所以这一代孩子会觉得："哦，是的，每个人都戴着口罩，不是吗？"

我们有了闪电，所以要有雷声，然后"thunder drowns the trumpets' blast"（雷声淹没了号角的轰鸣）。这有点像电影；预言式的配乐正在奏响，而雷声把它淹没，所以这就像电影的配乐。我是用钢琴创作的曲子，所以写的时候没有太多架构，而是在录音时进行了填充。我会想："好吧，应该更戏剧化一些，伴奏应该更戏剧化一点，我们应该以这种方式来架构它。"我们现场演过这首歌，但我们必须喝一大杯威士忌，拍着自己的后脑勺来记住它。这首歌喜怒无常。我喜欢演奏它，乐队喜欢演奏它，观众中有些人喜欢听它被演奏。

一般来说，这样的歌不会出现在你的曲目单中，因为你意识到，人们会在这类歌上演时走开去买酒，你会想："好吧，我用《麦当娜夫人》把他们拉回来。"我看过王子，对他没有演《紫雨》（Purple Rain）很不高兴，但他也许是被《紫雨》的关注度惹恼了。作为一名表演艺术家，这是一个你必须做的重要决定——是否只是追随自己一时的心血来潮："小伙子们，今晚我们只用原声乐器，我们要用没人听过的方式来演唱所有歌。"当你面对五万名巴西人时，你不会觉得那是最好的选择，你会想："好吧，要不这样吧，我们就演一些金曲吧。"我确实倾向于这么做。但如果我们在一个小俱乐部演出，就可以拿出一些不太知名的东西，让诸如《蜡像馆》这样的歌曲焕发生机。

现在，准备巡演时或是两场演出的间歇中，我们仍会有意做一些小场地演出。几年前我们参加了科切拉音乐节，在加州沙漠里分两个周末进行。你在星期六演出，接着有一个星期的休息时间，然后你在下个星期六演出。我们想保持一个节奏，于是订了一个叫帕皮和哈丽特（Pappy & Harriet）的小场地，在约书亚树（Joshua Tree）地区，靠近科切拉举办的地方，所以我们的设备就在附近。那只是一个小小的地方，有点像下流酒馆俱乐部，能容纳三百人，很有意思。这不是收费的演出。我们只是当天才告诉人们。

我们把大卫·霍克尼[1]请了过来。我告诉他："我要去这个地方，大卫，你可能会喜欢这个。"他带着他的 iPad 画了一点草图。他只有八十三岁。

1　大卫·霍克尼（David Hockney，1932—），英国艺术大师。

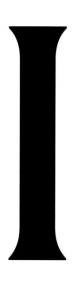

I Don't Know

我不知道

作 者 WRITER	保罗·麦卡特尼　Paul McCartney
艺术家 ARTIST	保罗·麦卡特尼　Paul McCartney
录 音 RECORDED	洛杉矶汉森录音棚、萨塞克斯郡猪山磨坊、伦敦阿比路录音棚
	Henson Studios, Los Angeles; Hog Hill Mill, Sussex and Abbey Road Studios, London
发 行 RELEASED	《亲近我》/《我不知道》双 A 面单曲，2018 年　'Come On to Me'/'I Don't Know' double A-side single, 2018
	《埃及站》，2018 年　Egypt Station, 2018

I got crows at my window
Dogs at my door
I don't think I can take any more
What am I doing wrong?
I don't know

My brother told me
Life's not a pain
That was right when it started to rain
Where am I going wrong?
I don't know

But it's alright, sleep tight
I will take the strain
You're fine, love of mine
You will feel no pain

Well I see trouble
At every turn
I've got so many lessons to learn
What am I doing wrong?
I don't know

Now what's the matter with me?
Am I right, am I wrong?
Now I've started to see
I must try to be strong

I tried to love you
Best as I can
But you know that I'm only a man
Why am I going wrong?
I don't know

But it's alright, sleep tight
I will take the strain
You're fine, little love of mine
You will feel no pain

I got crows at my window
Dogs at my door
But I don't think I can take any more
What am I doing wrong?
I don't know

Now what's the matter with me?
I don't know, I don't know
What's the matter with me?
I don't know, I don't know
What's the matter with me?
I don't know, I don't know

　　为人父母是件有趣的事。我们生孩子纯粹是为了把一个小生命带到这个世界上，以及随之而来的所有事情。但有时你忘记了他们总有一天会长大。我知道有人会说："噢，我不喜欢他们小时候的样子。我喜欢他们长大一点。"我不同意。我喜欢他们还是婴儿的时候，不过随着他们的成长，孩子也会变得更有趣，因为"咕咕"和"妈妈"之外的其他东西也会出现在谈话中。词汇量扩大了一点。就像他们所说的，这有时候是"挑战"，而这正是那些时刻之一。

　　有好几天我对发生在我家门前的事情有点紧张——发生在我们所有人身上的事情。这首歌以"I got crows at my window / Dogs at my door"（乌鸦在我的窗前 / 狗在我的门口）开始，因为这就是我当时的感觉，它脱口而出，就好像"上帝呵，我感觉很糟糕，我要告诉所有人"。这首歌写完后，我觉得自己就好像在心理医生的沙发上进行了一次治疗。

　　我不是经常感到如此沮丧，但在这种情况下，我真的有压力。有一两段主歌是在自言自语，把雨作为悲伤的象征，然后我想，"它的反面是什么呢？是会越来越糟，还是我仍能找到一些安慰呢？"作为一个家长，我想说，"没事，没事，别担心。"然后这个桥段就来了："But it's alright, sleep tight / I will take the strain / You're fine, love of mine / You will feel no pain"（但是没关系 / 好好睡觉 / 我能承担这压力 / 你不会有事的，我的爱 / 你不会感受到痛苦）。

　　这就是这首歌的出发点。我倾诉我的烦恼，就像在布鲁斯歌曲里那样。"Well I see trouble / At every turn / I've got so many lessons to learn"（而我看见困难 / 在每一个拐角 / 生活有太多教训仍待学习）。当你感到忧伤，你有布鲁斯音乐。如果我要唱一首关于悲伤的歌，考虑到我多年来的音乐品位，它经常会倾向于布鲁斯——摇滚乐的基础形态。用那样的方式唱歌感觉很好。体现一种悲伤而不是仅仅说"我今天很悲伤"的感觉也很好。

在很多方面，这就是和诗歌或音乐相关的一切——通过艺术本身投射或表现某种事物的能力，将所有这些情感提升到一个更高的水平，就像一个好的写作老师有时会要求你"表现"而不是"说"。

　　这是一首我们还没有在演唱会上演过的歌，因为它有点复杂，我要谨慎地选择，要么演奏非常简单的音乐——三个和弦，最多四个和弦的摇滚乐，极简派——要么是我父辈时代的音乐，那些歌曲中的旋律、和声和技巧。我想着父辈时代标准的伟大的作曲家，比如哈罗德·阿伦（Harold Arlen）、科尔·波特、格什温兄弟，他们都是那种传统的产物。那是一个百老汇大爆炸和好莱坞大爆炸的时代，所以这些人相当擅长设计巧妙的小韵脚，并使之成为一个美国的重要传统。

　　我一直对那个时期非常感兴趣，那是大概持续到我出生后的一个时代，那时每个家庭都有一架钢琴，当时很多家庭都有为某人的生日编首小曲的传统。那时每个人某种程度上都是词曲作者。所以，有时候我会抛开三四个和弦，去探索其他形式。

　　《我不知道》是我走出舒适区的歌曲之一。它不仅仅是 C，F，G。里面还有降 A 和降 E。更多的色彩。我喜欢尝试不同的东西和实验。

　　我常说写一首歌就像和一个心理医生交谈，这首歌就是这样。我把我的烦恼和想法都发泄出来，并且疑惑我做错了什么。而答案是，《我不知道》。

保罗画作，《埃及站 II》油画。

上图:《埃及站》录音期间。
洛杉矶汉森录音棚，2016 年
2 月 22 日。

右图:《我不知道》限量版七寸
白色标签宣传单曲碟。

I Lost My Little Girl

我失去了我的小女孩

作　者 WRITER	保罗·麦卡特尼　Paul McCartney	
艺术家 ARTIST	保罗·麦卡特尼　Paul McCartney	
录　音 RECORDED	伦敦莱姆豪斯录音棚　Limehouse Studios, London	
发　行 RELEASED	《不插电》（官方私录），1991 年　*Unplugged (The Official Bootleg)*, 1991	

写于 1956 年，1991 年首次发行　Written in 1956 but unreleased until 1991

Well I woke up late this morning
My head was in a whirl
And only then I realised
I lost my little girl
Uh huh huh huh

Well her clothes were not expensive
Her hair didn't always curl
I don't know why I loved her
But I loved my little girl
Uh huh huh huh huh huh

你不用成为西格蒙德·弗洛伊德就能意识到，这首歌是对我母亲去世的直接回应。1956 年 10 月，她四十七岁，非常年轻时就去世了。同一年的晚些时候，我写了这首歌。当时我十四岁。

因为我爸爸吹小号，我也学会了一点。我放弃是因为，嘴巴里有一个吹口使我没法唱歌。关键是我喜欢唱歌，我见过无数人出现在音乐场景中。当你回过头想想，摇滚乐那时只是刚刚诞生。

鉴于小号在摇滚乐中确实不太行得通，所以我勉强地从吉他开始了。一把泽尼斯牌木吉他。这是把右手琴，因为他们不卖左手吉他，所以我不得不做一个拙劣的工作，把它反过来，这样的话，粗一些的低音弦要穿过细细的琴孔，而细的高音弦要穿过粗的琴孔。我不得不把小孔刨开让粗弦穿过去，然后在每个大孔里放一小截火柴好让细弦安在上面。现在，我差不多有了一把左手吉他，还学会了一些和弦 —— 非常基本的和弦，和我们所有人一样。

《我失去了我的小女孩》中的和弦从 G 到 G7 再到 C，这是下降的，于是我们有了一种叮叮叮的效果。我希望旋律随着和弦的下行而上升。所以，我在十四岁时就开始思考这种事情了，也许是因为我爸爸，他的朋友或者我们的阿姨们总是在家里玩音乐，我也许也见过他们偶尔的即兴表演。所以，我决定当吉他下行时，让唱声上行。

开头的"Well I woke up late this morning"（今早我很晚醒来），或者其他类似的歌词，是美国布鲁斯音乐的重要成分。我一点也不确定我脑子里是否有一首特别的布鲁斯歌曲。这是一个非常类似的设置。布鲁斯一〇一首。"Her hair didn't always curl"（她的头发并不总是卷曲）这句歌词让我尴尬了好几年，不过算了吧，我才十四岁。而正如他们所说，这只是开始。

上图：采石人的早期照片，保罗和阿瑟·凯利（Arthur Kelly）、乔治·哈里森及约翰·列侬。

不用说，当我遇到约翰·列侬时，事情真的开始了。我们由一个共同的朋友伊万·沃恩介绍相识，他带我到圣彼得教堂的沃尔顿乡村市集去看约翰的演出。舞台是一辆平底卡车，而我觉得他相当不错。他唱了一首《和我一起》（Come Go With Me），德尔维京人乐队[1]的歌，我大概知道这首歌。显然，他也只是对这首歌有些模糊的了解，并且边演边编。他唱着像"来，来，来，来，跟我一起去，去到监狱里"之类的东西。这些肯定不是歌词，但他一定是从铅肚皮[2]或者其他人那里扯出来的。我觉得他很聪明。

约翰和我在他日场和晚场的演出之间见面，那是在村礼堂——教堂大厅——那里有一个很小的后台区。我记得有架钢琴，我带着吉他。所以我弹了《二十次飞行摇滚》，那是我的聚会保留曲目。显然他对我知道所有的歌词印象深刻。

我感觉他真的不想和我交往，因为我比他小一点，但他不得不承认，我有点天赋。

我去了他的晚场演出，与伊万和他混在一起。他们不是一支很棒的乐队，但约翰很不错。大约一周后，约翰的一个朋友，皮特·肖顿，在我骑自行车外出时跟过来对我说："他们想让你加入乐队。"我停下来说："我会考虑一下的。"

我不是很努力。但我是个细心的年轻人。我怀疑自己是否真的想加入乐队。这是不是件好事，或者我应该努力去上学？

不管怎样，我还是答复他们说："好的。"

不用说，当我遇到约翰·列侬时，事情真的开始了。
我们由一个共同的朋友伊万·沃恩介绍相识，
他带我到圣彼得教堂的沃尔顿乡村市集去看约翰的演出。
舞台是一辆平底卡车，
而我觉得他相当不错。

1　德尔维京人乐队（The Del-Vikings），1950年代美国摇滚乐队。
2　铅肚皮（Lead Belly，1885—1949），美国布鲁斯歌手。

Woolton Parish Church
Garden Fete
and
Crowning of Rose Queen
Saturday, July 6th, 1957

To be opened at 3p.m. by Dr. Thelwall Jones

PROCESSION AT 2p.m.

LIVERPOOL POLICE DOGS DISPLAY
FANCY DRESS PARADE
SIDESHOWS   REFRESHMENTS
BAND OF THE CHESHIRE YEOMANRY
THE QUARRY MEN SKIFFLE GROUP

ADULTS 6d., CHILDREN 3d.   OR BY PROGRAMME

GRAND DANCE
at 8p.m. in the Church Hall
GEORGE EDWARDS' BAND
THE QUARRY MEN SKIFFLE GROUP
Tickets 2/-

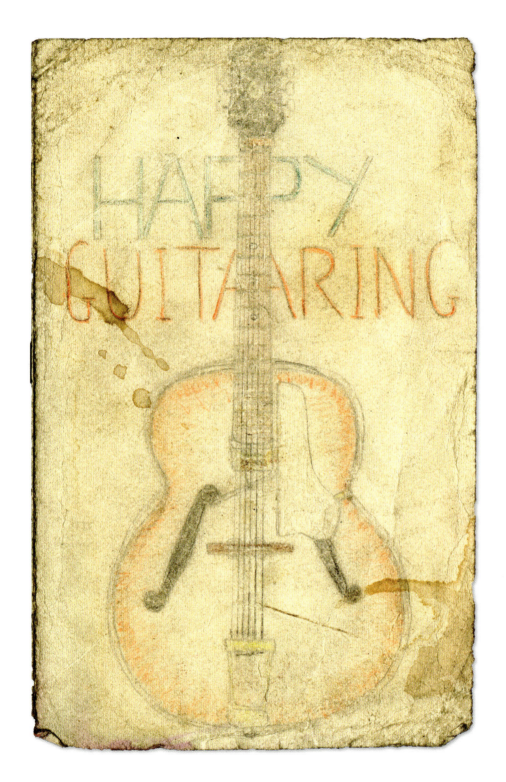

上图：在《哈姆雷特》的教材副
本上发现的手绘泽尼斯吉他，
1950 年代末。

右图：伊万·沃恩与保罗，伦敦，
1968 年。

在《早期时光》（Early Days）
音乐录影带里弹着泽尼斯吉他。
洛杉矶，2014 年 3 月 5 日。

I Saw Her Standing There

我看见她站在那里

作 者 WRITERS	保罗·麦卡特尼和约翰·列侬	Paul McCartney and John Lennon
艺术家 ARTIST	披头士乐队 The Beatles	
录 音 RECORDED	伦敦阿比路录音棚 Abbey Road Studios, London	
发 行 RELEASED	《请让我快乐》，1963 年 *Please Please Me*, 1963	
	《我想牵你的手》美国单曲 B 面，1963 年 B-side of 'I Want to Hold Your Hand' US single, 1963	
	《介绍……披头士乐队》，1964 年 *Introducing... The Beatles*, 1964	

Well she was just seventeen
You know what I mean
And the way she looked was way beyond compare
So how could I dance with another
Ooh when I saw her standing there

Well she looked at me
And I, I could see
That before too long I'd fall in love with her
She wouldn't dance with another
Ooh when I saw her standing there

Well my heart went boom
When I crossed that room
And I held her hand in mine

Oh we danced through the night
And we held each other tight
And before too long I fell in love with her
Now I'll never dance with another
Ooh when I saw her standing there

Well my heart went boom
When I crossed that room
And I held her hand in mine

Oh we danced through the night
And we held each other tight
And before too long I fell in love with her
Now I'll never dance with another
Ooh since I saw her standing there
Since I saw her standing there
Since I saw her standing there

我写过很多首歌，但有些歌很突出，如果必须选出我认为自己这些年来最好的作品，我可能会选《我看见她站在那里》。不，我绝对会选这首。

我第一次把它弹给约翰听的时候，我们正在用我爸爸的烟斗抽茶叶。（当我说茶叶的时候，我指的就是茶叶。）我说："她刚刚十七岁。她从来没有当过选美皇后。"约翰说："我不确定。"所以我们的首要任务是去除选美皇后。我们挣扎了一番，然后这首歌就来了。

现在唱这首歌，我意识到自己是在回顾一个十八岁到二十岁的男孩的作品——这会发生在我唱所有披头士歌曲时，尤其是早期歌曲。我觉得这很有趣，因为它有一种幼稚，某种纯真，那是你无法发明的。

提醒你一下，杰瑞·森菲尔德[1]狠狠地讽刺过这首歌。我们去了白宫，杰瑞说："保罗，你知道吗，我一直在看'她刚刚十七岁／你知道我的意思'这句歌词，我不确定我们是否真的明白你的意思，保罗！"

不管怎么说，我们都听过所有这些东西——我二十岁左右，我们在福特林路我爸爸家写了这首歌——现在我们要写，"She was just seventeen / You know what I mean / And the way she looked was way beyond compare"（她刚刚十七岁／你知道我的意思／她看上去无与伦比）。这种节奏与斯坦利·霍洛威[2]版本的《狮子与阿尔伯特》(The Lion and Albert) 如出一辙。那是马里奥特·埃德加[3]写的一首打油诗，有着相似的韵律。

我心中满载所有这些我听过的曲调。霍吉·卡迈克尔、哈罗德·阿伦、乔治·格什温、约翰尼·默瑟[4]，我听着这些东西长大。我自己写的东西不多，但都在里面了。而且在学校里，我听到我的英语老师，艾伦·杜邦德讨论莎士比亚十四行诗结尾的押韵对句。我不知道"无与伦比"是从哪里来的，但它可能来自第十八首十四行诗："我能否把你比作夏日？"当我还是孩子时，我甚至可能就已经意识到爱尔兰歌曲的传统——将一个女人描述为"无与伦比"。

无论如何，这不是你在摇滚乐中所期望的。就像我说的，我不知道我从哪里挖出来的，但是在我年轻时的大拖网里，这首歌就像海豚一样被抓了起来。

上图：艾伦·杜班德，利物浦学院男子高中的英语系主任。

1　杰瑞·森菲尔德（Jerry Seinfeld，1954—），美国脱口秀演员、作家、编剧、导演。
2　斯坦利·霍洛威（Stanley Holloway，1890—1982），英国演员。
3　马里奥特·埃德加（Marriott Edgar，1880—1951），英国编剧。
4　约翰尼·默瑟（Johnny Mercer，1909—1976），美国音乐家。

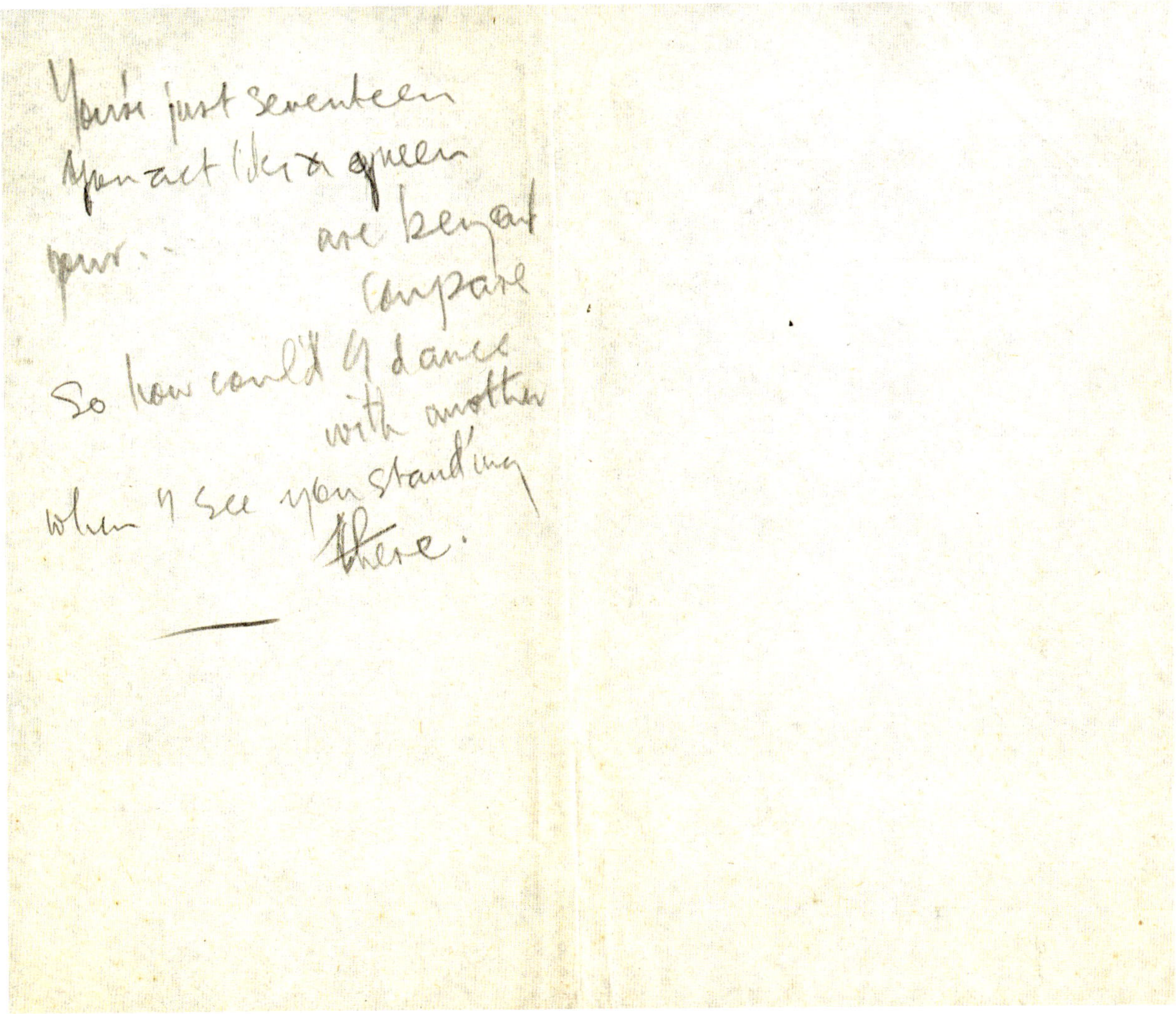
You're just seventeen
you act like a queen
your .. are beyond
compare
So how could I dance
with another
when I see you standing
there.

左图：和约翰 · 列侬一起。
利物浦，1950 年代末。

和约翰·列侬一起创作《我看见
她站在那里》。利物浦福特林路，
1962 年。

和约翰·列侬一起创作，弟弟迈克拍摄。利物浦福特林路，1960年代初。

I Wanna Be Your Man
我想成为你的男人

作　者　WRITERS 　　保罗·麦卡特尼和约翰·列侬 Paul McCartney and John Lennon
艺术家　ARTIST 　　披头士乐队 The Beatles
录　音　RECORDED 　伦敦阿比路录音棚 Abbey Road Studios, London
发　行　RELEASED 　《和披头士一起》，1963 年 *With The Beatles*, 1963

I wanna be your lover, baby
I wanna be your man
I wanna be your lover, baby
I wanna be your man

Love you like no other, baby
Like no other can
Love you like no other, baby
Like no other can

I wanna be your man
I wanna be your man
I wanna be your man
I wanna be your man

Tell me that you love me, baby
Let me understand
Tell me that you love me, baby
I wanna be your man

I wanna be your lover, baby
I wanna be your man
I wanna be your lover, baby
I wanna be your man

I wanna be your man
I wanna be your man
I wanna be your man
I wanna be your man

I wanna be your lover, baby
I wanna be your man
I wanna be your lover, baby
I wanna be your man

Love you like no other, baby
Like no other can
Love you like no other, baby
Like no other can

I wanna be your man
I wanna be your man
I wanna be your man
I wanna be your man

我们总会在每一张专辑中为林戈写一首歌,因为他很受歌迷的欢迎,就像基思·理查兹[1]曾经对我说的那样:"你们乐队有四位歌手,我们只有一个。"确实是这样。林戈不是乐队里最好的歌手,但毫无疑问,他能搞定一首歌。他总是唱一首名为《男孩们》(Boys)的歌,这首歌最初是由雪莉乐队[2]唱的。

同性恋观众一定很高兴听到披头士的鼓手唱关于男孩的歌,但我们从来没有真正考虑过这一点。对于那些对歌词大惊小怪的人,我们常说:"没人听歌词。这只是歌曲里的一种声音。"

现在我不太确定了。我想时代变了。但在早期,我们不会总是太在意词句或者它们的细微差别。"I wanna be your lover, baby / I wanna be your man / I wanna be your lover, baby / I wanna be your man"(我想成为你的爱人,宝贝 / 我想成为你的男人 / 我想成为你的爱人,宝贝 / 我想成为你的男人)。非常简单,但这是一首足够酷的小歌,而且林戈唱得非常好。

大约在 1963 年夏天我们从利物浦搬到伦敦的时候,有一天,约翰和我在查令十字街,那里是吉他中心,我们会叫辆出租车去那里看看吉他。1960 年代初,那里整个地

披头士参加《谢谢你的幸运星》。
伯明翰,1964 年。

1　基思·理查兹(Keith Richards,1943—),滚石乐队吉他手。
2　雪莉乐队(The Shirelles),1960 年代成立于美国的女子组合。

331

方都是吉他店，我们整个下午都在那里热切地注视着我们买不起的吉他。

另外，迪克·詹姆斯（Dick James）的办公室也在那里。他那时是我们的出版商。这可能是我们去那里的真正原因。不管怎样，有一天我们在看吉他时，一辆黑色的伦敦出租车经过，我们注意到米克·贾格尔和基思·理查兹在车里。于是我们大叫："嘿！"他们看见我们挥手，就把车停在路边。我们跑上去说："嘿，载我们一程。""好的，没问题。你要去哪里？""我们要去北伦敦。"

于是，我们就在车里聊聊我们在做什么。"我们拿到了唱片合同。"米克告诉我们。我们已经知道了，因为是乔治·哈里森帮助他们拿到的。迪克·罗（Dick Rowe）是那个拒绝了披头士，并且不想让我们签到德卡唱片（Decca）的家伙，我不得不说，如果你听听我们的试听带，它并不算太好，不过确实有些东西。所以，乔治在一个鸡尾酒会上，迪克·罗说："你认识什么好的乐队吗？我犯了一个错误，我想签一个好的。"乔治说："有啊，滚石乐队。你应该试试签下他们。"他告诉罗，滚石乐队在里士满的车站旅馆，他们经常在那里演出，罗去看了他们，几乎当场就签了他们。

回到出租车上那段聊天，米克说："唯一的问题是，我们没有新单曲。"他们问我们有没有歌，我说："嗯，我们最近的唱片《和披头士一起》上有一首歌，但这是专辑曲目。它还没做成单曲，也不会做成单曲了，因为它是林戈唱的。不过我觉得这对你们很有用。"于是，我们把《我想成为你的男人》给了他们，他们进行了录制。我们的版本有点博·迪德利[1]式的跳跃感；他们的版本相当原始和扭曲，几乎是朋克式的，这是他们的第一首金曲。

在那之后，我们会一起出去玩，我们会谈论他们在做什么音乐。我会去基思的公寓，所以我们的关系很好。约翰和我唱了他们的一首歌——《我们爱你》（We Love You）——在1967年。我们有很多互动。我们是对手的观念只是由媒体发起的话题，然后人们开始问："你喜欢谁，披头士还是滚石？"这就变成了非此即彼的事情。在最初的几年里并不是这样的，但是当我们越来越成功时，它被媒体塑造出来了。但这不是真的。米克过去常到我伦敦的家里来，让我给他播放所有最新的美国唱片，而同时媒体正在写关于"我们是对手"的闲话。

所以，这就是我们之间的关系。至于媒体，你需要他们，他们也需要你，这是我们在职业生涯中学到的，但是说出来的话是会伤人的。比如说，他们把我们的作品叫作"默西之声"（Mersey Beat）——这个名字取自当地一家娱乐报纸——我们想："呃，该死的。那太过时了。"我们从来没有把自己看作默西人，我们认为自己是利物浦人，如果你来自那里的话，这是一个重要的区别。但是"默西之声"和"拖把头"——所有这些流行语挡在那里，并且非常烦人。你要做一些你想都不敢想的事情，不过，之后，那会是一个宏大的故事。

滚石乐队，披头士——我们是老朋友，永永远远，但是歌迷们开始相信这场人造的竞争中有一些真实成分。从来没有。

1　博·迪德利（Bo Diddley，1928—2008），美国早期摇滚乐先驱之一。

I Want to Hold Your Hand

我想牵你的手

作 者 WRITERS	保罗·麦卡特尼和约翰·列侬 John Lennon and Paul McCartney	
艺术家 ARTIST	披头士乐队 The Beatles	
录 音 RECORDED	伦敦阿比路录音棚 Abbey Road Studios, London	
发 行 RELEASED	单曲，1963 年 Single, 1963	
	《遇见披头士！》，1964 年 *Meet The Beatles!* 1964	

Oh yeah I'll tell you something
I think you'll understand
When I say that something
I want to hold your hand

I want to hold your hand
I want to hold your hand

Oh please say to me
You'll let me be your man
And please say to me
You'll let me hold your hand

Now let me hold your hand
I want to hold your hand

And when I touch you I feel happy inside
It's such a feeling that my love
I can't hide
I can't hide
I can't hide

Yeah you got that something
I think you'll understand
When I say that something
I want to hold your hand

I want to hold your hand
I want to hold your hand

And when I touch you I feel happy inside
It's such a feeling that my love
I can't hide
I can't hide
I can't hide

Yeah you got that something
I think you'll understand
When I feel that something
I want to hold your hand

I want to hold your hand
I want to hold your hand
I want to hold your hand

这一切的背后是一种情欲。如果我在十七岁时听到自己用这个词，一定会狂笑不止，但情欲确实是我所做的每一件事背后的驱动力。这是一种非常强大的东西。而且，你知道，这就是很多情歌背后隐藏的东西。"I want to hold your hand"（我想牵你的手），[可能还会做更多！]

写这首歌的时候，我大约二十一岁，我们已经来到伦敦。我们的经纪人给披头士弄了一套公寓：梅费尔区格林街 57 号 L 公寓。一切都很令人兴奋，梅费尔是伦敦的一个时髦区。出于某种原因，我是最后一个去那里看的人，他们给我留了一个小房间。其他人把所有大房间都承包了。他们把这个小破房间留给了我。

但那时我有了一个女朋友，简·阿舍，她是一个非常优雅的女孩，她的父亲是温波尔街的医生，母亲是一位很有教养的女士，一位音乐老师，名叫玛格丽特·阿舍。所以我会去他们家玩。我喜欢那里，因为那真是一个"家庭"。玛格丽特和我相处得很好。对我来说，她有点像母亲。那是在我十四岁，母亲去世之前，我所习惯的生活，尽管我从未见过这样的家庭。我只见过利物浦的工人阶级，这是上流社会的伦敦。他们所有人的记事本都从早上八点延伸到晚上六七点，被塞得满满的。每一秒都是数着过。简会去找她的经纪人，然后读剧本，然后和某人共进午餐，然后让念白指导为她的下一部戏教她诺福克口音。我很迷恋这一切。这就像一个故事，就像我生活在其中的一部小说。

最终，我和阿舍一家住在了一起。我其实已经经常在那里留宿了，但玛格丽特一定说过，"嗯，你知道，我们可以让你住阁楼。"所以我就去了，他们在那间屋子里放了一架钢琴。

当约翰来拜访时，地下室里也有一架钢琴——我想那是玛格丽特教学生的一个小音乐室。所以，我们会在地下室写歌，用钢琴，或者面对面弹吉他。

《我想牵你的手》不是关于简的，但肯定是我和她在一起时写的。说实话，我想我们更多的是面向普通的听众。我可能是在借鉴我和一个我当时爱的人在一起时的经历——有时是非常具体的——但大多数情况下我们是写给这个世界的。

I WANNA HOLD YOUR HAND

Oh yea, I'll tell you something
I think you'll understand
When I say that something
I wanna hold your hand
Repeat twice

Oh please say to me
you'll let me be you man
And please say to me
you'll let me hold your hand

And when I touch you
I feel happy inside
It's such a feeling
That my love
— I can't hide
I can't hide

Oh you got that something
I think you understand
When I feel that something
I wanna hold your hand

右图：与简·阿舍于《我如何赢得战争》[1] 首映式上，伦敦帕维侬剧院，1967 年 10 月 18 日。

---

1 《我如何赢得战争》(How I Won the War)，英国电影，由理查德·莱斯特导演，约翰·列侬主演。1967 年上映。

I Will

我愿意

作　者　WRITERS　　　　保罗·麦卡特尼和约翰·列侬　Paul McCartney and John Lennon
艺术家　ARTIST　　　　　披头士乐队　The Beatles
录　音　RECORDED　　　伦敦阿比路录音棚　Abbey Road Studios, London
发　行　RELEASED　　　《披头士》，1968 年　*The Beatles*, 1968

Who knows how long I've loved you
You know I love you still
Will I wait a lonely lifetime
If you want me to I will

For if I ever saw you
I didn't catch your name
But it never really mattered
I will always feel the same

Love you forever and forever
Love you with all my heart
Love you whenever we're together
Love you when we're apart

And when at last I find you
Your song will fill the air
Sing it loud so I can hear you
Make it easy to be near you
For the things you do endear you to me
You know I will
I will

艾伦·戴尔（Alan-A-Dale）。罗宾汉传奇中游荡在舍伍德森林里的吟游诗人。那就是我。这首歌让我找到了游吟诗人的方式。

有一种理论认为最有趣的情歌是那些关于爱情出了问题的歌曲。我不同意这一点。这是一首关于爱的喜悦的歌。有时，这种感情会被视作多愁善感、太甜，或者故作多情。是的，我明白这一点，但爱情是这个星球上最非凡、最强大的力量。现在在越南，或者巴西，都有人坠入爱河。他们大多想要孩子。这是一种强大的、宇宙性的力量。一点也不多愁善感。

当我坐下来试着写一首歌的时候，我经常想："希望我能捕捉到初恋的感觉。"这首歌是 1968 年 2 月开始写的，当时我和简·阿舍在印度。我还记得，我先写出了一段旋律，音乐很快就合在一起。它仍然是我写过的最喜欢的旋律之一。歌词花了些时间。那似乎有点奇怪，我知道，因为这是一套相当简单的构思。民谣歌手多诺万（Donovan）在去拜访玛哈里希·玛赫西·优济的旅程中和我们在一起，他为歌词的一个早期版本提供了一些帮助，但是并不合适，它更简单，全是月亮 / 六月之类的。

再说一次，仅仅因为我当时和简在一起，并不意味着这首歌是写给或是关于简的。当我写作的时候，就好像我在脑海里为我正在看的电影设定歌词和音乐。这是爱情的宣言，是的，但并不总是针对某个特定的人。除非是对一个正在听这首歌的人。他们必须为这首歌做好准备。几乎可以肯定不会有人说："他又来了，又写了一首愚蠢的情歌。"所以，这就是在我的吟游诗人方式中的我。

上图：保罗与简·阿舍及玛哈里希。印度瑞诗凯诗，1968 年 4 月。

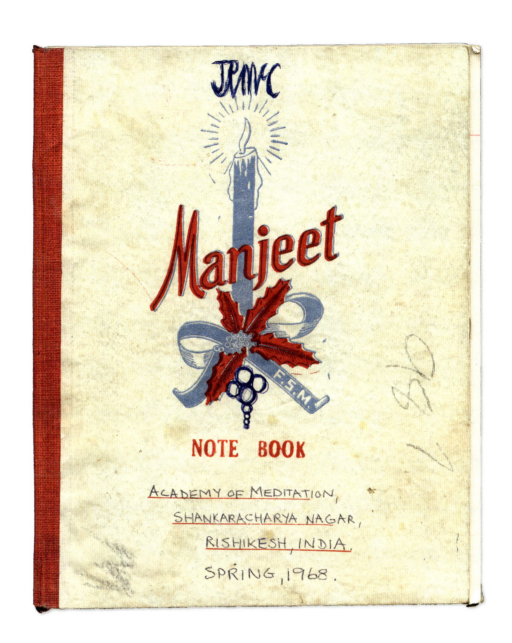

这是一首关于爱的喜悦的歌。
有时，这种感情会被视作多愁善感、太甜，或者故作多情。
是的，我明白这一点，但爱情是这个星球上最非凡、
最强大的力量。现在在越南，或者巴西，都有人坠入爱河。
他们大多想要孩子。
这是一种强大的、宇宙性的力量。一点也不多愁善感。

I'll Follow the Sun

我将跟随太阳

作 者 WRITERS	保罗·麦卡特尼和约翰·列侬	Paul McCartney and John Lennon
艺术家 ARTIST	披头士乐队	The Beatles
录 音 RECORDED	伦敦阿比路录音棚	Abbey Road Studios, London
发 行 RELEASED	《待售的披头士》，1964 年	*Beatles for Sale*, 1964
	《披头士'65》，1964 年	*Beatles '65*, 1964

One day you'll look
To see I've gone
For tomorrow may rain, so
I'll follow the sun

Some day you'll know
I was the one
But tomorrow may rain, so
I'll follow the sun

And now the time has come
And so, my love, I must go
And though I lose a friend
In the end you will know, oh

One day you'll find
That I have gone
But tomorrow may rain, so
I'll follow the sun

Yes tomorrow may rain, so
I'll follow the sun

And now the time has come
And so, my love, I must go
And though I lose a friend
In the end you will know, oh

One day you'll find
That I have gone
But tomorrow may rain, so
I'll follow the sun

我在利物浦住的最后一所房子是福特林路 20 号。那时我们已经出名了。我妈妈对我们有很高的期望，她在一个相对比较好的区域找到了这所房子。房子里有蕾丝花边窗帘，这可能就是为什么我仍然在每一个住所都挂上蕾丝花边窗帘。或许是一种爱尔兰式的乡愁。人们无法窥视屋内。我记得我拿着吉他站在客厅里，唱着这首歌。仔细想想，这是一首"离开利物浦"的歌。我要离开这个多雨的北方城市，去一个发生更多事情的地方。

　　这首歌也有一段有意思的旋律。我一直在寻找音符之间引人注目的新组合。这首歌有相当根源性的东西。我最喜欢的父辈歌曲之一是《脸贴脸》（Cheek to Cheek），弗雷德·阿斯泰尔的歌，我喜欢它的地方是它是以"Heaven, I'm in heaven"[1] 开始，它穿过两段主歌，在桥段的结尾又回到了"天堂"。一个简单的句子。就像我们在福特林路的房子。你走进前门，继续穿过客厅，餐厅，厨房，大厅，最后回到了起点。《我将跟随太阳》也是这样。

　　尽管我们开放地接受各种影响，不过披头士乐队的一个伟大之处就是我们对重复自己的厌恶。我们是聪明的年轻人，我们不喜欢无聊。我们在汉堡演出时，有时要填满八个小时的时间。我们试着学习足够多的歌，这样就不用重复了。有些乐队只有一个小时的演出曲目，休息一个小时，然后从头再演一个小时。我们试图改变这些，因为我们已经认定，若非如此，我们实在无法幸存。当我们回到英国时，我们有了大量曲目，我想，当我们开始录唱片时，这种想法也一直存在。为什么重复自己？为什么要做两次相同的录音？

　　确实是，正如我所说，在早期的一些歌曲中有一个特定的公式 ——人称代词"我""你""他""她的""我的""她"的重复出现 ——不过，那是因为我们希望与歌迷产生联系，与他们接触。但它们不是公式化的。披头士之所以成为如此伟大的乐队，是因为没有两首歌是相似的。考虑到我们的产出，这确实非常令人惊讶。另一件事是，约翰和我在每次几个小时或者一整天这样的持续录音期间，一共写了将近三百首歌，我们从来没有，从来没有在一个写歌时段结束时却没有完成一首歌。每当我们坐下来写一首歌的时候，直到写完，我们才会离开那个房间。

1　"天堂，我在天堂"。

上图：歌单，1950 年代末。

左图：在利物浦福特林路 20 号的花园里，弟弟迈克拍摄，1960 年代初。这张照片后来被用作 2005 年的专辑《在后院的混乱和创造》（ *Chaos and Creation in the Backyard* ）的封面。

I'll Get You

我将得到你

作　者 WRITERS	保罗·麦卡特尼和约翰·列侬　Paul McCartney and John Lennon
艺术家 ARTIST	披头士乐队　The Beatles
录　音 RECORDED	伦敦阿比路录音棚　Abbey Road Studios, London
发　行 RELEASED	《她爱你》B 面单曲，1963 年　B-side of 'She Loves You' single, 1963
	《披头士的第二张专辑》，1964 年　*The Beatles' Second Album*, 1964

Oh yeah, oh yeah
Oh yeah, oh yeah

Imagine I'm in love with you
It's easy 'cause I know
I've imagined I'm in love with you
Many, many, many times before
It's not like me to pretend
But I'll get you, I'll get you in the end
Yes I will, I'll get you in the end
Oh yeah, oh yeah

I think about you night and day
I need you and it's true
When I think about you, I can say
I'm never, never, never, never blue
So I'm telling you, my friend
That I'll get you, I'll get you in the end
Yes I will, I'll get you in the end
Oh yeah, oh yeah

Well there's gonna be a time
When I'm gonna change your mind
So you might as well resign yourself to me
Oh yeah

Imagine I'm in love with you
It's easy 'cause I know
I've imagined I'm in love with you
Many, many, many times before
It's not like me to pretend
But I'll get you, I'll get you in the end
Yes I will, I'll get you in the end

Oh yeah, oh yeah
Oh yeah, oh yeah, oh yeah

这首歌是在利物浦的门洛夫大街写的，约翰和他的咪咪姑妈住在那里。她是一个善良而固执的女人，她很清楚自己的想法。奇怪的是咪咪不太喜欢我们的音乐，而且巴不得我们不在周围出现，因为她认为我们是在鼓励约翰把更多时间花在吉他上而不是学习上。咪咪总是说："吉他作为一种业余爱好是可以的，约翰，但你永远不能靠它谋生！"

"想象"这个词和概念将在约翰自己的歌曲《想象》（Imagine）中稍作调整。这也有一点像《露西在镶满钻石的天空中》（Lucy in the Sky With Diamonds）的开场，用敦促的口吻说"想象你自己……"。所以，这是电影的东西，也是文学的东西。当我说"文学"时，我想到了我和约翰都非常喜欢的刘易斯·卡罗尔的幻想世界。卡罗尔对我们俩都有很大的影响，这一点在约翰的书《他自己的写作》（*In His Own Write*）和《作品中的西班牙人》（*A Spaniard in the Works*）都可以看到。

就音乐结构而言，那是一个非常有效的开场——D 大调和弦伴随着我们以八度音阶唱"噢耶"。我们已经学会了 C、Am、F、G，以及 D 的排列——很直接，三和弦的东西。而随后你将它们稍加排列，《我将得到你》的开头就是一个例子。原本，这些是相当标准的和弦，直到你进行到"It's not like me to pretend"（我不喜欢伪装）。"伪装"用的是一个古怪的和弦。不太适合这个地方，而那就是这首歌的秘密。

如果说那个和弦是在评判"伪装"这个词，可能有点过分——这暗示着人们不能从表面看待这首歌中的角色，他实际上是在伪装感受，来表达一种他没有真正投入的感觉。他可能只是在玩。不过，一般来说，这些早期歌曲中的情感是相当直接的，讽刺意味不大。这就是为什么人们曾经喜欢，而且一直喜欢这些歌。它们表达出来的就是本意。"It's not like me to pretend / But I'll get you, I'll get you in the end"（我不喜欢伪装 / 但是我将得到你，我最终将得到你）。请注意，我觉得公平地说，这个想法也许萦绕着一些学生式的幽默感。

John.
I have to
go for Mimi about
1-30pm so I have left
her clothes here. Will
be back in an hour 12.30pm
Mami.

咪咪姑妈写给约翰·列侬的纸条，
1950 年代末。

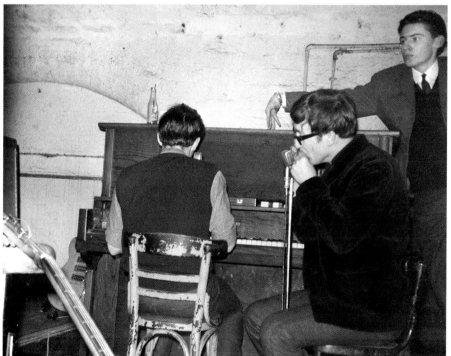

上图：披头士在排练。利物浦洞穴俱乐部，1960 年代初。

右图：和约翰·列侬及弟弟迈克在一起，乔治·哈里森拍摄。利物浦洞穴俱乐部，1960 年代初。

I'm Carrying

我带着

作 者 WRITER	保罗 · 麦卡特尼　Paul McCartney	
艺术家 ARTIST	羽翼乐队　Wings	
录 音 RECORDED	维京群岛费尔卡罗号、伦敦阿比路录音棚　*Fair Carol*, Virgin Islands and Abbey Road Studios, London	
发 行 RELEASED	《伦敦城》，1978 年　*London Town*, 1978	
	《伦敦城》B 面单曲，1978 年　B-side of 'London Town' single, 1978	

By dawn's first light I'll come back to your room again
With my carnation hidden by the packages
I'm carrying
Something
I'm carrying something for you

Ah long time no see, baby, sure has been a while
And if my reappearance lacks a sense of style
I'm carrying
Something
I'm carrying something for you

I'm carrying
Can't help it
I'm carrying something for you

I'm carrying
Something
I'm carrying something for you

追随披头士总是很困难。在很多人看来，我会有很多负担。但是发行了几张个人专辑后，我想回到乐队那种友爱氛围中。我有两种呈现羽翼乐队的方式：我可以作为披头士乐队的一员和以前的小脸乐队[1]或奶油乐队[2]的成员在一起，组成他们过去所谓的"超级乐队"；我也可以开始做一些感觉不错的事，并试着像披头士曾经那样慢慢成长。我选择了后者。唯一的问题是，这次我们不得不在公众面前犯错误。对披头士来说，这一切都是私下进行的，因为在汉堡的俱乐部里，并没有太多人听到我们犯错。

一开始很辛苦，因为羽翼乐队没歌，而我不想演披头士的任何东西。我想有个清楚的分割。当时所有的大牌宣传人员都说："你会演《昨天》吗？"从他们的表情就可以看出，这是他们所希望的，这也是我们必须对抗的。我就是这样的人；我不愿意复制任何东西或任何人，所以我期盼着羽翼乐队自身的成功。然而，从一开始，我们显然不得不接受成功需要时间这一事实。我们从小事做起，慢慢出了点名，去了国外。我们一开始不是一支很好的乐队，有一些瑕疵。在这儿那儿有一些小演出，在大学里出现，请求那天晚上在学生会演一些人们不知道的歌。但后来我们开始变得好一些了，我们开始更习惯彼此。然后，到了1970年代中期，我们突然有了金曲，比如《逃亡乐队》《愚蠢的情歌》，以及足够多我们自己的广为人知的东西，而不是披头士的。

人们会问："这首歌是什么意思？"我会回答："呃，这取决于你。"这首歌可以有无数种意思。我带来了什么？我说得很清楚，是包裹。我就像达帕·丹[3]，把我的康乃馨藏在包裹里。我给你带来了礼物，我为你带来一些东西，但是同时，当一个女人有孕的时候，她也会"带着"宝宝。有几个其他含义是可以排除的：一个是带着枪，一个是带着毒品。一个可能有点吸引力的意思是一个人"带着"一支乐队，其他人跟随着。我对它不太确定。我只是在玩"带着"这个词。这是一首模棱两可的小歌，但那是羽翼乐队的某种自由，做一些有点模棱两可的事。

有人说这首歌听起来像列侬风格。如果确实如此，我会承认；但对我来说，这听起来更像麦卡特尼风格：只是细微的声音。我无法想象约翰会发出这么细微的声音。但你知道，如果它被视为列侬式的，那也不是什么大问题。毕竟，我们确实学着如何一起写歌。

人们会问："这首歌是什么意思？"
我会回答："呃，这取决于你。"这首歌可以有无数种意思。

1　小脸乐队（Small Faces），成立于1965年的英国迷幻乐队。
2　奶油乐队（Cream），成立于1969年的英国乐队。
3　达帕·丹（Dapper Dan，1944— ），美国时装设计师。

左图:《伦敦城》录音期间。
维京群岛，1977 年。

上图：羽翼乐队出发去进行大学
巡演，1972 年。

下图:《伦敦城》的双开面折页
的图片，1979 年。

I'm Down

我很失落

作　者	WRITERS	保罗·麦卡特尼和约翰·列侬　Paul McCartney and John Lennon
艺术家	ARTIST	披头士乐队　The Beatles
录　音	RECORDED	伦敦阿比路录音棚　Abbey Road Studios, London
发　行	RELEASED	《救命!》B 面单曲，1965 年　B-side of 'Help!' single, 1965

You tell lies thinkin' I can't see
You can't cry 'cause you're laughing at me

I'm down (I'm really down)
I'm down (down on the ground)
I'm down (I'm really down)
How can you laugh when you know I'm down?
(How can you laugh?) When you know I'm down?

Man buys ring
Woman throws it away
Same old thing
Happen every day

I'm down (I'm really down)
I'm down (down on the ground)
I'm down (I'm really down)
How can you laugh when you know I'm down?
(How can you laugh?) When you know I'm down?

We're all alone
And there's nobody else
You still moan
Keep your hands to yourself

I'm down (I'm really down)
Oh babe, I'm down (down on the ground)
I'm down (I'm really down)
How can you laugh when you know I'm down?
(How can you laugh?) When you know I'm down?

Oh babe, you know I'm down (I'm really down)
Oh yes I'm down (I'm really down)
I'm down on the ground (I'm really down)
I'm down (I'm really down)
Ah baby, I'm upside down
Oh yeah, yeah, yeah, yeah, yeah

一个摇滚乐尖叫者，而这声音属于小理查德。很早的时候，我在学期末派对上唱过《高个子莎莉》。你可以在最后一天把吉他带到学校。我们有一位历史老师叫沃尔特·艾奇（Walter Edge），不过我们叫他"悬崖边缘"（Cliff Edge），因为我们觉得那真的很有趣。他是我们最喜欢的老师之一。我会当着班上所有同学的面站在课桌上，弹着我的吉他唱《高个子莎莉》，因为他允许我们这么做。

我真的从未过多考虑过我的嗓音。我很幸运不必这么做。人们问我："你用的是头腔共鸣还是胸腔共鸣？"我回答："恐怕我不知道有什么区别。"我没分析过。

唱小理查德的歌得全身心投入，你不能真的去思考它。有一次，我们和披头士一起录制《堪萨斯城》（Kansas City）时我就在想这个问题。在那几周前，约翰问过我，我是怎么唱小理查德那种歌的。我说："它就从我的头顶出来了。"我在录《堪萨斯城》时遇到了麻烦，因为现在我在想，"这一定是我有史以来最好的表演"，但我做得不太好。我在录音间里录唱时，约翰和其他人都在上面的控制室里，他下来了一会儿，走进来在我耳边低声说："从你头顶出来。还记得吗？"

在写第一段主歌的过程中，你已经基本上架构了往下进行的东西。你只要详细加工一下。而且，当你嘶喊一首摇滚歌曲时，你想要瞬间爆发；你不想变得太花哨。你自然的押韵模式就是试着去找到两个韵脚。"Man buys ring / Woman throws it away / Same old thing / Happen every day"（男人买戒指 / 女人把它扔掉 / 同样的老故事 / 每天都在发生）。这就像电报。

摇滚乐和布鲁斯的优点之一是它非常节约。在第一段主歌中，你找到一点押韵的模式，然后一般来说，在接下来的主歌中你也会持续用。这将是一首三分钟的歌，没时间太过花哨。我们必须把它弄出来并且说清楚，有力而且迅速，在两分半或者三分钟内。当然，从那以后，歌曲开始变得有一点点长了。它们长达三分钟，或者三分十秒，或者三分三十秒。

356—357 页：披头士和小理查德。默西塞德郡新布莱顿塔楼舞厅，1962 年 10 月 12 日。

In Spite of All the Danger
不顾一切危险

作　者　**WRITERS**　　保罗·麦卡特尼和乔治·哈里森　Paul McCartney and George Harrison
艺术家　**ARTIST**　　采石人乐队　The Quarry Men
录　音　**RECORDED**　　利物浦菲利普斯录音服务公司　Phillips Sound Recording Service, Liverpool
发　行　**RELEASED**　　《选集 1》，1995 年　*Anthology 1*, 1995

原始录音录制于 1958 年的夏天　Originally recorded in summer 1958

In spite of all the danger
In spite of all that may be
I'll do anything for you
Anything you want me to
If you'll be true to me

In spite of all the heartache
That you may cause me
I'll do anything for you
Anything you want me to
If you'll be true to me

I'll look after you
Like I've never done before
I'll keep all the others
From knocking at your door

In spite of all the danger
In spite of all that may be
I'll do anything for you
Anything you want me to
If you'll be true to me

In spite of all the heartache
That you may cause me
I'll do anything for you
Anything you want me to
If you'll be true to me
I'll do anything for you
Anything you want me to
If you'll be true to me

我们总是遇到"鼓手麻烦"。在很早的时候，我们还只是刚开始组乐队的天真男孩时，约翰和乔治非常确定我们三个要在这个乐队里，但我们一直不确定谁会为我们打鼓。有一段时间，我们甚至开始告诉人们节奏来自吉他。

我们经常向一个鼓手的窗户扔小石子，说"我们星期二有一场演出"，他则昏昏欲睡，或者他的妻子女友之类的会对我们大喊大叫。在那些年里，也很难找到一个真正拥有一套鼓的人。吉他更容易携带，也更容易得到。不过，有一个比我们大一点，叫科林·汉顿（Colin Hanton）的家伙，是约翰的乐队采石人的成员；他和我们在一起有一段时间了。所以这就是披头士的开始：我、约翰、乔治，科林·汉顿打鼓，还有我的一个校友，约翰·"达夫"·洛（John 'Duff' Lowe），他会弹钢琴。

杰瑞·李·刘易斯的《卑鄙的女人布鲁斯》（Mean Woman Blues）的开头有一个琶音，我后来才学会这个叫法。这是一个连续的琶音——基本上是指你把一个和弦的音符分开来弹，而不是同时演奏，而且要真的快速跨越几个八度——我们没有人能做到这一点，但达夫能做到，我们对此印象深刻，仅凭这一点，我们就让他加入了乐队。

"采石人"这个名字来自约翰的文法学校，采石场河岸高中。乔治和我去了一所我认为更好的文法学校，利物浦学院男子高中，现在是利物浦表演艺术学院。约翰在采石场河岸高中时组建了一支乐队，称他们为采石人，所以，我们差不多算是继承了这个头衔，我们并不介意。这只是个名字。

在 1958 年的某个时候，我们想录制一张唱片，告诉大家"看，这是我们"，来展示我们的东西。我们发现了一个小录音棚的广告，在肯辛顿的珀西·菲利普斯（Percy Phillips）——是利物浦的肯辛顿，没有伦敦的肯辛顿那么时髦，乘公共汽车大约半小时就到。制作一张醋酸酯唱盘的样带要花五英镑，那是老式的做法。我们每个人都凑了一英镑，一旦下定决心，这并不很困难。如果是每个人五英镑，那可能会更具挑战性。

于是，我们去了珀西·菲利普斯的录音棚，那里基本上是一个只有一支话筒的小房间。我们还是小孩子，带着自己的设备，你得等着轮到你，就像在医生的办公室一样。轮到我们时，他只是说："好吧，你们进去，我们走一遍这首歌，你们就可以录了。告诉我你们想把什么录在 A 面和 B 面之类的。"我们说 OK。

有一首巴迪·霍利的歌，现在是一首真正的经典，叫作《终有一天》（That'll Be the Day），我们非常喜欢这首歌，决定录这首。然后，我们有一首自创的史诗作为 B 面歌曲，叫作《不顾一切危险》。约翰和我已经开始了创作生涯，那时我们有几首歌。他有两首，我有两首，我们在一起时相互完善对方的歌，事实上，现在它们仍未被正式录制，这也许是件好事，因为它们不是很好。但我们确实带着这两首歌——《终有一天》和《不顾一切危险》——我们在这间小小的、黑暗的录音棚里录了它们，然后我们付了五英镑。

唯一的问题是只有一份拷贝，所以我们很高兴分享它，协议是我们每人保存一周。我们会为我们所有的亲属播放，然后说："看这个。这就是我们做的。"仅仅在一张唱片里听到我们的声音，就让我们相当激动，因为我们之前从未做过。结果是，约翰拥有了一个星期，然后把它给了我。我拥有了一个星期，乔治拥有了一个星期，科林拥有了一个星期，达夫·洛拥有了二十三年。

当我们每个人都听了一个星期后，大家或多或少都忘记了这件事。它没什么大不了的。我们没有任何宣传人员或经纪人来推广它。这真的只是为了我们自己和我们的家人。我在 1981 年拿回它，并为朋友和家人复刻了几份。你不能真正播放原始的醋酸酯唱片，因为虫胶会磨损。据说这是世界上最有价值的唱片之一，但说真的，对我来说，这是关于那些凹槽纹路中的记忆。

《不顾一切危险》经常被认为是一种呼救，它在某种程度上反映了约翰对一切的焦虑，他的母亲朱莉亚在我们录下这首歌后不久，可能只是几天后就去世了，彼时他的焦虑变得越发严重。但是这首歌，约翰没有从一开始就参与。我意识到我们的很多歌，尤其是那些很老的歌，都被认为出自我，比如《我看见她站在那里》，这首歌确实是从我开始的，约翰帮我加了几句歌词。

这些歌曲中有一些确实是从我开始的，还有一些是从约翰或我们合作开始的，关于《不顾一切危险》最重要的一点是，这是唯一的一首署名麦卡特尼-哈里森的作品。这是在我们理解创作署名是怎么回事之前。乔治编了独奏，但是有一部分确实来自约翰。这是我们录制的第一首歌，出现我们名字的第一首歌，后来变成披头士乐队的第一首官方录音。

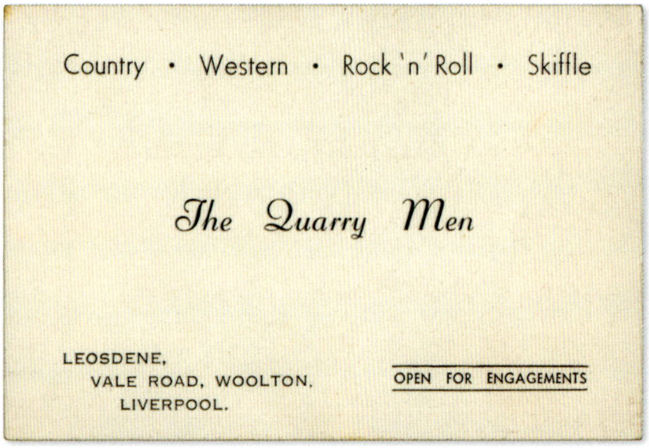

Country · Western · Rock 'n' Roll · Skiffle

The Quarry Men

LEOSDENE,
VALE ROAD, WOOLTON,
LIVERPOOL.

OPEN FOR ENGAGEMENTS

右图：约翰·列侬写的早期歌单。

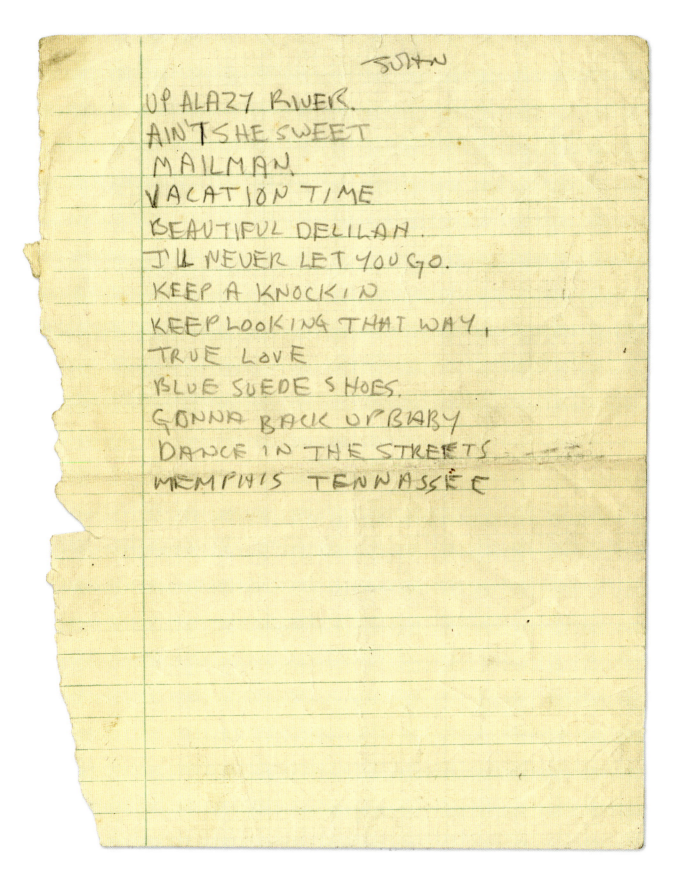

JOHN

UP A LAZY RIVER.
AIN'T SHE SWEET
MAILMAN.
VACATION TIME
BEAUTIFUL DELILAH.
I'LL NEVER LET YOU GO.
KEEP A KNOCKIN
KEEP LOOKING THAT WAY,
TRUE LOVE
BLUE SUEDE SHOES.
GONNA BACK UP BABY
DANCE IN THE STREETS
MEMPHIS TENNASSEE

上图：《不顾一切危险》1958 年
的原始醋酸酯唱片。

I've Got a Feeling

我有种感觉

作　者　WRITERS　　保罗·麦卡特尼和约翰·列侬　Paul McCartney and John Lennon
艺术家　ARTIST　　披头士乐队　The Beatles
录　音　RECORDED　伦敦苹果唱片公司屋顶　Apple Corps rooftop, London
发　行　RELEASED　《顺其自然》，1970 年　*Let It Be*, 1970

I've got a feeling
A feeling deep inside, oh yeah
I've got a feeling
A feeling I can't hide, oh no
I've got a feeling

Oh please believe me
I'd hate to miss the train, oh yeah
And if you leave me
I won't be late again, oh no
I've got a feeling

All these years I've been wandering around
Wondering how come nobody told me
All that I've been looking for was
Somebody who looked like you

I've got a feeling
That keeps me on my toes, oh yeah
I've got a feeling
I think that everybody knows, oh yeah
I've got a feeling

Everybody had a hard year
Everybody had a good time
Everybody had a wet dream
Everybody saw the sunshine
Oh yeah

Everybody had a good year
Everybody let their hair down
Everybody pulled their socks up
Everybody put their foot down
Oh yeah

Everybody had a good year
　　(I've got a feeling)
Everybody had a hard time
　　(A feeling deep inside, oh yeah)
Everybody had a wet dream
　　(Oh yeah)
Everybody saw the sunshine

Everybody had a good year
　　(I've got a feeling)
Everybody let their hair down
　　(A feeling deep inside, oh no)
Everybody pulled their socks up
　　(Oh no)
Everybody put their foot down
Oh yeah
I've got a feeling

　　这首歌是我自己的《我有种感觉》和约翰写的一首名为《每个人都经历了艰苦的一年》（Everyone Had a Bad Year）的歌曲片段之间的一场强制婚姻。与约翰一起写歌最令人兴奋的方面之一是，他经常从另一个角度切入。如果我说"情况一直在好转"，约翰很可能说"不会更糟了"，这就立刻把这首歌打开了。

　　对约翰来说，这一两年很波折。他婚姻的破裂，他与朱利安的疏远，海洛因的问题。并且在这个时候，乐队的整体状况很糟糕。那些被概括在"Everybody pulled their socks up"（每个人都打起了精神）和"Everybody put their foot down"（每个人都坚定了立场）这两个短句的组合中。这些歌词在某种程度上指的是国家的状况，或者是披头士的状况。

　　当我继续写自己的歌时，我很清楚他不在我的身边，但过去这么多年之后，他仍会在我耳边低语。我经常在事后猜测约翰会怎么想 —— "这太多愁善感了" —— 或者他会怎么用不同的方式来说，所以我有时会改变想法。但这就是词曲作者的意义所在，你必须能够纵观全局。

　　这些年我不得不自己做这件事。如果有人问我，和约翰一起工作是什么感觉，事实是那会更容易 —— 会容易得多，因为有两个头脑在工作。我的头脑会做这个，他的头脑会做那个，互动简直神奇。这就是为什么人们还在听我们写的歌。它们不像你平常听的流行歌曲那样消失了。我们两个写歌时创造的氛围不是一种矫情的流行歌曲氛围。我们创造了一个我们在其中可以成长、尝试新事物，甚至可以学到一两样东西的环境。

　　但约翰去世了，而我不能干坐在那里感叹过去的日子。我不能坐在那里希望他还在这儿。我不仅不能取代他，而且从某种意义上说，我也不需要取代他。有一次，有鲍勃·迪伦被问到为什么不写另一首《铃鼓先生》（Mr. Tambourine Man），他说："我不再是那个人了。"我也是一样。

上图：拍摄《顺其自然》纪录片，1969 年。

<u>I've Got a feeling</u> .

I've got a feeling
a feeling deep inside Oh yea .

I've got a feeling
a feeling I can't hide .

Oh please believe me
I'd hate to miss the train
And if you leave me
I won't be ~~here~~ late again .

All these years I've been wandering around
wondering how come nobody told me
All that I was looking for was somebody
who looked like you .

I've got a feeling
(that everybody knows) oh yea
I've got a feeling
(that keeps me on my toes) oh k

know
knows

366

右图：于《披头士》录音期间和
约翰·列侬一起创作。伦敦阿比
路录音棚，1968 年。

Jenny Wren

鹪鹩珍妮

作　者　WRITER	保罗 · 麦卡特尼　Paul McCartney	
艺术家　ARTIST	保罗 · 麦卡特尼　Paul McCartney	
录　音　RECORDED	伦敦 AIR 录音棚、洛杉矶航道录音棚　AIR Studios, London and Ocean Way Recording Studios, LA	
发　行　RELEASED	《在后院的混乱和创造》，2005 年　*Chaos and Creation in the Backyard*, 2005	
	单曲，2005 年　Single, 2005	

Like so many girls
Jenny Wren could sing
But a broken heart
Took her song away

Like the other girls
Jenny Wren took wing
She could see the world
And its foolish ways

How we spend our days
Casting love aside
Losing sight of life
Day by day

She saw poverty
Breaking up a home
Wounded warriors
Took her song away

But the day will come
Jenny Wren will sing
When this broken world
Mends its foolish ways

Then we'll spend our days
Catching up on life
All because of you
Jenny Wren
You saw who we are
Jenny Wren

洛杉矶有个峡谷，我特别喜欢去那里散步。到那儿需要开车，所以我经常自己去，写这首歌的那天，我在一个偏远的地方发现了一个安静的停车位，我没有去散步，我想："我要写首歌。"

人们常常认为利物浦是一个工业城市，但在我小时候，要进行鸟类观察并不困难。我喜欢能够离开日常的世界，这并不困难，因为我们住在利物浦南部的斯皮克，离真正的乡村只有一英里远。我有一本小口袋书，是《鸟类观察指南》（*The Observer's Book of Birds*），我过去常常独自一人出去散步，单独待一会儿。我喜欢远离正常的生活——学校、家庭生活、广播、电视、跑腿，无论如何——只要独自一人，能够漫步和冥想。很快，我就可以认出这些鸟了，而鹪鹩可能成了我最喜欢的鸟。非常小，非常隐秘，非常可爱的小东西。你不会经常看到它，不过突然间，你会看到它从一个小灌木丛飞到另一个。所以，当我们谈起鸟类——黑鸟也属于我最喜爱的鸟类，或者云雀或鹪鹩——谈的是长久以来我一直喜欢的东西。

当你要写点什么的时候，写一个关于你喜欢的世界，总是好的。所以，说到鹪鹩珍妮时，我首先想到的是小说，狄更斯的《我们共同的朋友》（*Our Mutual Friend*）中那个勇敢的女孩，她积极的态度让她克服了痛苦的畸形，然后我看到了那只鸟，但是后来我又看到了一个人，在这个故事中她是一位伟大的歌手。孩子们可能已经没听说过她了，但我父母和祖父母那一代人都知道伟大的瑞典歌剧演唱家珍妮·林德（Jenny Lind），他们过去称她为"鹪鹩珍妮"。

在我的讲述中，结局是鹪鹩珍妮的灵魂已被夺走，她将停止歌唱作为一种抗议。于是这首歌多少有些影射我们的社会：我们是如何把事情搞砸的，以及我们是如何与抗议者产生共鸣的。她看到了我们愚蠢的方式，我们抛弃爱的方式，我们忽视生命的方式——贫穷摧毁家园，创造受伤的战士。她知道我们是谁，和其他人一样，她只是在寻找更好的方法。比方说，如果这是一个选举年，它可能是世界上的任何地方，你希望混乱——我们现在所在的"this broken world"（这个破碎的世界）——会消失，制造混乱的人也一并消失，更好的人将会出现，这样我们就可以回到自己更好的一面，纠正我们的愚蠢行为。你知道更好的一面就在那里，但并不总是那么容易接近。

仍然，我还是要保持乐观主义——因为我是一个战争婴儿，而英国已经走出第二次世界大战最黑暗的日子。所以我仍然深信这是一个美好的旧世界，真的，不过我确实认为我们搞砸了。这相当明显：海里充斥着塑料，它们可不是自行进入海中的。认为气候变化是一个骗局则是另一个错误，我希望我们仍然可以为我们的孩子和我们孩子的孩子修复这个错误。

我意识到，我是在为那些也许生活艰难的人唱歌，因为在我的家乡，很多人都因为缺钱而过得艰难；而我永远不会忘记，如果没有钱，有很多东西你是得不到的。我一直非常清楚一首美妙的歌曲能带来的力量，因为我记得在利物浦成长的过程中，当我听到一首歌时——即使是一只小鸟的歌声——它会给我希望，并让我快乐。我明白那种感觉对我有多重要。但我现在说的是："瞧，事情并不总是糟糕。"这给了我一首歌的方向，也给了我一个我希望的方向。这真的很像查理·卓别林的歌曲《微笑》[1]。这是 OSS —— 乐观歌曲综合征（Optimistic Song Syndrome）。

歌曲经常与其他歌曲对话，而这首歌很显然是与《黑鸟》的对话。我认为，当你拿着一把木吉他坐下来，有几个方向可以走。《黑鸟》，吉他部分和唱是对立的，而不是弹奏和弦，我认为《鹪鹩珍妮》也是同样的概念。我想我可能是在写另一首《黑鸟》，而且是故意这样做的。如果我不是在写这本书"追忆人生"的话，我是不会向任何人承认这一点的，这一切都是因为鹪鹩珍妮。

1　《微笑》（Smile），卓别林为 1936 年自导自演的电影《摩登时代》创作的主题歌。

下图：牙买加，1979 年。

右图：在英国萨塞克斯郡开车，1978 年。

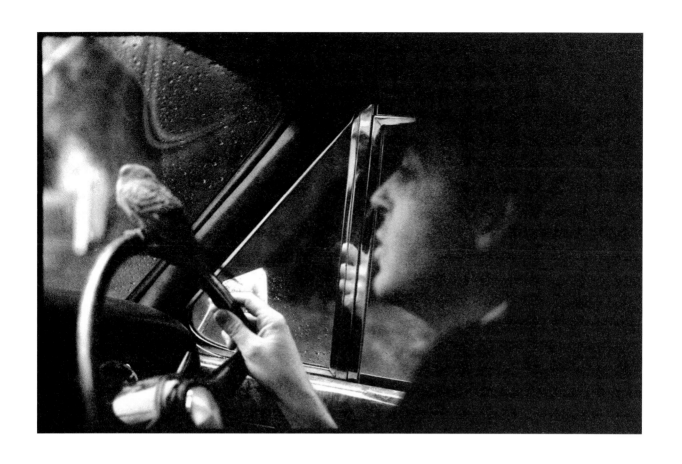

歌曲经常与其他歌曲对话，
而这首歌很显然是与《黑鸟》的对话。
我认为，当你拿着一把木吉他坐下来，
有几个方向可以走。
《黑鸟》，吉他部分和唱是对立的，而不是弹奏和弦，
我认为《鹩哥珍妮》也是同样的概念。

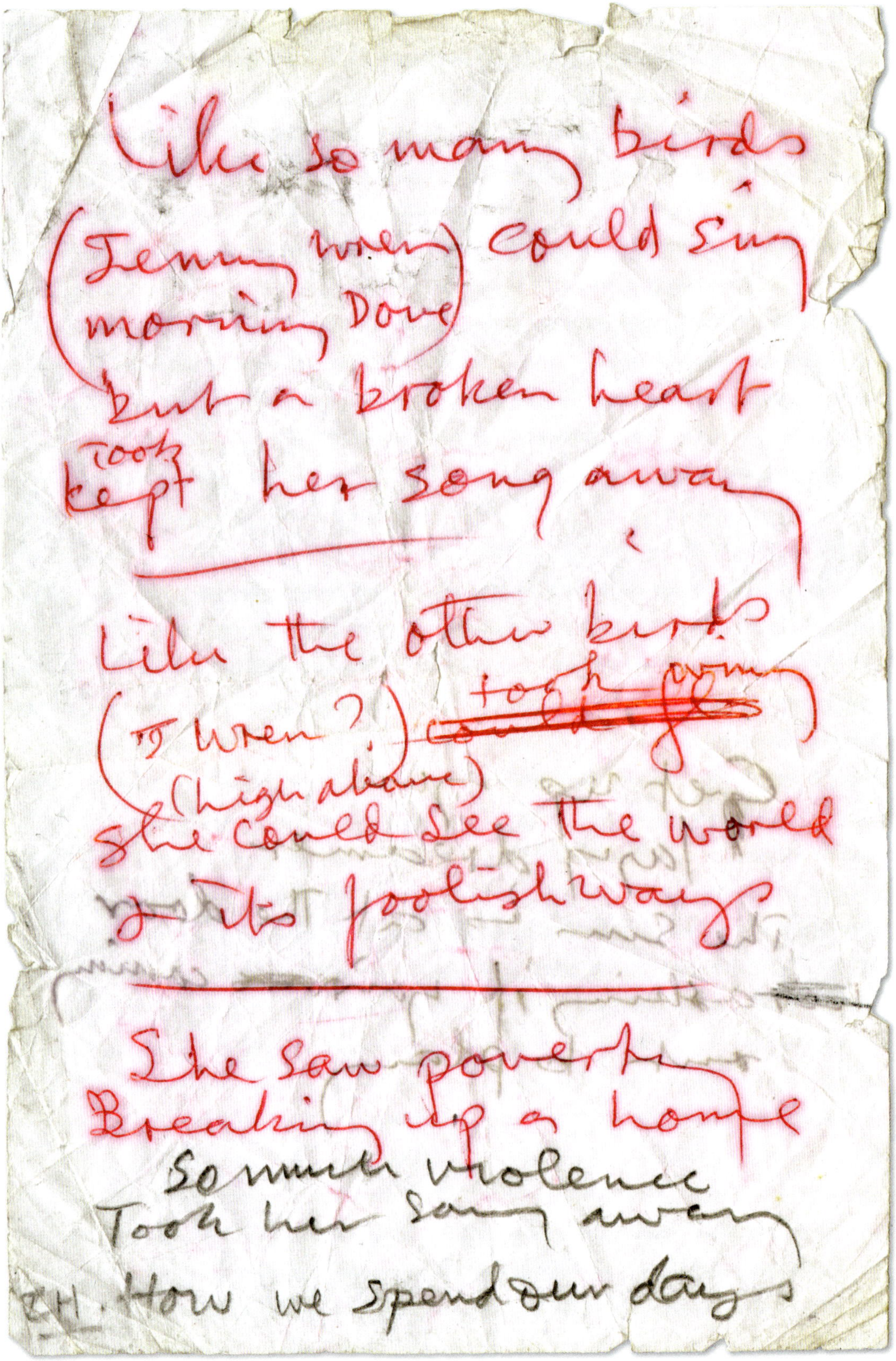

Like so many birds
(Jenny wren) could sing
(morning Dove)
But a broken heart
took
~~kept~~ her song away

Like the other birds
(Jenny wren?) took away
~~could fly~~
(high above)
She could see the world
& its foolish ways

She saw poverty
Breaking up a home
So much violence
Took her song away
EH. How we spend our days

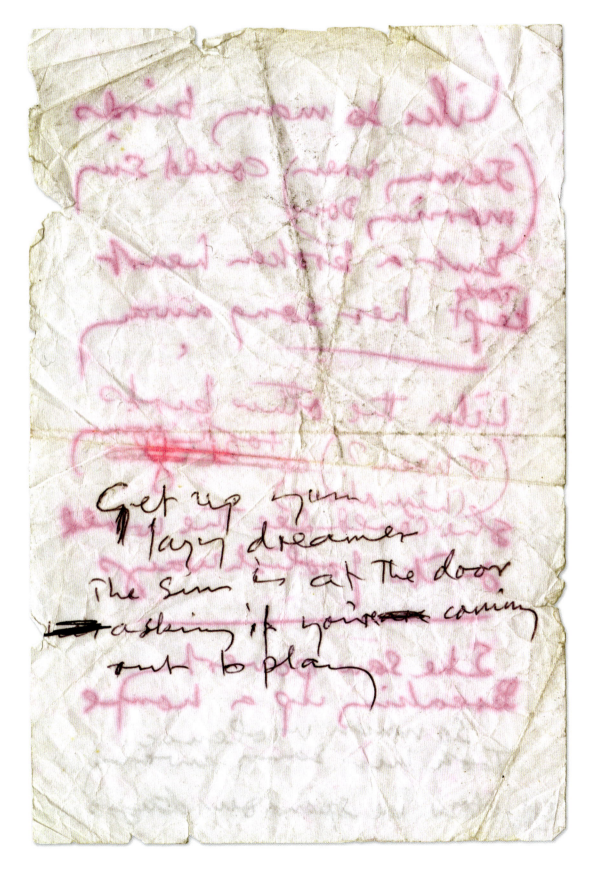

Get up you
lazy dreamer
the sun is at the door
asking if you're ~~~~ coming
out to play

375

Jet
喷气机

作　者	WRITERS	保罗·麦卡特尼和琳达·麦卡特尼　Paul McCartney and Linda McCartney
艺术家	ARTIST	保罗·麦卡特尼和羽翼乐队　Paul McCartney and Wings
录　音	RECORDED	拉各斯百代录音棚、伦敦 AIR 录音棚　EMI Studios, Lagos and AIR Studios, London
发　行	RELEASED	《逃亡乐队》，1973 年　*Band on the Run*, 1973
		单曲，1974 年　Single, 1974

Jet
Jet
Jet, I can almost remember their funny faces
That time you told them that you were going to be
    marrying soon
And Jet, I thought the only lonely place was on the
    moon
Jet
Jet

Jet, was your father as bold as the sergeant major
How come he told you that you were hardly old
    enough yet
And Jet, I thought the major was a lady suffragette
Jet
Jet

Ah Mater
Want Jet to always love me
Ah Mater
Want Jet to always love me
Ah Mater
Much later
Jet

And Jet, I thought the major was a lady suffragette
Jet
Jet

Ah Mater
Want Jet to always love me
Ah Mater
Want Jet to always love me
Ah Mater
Much later

Jet, with the wind in your hair of a thousand laces
Climb on the back and we'll go for a ride in the sky
And Jet, I thought that the major was a little lady
    suffragette

Jet
Jet
And Jet, you know I thought you was a little lady
    suffragette
Jet

A little lady
My little lady, yes

我们还是披头士时，学会了写金曲。毕竟，我们是披头士，所以我们必须这样。我们不能写砸了。那对披头士来说是不对的。

所以，我已经掌握了写一首流行歌或者金曲的诀窍。现在，我有意计羽翼乐队的声音不同于披头士，但诀窍和技巧仍然适用，所以写《喷气机》时，我有很多技巧可以使用。其中一个是喊叫；这很管用。大声喊叫总是一个很好的歌曲开场。

"喷气机"实际上是一匹小马的名字，我们在农场里给孩子们养的一匹设得兰小马。我的女儿玛丽出生于 1969 年，所以在 1973 年，写这首歌的时候，她四岁，斯特拉两岁。她们还小，但是知道喷气机是一匹小马，就像知道《我亲爱的玛萨》（Martha My Dear）里的玛萨是一只牧羊犬一样重要，或者不重要。

我清楚地记得这首歌是怎么开始的。我们在苏格兰。我带着我的吉他，惊喜，惊喜。有一个要塞在一座山上，一个古老的凯尔特堡垒。它现在主要是一个军事测量标地。这是一个非常好的有利位置。是那种你可以想象维京人冲上山来，而我们往他们身上倒油的地方，或者，如果那不起作用，就向他们扔长矛。山坡上有一些可爱的小土包，我们都喜欢在那里闲逛。

我告诉琳达我要离开一段时间。在这个美丽的夏日躺在那里时，我放任自己的思绪漫游。一些意象来自琳达和她父亲之间的关系。他是一个很酷的人，非常有才华，但从我的喜好来说，他有点太父权。我和他相处得很好，但他有点严格。"Sergeant major"（军士长）有一部分就来自这里。还有一部分来自吉尔伯特和沙利文以及《现代少将的典范》，也部分来自英国的电视情景喜剧《布西和斯努奇》（Bootsie and Snudge），剧中有一个名叫克劳德·斯努奇军士长（Sergeant-Major Claude Snudge）的角色。

上图：玛丽、斯特拉及喷气机。苏格兰，1975 年。

"Mater"（母舰），或说"母亲"，回到了我在学校的拉丁语课上。这是一个想象中的母亲形象，尽管我认为公平地说，我真正母亲的幽魂总是隐约地出现在背景的某个地方。

不管怎样，我都编好了，在吉他上弹出这首歌，回到农舍后弹给琳达听。我问她是怎么想的。她喜欢！这就是我下午在山上弄出来的东西。这不是西奈山，我也没有带着"十诫"回来，但我带着《喷气机》回来了。

ready for take off...

JET

PAUL McCARTNEY and WINGS

Apple Single 1871

380

Junior's Farm

少年农场

作　者　WRITERS　　保罗·麦卡特尼和琳达·麦卡特尼　Paul McCartney and Linda McCartney
艺术家　ARTIST　　保罗·麦卡特尼和羽翼乐队　Paul McCartney and Wings
录　音　RECORDED　纳什维尔生意商店录音棚　Soundshop Recording Studios, Nashville
发　行　RELEASED　单曲，1974 年　Single, 1974

You should have seen me with the poker man
I had a honey and I bet a grand
Just in the nick of time I looked at his hand
I was talking to an Eskimo
Said he was hoping for a fall of snow
When up popped a sea lion ready to go

Let's go, let's go, let's go, let's go
Down to Junior's Farm where I want to lay low
Low life, high life, oh let's go
Take me down to Junior's Farm

At the Houses of Parliament
Everybody's talking 'bout the President
We all chip in for a bag of cement
Ollie Hardy should have had more sense
He bought a gee-gee and he jumped the fence
All for the sake of a couple of pence

Let's go, let's go, let's go, let's go
Down to Junior's Farm where I want to lay low
Low life, high life, oh let's go
Take me down to Junior's Farm
Let's go, let's go
Down to Junior's Farm where I want to lay low
Low life, high life, oh let's go
Take me down to Junior's Farm
Everybody tag along

I took my bag into a grocer's store
The price is higher than the time before
Old man asked me, why is it more?
I said, you should have seen me with
the poker man
I had a honey and I bet a grand
Just in the nick of time I looked at his hand

Let's go, let's go, let's go, let's go
Down to Junior's Farm where I want to lay low
Low life, high life, oh let's go
Take me down to Junior's Farm
Let's go, let's go
Down to Junior's Farm where I want to lay low
Low life, high life, oh let's go
Take me down to Junior's Farm
Everybody tag along
Take me down to Junior's Farm

Take me back
Take me back
I want to go back
Yeah, yeah, yeah

上图：和斯特拉及詹姆斯在一起。
苏格兰，1982 年。

　　琳达和我私奔了——越过苏格兰边境，绕过了格雷特纳格林，那实际上在半路上——然后去了我几年前购买的农场。说实话，我对它不是很感兴趣，但琳达感兴趣。她让我见识到那里有多么美。

　　我们花了很多时间在农场，只是抚养孩子和种田。它成了某种程度上的避难所，离开伦敦及伴随着这座城市的一切——无论是好是坏——都很不错。我会开一辆麦赛福格森牌 315 型拖拉机来割干草，我喜欢这样，是因为我小时候就是一个大自然狂热爱好者，而这种自由让我有时间思考——"Down to Junior's Farm where I want to lay low"（去到少年农场在那里我想躺倒）。如此轻松地从那些西装革履的商务会议中解脱，那些人每时每刻都是那么严肃，然后去苏格兰，并且可以只穿着 T 恤和灯芯绒裤坐在那里。当我写这首歌的时候，我就是这样的心态。基本信息是，让我们离开这里。你可能会说，这是我的后披头士时代的逃离城市之歌。

　　羽翼乐队为了加强乐队的团结去了纳什维尔。我们在录制《逃亡乐队》前失去了一个吉他手和一个鼓手，有了两位新成员。所以，我的想法是排练和录制几首歌，这是其中一首。我们住在一个名叫科利·普特曼（Curly Putman）的词曲作者家里，他写了《家乡的绿色，绿色的草地》（The Green, Green Grass of Home）。我想他和他妻子去度假了，所以我们有了自己的地方。

我自己的农场离得很远，在这里，我们住的是一个大牧场，非常美国，并且和苏格兰非常不同。平坦的平原，而不是起伏的丘陵，还有走廊上的摇椅。所以我决定在主歌部分加入一些幻想的成分。鲍勃·迪伦的《麦琪的农场》（Maggie's Farm）是在将近十年前发行的，在 1965 年，这无疑对这首歌产生了影响。"因纽特人"可能来自迪伦歌曲《因纽特人奎因》（Quinn the Eskimo）中的强人奎因。主歌的"I took my bag into a grocer's store / The price is higher than the time before"（我带我的包走进杂货店 / 价格比以前更高了）——这句话很贴切，因为很多人都感到手头拮据，1970 年代初对很多人来说是一个财政困难的时期，资金紧张。为什么每样东西都比以前贵得多？

　　至于第二段主歌。我们现场演奏这首歌时，我并不总是唱得一模一样，所以有时歌词里不包括这些："At the Houses of Parliament / Everybody's talking 'bout the President / We all chip in for a bag of cement"（在议会大厦 / 每个人都在谈论总统 / 我们所有人凑钱买了一袋水泥）。这首歌录制于 1974 年夏天，并在同年 10 月发行。大约是在理查德·尼克松和他的弹劾听证会的同一时间；事实上，我想那个夏天他不得不灰溜溜地辞职了。这首歌的想法是给他所谓的黑手党送行。我觉得我们现在没有理由不表演那段主歌。可能只是因为这首歌太长了，而我们在演出时要唱大约四十首歌。

　　音乐和歌曲中都有时髦的东西，紧接这首歌之前的，专辑《逃亡乐队》的那段时间，亡命之徒的概念也很时髦，部分原因是老鹰乐队所唱的同名歌——更别提《虎豹小霸王》有多受欢迎了。我们只是把它带到更大以及更个人的层面。当时的想法是，我们所有人都在逃避法律。当你抽大麻的时候，警察成了你不得不担心的事情，害怕他们会说："那是什么味道？"你认为你会被指控犯有轻罪，他们会因此逮捕你。我小时候就不一样了；对我来说，那时候的警察只是日常巡逻的友善老伙计，与警察之间也没有太多负面的联系。不过，有那么一两次，我开着一辆新车被拦下来，那是我的第一辆车，一辆福特领事经典款。我有点太年轻了，不应该开一辆这么闪亮的车，警察拦住了我："你从哪儿弄来的这辆车？"你知道，我是利物浦人，我看起来好像刚偷了车。我说："这是我的。我买的。"

　　《少年农场》一直是很棒的现场歌曲，我们通常会把它放在演出的开场。它有很多有用的元素——容易辨认的前奏和好听的、持续稳定的摇滚节奏，然后是这些有趣的、有点超现实的歌词，和振奋人心的合唱"Let's go, let's go"（我们走吧，我们走吧）。这让人们开始兴奋，"just in the nick of time"（就在关键时刻），为了他们自己版本的《少年农场》，无论那是什么——无论他们想消失在哪里，在哪里躲藏，以及在哪里躺下。

1. You should have seen me with the Poker man
I had a honey and I bet a grand
Just in the nick of time I looked at his hand
I was talking to an Eskimo
Said he was hoping for a fall of snow
When up popped a sea-lion ready to go

2. At the Houses of Parliament
Everybody's talking 'bout the President
We all chip in for a bag of cement
Ollie Hardy should have had more sense
He bought a gee-gee and he jumped the fence
All for the sake of a couple of pence

3. I took my bag into a grocer's store
The price is higher than the time before
Old man asked me "Why is it more?"
You should have seen me with the Poker man
I had a honey and I bet a grand
Just in the nick of time I looked at his hand

Chorus: Let's go, let's go, let's go, let's go
Down to Junior's Farm where I want to lay low
Low life, high life, let's go, let's go
Take me down to Junior's Farm
Everybody tag along
Take me down to Junior's Farm

apple single R 5999
Marketed by EMI Records
20 Manchester Square, London, W1A 1ES.

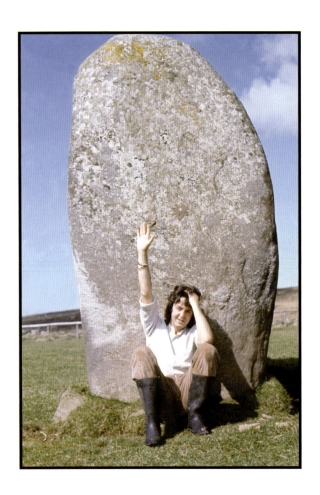

上左：苏格兰，1974 年。

上右：纳什维尔，1974 年。

But just in the nick of time I looked at his hand.

lets go, lets go -

② I was talking to an Eskimo —
said he was hoping for a fall of snow -
And up popped a sea lion ready to go

CHORUS   lets go ~~ ~~ ~~ down to juniors farm
                                    where I wanna lay low
                                    when
low life ~~high~~ high life   oh lets go (go life, go!)
                        Take me
                    heading down to Juniors Farm

~~~ students union ~ ~ ~~~

③ At the houses of Parliament,   ④ Ollie Hardy should have had
Everybodys talkin bout the ~~President~~   more sense
All chip in for a bag of cement.   He bought a gee gee and he
            (Everybody tags along.)   All for the sake of a couple
                                             3- of pence.

③ Took my bag into a grocery store (gross restore)
The prices were higher than the time before
Old man asking coln is it more ? (Everybody tags along)

Junk

破 烂

作 者 WRITER   保罗·麦卡特尼 Paul McCartney
艺术家 ARTIST   保罗·麦卡特尼 Paul McCartney
录 音 RECORDED   伦敦家中及伦敦摩根录音棚 At home, London and Morgan Studios, London
发 行 RELEASED   《麦卡特尼》，1970 年 *McCartney*, 1970

Motor cars, handlebars, bicycles for two
Broken-hearted jubilee
Parachutes, army boots, sleeping bags for two
Sentimental jamboree

Buy, buy, says the sign in the shop window
Why? Why? says the junk in the yard

Candlesticks, building bricks, something old and new
Memories for you and me

Buy, buy, says the sign in the shop window
Why? Why? says the junk in the yard

　　威尔弗里德·布朗贝尔（Wilfrid Brambell）是一名爱尔兰演员，他在披头士的电影《一夜狂欢》中扮演了我的"异常整洁"的祖父角色。他也是《斯特普托与儿子》（*Steptoe and Son*）中的明星之一，那是英国广播公司的著名情景喜剧。这部连续剧聚焦于常被称为"脏老头"的阿尔伯特·斯特普托（Albert Steptoe）和他儿子哈罗德（Harold Steptoe）之间不断的冲突，后者注定要有一个似乎从未具体化的社会抱负。我想我们都很熟悉这样的剧本！

　　如果我可以用一个花哨的词，人环境，来形容的话，"破烂"是受了二手店，或者垃圾场的影响，那也是《斯特普托与儿子》的主要背景。1960 年代和 1970 年代的英国观众对这个垃圾场的熟悉程度，就如熟悉《伯南扎的牛仔》[1] 里的牧场或《贝弗利山人》[2] 里的豪宅一样。

　　这首歌像很多歌曲一样，以我喜欢的和弦序列开始，然后是旋律。我知道这也许听起来很奇怪，但这首歌开始的和弦让我想到了废品场或者商店的后院。如果要写一部小说的话，我想我会把场景设置在那种氛围中。狄更斯经常那么做。商店的后院或者一间地下室，甚至《荒凉山庄》里的朗斯韦尔钢铁厂。而这首歌里我们有"Motor cars, handlebars, bicycles for two"（摩托车、车把手、双人自行车）。许多人会认出这最后一个短句是从歌曲《戴茜·贝尔（双人自行车）》[Daisy Bell (Bicycle Built for Two)] 中回收再利用的，那首歌里有这样的歌词："Daisy, Daisy, / Give me your answer do !"[3] 这是哈里·戴克雷创作于（Harry Dacre）1892 年的歌，在 1963 年，纳特·金·科尔让这首歌成为畅销金曲。

上图：保罗与威尔弗里德·布朗贝尔。《一夜狂欢》，1964 年。

1　《伯南扎的牛仔》（*Bonanza*），美国第一部彩色西部牛仔连续剧，1959 年首播。
2　《贝弗利山人》（*The Beverly Hillbillies*），美国电视喜剧片，1993 年上映。
3　"戴茜，戴茜，/ 给我你肯定的答案！"

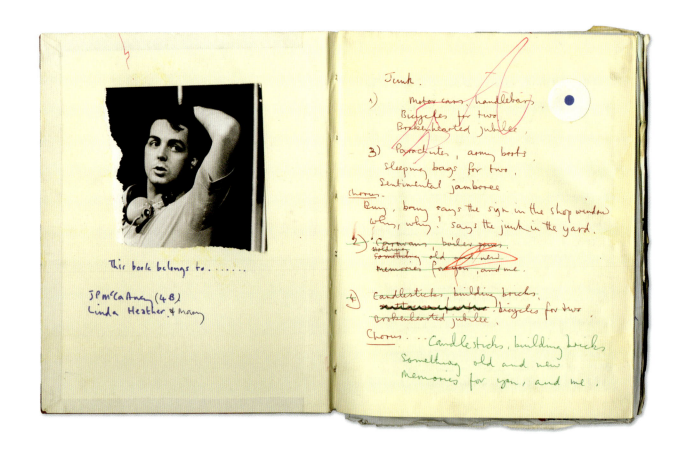

回到 1960 年代，回收再利用并不是一个很重要的特征。这在一定程度上是因为"内在性陈旧"[1] 这个概念还没有完全流行起来。在那些日子里，如果你买了一辆车，意味着会使用很长时间，它甚至可能在一个家庭中流传。当我还是个孩子的时候，你一直使用这些物品。我现在有一种坚守物品的本能，不仅如此，我希望事物能持续下去。所以，这是对消费社会的评论。这是作为创作者该做的一件事：你评论社会，并且表达观点。我在歌曲中加入了自己的观点——并不总是我持有的观点，而只是我听过的，或者喜欢的，或者让我感兴趣的观点。所以，认为东西买完就没用了的想法是对消费社会的一种评论。实际上，正是在 1960 年代，我们跨越了需要和欲望之间的那条界限，并根据这些欲望来采取行动。所以，这首歌就是一首这样的曲子。

不过它更多的是一首情歌。"双人自行车"汇合着"双人睡袋"。然后是"Buy, buy, says the sign in the shop window"（买，买，商店橱窗里的招牌说着）这句歌词，听起来就像一个情人说"再见"，然后另一个哀怨地问"为什么，为什么?"，甚至"院子里的破烂"也在要求解释为什么要买新的东西，或者新的人。

1　内在性陈旧（built-in obsolescence），指制造商在设计商品时人为设定使用寿命，令产品在一段时间后就会过时或出现故障，以鼓励消费者购买新产品。

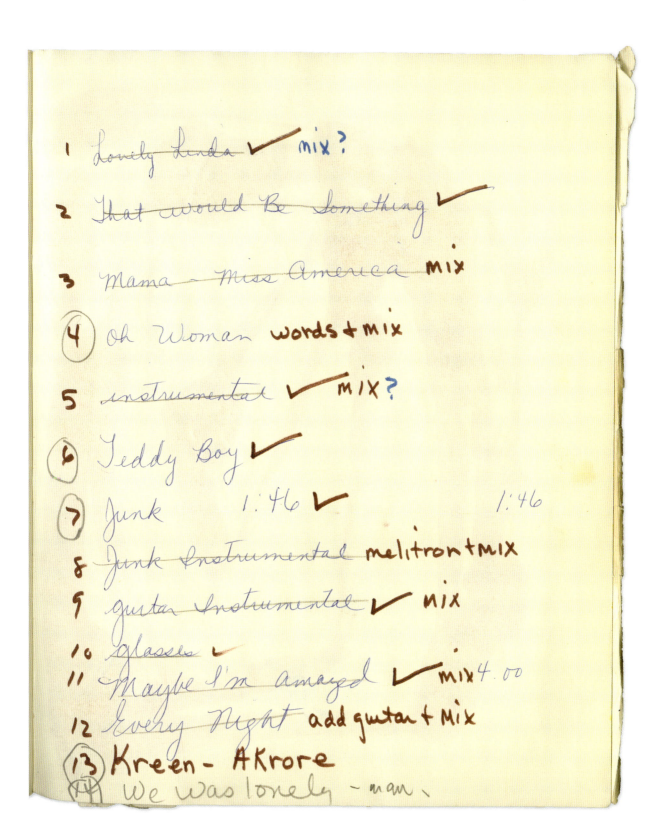

1 Lovely Linda ✓ mix?

2 That would Be Something ✓

3 Mama - Miss America mix

④ Oh Woman words + mix

5 instrumental ✓ mix?

⑥ Teddy Boy ✓

⑦ Junk   1:46 ✓   1:46

8 Junk Instrumental melitron + MIX

9 guitar Instrumental ✓ nix

10 Glasses ✓

11 Maybe I'm Amazed ✓ mix 4.00

12 Every Night add guitar + Mix

⑬ Kreen - Akrore

⑭ We was lonely - man.

麦卡特尼的笔记，1970 年。

391

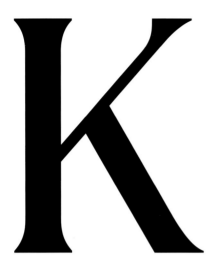

The Kiss of Venus

394

维纳斯之吻

The Kiss of Venus

维纳斯之吻

作　者 WRITER	保罗·麦卡特尼	Paul McCartney
艺术家 ARTIST	保罗·麦卡特尼	Paul McCartney
录　音 RECORDED	萨塞克斯郡猪山磨坊	Hog Hill Mill, Sussex
发　行 RELEASED	《麦卡特尼 III》，2020 年	*McCartney III* , 2020

The kiss of Venus
Has got me on the go
She scored a bullseye
In the early morning glow
Early morning glow

Packed with illusions
Our world is turned around
This golden circle has a
Most harmonic sound
Harmonic sound

And in the sunshine
When we stand alone
We came together with
Our secrets blown
Our secrets blown

Now moving slowly
We circle through the square
Two passing planets in the
Sweet, sweet summer air
Sweet summer air

And in the sunshine
When we stand alone
We came together with
Our secrets blown
Our secrets blown

Reflected mountains in a lake
Is this too much to take?
Asleep or wide awake?
And if the world begins to shake
Will something have to break?
We have to stay awake

Packed with illusions
Our world is turned around
This golden circle has a
Most harmonic sound
Harmonic sound

And in the sunshine
When we stand alone
We came together with
Our secrets blown
Our secrets blown

The kiss of Venus
Has got me on the go
She scored a bullseye
In the early morning glow
Early morning glow

The kiss of Venus
Has got me on the go

有一本关于太阳系中偶然性的小册子，由约翰·马蒂诺（John Martineau）所写，是一本关于行星及其轨道，以及太阳和月亮运行的小论文。我最近读过，这绝对是一次引人入胜的阅读，因为设计这本书的人把那些轨道和运行视觉化了。比如说，以地球为中心来看，金星绕地球的轨迹每八年会画出一个五角星。

第一次读这本书的时候，我惊讶地看到宇宙中这些复杂的设计，它让我去想，"是的，这是奇迹——这种生命，万物的相互依存，树木提供氧气；有太多神奇的事物在发生。"

说到神秘，当我在 2004 年参加格拉斯顿伯里音乐节时，我很喜欢这样一个想法，我们很可能处在能量线的交汇处，这些能量线纵横交错在地球上，并且我们的祖先被认为沿着这些线建造了重要的遗址。我喜欢那样的历史。格拉斯顿伯里据说也是安葬亚瑟王的地方。所以，不管怎样，这是一个非常特殊的地方，并且有着非常明确的氛围。不可否认，那里有一种不同寻常的气场。

自 1960 年代起，我就对星座和宇宙学，以及宇宙之声很感兴趣。马蒂诺的书中还探讨了声音——球体的音乐——每一个行星听起来都是不同的音符。这些，对我来说，是非常"嬉皮"的——整个概念就是享受生活中的简单事物并与自然和谐相处。"We came together with / Our secrets blown"（我们走到一起 / 吹散我们的秘密）——我们没有试图隐藏任何东西，我们在大雨中赤身裸体，而宇宙正在忙它自己的事。

当你思考这些更大的事情时，这一切都是如此卑微。我们在这里，这个星球上的这些小点，而星球本身也是宇宙中的一个小点，而在它的核心，你可以看到这个莲花图案，至少有两个宗教——佛教和印度教——把它视为重要的象征。

从马蒂诺的书中，我学到的另一件事是金星经常离地球很近，这种现象被称为"维纳斯之吻"。这足以激发我的想象力。这才是我真正的动力。

"Two passing planets in the / Sweet, sweet summer air"（两颗经过的星球 / 在甜蜜的，甜蜜的夏日气息中）。这就好像，作为人类，我们是擦肩而过的行星——有点像夜晚经过的船只。"Now moving slowly / We circle through the square"（现在缓缓移动 / 我们绕着广场转圈）这句话让我想起了"穿过市集"，这是很多歌谣中都使用过的一个短语，包括传统的爱尔兰小歌谣《她穿过市集》(She Moved Through the Fair)。"把事情搞定"(squaring the circle) 的概念——做一些不可能的事情——也潜藏在这句短语之下。每一首歌都要克服巨大的困难去完成，就是这样一种感受。

HARMONIC SOUND

1. Packed with illusion
   my world is ~~turning~~ turned around
   ~~The~~ This golden circle
   ~~The kiss of Venus~~
   Has a most harmonic sound
   (harmonic sound)

   ~~This golden circle~~

2. The kiss of Venus
   ~~Has~~ got me on the go
   ~~She scored a bulls eye~~
   In the early morning glow
   (~~early morning~~ glow)

CH And in the Sunshine
    where we stand alone
    we came ~~together~~
    with our secrets blown
    (secrets blown)

3. Now moving slowly
   we circled in the square
   ~~Two passing planet~~
   ~~and came together~~ in the
   sweet sweet summer air
   (sweet summer air)

   CH. And in the Sunshine ... etc.

[MID] Reflected mountains
      in a lake
      Is this too much to take.
      Asleep or wide awake

1. Packed with illusion
   my world is turned around
   This golden circle
   Has a most harmonic sound.

THE KISS OF VENUS

①   The kiss of Venus
Has got me on the go
She scored a bullseye
In the early morning (glow) (show)
(" " ")

②   Packed with illusion
Our world is turned around
This golden circle has a
Most harmonic sound
(" / ")

(Bridge) And in the sunshine
When we stand alone
We came together with
Our secrets blown
(" ")

③   Now moving slowly
We circle through (IN) the square
Two passing planets in the
Sweet sweet summer air
(" " ")

(Bridge) And in the sunshine when we stand alone
We came together with our secrets blown ("our ")

[MID] Reflected mountains in a lake / is this too much to take?
Asleep or wide awake / REPEAT
And if the world begins to shake / Will something have to
We have to stay awake.   break?

④   The kiss of Venus
Has got me on the go
She scored a bullseye
In the early morning (show) (glow)
(" " ")

V1
V2
① B
V3
② B
m
V2 | B ③
m
V1
end

在格拉斯顿伯里音乐节的压轴
演出，2004 年 6 月 26 日。

THE LYRICS

VOLUME 2

第二卷

Paul McCartney

THE LYRICS

1956 TO THE PRESENT

保罗·麦卡特尼

歌抒人生

L-Z

［英］保罗·麦卡特尼 著

［爱尔兰］保罗·马尔登 编

杨海崧 译

中信出版集团 | 北京

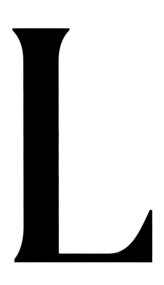

Lady Madonna
麦当娜夫人

作　者　WRITERS　　　保罗·麦卡特尼和约翰·列侬　Paul McCartney and John Lennon
艺术家　ARTIST　　　　披头士乐队　The Beatles
录　音　RECORDED　　伦敦阿比路录音棚　Abbey Road Studios, London
发　行　RELEASED　　单曲，1968 年　Single, 1968

Lady Madonna, children at your feet
Wonder how you manage to make ends meet
Who finds the money when you pay the rent?
Did you think that money was heaven sent?

Friday night arrives without a suitcase
Sunday morning creeping like a nun
Monday's child has learned to tie his bootlace
See how they run

Lady Madonna, baby at your breast
Wonders how you manage to feed the rest

See how they run

Lady Madonna, lying on the bed
Listen to the music playing in your head

Tuesday afternoon is never-ending
Wednesday morning papers didn't come
Thursday night your stockings needed mending
See how they run

Lady Madonna, children at your feet
Wonder how you manage to make ends meet

我妈妈玛丽在我十四岁时去世是我从未跨过去的坎。一首描绘一位非常鲜活的家庭主妇的歌曲必然会受到那种可怕的失落感的影响。关于麦当娜夫人如何"to feed the rest"（养活其他的人）这个问题对我来说尤其尖锐，因为你不必是一个精神分析学家就能知道，我自己就是"其他的人"之一。我一定觉得被冷落了。这真的是对母亲形象的致敬，对女性的致敬。

我最喜欢这首歌的地方是一再出现的短语"See how they run"（看看他们如何奔跑）。它出自童谣《三盲鼠》（Three Blind Mice），童谣里农场主的那位不怎么称职的家庭主妇用一把雕刻刀砍掉了老鼠的尾巴。这个引用为这首歌增添了一点阴暗的色彩。无论如何，"奔跑"一词同样指向长袜。我在成长过程中难以忘怀的记忆之一是，除非还有更重要的事情，女性面对的难题总是长筒袜的滑丝——"Thursday night your stockings needed mending"（周四的晚上你的长袜需要缝补）。

"看看他们如何奔跑"的这种重复是歌曲创作中最有力的组成部分之一，这种重复在术语中称为"迭句"（refrain）。同一时期的另一首歌曲《嘿，裘德》中，在那句劝诫的歌词里，我们就"refrain"这一动机开了一个小玩笑："And anytime you feel the pain / Hey Jude, refrain"[1]。

对于披头士乐队，我们总是游走于两者交汇的边缘，一方面是意识到"迭句"对于一首歌的贡献，另一方面是基本上不知道我们在做什么。我一直认为披头士乐队的秘密之一是：我们的音乐是自学的。我们从来没有有意识地思考过我们在做什么，我们所做的一切都是自然而然的。不会出现什么惊人的和弦变化，因为我们知道那个和弦是如何与另一个和弦相关联的。我们不会读乐谱，也没法记谱，所以我们只是把它编出来。我爸爸也一样。如果你不是刻意的，如果你没有试图让它发生，并且它是自然出现的，你的东西中就会有某种快乐。这有某种魔力。我们所做的很多事情都出自深深的好奇，而非学习。我们根本没有真正学习过音乐。

1　"任何时候你感受到痛苦／嘿，裘德，忍住"，出自《嘿，裘德》（Hey Jude）。refrain 既有"副歌；迭句"之意，又有"克制；避免"之意。

右图和下图：家庭照片，和妈妈
玛丽及弟弟迈克在一起。

Let 'Em In
让他们进来

作 者 WRITERS　　保罗·麦卡特尼和琳达·麦卡特尼　Paul McCartney and Linda McCartney

艺术家 ARTIST　　羽翼乐队　Wings

录 音 RECORDED　　伦敦阿比路录音棚　Abbey Road Studios, London

发 行 RELEASED　　《以音速》，1976 年　*At the Speed of Sound*, 1976

　　　　　　　　单曲，1976 年　Single, 1976

Someone's knocking at the door
Somebody's ringing the bell
Someone's knocking at the door
Somebody's ringing the bell
Do me a favour
Open the door and let 'em in
Let 'em in

Sister Suzy, Brother John
Martin Luther, Phil and Don
Brother Michael, Auntie Jin
Open the door and let 'em in
Oh yeah

Sister Suzy, Brother John
Martin Luther, Phil and Don
Uncle Ernie, Auntie Jin
Open the door and let 'em in
Oh yeah, yeah

Someone knocking at the door
Somebody ringing the bell
Someone's knocking at the door
Somebody's ringing the bell
Do me a favour
Open the door and let 'em in
Oh yeah, yeah, let 'em in now

Sister Suzy, Brother John
Martin Luther, Phil and Don
Uncle Ernie, Uncle Ian
Open the door and let 'em in
Yeah, yeah

Someone's knocking at the door
Somebody's ringing the bell
Someone's knocking at the door
Somebody's ringing the bell
Do me a favour
Open the door and let 'em in
Yeah, yeah, yeah, yeah, ycah

　　一些歌曲对我来说像是塞进圣诞袜的小礼物，它是有趣的小东西，但不会是你的圣诞节大礼。我在音乐这事上可能有点完美主义，我会想"这可不算我的杰作"，然后对它们略感失望。我记得自己对一首名为《比普波普》(Bip Bop)的歌非常失望，我想："天哪，你能变得多么平庸？"但我对一位名叫特雷弗·霍恩(Trevor Horn)的制作人说起这事时——他制作了弗兰基去好莱坞[1]、格雷斯·琼斯[2]和许多很酷的音乐家的唱片——他说："这是我最喜欢的你的歌之一！"于是，我得以明白他在歌中看到了什么，那就是我创作它、想把它录下来时所看到的，所以他让我对此感觉好多了。

　　"Someone's knocking at the door / Somebody's ringing the bell"（有人在敲门 / 有人按响门铃）——我想象这是在利物浦，一个聚会之类的。我们在牙买加时，所有牙买加男人都会对金发的琳达说："嘿，苏西，苏西！"对他们来说，一个金发的白人女性就是"苏西"。于是，琳达成立了一个乐队，命名为"苏西和红条纹"(Suzy and the Red Stripes)，名字来自一个啤酒品牌。"Sister Suzy"是琳达；"Brother John"是她的兄弟约翰·伊斯曼，或者约翰·列侬；"Martin Luther"是马丁·路德·金；"Phil and Don"是埃弗利兄弟；然后还有"Brother Michael"，那是我的弟弟，或者可能是迈克尔·杰克逊——时间正好，因为前一年我们邀请杰克逊五兄弟[3]参加了在玛丽女王号游艇上举办的《金星和火星》(Venus and Mars)的专辑派对。然后是"Auntie Jin"，拼写为 J

1　弗兰基去好莱坞（Frankie Goes to Hollywood），英国舞曲组合，1980 年成立于利物浦。
2　格雷斯·琼斯（Grace Jones，1948— ），牙买加演员、歌手。
3　杰克逊五兄弟（The Jackson 5），成立于 1965 年的美国五兄弟乐队，迈克尔·杰克逊是其中最小的弟弟。

而不是 G，因为她的名字是简，但在利物浦，这听起来太正式了，所以她会说"就叫我金妮（Jinny）吧"。随后的"Uncle Ernie"——我表弟的名字实际上是伊恩，但他们叫他厄恩，对此我并没有太在意，我只是在玩文字游戏。"Uncle Ian"？哦，伙计们，你只是没注意而已。算了吧，并没有伊恩叔叔……他当然没有和金阿姨结婚。

然后是最奇怪的事情：快进一百万年，我娶了南希·谢维尔，她的姐姐叫苏西，哥哥叫乔恩。所以，突然之间，我唱的似乎是南希的家庭——"苏西姐姐，约翰哥哥"。这非常巧合。

有人认为歌中出现"马丁·路德"是因为他和敲门有关，把信条钉在门上。这不是我在写这首歌时所意识到的，但在集体无意识中，也许这是可能的。的确，歌曲可以来自某个神秘的地方。很多时候，如果你幸运的话，歌词和音乐会结合在一起。你就坐下来开始。你用各种各样的声音勾画出事物，终于，你听到一个开始奏效的乐句，于是跟随那条轨迹。作为艺术家，我们似乎本能地知道，如果我们对它持开放态度，如果我们反复琢磨这一堆文字或音符，它会带来一些东西。会有东西进来。你甚至不用让它进来。

上图：和苏西·谢维尔、南希及玛丽萨·西蒙（Merissa Simon）在一起，2011 年。

右图：为苏西和红条纹《海边的女人》（Seaside Woman）单曲发行拍摄的照片，1977 年。

408

的确，歌曲可以来自某个神秘的地方。
很多时候，如果你幸运的话，歌词和音乐会结合在一起。
你就坐下来开始吧。你用各种各样的声音勾画出事物，
终于，你听到一个开始奏效的乐句。

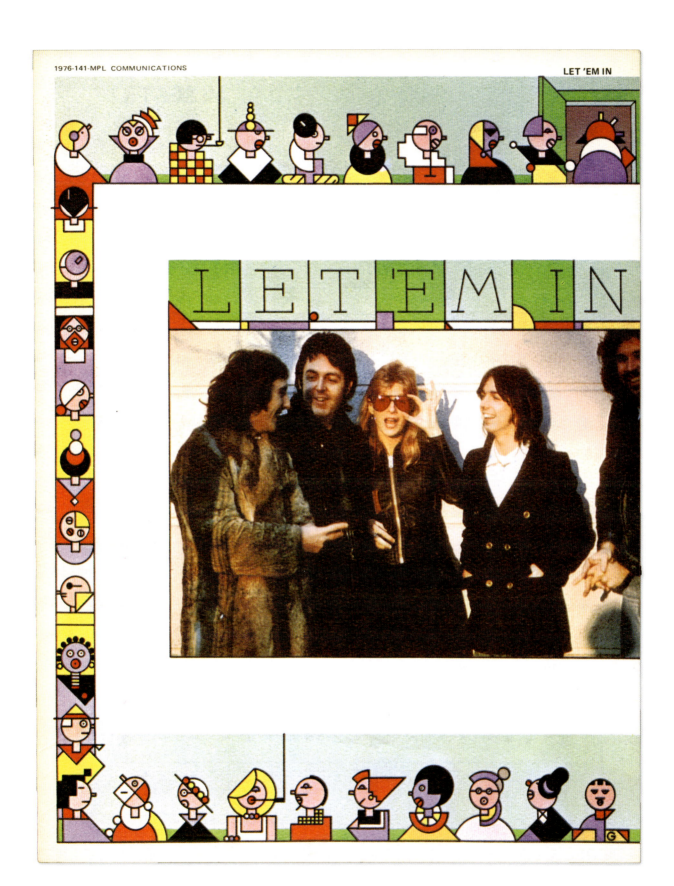

Let It Be

顺其自然

作　者　WRITERS　　保罗·麦卡特尼和约翰·列侬　Paul McCartney and John Lennon

艺术家　ARTIST　　披头士乐队　The Beatles

录　音　RECORDED　伦敦苹果录音棚　Apple Studio, London

发　行　RELEASED　单曲，1970 年　Single, 1970

　　　　　　　　　《顺其自然》，1970 年　*Let It Be*, 1970

When I find myself in times of trouble
Mother Mary comes to me
Speaking words of wisdom
Let it be
And in my hour of darkness
She is standing right in front of me
Speaking words of wisdom
Let it be

Let it be, let it be
Let it be, let it be
Whisper words of wisdom
Let it be

And when the broken-hearted people
Living in the world agree
There will be an answer
Let it be
For though they may be parted
There is still a chance that they will see
There will be an answer
Let it be

Let it be, let it be
Let it be, let it be
There will be an answer
Let it be
Let it be, let it be
Let it be, let it be
Whisper words of wisdom
Let it be

Let it be, let it be
Let it be, let it be
Whisper words of wisdom
Let it be

And when the night is cloudy
There is still a light that shines on me
Shine until tomorrow
Let it be
I wake up to the sound of music
Mother Mary comes to me
Speaking words of wisdom
Let it be

Let it be, let it be
Let it be, let it be
There will be an answer
Let it be
Let it be, let it be
Let it be, let it be
There will be an answer
Let it be
Let it be, let it be
Let it be, let it be
Whisper words of wisdom
Let it be

斯汀[1]曾经对我说，我在"拯救生命"演唱会[2]上唱《顺其自然》并不是个好选择。他觉得"拯救生命"毫无疑问是需要行动的，而各人自扫门前雪对于"拯救生命"所代表的大规模行动的号召并不是一个适当的信息。但是《顺其自然》并不是自满，或者共谋。这首歌说的是感受全貌，对于全球视野的顺应。

　　这首歌所描写的语境来自某种压力。那是一段艰难的时期，因为披头士乐队正走向解散。这是一个变化的时期，部分原因是约翰和洋子走到了一起，这对乐队的互动产生了影响。洋子出现在录音场合中，那是一种挑战，而我们必须应对。除非真有什么非常严重的问题——除非我们中的一个说"她在这里我唱不了"——我们只能随它去。我们不是很有对抗性，所以我们只是忍气吞声，继续做事。我们是北方的小伙子，这是我们文化的一部分。笑着并忍受。

　　我最近才想起《顺其自然》的一个有趣之处。当我随我最喜欢的老师艾伦·杜邦德在利物浦学院男子高中学习英国文学时，我读了《哈姆雷特》。在那些日子里，你必须学习背诵演讲，因为在考试中会用到，并且你必须能够在考试中引用它们。这出剧的结尾处有这样几句台词：

　　　　噢，我可以告诉你——
　　　　不过顺其自然吧。——霍雷肖，我死了。

　　我怀疑那些台词下意识地扎根于我的记忆中。写《顺其自然》时，我做了太多的事情，筋疲力尽，而这一切当然产生了影响。乐队，我　　正如歌中所说，我们都经历了麻烦，似乎没有任何办法摆脱困境。有一天，我累得睡着了，做了一个梦，在梦中，我的妈妈（她去世差不多十年了）真的来找我了。当你梦见你失去的人时，即使有时只是几秒钟，但你真的觉得他们就在你的身边，好像他们一直都在那里。我想，任何失去亲人的人都明白这一点，尤其在他们刚刚去世的那段时间里。直到今天，我仍然会梦见约翰和乔治，并与他们交谈。但是在这个梦里，看着我妈妈美丽善良的脸，和她一起在一个祥和的地方，让我备受安慰。我感觉自在，感觉被爱着、被保护着。我的妈妈很让人安心，并且像很多女人一样，她是我们家的动力之源，她让我们精神振作。她似乎意识到我很担心生活中正在和将要发生的事情，而她对我说："一切都会好起来的。顺其自然。"

　　我醒来时想，这对于一首歌会是一个很棒的主题。于是，我从我周围的情况开始——"当下的麻烦"。

　　在我们录制《顺其自然》的那段时间，我一直在推动乐队进行一些俱乐部场地的演出——回到根源，并且作为一支乐队再次紧密联系在一起，就像我们开始时那样，为这十年做个总结，只是为了热爱而演奏。我们没有作为披头士乐队做到这些，但是

1　斯汀（Sting，1951—），英国摇滚歌手。
2　"拯救生命"演唱会（Live Aid），1985年7月13日，在英国伦敦和美国费城同时举行的两场演唱会，由鲍勃·吉尔多夫发起，旨在为发生在埃塞俄比亚的饥荒筹集资金。

这个想法确实预示了《顺其自然》专辑的方向。我们不想要录音棚的花招。这张专辑应该是一张诚实的、没有叠录的专辑。结果并不是这样，但这是我们的计划。

可惜的是，此前披头士从未在现场演出过这首歌。因此，对许多人来说，在"拯救生命"上的表演可能是他们第一次看到它在舞台上被演唱。

不过，现在《顺其自然》已经在现场演出中出现好一阵子了。这一直是一首关于接受逆境的"合唱曲目"，而且我觉得，它真的很适合人群。你会看到很多人手挽着伴侣、朋友或家人一起跟着唱。早年间，演唱这首歌时，会有成千上万的打火机被举到空中；但你现在不能在演出中抽烟了，于是灯光来自人们的手机。你总是可以知道哪些歌曲不那么流行，因为人们会收起手机；而《顺其自然》，手机会被举起。

几年前，我们在日本东京武道馆演出。我们刚刚在东京巨蛋演了三个晚上，这是一个拥有五万五千个座位的大型棒球场。为了平衡，我们在武道馆进行巡演的最后一场，相比之下，这是一个更私密的夜晚。披头士乐队在那里的演出差不多是五十年前的事情了，但那是一场特别的演出，场地充满了回忆。我的巡演团队喜欢给我准备一些惊喜，比如，他们向现场的每个人分发腕带。我不知道会这样，但演唱《顺其自然》时，整个场地都被这些摆动的手臂照亮了。在那样的时刻，有时很难继续唱下去。

有人说《顺其自然》有轻微的宗教含义，听起来确实有点像福音歌曲，尤其是钢琴和风琴。"Mother Mary"（母亲玛丽）一词可能首先可以理解为是指圣母玛利亚。你可能还记得，我的母亲玛丽是天主教徒，而我的父亲是新教徒，我的弟弟和我都接受过洗礼。所以，就宗教而言，我显然受到基督教的影响，但所有宗教中都有许多伟大的教义。我并不特别信奉任何传统意义上的宗教，但我确实相信有某种更高的力量可以帮助我们。

因此，这首歌变成了一个祈祷文，或短祈祷文。在这首歌的核心里有一种渴望。而"阿门"这个词本身的意思就是"就这样吧"——或者"顺其自然"。

这一直是一首关于接受逆境的"合唱曲目"，
而且我觉得，它真的很适合人群。
你会看到很多人手挽着伴侣、朋友或家人一起跟着唱。

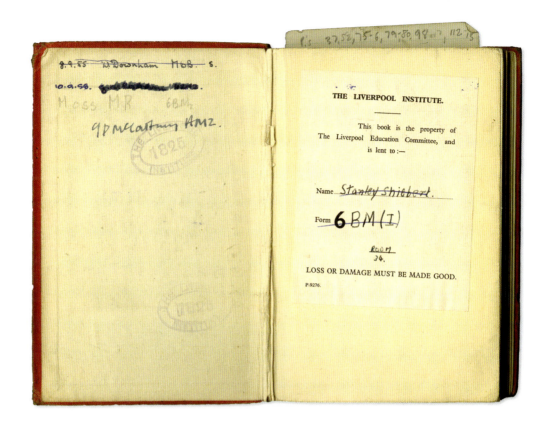

P.s 37,52, 75-6, 79-80, 98 or 7, 112-73

What dramatic device
is specially employed in
Hamlet to let the audience
into the innermost working
of the heroes mind. Describe
and illustrate its use.

Clutton Brook, A. Shakespeares
"Hamlet" M5139.

Joseph, Bertram "Hamlet"
LR 822.3
JOS.

~~crossed out~~
"Hamlet" once more
Robertson JM. M8695.

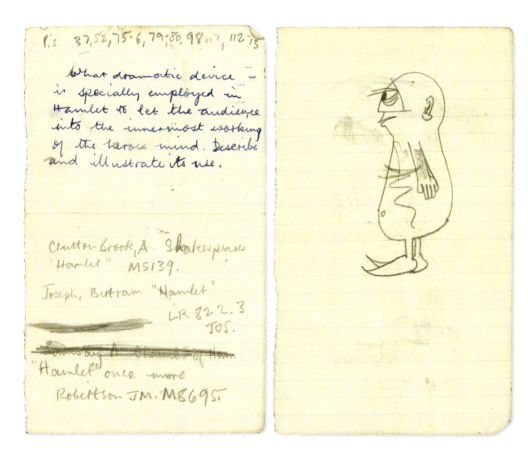

左图：妈妈，玛丽·麦卡特尼。

右图：录音，伦敦苹果录音棚，
1969 年。

418—419 页："外出"巡演东京
武道馆站，演唱《顺其自然》。
2015 年 4 月 28 日。

我的妈妈很让人安心，并且像很多女人一样，
她是我们家的动力之源，她让我们精神振作。
她似乎意识到我很担心生活中正在和将要发生的事情，
而她对我说："一切都会好起来的。顺其自然。"

Let Me Roll It
让我滚动它

作 者 WRITERS 保罗·麦卡特尼和琳达·麦卡特尼 Paul McCartney and Linda McCartney

艺术家 ARTIST 保罗·麦卡特尼和羽翼乐队 Paul McCartney and Wings

录 音 RECORDED 拉各斯百代录音棚、伦敦 AIR 录音棚 EMI Studios, Lagos and AIR Studios, London

发 行 RELEASED 《逃亡乐队》，1973 年 *Band on the Run*, 1973

《喷气机》B 面单曲，1974 年 B-side of 'Jet' single, 1974

You gave me something
I understand
You gave me loving in the palm of my hand

I can't tell you how I feel
My heart is like a wheel
Let me roll it
Let me roll it to you
Let me roll it
Let me roll it to you

I want to tell you
And now's the time
I want to tell you that
You're going to be mine

I can't tell you how I feel
My heart is like a wheel
Let me roll it
Let me roll it to you
Let me roll it
Let me roll it to you

沼泽回声。我们总是叫它沼泽回声,因为它就像厕所 —— 我们称之为"沼泽"——里的回声。我们会向控制室喊:"我们能来点沼泽回声?"然后他们会问:"你们想要每秒 7.5 英寸还是每秒 15 英寸的?"我们会说:"我们不知道。两个都放一下。"那时候回声是录在磁带上的。短沼泽回声,长沼泽回声。非常吉恩·文森特,非常猫王。

约翰喜欢这种磁带回声,而且用的比我们任何人都多,因此,它成了他个人唱片中的标志性声音。我承认我在这里用了它。我记得第一次唱《让我滚动它》时,我想:"对,这很像约翰的歌。"不用说,这是约翰的音域,但最像列侬风格的是回声。

然而,这首歌中最重要的元素不是回声,不是音域,不是歌词,而是吉他连复段。我能想到的词是"灼热"。这是一个灼热的小东西。我们可以无休止地谈论歌词,但好的连复段有一种罕见的美。这个连复段非常戏剧化,足以令观众听到时大吃一惊。因为它停得如此突然,感觉一切都冻结了。时间冻结了。

当我们谈论歌词时,可以说"滚动"与卷大麻有关,我想这不会让任何人感到惊讶。演出场地仍然允许抽烟的时候,观众中会有很多人抽大麻。现在,我现场演出时,有时会觉得观众是否有点拘谨;然后,我会闻到大麻的味道。不过这可能更多发生在音乐节上。

《让我滚动它》本质上是一首情歌。另一种滚动的感觉,情欲,是摇滚乐的一部分,也是这首歌重要的一部分。"My heart is like a wheel"(我的心像一个轮子),所以任何人都可以联想到"Let me roll it to you"(让我滚着它去向你)。任何人都能理解,当你把心奉献给另一个人,或表达对另一个人的感情时,你的感受完全暴露在外。这很难。

在这种情况下,我们感到的犹豫 —— 想伸出手但又不愿完全敞开 —— 在这个连复段的突然开始和停止中展现得淋漓尽致。这首歌用不断地缓冲来模仿主题。我们都经历过这种状况。一两年前,我看了一部由乔·伊科尼斯(Joe Iconis)和乔·特雷茨(Joe Tracz)主演的音乐剧《放松一点》(Be More Chill),关于一个书呆子说不出他爱某个人的故事。他说话有障碍,一种神经性口吃。《让我滚动它》就是一种拉长的、拖沓的口吃。

Rock 17

(1) You gave me something
I understand
You gave me loving
in the palm of my hand

(2) I want to tell you
And now's the time
I want to tell you
That you're going to be mine

Chorus
I can't tell you how I feel
My heart is like a wheel
Let me roll it to you

LET ME ROLL IT.

① You gave me something,
I understand,
You gave me loving in the palm of hand

Refrain
I can't tell you how I feel
my heart is like a wheel
LET ME ROLL IT
Let me roll it to you
Let me roll it
Let me roll it to you.

② I want to tell you
And now's the time,
I want to tell you that
You're going to be mine

Refrain.

LET ME ROLL IT

Words & Music by Paul & Linda McCartney

As Recorded by
PAUL McCARTNEY
and
WINGS

MUSIC PUBLISHING COMPANY OF AFRICA (PTY.) LTD
McCARTNEY MUSIC LTD.

Sole Selling Agents for the Republic of South Africa and Rhodesia.
GALLO (AFRICA) LIMITED
P.O. Box 6216, JOHANNESBURG CAPE TOWN: 43 Somerset Road DURBAN: 593 Smith Street.

60c PA 4245

沼泽回声。
我们总是叫它沼泽回声，
因为它就像厕所 —— 我们称之为"沼泽" —— 里的回声。
我们会向控制室喊："我们能来点沼泽回声？"
然后他们会问："你们想要每秒 7.5 英寸还是每秒 15 英寸的？"
我们会说："我们不知道。两个都放一下。"
那时候回声是录在磁带上的。短沼泽回声，长沼泽回声。

Live and Let Die
你死我活

作 者 WRITERS	保罗 · 麦卡特尼和琳达 · 麦卡特尼	Paul McCartney and Linda McCartney
艺术家 ARTIST	保罗 · 麦卡特尼和羽翼乐队	Paul McCartney and Wings
录 音 RECORDED	伦敦 AIR 录音棚	AIR Studios, London
发 行 RELEASED	单曲，1973 年	Single, 1973

When you were young
And your heart was an open book
You used to say live and let live
You know you did
You know you did
You know you did
But if this ever-changing world in
    which we're living
Makes you give in and cry

Say live and let die
Live and let die
Live and let die
Live and let die

What does it matter to ya?
When you got a job to do
You got to do it well
You gotta give the other fellow hell

You used to say live and let live
You know you did
You know you did
You know you did
But if this ever-changing world in
    which we're living
Makes you give in and cry

Say live and let die
Live and let die
Live and let die
Live and let die

大多数歌曲都是自我委托的：你写这些歌是为了自己的乐趣或是让自己走出困境；但有时候别人会委托你写首歌，这是件好事，此时，技巧便有了用武之地。在某些方面，我喜欢把自己看作兼职作家。我是那种人，如果我们需要一张桌子，我会说，"好吧，我会做一个"，这会给我带来几周甚至几个月的乐趣——画草图，弄清楚我该怎么做。

就《你死我活》来说，罗恩·卡斯（Ron Kass）有一阵子担任苹果唱片公司负责人，我非常喜欢他，与他相处得也很好。他认识一个与007电影专营权有关的人，1972年10月的一天，他给我打电话，聊着聊着，他说："你对给007电影写歌有兴趣吗？"我回答："是的，我可能会感兴趣"——你知道，尽量不要显得太热情。

写一首007歌曲是一种荣誉，我私下里一直有野心想去写一首。罗恩告诉我这部电影叫《007之你死我活》。那个时候剧本还没有写完，我拿到了伊恩·弗莱明[1]的那本书，它真是扣人心弦。那天下午，我完全沉浸在这本书里，所以当我坐下来写这首歌时，我知道如何呈现它。我不希望这首歌成为那种"你有枪。现在去杀人吧。你死我活"之类的东西，那不是我；我希望它讲述的是"随它去吧。别担心。当你有麻烦时，就是你死我活"。一旦我脑子里有了这个想法，这首歌几乎就是自动写成的。我想我是在一个周六读了这本书，在那个周日，我坐在起居室的钢琴前把想法整理到一起，琳达帮忙弄了一些雷鬼乐的东西。完成得真的很快。

然后我把它交给乔治·马丁，他正在为这部电影配乐。我向他展示了和弦及歌曲的结构，还有核心的连复段。我知道电影里会有不少爆炸场面，但我把007式的编曲完全留给了他。这是自披头士乐队之后我们的第一次合作，这是一种快乐。他的编排是纯粹乔治式的——完美地阐释了宏伟而不浮夸的平衡。我对此感到非常高兴。

在那个时候，你会有一个醋酸酯样带，一个少量压制的录音，乔治去了加勒比海，电影正在那里拍摄。他带了一个小唱机给电影制作人之一库比·布鲁科利（Cubby Broccoli）播放，库比·布鲁科利听了之后说："太好了，乔治。这是一个很好的样带。你打算什么时候制作最终版的录音？"乔治回答："这个就是。"他们以为我要写给其他人来唱。

我并没有把它和以前的一些007主题联系在一起，比如《007之俄罗斯之恋》或者《007之金手指》，它们都是典型的邦德式的。我不确定我的歌是否如此，或者它是否能和那些经典并肩，不过很多人都把它列入了他们的最佳007歌曲名单。然后，当它发行时，它成了迄今为止最成功的007主题曲，并获得奥斯卡最佳原创歌曲提名——"When you got a job to do / You got to do it well"（当你有份工作要做 / 你尽力做好）。

1990年代初，枪炮与玫瑰[2]翻唱了这首歌，有趣的是，我的孩子们去学校说，"这是我爸爸写的"，而他们的朋友说："不，不是他写的。是枪炮与玫瑰。"没人相信他们。不过我很高兴枪炮与玫瑰翻唱了这首歌。实际上，我觉得这是一个非常好的版本。我

1　伊恩·弗莱明（Ian Fleming，1908—1964），英国作家，007系列小说的作者。
2　枪炮与玫瑰（Guns N' Roses），美国摇滚乐队，1985年成立于洛杉矶。

左图:《你死我活》单曲碟，
1973 年。

右图：乔治·马丁的《你死我活》
乐谱手稿，1972 年。

430—431 页：《你死我活》
演出现场，2016—2019 年。

很惊讶他们会这么做————一个年轻的美国乐队。我总是喜欢人们唱我的歌。这是一种
伟大的敬意。

在今天，对我们来说，这首歌仍然是一首大场面的歌曲。演唱它时，会有烟火出
现，我想我最喜欢这首歌的地方是，我们知道爆炸即将发生，演出中的第一场大爆炸。
我通常会看着那些人，尤其是前排的人，他们正愉快地与歌曲同行："你死我……"砰！
观察他们真是太好了，他们被惊到了。

一天晚上，我注意到前排有一位年纪很大的女士，我想，"哦，见鬼，我们会杀了她。"
但是停不下来，我无法停下这首歌说："捂住你的耳朵，亲爱的！"因此，到了那句歌
词时，我把目光移开了。"你死我……"砰！我回头看着她，反正她没有死。她很喜欢，
而且笑得合不拢嘴。

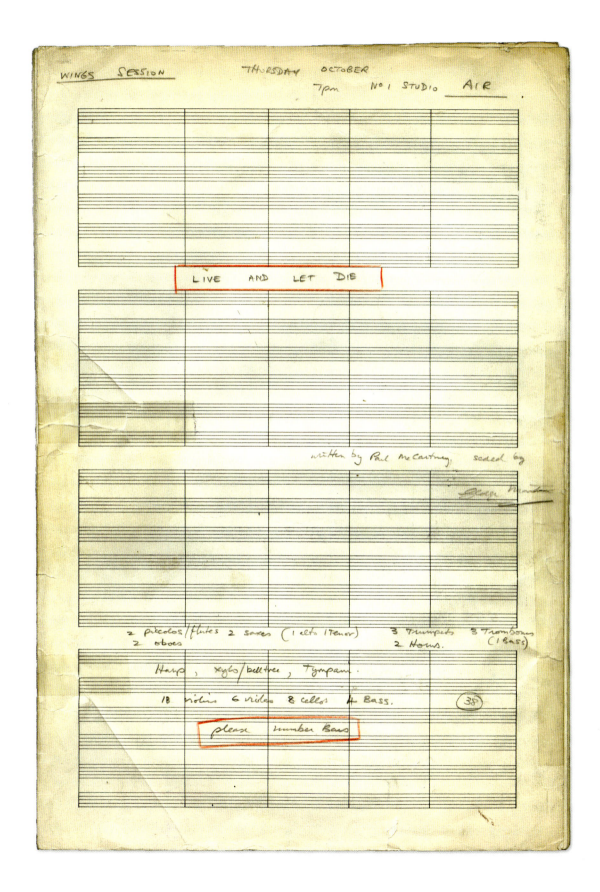

WINGS SESSION   THURSDAY OCTOBER

7pm   N°1 STUDIO   AIR .

LIVE   AND   LET   DIE

written by Paul McCartney, scored by

George Martin

2 piccolos/flutes 2 saxes (1 alto 1 tenor)   3 Trumpets 3 Trombones
2 oboes   2 Horns.   (1 Bass)

Harp , xylo/belltree , Tympani.

18 violins 6 violas 8 cellos 4 Bass.   (35)

please number Bars

429

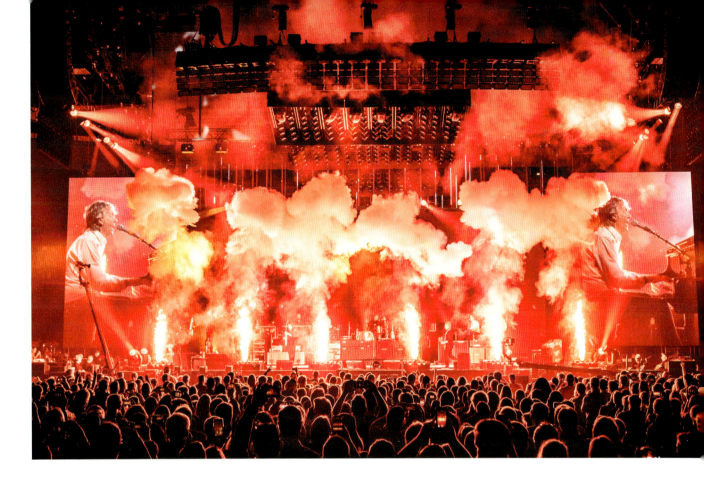

London Town
伦敦城

作　者	WRITERS	保罗·麦卡特尼和丹尼·莱恩　Paul McCartney and Denny Laine
艺术家	ARTIST	羽翼乐队　Wings
录　音	RECORDED	伦敦阿比路录音棚　Abbey Road Studios, London
发　行	RELEASED	《伦敦城》，1978 年　*London Town*, 1978
		单曲，1978 年　Single, 1978

Walking down the sidewalk on a purple afternoon
I was accosted by a barker playing a simple tune
Upon his flute
Toot toot toot toot

Silver rain was falling down
Upon the dirty ground of
London Town

People pass me by on my imaginary street
Ordinary people it's impossible to meet
Holding conversations that are always incomplete
Well I don't know

Oh where are there places to go?
Someone somewhere has to know
I don't know

Out of work again the actor entertains his wife
With the same old stories of his ordinary life
Maybe he exaggerates the trouble and the strife
Well I don't know

Oh where are there places to go?
Someone somewhere has to know

Crawling down the pavement on a
    Sunday afternoon
I was arrested by a rozzer wearing a pink balloon
About his foot
Toot toot toot toot

Silver rain was falling down
Upon the dirty ground of
London Town

Someone somewhere has to know
Silver rain was falling down
Upon the dirty ground of
London Town

　　我的歌曲经常是这样创作的：我是一位水彩画家，我只是画出一个场景。在这首歌中，我在一个紫色的下午走在人行道上，被一个酒吧招待搭讪，他用笛子演奏着简单的曲调——"嘟嘟嘟嘟"。我只是疏导着我的幻想，说着："好的,我们现在要做什么？"

　　我知道，"sidewalk"是美国的叫法。现在看着这首歌时，我在想："为什么不用'pavement'[1]？"不过我喜欢这个词。在音乐方面，美国在我的思维过程中占据了很大的位置。那时我娶了一位美国女人，现在娶的也是一位美国女人。我经常待在纽约。很明显，我知道我有机会选择"sidewalk"或者"pavement"，不过"pavement"恰好冒出来，而我想，"是的，就是那个。"

　　"Ordinary people it's impossible to meet"（不会相识的普通人）有双重含义。几乎不会遇见任何人，不会认识新的人。你也可以说不会遇见你认识的人。"The dirty ground of London Town"（伦敦城泥泞的地上）——那是布鲁斯式的东西，同时也是民谣式的。于是，现在，在这个画面中，人群和我擦肩而过，它变得有些哲学意味，我意识到我们在生命中彼此擦肩而过，就像夜航的船只。从关于人群的哲学角度出发——"Oh where are there places to go? / Someone somewhere has to know"（噢有什么地方可以去？/ 某个地方某个人一定知道），接下来"Out of work again"（再次失业），我们又有了一条故事线。演员给妻子讲述他们平凡生活的故事，这几乎像是在挖苦他：他失业了，他娱乐他的妻子而不是娱乐大众。

　　一首歌里穿插着两条平行线。你设置了一个模式，而不必紧随着它，不过紧随着也不错。比如说，在《无处不在》中，模式是通过歌曲名来表现的。那三个词在歌曲

上图：伦敦，1978年。　　　　　1　"sidewalk"和"pavement"均指"人行道"，前者为美式英语，后者为英式英语。

的特定地方按照顺序出现，使故事进行下去。所以，在《伦敦城》中，鉴于之前我走上人行道，如今我做了这样的变化：我在一个阳光灿烂的下午在人行道上爬行。这是同样的韵脚模式，不过现在故事往前进行了。听上去像是我喝醉了，然后我被一个腿上绑着粉色气球的警察逮捕了，而这只是胡闹，不过你也可以读懂，粉色可能意味着某种同性恋式的东西。"Rozzer"是对警察或条子的另一种称呼，不过"嘟嘟嘟嘟"指的是可卡因。这就是羽翼乐队的自由：我可以抛出一段超现实的歌词，因为我喜欢绘画中的超现实主义，比如马格里特，自从我在1960年代了解他的作品之后，他对我产生了很大的影响。我喜欢这样的自由，能够毫无理由地在一首歌里抛出这个。

　　无论什么时候，你提到药物，就和一群人联系到了一起；你有点像是在说你了解他们在做什么，而这并不意味着你也在做同样的事情，或者你提倡这样的事情，但是，你是在观察一个秘密的小团体，秘密的一小群人。当约翰和我写下"I'd love to turn you on"[1]，我们知道这个短句完全无害，但我们也知道这会吸引提莫西·利里[2]一群人。这是有点顽皮的、中学男生式的东西。有一些老歌也提到过它——科尔·波特的《我从你身上得到了乐趣》（I Get a Kick Out of You），或者《可卡因布鲁斯》（Cocaine Blues）（被约翰尼·卡什和鲍勃·迪伦翻唱过）。这是某种点点头、眨眨眼的暗示，因为当你谈论一个家伙用笛子吹奏出"嘟嘟嘟嘟"时，那就是笛子的声音，你用的完全是普通的词句；不过你同样开了一点小玩笑。

1　"我希望让你神魂颠倒"，出自《生命中的一天》（A Day in the Life）。
2　提莫西·利里（Timothy Leary，1920—1996），美国心理学家，因公开支持合法使用LSD而饱受争议。

上左：琳达为《伦敦城》手写的歌词，出现在单曲海报中。

右图：南希，纽约，2019年。

The Long and Winding Road
漫长而曲折的路

作 者	**WRITERS**	保罗·麦卡特尼和约翰·列侬　Paul McCartney and John Lennon
艺术家	**ARTIST**	披头士乐队　The Beatles
录 音	**RECORDED**	伦敦苹果录音棚及阿比路录音棚　Apple Studio, London and Abbey Road Studios, London
发 行	**RELEASED**	《顺其自然》，1970 年　*Let It Be*, 1970
		美国单曲，1970 年　US single, 1970

The long and winding road that leads to your door
Will never disappear, I've seen that road before
It always leads me here, lead me to your door

The wild and windy night that the rain washed away
Has left a pool of tears crying for the day
Why leave me standing here?
Let me know the way

Many times I've been alone and many times I've cried
Anyway you'll never know the many ways I've tried
But still they lead me back to the long winding road
You left me standing here a long, long time ago
Don't keep me waiting here, lead me to your door

从位于阿盖尔郡琴泰岬半岛的农场卧室窗户望出去，我可以看到一条遥遥通向远处主干道的蜿蜒小路。那是你进城的路。准确地说，是去坎贝尔敦的路。

1966 年，我买下了高公园农场。那是一次特意远离的逃避，这座农舍实际上是被遗弃的，如果琳达没有说我们应该把它修好的话，它可能会一直这样。直到两年后，这条远远的，蜿蜒道路的形象才完全发展成为一首歌。它于 1970 年发行，成为披头士乐队第二十支美国冠军单曲。这也是我们最后一支冠军单曲。

这首歌的迷人之处是，它似乎以非常强大的方式产生了共鸣。对那些当时在场的人来说，似乎有一种极度悲伤同时也抱有希望的双重联想，特别是在那条道路"leads to your door / Will never disappear"（通往你的门口 / 永远不会消失）的断言中。

通常当我写一首歌时，我自己会做一些消失的把戏。比如说，我想象它已经被其他人录过 —— 在这个例子中是雷·查尔斯。像往常一样，我最不想写的是保罗·麦卡特尼的歌。这是一种保持新鲜感的策略。

我画画时也有类似的经历。多年来，我就是不能让自己沉浸于绘画，尽管我喜欢画画，而且有一点天赋。我甚至在学校里获得了一个小小的艺术奖。但是一想到这张空白的画布，就让我气馁。然后我碰巧在威廉·德·库宁的工作室遇到了他。他给了我们一张小图片，我鼓足勇气说："比尔，这是什么？"我猜你不应该问一位抽象表现主义者这样的问题！不过他是个很有耐心的人，他说："哦，我不知道。看上去像一个沙发。"而我意识到，所有这些关于一幅画也许该有什么意义的担忧根本就不是问题。

于是，我出去买了一大堆画布、颜料、画笔，以及其他东西，然后开始画了大约 500 幅画。我想象一个开餐馆的朋友让我为他的壁龛画一幅画。所以，我可以想象正在为路易吉[1]的壁龛画一幅画 —— 没什么压力。或者，当我调色时，我变成了一个确信无疑的"混合迪尼先生"。这都是小伎俩。

在写歌方面我也有类似的伎俩。在最初的日子里，我们假装是巴迪·霍利，然后我们写得像摩城，接着我们像鲍勃·迪伦那样写歌。

你总是可以引用其他人。当你创作的时候，你可以戴上面具和斗篷，这样可以消除很多焦虑。它让你自由。你会发现当你完成它时，它无论如何也不是一首雷·查尔斯的歌；那是你的。这首歌有它自己的特点。这条路并非通向坎贝尔敦，而是通往你从未想到的地方。

1　路易吉·诺诺（Luigi Nono，1924—1990），意大利前卫作曲家。

苏格兰，1969 年。

通常当我写一首歌时，我自己会做一些消失的把戏。
比如说，我想象它已经被其他人录过 ——
在这个例子中是雷·查尔斯。
像往常一样，我最不想写的是保罗·麦卡特尼的歌。
这是一种保持新鲜感的策略。

Love Me Do

爱我吧

作　者	WRITERS	保罗·麦卡特尼和约翰·列侬　Paul McCartney and John Lennon
艺术家	ARTIST	披头士乐队　The Beatles
录　音	RECORDED	伦敦阿比路录音棚　Abbey Road Studios, London
发　行	RELEASED	英国单曲，1962 年　UK single, 1962
		《请让我快乐》，1963 年　*Please Please Me*, 1963
		《介绍……披头士乐队》，1964 年　*Introducing... The Beatles, 1964*
		美国单曲，1964 年　US single, 1964

Love, love me do
You know I love you
I'll always be true
So please
Love me do
Whoa love me do

Love, love me do
You know I love you
I'll always be true
So please
Love me do
Whoa love me do

Someone to love
Somebody new
Someone to love
Someone like you

Love, love me do
You know I love you
I'll always be true
So please
Love me do
Oh love me do

Love, love me do
You know I love you
I'll always be true
So please
Love me do
Whoa love me do
Yeah love me do
Whoa love me do

对我和约翰影响最大的是埃弗利兄弟。直到今天，我依然觉得他们是最伟大的。他们与众不同。你听过理发店四重唱，听过埃弗利姐妹——三个女孩——你听过所有这些。不过只有两个男孩，两个很帅的男孩？所以你崇拜他们，我们希望像他们一样。

然后，我们十五六岁的时候，巴迪·霍利出现了。巴迪的样子符合约翰戴眼镜的实际情况，约翰有了一个完美的理由把他的眼镜从口袋里掏出来重新戴上。巴迪·霍利也是一位词曲作者、主音吉他手及歌手；猫王不是创作者或主音吉他手，他只是一位歌手；杜安·艾迪是一位吉他手但不是歌手。而巴迪身兼以上所有，还有那个名字，蟋蟀乐队。我们也希望有双重含义的名字。

"披头士"这个名字的实际来源被笼罩在某种神秘中，但我记得我们努力找到一个像"蟋蟀"那样有双重含义的名字；你可以理解为板球运动，也可以理解为小昆虫蟋蟀。如果我们能找到一种同样有双重含义的小昆虫会怎么样？当你把"Beatles"从文本中抽离出来，并把它想象成只是一种昆虫，这并不能立刻吸引人。但是现在，经过了这么漫长的一段时间，你完全接受了它，你甚至不会联想到令人毛骨悚然的爬虫。

《爱我吧》是我们在福特林路 20 号写出的一批歌曲之一。在那里，沿着一条花园小径上去，经过我爸爸的薰衣草篱笆，到达前门，我爸爸在那里种了一棵花楸树，那是他最喜欢的树。你可以穿过前门，进入门左边的一个小客厅，然后你可以穿过客厅

上图：披头士乐队，利物浦，1962 年。

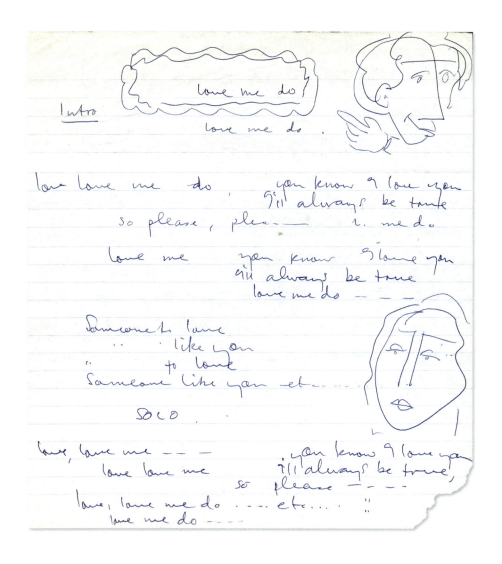

去后面的餐厅，那里是我们年轻时创作了大部分作品的地方。我一次又一次地想象着它。约翰写出了一个连复段，一小段口琴即兴。它如此简单。这轻而易举，这是一首轻声许愿的歌。不过桥段里有着强烈的渴望感，它与那段口琴合在一起，以某种方式触动灵魂。

我觉得，我们作为披头士的形象和能量，只有四个人在一起时才会产生这样的效果。《爱我吧》不是主打金曲，它只是悄悄地进入排行榜。自从 1960 年的夏天以来，我们已经演遍全国，所以我们在英国有很多歌迷。我们的声音非常新鲜，那是会被人注意到的声音。我们的形象也很新鲜。

没有人的外表和我们看起来一样。当然，不久之后，所有人看起来都和我们一样。

"BUDDY AT 60"
by Jeff Cummins
Commissioned by Paul McCartney

Lovely Rita

可爱的丽塔

作　者　WRITERS　　　保罗·麦卡特尼和约翰·列侬　Paul McCartney and John Lennon
艺术家　ARTIST　　　　披头士乐队　The Beatles
录　音　RECORDED　　伦敦阿比路录音棚　Abbey Road Studios, London
发　行　RELEASED　　《佩珀军士孤独之心俱乐部乐队》，1967 年　Sgt. Pepper's Lonely Hearts Club Band, 1967

Lovely Rita, meter maid
Lovely Rita, meter maid

Lovely Rita, meter maid
Nothing can come between us
When it gets dark I tow your heart away

Standing by a parking meter
When I caught a glimpse of Rita
Filling in a ticket in her little white book
In a cap she looked much older
And the bag across her shoulder
Made her look a little like a military man

Lovely Rita, meter maid
May I enquire discreetly
When are you free to take some tea with me, Rita?

Took her out and tried to win her
Had a laugh and over dinner
Told her I would really like to see her again
Got the bill and Rita paid it
Took her home I nearly made it
Sitting on the sofa with a sister or two

Lovely Rita, meter maid
Where would I be without you?
Give us a wink and make me think of you

Lovely Rita, meter maid
Lovely Rita, meter maid

　　在那个落后的时代，没有人喜欢泊车员或者开违停罚单的女交警。所以，写一首关于爱上一个没有其他人喜欢的女交警的歌，本身就很有趣。在波特兰广场，有一个特别的女交警，丽塔就是以她为蓝本的。她看上去有点像军人。我知道这听起来令人不快，不过那些女交警向来不好看。你从来没听过有人说："天哪，那是一个魅力惊人的泊车员。"

　　无论如何，我瞥见了波特兰广场中国大使馆对面的丽塔。她正在往她的白色小本子上填表。帽子，还有搭在她肩上的包。这是纯粹的观察，就像画出空气中的光线。我以前说过，现在我要再说一遍：成功写歌的秘诀是画一幅图像的能力。

　　这幅图像的复杂因素之一就是叙述者如何看待丽塔。你可能还记得她的追求者拿到了账单，但丽塔付了钱。在那个时代，让女士付钱会被认为不礼貌。与此相反的是，叙述者似乎对他和丽塔最终与一两个姐妹坐在沙发上的事实有点恼火。这段歌词表明，他可能很想和她单独在一起，而不是让一两个姐妹当电灯泡。当然，另一种含义是不仅有可能和丽塔"做"，还有可能和拖在后面的一两个姐妹"做"。"When it gets dark I tow your heart away"（天黑时我拖走你的心）这句歌词里的这种模棱两可已经勾起了我的兴趣。

　　最终，我无法完全抑制我顽皮的弱点。比如说，在短语"Give us a wink"（给我们递个眼色）中，递个眼色可能会让人联想到"挤眉弄眼"之类的概念，但我承认这也是一种委婉说法。我们总是喜欢在歌里加入"finger pie"（手指派）[1] 这类词，你可以在《便士巷》里找到这个。我们知道人们会懂。英国广播公司不会禁止这样的歌曲，因为他们不能确定你说"Give us a wink and make me think of you"（给我们递个眼色让我思念你）时，究竟是什么意思。一想到英国广播公司，那个令人尊敬的堡垒，也在波特兰广场，离我第一次看见丽塔的中国大使馆不远，就让我发笑。

上图：在伦敦阿比路录音棚。

1　利物浦俚语，含有性意味，意指亲密的爱抚。

右图：约翰·列侬的《可爱的丽塔》歌词手稿及保罗的注释。写在伦敦圆形剧场"百万伏特声光"派对邀请函背面，1967 年。

I'm real, in a world that inte
And sunlight is filtered away
of our misfortune.

I'm grey, in a ~~day~~ that is cha
And memory means living righ
of our misfortun

BINDER   EDWARDS   VAUGHAN

invite you to share a new experience.

London's first Light and Sound Show, at the

Round House.

The first showing is on the 28th January from

8:30 pm. Please come in something white or

wear a sheet.

This admits two.

HARANHURST LTD. 13 WIGMORE ST. LONDON W1 LAN 3824 N. SHULMAN, Secy.

to grey
the veils

t night
ng rules

②

Standing by a parking meter
when I caught a glimpse of Rita
filling in a ticket in her
little white book.

① Lovely Rita, meter maid
Nothing can come between us
when it gets dark ~~night~~ I'll
~~tow~~ your heart away.

③ in a cap she looked ~~so stunning~~ much older
~~with~~ a bag across her shoulder
made her look a little like a military man.

④ Lovely Rita ~~watermaid~~
May I inquire discretely
when ~~are you are~~ free to take some tea with me
what would I do without you

449

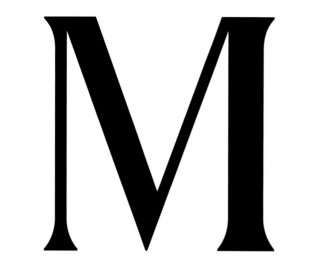

M

Magneto and Titanium Man
万磁王和钛甲人

作 者 WRITERS　　保罗·麦卡特尼和琳达·麦卡特尼　Paul McCartney and Linda McCartney

艺术家 ARTIST　　羽翼乐队　Wings

录 音 RECORDED　　新奥尔良海圣录音棚　Sea-Saint Recording Studio, New Orleans

发 行 RELEASED　　《金星和火星》，1975 年　*Venus and Mars*, 1975

《金星和火星》/《摇滚演出》B 面单曲，1975 年　B-side of 'Venus and Mars' / 'Rock Show' single, 1975

Well I was talking last night
Magneto and Titanium Man
We were talking about you, babe
They said

You was involved in a robbery
That was due to happen
At a quarter to three
In the main street

I didn't believe them
Magneto and Titanium Man
But when the Crimson Dynamo
Finally assured me, well I knew

You was involved in a robbery
That was due to happen
At a quarter to three
In the main street

So we went out
Magneto and Titanium Man
And the Crimson Dynamo
Came along for the ride

We went to town with the library
And we swung all over that
Long tall bank
In the main street

Well there she were
And to my despair
She's a five-star criminal
Breaking the code

Magneto said, now the time has come
To gather our forces and run
Oh no
This can't be so

And then it occurred to me
You couldn't be bad
Magneto was mad
Titanium too
And the Crimson Dynamo
Just couldn't cut it no more
You were the law

　　1975 年，大约在写《万磁王和钛甲人》的那段时间，我读了很多漫画书，我现在依然对漫画很感兴趣，那是真正的艺术。完成这些插画需要一些技巧，更别说洞察力和想象力了。所以，我觉得把这两本漫画书中的人物写进一首歌里是个好主意。万磁王是 X 战警的主要对手，迈克尔·法斯宾德在最近的漫威系列电影里扮演了他，钛甲人是钢铁侠的敌人之一，绯红机甲也在歌里出现，他也是坏人。所以我们有了三个哥们儿，而我架构了一个故事，也许可以成为这些漫画书的其中一本。

　　1970 年代中期同时标志着华丽摇滚的兴起——譬如大卫·鲍伊、暴龙乐队[1]。相比从前一支乐队只是站在舞台上简单地演奏乐器，我们进入了一个演出需要用到剧院灯光和大量舞台效果的时代。平克·弗洛伊德这样的乐队举办了巨大的、场面惊人的演出。所以当我们在台上表演这首歌时，我们背后的屏幕上有一个巨大的漫画角色万磁王和钛甲人的画面。

　　在我看来，这些漫画人物画得非常好。我一直觉得波普艺术和漫画艺术近乎疯狂。在学生还要读约翰·德莱顿[2]这类诗人作品的时代，我在学校里研究过约翰·德莱顿，而且总是被他的这几句诗击中：

　　　　伟大的智者必与疯狂为伍
　　　　细枝末节则划分其边界

　　波普艺术在 1960 年代确实到达了顶峰。罗伊·利希滕斯坦[3]在创作漫画书里的人物，彼得·布莱克[4]在画他的摔跤手，而披头士贡献了《佩珀军士》。这有很多面——那真是同一个对话的一部分，人们带来了你称之为工人阶级的快乐、工人阶级的主题、汤罐头之类的东西，并且在艺术画廊和美术馆里占有一席之地。

1　暴龙乐队（T. Rex），英国华丽摇滚乐队，活跃于 1960 年代及 1970 年代。
2　约翰·德莱顿（John Dryden，1631—1700），英国古典主义诗人。下文所引诗歌原句为："Great wits are sure to madness allied / And thin partitions do their bounds divide"。
3　罗伊·利希滕斯坦（Roy Lichtenstein，1923—1997），美国波普艺术家。
4　彼得·布莱克（Peter Blake，1932— ），英国波普艺术家。

上图：保罗与彼得·布莱克及克丽茜·布莱克（Chrissy Blake）。伦敦，1985 年。

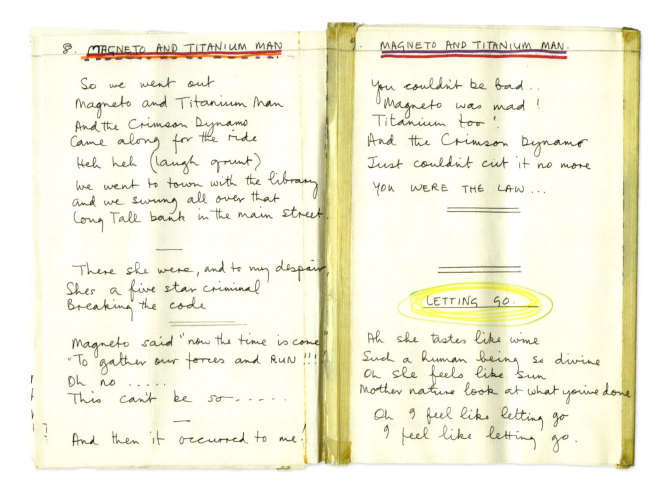

So we went out
Magneto and Titanium Man
And the Crimson Dynamo
Came along for the ride
Heh heh (laugh grunt)
we went to town with the library
and we swing all over that
Long Tall bank in the main street.

―――

There she were, and to my despair,
Shes a five star criminal
Breaking the code

―――

Magneto said "now the time is come"
"To gather our forces and RUN !!!"
Oh no . . . . .
This can't be so . . . . .

―――

And then it occurred to me !

You couldn't be bad . .
Magneto was mad !
Titanium too !
And the Crimson Dynamo
Just couldn't cut it no more
YOU WERE THE LAW . . .

―――

―――

LETTING GO.

Ah she tastes like wine
Such a human being so divine
Oh She feels like Sun
Mother nature look at what you've done

Oh I feel like letting go
I feel like letting go.

对我来说，那是一个迷人的时代，能够见到这些艺术家，看到他们的作品，甚至和他们中的一些人一起工作。在利物浦读书时，大约在十岁或者十一岁，我曾获得一个小小的散文奖。奖品是一本现代艺术图书，很可爱的一本书。它吸引了我，所以当我生活在伦敦并有了一点钱时，我会去画廊买一些小艺术品。我在 1966 年遇见了罗伯特·弗雷泽（Robert Fraser），他是一家画廊的老板，对我的艺术影响相当大。我们最终成为合作者。不之后，他在《佩珀军士》上帮了我们很大的忙，介绍了很多人给我，譬如彼得·布莱克和理查德·汉密尔顿[1]，我们经常和他们一起闲逛或者去俱乐部。

大约在同一段时间，我通过罗伯特认识了安迪·沃霍尔，他常来伦敦，我们会偶尔在一家名叫"巴格达之家"的地方一起吃饭，那里的咖喱很不错。有一天晚上，我们一起回了我在北伦敦的家。我们为安迪举办了一场他自己电影的放映会，《帝国大厦》（Empire），他几年前拍摄的电影，只有一个摄像机对着帝国大厦建筑的镜头，长达八个小时。我们都看了。我们大多是走来走去，不过我是和安迪一起看的。他说话不多，所以不太容易了解他，而且电影里的谈话也很少，所以那确实说不上是热闹的一夜。

所以，这首歌是我向漫画成为高雅艺术的致意。

―――――――

1　理查德·汉密尔顿（Richard Hamilton，1922—2011），英国艺术家，被称为"波普艺术之父"。

保罗与罗伯特·弗雷泽。
伦敦，1981年。

我在 1966 年遇见了罗伯特·弗雷泽，他是一家画廊的老板，
对我的艺术影响相当大。我们最终成为合作者。
不久后，他在《佩珀军士》上帮了我们很大的忙，
介绍了很多人给我，譬如彼得·布莱克和理查德·汉密尔顿，
我们经常和他们一起闲逛或者去俱乐部。

上图：1975 年，《万磁王和钛甲人》
作为《金星和火星》/《摇滚演出》
的 B 面单曲发行。绯红机甲这个
角色同时出现在封套和歌词中。

右图："羽翼乐队穿越世界"巡演，
底特律，1976 年。

Martha My Dear

我亲爱的玛萨

作　者　WRITERS　　　　保罗·麦卡特尼和约翰·列侬　Paul McCartney and John Lennon

艺术家　ARTIST　　　　　披头士乐队　The Beatles

录　音　RECORDED　　　伦敦三叉戟录音棚　Trident Studios, London

发　行　RELEASED　　　《披头士》，1968 年　*The Beatles*, 1968

Martha my dear
Though I spend my days in conversation
Please remember me
Martha my love
Don't forget me
Martha my dear

Hold your head up, you silly girl
Look what you've done
When you find yourself in the thick of it
Help yourself to a bit of what is all around you, silly girl

Take a good look around you
Take a good look, you're bound to see
That you and me were meant to be
For each other, silly girl

Hold your hand out, you silly girl
See what you've done
When you find yourself in the thick of it
Help yourself to a bit of what is all around you, silly girl

Martha my dear
You have always been my inspiration
Please be good to me
Martha my love
Don't forget me
Martha my dear

因为我的爸爸妈妈每天都要出去工作，我和弟弟迈克要去上学，所以没人能照顾一条狗。我记得有一次，我们听说旁边那条街上有一些小狗待人收养，便跑到街角，那里有一窝小狗。我们挑了一只非常可爱的回家，但妈妈说我们不能留着它，我们非常沮丧，十分受打击。

长大并加入披头士后，我在伦敦有了自己的房子。不仅如此，我还请了位管家来照料房子。现在已经可以养狗了。我一直喜欢英国古代牧羊犬的样子，于是我去了位于米尔顿凯恩斯的一个地方，离北伦敦大约一小时路程，挑选了这只小狗。我给她起名叫玛萨。

我相当确定我被英国古代牧羊犬吸引，完全是因为那些多乐士油漆的广告。在1961年，多乐士开始用英国古代牧羊犬作为他们的品牌吉祥物。承认这个很难，不过我确实是个广告迷。多乐士小狗看上去可爱极了。这不是唯一的我因为所谓的植入式广告而做的选择。比如说，之前我提过我给自己买了一辆阿斯顿·马丁，是因为我看了第一部007电影，对里面的车印象深刻。

不管怎么说，我有了玛萨，她是一条可爱的小狗。我很喜欢她。让人意外的是约翰开始对我极有同情心。当他来我家看见我和玛萨一起玩的时候，我看得出，他也喜欢她。约翰是一个非常有戒备心的人，他的全部才智有一部分也是因此而来，他的成长很艰难，他的父亲离家出走，叔叔去世，妈妈被一场交通事故夺去了生命。我认识他的时候，他总是爱讽刺和挖苦。我也有可能会是那样。我希望，我也能用这样的方式来应对我妈妈的去世。我们两个之间都巧妙地说些令人难堪的话。但是看着我和玛萨在一起，放下了我的戒备心，突然之间，他就开始友好地对待我，就这样，他也放下了他的戒备心。

好玩的是，那个时候听这首歌的人都不知道玛萨是一条狗。实际上，随着歌曲的进行，玛萨变成了一个人。碰巧，我的一个亲戚来伦敦告诉我一些他婚外恋的事情。也许是想寻求一些慰藉。如果你想想，会发现在1968年，我代表着自由的气息。现在我微微脱离了这个圈子。这位亲戚可以向我袒露心声——对这个爱传闲话的利物浦家庭的其他成员倾诉是不人可能的。我是唯一知道这首歌说的是某个人的婚外恋的人，这让类似"When you find yourself in the thick of it"（当你发现自己深陷其中）这样的歌词有了一层感伤的意味。

左图：保罗与玛萨及埃迪。
伦敦，1968 年。

上图：保罗与玛萨。
伦敦，1969 年。

下图：录制《我亲爱的玛萨》。
伦敦三叉戟录音棚，1968 年。

Maxwell's Silver Hammer
麦克斯韦的银锤

作 者 **WRITERS**	保罗·麦卡特尼和约翰·列侬	Paul McCartney and John Lennon
艺术家 **ARTIST**	披头士乐队	The Beatles
录 音 **RECORDED**	伦敦阿比路录音棚	Abbey Road Studios, London
发 行 **RELEASED**	《阿比路》，1969 年	*Abbey Road*, 1969

Joan was quizzical, studied pataphysical
Science in the home
Late nights all alone with a test tube
Oh oh oh oh
Maxwell Edison majoring in medicine
Calls her on the phone
Can I take you out to the pictures, Joan?
But as she's getting ready to go
A knock comes on the door

Bang bang Maxwell's silver hammer
Came down upon her head
Clang clang Maxwell's silver hammer
Made sure that she was dead

Back in school again, Maxwell plays the fool again
Teacher gets annoyed
Wishing to avoid an unpleasant scene
She tells Max to stay when the class has gone away
So he waits behind
Writing fifty times I must not be so
Oh oh oh
But when she turns her back on the boy
He creeps up from behind

Bang bang Maxwell's silver hammer
Came down upon her head
Clang clang Maxwell's silver hammer
Made sure that she was dead

PC Thirty-One said, we've caught a dirty one
Maxwell stands alone
Painting testimonial pictures
Oh oh oh oh
Rose and Valerie screaming from the gallery
Say he must go free
The judge does not agree and he tells them so
Oh oh oh
But as the words are leaving his lips
A noise comes from behind

Bang bang Maxwell's silver hammer
Came down upon his head
Clang clang Maxwell's silver hammer
Made sure that he was dead

Silver hammer man

开着此前提到的阿斯顿·马丁沿着高速公路从伦敦到利物浦，我调着收音机想听点什么，碰巧听到了英国广播公司三台制作的《愚比龟》。它在 1965 年 12 月 21 日首次播出，1966 年 1 月 10 日重播。这是法国剧作家阿尔弗雷德·贾里的三部戏剧之一（其中最著名的是《乌布王》），副标题为"一场荒诞玄学的盛会"。"荒诞玄学"是贾里编造的一个无意义的词，用来取笑目空一切的学院派。在这首歌中把"quizzical"（怪人）和"pataphysical"（荒诞玄学）押韵时，我激动到发抖。这种机会可遇不可求！人们不一定知道什么是"荒诞玄学"，我喜欢这一点，所以我故意把歌词弄得有点晦涩。

麦克斯韦可能派生自电磁学先驱詹姆斯·克拉克·麦克斯韦，爱迪生显然指涉托马斯·爱迪生；他们是两种不同类型的发明家。这里有意思的部分在于爱迪生发明了电灯泡和留声机，而我们制作了一张留声机唱片。说到灯泡，它们总是会像小钟一样"叮"的一声，特别是当那些押韵的灵感出现时：Edison / medicine（"爱迪生"和"医学"），Valerie / gallery（"瓦莱丽"和"旁听席"）。

麦克斯韦是一个连环杀手，他的锤子不是普通的家用锤子，而是，正如我想象的那样，是医生用来敲打你的膝盖的那种锤子。不过不是橡胶制品，而是银制的。

这首歌同时提及了童谣的世界，里面的人们总是被砍头 —— 当然，还有《爱丽丝梦游仙境》中的红桃皇后，她总是说，"砍下他们的头！"1966 年，两个摩尔人杀人犯伊恩·布雷迪（Ian Brady）和迈拉·辛德利（Myra Hindley）因犯下连环杀人案被终身监禁。这个案件很有可能也浮现在我的脑海里，因为这是英国的头条新闻。

我非常喜欢这首歌，但录制这首歌花了很长时间，其他人都对我很生气。录音期间，正好穆格合成器的发明者罗伯特·穆格来参观阿比路，我对这些新声音能做些什么很是着迷。这就是它比我们的大部分歌曲花费了更长时间的原因之一。与今天的标准相比并不疯狂 —— 大约是三天 —— 但按照当时的标准，已经很长了。这首歌也是一种"突然出现问题"的比拟，大约就在这个时候，我开始发现我们的商业事务中发生了一些事情。录音总是很好的，因为无论我们有怎样的个人麻烦,无论在商业领域发生了什么，我们坐下来做一首歌的那一刻，大家的状态都很好。直到最后，在录音棚里一起工作总是充满了快乐。

所以我们就这样，录制了一首《麦克斯韦的银锤》这样的歌曲，并且知道我们永远没有机会表演它。这种可能性已经过去了，就像麦克斯韦的受害者之一那样被击中头部。砰砰。

Back in school again Maxwell plays the fool again
Teacher gets annoyed.
Wishing to avoid an unpleasant scene
She tells Max to stay when the class has
gone away so he waits behind, no no no
writing 50 times I must not be so, oh oh oh
~~And as she turns her back to the board,~~
~~But when she turns her back~~ on the boy
he creeps up from behind. - - - - -
Bang Bang — Maxwells . . . . .

P.C. thirty one
says " we caught a dirty one"
Maxwell stands alone
Painting testimonial pictures - o oh oh oh
Rose & Valerie, screaming from the gallery
say he must go free,
The judge cannot agree and he tells them so,
But as the words are leaving his lips,
a noise comes from behind.

Maxwell's Silver Hammer

① Joan was quizzical
Studied pataphysical
Science in the home
Late nights all alone with a test tube
Oh Ho ho ho

Maxwell Edison majoring in medicine
Calls her on the phone
Can I take you out to the pictures
Joa — oa — an now
But as she's getting ready to go,
a knock comes on the door . . . .
Bang Bang Silver Hammer
Maxwells Silver Hammer

② Back in school again,
Maxwell plays the fool again
teacher gets annoyed
~~Now on she avoid him third time?~~
~~Wishing to avoid an~~
How can she avoid unpleasant scene

左图：演奏迷你穆格合成器。
拉各斯，1973 年。

464

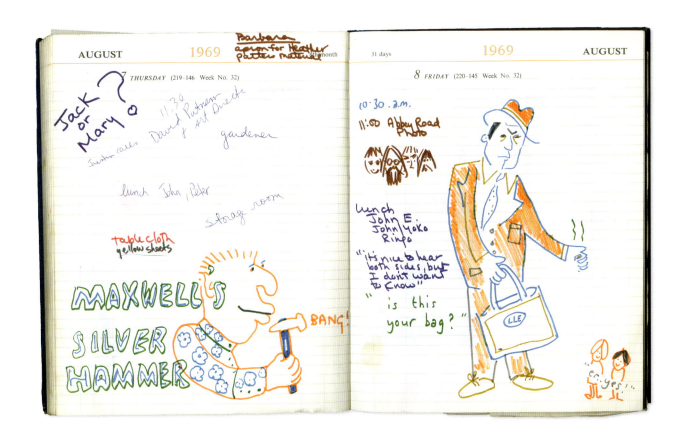

日记条目，包括《阿比路》专辑封套拍摄时间，1969 年 8 月。

所以我们就这样，
录制了一首《麦克斯韦的银锤》这样的歌曲，
并且知道我们永远没有机会表演它。
这种可能性已经过去了，
就像麦克斯韦的受害者之一那样被击中头部。砰砰。

Maybe I'm Amazed
也许我惊讶

作　者 WRITER	保罗·麦卡特尼 Paul McCartney
艺术家 ARTIST	保罗·麦卡特尼 Paul McCartney
录　音 RECORDED	伦敦阿比路录音棚 Abbey Road Studios, London
发　行 RELEASED	《麦卡特尼》，1970 年 *McCartney*, 1970

Baby, I'm amazed at the way you love me all the time
And maybe I'm afraid of the way I love you
Maybe I'm amazed at the way you pulled me out of time
You hung me on a line
Maybe I'm amazed at the way I really need you

Baby, I'm a man
Maybe I'm a lonely man who's in the middle of something
That he doesn't really understand
Baby, I'm a man
And maybe you're the only woman who could ever help me
Baby, won't you help me to understand

Maybe I'm amazed at the way you're with me all the time
Maybe I'm afraid of the way I leave you
Maybe I'm amazed at the way you help me sing my song
You right me when I'm wrong
And maybe I'm amazed at the way I really need you

据说这是丽莎·明妮莉[1]最喜欢的我的歌。我以为她会更喜欢一些有点歌谣化的歌曲，但是她真的喜欢这首歌。回溯到那个时代，在1960年代末，当时琳达和我刚刚住在一起。在很大程度上是因为琳达想要逃离纽约社会——公园大道和斯卡斯代尔的束缚——而我想要逃离披头士将要面对的事情。我渴望逃离，她也渴望逃离。所以我们感觉我们两个都在将对方"推离时间"。

尽管这首歌是在披头士解散之后很快写出来的，它仍然被署在列侬-麦卡特尼的名下，其实不应该是这样。这是我的第一首个人歌曲，但是囿于合约，它在发行时用了这个署名。那很让人生气。

实际上，写这首歌时琳达和我可能已经结婚了，因为现在我能勾勒出坐在一架可爱的黑色斯坦威钢琴前的场景，那是在我们婚礼之后收到的。有一天我弹着它，而这首歌就出现了——核心的动机关于内在和外在之间经常会有的分裂。比如说，今天早上我在健身房，看着电视上的女孩们，而我想："噢天哪，我真的不应该这么做，因为我已经结婚了。如果人们知道我脑子里在想什么，我就完蛋了。"你可以想任何事情，于是你确实在想任何事情，然后你的良心会来检查和控制。

我用这作为一个极端的例子，来描述这首歌中发生的某种强烈的、内在的对话。恐惧和孤独的元素非常突出。"Maybe I'm afraid of the way I love you"（也许我担心我爱你的方式）本身就是一个令人不安的想法。

然而琳达确实是我与之对话的人，同时我确实也在处理虚构事物。出现在我歌曲中的角色，都始于自我的想象。我已经不能说再多了。我知道在某些方面，你似乎不能描写同性恋，除非你自己就是个同性恋；你也不能描写亚裔美国人，除非你自己就是亚裔美国人。

我觉得这很蠢。就好像说因为詹姆斯·乔伊斯不是犹太人，他就不应该写利奥波尔德·布卢姆[2]。作为一位作家的重点在于，你应该自由地描写任何东西。事实上，进入一个别人也许感觉不舒服的地方，正是你的工作的一部分。

不管怎么样，这首歌不是用一种传统的方式来呈现一段关系，或者恋爱中可能产生的矛盾。那也许就是丽莎·明妮莉那么喜欢它的原因。它呈现了爱情的脆弱性。

---

1   丽莎·明妮莉（Liza Minelli，1946—），美国歌手、演员。
2   利奥波尔德·布卢姆（Leopold Bloom），詹姆斯·乔伊斯的小说《尤利西斯》中的主人公。

(13) <u>Maybe I'm Amazed</u>

Baby I'm Amazed at the way you
            love me all the time,
   and maybe I'm afraid of the way I love you
Maybe I'm amazed at the way you pulled
   me out of time, hung me on a line
and maybe I'm amazed at the way I really
                        need you.

<u>MIDDLE</u>
      Baby I'm a man, maybe I'm a lonely man
whose in the middle of something
that he doesn't really understand
   Baby I'm a man maybe you're the
only woman who could ever help me,
Baby won't you help me to understand,

   Maybe I'm amazed at the way you're
with me all the time,
+ maybe I'm afraid of the way I leave you.
   maybe I'm amazed at the way you

(13) maybe I'm amazed (cont....)

help me sing my song,
right me when I'm wrong,
and maybe I'm amazed at the way I
                              really need you.

MIDDLE
     Baby I'm a man, (REPEAT,) _ _ _ _ _

(14)   Kreen - Akrore

        — instrumental.

MAYBE I'm amazed

Maybe I'm amazed at the way you
    love me all the time
  Maybe I'm afraid of the way I love you
Baby I'm amazed at the way you pulled me
    out of time
  hung me on a line
  Maybe I'm amazed at the way
    I really need you.

MIDDLE
  Baby I'm a man
    maybe I'm a lonely man
whose in the middle of something
That he doesn't really understand.
  Baby I'm a man
    maybe you're the only woman
  who could ever help me
Baby won't you help me understand . . .

  Maybe I'm amazed at the way you're
    with me all the time,
  Maybe I'm afraid of the way I leave you
maybe I'm amazed at the way you

help me sing my song
right me when I'm wrong
maybe I'm amazed at the way I really
    need you.

middle. Baby I'm a man . . . . .

- - , , , , ,

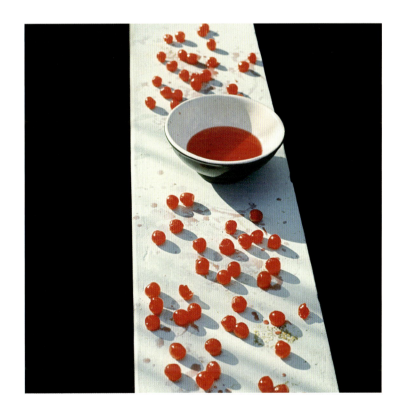

TAKING THINGS EASY.

左图：琳达。安提瓜岛，1969 年。
她拍摄的右手边樱桃后来成为
1970 年的《麦卡特尼》专辑封面。

恐惧和孤独的元素非常突出。
"也许我担心我爱你的方式"本身就是一个令人不安的想法。

Michelle

米歇尔

作　者	WRITERS	保罗·麦卡特尼和约翰·列侬　Paul McCartney and John Lennon
艺术家	ARTIST	披头士乐队　The Beatles
录　音	RECORDED	伦敦阿比路录音棚　Abbey Road Studios, London
发　行	RELEASED	《橡胶灵魂》，1965 年　*Rubber Soul*, 1965

Michelle, ma belle
These are words that go together well
My Michelle

Michelle, ma belle
Sont les mots qui vont très bien ensemble
Très bien ensemble

I love you, I love you, I love you
That's all I want to say
Until I find a way
I will say the only words I know that
    you'll understand

Michelle, ma belle
Sont les mots qui vont très bien ensemble
Très bien ensemble

I need to, I need to, I need to
I need to make you see
Oh what you mean to me
Until I do I'm hoping you will know what I mean
I love you

I want you, I want you, I want you
I think you know by now
I'll get to you somehow
Until I do I'm telling you so you'll understand

Michelle, ma belle
Sont les mots qui vont très bien ensemble
Très bien ensemble

And I will say the only words I know that
    you'll understand
My Michelle

约翰在艺术学校上学，并且年纪稍大，他会带我去艺术学校的派对。我记得在一次派对上，我穿着黑色高领毛衣坐在角落里，试图让这群年长的人产生兴趣。我带着我的木吉他，弹起一首法国风味的曲子随便哼唱。我有点希望有人会觉得我是一个法国人，也许甚至是个法国知识分子。

所以，这就是这首歌如何开始的。回溯记忆，这首伪法国歌曲大抵受到了1959年的金曲，伊迪丝·皮雅芙[1]的《先生》（Milord）的影响。《先生》这首歌有意思的地方是它很怪诞，不像其他歌曲那样可以轻松定义风格。在《先生》里，皮雅芙用了一个老式的技巧，就是在歌曲的过程中放慢速度。我的大脑存储器中想必存下了这段记忆。

另一个元素是乔治·哈里森和我喜欢学习新的和弦，并想办法把它们加进歌里。我们认识一个叫作吉姆·格莱蒂（Jim Gretty）的家伙，他在利物浦的海希吉他店工作。我们挺喜欢去这家店，尽管这意味着我们必须支付记在小本子上的欠款，因为，当然，我们是分期付款买了各自的吉他。吉姆·格莱蒂通常就站在海希吉他店的柜台后面，弹弹吉他，就像乐器店的店员经常做的那样。我们真的很羡慕他的技巧——远胜我们。我们听到他弹的一个特别华丽的和弦，而他也不厌其烦地弹给我们看。我们所知道的F和弦——一个简单的F和弦手型，在指板下面第一品的位置；但是吉姆用他的另外两根手指罩住了上面两根弦第四品的地方，那应该是降A和降E，于是这让F和弦有了特别的成分。他弹给我们俩看的好处是，我们总是会记住它，因为如果乔治忘记了，我还会记得，反过来一样。我们把吉姆这个华丽的F和弦称作"躁狂F"。

在披头士时期，我们在寻找新的歌曲，约翰有一次对我说："还记得你在派对上的那首瞎胡闹的法国歌吗？"我正好遇见伊万·沃恩，他可能是我在学校里最好的朋友。那时他去了伦敦大学学院学习。他和妻子简生活在伊斯林顿，我经常去拜访他们。简教法语，所以我问她是否可以想到一个和"米歇尔"押韵的词，两个音节的。她说"我的姑娘"。那么，我要怎么用法语说"这些词语搭配在一起"？于是简给了我"sont les mots qui vont très bien ensemble"。我总是不发 ensemble 的"b"这个音。

"躁狂F"，它正式的和弦名称应该是F挂九和弦或者什么，除了这个，我还加进了第二个好玩的和弦。再一次，我不知道它的名称——也许是D减和弦？我是从杯垫乐队[2]的唱片《琼斯来了》（Along Came Jones）里扒下来的。我用了这两个和弦，以及这个旋律，并且嘀嘀咕咕地，像一个假法国人，而这就是《米歇尔》。

1　伊迪丝·皮雅芙（Édith Piaf，1915—1963），法国香颂女歌手、演员。
2　杯垫乐队（Coasters），1950 年代美国乐队。

左图：保罗与伊万·沃恩父子。
伦敦，1968 年。

上左和上右：在利物浦的家里，
弟弟迈克拍摄，1950 年代末。

Mother Nature's Son
自然之子

作　者　WRITERS　　　保罗·麦卡特尼和约翰·列侬　Paul McCartney and John Lennon

艺术家　ARTIST　　　披头士乐队　The Beatles

录　音　RECORDED　　伦敦阿比路录音棚　Abbey Road Studios, London

发　行　RELEASED　　《披头士》，1968 年　*The Beatles*, 1968

Born a poor young country boy
Mother Nature's son
All day long I'm sitting singing songs
For everyone

Sit beside a mountain stream
See her waters rise
Listen to the pretty sound of music
As she flies

Find me in my field of grass
Mother Nature's son
Swaying daisies
Sing a lazy song beneath the sun

Mother Nature's son

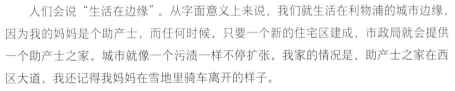

顶图和上图：和弟弟迈克及妈妈
玛丽在一起，1940 年代末。

人们会说"生活在边缘"。从字面意义上来说，我们就生活在利物浦的城市边缘，因为我的妈妈是个助产士，而任何时候，只要一个新的住宅区建成，市政局就会提供一个助产士之家。城市就像一个污渍一样不停扩张。我家的情况是，助产士之家在西区大道，我还记得我妈妈在雪地里骑车离开的样子。

我们搬到位于斯皮克地区阿德维克路 12 号的新家之后，路上骑车只要十分钟，坐公共汽车只要五分钟。出现了许多房子。到处都是建筑工地，马路还没有完全修好，所以到了冬天就很泥泞。我们在建筑工地上玩耍，那确实有点危险。我有一次把我弟弟从石灰坑里拉出来，因为他爬不上陡峭光滑的坡道。这有点吓人，不过我们是孩子，而且我们知道没别的地方比那里更好玩。那就是我们的游乐园。

如果我们从家走大约一英里，就会突然就置身于兰开夏郡的乡村，这就好像你从地球的尽头跌落了下去。全是森林、溪流和晃动着的金色玉米的天地——你热爱的乡村的每一样东西都有。有很多鸟类生活在那里，因为在那时候，东西多多少少都是有机的。他们只是还没来得及购买昂贵的杀虫剂和化肥，大自然更加平衡。

所以，那是我经常会做的事情——只是走路，要么到森林里去，要么在小溪上筑坝，或者爬树，或者在田野里漫步，被农民追赶。甚至现在，当我漫步在自己的田地上，或者骑马穿过它们时，我经常想起那些农民："从这里滚开！你在破坏我的田地！"

那是一种很强烈的乡村感，而我很幸运那么容易就得到了。我有幸去观察一只云雀起飞——真的很愉悦。在田地的中间有一只正在起飞的鸟，垂直地，鸣叫着，就好像它的生命完全取决于此，它沿着空气柱上升，直到升到顶部，然后它停止鸣叫并开

始滑翔。这就是它引导你离开它的巢穴的方式，翩然如同拉尔夫·沃恩·威廉姆斯[1]的美妙作品《云雀高飞》（*The Lark Ascending*）中的小提琴独奏。现在这是一段美好的回忆。那时候我遇见的大部分人没见过云雀的这种行为，但那对我产生了极大的震撼，大自然的纯粹的荣耀。我生活在伦敦时想象着它，试着去像一个乡村男孩一样思考。自然之子。

"Sit beside a mountain stream"（坐在山涧旁）——那是不可能的，那其实是一条沟渠或者森林小溪。"See her waters rise / Listen to the pretty sound of music / As she flies"（看着她的水流升起 / 倾听完美的音乐之声 / 当她飞翔时）。溪流对我非常有吸引力，现在仍是。我只是喜欢看着它们找到流向大海的道路，或者任何它们要去的地方。"My field of grass"（我的草地）明确地示意大麻，也许你也还记得，我总喜欢稍微提及一下这个。我只是组合了这个短句，因为我喜欢说一点圈子里的玩笑。

这首歌受到的部分影响来自和玛哈里希在瑞诗凯诗的经历，以及纳特·金·科尔的《自然男孩》（Nature Boy），但是我依稀记得，它是在利物浦我爸爸的家里写就的。我当时是在我的"加州"民谣唱法的心态里，不过歌中的地点是在斯皮克，或者后来的苏格兰。摇曳的雏菊、毛茛——这是美丽田野上的夏日的记忆。这是一首情歌——一首给自然世界的情歌。

1　拉尔夫·沃恩·威廉姆斯（Ralph Vaughan Williams，1872—1958），英国作曲家。

左图：爱尔兰，1971 年。

右图：保罗和弟弟迈克在马背上。
威尔士，1940 年代末。

③

MOTHER NATURES SON.

1. Born a poor young country boy
Mother Natures son,
All day long I'm sitting singing songs
For everyone.

2. Sit beside a mountain stream
See her waters run,
Listen to the pretty sound of music
As she flies ....
Mother Natures son

在萨塞克斯郡骑马，
女儿玛丽拍摄，2020 年。

Mrs. Vandebilt

温德比夫人

作　者	WRITERS	保罗·麦卡特尼和琳达·麦卡特尼　Paul McCartney and Linda McCartney
艺术家	ARTIST	保罗·麦卡特尼和羽翼乐队　Paul McCartney and Wings
录　音	RECORDED	拉各斯百代录音棚、伦敦 AIR 录音棚　EMI Studios, Lagos and AIR Studios, London
发　行	RELEASED	《逃亡乐队》，1973 年　*Band on the Run*, 1973

Down in the jungle, living in a tent
You don't use money, you don't pay rent
You don't even know the time
But you don't mind

Ho hey ho

When your light is on the blink
You never think of worrying
What's the use of worrying?
When your bus has left the stop
You'd better drop your hurrying
What's the use of hurrying?
Leave me alone Mrs. Vandebilt
I've got plenty of time of my own

What's the use of worrying?
What's the use of hurrying?
What's the use of anything?

Ho hey ho

When your pile is on the wane
You don't complain of robbery
Run away, don't bother me
What's the use of worrying?
What's the use of anything?
Leave me alone Mrs. Washington
I've done plenty of time on my own

What's the use of worrying?
What's the use of hurrying?
What's the use of anything?

Ho hey ho

披头士乐队初期，我们常常被问起是否担心自己可能加入"机构"（Establishment）。我们觉得"机构"是伦敦的一家俱乐部——确实是的。我们并不是特别准确地了解那是什么意思，只知道我们已是现状的一部分。当然，我们坚持我们不会成为任何时髦事物的一部分。我们认识一些时髦的人物，不过就是这样。

如果你是在一场智力竞猜节目上，并且必须列出一份包含巨大财富的清单，你可以写洛克菲勒、格蒂、温德比。这些都是你确定的名字，因为他们永远都会出现在报纸上——超级富豪。

有钱的问题是伴随而来的通常都是烦恼。比如说，我买了一艘可以让我独自出海的小帆船。我自己就可以把它推下水拉上岸。不过有一天，有人提醒我这不过是艘儿童船。我会说："好吧，我就是个孩子。"我不确定他们是否能理解这个，而我就是不想要大船，那种"成人"的。如果有艘大船，我将需要一个团队，而我不想要一个团队。

和温德比夫人打交道的问题是，许多社交规则伴随而来。我要邀请那些我不喜欢的人来参加鸡尾酒会。我是那种会去参加温德比夫人的鸡尾酒会的人——曾经。

这就是我的生活方式。我喜欢这样的想法，替换标准，然后进入，或者周旋于另一个我不喜欢并永远不会属于的世界。"Down in the jungle, living in a tent / You don't use money, you don't pay rent"（走进丛林，住在帐篷里 / 你不用花钱，你不用付租金）是英国喜剧演员查理·切斯特（Charlie Chester）写的一首歌中的连复段，在我小时候，他是电台的中流砥柱。这同时也是一种我觉得很有吸引力的世界观。嬉皮世界。退出。

我不希望温德比夫人或者她的嗜好打扰我的宁静时光。她会毁了我。她会让我遵守那些我不愿意遵守的规则。她会把我拉到她的金钱、影响力和权威的云朵上，而我宁愿和世界上的埃莉诺·里格比们度过我的时间。

就像温德比夫人变成了代表美国政治首都的华盛顿夫人（Mrs Washington）那样，短句"I've got plenty of time of my own"（我有太多的时间）也变成了"I've done plenty of time on my own"（我花了太多的时间）。尽管1980年我在日本被逮捕时，这首歌早已写好良久，当时我因为携带大麻在监狱待了九个晚上，以前我在汉堡也被监禁过几次。只有一天，或者一个晚上。所以这种感觉很熟悉。

简单地说，温德比夫人代表权力、财富、规则和金钱，而这些是这首歌的主角并不想了解的。他想要一个人待着。而那就是我，非常地我。没有什么比得上在森林中骑着马、留下足迹更能让我快乐，一旦有任何机会，我都喜欢自己去森林里。

MRS. VANDEBILT

Down in the jungle living in a tent
You don't use money you don't pay rent
" " even know the time
But you don't mind

CHORUS HO HEY HO
" " "
" " "
" " "

When you light is on the blink
You never think of worrying
What's the use of worrying?)
When your bus has left the stop
You'd better drop your hurrying
What's the use of " "?
Leave me alone Mrs. Vandebilt
I've got plenty of time of my own
What's the use of worrying?)
" " " " hurrying?
" " " " anything)?

CHORUS HO HEY HO

What's the use of worrying?
hurrying)?
anything?

HO HEY HO

486

When your pile is on the wane
You don't complain of robbery
Run away don't bother me
What's the use of worrying?
                    anything?
Leave me alone Mrs. Washington,
I've don't plenty of time on my own

what's the use of worrying?
                  hurrying? (no use!)
            anything?

CHORUS HO HEY HO

上图：骑马，萨塞克斯郡，1992 年。

左图：太阳鱼号帆船。1990 年。

右图：梅诺卡岛，1986 年。

Mull of Kintyre

琴泰岬

作 者	WRITERS	保罗·麦卡特尼和丹尼·莱恩　Paul McCartney and Denny Laine
艺术家	ARTIST	羽翼乐队　Wings
录 音	RECORDED	苏格兰拉那坎精神录音棚　Spirit of Ranachan Studio, Scotland
发 行	RELEASED	《琴泰岬》/《女子学校》双 A 面单曲，1977 年　'Mull of Kintyre' / 'Girls' School' double A-side single, 1977

Mull of Kintyre
Oh mist rolling in from the sea
My desire is always to be here
Oh Mull of Kintyre

Far have I travelled and much have I seen
Dark distant mountains with valleys of green
Past painted deserts, the sunset's on fire
As he carries me home to the Mull of Kintyre

Mull of Kintyre
Oh mist rolling in from the sea
My desire is always to be here
Oh Mull of Kintyre

Sweep through the heather like deer in the glen
Carry me back to the days I knew then
Nights when we sang like a heavenly choir
Of the life and the times of the Mull of Kintyre

Mull of Kintyre
Oh mist rolling in from the sea
My desire is always to be here
Oh Mull of Kintyre

Smiles in the sunshine and tears in the rain
Still take me back where my memories remain
Flickering embers grow higher and higher
As they carry me back to the Mull of Kintyre

Mull of Kintyre
Oh mist rolling in from the sea
My desire is always to be here
Oh Mull of Kintyre

这首歌是在苏格兰一个小农场的一间小录音棚里录制的，那是我们建的一个移动录音房间。不走运的是，那里的空间太小了，没办法塞进一整个风笛乐队。如果你要录一个乐团，音乐家们会数"一二三四，二二三四……"，但是苏格兰风笛乐队不会这样，他们会数"一二三四五六七八九十十一十二……"，那很了不起。英国人只能数到四！

1970 年代中期，我们已经在我的苏格兰农场里待了很长时间。碰巧，那是在琴泰，实际上并不是在琴泰岬。我想，很多英国人或非盖尔语系的人都有个盖尔人的梦，关于浪漫的苏格兰历史，或者爱尔兰历史的概念；而如果你的祖先来自爱尔兰，就像我这样，那对你甚至更为重要，因为你有权进入这个梦。很早之前，约翰有一些苏格兰亲戚，他会去那里待在某个小农场里，而我想："哇，那真是非常浪漫。"所以这首歌是一种接入这种感觉的方式，也是为我居住的这个地区自豪的方式。有一天，我突然意识到不再有新的苏格兰歌曲；有很多风笛演奏的非常好的老歌，但是没人写新的东西。于是，那是一个好机会，看看我能不能写。由一个撒克逊人写的一首新的苏格兰歌曲？那会很有意思。

你作为艺术家所做的事情之一是尝试去理解——或者甚至说是尊重——你所处的位置。你这么做是为了你的故乡，我总是试着为利物浦而做，因为我为它自豪。我真的喜欢回忆我从哪里来；这不仅是对故乡的致敬，同时也提醒着我，自己走得有多远。这和英国的阶级体系有关——从一个被认为比较底层的地方走出来是一个了不起的成就，而相比之下，从其他阶层走出来则不会。这其中有巨大的满足感。

当琳达和我第一次相遇并开始互相了解时，她说："你在苏格兰买了块地吗？我听说你买了。"我确实买了，尽管实话说，那个时候我并不是那么喜欢那块地，但是当我们到那里时，她说："噢，太棒了，我爱这里！"我也发现这里非常可爱，所以我很乐意把它浪漫化。游子，回家的士兵，梦想回到美丽的乡村，美丽的村庄，我用这样的方式来思考。返乡的观念深深地扎根在每个人的灵魂里。有时当我们在加拿大和新西兰这样的移民国家演出，我们会在现场表演这首歌。我们会有一些苏格兰保安，你可以看到他们热泪盈眶。

录音的时候，我找来一个当地的风笛大师来我家，一个名叫托尼·威尔森（Tony Wilson）的绅士。房间很小，他演奏时音量非常大，于是我提议："我们去花园吧。"花园同样很小，我们随便玩了一下，然后我有了一些构思。我找出一些可以和他演奏的东西配合的和弦——配合他用的调式，因为你没办法在风笛上变调：所听即所得。我写了这首歌，我们一起录了基础音轨。接下来，几天之后，我们在晚上安排了一个录音时段，为乐队的人准备了很多麦克尤恩牌啤酒，尽管要在结束后他们才被允许喝酒，因为他们中的一些人相当年轻，可能会把事情搞砸。他们都穿上了风笛手的服装。听着乐队演奏，我激动极了；声音非常大，他们演奏了几次。那是一个非常好玩的夜晚，而且他们喜欢这首歌。"哦，是的，这是冠军歌曲！"

我，以及其他人都认为：这是 1977 年，我们不能在朋克的时代发行这首歌。我的意思是，那太疯狂了，不过我又想："呃，去他妈的。"但是，虽然我是撒克逊人，这首歌仍然成了一首伟大的苏格兰歌曲。它在榜首的位置待了九周，而且我觉得，它好像仍然是英国有史以来销量第四高的单曲。奇怪的是，甚至朋克们也喜欢它。有一天，琳达和我被堵在伦敦西区的某个地方，有一帮看上去非常有侵略性的朋克，我们有点躲躲闪闪，尽量不引人注意，并且想着："天哪，我们要怎么办？"然后他们注意到了我们，其中一个人来到我们的车前，于是我摇下一点车窗，而他说："噢，保罗，那首《琴泰岬》真他妈的好！"

上图：与风笛大师托尼·威尔森在一起。苏格兰，1977 年。

右图：坎贝尔顿风笛乐队。苏格兰，1977 年。

上图、左图和右上：保罗和羽翼乐队及坎贝尔顿风笛乐队在一起，苏格兰拉那坎精神录音棚，1977 年。

右下：玛丽和斯特拉在为风笛乐队准备录音结束后的茶点，1977 年。

MULL OF KINTYRE.

Chorus. —————

Mull of Kintyre

Oh mist rolling in from the sea
My desire is always to be here
Oh mull of Kintyre.

(1) Far have I travelled & much have I seen
Dark, distant mountains with vallies of green
Past painted deserts the sun sets on fire
as he carries me home to the mull of Kintyre.

— CHORUS   Mull of Kintyre.

※ 4 Bars PIPE BAND — drone starting.
KEY CHANGE TO D — PIPE SOLO (chorus.)

(2) Sweep through the heather, like deer in the glen
Carry me back ~~where my memories remain~~ to the days I knew then.
Nights when we sang like a heavenly choir
of the life and the times of the mull of Kintyre.

CHORUS ——▶ PIPE RIFF   D — to A
                                    Repeat. once.

(3) (BACK IN **A**)
        Smiles in the sunshine – tears in the rain
Carry me back where my memories remain
Flickering embers grow higher & higher
  as they carry me back to the mull of Kintyre.
  CHORUS Mull of Kintyre.   (TWICE) CHORUS in D ...
        PIPE RIFF — D to A ∧ ~~fade out~~ END.

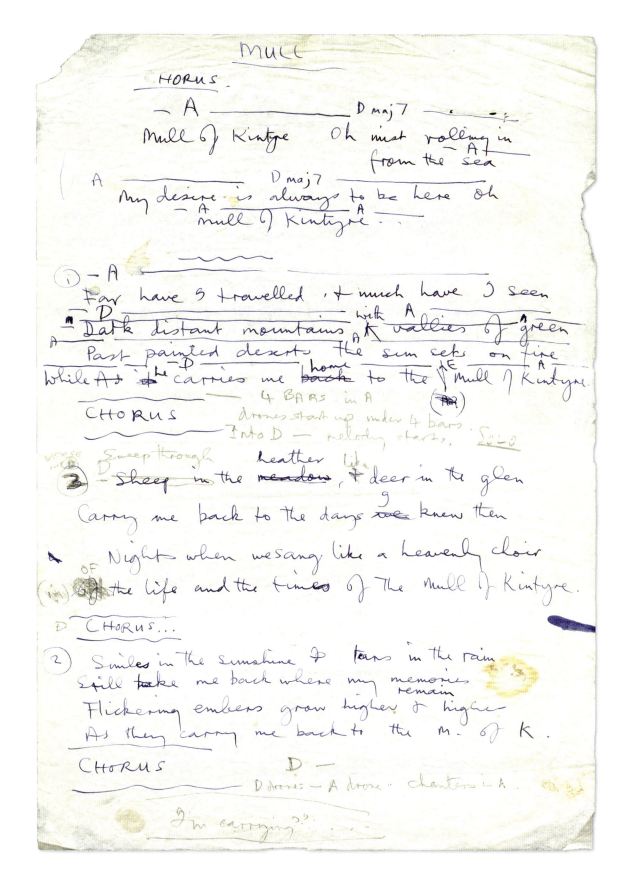

MULL

CHORUS.

~ A _____ D maj 7 — . —
Mull of Kintyre   Oh mist rolling in
                          ~ A
                          from the sea

A _____ D maj 7 _____
My desire is always to be here   Oh
~ A   A
mull of Kintyre...

① ~ A _____
Far have I travelled, + much have I seen
~ D
Dark distant mountains with valleys of green
Past painted deserts the sun sets on fire
While A + the carries me home to the Mull of Kintyre.

4 BARS in A
CHORUS   drones start up under 4 bars.
            Into D — melody starts. SOLO

VERSE Sweep through heather like
③ D Sheep in the meadow, + deer in the glen
Carry me back to the days we knew then

Nights when we sang like a heavenly choir
OF the life and the times of The Mull of Kintyre.

D CHORUS...

② Smiles in the sunshine + tears in the rain
Still take me back where my memories remain
Flickering embers grow higher + higher
As they carry me back to the M. of K.

CHORUS   D —
D drones — A drone. chanters in A.

I'm carrying?.

497

My Love

我的爱

作　者 WRITERS	保罗·麦卡特尼和琳达·麦卡特尼	Paul McCartney and Linda McCartney
艺术家 ARTIST	保罗·麦卡特尼和羽翼乐队	Paul McCartney and Wings
录　音 RECORDED	伦敦阿比路录音棚	Abbey Road Studios, London
发　行 RELEASED	单曲，1973 年	Single, 1973
	《红玫瑰高速公路》，1973 年	*Red Rose Speedway*, 1973

And when I go away
I know my heart can stay with my love
It's understood
It's in the hands of my love
And my love does it good
My love does it good

And when the cupboard's bare
I'll still find something there with my love
It's understood
It's everywhere with my love
And my love does it good
My love does it good

I love
My love
Only my love holds the other key to me
My love
My love
Only my love does it good to me
My love does it good

Don't ever ask me why
I never say goodbye to my love
It's understood
It's everywhere with my love
And my love does it good
My love does it good

I love
My love
Only my love does it good to me

斯蒂芬·桑德海姆[1] 和我曾经花了非常愉快的几个小时闲聊，最后总结出一些写歌的方法。他问我我是怎么进行的，我告诉他我是从找和弦开始的。哪一个和弦和相近的和弦配合得好，哪一种发展可以带来新的旋律。他看起来对我的创作完全以和弦为基础有些惊讶。对他来说，一切都与旋律和对位有关，不同的旋律如何在一起配合并互相补充。我从未意识到他的音乐及古典音乐并不是以和弦为基础的，因此对于古典音乐是如何创作的，我有了一个有趣的理解。

在阿比路录音棚录制《我的爱》真的很酷，我们的吉他手亨利·麦卡洛（Henry McCullough），一个北爱尔兰的孩子，在这首歌里扮演了重要的角色。因为需要和一支管弦乐团同步录音，所以在排练时，我们写了一段独奏。我记得亨利在听其中一遍录音时，在录音棚里走来走去，并小声对我说他有个独奏的主意，我介意他试一下吗？我可以说不，我也可以说我觉得他已经很贴合编好的东西了，但是我说："好啊，当然。"

于是，这段独奏就出乎意料地出现了。所有人在之前都没听过。绝对是一段美妙的独奏，我觉得对我来说，能够让亨利自由发挥真是太好了，而他在乐队里只不过才一年的时间。对他来说，能够大胆地提出想法，而且如愿完成，这也很了不起。

提醒一下，这是一种有限度的自由。亨利选择的独奏和音符仍然需要在那些基础和弦的框架内操作，在歌曲中配合。从这个意义上来说，音乐在告诉他 —— 或者甚至是指引他。

甚至在 "My love does it good"（我的爱完美无缺）这样的句子后面也隐藏有大量的

上图：与丹尼·塞维尔（Denny Seiwell）及亨利·麦卡洛在《我的爱》录音期间。伦敦阿比路录音棚，1972 年。

1　斯蒂芬·桑德海姆（Stephen Sondheim，1930—2021），美国作曲家，概念音乐剧的奠基人。

音乐史。那样的句子是典型的"尽管是完美的选择但不合语法"的例子。这是从布鲁斯音乐开始的，不过我经常想到的是猫王在"You ain't nothing but a hound dog"[1] 中的双重否定。那种双重否定的效果非常好，因为它听上去就像是人们的日常说话。比如说，在《佩珀军士》中的《越来越好》里，我们用了"it can't get no worse"[2] 这样的句子。我们对这个句子很是骄傲，特别是因为那首歌的场景设置有一部分是课堂。颠覆语法规则总是让人很满足。相比于去写"我的爱干得不错"或者"我的爱不可思议"或者"我的爱神气十足"或者甚至"我的爱是个好人"，我们让她"完美无缺"。这留下了很多想象空间。

我喜欢去发现一些有意思的和弦，然后发现一些在这些和弦之上进行的旋律，以及找到一些和它们两者配合的歌词，也许甚至是互相启发。然后我希望它能扩散，不仅启发我，而且启发其他人。

这首歌是一首写给琳达的单纯的情歌，重申我对她的爱。不过一如既往地，不会简单地说"我的琳达"。它说的是"我的爱"，所以其他人也可以和这首歌产生联系。这首歌特别让我高兴的一件事情是，它在美国的节奏布鲁斯排行榜上很成功，这对我来说非常特别，因为这事对我可不常见。我经常会出现在白人音乐的排行榜上，但是出现在黑人音乐排行榜，带给他们影响，这对我总是非常重要。对于这首歌，一对黑人情侣会想，"是啊，我认同那个"，想到这个就让我激动得发抖。

---

1 "除了猎犬你什么都不是"，出自《猎犬》（Hound Dog）。
2 "不会再糟了"，出自《越来越好》（Getting Better）。

My Love

1. And when I go away, I know my
                                    heart can stay with
                                    my love
   'its understood, 'its in the hands of
          my love, + my love does it good
   w-oh!... my love does it good,

2. And when the cupboards bare, I'll still
   find something there with my love, its
   understood 'its everywhere with my love,
   my love does it good. Woh!

MIDDLE: I love, oh my love
   oh ~~No~~
   only my love holds the other key
   TOme
   Oh my love oh my love
   only my love does it good to me.
                    Solo
   Don't ever ask me why
   I never say goodbye to my love
   'its understood 'it everywhere with
   my love
        And my love does it good,
        only my love does it good to...me!

《我的爱》音乐录影拍摄现场。
伦敦，1973 年。

我喜欢去发现一些有意思的和弦，
然后发现一些在这些和弦之上进行的旋律，
以及找到一些和它们两者配合的歌词，也许甚至是互相启发。
然后我希望它能扩散，不仅启发我，而且启发其他人。

My Valentine

我的情人

作 者 WRITER	保罗·麦卡特尼	Paul McCartney
艺术家 ARTIST	保罗·麦卡特尼	Paul McCartney
录 音 RECORDED	纽约阿凡达录音棚	Avatar Studios, New York
发 行 RELEASED	《爱的签名》，2012 年	*Kisses on the Bottom*, 2012

What if it rained
We didn't care
She said that someday soon the sun was gonna shine
And she was right, this love of mine
My valentine

As days and nights
Would pass me by
I'd tell myself that I was waiting for a sign
Then she appeared, a love so fine
My valentine

And I will love her for life
And I will never let a day go by
Without remembering the reasons why
She makes me certain that I can fly

And so I do
Without a care
I know that someday soon the sun is gonna shine
And she'll be there, this love of mine
My valentine

事情是这样的。我爱上了南希，不过我们还没有上过床。我们去了摩纳哥度假，去了一家我知道的安静的小酒店，不过因为我们还没有上过床，所以我们没有住在同一个房间里。

南希一个房间，我一个房间，和我们一起度假的我弟弟迈克和他的妻子在一个房间。但是每天都在下雨，我们花了这么多钱来到这样的天堂，或许还不如待在曼彻斯特呢！

雨一直不停，不过我们过得还算愉快，美妙的是我开始了解南希，就像你在那种情况下会做的那样。我不停地因为下雨向她道歉，就好像这是我的错。我说："我真的为这些雨感到抱歉，亲爱的。"而她说："没关系。"那种甜蜜的态度让我产生了共鸣。我想："那真好。"

酒店的门厅有一架钢琴，每天晚上，我们会去那里喝点东西，听一个人弹一些歌曲。他曾是一位爱尔兰军人，后来因为某种原因留在了摩纳哥——我们甚至不敢想象是什么原因——不过他人很好。他钢琴弹得也特别好，他弹的曲目有点像我父亲，都是老歌，是那些把我带回过去的歌曲。我们真的很享受，他也接受点歌，然后我们离开去吃晚餐。

钢琴就摆在门厅里，演奏者会在晚上的鸡尾酒时间到来，而因为雨一直不停，有时候我会过去随便弹点东西。一些服务员会打扫卫生，但是周围人很少，所以很不错。这就像我一直喜欢躲在里面写歌的橱柜。我只是随便弹，尽管在那个时候我还不知道，但我想我被他影响了，那个饭店的演奏者，或许甚至也被我父亲所影响——我用的和弦开始进入某种老派的方向。那天正是情人节。

就像通常当我有了一些好东西时那样，我想："我他妈的要怎么才能记住这个？"所以我冲回我的房间，拿起我的手提摄像机——那是在苹果手机之前，不过我确实有个小摄像机——在钢琴上架好，并开始唱这首歌，这样至少我还有个配乐可以提醒我。

所有的一切都很浪漫。我想着所有这些对南希的爱，当我坐在钢琴前时，我可以看见打扫卫生的服务员在聆听。当某人在偷听你的时候，你是能感觉到的，就算他们在假装忙着做他们的工作。但是这很美好，浪漫，这是个完美的时刻，我对自己说，今晚我们不会再住在分开的房间了。

我一直很喜欢那样的态度：不要担心，一切都会好。"As days and nights / Would pass me by / I'd tell myself that I was waiting for a sign"（当日日夜夜 / 从我身边流逝 / 我告诉自己我在等待一个征兆）。这是我的人生哲学，这是在我遇见南希之前的事情；我总是想，"我会看见什么东西，会告诉我，'噢，这是你的女人。'"我曾在巴黎参加女儿斯特拉的时装秀，我买了一套挂在商店橱窗里的粉色套装，并想，"这是给我的下一个女人的"，最后我把它送给了南希。

我从一开始就知道这段和南希的关系会持续下去，但是我们不得不遮遮掩掩——至少在一段时间之内。我总是要回头看看有没有狗仔队，所以我们做一些事情的时候，南希不得不避开。

我们只是想以我们自己的节奏和方式来宣布我们之间的关系，但是他们总是会抓住你。他们最后总是把你挖出来。你们会在一个地中海的海滩上，手牵手走在那些纯真美丽的春日里，并且想，"真是太好了，周围几英里都没人。"然后第二天你上网，看见你自己以各种难看的姿势在海滩上被抓拍。

如果要用一个词来形容南希，那就是真实。我有一张我们去白宫时的漂亮照片。是我和南希与奥巴马总统夫妇谈话的照片，我们正为总统说的什么事情大笑，而南希的表情如此专注。她是个了不起的人。她多才多艺。她运营着一家卡车公司，所以那是她的另一面，非常蓝领风格。南希有那种极务实的管理能力，和她聊天非常有趣。她很贴心 —— 真的，就像这首歌里唱的，"我的情人"。

这首歌里的"for life"（一生）这个词也是南希所关注的事情。我们认识埃德·拉斯查（Ed Ruscha），这位画家经常把字母用在他的画作中，于是她问他是否可以为我的生日做一幅画：那是埃德最美的画作之一，说的就是，"一生"。

上图：南希，2008 年。

MY VALENTINE.

FEB 10 · 11 ·

① What if it rained
we didn't care
 She said that someday soon
The sun was going to shine
 And she was right
 This love of mine
 my valentine.

② As days and nights
 would pass me by
I'd tell myself that I
was waiting for a sign
 Then she appeared.
 A love so fine.
 my valentine

[MIDDLE] And I will love her
 for life
 I know I'll never
 let a day go by
without remembering the reasons why
she makes me certain that I can fly

③ And so I do
 without a care
 I know that someday soon
The sun is going to shine
 And she'll be there
 this love of mine
 my valentine

SOLO
(MIDDLE)

VERSE
①

507

所有的一切都很浪漫。

我想着所有这些对南希的爱，当我坐在钢琴前时，

我可以看见打扫卫生的服务员在聆听。

当某人在偷听你的时候，你是能感觉到的，就算他们在假装忙着做他们的工作。但是这很美好，浪漫，这是个完美的时刻。

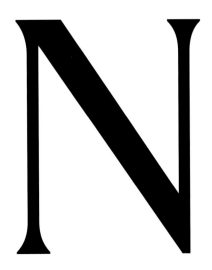

Nineteen Hundred and Eighty Five
一九八五

作　者　WRITERS　　保罗·麦卡特尼和琳达·麦卡特尼　Paul McCartney and Linda McCartney

艺术家　ARTIST　　保罗·麦卡特尼和羽翼乐队　Paul McCartney and Wings

录　音　RECORDED　拉各斯百代录音棚、伦敦 AIR 录音棚　EMI Studios, Lagos and AIR Studios, London

发　行　RELEASED　《逃亡乐队》，1973 年　*Band on the Run*, 1973

　　　　　　　　　《逃亡乐队》美国单曲 B 面，1974 年　B-side of 'Band on the Run' US single, 1974

Oh no one ever left alive
In nineteen hundred and eighty five
Will ever do
She may be right
She may be fine
She may get love but she won't get mine
'Cause I got you

Oh I oh I
Well I just can't get enough of that sweet stuff
My little lady gets behind

Oh my mama said the time
Would come when I would find myself
In love with you
I didn't think
I never dreamed
That I would be around to see it
All come true

Woh I oh I
Well I just can't get enough of that sweet stuff
My little lady gets behind

读乔治·奥威尔的《1984》时，我还是个孩子，觉得那是过于遥远的未来，而我
恐怕活不到目睹的那一天。就像电影《2001：太空漫游》——遥不可及。而现在，它
们被我们甩在了后面。

这首歌背后的理念是，这是一段始终命中注定的关系。在遥远的未来，没有人会
让我关注，因为我有了你。不过在我写这首歌的时候，离 1985 年只有十二年；那不
是非常遥远的未来——在这首歌里只有这个未来。所以，这基本上是一首关于未来的
情歌。

你试着避免在一首歌里用"爱"这样的字眼，不过我也写过一首歌，来探讨愚蠢
的情歌有什么错。这就是我想的东西。"爱"是一个非常重要的词，以及一种非常重
要的感受。因为它在任何地方发生，在全部的存在中，在现在。我想的是这整个星球
以及全人类。我想的是现在在中国两个彼此相爱的人，他们结婚并许下共度余生的诺
言，或者现在在南美一位母亲有了孩子并爱着这个孩子，父亲也爱这个孩子。我的观
点很明显——这"爱情的东西"是全球化的，真的是宇宙性的。不仅人类，而且包括
动物，我们经常会忘了它们，这种共性超过了它可能令人多愁善感的事实。但是你总
是试着用一种不那么多愁善感的方式来表达。那就是我写这首歌的原因。

你试着避免在一首歌里用"爱"这样的字眼，
不过我也写过一首歌，来探讨愚蠢的情歌有什么错。
这就是我想的东西。
"爱"是一个非常重要的词，以及一种非常重要的感受。
因为它在任何地方发生，在全部的存在中，在现在。
我想的是这整个星球以及全人类。

NINETEEN HUNDRED AND
EIGHTY FIVE.

(1) Oh No one ever left alive in 1985, will ever
     She may be right   do
     "   ")   "   fine
     She may get love but she won't get mine
     Cos I got you
     Oh 9 9 — Oh 9
Well 9 just cant get enough of that sweet
     Stuff my little lady gets behind

INTERLUDE

   Oh my mama said the time would come when 9 would
(2) → In love with you   find myself
     9 didnt think
     9 never dreamed ~~that 9 would be around~~
That 9 would be around to see it all come
     with 9 — Oh 9   true
Well 9 just cant get enough of that sweet stuff
     My little lady gets behind,

INTERLUDE

Repeat (1)

FINALE

515

No More Lonely Nights
不再有孤独的夜晚

作　者　WRITER	保罗·麦卡特尼	Paul McCartney
艺术家　ARTIST	保罗·麦卡特尼	Paul McCartney
录　音　RECORDED	伦敦 AIR 录音棚	AIR Studios, London
发　行　RELEASED	单曲，1984 年	Single, 1984
	《代我问候百老汇大街》，1984 年	*Give My Regards to Broad Street*, 1984

I can wait another day
Until I call you
You've only got my heart on a string
And everything aflutter

But another lonely night
Might take forever
We've only got each other to blame
It's all the same to me, love
'Cause I know what I feel to be right

No more lonely nights
No more lonely nights
You're my guiding light
Day or night I'm always there

May I never miss the thrill
Of being near you
And if it takes a couple of years
To turn your tears to laughter
I will do what I feel to be right

No more lonely nights
Never be another
No more lonely nights
You're my guiding light
Day or night I'm always there

And I won't go away until you tell me so
No I'll never go away

Yes I know what I feel to be right

No more lonely nights
Never be another
No more lonely nights
You're my guiding light
Day or night I'm always there

And I won't go away until you tell me so
No I'll never go away
I won't go away until you tell me so
No I'll never go away

No more lonely nights

我称之为"文字舞蹈"。你从一个动机开始，然后跳文字舞蹈，然后一步，一步，一步。这是一首直白的情歌，真的，关于一个孤独的人，他说："等不及和你在一起。"还有几句歌词强化了这一构思："Cause I know what I feel to be right"（因为我知道我的感觉是对的）和"You're my guiding light"（你就是我的指路明灯）。这首歌关于与你所爱的人分离的心痛，以及当你们重归于好时，不希望再次与之分离 —— "May I never miss the thrill / Of being near you"（但愿我永远不会错过 / 靠近你时的兴奋颤抖）。

大卫·吉尔摩[1]在录制时弹了主音吉他独奏。我从平克·弗洛伊德乐队刚起步时就认识他了。大卫是个天才，所以我要竭尽全力。我非常欣赏他的演奏，我经常见到他。我记得他刚刚完成了个人专辑《向后转》（*About Face*），所以我给他打电话说："你可以在这首歌里演奏吗?"这首歌听起来像是他那一类的东西。

这首歌是我专门为一部电影创作的——《代我问候百老汇大街》，电影也是我写的，而这首歌比这部电影好。最初，电影的开场是我在百老汇大街车站走来走去，并配上了一些夸张的音效。但是我想做一部电影配乐，于是写了这首歌来配合音乐。后来我把它重新编排成一个快节奏的版本，这样，当它在结尾播放时，就会有一个舞曲的版本。

电影的片名戏仿了一首老流行歌，《代我问候百老汇》（*Give My Regards to Broadway*）。电影和我的个人专辑《和平管乐》差不多是同时做的，我想，我在萨塞克斯郡和伦敦之间的火车上写了一部分剧本。情节有点滑稽。一个阴沉、潮湿的日子，我在去开会的路上睡着了，梦见丢失一张新专辑的母带。我们认为是哈里，一个改过自新的罪犯，又回到了他的老路上，打算把它做成盗版。我们必须在午夜前找到磁带，否则，电影中的坏蛋拉思先生将接管唱片公司。

制作这部电影充满了乐趣。林戈和他的妻子芭芭拉参与其中，琳达也去了，还有乔治·马丁和崔茜·尤玛（Tracey Ullman），摔跤手巨人海斯塔克斯（Giant Haystacks）也在片子里，还有布莱恩·布朗（Bryan Brown）。我们有一些不错的桥段，为歌曲《舞厅交际舞》（Ballroom Dancing）重新创作了1950年代的老派利物浦舞蹈，在皇家阿尔伯特音乐厅的

上图：《代我问候百老汇大街》拍摄现场。伦敦，1983年。

下图：保罗与拉尔夫·理查森爵士，1983年。

1　大卫·吉尔摩（David Gilmour，1946—），平克·弗洛伊德乐队吉他手、主唱。

舞台上表演《埃莉诺·里格比》也很有趣。

　　影片中，就在事情变得越来越糟糕，我们找不到哈里或是丢失的磁带时，我突然走进酒吧去看拉尔夫·理查森（Ralph Richardson），他扮演吉姆，一个有点波洛涅斯[1]式的父亲。拉尔夫爵士是一位令人难以置信的莎士比亚剧演员，所以和他在同一个场景中表演非常棒，我想这是他发行的最后一部电影。拉尔夫的角色吉姆责备我到处瞎跑，不过随后，他赠与我一些智慧的话语，借用自 W.H. 戴维斯[2]的诗《闲暇》（Leisure）：

> 生活是什么倘若，充满思虑
> 以至无暇驻足欣赏

　　我想我曾经在学校的英语课上读到过这首诗。无论如何，我不能慢下来，因为我必须去百老汇大街车站，车站在故事情节中起着重要作用。这就是电影名字的来源。

　　那会儿是音乐录像的爆发期，我们为这首歌做了两个 MV。一个是在夜晚的火车站拍摄的，另一个有点像是电影镜头的集锦剪辑。这首单曲做得不错，但错过了榜首的位置，我想第一名是威猛乐队[3]的《自由》（Freedom）。

　　不过吉尔摩在弹主音吉他时真的很投入，特别是在专辑版本中，这个版本更长，也给了他更多的演奏空间。这是一段非常优美的主音独奏，有着他标志性的芬达斯特拉特卡斯特吉他（Fender Stratocaster）的音色。1999 年 12 月，我在洞穴俱乐部的一场演出中，他弹了吉他，他们重新开张了，就在当初披头士最早表演的那条街上。所以，这是一个看待 20 世纪的相当不错的角度。

1　波洛涅斯（Polonius），莎士比亚戏剧《哈姆雷特》中的人物，人们普遍认为，在整个戏剧过程中，波洛涅斯的每一个判断都是错误的，但他是一位真诚的父亲。

2　W.H. 戴维斯（W. H. Davies，1871—1940），英国诗人。此处所引诗歌原句为："What is this life if, full of care / We have no time to stand and stare"。

3　威猛乐队（Wham!），英国 1980 年代流行乐队，是第一支来中国大陆演出的西方流行乐队。

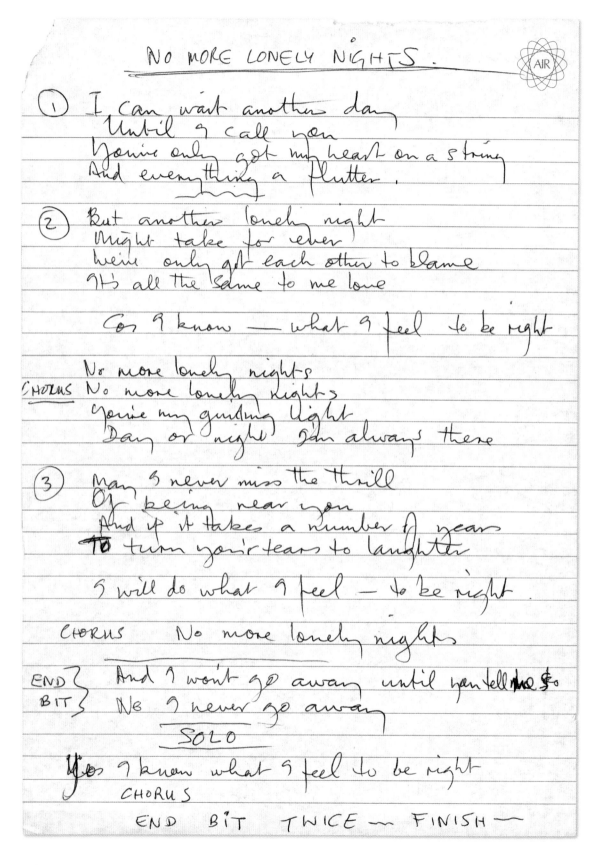

NO MORE LONELY NIGHTS.

(1) I can wait another day
Until I call you
You've only got my heart on a string
And everything a flutter.

(2) But another lonely night
Might take for ever
We've only got each other to blame
It's all the same to me love

Cos I know ― what I feel to be right

CHORUS No more lonely nights
No more lonely nights
You're my guiding light
Day or night I'm always there

(3) Man I never miss the thrill
Of being near you
And if it takes a number of years
To turn your tears to laughter

I will do what I feel ― to be right.

CHORUS No more lonely nights

END BIT And I won't go away until you tell me so
No I never go away

SOLO

Yes I knew what I feel to be right
CHORUS
END BIT TWICE ― FINISH ―

520

(1) I can wait another day
Until I ~~see~~ call you
You've only got my heart on a string
And everything a flutter ....

(2) But another lonely night
~~Could~~ Could BE take for ever ⸻ (could break the camel)
We'd only have each other to blame
~~It seems, A SHAME TO ME LOVE~~ ....
~~It's all the same to me love,~~
~~But~~ I know
What I feel
to be right ....

CHORUS. You're my guiding light
          (Let the world know)

You're my guiding light-
You're my guiding light
Day or night you're always there.

(3) May I never miss the thrill
Of being NEAR you

But I know
What I feel
To be right

CHORUS   You're my guiding light
          "   "   "   " (never need
                                   another)
(N.B.   day or night you're always there.
goes through...

521

The Note You Never Wrote
你永远不会写的便条

作　者　WRITERS　　　保罗·麦卡特尼和琳达·麦卡特尼　Paul McCartney and Linda McCartney
艺术家　ARTIST　　　　羽翼乐队　Wings
录　音　RECORDED　　伦敦阿比路录音棚　Abbey Road Studios, London
发　行　RELEASED　　《以音速》，1976 年　*At the Speed of Sound*, 1976

Later on the story goes
A bottle floated out to sea
After days when it had found the perfect spot
It opened up

And I read the note
That you never wrote to me

After all I'm sure you know
The Mayor of Baltimore is here
After days now he can finally appear
Now at last he's here

But he never is gonna get my vote
'Cause he never is gonna get a quote
From the little note
That you never wrote to me

Further on along the line
I was arrested on the shore
Holding papers of governments galore
I was taken in

But I read the note that you never wrote
Yes I read the note that you never wrote
Oh I read the note that you never wrote to me
To me

主音吉他是吉米·麦克洛赫（Jimmy McCulloch）——不要跟亨利·麦卡洛弄混了——他的主音独奏棒极了。有点让人想起大卫·吉尔摩。整个编排有点梦幻，和平克·弗洛伊德有些相似。我们称之为"弗洛伊德似的滑移"。

平克·弗洛伊德在 1970 年代做了一些伟大的唱片。《月之暗面》(*Dark Side of the Moon*)是 1973 年发行的，羽翼乐队很自然地就会去做一些类似他们风格的东西。许多人都这么做。几年前，贝克[1]的专辑《晨相》(*Morning Phase*)就非常像一张弗洛伊德的唱片，它获得了格莱美年度最佳专辑奖。我边听边想："这很大程度上是平克·弗洛伊德的功劳。"平克·弗洛伊德的世界几乎是个外星世界，所以是个该去的好地方。当然，我不得不虚构巴尔的摩市长的角色。为什么？因为这听上去不错。我不太担心意义。也许这首歌会在某个时候自己构造出一个意义；或者，也许某些人会发现它的某种意义。

就像童谣，我们不必知道它们的含义。我们甚至都不知道它们所指的观点，它们只是一代一代地传下来。它们指的是这个或者那个，或者在某些情况下它们完全没有意义，但是真的没什么关系。我们总是觉得一切都要有意义，一切背后必定都有逻辑，而那根本不是真的。你必须投入被称为灵感的那股能量之中。

我创作一首歌通常要花几个小时，有时候它们出来得更快。不过一般来说，这个过程大约是坐在那里琢磨三四个小时，然后第一段主歌出现了，接着是第二段主歌。在最初，当约翰和我刚开始写歌的时候，想的都是这首歌要多长。我去他家，我们面对面坐着，从十二点，一点，我们开始写，我会在大约三点或四点回去。你可能会觉得总有那么几次我们会遇到那样的情况："写不出来，不好意思，哥们儿，我觉得有一点白费功夫"——不会的。每一次我们坐下来，就有一首歌出来。那真是非常神奇。我发现基本上真的是这样。现在的危险是有像苹果手机这样的设备，让你觉得一个草稿就是一首歌，从某些方面来说来得太容易了。或者你会把它记下来，想着"我之后再完成它"，但是约翰和我从不会这样做。假如我们见面后一起写了几句歌，"让我带你去 / 因为我将要……"然后说，"好吧，明天见"或者"我们之后再完成它"，那这之于我们就没有意义了。简直毫无意义。

所以我们会说，"草莓田，对，就是它"，而我们只是抓着一个小本子，那就是我们的手稿，那就是音乐。我们知道接下来是这句歌词，而且无论是谁写的，都在本子上。三四个小时之后，你会觉得有点疲倦并且失去耐心，于是你就该结束了。我在《利物浦清唱剧》项目中合作过的卡尔·戴维斯曾说，你的大脑大约在三个小时之后就会变得有点晕，那样的话那就停下来。我一直觉得确实是这样的。

我在羽翼乐队的职业生涯很幸运。唱片公司没有给我们任何压力，羽翼乐队的唱片公司在英国是帕洛风唱片（Parlophone），在美国是国会唱片，有很短的一段时间是哥伦比亚唱片。我让我的经纪人或商业同事只签订三四张唱片的合约。所以，我知道

1　贝克（Beck，1970—），美国摇滚歌手，其音乐风格极具独创性。

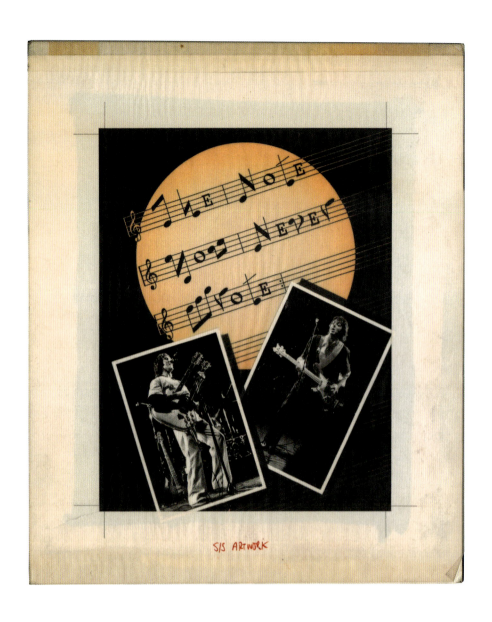

《你永远不会写的笔》的乐谱
封面设计。

那将会是五年左右的时间，我会每一两年做一张唱片。能够有那样的自由十分幸运，所以我会在任何我想写的时候去写，基本上都是我休假的时候，我在我的家庭计划之间见缝插针。我会写点东西，而不是闲坐着。创作时用的都是吉他或者钢琴，从没用过其他乐器，然后，还有一个本子和一支笔头带橡皮的铅笔（即使那个时候，我也是老派的）。当你写够了，就该把这些歌放进一个瓶子里，于是你就可以写得更多。我喜欢把它们放出来，让它们离开并清理书桌，让它们"漂向大海"。

And I read the note
That you never wrote
To me.

保罗与吉米·麦克洛赫。
伦敦阿比路录音棚，1977 年。

Nothing Too Much Just Out of Sight

事情不多只是看不见而已

作 者 WRITER	保罗·麦卡特尼	Paul McCartney
艺术家 ARTIST	消防员乐队	The Fireman
录 音 RECORDED	萨塞克斯郡猪山磨坊	Hog Hill Mill, Sussex
发 行 RELEASED	《电参数》，2008 年	Electric Arguments, 2008

Yeah na
Oh na na na na na
Yeah road too all bright

Now nothing too much just outta sight
You say you love me this is true
The best thing to do is to lie down beside me
I said I love you
Now nothing too much just outta sight

Yeah na na na na na
Oh don't you want to be fair
In the beautiful air in the twilight
Of the half-night
It was all bright all bright

I said I love you
I thought you knew
The last thing to do was to try to betray me
The new morning light, I'll never forget it
That's just outta sight

Yeah na na na na na
Twilight of the half-night
Southwest
I was barely obsessed
Nothing too much all bright

All I can remember the beautiful air
I can't remember why did you take me there
Don't you try to betray me
You don't wanna betray me
I was barely obsessed
I was barely obsessed
With the way she undressed

Bright nothing too half-night
It was all right all bright
Now nothing too much just outta sight

Now nothing too much just outta sight
In the beautiful air

Oh don't you wanna be frightened of the half-night
Beautiful air
On the road to the west
I was barely obsessed
By the way she undressed in the moonlight
In the twilight of the half-night
It was all right all bright

All bright
Well nothing too much
It was all right
Just outta sight

The last thing to do was to try to betray me

"Nothing too much, just out of sight"（事情不多，只是看不见而已）是一位尼日利亚朋友吉米·斯科特（Jimmy Scott）教我的。1960 年代那会儿，我们常在伦敦的俱乐部里见面，他有很多很棒的口头禅。"噢布～啦～迪"也是吉米教我的，所以你可以说他是个传奇人物。"事情不多，只是看不见而已"是他另一个口头禅。那时候，口头禅就像是一种时尚。我猜每个时代都是这样，但我认为就是在 1960 年代的时候，语言开始变得有点不正规，特别是在歌词里。我们有像"离谱"这样的口头禅，还有另一个，"多了"。我记得自己说"呃哦，多了"时，吉米会说："事情不多，只是看不见而已。"我想，"我喜欢这个，这非常好。"

这首歌是分支乐队消防员的作品。我有一个化名"青年"的制作人朋友，他是杀戮玩笑 [1] 的成员，真名是马丁·格洛弗。他几年前帮我做了一次重新混音。我常常拿一首歌给某个人听，他们会有新鲜的视角。我和"青年"关系变得越来越近，于是我说："来我的录音棚吧，我们可以做点什么。"

我们做了非常即兴的东西，这是一次惊喜。我真的非常喜欢这样的工作方式。如果想创作《麦当娜夫人》或者《埃莉诺·里格比》，你就不能这么做，你不能在录音棚里当场考虑如何编排那样的歌曲；你必须更自律一些。但是他过来了，而我们开始了这个分支计划。我们决定叫自己消防员乐队，并在 1993 年发行了我们的第一张专辑，《草莓海洋船只森林》（*Strawberries Oceans Ships Forest*），是那类氛围迷幻音乐。他好像一直熬到天亮做完了混音。我们发行了这首歌，它几乎默默无闻，那是我们想要的；人们认为我总是努力创作榜首金曲，但事实是，我也真的很喜欢地下的计划，在那里，人们不得不自己挖掘。"消防员乐队是谁？"我们会说，"我们不知道。"这种匿名有相当的自由感，也很好玩。

1　杀戮玩笑（Killing Joke），英国后朋克乐队，成立于 1980 年代初。马丁·格洛弗（Martin Glover）为杀戮玩笑的贝斯手，以艺名"青年"（Youth）活跃。

实际上我们还做了第二张专辑，《急促》（Rushes），现在我们完成了第三张。前两张是器乐，不过其实我们有一首歌，"青年"对我说："去话筒那里。想象你是亚利桑那的一个晨间 DJ，唱一些说唱。就那样继续。"他会选择最好的部分，做成循环，剪切，然后用在歌里。于是我拿起话筒："好吧，大家好，这是一个美丽的清晨，阳光普照，普照，普照！"然后他剪切并拼接在一起。在那之前，我们从来没写过有歌词的歌。

在最近的一张专辑里 —— 2008 年，这首歌也收录其中 ——"青年"对我说："对了，保罗，你为什么不唱点歌词呢？"我说："呃，我没歌词。"他给了我一个心照不宣的眼神，意思是："得了吧！你可以的。"然后我想："噢，该死，好吧。"于是我走向话筒，对房间里的所有人说 ——只是录音师和巡演助理及一些朋友 ——"好吧，我先申明：我不知道会唱些什么，所以可能会有点尴尬。可能是我的职业生涯中最尴尬的时刻。"

我有一个主意是用我朋友吉米·斯科特的口头禅"事情不多，只是看不见而已"。我们都觉得这是一个好起点。然后，我将在话筒上漫游，在我唱人声之前，我们已经有一些基础音轨 ——这首歌里有持续的鼓和失真滑棒吉他 ——然后我知道我应该稍作嘶吼了。

一般来说，我知道我要唱什么，但是我不太擅长这样的事情。也许我要在一张纸上随便写下来，然后唱一下看看后面会有什么。在我通常的歌曲写作的方式中，我要遵从我给自己设置的节奏和律动，但是意识流很明显限制更少，所以你就看到了这样的东西，读起来有点像是某种垮掉派诗歌。我想我只是试了几遍并喊出来，只是自由流动并试着抓住韵脚。当你坐下来写歌时，你会想："呃，我可以比这个写得更好。"但是这里要做的是自由联想，所以没有任何准备的时间。你只是抓住第一个出现的韵脚。

专辑的名字《电参数》出自艾伦·金斯堡的诗《堪萨斯城到圣路易斯》（Kansas City to St. Louis）里面的一句。艾伦，我了解得不多，他经常说："第一个念头，就是最好的念头。"不过我却注意到，他在不停地修改他的诗！

在我通常的歌曲写作的方式中，
我要遵从我给自己设置的节奏和律动，
但是意识流很明显限制更少，所以你就看到了这样的东西，
读起来有点像是某种垮掉派诗歌。

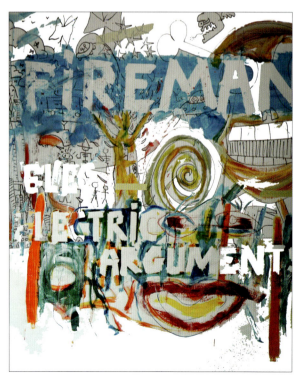

上图和左图：《电参数》设计图。

右图："青年"与保罗。
伦敦，2008 年。

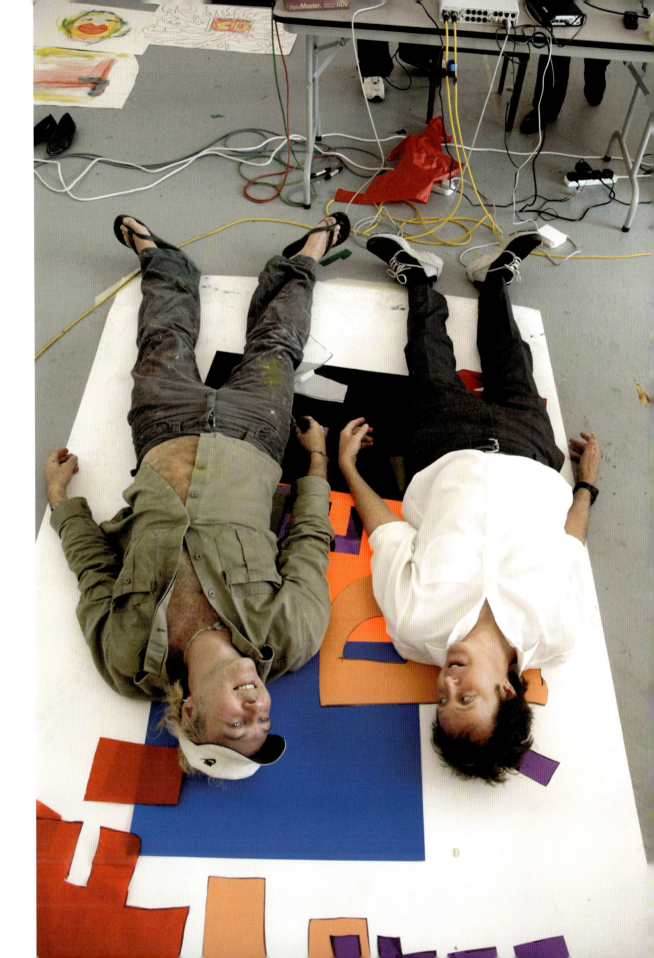

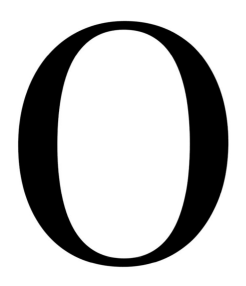

Ob-La-Di, Ob-La-Da

噢布 ~ 啦 ~ 迪，噢布 ~ 啦 ~ 哒

作　者　WRITERS　　保罗·麦卡特尼和约翰·列侬　Paul McCartney and John Lennon
艺术家　ARTIST　　披头士乐队　The Beatles
录　音　RECORDED　　伦敦阿比路录音棚　Abbey Road Studios, London
发　行　RELEASED　　《披头士》，1968 年　*The Beatles*, 1968

Desmond has a barrow in the market place
Molly is the singer in a band
Desmond says to Molly, Girl, I like your face
And Molly says this as she takes him by the hand

Ob-la-di, Ob-la-da, life goes on
Bra, la-la how the life goes on
Ob-la-di, Ob-la-da, life goes on
Bra, la-la how the life goes on

Desmond takes a trolley to the jeweller's store
Buys a twenty carat golden ring
Takes it back to Molly waiting at the door
And as he gives it to her she begins to sing

Ob-la-di, Ob-la-da, life goes on
Bra, la-la how the life goes on
Ob-la-di, Ob-la-da, life goes on
Bra, la-la how the life goes on

In a couple of years
They have built a home sweet home
With a couple of kids running in the yard
Of Desmond and Molly Jones

Happy ever after in the market place
Desmond lets the children lend a hand
Molly stays at home and does her pretty face
And in the evening she still sings it with the band

Ob-la-di, Ob-la-da, life goes on
Bra, la-la how the life goes on
Ob-la-di, Ob-la-da, life goes on
Bra, la-la how the life goes on

In a couple of years
They have built a home sweet home
With a couple of kids running in the yard
Of Desmond and Molly Jones

Happy ever after in the market place
Molly lets the children lend a hand
Desmond stays at home and does his pretty face
And in the evening she's a singer with the band

Ob-la-di, Ob-la-da, life goes on
Bra, la-la how the life goes on
Ob-la-di, Ob-la-da, life goes on
Bra, la-la how the life goes on
And if you want some fun
Take Ob-la-di-bla-da

问题在于，我们的演出结束得都太晚了，当我们回去时，伦敦的餐馆和酒吧都关门了，所以唯一能吃点东西、喝点什么的办法是"去一家俱乐部"，就像他们经常说的那样。那成了一种生活方式。我们会在演出结束后开车回来，直接去一家俱乐部。口袋钉子（The Bag O'Nails）是我最喜欢的俱乐部之一，还有扬声器（The Speakeasy）、革命（The Revolution）、苏格兰的圣詹姆斯（The Scotch of St James）、克伦威尔人（The Cromwellian）。后来，当其他人都结婚并住到郊区时，我经常自己一个人去那些地方。

　　我就是在其中一家俱乐部遇见了吉米·斯科特——一个我非常喜欢的尼日利亚康佳鼓手。吉米有许多口头禅，有一句是"Ob-La-Di, Ob-La-Da, life goes on, bra"（噢布~啦~迪，噢布~啦~哒，生活在继续，布啦）。有些人觉得这是一句约鲁巴语，有点像法语里"这样，那样"的意思。有些人认为这是吉米·斯科特自己发明的。还有一些人觉得"布啦"指的是胸罩，而不是非洲语的"哥们儿"。

　　我喜欢理解成"这样，那样，会是什么"。所以我打算写一首幽默的"人物歌曲"，关于戴斯蒙德和茉莉及他们的孩子。里面混合了非洲和牙买加元素。我相当确定，戴斯蒙德这个名字来自牙买加斯卡乐和雷鬼音乐家戴斯蒙德·德克尔（Desmond Dekker），他的《以色列人》（Israelites）后来成为1969年的金曲。1967年，他在英国已经有了一首金曲，叫《007》。

　　当戴斯蒙德坐上"电车"时，我可能想到的是旧金山的有轨电车系统。旧金山是披头士乐队举办最后一场演出的地方。但"戴斯蒙德坐上有轨电车"和"戴斯蒙德坐上电车"之间有天壤之别。有些东西要么符合节奏，要么没有；"有轨电车"（tram）在一首歌里显得有点笨拙，"电车"（trolley）却允许有节奏上的更多可能性。约翰和我曾经讨论过试着写一首非常口语化的歌。"Desmond takes a trolley to the jeweller's store"（戴斯蒙德坐上电车去了珠宝店）不是那么华丽。这是现实中你可以听到人们在说的话。这可能就是披头士的作品仍然很容易为人接受的秘密所在。因为我们说得很直接。

　　不过，不管你说得有多直接，仍然有诠释的空间。回到"电车"这个词，我明白实际上有很多人会把它解读成"购物车"。推着一辆购物车去珠宝店买东西这个主意非常有趣，特别是回来时带着一枚"十二克拉"的订婚戒指。无论如何，这很平常。

　　那是我仍然在追求的东西。我对平凡事物的力量非常感兴趣。我的镜头环顾四周，为了我的故事，搜寻生活中的线索。当我在公共汽车上、飞机上或者火车上，我的想象就开始了。我喜欢简单的事实。我喜欢大部分的人，不管他们是蒙古人、印度人或是美国人，直接可以联想到家庭、家庭生活，以及几个孩子在院子里玩耍的画面。如果我接通进去，我就会和人们产生联系。

<u>SONG TITLES.</u>

I'M SO TIRED, John in bed.

DON'T PASS ME BY, Ringo as fiddler (c+w handout.)

BLACKBIRD, Blackbird from bird book.

EVERYBODYS GOT SOMETHING TO HIDE EXCEPT FOR ME AND MY MONKEY, Black space.

GOODNIGHT, Ringo saying goodnight to his kids.

YER BLUES, Blues.

OB LA DI, OB LA DA, Jimmy Scott and wife in market

ROCKY RACCOON, Mal as Rocky being shot by Dan while

WILD HONEY PIE, (Hollywood handout) Lil sits on 4 poster.

MOTHER NATURES SON, Paul by stream.

BACK IN THE U.S.S.R. Paul throwing flowers to fat Russian (BOAC.)

SEXY SADIE, Black vinyl special.

WHILE MY GUITAR GENTLY WEEPS, Guitar rain splashed window

NOT GUILTY, George smiling behind bars.

HELTER SKELTER, Beatles on helter skelter

CRY BABY CRY, Alice fancy dress party on lawn.

REVOLUTION NO. 9, White space

WHAT'S NEW MARY JANE, Alexis machine

CHILD OF NATURE, John standing in hot sun.

HAPPINESS IS A WARM GUN, Johns hand on steel gun.

THE CONTINUING STORY OF BUNGALOW BILL, Ringo as tiger. John as heavily armed Bill.

JULIA, Picture of Julia — or of cloud.

POLYTHENE PAM, In person.

MAXWELLS SILVER HAMMER,

538

Desmond has a barrow in the market place
Molly is the singer in a band
Desi says to Molly girl I like your face
And Molly says this as she takes him by the hand
CHORUS   Obla dee Obla da, life goes on, bra,
         la-la how the life goes on. -
Desmond takes a trolley to the jewellers store
Buys a twenty. carat golden ring,
Takes it back to Molly waiting at the door
And as he gives it to her, she begins to sing

CHORUS. _ _ _ _ _ _

    In a couple of years they have built a home sweet home
With a couple of kids running in the yard of
    Desmond & Molly Jones - - - -
~~Desmond~~   Happy ever after in the market place
    Desmond lets the children lend a hand
Molly stays at home & does her pretty face
And in the evening she still sings this with the band
    CHORUS - - - - - - - -

左图：保罗和约翰写的专辑笔记，
1968 年。

Oh Woman, Oh Why

噢女人，噢为什么

作 者 WRITER	保罗·麦卡特尼	Paul McCartney
艺术家 ARTIST	保罗·麦卡特尼	Paul McCartney
录 音 RECORDED	纽约 CBS 录音棚	CBS Studios, New York
发 行 RELEASED	《又一天》B 面单曲，1971 年	B-side of 'Another Day' single, 1971

Woman, oh why why why why why
What have I done?
Oh woman, oh where where where where where
Did you get that gun?
Oh what have I done?
What have I done?

Well I met her at the bottom of a well
Well I told her I was tryin' to break a spell
But I can't get by, my hands are tied
Don't know why I ever bother to try myself
'Cause I can't get by, my hands are tied

Oh woman, oh why why why why why
What have I done?
Oh woman, oh where where where where where
Did you get that gun?
Oh what have you done?
Woman, what have you done?

Well I'm fed up with your lying cheating ways
But I get up every morning and every day
But I can't get by, my hands are tied
Don't know why I ever bother to try myself
'Cause I can't get by, my hands are tied

Oh woman, oh why why why why why
What have I done?
Oh woman, oh where where where where where
Did you get that gun
Woman, what have I done?
What have you done?
Woman, what have I done?
Oh woman, oh why

我特别喜欢的一种布鲁斯音乐是"女人，你待我太坏了"这样主题的歌。我不知道所有这些糟糕的事情是否真的曾发生在所有这些布鲁斯歌手身上。看上去似乎外面有很多可怕的做坏事的女人。我怀疑也许也有很多做坏事的男人！

这首歌的情绪有点接近《弗兰基和约翰尼》（Frankie and Johnny），那是一个有着无数表现形式的肮脏行为的故事，被无数歌手唱过，包括 1935 年铅肚皮的版本：

> 不是一级谋杀
>
> 不是三级谋杀
>
> 一个女人只是抛弃了她的男人
>
> 就像猎人抛弃一只鸟
>
> 他是她的男人，但她把他射杀 [1]

当我写这首歌的时候，我就进入了那个意象的体系，"I met her at the bottom of a well"（我在井底遇见她）。我觉得比起比如说"我在波旁大街遇见她"或者"我在巴黎的妓院遇见她"，那是一个更有意思的画面。我喜欢直截了当，不过不一定是从字面上来说。

水井本身更多是与民谣传统联系在一起。有一个关于水井形象的色情潜台词。我想的是威廉·贝尔[2]的《你不会思念你的水》（You Don't Miss Your Water）。我被这些歌曲吸引的另一个原因是，我在寻找一种手法来表现我的嗓音。我希望我的声音脏一点，我希望表现出一点美好的肮脏背景。我试着让我的嗓音在唱歌时更布鲁斯一些，而不是试着去抓住一段旋律。唱歌时放松很不错。

认真地想一下，在我做的每一件事情中——披头士乐队、羽翼乐队、个人计划——都有黑人音乐的暗流。你可以说这是布鲁斯，不过这更像是灵魂乐。那么多的白人乐队通过看黑人乐手和歌手来获得灵感。如果你想想披头士早期的东西，更像是翻唱黑人的《你真的俘获了我》（You Really Got a Hold on Me）、《扭摆和尖叫》。我们热爱查克·贝里、胖子多米诺、小理查德。然后开始有白人出现——猫王、吉恩·文森特、巴迪·霍利、卡尔·帕金斯[3]、杰瑞·李·刘易斯——他们也已经受到了黑人的影响。所以，尽管我们仰慕这些白人，我们仰慕的是仰慕黑人的白人。那绝对是我所做的几乎一切事情的基础。

1　原句为 "It was not murder in the first degree / It was not murder in the third / A woman simply dropped her man / Like a hunter drops a bird / He was her man, but she shot him down"。

2　威廉·贝尔（William Bell，1939— ），美国灵魂乐歌手。

3　卡尔·帕金斯（Carl Perkins，1932—1998），美国早期摇滚乐先驱之一。

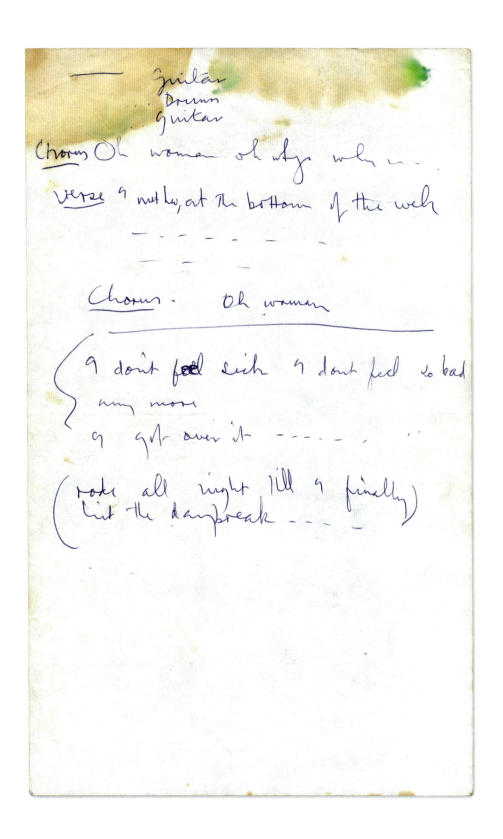

右图：歌单，1950 年代末。

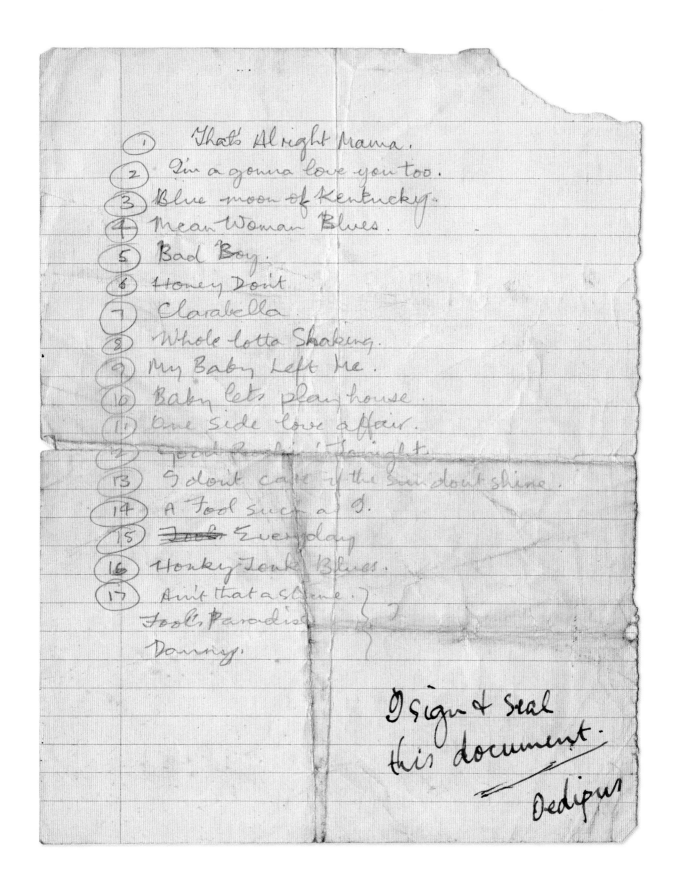

1. That's Alright Mama.
2. I'm a gonna love you too.
3. Blue moon of Kentucky.
4. Mean Woman Blues.
5. Bad Boy.
6. Honey Don't
7. Clarabella
8. Whole lotta Shaking.
9. My Baby Left Me.
10. Baby lets play house.
11. One side love affair.
12. ~~Good Rockin' tonight.~~
13. I don't care if the sun don't shine.
14. A Fool such as I.
15. ~~Fool~~ Everyday
16. Honky Tonk Blues.
17. Ain't that a shame.
    Fools Paradise
    Donny.

I sign & seal
this document.

Oedipus

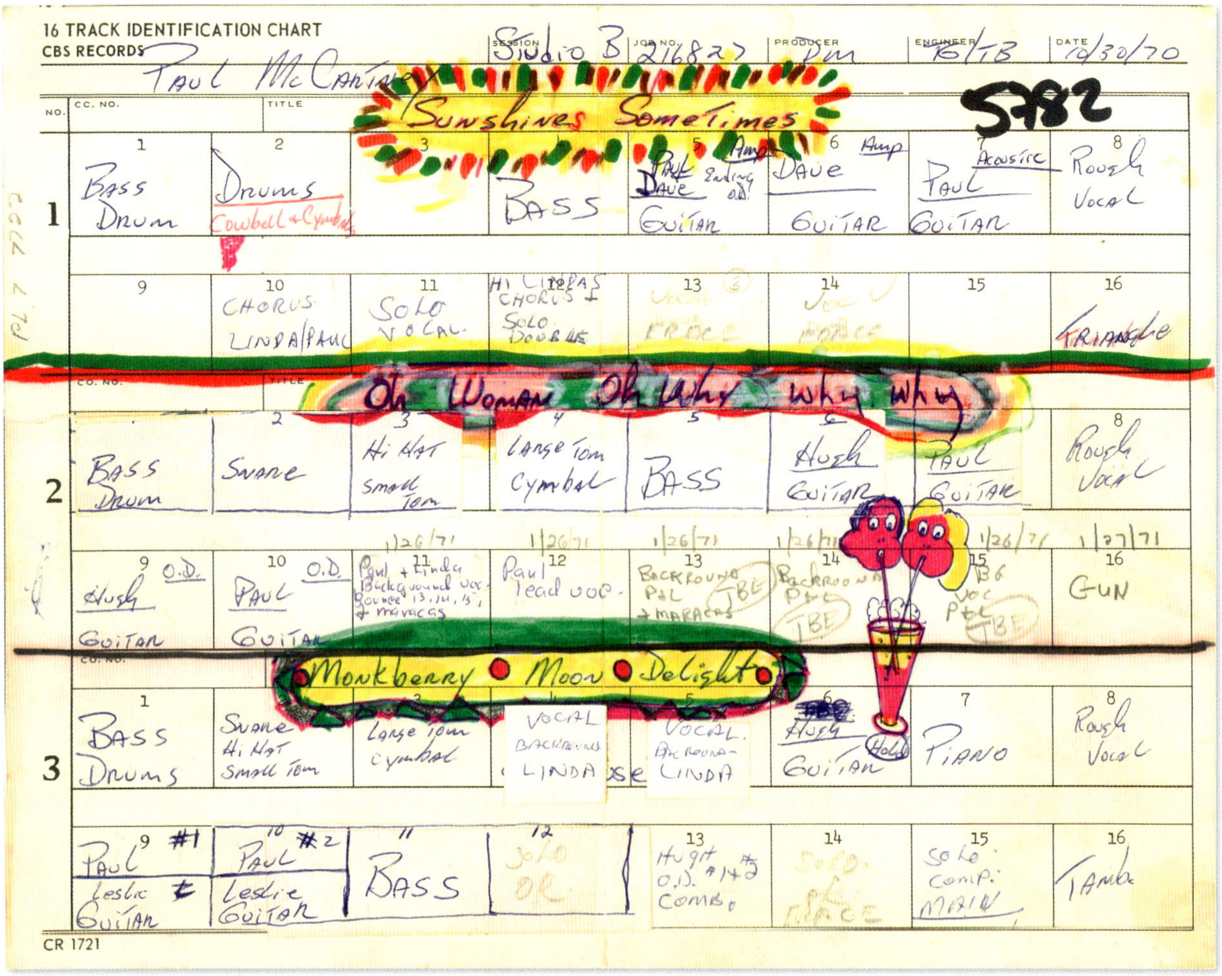

当我写这首歌的时候，我就进入了那个意象的体系，
"我在井底遇见她"。
我觉得比起比如说"我在波旁大街遇见她"
或者"我在巴黎的妓院遇见她"，
那是一个更有意思的画面。
我喜欢直截了当，不过不一定是从字面上来说。

上图：《拉姆》录音时段的声音
轨道表，1970 年。

右图：为《噢女人，噢为什么》
叠录枪声，纽约 A&R 录音棚，
1970 年。

披头士乐队与胖子多米诺。
新奥尔良，1964 年。

Old Siam, Sir

古老暹罗，先生

作　者　WRITER　　　保罗·麦卡特尼　Paul McCartney

艺术家　ARTIST　　　羽翼乐队　Wings

录　音　RECORDED　　苏格兰拉那坎精神录音棚　Spirit of Ranachan Studio, Scotland

发　行　RELEASED　　单曲，1979 年　Single, 1979

　　　　　　　　　　《回到蛋中》，1979 年　*Back to the Egg*, 1979

In a village in old Siam, sir
Lived a lady who lost her way
In an effort to find a man, sir
She found herself in the old UK

She waited round in Walthamstow
She scouted round in Scarborough
She waited round in Walthamstow
She scouted round in Scarborough

In a village in old East Ham, sir
She met a fellow who made her reel
Took her rushes to show his mam, sir
Met his dad at the wedding meal

In a letter from old Siam, sir
Came a terrible tale of woe
She decided the only answer
Was to get up a pile of dough

She waited round in Walthamstow
She scouted round in Scarborough
She waited round in Walthamstow
She scouted round in Scarborough

When a relative told her man, sir
He directed her not to stay
In a village in old Siam, sir
Lives a lady who lost her way

In a village in old Siam, sir
Lived a lady who lost her way
In an effort to find her man, sir
She found herself in the old UK

She waited round in Walthamstow
She scouted round in Scarborough
She waited round in Walthamstow
She scouted round in Scarborough

拉那坎精神录音棚听起来相当花哨，不过它基本上就是一个谷仓，一面墙上开了一扇控制室的窗户。古怪是那段时间的时代风尚——艳俗的外套和朋克迪斯科的时代——不过它们不会比《古老暹罗，先生》更古怪。如果我必须对这首歌曲中元素的古怪级别进行评级，我认为根据歌曲的感觉，歌词会排在第三位，排在第二的是人声的攻击性。我在这里用了一点点头韵，玩弄文字游戏——waited / Walthamstow（"等候"和"沃尔瑟姆斯托"），scouted / Scarborough（"搜索"和"斯卡波罗"）。我想我对此感觉有点尴尬的原因是，这其实没有什么意义。

不过，也许我应该放松一点，因为它并不是必须要有意义。这首歌有无意义的一面，不过当你读到像刘易斯·卡罗尔的《炸脖龙》[1]那样的东西时，它让你觉得做任何事情都是可以的。另一种考虑是，这首歌描绘的是一个在英国的亚洲移民，这首歌说的是对她的文化冲击。

我的歌曲有百分之九十八来自音乐性的动机，而不是歌词的动机，这首歌好像是从连复段开始的。有时候，我写歌时歌词就自动出现了，特别是围绕连复段创作的段落，它们会配合歌曲以及人声。即便在这个开明的时代，它们也会被叫作"愚蠢的"歌词，是当你绘制整首歌的结构时占位的歌词。我想这些实际上仍然是愚蠢的歌词。

在我的记忆里，只有一首歌是先写出歌词的——《我所有的爱》，因为我当时在巡演大巴上。大部分情况下，我都会用一个乐器开始创作。甚至《埃莉诺·里格比》都是从一个 E 小调和弦开始的，我从那个和弦中发展出动机，要么写一些轻柔的旋律，要么我会站起来尖叫——就看哪一种更适合。而有的时候，歌词会无意中出现，然后接下来你就有了《古老暹罗，先生》。

回到最开始，约翰和我听唱片时，我们在很多时候并不真的在乎歌词——只是一种声音。人们会说："那么，那些歌词呢？"我们意识到我们甚至没有注意到其他人注意到的一些细节差异，我们会说："噢是的，是这样的。"吉姆·里弗斯[2]有一首叫作《只是路过》（Just Walk On By）的歌，在 1960 年代初是一首金曲，我记得有一位牧师抱怨这首歌，说它是关于离婚或是一个男人有了外遇的。我们说："什么？他疯了！"我们从来没想过歌词。我们绝对不关心这首歌写的是什么。我们只是喜欢这首歌的声音。

1　《炸脖龙》（Jabberwocky），刘易斯·卡罗尔创作的诗歌，出自《爱丽丝镜中奇遇记》第一章。
2　吉姆·里弗斯（Jim Reeves，1923—1964），美国著名乡村乐／流行乐歌手。

左图：《古老暹罗，先生》单曲碟和封套设计，1979 年。

右图：肯特郡林普恩城堡，1979 年。

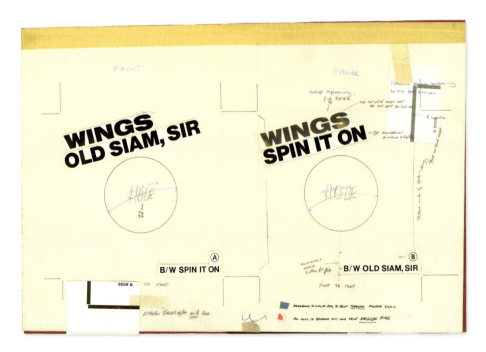

OLD SIAM, SIR.

In a village in Old Siam, Sir
Lived a lady who lost her way
In an effort to find a man, Sir
Found herself in the Old U.K.

She waited round in Walthamstow
She scouted round in Scarborough

Repeat.

In the village of Old East Siam, Sir
MET a fella that made a reel
Took her rushes to show his mam, Sir
Met his dad at the wedding meal

In a letter from Old Siam, Sir
Came a terrible tale of woe
She decided the only answer
Was to get up a pile of dough
She waited round in Walthamstow
She scouted " " Scarborough.

Repeat.

When a relative told her man, Sir,
He directed her not to stay
In a village in Old Siam, Sir
Lives a lady who lost her way

She waited round in Walthamstow

552

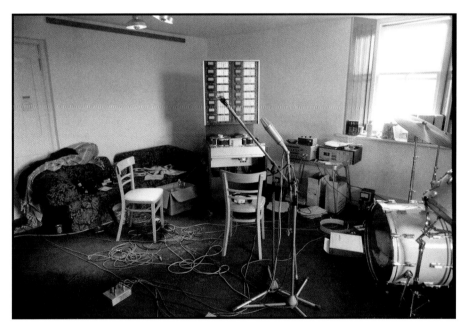

这首歌有无意义的一面，
不过当你读到像刘易斯·卡罗尔的《炸脖龙》那样的东西时，
它让你觉得做任何事情都是可以的。

On My Way to Work

在我上班的路上

作　者　WRITER	保罗·麦卡特尼　Paul McCartney	
艺术家　ARTIST	保罗·麦卡特尼　Paul McCartney	
录　音　RECORDED	萨塞克斯郡猪山磨坊、伦敦阿比路录音棚、洛杉矶汉森录音棚、伦敦 AIR 录音棚	
	Hog Hill Mill, Sussex; Abbey Road Studios, London; Henson Studios, Los Angeles and AIR Studios, London	
发　行　RELEASED	《新》，2013 年　*NEW*, 2013	

On my way to work
I rode a big green bus
I could see everything
From the upper deck
People came and went
Smoking cigarettes
I picked the packets up
When the people left

But all the time I thought of you
How far away the future seemed
How could I have so many dreams
And one of them not come true?

On my way to work
I bought a magazine
Inside a pretty girl
Liked to waterski
She came from Chichester
To study history
She had removed her clothes
For the likes of me

But all the time I thought of you
How would you know that I was there?
How could a soul search everywhere
Without knowing what to do?

On my way to work
As I was clocking in
I could see everything
How it came to be
People come and go
Smoking cigarettes
I pick the packets up
When the people leave

But all the time I think of you
How far away the future seems
How could I have so many dreams
And one of them not come true?

On my way to work

But all the time I thought of you
How would you know that I was there?
How could a soul search everywhere
Without knowing what to do?

On my way to work
On my way to work

上图：从皇家利物浦大厦上看到的景象，1955 年。

我的爸爸来自那样一个阶层，他相信在你十几岁的年纪不应该游手好闲。待在家里不付房租也不是一个好主意。那个时候，我的妈妈刚刚去世，只剩下他、我和我的弟弟，所以家庭收入不算太多。

我的第一份工作在一个叫作 SPD 的地方，快速交货（Speedy Prompt Deliveries），就在利物浦老码头的后面。我就是人们所说的运货车里的"二把手"，听上去是个很重要的位置。但就我来说，我真的不是那么重要。我问司机，那位货车里显而易见的"一把手"："作为货车里的二把手，我的工作是什么？"而他回答："呃，当我们到了要送货的地点，你要帮我搬东西。"送货的地点一般是商店和工厂。所以，那就是我的工作。

我记得和我交朋友的那个司机很酷，而且他知道我是个少年懒汉，所以当他开车去送货地点时，他会让我在车里睡觉，当我们到达时他才叫醒我。我们下车，他打开货车的后厢，拿出包裹，而我要把这些包裹送进去，或者我们一起把包裹送进去。

年轻时我总是在想："我究竟要怎么样做才能在地球上数十亿人里找到合适的人呢？一颗灵魂怎么能四处寻找，却不知道该做什么呢？我怎么才能遇见对的那个人呢？"这是我青春期时的困扰。其他还有："我要找什么样的工作？"送货车这个工作，或者在工厂的流水线上工作（我的另一份工作），或者像我爸爸一样去棉花交易所，我从中看不到任何前途。

我能明白如今那些有着同样困扰的孩子，他们是真的很困扰，非常像我在这首歌里描述的那样。"On my way to work / I bought a magazine / Inside a pretty girl / Liked to waterski / She came from Chichester"（在我上班的路上 / 我买了一本杂志 / 里面有一位

上图：约翰·列侬和采石人乐队在圣彼得教堂集市上的演出，1957 年 7 月 6 日。

左图：利物浦独特的绿色公交车，《便士巷》宣传片里的画面。

美丽姑娘／她喜欢滑水／她来自奇切斯特）。我很高兴把这些细节写在歌里。有时候在去 SPD 的路上我会这么做。我会买裸体杂志，现在我是个工人，而且被允许买它们！除此之外，几年后《太阳报》开始在第三版刊登这些："珍妮特来自海灵岛。她的喜好包括……"我喜欢这些传记体的细节，那是很好的背景——充实了故事。

关于那个时期，有一段深刻的记忆——从家里去往海边巨大而繁华的码头。坐公交车需要大概半个小时。那时候利物浦的公交车都是绿色的，有可能是 80 路或者 86 路，进城的线路之一。我总是喜欢坐在上层，因为我喜欢更好的视野，以及在上面发生的一些好玩的事情。那时候每个人都抽烟，坐在上面你就可以抽烟。当汽车到站时，我和朋友会捡起被丢下的烟盒。我知道这说起来似乎有点奇怪，不过在贫穷中有一种特殊的快乐——至少如果你还是个孩子，对贫穷了解不多时。然而长大成人后，你就不能谈论太多贫穷的快乐，因为人们会说："噢，不，这是可怕的事情。"但是当你很年轻时，你所看见的一切，确实都可以变成快乐的事情，因为你一无所有，从那里开始创造所有有趣的场景，并使它们成为你每天的现实，成为一种日常。

我们会收集丢在车上的烟盒，然后整理好，就像你在美国看见的那些棒球卡，这样你就有了一大卷烟盒——高级专供、运动员海军刀、俄罗斯寿百年、浮云、吉卜赛女郎、黑猫、罗宾、忍冬。有那么多香烟牌子，几乎成为极棒的藏品。而一旦你的朋友也开始收藏，你就可以说，"我用三张忍冬换你一张浮云。"结果，这全都是在宣传癌症。

我第一次见到约翰·列侬就是在一辆公交车上。那时候我还不认识他，他就是那种年纪稍微大一点的家伙，留着摇滚发型，很多头油，黑夹克，大鬓角（我们说连鬓胡了，"鬓角"是美国人的说法）。我记得我当时想："呃，他真酷。"我们认识之后，我认出他就是那个公交车上的奇怪的泰迪男孩。约翰总是设法显得比我年长一些，我一直赶不上他。

那个时候我不知道他是谁，但我一直记得那个第一印象。

我第一次见到约翰·列侬就是在一辆公交车上。
那时候我还不认识他，
他就是那种年纪稍微大一点的家伙，
留着摇滚发型，很多头油，黑夹克，大鬓角。

Once Upon a Long Ago
很久以前

作　者　WRITER　　　保罗·麦卡特尼　Paul McCartney

艺术家　ARTIST　　　保罗·麦卡特尼　Paul McCartney

录　音　RECORDED　萨塞克斯郡猪山磨坊及伦敦阿比路录音棚　Hog Hill Mill, Sussex and Abbey Road Studios, London

发　行　RELEASED　英国单曲，1987 年　UK single, 1987

Picking up scales and broken chords
Puppy dog tails in the House of Lords
Tell me darling, what can it mean?

Making up moons in a minor key
What have those tunes got to do with me?
Tell me darling, where have you been?

Once upon a long ago
Children searched for treasure
Nature's plan went hand in hand with pleasure
Such pleasure

Blowing balloons on a windy day
Desolate dunes with a lot to say
Tell me darling, what have you seen?

Once upon a long ago
Children searched for treasure
Nature's plan went hand in hand with pleasure
My pleasure

Playing guitars on an empty stage
Counting the bars of an iron cage
Tell me darling, what can it mean?

Picking up scales and broken chords
Puppy dog tails in the House of Lords
Help me darling, what does it mean?

Once upon a long ago . . .

威廉·S. 巴勒斯有那种我们所说的"拼贴技巧"。我则时不时成为这方面的爱好者 —— 只是把文字拖来拖去，扔到半空中，看看它们会落在哪里。你会觉得："好吧，那没什么意思。"但是当你读它时，看起来就有了些意思。

我知道我曾经说过这个故事，但是当我开始画画时，我的想法是，我所画的必须有意思，它必须要有深远的意义。这彻底拦住了我的脚步。我画不了任何东西。然后我遇见了威廉·德·库宁，我问起他的一幅绘画以及其中的"意义"，他说："我不知道。看起来像是一个沙发，哈？"而我想，"天哪。"这把我的头脑打开了。

在这首歌的文本中，不需要有任何意义的理念解放了我。我可以编一个故事。几乎不费吹灰之力，我就开始行动了。所以，"Picking up scales and broken chords"（拾起音阶和破碎的和弦）再一次提及我为什么从来不想学习音乐，因为那是"哒-哒-哒-哒-哒，哒-哒-哒-哒"——一个接一个的五指练习。我受不了那个，对我来说太无聊了。这使我推迟了学习记谱法。而"Puppy dog tails in the House of Lords"（上议院的小狗尾巴）这一句，上议院有一群小孩子的想法出自——如果你还记得——小孩子是由小狗尾巴做成的。这有点尖刻，我知道，但是我觉得跟上议院有关的任何事情可能都有点愚蠢。

这首歌里的许多其他意象来自我的童年，来自我们住宅区附近的田野。"Blowing balloons on a windy day"（在起风的日子里吹气球）是真的发生过的，同时"Desolate dunes with a lot to say"（荒凉的山丘有许多话要说）这个意象出自童年时去海边的记忆。

至于"Playing guitars on an empty stage"（在空无一人的舞台上弹吉他），我没有演出焦虑症，不过在梦里有过。他们说所有表演者都会有。演员登上舞台准备说他们的第一句台词，而他们不知道他们演的是哪一部戏。他们冒着冷汗醒来。我曾经做过试图阻止观众成群结队地离开的梦。

在我的梦里，如果在一场演唱会上，我看见观众中的人群不停走动或离开他们的座位，我不会去想，"这些人怎么了？他们为什么不坐着好好听呢？"我会想，"我们做错了什么吗？我们显然唱错了歌。"于是我转成《高个子莎莉》，心想，"这下子可以抓住你们了"，或者"让我们演个快速热烈的《昨天》"。无论是在纸页上，还是在舞台上，我总是试着找到能够让观众兴趣的东西。

ONCE UPON A LONG AGO

PICKING UP SCALES AND BROKEN CHORDS.
PUPPY DOG TAILS IN THE HOUSE OF LORDS
TELL ME DARLING — WHAT CAN IT MEAN?

MAKING UP MOONS IN A MINOR KEY,
WHAT HAVE THOSE TUNES GOT TO DO WITH ME?
TELL ME DARLING — WHERE HAVE YOU BEEN?

ONCE UPON A LONG AGO
CHILDREN SEARCHED FOR TREASURE.
NATURE'S PLAN WENT HAND IN HAND
WITH PLEASURE, ... MY PLEASURE ..... SOLO ..

BLOWING BALLOONS ON A WINDY DAY,
DESOLATE DUNES WITH A LOT TO SAY,
TELL ME DARLING — WHAT HAVE YOU SEEN?

PLAYING GUITARS ON AN EMPTY STAGE,
COUNTING THE BARS **OF** AN IRON CAGE
TELL ME DARLING — WHAT CAN IT MEAN?

ONCE UPON A LONG AGO
CHILDREN SEARCHED FOR TREASURE.
NATURE'S PLAN WENT HAND IN HAND.
WITH PLEASURE .... SUCH PLEASURE ... .

560

《很久以前》音乐录影带，
1987 年。

这首歌里的许多其他意象来自我的童年，
来自我们住宅区附近的田野。
"在起风的日子里吹气球"是真的发生过的，
同时"荒凉的山丘有许多话要说"这个意象
出自童年时去海边的记忆。

左图：和威廉·德·库宁在一起，东汉普顿，1984 年。

右图：保罗画作《天空中的花马和罂粟沙漠》(*Pintos in the Sky with Desert Poppy*)，1991 年。

当我开始画画时，我的想法是，我所画的必须有意思，
它必须要有深远的意义。
这彻底拦住了我的脚步。我画不了任何东西。

Only Mama Knows

只有妈妈知道

作 者 WRITER	保罗·麦卡特尼	Paul McCartney
艺术家 ARTIST	保罗·麦卡特尼	Paul McCartney
录 音 RECORDED	伦敦阿比路录音棚	Abbey Road Studios, London
发 行 RELEASED	《记忆将满》，2007 年	*Memory Almost Full*, 2007

Well I was found in the transit lounge
Of a dirty airport town
What was I doing on the road to ruin?
Well my mama laid me down
My mama laid me down

Round my hand was a plastic band
With a picture of my face
I was crying, left to die in
This godforsaken place
This godforsaken place

Only mama knows why she laid me down
In this godforsaken town
Where she was running to, what she ran from
Though I always wondered, I never knew
Only mama knows
Only mama knows

I'm passing through, I'm on my way
I'm on the road, no ETA
I'm passing through, no fixed abode
And that is why I need to try
To hold on, I've gotta hold on, gotta hold on

Was it planned as a one-night stand
Or did she leave in disgrace?
Well I never, will I ever
See my father's face?
See my father's face?

Only mama knows why she laid me down
In this godforsaken town
Where she was running to, what she ran from
Though I always wondered, I never knew
Only mama knows
Only mama knows

I've gotta hold on
I've gotta hold on
You've gotta hold on

我的一个朋友在他还是婴儿时就被收养了。他和他的兄弟被丢在孤儿院。他们在孤儿院长大，从不知道母亲是谁。他成功消化了这段经历，他的兄弟却很挣扎。我用这段"真实的故事"来创作一个想象的场景，这是这首歌的基石。这首歌是用被丢下的某个人的视角来写的。被抛弃的某个人。

我写这首歌的时候，我的朋友和我在一起；我录这首歌时，他也在我的身边。我们开诚布公地讨论过这些。他总是会疑惑为什么他的妈妈要丢下他。他隐约知道这个故事，她因为某个路过的家伙而怀孕。在那个年代，这是非常丢人的——一个女人如果还没有结婚，是不应该有孩子的——然后还有抚养孩子的经济困难。

从某种程度上，我在给自己做心理测试，进入那个让她怀孕的男人的视角。"I'm passing through, I'm on my way / I'm on the road, no ETA"（我正路过，我在路上 / 我在路上，没有预计到达的时间）。我喜欢这两句歌词，它们总结了很多旅行生活的样子。"I'm passing through, no fixed abode"（我正路过，没有固定住所）。在这首歌里，孩子被留下来，而他正走开，他在上路。他的行为和他爸爸一样，所以生活就是一个固定的轮回。一旦我开始写这些，我显然是从自己的角度来看待它的。我承认，比起普通人，那个被妈妈遗弃的孩子在生活中遭遇的麻烦更多。他要坚持，他要沉着。但是真的远不止于此。当我越来越成熟，就越来越觉得我们所有人都不得不坚持。没有人确切地知道我们会遇到什么，但是我们一起深陷其中。

桥段给了你一个机会，去用不同的角度探讨一个主题。因为旋律变化了，音乐已经去往一个不同的地方，所以这是一个歌词去往别处的好机会。你可以用一些重要的表达来帮助这首歌前进，或者你可以做个随便的观察：这是非常棒的事情——你可以自由地做你想做的。你基本上只是试图在重新进入高速公路之前，在出口匝道上停留几分钟。

我们把这叫作"桥段"（middle eight），因为其他人就这么叫它，它往往是八个小节，当然，你希望颠覆它，你不想要八个小节，你想要十个小节。我们从来没有做过我一直想做的事，那就是布鲁斯乐手所做的：他们会做七个小节，而就在你觉得它不会变化的时候，它变化了；或者他们会做九个小节，当你想"就是现在"时，他们会继续："不，还多一点。"

我喜欢你可以自由地做任何你想做的事情这个想法。任何写歌的人都知道，如果你有追随者，人们会了解你的风格。我的风格之一是，"好了，好了，一切都会好起来"，不过颠覆这个也很好。你知道你的歌迷想要什么，所以你也许试着戏弄他们一下，不要以他们期待的方式给予。我觉得很多我的歌曲，很多披头士的歌曲，就是这么做的：你期待它走这里，而它并没有——它去了那里。已经有不少人说过这是我们歌曲最好的特性之一。《一夜狂欢》和《救命！》的导演理查德·莱斯特（Richard Lester）就是其中之一，他是个爵士乐迷，他说："我喜欢它们的出其不意。"

所以，这成为我们一条有意思的规则：试着走他们没料到你会走的路。

《记忆将满》录音期间，2007 年。

ONLY MAMA KNOWS

INTRO

(E min)   (D)

① I WAS FOUND IN THE TRANSIT LOUNGE
(E min)   (D)
OF A DIRTY AIRPORT TOWN
(E min)   (D)
WHAT I WAS DOING ON THE ROAD TO RUIN
(E min)   (F# min)
WELL, MY MAMA LAID ME DOWN
(E min)   (D)
MAMA LAID ME DOWN

(E min)   (D)
② ROUND MY HAND WAS A PLASTIC BAND
(E min)   (D)
WITH A PICTURE OF MY FACE
(E min)   (D)
I WAS CRYING, LEFT TO DIE IN
(E min)   (F# min)
THIS GOD FORSAKEN PLACE
(E min)   (D)
GOD FORSAKEN PLACE   CHORDS D A E
                                              B

(CHORUS)   (B)   (Eb min)   (C# min)
ONLY MAMA KNOWS, WHY SHE LAID ME DOWN
(E min)   (B)
IN THIS GOD FORSAKEN TOWN
(B)   (Eb min)   (C# min)
WHERE SHE WAS RUNNING TO, WHERE SHE RAN FROM
                              (E min)
THOUGH I ALWAYS WONDERED, I NEVER KNEW
(E min) ONLY MAMA KNOWS —

MIDDLE   (E min 7) —
PASSING THROUGH, I'M ON MY WAY
ON THE ROAD, NO E.T.A.
PASSING THROUGH NO FIXED ABODE
AND THAT IS WHY I NEED TO TRY, TO HOLD ON....

③ (E min)   (D)
WAS IT PLANNED AS A ONE NIGHT STAND
(E min)   (D)
OR DID SHE LEAVE IN DISGRACE
(E min)   (D)   (E min)   (F# min)
WELL I NEVER, WILL I EVER SEE MY FATHER'S FACE
                              (E min) " " (D) "
[CHORUS]
(B)   (Eb min)   (C# min)   (E min)   (B)
ONLY MAMA KNOWS WHY SHE LAID ME DOWN IN THIS GOD FORSAKEN TOWN
(B)   (Eb min)   (C# min)
WHERE SHE WAS RUNNING TO, WHERE SHE RAN FROM THOUGH I ALWAYS
(E min)   (E min)
WONDERED, I NEVER KNEW ONLY MAMA KNOWS.
                    (E min 7)

The Other Me
另一个我

作　者 WRITER　　　保罗·麦卡特尼　Paul McCartney
艺术家 ARTIST　　　保罗·麦卡特尼　Paul McCartney
录　音 RECORDED　　伦敦 AIR 录音棚　AIR Studios, London
发　行 RELEASED　　《和平管乐》，1983 年　*Pipes of Peace*, 1983

I know I was a crazy fool
For treating you the way I did
But something took a hold of me
And I acted like a dustbin lid

I didn't give a second thought
To what the consequence might be
I really wouldn't be surprised
If you were trying to find another me

'Cause the other me would rather be the glad one
The other me would rather play the fool
I want to be the kind of me
That doesn't let you down as a rule

I know it doesn't take a lot
To have a little self-control
But every time that I forgot
Well I landed in another hole

But every time you pull me out
I find it harder not to see
That we can build a better life
If I can try to find the other me

The other me would rather be the glad one
Yeah the other me would rather play the fool
Said I want to be the kind of me
That doesn't let you down as a rule

But if I ever hurt you
Well you know that it's not real
It's not easy living by yourself
So imagine how I feel

I wish that I could take it back
I'd like to make a different mood
And if you let me try again
I'll have a better attitude

Well I know that one and one makes two
And that's what I want us to be
I really would appreciate it
If you'd help me find the other me

And the other me would rather be the glad one
The other me would rather play the fool
But I want to be the kind of me
That doesn't let you down as a rule

如果我没有加入一支像披头士那样成功的乐队——一个生命长久的乐队，那么我也许不得不去找一些其他工作。我几乎肯定会成为一位英语教师，那个"另一个我"。

但是，作为音乐家、表演者、歌手、词曲作者，我过的生活不可思议，我仍然觉得好像我是在扮演它。我有点"冒名顶替综合征"——我猜，就像许多"成功"人士那样。我过的生活是我自己找的，因为被它吸引，因为对一些永远无法解决的问题的爱。而每一首歌，都是解决方案的一部分。我自己一个人不一定能找到这个解决方法。

我们全都陷入了进退两难的境地。我们会说一些我们不想说的话，或者说一些会产生误解的话。所以这首歌是个道歉："I know I was a crazy fool / For treating you the way I did / But something took a hold of me / And I acted like a dustbin lid"（我知道从前对待你的方式 / 像个疯狂的白痴 / 但有些东西控制了我 / 我表现得极其幼稚）。发生了一些事情，而我表现得很幼稚——"dustbin lid"是利物浦孩子的俚语。通常在一场争吵之后，人们离开时会带着许多强烈的、无处发泄的能量。如果你是个词曲作者，你可以利用它。在写像《另一个我》这样的歌时，你可以成为你自己的精神病学家。你回顾你的表现，承认自己的错误，然后下一次寻找一个更好的解决方法。

当然，在披头士乐队成立初期，我们甚至没考虑过写歌，只是将它当作副业。我们主要是喜欢其他人录制的完整的歌曲，所以我们会唱一首查克·贝里的歌，或者唱一首卡尔·帕金斯的歌，或者猫王的歌。约翰和我相遇时，我们友谊的第一年就是在谈论这些翻唱版本歌曲、我们喜欢的唱片，并且把它们演奏了一遍又一遍。开始互相了解对方时，我们排练了大量这些翻唱歌曲，直到有一天出现这样的对话——"你知道吗，我写了一两首歌。"然后他说："好啊，我也有一两首。"

上图：高个子约翰和银色甲壳虫乐队为拉里·帕内斯试演时，和斯图尔特·萨克利夫、约翰·列侬、约翰尼·哈金森（Johnny Hutchinson）及乔治·哈里森一起。利物浦翼龙社交俱乐部（后来的蓝色天使），1960 年 5 月。

这给了我们一些共同点，这些共同点本身就完全不同寻常。我的学校有一千名学生，而我从来没遇见过谁说他写了一首歌。我的歌就在我的脑海里，约翰也是。我们彼此都大吃一惊。然后合乎逻辑的发展是："好吧，也许我们可以一起写一首。"我们就是这样开始的。我们成了彼此的翻版。

在 1960 年左右，我们为一个伦敦经纪人和演出推广人拉里·帕内斯（Larry Parnes）进行了一次试演，他那时候很有名，他签了一批年轻的摇滚男孩。老拉里是个通情达理的人，而他要到利物浦来安排试演，所以这真的是个大新闻，我们很兴奋，你完全可以想象。试演在一个叫翼龙社交俱乐部的地方进行，这个地方后来改名叫蓝色天使。当时还叫"卡斯和卡萨诺瓦斯"（Cass and the Cassanovas）的三巨头乐队（The Big Three）、德里和老头乐队，以及后来因为《穿越默西河的渡船》（Ferry Cross the Mersey）成名的杰瑞和领跑者乐队 —— 我们全都在那天试演。

我们试演时的贝斯手是斯图尔特·萨克利夫。斯图尔特是约翰在艺术学院时的一个朋友，他是一位真正的画家，不过他赢得了六十五英镑的艺术奖金，那正巧是买一把霍夫纳贝斯所需要的钱。斯图尔特说："没门，我不会去干这个。"但是约翰很有说服力，于是，斯图尔特买了这把他真的不知道怎么弹的贝斯，不过只要在 A 调上，他就这样"咚-咚-咚"，将低音元素加入我们的吉他和弦中。

乔治弹主音吉他，约翰和我弹节奏吉他。斯图尔特转身背对着镜头和拉里，因为我们想："如果他们看见他的手指，就会发现他不会弹。"所以我们非常外交式地建议他："转过身去，看起来忧郁点。"于是，在早期的照片上，你会看到斯图尔特没有面对镜头，而他看上去确实很忧郁。

拉里·帕内斯说："你们叫什么名字？乐队叫什么名字？"我们不想用"采石人"，便说："我们还不确定。"他说："好吧，你们应该有个名字。"约翰表现得像乐队领头人，所以拉里问他："你叫什么名字？"约翰回答"高个子约翰·希尔弗"（Long John Silver）。然后，我说我的名字是"保罗·雷蒙"（Paul Ramone），我也不知道为什么。或许当时我觉得"雷蒙"很有法国味，而且老练。随后乔治说自己叫"卡尔·哈里森"（Carl Harrison），来自卡尔·帕金斯。之后，我们大概说了"我们叫自己'甲壳虫乐队'（The Beetles）"或者类似这样的名字，不过我想我们确实说的是两个 e。然后那个家伙说："天哪，这个名字真糟糕。我们就叫你们'高个子约翰和银色甲壳虫乐队'吧。"我们回答："没问题。"

所以，我们实际上跟随拉里·帕内斯，以银色甲壳虫乐队的名字做了一个巡演。拉里旗下的歌手都有一些夸张的名字。比利·愤怒（Billy Fury）、马蒂·狂野（Marty Wilde）、迪基·骄傲（Dickie Pride），有点像是漫画书里的动作角色。我们跟他旗下的另一个人一起巡演 —— 某个叫"约翰尼·温柔"（Johnny Gentle）的人。我们想："这他妈的是什么意思？"苏格兰巡演时，我们排在他的后面，我们有点失望，没有人有听起来更激烈的名字。

约翰尼·温柔其实是带着一位年轻女士一起巡演的，他介绍说是他的妻子，而作为天真的年轻利物浦男孩，我们会说，"当然，温柔夫人。"我们真的相信她，但是随歌迷杂志《俱乐部三明治》（*Club Sandwich*）里的海报，1996 年第 77 期。

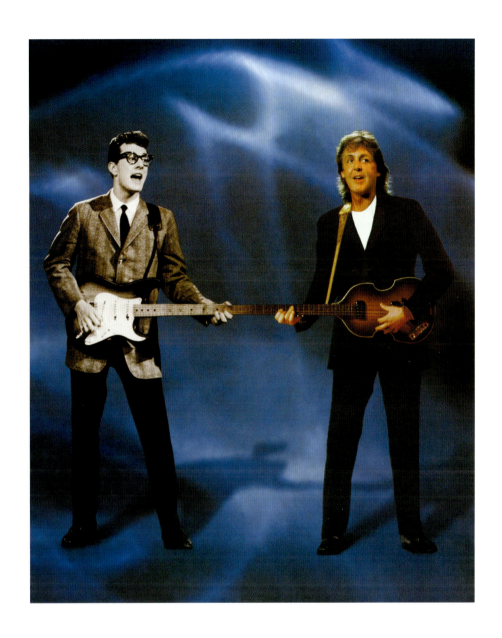

后。怀疑主义开始抬头。我们恍然大悟，如果你要在汉堡待一段时间，或者在苏格兰巡演，你可以做的是带上一个女朋友和你住同一家酒店房间，并且告诉乐队成员她是你的妻子。

在最初，巴迪·霍利对我们来说是大明星。我们在电台听过他，以为他是一位黑人音乐家。《终有一天》（That'll Be the Day）是首伟大的歌曲，我们爱这首歌，它有一个了不起的短前奏。我们用了几年的时间来学习那段前奏，我们最终学会了。然后我们看着 B 面，看看他做的其他歌。《佩吉·苏》（Peggy Sue）——哇，我们也爱那首歌；《也许宝贝》（Maybe Baby）——很迷人。很明显他自己写歌，几乎没有其他人这么做。我们年轻，但我们总是看创作名单，因为我们对整个过程很感兴趣。那是披头士了不起的地方之一：我们从不错过一个戏法；我们知道谁写了什么，试着去找出他们是谁。

在一些我们喜欢的金曲的下面，我们看到"戈芬／金"这个署名。我们觉得这可能是两个男人，结果是一个女人和一个男人：卡罗尔·金（Carole King）和她的第一任丈夫杰瑞·戈芬（Gerry Goffin）。他们在曼哈顿的布里尔大厦外工作。我们看见"霍利"这个名字署在巴迪·霍利的歌曲下面，我们想："哇，他写了这首歌。"然后我们在伦敦帕拉丁的电视上看到了他，他弹吉他唱歌。但是猫王自己不写歌，他也不会弹吉他；我们观察他的手指，就明白他弹得很糟糕。在《温柔地爱我》（Love Me Tender）中，我们确实能看出他不是真弹。当然，他是一位迷人的表演者，但是他只能弹一些基础的和弦。

所以，因为这些原因，我们喜欢巴迪和蟋蟀乐队。我们喜欢他的乐队，但是我们爱的还是巴迪，他的嗓音和他的吉他演奏，更别提那副眼镜了，以及他写歌的事实。如果你考虑到这些，那正是披头士所做的：我们自己创作，我们在台前弹吉他，而且我们唱。我们就是这样成了我们应该成为的样子。

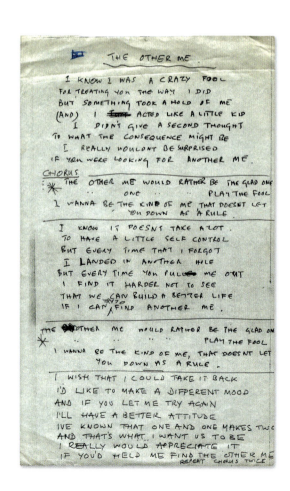

THE OTHER ME.

1. I KNOW I WAS A CRAZY FOOL
FOR TREATING YOU THE WAY I DID
BUT SOMETHING TOOK A HOLD OF ME
(AND) I ~~JUST~~ ACTED LIKE A LITTLE KID
I DIDN'T GIVE A SECOND THOUGHT
TO WHAT THE CONSEQUENCE MIGHT BE
I REALLY WOULDN'T BE SURPRISED
IF YOU WERE LOOKING FOR ANOTHER ME.

CHORUS
THE OTHER ME WH**O**'D RATHER BE THE GLAD ONE
ME WHO WOULDN'T ~~PLAY~~ BE THE FOOL
I WANNA BE THE KIND OF ME THAT DOESNT LET
YOU DOWN AS A RULE.

2. I KNOW IT DOESNT TAKE A LOT.
TO HAVE A LITTLE SELF CONTROL
BUT EVERY TIME THAT I FORGOT
I LANDED IN ANOTHER HOLE
AND EVERY TIME YOU PULL~~ED~~ ME OUT
I FIND IT HARDER NOT TO SEE
THAT WE CAN BUILD A BETTER LIFE
IF I CAN TRY TO FIND THE ~~OTHER~~ OTHER ME.

CHORUS.
THE ~~OTHER~~ OTHER ME WHO'D RATHER BE THE GLAD ONE.
WHO WOULDN'T BE ~~THE~~ THE FOOL
I WANNA BE THE KIND OF ME, THAT DOESNT LET
YOU DOWN AS A RULE.

MIDDLE.
AND IF I EVER HURT YOU, PLEASE IMAGINE HOW I FEEL
~~LIVING WITH~~
~~ITS NOT EASY TO RESPECT YOURSELF WHEN~~ ~~BREAKING ALL~~
~~WHEN YOU NEED~~ TO MAKE A DEAL ~~YOUR IDEAS~~.

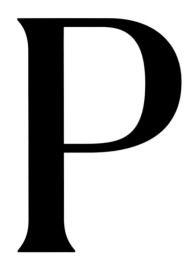

Paperback Writer

平装书作家

作　者　WRITERS　　保罗·麦卡特尼和约翰·列侬　Paul McCartney and John Lennon
艺术家　ARTIST　　披头士乐队　The Beatles
录　音　RECORDED　伦敦阿比路录音棚　Abbey Road Studios, London
发　行　RELEASED　单曲，1966 年　Single, 1966

Paperback writer
　(Paperback writer)

Dear Sir or Madam, will you read my book?
It took me years to write will you take a look?
It's based on a novel by a man named Lear
And I need a job so I want to be a
Paperback writer, paperback writer

It's a dirty story of a dirty man
And his clinging wife doesn't understand
His son is working for the Daily Mail
It's a steady job but he wants to be a
Paperback writer, paperback writer

Paperback writer
　(Paperback writer)

It's a thousand pages give or take a few
I'll be writing more in a week or two
I can make it longer if you like the style
I can change it round and I want to be a
Paperback writer, paperback writer

If you really like it you can have the rights
It could make a million for you overnight
If you must return it you can send it here
But I need a break and I want to be a
Paperback writer, paperback writer

Paperback writer
　(Paperback writer)

事实是我们发现了大麻。我们意识到歌曲不仅仅是"谢谢你姑娘，我对你的，她爱你"，不再是那么简单了。我们开始寻找一些之前从未真正在流行歌曲里出现过的主题。

　　这种意识让我一头栽进了作家的大杂烩，比如金斯利·艾米斯（Kingsley Amis）、约翰·莫蒂默（John Mortimer）、佩内洛普·莫蒂默（Penelope Mortimer）、哈罗德·品特（Harold Pinter）。我在读他们的书，也在读他们的人。小的时候，我会去利物浦当地的一家书店，菲利普儿子和侄子书店（Philip Son & Nephew）。伦敦的书店几乎和吉他店一样好，在里面可以找到很多书。

　　我有了动机：一个有抱负的作家，我想象写一封信给出版公司来称赞自己的优点，并试着推销自己。这就是为什么歌曲是以"Dear Sir or Madam"（亲爱的女士或先生）开头的，那个时候，你都是那样开始写信的。我把这设置在音乐中。我那时刚买了一把新的电吉他，一把 Epiphone Casino，我现在演出时还会用它。我把它接上我的 Vox 音箱，调到好听又大声，然后我写了这个连复段。这个连复段不错，很容易弹。实际上，我大部分音乐上的构成，都有一个简单的技巧，因为我不是特别精通于乐器。比如说，我没办法在钢琴上总是按出正确的键。所以，几乎总是有一些变通。我只是稍作改变。我表面上改动了一些，但是离核心不会走得太远。

　　沙滩男孩对这首歌的音色有着直接的影响。他们的和声特别吸引我们。不过更早之前，实际上，我爸爸就教过我弟弟和我一些和声的基础。比沙滩男孩更早的，埃弗利兄弟也用和声，所以我弟弟迈克和我也这么做。我们甚至参加过一次巴特林度假营[1]的才艺比赛。那时候我大约十五岁，我们唱了《再见爱情》（Bye Bye Love），这是我们从埃弗利兄弟那里听来的。当然，没赢。对巴特林度假营的观众来说，我们还不够才华出众！

　　我们也许是从沙滩男孩的和声书里偷拿了一两页，但我们就像调皮的学校学生一样做了一些变化。我们会告诉别人我们唱的是"嘀，嘀，嘀，嘀"，不过我们的傻笑泄露了真相，实际上我们唱的是"踢，踢，踢，踢"。

　　在所有的文字游戏中，我们最爱双关语。我们喜欢无厘头。我们喜欢无稽之谈，特别是爱德华·李尔的作品。那就是为什么你在《平装书作家》里面能找到他的名字。

左图：和弟弟迈克在巴特林度假营，1940 年代。

1　比利·巴特林（Billy Butlin）于 1930 年代开设的公众连锁度假村，后来成为英国中产阶级一家每年度假的首选地。

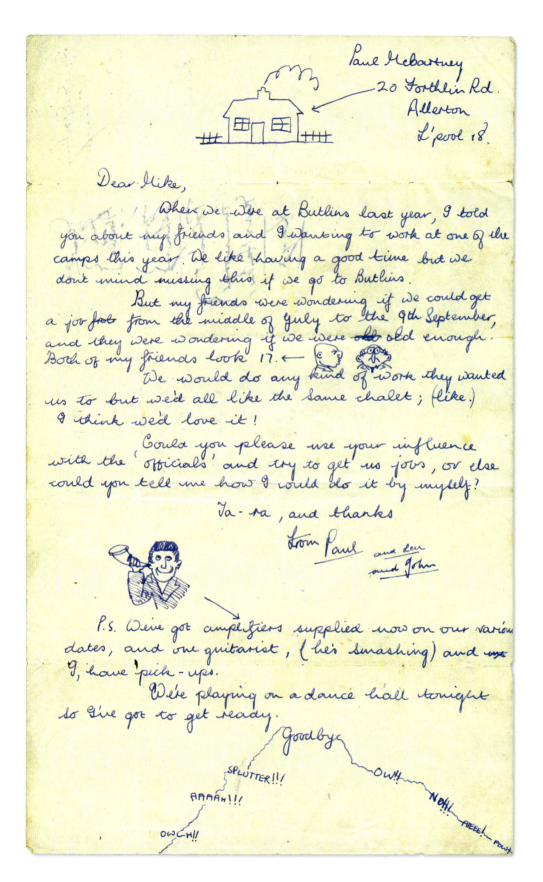

Paul McCartney
20 Forthlin Rd.
Allerton
L'pool 18.

Dear Mike,

When we were at Butlins last year, I told you about my friends and I wanting to work at one of the camps this year. We like having a good time but we don't mind missing this if we go to Butlins.

But my friends were wondering if we could get a job from the middle of July to the 9th September, and they were wondering if we were old enough. Both of my friends look 17. ←

We would do any kind of work they wanted us to but we'd all like the same chalet; (like.) I think we'd love it!

Could you please use your influence with the 'officials' and try to get us jobs, or else could you tell me how I could do it by myself?

Ta-ra, and thanks

from Paul and Len and John

P.S. We've got amplifiers supplied now on our various dates, and one guitarist, (he's smashing) and we, I, have 'pick-ups.

We're playing on a dance hall tonight so I've got to get ready.

Goodbye

SPLUTTER!!!   OW!!

AAAAH!!!   NO!!!

OWCH!!   AIEEE! POW!

披头士乐队在《流行之巅》节目
上表演《平装书作家》，1966 年。

在罗宾汉义演（*Robin Hood Benefit*）
上弹奏 Epiphone Casino。纽约，
2015 年。

Penny Lane

便士巷

作 者	WRITERS	保罗·麦卡特尼和约翰·列侬　Paul McCartney and John Lennon
艺术家	ARTIST	披头士乐队　The Beatles
录 音	RECORDED	伦敦阿比路录音棚　Abbey Road Studios, London
发 行	RELEASED	《便士巷》/《永远的草莓田》双 A 面单曲，1967 年　'Penny Lane' / 'Strawberry Fields Forever' double A-side single, 1967

In Penny Lane there is a barber showing
    photographs
Of every head he's had the pleasure to know
And all the people that come and go
Stop and say hello

On the corner is a banker with a motorcar
The little children laugh at him behind his back
And the banker never wears a mac
In the pouring rain, very strange

Penny Lane is in my ears and in my eyes
There beneath the blue suburban skies
I sit and meanwhile back

In Penny Lane there is a fireman with an hourglass
And in his pocket is a portrait of the Queen
He likes to keep his fire engine clean
It's a clean machine

Penny Lane is in my ears and in my eyes
A four of fish and finger pies
In summer, meanwhile back

Behind the shelter in the middle of the roundabout
The pretty nurse is selling poppies from a tray
And though she feels as if she's in a play
She is anyway

In Penny Lane the barber shaves another customer
We see the banker sitting waiting for a trim
And then the fireman rushes in
From the pouring rain, very strange

Penny Lane is in my ears and in my eyes
There beneath the blue suburban skies
I sit and meanwhile back

Penny Lane is in my ears and in my eyes
There beneath the blue suburban skies
Penny Lane

《便士巷》有一部宣传片，不过最好把它看作一部纪录电影。这并不让人惊讶，因为，当我去利物浦的约翰家时，要在便士巷环岛转乘公车，那里是教堂路和史密斯顿路的路口。不仅是一个汽车站，也是在我和约翰的生活中非常重要的一个地方——我们经常在那里见面——那里靠近圣巴拿巴教堂，而我是唱诗班男孩。所以它在很多方面都能引发我的联想，它仍然"in my ears and in my eyes"（在我的耳朵和眼睛里）。

关于"a barber showing photographs"（理发师展出照片）的歌词仍然让我觉得很有趣，仿佛理发店是一个展览绘画的画廊，他的橱窗里有一个展览。你看着理发店橱窗里的照片，并且走进去说，"我想剪个托尼·柯蒂斯的发型"或者"我想剪个平头"。我觉得"展出照片"这句用得不错。我想表达的就是有一个理发店，理发师在他的橱窗里展示了一些发型照片，但是那样就太平常了。

便士巷上的那个店属于哈里·比奥莱蒂（Harry Bioletti）。那是一家意大利理发店，外面有一根条纹柱子。披头士的所有成员至少有一次或者好几次在那里理过发。"Of every head he's had the pleasure to know"（关于他很高兴认识的每一个人）这句歌词使用了一种我的英语老师会称之为"自由间接引语"的手法。你能听见理发师说，"很高兴认识你"以及类似的话。所以，这是一种非常简洁的信息传递方式。它把许多东西塞了进去。

这首歌当然也受到了狄兰·托马斯的《在牛奶森林下》的巨大影响。那是一部广播剧，一幅威尔士小镇的肖像画。这部剧最初是在 1953 年完成的，不过在 1963 年有一个全新的电台版本，以及 1964 年的电视版本。所以，这部剧流传甚广。

《便士巷》中的人物对我来说仍然栩栩如生。时至今日，我仍会开车路过那里，向别人介绍理发店、银行、消防站、我唱歌的教堂，以及我等公交车时站在那里拿着托盘卖罂粟花的姑娘。那个漂亮护士，我清楚地记得她。那是阵亡将士纪念日，她拿着一个装满了纸做的罂粟花和徽章的托盘。有趣的是，许多美国人认为她卖的是小狗，那是另一幅有趣的画面，装满小狗的盘子。但不是的，她卖的是罂粟花，并且"she feels as if she's in a play / She is anyway"（她觉得似乎是在演戏 / 然而她就是这样）。

这句"然而她就是这样"非常 1960 年代——对自身方式的一种评论。如果我要为这些角色写一部戏，我宁愿让它像一部哈罗德·品特的戏剧，也不愿让它更直白一点。对于所有这些角色，我喜欢他们有点不确定的感觉。他们身上有一点奇怪的东西。而且，当然，我不仅仅在舞台上欣赏品特的作品，我还去过他在摄政公园的家。我们有一次去参加一个派对，而浴缸里倒满了香槟。

584—585 页：保罗和约翰
手写的《便士巷》歌词。

583

1. In Penny ~~Lane~~ there is a barber showing photograph
of every head he had the pleasure to know

A. & all the people that come and go
        stop and say hello

On the corner
2. ~~In Penny Lane there~~ is a banker with a motor car
the ~~and~~ little children laugh at him behind his back

A and ~~for~~ the banker never wears a mac
        in the pouring rain, very strange

Penny Lane, is in my ears, and in ~~my~~ eyes,
B ~~Penny Lane~~
There beneath the blue suburban skies I sit and

A Meanwhile back in Penny Lane.

A There is a fireman with an hour glass
A . And in his pocket is a portrait of the Queen
B He likes to keep his engine clean
A Its a clean machine (Ah Ah it)
A ~~Penny Lane is in my~~ ears and in my eyes
A Four of fish and finger pies in summer
B. (THEN B IN C)

In Penny Lane there was a barber
                              Showing photographs
Of every head he'd had the pleasure to know
 It was easy not to go - he was very slow

Meanwhile back in ~~Penny Lane~~ behind the shelter
in the middle of the roundabout
A pretty nurse is selling poppies from a tray
And though she feels as if she's in a play
She is anyway.

In Penny Lane the barber shaves another customer
We see the banker sitting for a trim
And then the fireman rushes in
From the pouring rain — very strange

Penny Lane is in my ears and in my eyes
There beneath the blue suburban ~~skies~~ skies
And meanwhile back at.
Penny Lane is in my ears a in my eyes
There beneath the blue suburban skies) Penny Lane

585

上图：《便士巷》宣传片，1967 年。

右图：在《便士巷》宣传片中所穿
的套装，由服装设计师蒙蒂·伯曼
（Monty Berman）设计。

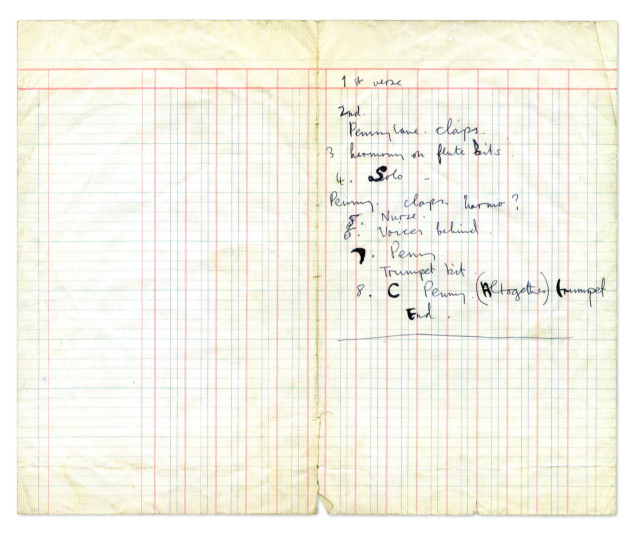

1 st verse

2nd.
    Penny Lane. claps.
3 harmony on flute bits.
4. Solo —
Penny. claps. harmo ?
5. Nurse.
6. Voices behind.
7. Penny.
    Trumpet bit.
8. C Penny (Altogether) trumpet
    End.

上图：保罗的录音笔记。

右图：在《便士巷》宣传片中出现的比奥莱蒂理发店，1967 年。

Picasso's Last Words (Drink to Me)

毕加索的遗言（为我干杯）

作　者	WRITERS	保罗·麦卡特尼和琳达·麦卡特尼　Paul McCartney and Linda McCartney
艺术家	ARTIST	保罗·麦卡特尼和羽翼乐队　Paul McCartney and Wings
录　音	RECORDED	拉各斯百代录音棚、拉各斯 ARC 录音棚，以及伦敦 AIR 录音棚
		EMI Studios, Lagos; ARC Studio, Lagos and AIR Studios, London
发　行	RELEASED	《逃亡乐队》，1973 年　*Band on the Run*, 1973

The grand old painter died last night
His paintings on the wall
Before he went, he bade us well
And said goodnight to us all

Drink to me, drink to my health
You know I can't drink any more
Drink to me, drink to my health
You know I can't drink any more

Three o'clock in the morning
I'm getting ready for bed
It came without a warning
But I'll be waiting for you, baby
I'll be waiting for you there

So drink to me, drink to my health
You know I can't drink any more
Drink to me, drink to my health
You know I can't drink any more

《毕加索的遗言》源自一次挑战。我在牙买加遇见了达斯汀·霍夫曼，他正在参加电影《巴比龙》（*Papillon*）的拍摄，我们去了他在蒙特哥湾的家里。

他问我："任何事情你都可以写成一首歌吗？"我答道："呃，我不知道，也许吧。"他说"等一下"，然后他上楼去，回来时带着本《时代》杂志，上面有一篇关于毕加索去世的文章。

他接着说："看看毕加索的遗言是什么？"文章说毕加索于 1973 年 4 月去世，一些朋友陪着他，而他的最后遗言是对朋友们说："为我干杯。为我的健康干杯。你们知道我再不能喝了。"

达斯汀问我："你能为这个写一首歌吗？"我不确定，不过我带着吉他，于是我拨弄着和弦，为这段文字唱出一段旋律，他惊呆了。他对他当时的妻子安妮说："快来！听听这个！我只是给了保罗这个，而他已经写了一首歌。"我当时一心想着接受达斯汀的挑战，所以我只是专注于放在我面前的这段文字。我觉得不错的一点是，他显然也把这段文字看作旋律。他是一个演员，所以他理解文字的节奏，而且我觉得当他读到这段话时，他也许会想，"这有很优美的起伏。"写这首歌非常高兴，有一点自我表现。我很幸运，某些东西很自然地就出现了。

我认为歌词本身的节奏会影响旋律的走向。你希望写出一些既自然又有趣的东西，并且切合你听到的音乐。有时候，你不得不改变一个词，因为它合不上韵律，所以你会找其他意思相近的词来代替。也许现在是双音节的词来代替那个不合适的单音节的词，或者反过来。节奏听起来自然很重要。如果不是这样，就很扎眼。

当你在组织词语的时候，你真的不会考虑这些具体的事情，这并不难为情，但是当达斯汀挑战我时，我心说，"好吧，我要把它做好"——"The grand old painter died last night / His paintings on the wall / Before he went, he bade us well / And said goodnight to us all"（伟大的画家昨夜死去 / 他的绘画还在墙上 / 他离开之前，向我们告别 / 向我们所有人说晚安）。然后这首歌偏离了主题，就像我的很多歌曲那样，谁知道毕加索在凌晨三点做了什么，但是歌词听起来不错："Three o'clock in the morning / I'm getting ready for bed / It came without a warning / But I'll be waiting for you, baby / I'll be waiting for you there"（凌晨三点 / 我准备睡觉 / 它来得毫无征兆 / 但是我将等你，宝贝 / 我将在那里等你）。接下来我就可以用他的话了："为我干杯"。

正常来说，这大概就是毕加索所做的，这只是一件平常的事情，只是说起来有点郑重其事："为我干杯！"但是一旦出现在杂志上，就几乎就要成为一首诗了，像达斯汀这样的人读到的时候会想，"毕加索的遗言，了不起的一句话。"我也同意。我总是喜欢这样的事情。

左图：达斯汀·霍夫曼，头上戴着"碎布包"。牙买加，1973 年。

592—593 页:《毕加索的遗言（为我干杯）》的手写曲谱。

达斯汀问我："你能为这个写一首歌吗？"
我不确定，不过我带着吉他，于是我拨弄着和弦，
为这段文字唱出一段旋律，他惊呆了。

PICASSOS LAST WORDS (DRINK TO ME...)

The grand old painter died last night
His paintings on the wall
Before he went he bade us well
And said goodnight to us all

CHORUS Drink to me, drink to my health,
You know I cant drink any more
Drink to me, drink to my health,
You know I cant drink any more
MIDDLE 3 oclock in the morning
I'm getting ready for bed
It came without a warning
But I'll be waiting for you baby
I'll be waiting for you there
So Drink to me drink to my health
You know I cant drink any more
Drink to me drink to my health
You know I cant drink any more

FRENCH INTERLUDE.
(TEMPO CHANGE)
JET ———— Drink to me CHORUS
(TEMPO) DRUNKEN CHORUS
FRENCH (TEMPO) Drink to me - HO HEY HO

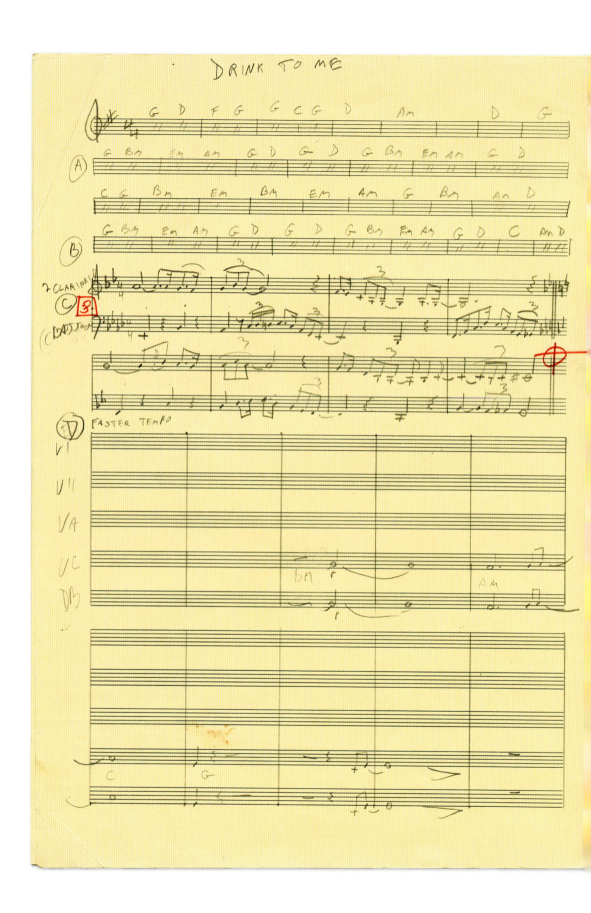

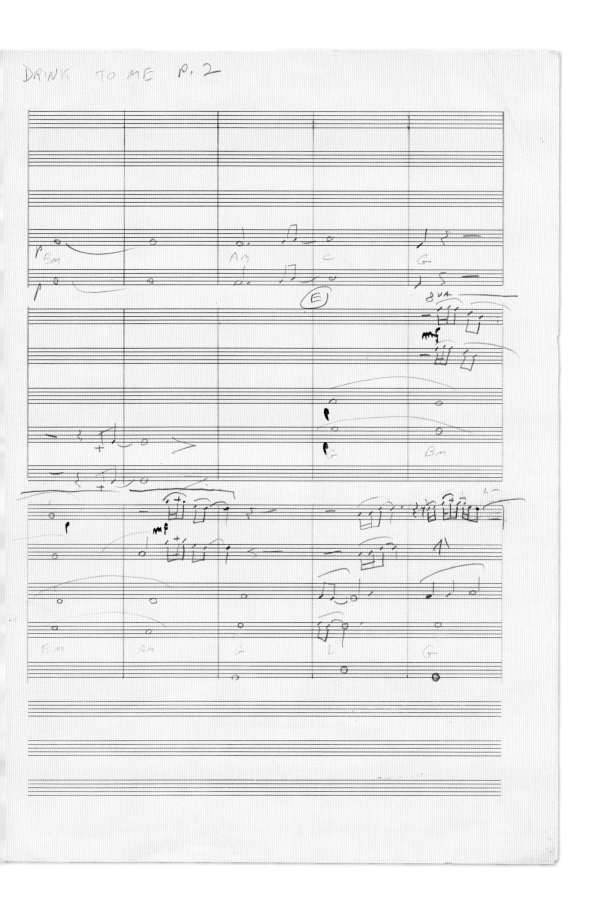

Pipes of Peace
和平管乐

作　者 WRITER	保罗·麦卡特尼	Paul McCartney
艺术家 ARTIST	保罗·麦卡特尼	Paul McCartney
录　音 RECORDED	伦敦 AIR 录音棚	AIR Studios, London
发　行 RELEASED	《和平管乐》，1983 年	*Pipes of Peace*, 1983
	单曲，1983 年	Single, 1983

I light a candle to our love
In love our problems disappear
But all in all we soon discover
That one and one is all we long to hear

All round the world
Little children being
Born to the world
Got to give them all we can
Til the war is won
Then will the work be done

Help them to learn
Songs of joy instead of
Burn baby burn
Let us show them how to play
The pipes of peace
Play the pipes of peace

Help me to learn
Songs of joy instead of
Burn baby burn
Won't you show me how to play
The pipes of peace
Play the pipes of peace

What do you say?
Will the human race
Be run in a day?
Or will someone save
This planet we're playing on
Is it the only one?
What are we going to do?

Help them to see
That the people here
Are like you and me
Let us show them how to play
The pipes of peace
Play the pipes of peace

I light a candle to our love
In love our problems disappear
But all in all we soon discover
That one and one is all we long to hear

名字古怪的菲利普儿子和侄子书店（如果我没记错的话）位于利物浦，我在那里度过了很多时光。从我还是小孩子时，我就喜欢书店。我喜欢它们的味道。我也喜欢所有这些作品集合在一个屋檐下的样子。

在 1980 年代初，创作《和平管乐》的那段时期，我在另一家最爱的书店，马里波恩大街上的东特书店，找到一本孟加拉语诗人泰戈尔的书，他获得过诺贝尔奖。泰戈尔的诗里有一句"点亮蜡烛"或类似的话，我被它打动了。那就是这首歌的开始。泰戈尔，有着凹陷的眼睛，和长长的、飘垂的胡须，在照片上看起来很有趣，所以这可能是吸引我的地方，我真的喜欢他的诗，于是我偷来了这一句。

我也许记错了这句。它也许只是一个为爱点亮蜡烛的概念，不过那就是我记得的。那就是我们所有人渴望听到的：在一起，互相友爱，"Little children being / Born to the world"（年幼的孩子们 / 出生），我们要尽可能给予他们一切，直到战争胜利——这场战争就是生活，这场战争，无论它如今发生在哪里，都在残害我们的星球。"Songs of joy instead of / Burn baby burn"（快乐的歌曲而不是 / 灼伤的婴儿）这个短句后来变得很有名，那是在洛杉矶瓦特区的骚乱摧毁了市中心的大部分地区之后。所以几年后写的这首歌，成为某种和平颂歌，非常令人鼓舞。同时振奋人心的是，在 1983 年 12 月，这首歌在英国成为冠军单曲。

我的乐观态度可以追溯到我在利物浦的成长经历。战后的人们惊人地乐观，他们只是很高兴能够脱离苦海。我们家一年一度的新年夜聚会是一件快乐的事情，每个人都围坐在一起唱歌。都是些积极乐观的歌曲——"把桶滚出来 / 我们就会有一桶快乐"，类似这样的调子。我的爸爸弹钢琴，每个人都有美好的过去。我很幸运地出生在这样一个快乐的家庭里。

爸爸吉姆和金阿姨在弹钢琴。
利物浦。

作为一个孩子，我以为每个人的家庭都是那样的，直到遇见了像约翰这样的人，我才意识到这不是真的，也许是我们不同观点的反差产生了一种魔力。不过我天生就是这样想问题的，最后一切都会好的。悲剧可能会发生，但是总会翻页，我喜欢这一点。意识到我在世界上有影响力，人们会听我的东西，让我觉得自己有责任保持乐观，乐观到极致（尽管也许我不会这么大胆地说出来）。那种态度很自然地溜进我的歌曲里，因为我知道这些歌曲会去往某个地方，如果它们能够让人们选择一条积极的道路，那就太好了。我会积极乐观，除非情况变得如同《银翼杀手》描绘的世界那般糟糕，我才会无力去想，"让我们唱一首歌……"

为这首歌制作音乐录影带也很有趣。导演叫基思·麦克米兰（Keith McMillan），我还和他做过其他一些事情，他曾在英国广播公司工作，离开后成为自由职业者。他和我一起讨论《和平管乐》，我记得小时候在电视上看到一部电影的片段，说的是 1914年的圣诞节，战壕里的士兵们在无人区互相问候，一起踢足球。那是《和平管乐》音乐录影带故事的地点，所以在其中，我既扮演英国士兵，也扮演德国士兵。

上图：《和平管乐》音乐录影带拍摄场景。萨里郡乔巴汉姆公共绿地，1983 年。

PIPES OF PEACE.

I light a candle to our love
In love our problems disappear
But all in all we soon discover
That one and one is all we want to hear.

1.   All round the world
     Little children being born to the world
     Got to give them all we can till the war is won
     Then will the work be done.

CHORUS.   Help them to learn, songs of joy instead of burn, baby, burn,
          Let us show them how to play — the pipe of peace.
          — Repeat —   (SINGLE END)
          —   Instrumental . —

CHORUS.   Help me to learn songs of joy instead of burn, baby, burn,
          Won't you show me how to play - the p. o. p.
              — Repeat —   (DOUBLE END.)

2.   What do you say? will the human race be run in a day
     Or will someone save this planet we're playing on
         Is it the only one?

     Help them to see, that the people here are like you and me,
     Let us show them how to play the p. o. p.

         — Repeat —   (DOUBLE END.)

     I light a candle to our love .
       In love our problems disappear
       And all in all we soon discover
       That one + one is all we want to hear
           C . — p. o. p. riff.
           A min. — E.   END.

《和平管乐》单曲海报，1983 年。

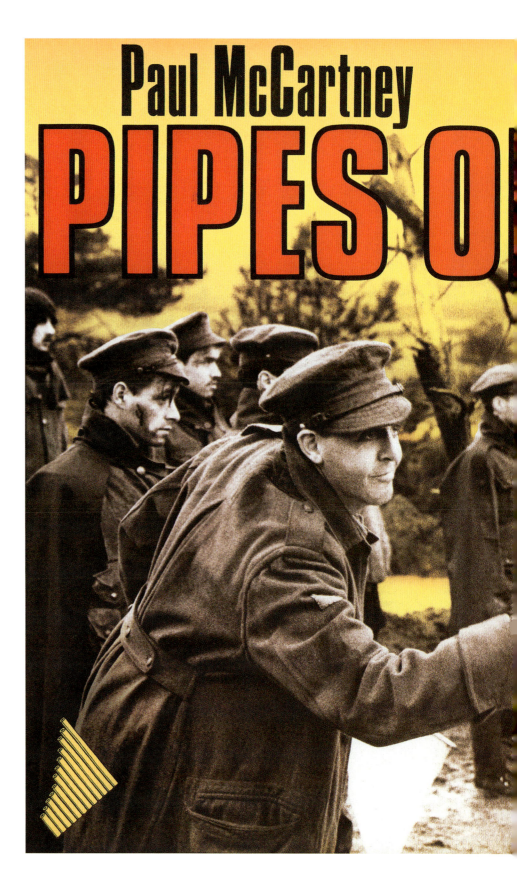

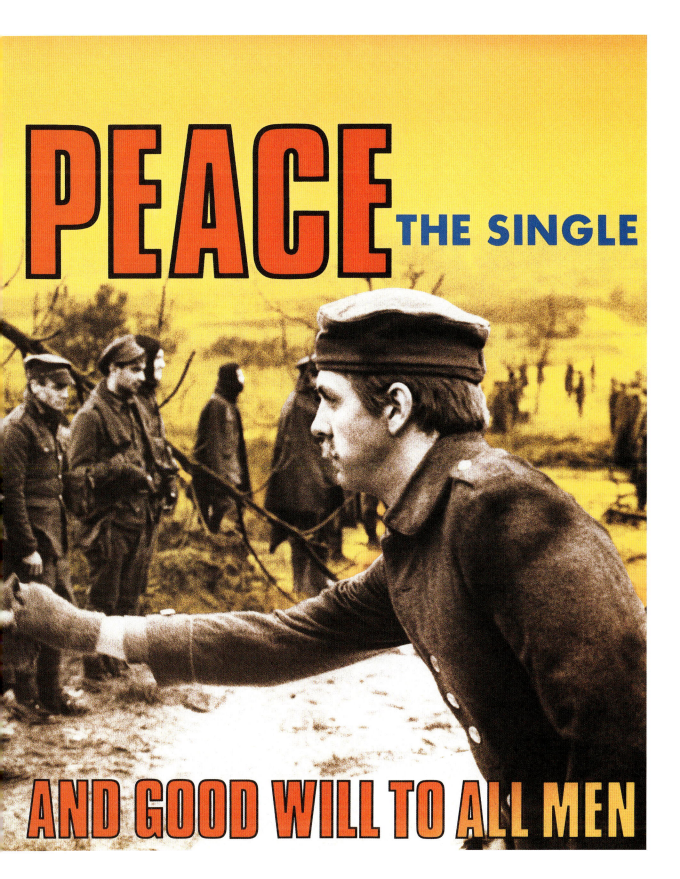

Please Please Me
请让我快乐

作　者	WRITERS	约翰·列侬和保罗·麦卡特尼	John Lennon and Paul McCartney
艺术家	ARTIST	披头士	The Beatles
录　音	RECORDED	伦敦阿比路录音棚	Abbey Road Studios, London
发　行	RELEASED	单曲，1963 年	Single, 1963
		《请让我快乐》，1963 年	*Please Please Me*, 1963
		《介绍……披头士乐队》，1964 年	*Introducing...The Beatles*, 1964

Last night I said these words to my girl
I know you never even try, girl

Come on (come on)
Come on (come on)
Come on (come on)
Come on (come on)
Please please me
Whoa yeah like I please you

You don't need me to show the way, love
Why do I always have to say, love

Come on (come on)
Come on (come on)
Come on (come on)
Come on (come on)
Please please me
Whoa yeah like I please you

I don't wanna sound complaining
But you know there's always rain in my heart
　(in my heart)
I do all the pleasin' with you
It's so hard to reason with you
Whoa yeah why do you make me blue?

Last night I said these words to my girl
I know you never even try, girl

Come on (come on)
Come on (come on)
Come on (come on)
Come on (come on)
Please please me
Whoa yeah like I please you
　(Please me)
Whoa yeah like I please you
　(Please me)
Whoa yeah like I please you

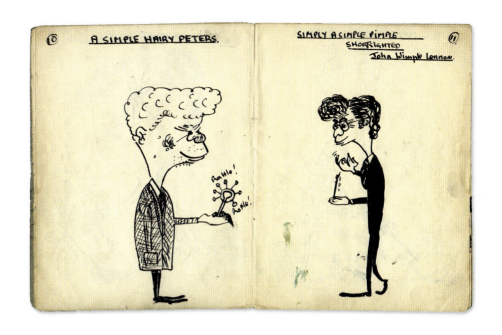

我们用两把吉他写了这首歌，约翰和我。还有，就像我之前提到过的，好玩的是我是左撇子，而他是右撇子，就好像我在照镜子，他也在照镜子一样。

我们会一直调试，抽根烟，喝杯茶，开始弹一些东西，找一个动机。一般来说，我或他会带来一首歌的片段。"请让我快乐"是约翰的动机。约翰喜欢"please"的双重含义——"请／取悦"。在这里，"please"是层层递进的"拜托了"。"请和我交往，拜托和我交往，求求你和我交往。"他喜欢这个，我也喜欢他喜欢这个。那是某种我们彼此心心相印的东西，某种我们相一致的东西。我们很同步。

有一首宾·克罗斯比的老歌叫作《请》，开始的歌词是"Please lend your little ear to my pleas"[1]。就算你之前没听过这首歌，也能听出——啊哈，好吧——两种含义。我们都喜欢文字游戏。我最近买了许多约翰的绘画和手稿。我把它们挂在墙上，所以就可以每时每刻看着它们，真是一座双关语的国度。那是约翰机智的一部分。任何可以变形的事物，都变形了。

当约翰带来这首歌的时候，《请让我快乐》还是一首非常慢的歌。我听了之后直接说："奥比森式的。"事实上，奥比森应该唱它。我不知道他是否唱过，但是这首歌处处可见罗伊的创作。如果你把这首歌放慢，并且对他的风格有印象，那真是合适。

但我们那时的制作人，乔治·马丁，做了一些改变。乔治喜欢我们带来的这首歌，不过他说："你们觉得我们可以把它加快一点吗？"我们的反应是："不，不，不。"但

上图：约翰·列侬在作业本上画的草图，1950 年代中期。

1　双关意为"请把你的小耳朵借我用来辩解"／"请你倾听我的请求"。

是乔治非常有说服力，他说："让我们试一下吧。如果你们不喜欢，我们就不这么做。"他还说，"我觉得这首歌会成为你们的第一首冠军单曲。"所以，我们勉勉强强地加快了速度，而这首歌确实成了我们的第一首冠军歌曲。

这是合作的好处之一。我会带来一些东西，约翰会修改它。他带来一些东西，我也会做一些修改。然后，如果我们两个都没注意到问题，乔治·马丁会做修改。那样的合作让披头士成为一支很幸运的小团体。

左图：《披头士》录音期间，乔治·马丁在弹钢琴。伦敦阿比路录音棚，1968 年。

右图：披头士在《谢谢你的幸运星》节目亮相之前，保罗和约翰在化妆间里。伯明翰，1963 年。

Pretty Boys

漂亮男孩

作　者　WRITER　　保罗·麦卡特尼　Paul McCartney
艺术家　ARTIST　　保罗·麦卡特尼　Paul McCartney
录　音　RECORDED　萨塞克斯郡猪山磨坊　Hog Hill Mill, Sussex
发　行　RELEASED　《麦卡特尼 III》，2020 年　*McCartney III*, 2020

Look into my lens
Give me all you got
Work it for me, baby
Let me take my best shot

Meet the Pretty Boys
A line of bicycles for hire
Objects of desire
Working for the squire
You can look but you'd better not touch

'Cause here come the Pretty Boys
They're gonna set your world on fire
Objects of desire
Preaching to the choir
They can talk but they never say much

Strike another pose
Try to feel the light
Hey the camera loves you
Don't put up a fight

There go the Pretty Boys
A row of cottages for rent
For your main event
They're what the angels sent
You can look but you'd better not touch

Look into my lens
Try to feel the light
Hey the camera loves you
It's gonna be alright

Oh here come the Pretty Boys
A line of bicycles for hire
Objects of desire
When they're working for the squire
You can look but you'd better not touch

The Pretty Boys
  (But you'd better not touch)
The Pretty Boys

这首歌是关于男模特的。我曾经读过一篇关于一群男模特的文章，他们起诉一两位摄影师，因为受到摄影师的虐待和羞辱。

他们说的一些摄影师我也认识。我并不确切地知晓在那些特别的拍摄过程中，那些摄影师做了什么，不过他们也拍摄过我，所以我确实知道这些摄影师工作的手法，他们会说，"来吧，宝贝。来吧，给我。来吧，噢，给我看看那个乳头……"

换句话说，他们往往非常粗俗，而且伴随着领地意识。你会说，"就是他。"他会说，"来吧，假装你在和小妞做爱。"这就是这些家伙工作的方式，让你不会呆站在那里看起来很无聊。他们试着刺激某些事情。就像许多专业人士那样——流行歌星、警察——他们对自己进行了漫画式的夸张。

因此我怀疑，是否这些模特只是不理解他们进入的其实是一个黑暗的领域。也或许确实是摄影师越过界限，不恰当地触碰了模特。我不知道，但是这首歌是一个虚构故事，我想象模特们因为这些摄影师所表现出的粗俗态度感到不安。

歌曲是从摄影师的话开始的："Look into my lens / Give me all you got / Work it for me, baby / Let me take my best shot"（看着我的镜头 / 用出你的全部本领 / 为我展现，宝贝 / 让我拍出最好的照片）。那是 1960 年代、1970 年代摄影师工作方式的温和写照——而现在他们要粗俗十倍。我想象排成一排的男模特，他们是等待出租的一排自行车，以及欲望的对象。他们试着让你对杂志内页里的他们产生欲望，但是他们为资本工作。在杂志的世界里，摄影师是个大人物。

上图：纽约，2020 年。

"They can talk but they never say much"（他们可以说但从来说得不多）。在大众看来，模特并不是聪明人的职业选择——我随便说的！——尽管我认识一些特别聪明的模特，而且对任何职业做一个概括总是很棘手。"There go the Pretty Boys / A row of cottages for rent"（漂亮男孩来了 / 等待出租的一排小屋）。我想象的是类似你在海滨可以租到的那种小简易房。后来，我渐渐明白，"小屋"指的是在公共厕所里进行的男同性恋行为，但是当我写这首歌的时候，我的脑海里还没有这个。

我写了一段非常简单的吉他旋律——只用两根手指按弦，其他的音符都是空弦。就是这样。

"You can look but you'd better not touch"（你可以看但最好不要触碰）。你可以在杂志上看见模特诱惑地盯着你。那是他们应该做的，因为你应该想去买他们身上穿的衣服，或者他们出售的商品。这首歌主要讲的是男模特们的经历，但女模特和她们所穿的胸罩也是一样；你应该去想，"我的女朋友穿上这个应该很美。"模特是用来出售商品的，而我怀疑他们自己也是商品本身。

创作《漂亮男孩》很有意思，这不是我创作时常用的视角，但这就是作为一位创作者的乐趣。许多人也许有同样的想法——在这首歌里，关于模特的待遇——但是没有机会表达。我很幸运，有机会把这些想法打磨成一首歌。模特被当作商品的想法也引发了与披头士乐队的有趣对比。我们是音乐家，不是模特，不过在披头士狂热最疯狂的时候，人们想把我们的名字和脸放在各式各样的东西上，有时候感觉完全失控了。

所以，那就是创建苹果唱片公司的起因之一，以及后来我自己的 MPL 同样如此。这对我们来说是一种解放，摆脱了以前掌权的穿着西装的人。我们不再为资本工作。现在，我们可以掌控我们的命运。2019 年，MPL 庆祝了它的五十周岁生日，所以看上去它运转得非常好。

右图：女儿玛丽拍摄的照片。
萨塞克斯郡，2020 年。

所以，那就是创建苹果唱片公司的起因之一，
以及后来我自己的 MPL 同样如此。
这对我们来说是一种解放，摆脱了以前掌权的穿着西装的人。

PRETTY BOYS

(Intro riffs)

(A) Look into my lens
Give me all you've got
Work it for me baby
Let me take my best shot

(1) Meet the Pretty Boys
A line of bicycles for hire
Objects of desire
Working for the squire
You can look but you'd better not touch
(short riffs)

(2) Here come the Pretty Boys
They gonna set your world on fire
Objects of desire
Preaching to the choir
They can talk but they never say much

(B) Strike another pose
Try to feel the light
Hey - the camera loves you
Don't put up a fight

(A2) Look into my lens
Try to feel the light
Hey the camera loves you
It's gonna be alright

SOLO (Verse)
(short riffs)

(3) There go the Pretty Boys
A row of cottages to rent
For your main event
They're what the angels sent
You can look but you'd better not touch
The Pretty Boys
Repeat A2/ Verse (1) END.

609

Pretty Little Head
漂亮的小脑袋

作　者 WRITERS	保罗·麦卡特尼和埃里克·斯图沃特	Paul McCartney and Eric Stewart
艺术家 ARTIST	保罗·麦卡特尼	Paul McCartney
录　音 RECORDED	萨塞克斯郡猪山磨坊	Hog Hill Mill, Sussex
发　行 RELEASED	《按下播放》，1986 年	Press to Play, 1986
	英国单曲，1986 年	UK single, 1986

Hillmen, hillmen, hillmen, hillmen
Oh, oh, oh, oh
Hillmen come down from the lava
Forging across the mighty river flow
Always forever
Only so you don't worry
Your pretty little head

Ursa Major
Ursa Minor
Ursa Major
Ursa Minor

Hillmen, hillmen, hillmen, hillmen
Oh, oh, oh, oh
Hillmen bring garments, spices
Carrying trinkets, silk and precious stones
Exotic legends
Only so you don't worry
Your pretty little head

Hillmen, hillmen, hillmen, hillmen
Oh, oh, oh, oh
Hillmen are sworn to allegiance
Living a life of silent dignity
For your protection
Only so you don't worry
Your pretty little head

Ursa Major
Ursa Minor
Ursa Major
Ursa Minor

The hillmen
Living in the higher reaches

"Hillmen"（山人）这个词我苦苦思索了很长时间。我有时候会被一首歌卡住，我会听见一个词，但我觉得"那没有任何意义"，然后我继续试着变化，不过这个词还是会不断回来，到最后，我会觉得，"噢，真讨厌，没关系。就它吧。我不知道这个是什么意思"。这个"山人"就是这种情况。我不知道它是从哪里冒出来的。

一想到古代部落成员，我就觉得很有乐趣，我叫他们"山人"；我对尼安德特人和维京人都有一点了解。我对埃及古物学和古代文明的研究很着迷，我确实读了很多关于这些东西的书，也看了很多相关的电视，所以创造一个我自己的部落和古代文明的想法一定非常吸引我。

接下来你知道，它变成了一首情歌。我刚创造了一个巨大的部落画面，然后就扔出一小段那样的歌词来让它漫游："…don't worry / Your pretty little head"（不会担心 / 你漂亮的小脑袋），这是非常现代的，也非常 1980 年代，但实际上和歌曲的其他部分形成了巨大的反差。我相信维京人也会有相同的说法。

我猜这和不同的文明都有关；所有这些琐碎的东西——中国的琐事、美国的琐事、英国的琐事、南美洲的琐事——都是让我们在乎的东西。用来保护我们。在某种程度上，正是文明的存在才让我们不用担心我们"漂亮的小脑袋"。当然，就文明本身而言，这个存在的简单理由并不是毫无危险。

我也许是在寻找一个不存在的部落。一个幻想出来的部落，而我很享受为他们创造一个属于我的历史。有点精神性的，像阿兹特克人，但是绝对位于北半球。我怎么看他们？长得有点像维京人，不过不戴头盔。他们跨过浩瀚的河流，仰望星空，并且交换货物。所以从这个角度说，我正在制造我自己的维京人，并把他们运到英国来。

"Living in the higher reaches"（生活在更上层）。我想的是更高层次的精神性，但是更高也可以解释成选择更高的道路，道德高地。或者从另一个角度来看，它也可以指涉药物。这首歌是幻想出来的，但是纵观我所有的歌词，我发现我的风格相当宽泛，并且我几乎允许自己做任何事情——包括在这首歌里科技舞曲的感觉，科技舞曲在那个时候很流行。

上图：萨塞克斯郡猪山磨坊，
1984 年。

611

ON THE MOVE
Tribe

"stampede" -- dust. C.U.

PRETTY LITTLE HEAD.

(Intro) troubadour / girl . (reflected in mirror)
in palace
tells story   reacts.   mood lighting.

① lava - (caravan, dust, C.U.'s)

(danger →) mighty river
drownings / fast current

(p. l. h.)

troubadour — girl.

Bridge.

"logo" △
blue (woad.)
great faces
horses, motor
cattle, bikes.
stampede, dust
spray, water
crossing

② garments, spices, trinkets
△

Exotic legends. (beards oiled)
things tied in...
(.. small ribbons)

(p. l. h.)

INT. tent.
jewellery,
clothes.
T.V.
card game
("stick.")

Charm bracelet.

african tribal
. make - ups.

Bridge   (troubadour / twirl.)

storytelling
kids at feet.

③ Palace attack (danger)
allegiance . ("new" martial arts moves.)
("branded" △)
with
... silent dignity (guards)

"new" hieroglyphics

(p. l. h.)
troub. walks off   → OFF - SET director walks in
                mime CUT — freeze cast -- walk off
" take care of you".

bracelet
on wrist

Hillmen   Unique race.

Tribe of Hill people. Traders.
                                 warriors.
                                 Priests.

Style. ⟶ mixture of many past tribes
                    (plus "modern aspect")
         Cossacks   (bikes/TVs (portables)

         Egyptians   Celtic races
                          Druids
         Afghanistans   Buddhist ("oranges")
                          Red Indian.   (–greens)
         Quest for fire primitives.
         Hippy colony

ie.

Have "raided" best of all cultures.
meditation . vegetarian (spices)
Candles

wall hangings
painters/paintings
     abstract –

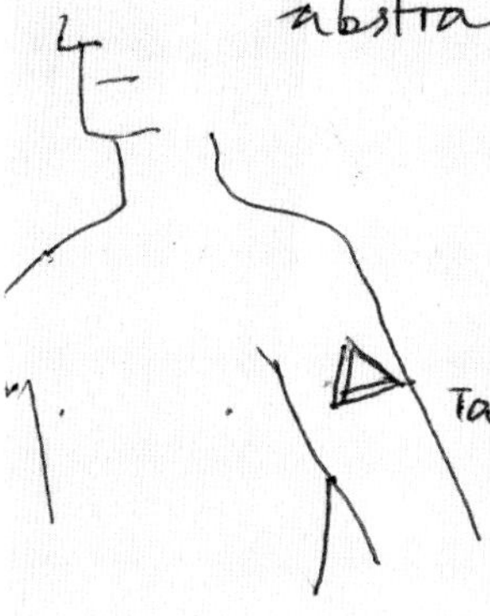

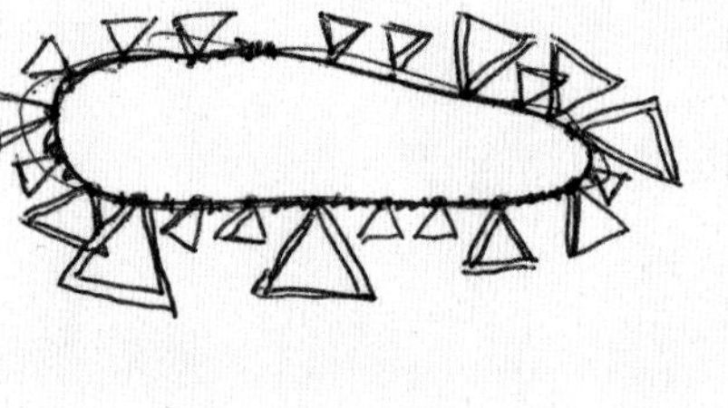

"giraffe neck"   gold.
women.

tattoos

triangle
"charm" bracelet

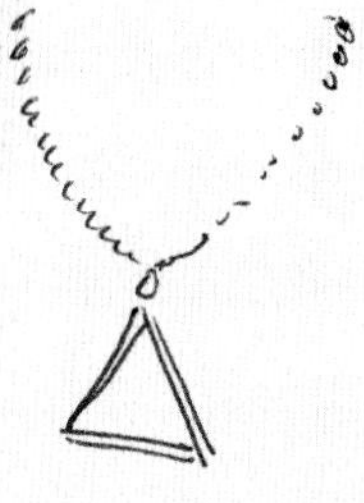

613

Army on the move ——————

African materials
morrocan
dreadlocks
American Indian

614

HILLMEN.

mud make-ups.

Tribe includes .....
All types · female/male
old / young
dignified / bandy

Put It There

放在那里

作　者　WRITER　　　保罗·麦卡特尼　Paul McCartney
艺术家　ARTIST　　　保罗·麦卡特尼　Paul McCartney
录　音　RECORDED　　萨塞克斯郡猪山磨坊　Hog Hill Mill, Sussex
发　行　RELEASED　　《泥土中的花朵》，1989 年　*Flowers in the Dirt*, 1989

　　　　　　　　　　单曲，1990 年　Single, 1990

Give me your hand, I'd like to shake it
I want to show you I'm your friend
You'll understand if I can make it clear
It's all that matters in the end

Put it there if it weighs a ton
That's what a father said to his young son
I don't care if it weighs a ton
As long as you and I are here, put it there
Long as you and I are here, put it there

If there's a fight, I'd like to fix it
I hate to see things go so wrong
The darkest night and all its mixed emotions
Is getting lighter, sing along

Put it there if it weighs a ton
That's what a father said to his young son
I don't care if it weighs a ton
As long as you and I are here, put it there
Long as you and I are here, put it there

"放在那里"是我爸爸吉姆经常说的一句口头语。他有丰富的表达方式，有许多利物浦人直到今天还是这样。他喜欢文字游戏，在脑子里变换语言，他也有很多小格言，有时候毫无意义，有时候很管用，不过总是很抒情。当他握住你的手的时候，他会说："Put it there if it weighs a ton"（如果它有一吨重就放在那里）。

有人多次指出，爱尔兰的首都其实是利物浦，利物浦也确实有庞大的爱尔兰社群。我们的幽默基本上都是爱尔兰式的。我们倾向于在事情中看到好笑的一面，部分是因为人们的生活常常笼罩在阴郁之中。

我爸爸那一代人经历了战争，尽管他们赢了，仍有许多心灵和肉体的创伤需要恢复，但是同时，空气中到处飘浮着乐观主义情绪。我的爸爸和叔叔们——杰克叔叔经常来我家——总是会有新的笑话。他会说："过来，孩子。你听说过人体模特的事吗？"接着他会说一些好玩的笑话，然后他会给你五毛钱，说："给你，孩子，犒劳一下你自己。"所以，我觉得，能参加那些聚会真是何其有幸，因为回看过去，这好玩极了。但是现在已经没有了，聚会结束了。

话说回来，我爸爸有一大堆这些风趣的话，我经常想，它们那么好，我要写一首关于它们的歌。另一个口头语是："海鸥的胸口不长毛发。"关于它真正的含义，你猜的跟我差不多，但这是一句优美的话，我非常确定我会把它放进最近的一首歌里。

奇怪的是，虽然我现在七十多岁了，而我前几天还在想，如果我们淘气的话，我爸爸会怎样打我们的腿。我们确实是淘气的孩子，我们会违反规则——大多是无意的——他就会打我们的腿，说："你疼，我更疼。"当然，虽然我们从不敢说，但我们会想："呃，如果你疼的话，那就停下来吧。"现在我明白了，作为父母，我明白他的意思。

上图：和弟弟迈克、妈妈玛丽，以及爸爸吉姆在一起。利物浦，1940 年代末。

617

"如果它有一吨重就放在那里。"我不确定我那时候想过这个，尽管这是在披头士乐队解散很久之后写的，但是我忍不住将这句话中的压抑感与披头士结束时的压抑感联系起来。并不是说披头士完全结束了，我们又不是那种永远出不了另一张唱片的小乐队，尽管我们中的一半人已经去世，但是这种感觉越来越强烈。我所做的一切似乎都被喷上"披头士"的标签，回声室总是会传来某种回声。我女儿玛丽开玩笑地说，"我逃不开你"，因为她会在地铁上看到我——我的照片，或者披头士的广告之类的——或者她打开电台，电台里在放披头士的歌。有些人可能会认为这是一种负担，而有些名人会隐居，譬如葛丽泰·嘉宝；但是我对这一切感觉很高兴，因为这是我们取得的伟大成就，我很是为此骄傲。与其把自己封闭起来，我更觉得我有一种真正的责任，把这些年来歌迷们给我们的一切都回报给他们。

我不禁意识到，我所做的很多事情仍然和我是披头士的一员这个事实纠缠在一起。事实上，我对人们说我仍然是披头士的一员。好吧，也许不是在披头士乐队里，但我仍然是个"披头士"。我们的哲学过去和现在都非常有吸引力，它是面对全世界的——坚持我们发现的，并且我仍然热爱的创造性思维的自由。在照片上，林戈总是做出和平的手势说"和平与爱"。这是一个老派的哲学，但总是合时宜。许多披头士的东西仍然神奇地合时宜，我很高兴沐浴其中。

我不知道自己是否希望把这首歌献给约翰，无论它是不是给一个早已去世的人的和平献礼——以它自己的方式。"If there's a fight, I'd like to fix it / I hate to see things go so wrong"（如果有争斗，我会来处理 / 我讨厌看到事情变得如此糟糕）。不过我是一个永远的乐观主义者："The darkest night and all its mixed emotions / Is getting lighter, sing along"（最黑暗的夜晚和所有复杂的情绪 / 正变得越来越明亮，一起唱吧）。《放在那里》的结尾是特别积极的："As long as you and I are here, put it there"（只要你和我在这里，就放在那里）。最后的一点小文字游戏。

我们会违反规则——大多是无意的——他就会打我们的腿，说："你疼，我更疼。"
当然，虽然我们从不敢说，但我们会想，
"呃，如果你疼的话，那就停下来吧。"
现在我明白了，作为父母，我明白他的意思。

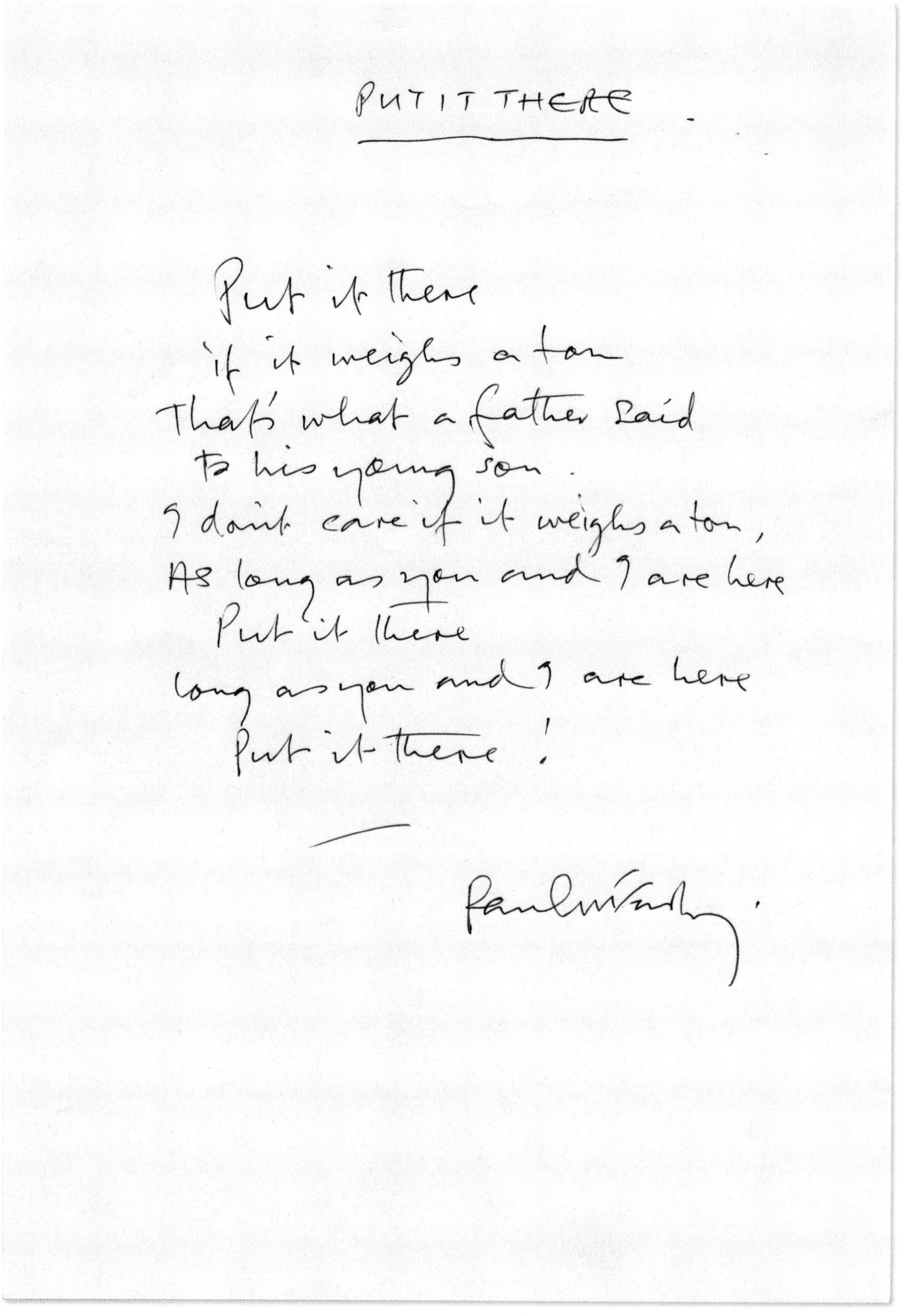

PUT IT THERE

Put it there
if it weighs a ton
That's what a father said
to his young son.
I don't care if it weighs a ton,
As long as you and I are here
Put it there
long as you and I are here
Put it there!

Paul McCartney.

有人多次指出，
爱尔兰的首都其实是利物浦，
利物浦也确实有庞大的爱尔兰社群。
我们的幽默基本上都是爱尔兰式的。
我们倾向于在事情中看到好笑的一面。

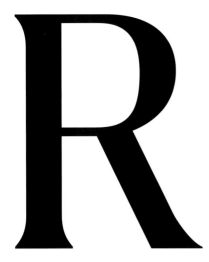

Rocky Raccoon

624

洛基 · 浣熊

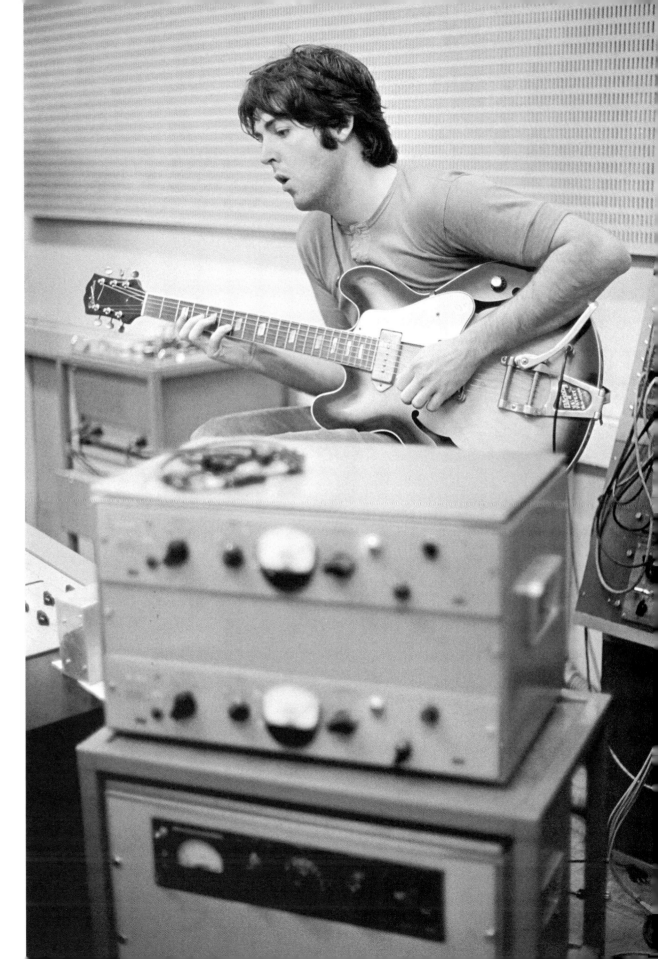

Rocky Raccoon

洛基·浣熊

作　者　WRITERS　　保罗·麦卡特尼和约翰·列侬　Paul McCartney and John Lennon

艺术家　ARTIST　　披头士乐队　The Beatles

录　音　RECORDED　伦敦阿比路录音棚　Abbey Road Studios, London

发　行　RELEASED　《披头士》，1968 年　*The Beatles*, 1968

Now somewhere in the black mountain
　　hills of Dakota
There lived a young boy named Rocky Raccoon
And one day his woman ran off with another guy
Hit young Rocky in the eye
Rocky didn't like that
He said, I'm gonna get that boy
So one day he walked into town
Booked himself a room in the local saloon

Rocky Raccoon checked into his room
Only to find Gideon's Bible
Rocky had come equipped with a gun
To shoot off the legs of his rival
His rival, it seems, had broken his dreams
By stealing the girl of his fancy
Her name was Magill and she called herself Lil
But everyone knew her as Nancy

Now she and her man who called himself Dan
Were in the next room at the hoedown
Rocky burst in and grinning a grin
He said, Danny boy, this is a showdown
But Daniel was hot he drew first and shot
And Rocky collapsed in the corner

Now the doctor came in stinking of gin
And proceeded to lie on the table
He said, Rocky, you met your match
And Rocky said, Doc, it's only a scratch
And I'll be better, I'll be better, Doc, as soon as I am able
Now Rocky Raccoon he fell back in his room
Only to find Gideon's Bible
Gideon checked out and he left it no doubt
To help with good Rocky's revival

这首歌最了不起的一点是，只有我一把吉他的时候，这首歌非常完美。想想看，它就是这样被写出来的。

当你拿着原声吉他坐下来时，通常最自然的创作就是有一点民谣味道。我在我听过的唱片的基础上做了一点滑稽的模仿，有点像念白布鲁斯。鲍勃·迪伦做过那样的东西，于是我开始想象南达科他州的布莱克山。我知道有首老歌《达科他的布莱克山》，开头是"Take me back to the black hills / The black hills of Dakota"[1]，那是桃乐丝·黛（Doris Day）在《野姑娘杰恩》（*Calamity Jane*）中唱的。所以，我们用了这样的念白，我恰好想出了一个叫"洛基·浣熊"的人物，因为大卫·克洛科特[2]和他的浣熊毛帽。我还是小孩子的时候，在电视上看过费斯·帕克主演的《大卫克罗传》（*Davy Crockett, King of the Wild Frontier*）。我看了那部电影，不过我主要关注的是影片同名主题歌，那真是一首很酷的歌。

我开始想象这个小故事，这对我来说有点像火车之旅之类的——头脑的火车之旅。而且，由于我创作时有点像是在开玩笑，所以写的时候、唱的时候都非常快乐。有些人——也许是喝醉的叔叔——会在聚会上朗诵诗歌，比如罗伯特·瑟维斯[3]的《丹·麦克格雷枪击案》（The Shooting of Dan McGrew）或是马里奥特·埃德加[4]的《狮子与阿尔伯特》（The Lion and Albert），后一首因斯坦利·霍洛威的舞台朗诵而闻名，那首诗里，狮子吃掉了阿尔伯特，而父母在向动物园管理员抱怨。就是那种黑色幽默。

在《洛基·浣熊》里，他的姑娘和另一个家伙私奔了，而洛基不喜欢这样。然后

1 "带我回到布莱克山 / 达科他的布莱克山"，出自《达科他的布莱克山》（The Black Hills of Dakota）。
2 大卫·克洛科特（Davy Crockett，1786—1836），美国政治家、战斗英雄。
3 罗伯特·瑟维斯（Robert Service，1874—1958），英裔加拿大诗人、作家。
4 马里奥特·埃德加（Marriott Edgar，1880—1951），英国剧作家、诗人。

他定了一个房间，只找到基甸版《圣经》[1]——美国的每个旅馆里都有，也许现在仍然有。我们在英国从未见过这个。所以我就想象这个画面——检查房间，查看桌子，打开抽屉，有一本基甸版《圣经》。洛基的女朋友名叫麦吉尔："…she called herself Lil / But everyone knew her as Nancy"（她称自己为莉莉 / 但每个人都知道她是南希）。这很不错，因为我最后和南希结婚了。

至于"The doctor stinking of gin"（满身酒气的医生），我确实在利物浦发生过一次事故，我从一辆轻便摩托车上摔下来，嘴唇裂开了，我们不得不找一位医生来我表姐贝蒂家。那差不多跟创作这首歌是在同一时期，当时我二十几岁，从我爸爸家骑了一辆小摩托车去贝蒂家。我带着一个朋友，塔拉·吉尼斯（Tara Guinness）。他后来在一场车祸中去世了。他是个很好的孩子。我在《生命中的一天》中写过他："He blew his mind out in a car / He didn't notice that the lights had changed"[2]。话说回来，我和塔拉在一起，发生了一起小事故——从摩托车上摔下来，我的嘴唇破了，到了贝蒂家，她说："叫个医生来，叫个医生来。需要缝针。"

所以他们叫来了这个家伙，他满身酒气地来了，醉得不成样子。"你好，保罗。你怎么样？""很好。""噢，需要缝针。我带着我的包来的。"于是他拿过他的黑包，开始试着穿针，一根弯曲的手术针，不过他看见的至少是三根针。

我大概提议"让我们来吧"，然后我们为他穿好了针。我问："你不用麻醉就做吗？"他说："呃，我没有麻醉剂。"我想我也许有一点苏格兰威士忌之类的东西，他就把针头放进去搅了搅。然后线掉出来了，他说："噢，不好意思，我要再来一次。"

所以，他需要第二次穿针，而我努力忍住尖叫。说实话，他真的没弄好，之后的很长一段时间里，我嘴唇上都有个肿块。我仍然能感觉到它。我全身青一块紫一块，真是一团糟，所以我决定留胡子。披头士的其他成员看见后都很喜欢，于是他们也都留起了胡子。约翰非常起劲，我想有人给他买了一个有小盖子的胡子杯，这样当你喝酒时，就不会弄湿胡子。我想这就是"满身酒气"这一形象的来由——来自这样一个有点小痛苦的回忆。

我一直想在演出中唱这首歌，因为很多人请求过，也许有一天我会的。

他们叫来了这个家伙，他满身酒气地来了，醉得不成样子。
"你好，保罗。你怎么样？""很好。"
"噢，需要缝针。我带着我的包来的。"
于是他拿过他的黑包，开始试着穿针，一根弯曲的手术针，
不过他看见的至少是三根针。

---

1 指美国福音派基督教组织"国际基甸会"自1908年起免费发放的《圣经》，起初安置在美国旅馆里。
2 "他在车里神志不清 / 他没有注意到信号灯已经变化"，出自《生命中的一天》（A Day in the Life）。

ROCKY RACOON.

1. Rocky Racoon checked into his room
Only to find Gideons bible.

2. Rocky had come, equipped with a gun,
To shoot off the legs of his rival,

3. His rival it seems had broken his dreams
By stealing the girl of his fancy.

4. Her name was McGill, she called herself
Lil,
But everyone knew her as Nancy

5. She and her man, who called himself
Dan,
were in the next room at the hoedown,

6. Rocky burst in, & grinning a grin
Said Danny boy, this is a showdown.

7. Daniel was hot, he drew first & shot
& Rocky collapsed in the corner.
SCREAM.... SOLO .....

S

San Ferry Anne

圣 · 费里 · 安

作 者 WRITERS	保罗·麦卡特尼和琳达·麦卡特尼	Paul McCartney and Linda McCartney
艺术家 ARTIST	羽翼乐队	Wings
录 音 RECORDED	伦敦阿比路录音棚	Abbey Road Studios, London
发 行 RELEASED	《以音速》，1976 年	*At the Speed of Sound*, 1976

You've got a lot
And from what you've got
I'd say you're doing well, dear

Dressed like a dream
And if things are what they seem
You're looking swell, dear

Your little man
Brings you trinkets when he can
But he can't stay, dear

That's very well
But inside your shiny shell
You dance all day, dear

So go, be gay
Let your feelings leap away
Into the laughter

San Ferry Anne
And the world keeps turning
Happy ever after

在战后，你听不到太多德语歌曲。或许这是有原因的！但是法语歌传到了英国，不仅因为我们是盟友，也因为法国离我们这么近，而且他们有优美的旋律。战后初期，作为一个孩子，我还记得伊迪丝·皮雅芙、莫里斯·舍瓦利耶 [1]、雅克·布雷尔 [2]，以及朱丽特·格蕾科 [3]。我们爱慕朱丽特，非常爱她。

我在学校里没学过法语。大多数英国孩子会学法语，约翰就学过，不过我得说他学得不太好。我选修的是西班牙语、德语和拉丁语。但是，因为那些法国金曲，几乎我那一代的所有孩子——包括我——都会几句法语短句，而在说或听那些法语短句的时候，我的想象力几乎不自觉地与它们嬉戏着。在这里，"圣·费里·安"是"ça ne fait rien"（没关系）的双关语。《圣·费里·安》是我尝试写法语歌的一个例证，就像我创作《米歇尔》。所以就有了圣·费里·安，她是一个姑娘。她很漂亮，她被人包养，一个"小男人"，他给她买首饰和东西，但是在她善良的外壳下，似乎一切都有问题。没关系。

我有另一首还没写的歌："演出的香肠"（Sausage on Show），或者"热香肠"（saucisson chaud）。说的是香肠在剧院里，一个戴着平顶帽的香肠。来吧，过来，看看演出的香肠。我们可能要过一段时间才能等到这首歌！

上图：《以音速》录音期间。
伦敦阿比路录音棚，1975 年。

1   莫里斯·舍瓦利耶（Maurice Chevalier，1888—1972），法国演员。
2   雅克·布雷尔（Jacques Brel，1929—1978），法国歌手。
3   朱丽特·格蕾科（Juliette Gréco，1927—2020），法国女演员。

东汉普顿，1975 年。

you get a lot
and from what you've got
I say your'e doing well, dear

Dress ~~up~~ like a dream
And if things are what
they seem ~~your're looking~~ swell, dear.
your're looking

Your little man
Brings you trinkets when
he can but he can't stay dear

Thats very well, ~~buts~~
t inside your shiny shell
you dance all day, dear

So go be gay
let your feelings leap away
into the laughter
an jerry ann
and the world keeps turning
happy ever after.

Say Say Say

说说说

作　者 WRITERS	保罗·麦卡特尼和迈克尔·杰克逊　Paul McCartney and Michael Jackson	
艺术家 ARTIST	保罗·麦卡特尼和迈克尔·杰克逊　Paul McCartney and Michael Jackson	
录　音 RECORDED	伦敦 AIR 录音棚、伦敦奥德赛录音棚、洛杉矶切诺基录音棚及纽约希格玛之声录音棚	
	AIR Studios, London; Odyssey Studios, London; Cherokee Studios, Los Angeles; Sigma Sound Studios, New York	
发　行 RELEASED	单曲，1983 年　Single, 1983	
	《和平管乐》，1983 年　*Pipes of Peace*, 1983	

Say say say
What you want
But don't play games
With my affection
Take take take
What you need
But don't leave me
With no direction

All alone
I sit home by the phone
Waiting for you, baby
Through the years
How can you stand to hear
My pleading for you, dear?
You know I'm crying

Now go go go
Where you want
But don't leave me
Here forever
You you you
Stay away
So long, girl, I
See you never

What can I do
Girl, to get through to you
'Cause I love you, baby
Standing here
Baptised in all my tears
Baby, through the years
You know I'm crying

You never ever worry
And you never shed a tear
You're saying that
My love ain't real
Just look at my face
These tears ain't drying

You you you
Can never say
That I'm not the one
Who really loves you
I pray pray pray
Every day
That you'll see things
Girl, like I do

What can I do
Girl, to get through to you?
'Cause I love you, baby
Standing here
Baptised in all my tears
Baby, through the years
You know I'm crying
Say say say

　　那是一个圣诞节，有人给我打电话，是一个我认不出的尖尖的声音："你好，保罗。"我想："这是一个女歌迷，她是怎么拿到我的号码的？"我非常生气。然后那个声音说："我是迈克尔。"我恍然大悟，不是什么女孩，是迈克尔·杰克逊。他说："你想做一首热门歌曲吗？"我回答："当然想啊，来我这边吧。"我们之前有过几次交集。迈克尔在他的专辑《突破界限》（*Off the Wall*）中翻唱过羽翼乐队的《女朋友》（*Girlfriend*），我也认识他的制作人昆西·琼斯[1]很长时间了。1971年，披头士的《顺其自然》获得奥斯卡最佳原创歌曲奖时，正是昆西代替我们去领的奖。

　　所以，迈克尔飞到英国，来了我在伦敦的办公室。我们上楼，那里有一架钢琴，然后开始写《说说说》。我让他做主导，我认为这首歌的很多感性成分都来自迈克尔。"Baptised in all my tears"（在泪水中接受洗礼）——我不会写那样的歌词。我的贡献在曲调上，他往里面填歌词。我们都对一起工作相当兴奋，这首歌很快就完成了：我们彼此契合。我把歌词记了下来，当我们离开办公室时，《说说说》已经完成了。我记得我们第一次把这首歌录成小样的时候，只有我们两个的人声和我弹的吉他。

　　对我来说，写一首歌就是追寻一条轨迹，然后偏离，并开辟出一条新的道路。我设置了类似地图的东西，有一些粗略的坐标，向那里前进，并在路上发现点什么，捡起一些恰好可以成为歌词和旋律的东西。这是一个发现的时刻，那也是我爱它的原因。在我写一首歌之前，有一种缺失的感觉，然后我拿起吉他或者走到钢琴边，然后——比如说，三个小时之后，如果在富有成效的氛围中的话——那个空洞就不存在了；有新的东西出现了。这是一种非常满足的感觉：你造了一辆车或者一件家具，或者于我来说，创造了一首歌。它不仅仅是在这个世界上占据空间的某个东西。如果幸运的话，它可以帮助定义世界。

上图：和乔治·马丁、迈克尔·杰克逊在一起。伦敦 AIR 录音棚，1983 年。

1　昆西·琼斯（Quincy Jones，1933— ），美国爵士／流行音乐家、制作人。

(1) SAY SAY SAY what you want.
but don't play _james_ with my affections

TAKE TAKE TAKE what you need
but don't leave me with no direction
cos all alone I sit home by
the phone, waiting for you baby)

All these years, how do you stand
to hear, my pleading for you dear
and hear me crying ooh oohwah
ooh ooh

(2) go go go where you want
But don't leave me here forever
But you you you stay away so long
girl I see you never.
it's plain to see girl that you
leaving me, for some other baby.
so here's a tear for a souvenir
cause if 'he's not sincere
you'll know I'm crying
ooh ooh ooh ooh oh.

对我来说，写一首歌就是追寻一条轨迹，然后偏离，
并开辟出一条新的道路。

SAY SAY SAY.

① PAUL
22
   Say say say what you want
But don't play games with my affection.

Take take take what you need
20   +13.
But don't leave me with no direction!.

8' MICHAEL All alone, I sit home by the phone.
15
Waiting for you .... baby. .. of 22
15 Through the years how can you stand to hear
My pleading for you dear — you know I'm
✝ crying.. OO H ..
PAUL EN

② PAUL
20 Go go go / where you want
But don't leave me.. here forever
But you you you stay away 77.
18 So long girl — 5 .... see you never
What can I do ... girl to get through to you
17 Cos I love you ... baby ...
Standing here — baptized in all my tears
Faithful through the years ....~~Ooh~~.....
You know I'm crying — ooh ...,
✝

= SOLO =

637

Sgt. Pepper's Lonely Hearts Club Band

佩珀军士孤独之心俱乐部乐队

作　者　WRITERS　保罗·麦卡特尼和约翰·列侬　Paul McCartney and John Lennon

艺术家　ARTIST　披头士乐队　The Beatles

录　音　RECORDED　伦敦阿比路录音棚　Abbey Road Studios, London

发　行　RELEASED　《佩珀军士孤独之心俱乐部乐队》，1967 年　*Sgt. Pepper's Lonely Hearts Club Band*, 1967

It was twenty years ago today
Sergeant Pepper taught the band to play
They've been going in and out of style
But they're guaranteed to raise a smile
So may I introduce to you
The act you've known for all these years
Sergeant Pepper's Lonely Hearts Club Band

We're Sergeant Pepper's Lonely Hearts Club Band
We hope you will enjoy the show
Sergeant Pepper's Lonely Hearts Club Band
Sit back and let the evening go
Sergeant Pepper's Lonely
Sergeant Pepper's Lonely
Sergeant Pepper's Lonely Hearts Club Band

It's wonderful to be here
It's certainly a thrill
You're such a lovely audience
We'd like to take you home with us
We'd love to take you home

I don't really want to stop the show
But I thought you might like to know
That the singer's going to sing a song
And he wants you all to sing along
So let me introduce to you
The one and only Billy Shears
And Sergeant Pepper's Lonely Hearts Club Band

披头士的特点之一是，我们会注意到意外，然后利用它。当我们用磁带回放出现意外时，我们会停下来说："那是怎么回事？"其他很多人会说："噢天哪，那是什么噪声？"但我们总是喜欢被这些想法改变主意。

这首歌的创作背景是，我去美国探望简·阿舍，她正在进行一部莎士比亚剧作的巡演，当时在丹佛。所以我飞到丹佛去和她待了两天，休息一下。

回来时，我和我们的巡演助理迈尔·伊文思同行，在飞机上，他说："你能把盐和胡椒递过来吗？"我没听清他说的话，问："什么？佩珀军士？"[1]

此前不久，我们在烛台公园做了一场演出。那是一场我们甚至听不见自己声音的演出；当时在下雨，我们几乎要触电了，走下舞台后，我们被塞进一辆小货车。小货车是空的，我们在里面被甩来甩去，我们都在想："真受够了。"

那天，我们决定停止巡演。我们决定做唱片，让唱片进行巡演。我们有一次听说，猫王曾经把他的镀金凯迪拉克带去巡演，我们觉得这真是绝妙。于是，我们想："我们将做一张唱片，那将是我们的镀金凯迪拉克。"

在从丹佛回来的路上，我向大家建议我们用不同的化身。概念是：我们不再是披头士，我们现在是另一支乐队。

我画了一张草稿，是我们四个人在花朵装饰的大钟前的画面。时间仿佛停滞了，因为钟是花做的。这很可爱。当时的想法是，乐队将接受伦敦市长之类的人颁发的奖杯。于是，我们在唱片封面的概念上取得了一致，然后去了索霍区，找服装设计师蒙蒂·伯曼为乐队配置服饰。

我必须承认，我在丹佛用了迷幻药，而这是我在那趟迷幻之旅之后的某种游戏。我画出草图，向其他人展示新的计划会是什么样。他们喜欢这个。这真是解放了我们。它给了我们一种匿名感，并让我们重获新生。

上图：披头士乐队在《佩珀军士孤独之心俱乐部乐队》媒体发布会上。伦敦，1967 年 5 月 19 日。

1　盐和胡椒（salt and pepper）和佩珀军士（Sergeant Pepper）发音相似。

左图：服装设计师蒙蒂·伯曼设计的外套，1967 年。

右上图：在《佩珀军士孤独之心俱乐部乐队》封套上出现的鼓皮设计。

642

It was 20 yrs ago today
when Sgt Peppers taught the band to play
They've been going in and out of style.
But they're guaranteed to raise a smile,
So may I introduce to you,
The act you've know for all these years,
Sgt. Peppers lonely hearts club band

Applause. Band — laughter and solo

CHORUS. We're Sgt. Peppers . . . .
We hope you will enjoy the show,
Sgt. Peppers . . . .
Sit back & let the evening go, Sgt Peppers lonely
~~really want to~~   THEN DRUMS

I Don't ~~~ me stop the show
It. I thought you might like to know
that the singers going to sing a song,
And he wants you all to sing along,
So let me introduce to you,
The one & only Billy Shears,
AND SGT. PEPPERS LONELY HEARTS CLUB BAND

Applause . . . . (different) into song.

It's wonderful to be here,
It's certainly a thrill.
You're such a lovely audience,
We'd like to take you home with us,
We'd like to take you home

SD.
The Sgt Peppers lonely hearts club band
we hope you've all enjoyed the show
Peppers etc . . . but once again we've got to go.

643

She Came in Through the Bathroom Window

她从浴室的窗户进来

作 者 WRITERS	保罗 · 麦卡特尼和约翰 · 列侬	Paul McCartney and John Lennon
艺术家 ARTIST	披头士乐队	The Beatles
录 音 RECORDED	伦敦阿比路录音棚	Abbey Road Studios, London
发 行 RELEASED	《阿比路》，1969 年	*Abbey Road*, 1969

She came in through the bathroom window
Protected by a silver spoon
But now she sucks her thumb and wonders
By the banks of her own lagoon

Didn't anybody tell her?
Didn't anybody see?
Sunday's on the phone to Monday
Tuesday's on the phone to me

She said she'd always been a dancer
She worked at fifteen clubs a day
And though she thought I knew the answer
Well I knew what I could not say

And so I quit the police department
And got myself a steady job
And though she tried her best to help me
She could steal but she could not rob

Didn't anybody tell her?
Didn't anybody see?
Sunday's on the phone to Monday
Tuesday's on the phone to me, oh yeah

我的妈妈是个护士，我爸爸喜欢文字，所以我是班上唯一可以正确拼写"痰"的人。尽管她只是个护士，或者助产士，而我的爸爸不过只是个棉花交易员，但我们一直把自己视为优雅的工人阶级。这是一种心理态度。我们的态度是优雅。我们渴望在每个部门都做得更好。

我们通常把"含着银汤匙出生"与高贵联系在一起，但即使在我的工人阶级家庭（虽然优雅），我受洗时也得到了一把银汤匙。我对此一无所知，直到几年后，我的迪尔阿姨（Auntie Dyl）告诉我，她一直为我保存着那把银汤匙。

从字面上和隐喻上来说，在我妈妈去世前，我一直有个幸运的童年。我是"protected by a silver spoon"（被银汤匙保护着的）。告诉你吧，我确实有一些非同寻常的想法。比如说，我过去常常用颜色表示一周的每一天。周一是黑色的，周二是黄色，周三是绿色，周四是深蓝色，周五是红色，周六是橙色，周日是白色的。当我看见周几的名字时，它们在我的想象中就是那样的。这是一种通感。

所以，我对"Sunday's on the phone to Monday / Tuesday's on the phone to me"（周日的电话一直打到周一 / 周二的电话打给了我）这句歌词特别有共鸣。在《麦当娜夫人》里，我使用了同样的策略，里面有"Friday night arrives without a suitcase"以及"Sunday morning, creeping like a nun"[1]。对我来说，这似乎是一块富饶的土地。

我觉得音乐真的可以成为非常视觉的艺术。它是由画面驱动的。我们能看见舞者"worked at fifteen clubs a day"（一天在十五个俱乐部工作），能看见角色"quit the police department"（从警察局辞职）。关于这个，我有一个讲过许多遍但仍然乐此不疲的故事：我在纽约坐出租车，出租车司机的身份卡上写的是"尤金·奎斯（Eugene Quits），纽约警察局"。我喜欢挖苦警察。调皮吧！关于这个女人"could steal but she could not rob"（会偷窃但她不会抢劫）的描述，仍然会把我逗乐。如果这其中有差别，这显然是个漂亮的差别。

而这可以追溯到一个事实：一个女人确实通过没关严的浴室窗户溜进我的房子。她显然是个歌迷——来自一个叫作"苹果渣"的歌迷团体。她在我伦敦的居所外发现了一架梯子。我能记起，她偷走了我的一幅画，画的是我的棉花交易员爸爸。也许她是从我这里抢走的。不过作为回报，我得到了这首歌。

1　"周五晚上到来时没带手提箱"及"周日清晨像修女一样爬行"，出自《麦当娜夫人》（Lady Madonna）。

左图：在伦敦家中。1969 年。

上图：等在门外的歌迷。
伦敦，1969 年。

这可以追溯到一个事实：
一个女人确实通过没关严的浴室窗户溜进我的房子。
她显然是个歌迷 —— 来自一个叫作"苹果渣"的歌迷团体。
她在我伦敦的居所外发现了一架梯子。
我能记起，她偷走了我的一幅画，
画的是我的棉花交易员爸爸。也许她是从我这里抢走的。
不过作为回报，我得到了这首歌。

BATHROOM WINDOW.

① She came in through the bathroom window
Protected by a silver spoon
But now she sucks her thumb & wonders
By the banks of her own lagoon

CHORUS
Didn't anybody tell her?
   "   "   see?
Sundays on the phone to Monday,
Tuesdays on the phone to me.

② She said she'd always been a dancer
She worked at 15 clubs a day
And though she thought I knew the answer
I just knew what I could not say.

CHORUS.

③ And so I quit the police department
And got myself a steady job
And though she tried her best to help me
She could steal but she could not rob,

CHORUS. and out.

Another Lennon + McCartney original.

648

Bathroom window

(1) She came in through the bathroom window
Protected by a silver spoon
But now she sucks her thumb and wonders
By the banks of her own lagoon

Chorus Didn't anybody tell her ......
        Didn't "   see
        Sundays on the phone to Monday
        Tuesdays ... . to me .

(2) She said she'd always been a dancer
     she worked at 15 clubs a day*
And though she thought I knew the answer
or just knew what I could not say.

Chorus ——— Didn't anybody tell her

(3) And so I quit the police department
And got myself a steady job,
And though she tried her best to help me
She could steal but she could not rob

        Chorus ... — repeated ,

                    End.

She Loves You

她爱你

作　者　WRITERS　　　保罗·麦卡特尼和约翰·列侬　Paul McCartney and John Lennon
艺术家　ARTIST　　　　披头士乐队　The Beatles
录　音　RECORDED　　 伦敦阿比路录音棚　Abbey Road Studios, London
发　行　RELEASED　　 单曲，1963 年　Single, 1963
　　　　　　　　　　　《披头士的第二张专辑》，1964 年　The Beatles' Second Album, 1964

She loves you
Yeah, yeah, yeah
She loves you
Yeah, yeah, yeah
She loves you
Yeah, yeah, yeah, yeah

You think you've lost your love
Well I saw her yesterday
It's you she's thinking of
And she told me what to say
She says she loves you
And you know that can't be bad
Yes she loves you
And you know you should be glad

She said you hurt her so
She almost lost her mind
But now she says she knows
You're not the hurting kind
She says she loves you
And you know that can't be bad
Yes she loves you
And you know you should be glad

She loves you
Yeah, yeah, yeah
She loves you
Yeah, yeah, yeah
And with a love like that
You know you should be glad
You know it's up to you
I think it's only fair
Pride can hurt you too
Apologise to her
Because she loves you
And you know that can't be bad
She loves you
And you know you should be glad

She loves you
Yeah, yeah, yeah
She loves you
Yeah, yeah, yeah
With a love like that
You know you should be glad
With a love like that
You know you should be glad
With a love like that
You know you should be glad

Yeah, yeah, yeah
Yeah, yeah, yeah, yeah

我们开始创作《她爱你》是在泰恩河畔纽卡斯尔的一场演唱会之后，那次演出我们跟罗伊·奥比森，以及杰瑞和领跑者乐队分摊开销。约翰和我坐在纽卡斯尔酒店房间的双人床上，但最后我们是在福特林路我爸爸家的饭厅里完成这首歌的。我父亲就坐在旁边的房间里抽着烟斗，看着电视，抱怨我们唱的"耶，耶，耶"，并且疑惑我们为什么不唱"是的，是的，是的"——他担心太多美式语法渗入英式英语中。如果我们那么做，我不确定这首歌是否还会成为我们在英国最畅销的单曲。

　　《她爱你》的动机之一来自鲍比·赖德尔[1]演唱的一首歌《原谅他》（Forget Him），它建立在一个呼应关系的结构上。这首歌就是这样开始的。我们打算让一个人唱，"她爱你"，另一些人回应，"耶，耶，耶"；不过那个想法成型时就被丢弃了。

　　就像我们的许多歌曲一样，《她爱你》这个歌名同样围绕着人称代词。不同的是，歌曲的叙述者是一个中间人，一个代理，一个传话者。我不能确定那个时候我是否听说过 L.P. 哈特利[2]的小说《送信人》。不过我很可能对哈特利有所了解。那时候他很有名，而这种对哈特利的熟悉很有可能影响了这首歌的创作。

　　我们也做了一首德语的版本，"Sie liebt dich"，由百代唱片的德国分支厂牌奥登唱片（Odeon Records）发行。当时我们觉得，如果我们在德国出唱片，就必须唱德语。考虑到我们和德国的关系，从某种角度来看，这很有趣，我们已经在利物浦工作了很长时间，基本上是一群有着古怪发型的摇滚歌手。我们和许多摇滚乐手一样去了汉堡，在那里变得有点"皮衣化"。后来，汉堡的一个朋友把我们的头发剪成和他同样的样式，于是我们发展出一种形象，然后在我们的经纪人布莱恩·爱泼斯坦的要求下，我们从皮衣改成了西装。我们都去了位于伯肯黑德的时髦裁缝店，贝诺·多恩（Beno Dorn）那里。我们之前从来没找过裁缝，更别说集体去裁缝店。我们全都去了，并且买了西装。

　　不过，比外表更重要的，是 1960 年代早期，我们在汉堡获得的所有音乐体验。马尔科姆·格拉德威尔（Malcolm Gladwell）在他的书《异类》（Outliers）中提到了著名的一万个小时理论，而我们的"一万个小时"在那里完成了不少。显然，1960 年至 1962 年之间，我们在汉堡演出了近三百场。所以，德语版的《她爱你》真的是用一种奇怪的方式为事情画上了句号。

1　鲍比·赖德尔（Bobby Rydell，1942— ），美国演员、歌手。
2　L.P. 哈特利（L. P. Hartley，1895—1972），英国作家、评论家。《送信人》（The Go-Between）为其代表作。

651

上图：早期的披头士乐队成员，
包括皮特·贝斯特（Pete Best）、
乔治·哈里森和约翰·列侬。
利物浦，1961 年。

右图：和爸爸吉姆在花园里。
利物浦福特林路。

She's a Woman

她是那样的女人

作 者 WRITERS	保罗·麦卡特尼和约翰·列侬	Paul McCartney and John Lennon
艺术家 ARTIST	披头士乐队	The Beatles
录 音 RECORDED	伦敦阿比路录音棚	Abbey Road Studios, London
发 行 RELEASED	《我感觉不错》B 面单曲，1964 年	B-side of 'I Feel Fine' single, 1964
	《披头士'65》，1964 年	*Beatles '65*, 1964

My love don't give me presents
I know that she's no peasant
Only ever has to give me
Love forever and forever
My love don't give me presents
Turn me on when I get lonely
People tell me that she's only foolin'
I know she isn't

She don't give boys the eye
She hates to see me cry
She is happy just to hear me
Say that I will never leave her
She don't give boys the eye
She will never make me jealous
Gives me all her time as well as lovin'
Don't ask me why

She's a woman who understands
She's a woman who loves her man

My love don't give me presents
I know that she's no peasant
Only ever has to give me
Love forever and forever
My love don't give me presents
Turn me on when I get lonely
People tell me that she's only foolin'
I know she isn't

She's a woman who understands
She's a woman who loves her man

My love don't give me presents
I know that she's no peasant
Only ever has to give me
Love forever and forever
My love don't give me presents
Turn me on when I get lonely
People tell me that she's only foolin'
I know she isn't

She's a woman
She's a woman

我们都有点喜欢节奏布鲁斯。现在的节奏布鲁斯在某种程度上是嘻哈，不过在那时候就是节奏加上布鲁斯音乐。在早期，我们都热爱黑人音乐。我们热爱这类音乐的自发性，或者看起来的自发性。

我们经常听的歌曲似乎都会提到"女人"。比如雷·查尔斯的《我有了一个女人》（I Got a Woman），或者小理查德的圣歌《高个子莎莉》和《天哪，莫莉小姐》（Good Golly, Miss Molly）。我们听到的很多东西已经在那里了，但是我想，我们所做的是接受它们，把它们扔进滚筒式干燥机，蒸馏它们，并从另一端推出来。

《她是那样的女人》称赞的是我的女孩的高尚品质，让我们说得清楚一点，她不是女孩，她是女人。这是件有趣的事情：一个女孩什么时候才能成为女人？对我们来说，在我们大概二十一岁前，她们都是女孩。那之后，她们或许仍是女孩，但我们可以大胆地将自己视为男人，也可以把女孩们想成女人。

通常，我们中的某个人会在录音中带来一些闪光点，我觉得《她是那样的女人》录音里的闪光点是约翰的节奏吉他和我的贝斯的结合。

我从来不用贝斯作曲。从来没有，现在也不会。所以我是怎么会在乐队里弹贝斯的呢？我的罗塞蒂牌实心 7 型吉他在汉堡摔坏之后，我必须找一件新的乐器。我们已经有了两把吉他，一个鼓手，以及贝斯手斯图尔特·萨克利夫。我们演出的舞台上正好有一架钢琴，我就用上了，在每首歌里面都弹点，于是，我成了乐队里的钢琴手。有意思的是，斯图尔特没有多余的贝斯弦，所以，如果他的某根弦断了，他就会突袭我的钢琴。他会拿着一支钳子剪下一根弦。

我们在汉堡的时候，斯图尔特和当地一位名叫阿斯特丽德的女孩坠入爱河，决定退出乐队。所以，现在我们没有贝斯手，我们不可能有三把吉他却没有贝斯。在那个时候，没人愿意当贝斯手，因为贝斯手总是个胖子。似乎贝斯上附带着某种耻辱感。总而言之，我买了一把霍夫纳贝斯，这个有着可爱的小提琴形状的东西吸引了我，因为作为左撇子，我知道我要把它倒过来弹。它的对称性对我极有吸引力，而且它像羽毛一样轻。

对于我变成贝斯手这个事实，我只能报以微笑，因为我爸爸过去总是指出我们所听的歌曲里面的贝斯声音。他是吉姆·麦克爵士乐队的一员，弹钢琴和吹小号，他在音乐欣赏方面对我和我的弟弟进行过教育。我们会听电台，而他会说："听见那个了吗？那是贝斯！"

在那个时候，没人愿意当贝斯手，
因为贝斯手总是个胖子。似乎贝斯上附带着某种耻辱感。
总而言之，我买了一把霍夫纳贝斯，
这个有着可爱的小提琴形状的东西吸引了我，
因为作为左撇子，我知道我要把它倒过来弹。
它的对称性对我极有吸引力，而且它像羽毛一样轻。

下图：和乔治·哈里森、约翰·列侬、皮特·贝斯特及斯图尔特·萨克利夫一起表演。汉堡英德拉俱乐部，1960 年。

右图：1960 年代早期。

She's Given Up Talking

她放弃了交谈

作　者 **WRITER**	保罗·麦卡特尼	Paul McCartney
艺术家 **ARTIST**	保罗·麦卡特尼	Paul McCartney
录　音 **RECORDED**	洛杉矶汉森录音棚	Henson Studios, Los Angeles
发　行 **RELEASED**	《倾盆大雨》，2001 年	*Driving Rain, 2001*

She's given up talking
Don't say a word
Even in the classroom
Not a dickie bird
Unlike other children
She's seen and never heard
She's given up talking
Don't say a word

You see her in the playground
Standing on her own
Everybody wonders
Why she's all alone
Someone made her angry
Someone's got her scared
She's given up talking
Don't say a word

But when she comes home
It's yap-a-yap-yap
Words are running freely
Like the water from a tap
Her brothers and her sisters
Can't get a word in edgeways
But when she's back at school again
She goes into a daze

She's given up talking
Don't say a word
Even in the classroom
Not a dickie bird
Unlike other children
She's seen and never heard
She's given up talking
Don't say a word

She's given up talking
She don't say a word
Don't say a word
Don't say a word

上图：斯派克·米利根在伊普尔
塔前，萨塞克斯郡。

　　"选择性缄默症"这个现象让我着迷。有一个我认识多年的家庭。我看着他们有
了孩子，我看着孩子们长大，有时候，我骑马外出时会带其中一个孩子同乘。

　　一天，这些孩子中一个不再说话了。在学校里，她不再交谈或者回答问题。某天
某人决定不再说话这个想法——有点疯狂，但是也很勇敢。所以，这首歌就是我对此
的想象。"Not a dickie bird"（不再是叽喳鸟）是押韵的俚语。我们在利物浦时就这么说。
和前面一句歌词"Don't say a word"（不发一言）合在一起很不错。

　　我喜欢普通人在运用语言时对花哨的拒绝，他们根据自己的需要来调整用语。他
们不理会词句的规则，用自己的方式梳理语句。在英国的南部海岸，有一座古老的纪
念碑，离我住的地方很近，那是法国人建的，来自伊普尔。它是一座塔，有点像小城堡，
叫作伊普尔塔。不说法语的当地人称之为"瓦普尔"。

　　我并没有和那个女孩讨论过她的沉默。但是我和她的家里人谈过，然后我说我会
为此写一首歌。几年后他们告诉我，这只是阶段性的。她长大了，现在她正常说话了。

　　也许这只是另一个阶段。

SHE'S GIVEN UP TALKIN'

①   SHE'S GIVEN UP TALKIN'
(SHE) DON'T SAY A WORD
    EVEN IN THE CLASSROOM
    NOT A DICKIE BIRD
    UNLIKE OTHER CHILDREN
    SHE'S SEEN AND NEVER HEARD
(SHE) GIVEN UP TALKIN'
    DON'T SAY A WORD

②   YOU SEE HER IN THE PLAYGROUND
    STANDIN' ON HER OWN
    EVERYBODY WONDERS
    WHY SHE'S ALL ALONE
    SOMEONE MADE HER ANGRY
    SOMEONE GOT HER SCARED
(SHE) GIVEN UP TALKIN'
    DON'T SAY A WORD

AH BUT WHEN SHE COMES HOME
    ITS YAP-A-YAP-YAP
(HER) WORDS ARE RUNNING FREELY
LIKE THE WATER FROM A TAP
    HER BROTHERS AND HER SISTERS
    CAN'T GET A WORD IN EDGE WAYS
    BUT WHEN SHE'S BACK AT SCHOOL AGAIN
    SHE GOES INTO A DAZE

    REPEAT ①

《倾盆大雨》专辑封面，使用卡西欧手腕相机拍摄，2001 年。

我喜欢普通人在运用语言时对花哨的拒绝，
他们根据自己的需要来调整用语。
他们不理会词句的规则，用自己的方式梳理语句。
在英国的南部海岸，有一座古老的纪念碑，
离我住的地方很近，那是法国人建的，来自伊普尔。
它是一座塔，有点像小城堡，叫作伊普尔塔。
不说法语的当地人称之为"瓦普尔"。

She's Leaving Home

她离开了家

作　者 WRITERS	保罗·麦卡特尼和约翰·列侬	Paul McCartney and John Lennon
艺术家 ARTIST	披头士乐队	The Beatles
录　音 RECORDED	伦敦阿比路录音棚	Abbey Road Studios, London
发　行 RELEASED	《佩珀军士孤独之心俱乐部乐队》，1967 年	*Sgt. Pepper's Lonely Hearts Club Band*, 1967

Wednesday morning at five o'clock as the day
    begins
Silently closing her bedroom door
Leaving the note that she hoped would say more
She goes downstairs to the kitchen clutching her
    handkerchief
Quietly turning the backdoor key
Stepping outside she is free

She
    (We gave her most of our lives)
Is leaving
    (Sacrificed most of our lives)
Home
    (We gave her everything money could buy)
She's leaving home
After living alone
For so many years
    (Bye-bye)

Father snores as his wife gets into her dressing
    gown
Picks up the letter that's lying there
Standing alone at the top of the stairs
She breaks down and cries to her husband,
    Daddy, our baby's gone
Why would she treat us so thoughtlessly?
How could she do this to me?

She
    (We never thought of ourselves)
Is leaving
    (Never a thought for ourselves)
Home
    (We've struggled hard all our lives to get by)
She's leaving home
After living alone
For so many years
    (Bye-bye)

Friday morning at nine o'clock she is far away
Waiting to keep the appointment she made
Meeting a man from the motor trade

She
    (What did we do that was wrong?)
Is having
    (We didn't know it was wrong)
Fun
    (Fun is the one thing that money can't buy)
Something inside
That was always denied
For so many years
    (Bye-bye)

She's leaving home
    (Bye-bye)

除了《西区故事》，约翰讨厌所有音乐剧。《西区故事》是我们一起去看的——一个巡演剧团在利物浦的演出。当然，我们也看了电影，开场镜头就是那个从直升飞机上拍摄的纽约。我们喜欢它，觉得它对我们来说算得上足够大胆。但是约翰在《南太平洋》[1] 的中途离场了——过于平淡，过于讲究，而且过于甜蜜。尽管"列侬和麦卡特尼"听上去像是"罗杰斯和哈默斯坦"，但从一开始，我们就很清楚我们永远不会去写音乐剧。

然而，我们确实写了叙事歌曲。这首歌是基于一则失踪女孩的新闻报道创作的。新闻的标题是"出身优越的女孩丢弃了汽车并且消失"之类的。于是，我开始想象可能发生的事情，事件的先后顺序。留下一张她"hoped would say more"（希望能说明更多）的纸条这一细节，是整首歌最有力量的时刻之一。（像许多创作者一样，我被那些缺失的部分深深吸引。我过去很喜欢在广播中听到观众无缘无故地大笑。喜剧演员并没有说笑话，不过也许他扮了一个鬼脸。你永远也不会知道他到底做了什么。）

除了新闻报道，我相当确定《周三剧场》（*The Wednesday Play*）也对这首歌有所影响。这是一个每周播出的系列时评片，经常包含一些"重要的"社会话题。而人们周四早上在公交车站等车时会讨论这个节目。这是一周里非常重要的一部分。最著名的几期之一是《凯茜回家》（*Cathy Come Home*），导演是肯·洛奇（Ken Loach）。这部片说的是无家可归者，1966 年 11 月播出时，全英国有四分之一的人在那个晚上收看了。

我们录制《她离开了家》时，它几乎就像《周三剧场》的分镜头脚本。"Clutching her handkerchief / Quietly turning the backdoor key"（紧紧抓着她的手绢 / 轻轻地转动后门的钥匙）。一方面，我们有一位叙述者在描述这些动作："她离开了家"；另一方面，还有聚光灯下的小型希腊合唱团穿插其中："We gave her most of our lives"（我们为她献出了大半人生）。本来有一句这样的歌词——"这就是我们得到的所有感激吗？"[2] 后来不知怎么地没用上。

现在我意识到，你能轻易地想象一个"man from the motor trade"（做汽车生意的人）和所有那些旅行推销员一起出现在菲利普·拉金[3] 的诗里。她见一个做汽车生意的人是为了买一辆车，还是为了一段浪漫的关系？这首歌留了一个开放的意象。

我不确定如今还能不能写出这样的歌。有趣的是，现在一部音乐剧的设想正是这类叙事歌曲的创作出发点。所以，也许列侬和麦卡特尼最终还是创作了音乐剧。

1　《南太平洋》（*South Pacific*），美国音乐剧，由乔舒亚·洛根（Joshua Logan）导演，1949 年首演。
2　原句为："Is this all the thanks that we get？"
3　菲利普·拉金（Philip Larkin，1922—1985），英国诗人。

SHE IS LEAVING HOME.

Wednesday morning at 5 o'clock as the day begins
Silently closing her bedroom door
Leaving the note that she hoped would say more
She goes downstairs to the kitchen clutching her handkerchief
Quietly turning the back door key
Stepping outside she is free

SHE,   we gave her most of our lives
IS LEAVING sacrificed most of our lives
HOME, we gave her everything money could buy
She's leaving home after living alone for so many years

Father snores as his wife gets into her dressing gown
Picks up the letter thats lying there
Standing alone at the top of the stairs
She breaks down and cries to her husband
Daddy our baby's gone
Why would she treat us so thoughtlessly
How could she do this to me,
SHE (Is this the thanks that we get) (We never thought of ourselves)
IS LEAVING (All of the thanks that we get) (Never a thought for
HOME, we struggled hard all our lives to get by   ourselves)

Friday morning at 9 o'clock she is far away
Waiting to keep the appointment she made
Meeting ~~the~~ A MAN from the motor trade

SHE   What did we do that was wrong?
IS HAVING We didn't know it was wrong
FUN   Fun is the one thing that money can't buy
Something inside that was always denied for so many
                                                years.

MIKE Iva 5605

《佩珀军士孤独之心俱乐部乐队》
封面早期草稿，画在歌词背面，
1967 年。

665

Silly Love Songs

愚蠢的情歌

作　者 WRITERS	保罗·麦卡特尼和琳达·麦卡特尼　Paul McCartney and Linda McCartney
艺术家 ARTIST	羽翼乐队　Wings
录　音 RECORDED	伦敦阿比路录音棚　Abbey Road Studios, London
发　行 RELEASED	《以音速》，1976 年　*At the Speed of Sound*, 1976
	单曲，1976 年　Single, 1976

You'd think that people
Would have had enough
Of silly love songs
But I look around me
And I see it isn't so
Some people want to fill the world
With silly love songs
And what's wrong with that?
I'd like to know
'Cause here I go again

I love you

Ah I can't explain
The feeling's plain to me
Now can't you see?
Ah she gave me more
She gave it all to me
Now can't you see?
What's wrong with that?
I need to know
'Cause here I go again

I love you

Love doesn't come in a minute
Sometimes it doesn't come at all
I only know that when I'm in it
It isn't silly
No it isn't silly
Love isn't silly at all

How can I tell you about my loved one?

I love you

Ah I can't explain
The feeling's plain to me
Say can't you see?
Ah he gave me more
He gave it all to me
Say can't you see?

You'd think that people
Would have had enough
Of silly love songs
But I look around me
And I see it isn't so, oh no
Some people want to fill the world
With silly love songs
And what's wrong with that?

在 1970 年代中期，出现了一种指责的声音——其中包括来自约翰的——说我只会写"愚蠢的情歌"。我猜大家的想法是我应该更强硬一点，更世界性一点。但后来我突然意识到，那实际上就是爱——它就是世界性的。"Some people want to fill the world / With silly love songs"（一些人希望填满世界 / 用愚蠢的情歌）。我已经有了这样的名声，我必须为它挺身而出。相比放弃情歌，更应该继续，投入其中，不要觉得尴尬，尽管你可能会说这是一个多愁善感的主题，实际上正相反：这是一种人们可以彼此感知并让生活更美好的事情。我觉得这是关键，如果你想成为一个愤世嫉俗的人，那很容易，你可以的。"Love doesn't come in a minute / Sometimes it doesn't come at all"（爱情不是瞬间到来 / 有时候它根本不来）。我觉得那些嘲讽爱的人，只是没有足够的运气去感受它。

如果你怨天尤人并且咒骂不休，你会更容易得到评论的认可，因为那让你看起来更强大。如果你说，"哦，天气不错，一切都好，我喜欢下雨"，那你就是个无聊的笨蛋。但是如果你说，"哦，这他妈的天气！真他妈的不敢相信！我他妈的讨厌打雷！我他妈的讨厌闪电！老天究竟在他妈的干什么？"评论家也许会说："真绝妙！"

了解我表演的人都知道，我不怎么在舞台上说"脏话"，我在生活中也不会。我们年轻时，时常咒骂很多事情。让我们现实一点，当你是个年轻人时，你更倾向于那么做，因为你没有被束缚。但是当你有了孩子，你会想，也许不该这么做了。这是一个几乎可以预测的生命循环。不过，我也有过那个骂天咒地的时期——"这他妈的，那他妈的"——我记得自己吓坏了我的晚餐客人，开始自省："我做了什么？"那只是虚张声势，假装很酷。

不过，约翰时常有那种咄咄逼人的姿态，那是他对抗世界的盾牌。我们曾经为某些事情争吵，他说了一些特别尖刻的话；我有一点受伤，而他拉下眼镜盯着我说："这就是我，保罗。"那就是约翰。"这就是我。"哦，好吧，你刚才气势汹汹，而那是另一个人，是吗？那是他防御性的交谈姿态。

他会说："我爸爸当着我的面离开了家，我妈妈被一个下班的警察开车撞倒在屋外，我的乔治叔叔去世了。对啊，我很怨恨。"他告诉我，他曾经觉得他是家里男性长辈的诅咒，因为他爸爸离家出走，然后他和咪咪姑妈、乔治叔叔一起生活，接着他很喜欢的乔治也去世了。他妈妈在探望他之后被撞倒。仅仅是要适应所有这些，你就会想建立一些防御。

关键是，大多数人不愿意表露他们的情感，除非是私下里，但是在内心深处，人们是很情绪化的，我在这首歌里真正想说的是，"爱一点也不愚蠢"。

羽翼乐队在柏林查理检查站[1]，1976 年。

1　柏林查理检查站（Checkpoint Charlie），东柏
　　林和西柏林交界处的一个检查岗，也是冷战
　　时期东西方世界对抗和交流的象征。

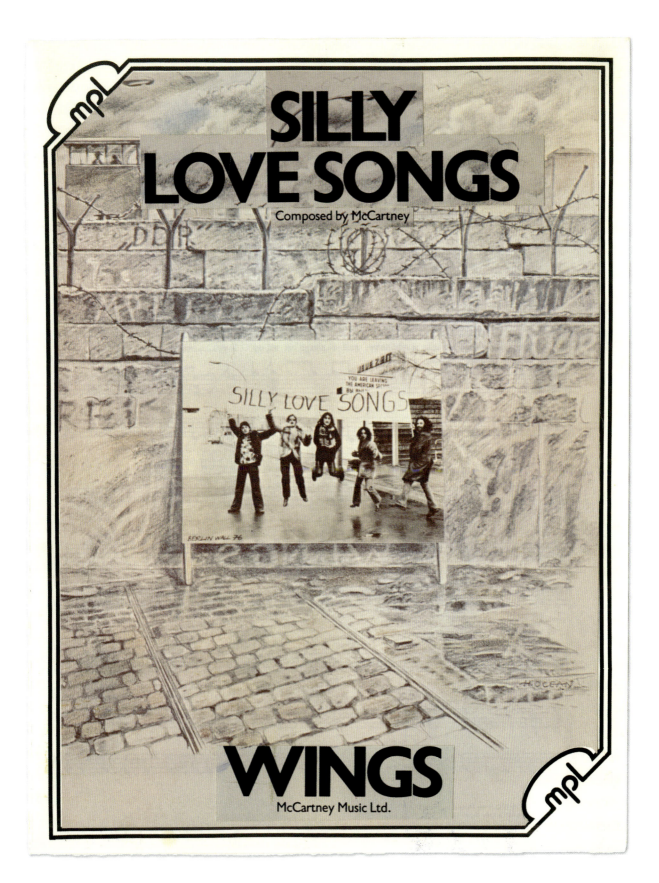

[SILLY LOVE SONGS]

You'd think that people
would have had enough
of silly love songs

HUSTLE
BEAT.

♩ ♪ ♩ ♩
♩ ♪ ♩♩
"OH YEAH"

But if I look around me
and I see it, isn't so

[HOOK]

Some people want to fill
the world with silly love songs

and what's wrong with that
I'd like to know (OR I'm ONE
of THEM!!)
(AND) cos here I go
Again.

Chorus   FIRST LINE
I love you

verse SECOND LINE.   Ah she gave me more
Ah — I can't explain   she gave it all to me.
the feeling, plain to me.
say — can't you see?

THIRD   How can I tell you about ?
LINE.   my loved one?

Chords

You'd think that people would have
had enough of silly love songs

But I look around me
and I see it isn't so

Some people want to fill the world
with silly love songs
and what's wrong with that?
I need to know   cos here I go - again

① I — love — you
   I — love — you
   I - love — you
   I — love — you

INSTRUMENTAL and what's wrong with that?
      I need to know   cos here I go - again!

        BREAK
② Ah I can't explain the feelings plain to me
      say cant you see
  Ah she gave me more it all to me say cant you see!
         she gave
      what's wrong with that -
INSTRUMENTAL going into E —
                out.

①+②

671

Simple as That

那么简单

作 者 WRITER	保罗·麦卡特尼	Paul McCartney
艺术家 ARTIST	保罗·麦卡特尼	Paul McCartney
录 音 RECORDED	萨塞克斯郡猪山磨坊	Hog Hill Mill, Sussex
发 行 RELEASED	《反海洛因计划：这是一个活生生的世界》，1986 年	*The Anti-heroin Project: It's a Live-in World*, 1986

I know it isn't easy to refuse
A lot of thoughts are flying through your head
Tell me this before you have to choose
Would you rather be alive or dead?

It's as simple as that
Would you rather be alive or dead?
It's as simple as that
It's so simple
It makes you wanna cry

They ask you if you wanna join in
You linger for a minute or so
Well now's a perfect time to begin
Are you gonna say yes or no?

It's as simple as that
Are you gonna say yes or no?
It's as simple as that
It's so simple
It makes you wanna cry

And if you love your life
Everybody will love you too
Yes if you love your life
Everybody will love you too

It's harder when you start to get around
I want you to remember what I said
I know you never like to let them down
But would you rather be alive or dead?

It's as simple as that
Would you rather be alive or dead?
It's as simple as that
It's so simple
It makes me wanna cry
So simple
It makes you wanna cry

Yes if you love your life
Everybody will love you too
And if you love your life
Everybody will love you too

Would you rather be alive or dead?
Would you rather be alive or dead?
It's as simple as that
It's as simple as that
It's as simple as that

And if you love your life
Everybody will love you too
Yes if you love your life
Everybody will love you too

在 1980 年代中期，英国广播公司请我为一个反海洛因的慈善活动做点什么。他们希望有一首歌能够告诉年轻人，海洛因并不是一个好选择。这就是我想到的："It's as simple as that"（就是那么简单）。

歌曲风格是我喜爱的风格之一——雷鬼乐。我清晰地记得我第一次对雷鬼乐感兴趣的场景。当时我在苏格兰粉刷我的屋顶，是一个夏日，我们正放着雷鬼乐唱片——《拧紧》（*Tighten Up*），那是一张原版的合集唱片，非常好听，很适合那个氛围：苏格兰的夏日，把屋顶刷成绿色，听着雷鬼乐。那让我感觉非常好。

我们一家人经常去牙买加度假。蒙特哥湾有一家我们很喜欢的酒店，我们会待在那里，无休止地听广播，牙买加有一个非常好的电台叫作 RJR，每天都放雷鬼乐。

镇子里有一家叫作托尼唱片店的小店，位于佛堤树路。这家店非常时髦。你浏览四十五转单曲唱片时，会看到一些你喜欢的东西。通常它只是醋酸酯唱片，一张样带唱片，它们不一定有公司的厂牌标签。所以我会问店员："这张是什么样的？""噢，哥们儿，那张非常棒。"我记得我买的一张唱片，那首单曲叫《舔我的烟斗》（Lick I Pipe），而我想："很好。不管是谁做的，不管它是什么意思，这首歌不错。"舔我的烟斗！

所以我买了一堆唱片，我们拿回家后，发现了一些非常好的歌曲。有一次，我们看见一张专辑，里面有一首歌叫作《毒药压力》（Poison Pressure），署名是列侬和麦卡特尼，于是我买下来听了，它一点也不像我们的歌。不过随后我想，好吧，这也许是鲍勃·列侬和查理·麦卡特尼，我要去跟谁吵呢？列侬和麦卡特尼写的《毒药压力》。一首金曲！

鲍勃·马利的出现巩固了雷鬼乐的风格，并把它带入主流。可惜的是，我从未见过马利。有一两次我非常接近他。有一天晚上，他在伦敦的兰心剧院演出，我们走在半路上，又改变了主意。我想的是也许我在观众中太引人注目了。这真的很蠢，因为看他的演出并和他见面真的很值得。

我们有一个家庭小传统，时不时为琳达的爸爸做一张唱片。所以在这首歌里，我有一个很棒的和声团：我的孩子们。全家人一起去录音棚胡闹总是很好玩。孩子们会在歌里演唱，每个人都有一句歌词，他们很喜欢这样。所以我说："瞧，这首歌是为一个慈善活动写的，而且这是一个了不起的慈善活动。"我觉得让孩子们加入这样一个反海洛因的计划，不会是坏主意。

我记得我买的一张唱片，那首单曲叫《舔我的烟斗》，而我想：
"很好。不管是谁做的，不管它是什么意思，这首歌不错。"
舔我的烟斗！

Single Pigeon

单身鸽子

作　者 **WRITERS**	保罗·麦卡特尼和琳达·麦卡特尼	Paul McCartney and Linda McCartney
艺术家 **ARTIST**	保罗·麦卡特尼和羽翼乐队	Paul McCartney and Wings
录　音 **RECORDED**	伦敦奥林匹克之声录音棚	Olympic Sound Studios, London
发　行 **RELEASED**	《红玫瑰高速公路》，1973 年	*Red Rose Speedway*, 1973

Single pigeon through the railings
Did she throw you out?
Sunday morning fight about Saturday night

Single seagull gliding over
Regent's Park canal
Do you need a pal for a minute or two?
You do?
Me too (me too, me too)

I'm a lot like you
Me too (me too, me too)
I'm a lot like you

Did she turf you out in the cold morning rain
Again?
Me too (me too, me too)

I'm a lot like you
Me too (me too, me too)
I'm a lot like you

Sunday morning fight about Saturday night

　　我的爱好之一是鸟类学。实际上，我是一个热心的鸟类学家，并且一直都是。就像我之前提到的，我小时候的业余爱好之一是带上我的《鸟类观察指南》，坐在田野里让自己迷失在大自然中。正如人们所说，我喜欢我的鸟儿们。

　　我看见过一只单身的鸽子，到处啄食——靠近栏杆的一只蓝灰色鸽子——我觉得这些词的组合相当迷人："单身鸽子"。我开始想，为什么这只鸽子会单身。

　　当你决定架构关于一只鸽子的故事，那就不仅是一只鸽子了。那是一出戏中的角色，是一个前一天晚上和女朋友吵架的家伙，他被赶出了屋子。所以就是这样，他现在单身了。都是因为"Sunday morning fight about Saturday night"（周日清晨为了周六晚上而争吵）。

　　第二段主歌总会很有趣，因为你会去往另一个地方，不过你也想保持第一段主歌的感觉。现在，我创造了一只单身的鸽子，第二段主歌介绍了一只"单身海鸥"——我的小戏剧中的另一个角色。我经常看见海鸥盘旋在摄政公园的河流上，不过也有可能他是从契诃夫那里飞来的。在契诃夫的戏剧里，海鸥不仅仅是海鸥，而是一个人物，康斯坦丁，以及他和妮娜的关系的象征。[1]

　　歌曲的主人公"a lot like you"（很像你）这个动机暗示了他，同样，是被赶出去的。他和鸽子与海鸥产生了联系，因为他，同样，被赶到了清晨寒冷的雨中。所以，我将这首歌从一个鸟类观察转变成自我描述。鸽子就是我，或者海鸥就是我，或者我的变体。

　　讽刺的是，创作这首歌时，我的个人生活非常幸福。人们听这首歌的时候，也许会意识到，我的嘴角因为微笑而轻快地上扬，因为我和琳达非常幸福，有她来和声"Me too / I'm a lot like you"（我也是 / 我很像你）是那么美好。

　　我之前说过，但是我要再说一次：许多创作者仅仅从他们日常自发的想法中汲取灵感，但是我喜欢天马行空地胡思乱想。那是作为任何一种艺术家的最好的事情之一。我喜欢用某种未知方式出现的歌曲和诗歌。这也许就是我那么羡慕鲍勃·迪伦的原因之一。你永远不知道他会做什么，或者他会跳到哪条路上。

1　指契诃夫经典剧作《海鸥》中的角色 Konstantin Tréplev 与 Nina。

歌曲的主人公"很像你"这个动机暗示了，他，同样，
是被赶出去的。
他和鸽子与海鸥产生了联系，因为他，同样，
被赶到了清晨寒冷的雨中。

Somedays

有些时候

作 者	WRITER	保罗·麦卡特尼　Paul McCartney
艺术家	ARTIST	保罗·麦卡特尼　Paul McCartney
录 音	RECORDED	萨塞克斯郡猪山磨坊、伦敦 AIR 录音棚　Hog Hill Mill, Sussex and AIR Studios, London
发 行	RELEASED	《火焰派》，1997 年　*Flaming Pie*, 1997

Somedays I look
I look at you with eyes that shine
Somedays I don't
I don't believe that you are mine

It's no good asking me what time of day it is
Who won the match or scored the goal
Somedays I look
Somedays I look into your soul

Sometimes I laugh
I laugh to think how young we were
Sometimes it's hard
It's hard to know which way to turn

Don't ask me where I found that picture
　on the wall
How much it cost or what it's worth
Sometimes I laugh
I laugh to think how young we were

We don't need anybody else
To tell us what is real
Inside each one of us is love
And we know how it feels

Somedays I cry
I cry for those who live in fear
Somedays I don't
I don't remember why I'm here

No use reminding me, it's just the way it is
Who ran the race or came in first
Somedays I cry
I cry for those who fear the worst

We don't need anybody else
To tell us what is real
Inside each one of us is love
And we know how it feels

Somedays I look
I look at you with eyes that shine
Somedays I don't
I don't believe that you are mine

It's no good asking me what time of day it is
Who won the match or scored the goal
Somedays I look
Somedays I look into your soul

　　这首歌的歌名来自第一句歌词，随后的第二句重复了首句的结尾。"Somedays I look / I look at you with eyes that shine / Somedays I don't / I don't believe that you are mine"（有些时候我看着 / 我看着你闪烁的眼睛 / 有些时候我不 / 我不相信你属于我）。字句的重复是一种小技巧，用来强调，那对歌词很管用。有一点像是电力驱动。我的文法学校教育告诉我，这是一种被称作"蝉联"的修辞手法，但是本质上，这是重复。你觉得你走在某条道路上，而后有点惊讶于它将你带到另一条路上。我喜欢字句游戏，和词语跳舞，像洗牌一样。

　　我经常觉得，当我写一首歌的时候，我是在追寻面包屑的踪迹。有人撒下了这些面包屑，而我看见了最初的一些，"有些时候我看着"，然后看见下一些。我更像是追寻着一首歌，而不是创作它。我会考虑将要出现的歌词，并且考虑如何切入，就像上下台阶。我的思考过程就像这样：我需要做那个去到达那里，这样继续。我非常享受，这是一个有趣的过程。我经常把它比作字谜游戏。我爸爸是字谜游戏的大玩家，也是一个话非常多的人。我觉得我从他那里继承了那种对词语和字谜游戏的热爱。那通常就是歌曲的本质——谜。试着去考虑一个字如何配合另一个字。于是，你如果那样把它们合在一起，并且把那个词转化一下，答案就是……

　　接下来就是填满空隙。

　　乔治·马丁说这首歌"极度简单"。他应该了解，因为他最擅长使复杂的东西看起来很简单。那也是我总是选择他来做编曲的原因。我已经认识他很长时间了——实际上，是我的大部分职业生涯——从披头士和他一起为百代公司做了我们的试听带开始，那时候，我离自己的二十岁生日还有几天。我已经跟他一起工作了那么久，如果我希望某件作品有一个好编曲，就会很高兴地给他打电话说："嗨，乔治，你有兴趣一起做点事情吗？"他是一位真正的绅士，就像我的第二个父亲，总是房间里的那个成年人，带着他讨人喜欢的纯正英国口音。如果我有机会和他而不是和其他人合作，

上图：乔治·马丁与保罗。
伦敦 AIR 录音棚，1982 年。

681

我就会打电话邀请他——除非涉及古典音乐，譬如《利物浦清唱剧》，我会和在古典乐领域更专业的人合作。无论如何，自从在 1962 年 6 月的那一天，他给了我们第一份录音合同，直到我们最后一次见面，乔治始终是我认识的最慷慨、最聪明、最有音乐天赋的人。

《有些时候》是一首很好的短歌，对我来说很有意义。探寻一个灵魂；这是你在一段关系中试图去做的事情，然而经常并不成功。歌词里包含了一些矛盾的想法，但目的是支撑这首歌，而不是体现歌词本身，这是一种解放。我知道这也许听起来古怪，但是歌词和歌曲是两种稍有点不同的东西。

一旦我将自己孤立（在这首歌的情况下是另一个小房间，而琳达在房子里的其他地方进行烹饪），一旦我真正动手写歌，我就会跟随这条印迹。我真的不知道目标是什么，甚至不知道我希望去向哪里，但是我确实喜欢到达那里，并在路上找到答案。你可以边走边试验，所以，在草率和停止之间有一道裂缝，如果你足够幸运，一些东西也许会无意中出现："I look at you with eyes that shine / Somedays I don't"（我看着你闪烁的眼睛 / 有些时候我不）。那就像是会在一个迷幻艺术家的作品中出现的一些想法。我用"I don't believe that you are mine"（我不相信你属于我）来做下一句，现在这儿出现了一个奇妙的模棱两可的含义。

保罗与乔治·马丁。
伦敦 AIR 录音棚，1983 年。

(B min — A)
SOMEDAYS I LOOK
(B min - A)
I LOOK AT YOU
WITH EYES THAT SHINE (X)
(E min)
(B min - A)
SOMEDAYS ~~SOMEDAYS~~ I DONT
I DONT BELIEVE
THAT YOU ARE MINE

ITS NO GOOD ASKING ME
WHAT TIME OF DAY IT IS
WHO WON THE MATCH
OR SCORED THE GOAL
SOMEDAYS I LOOK I
LOOK AT YOU WITH EYES THAT SHINE

①

SOMETIMES I LAUGH
I LAUGH TO THINK
HOW YOUNG WE WERE

SOMETIMES IT'S HARD
ITS HARD TO KNOW
WHICH WAY TO TURN
DONT ASK ME WHERE
I FOUND THAT PICTURE
ON THE WALL
HOW MUCH IT COST
OR WHAT ITS WORTH
SOMETIMES I LAUGH
I LAUGH TO THINK
HOW YOUNG
    WE WERE.

②

MIDDLE.
WE DONT NEED
ANYBODY ELSE
TO TELL US WHAT ▓▓▓
         IS REAL
INSIDE EACH ONE
OR US IS LOVE
AND WE KNOW
HOW IT FEELS.

        F# E C#
D C# B A F#
G A B C# A D .

repeat

③

F# B   C# D
SOMEDAYS I CRY
F# B C# D
I CRY FOR THOSE
C#   B   A B
WHO LIVE IN FEAR
(same.)
SOMEDAYS I DONT

I DONT REMEMBER
WHY im HERE
E E E E E E
NO USE REMINDING ME
E B B B B B
WHAT TIME OF DAY IT IS
(same)
WHO RAN THE RACE
OR CAME IN FIRST
SOMEDAYS I CRY
I CRY FOR THOSE
WHO LIVE IN FEAR.

④

SOMEDAYS

SOMEDAY'S I LOOK,
I LOOK AT YOU WITH EYES THAT SHINE
SOMEDAY'S I DON'T,
I DON'T BELIEVE THAT YOU ARE MINE
IT'S NO GOOD ASKING ME WHAT TIME OF DAY IT IS.
WHO WON THE MATCH OR SCORED THE GOAL
SOMEDAY'S I LOOK,
SOMEDAY'S I LOOK INTO YOUR SOUL.

SOMETIMES I LAUGH,
I LAUGH TO THINK HOW YOUNG WE WERE
SOMETIMES IT'S HARD,
IT'S HARD TO KNOW WHICH WAY TO TURN
DON'T ASK ME WHERE I FOUND THAT PICTURE ON THE WALL
HOW MUCH IT COST OR WHAT IT'S WORTH
SOMETIMES I LAUGH
I LAUGH TO THINK HOW YOUNG WE WERE.

WE DON'T NEED ANYBODY ELSE
TO TELL US WHAT IS REAL
INSIDE EACH ONE OF US IS LOVE
AND WE KNOW HOW IT FEELS

SOMEDAY'S I CRY
I CRY FOR THOSE WHO LIVE IN FEAR,
SOMEDAY'S I DON'T,
I DON'T REMEMBER WHY I'M HERE
NO USE REMINDING ME WHAT TIME OF DAY IT IS,
WHO RAN THE RACE OR CAME IN FIRST,
SOMEDAY'S I CRY,
I CRY FOR THOSE WHO LIVE IN FEAR.

SOMEDAY'S I LOOK,
I LOOK AT YOU WITH EYES THAT SHINE

WE DON'T NEED ANYBODY ELSE
TO TELL US WHAT IS REAL
INSIDE EACH ONE OF US IS LOVE
AND WE KNOW HOW IT FEELS.

SOMEDAY'S I LOOK
I LOOK AT YOU WITH EYES THAT SHINE
SOMEDAY'S I DON'T
I DON'T BELIEVE THAT YOU ARE MINE
IT'S NO GOOD ASKING ME WHAT TIME OF DAY IT IS
WHO WON THE MATCH OR SCORED THE GOAL
SOMEDAY'S I LOOK
SOMEDAY'S I LOOK INTO YOUR SOUL.

SOMEDAY'S I LOOK,
I LOOK AT YOU WITH EYES THAT SHINE......

乔治·马丁为《有些时候》手写
的乐谱，1996 年。

Spirits of Ancient Egypt
古埃及的精神

作　者 WRITERS　　　保罗·麦卡特尼和琳达·麦卡特尼　Paul McCartney and Linda McCartney
艺术家 ARTIST　　　　羽翼乐队　Wings
录　音 RECORDED　　新奥尔良海圣录音棚　Sea-Saint Recording Studio, New Orleans
发　行 RELEASED　　《金星和火星》，1975 年　*Venus and Mars*, 1975

You're my baby
And I love you
You can take a pound of love
And cook it in the stew
When you've finished doing that
I know what you'll want to do
'Cause you're my baby
And I love you

I'm your baby
Do you love me?
I can drive a Cadillac
Across the Irish Sea
But when I've finished doing that
I know where I'll want to be
'Cause I'm your baby
And you love me

Spirits of ancient Egypt
Shadows of ancient Rome
Spirits of ancient Egypt
Hung on the telly
Hung on the telly
Hung on the telephone

You're my baby
I know you know
You could sell an elevator
To Geronimo
And when you're finished doing that
I know where you'll want to go
'Cause you're my baby
I know you know

Spirits of ancient Egypt
Echoes of sunken Spain
Spirits of ancient Egypt
Hung on the phone
A-hung on the phone
A-hung on the phone again

我们在利物浦时就认识乔治·梅利（George Melly）。乔治是个非常时髦的利物浦人，曾经在默西西比爵士乐队（Merseysippi Jazz Band）中担任歌手。他人很好，喜欢卖弄，稍微有点古怪。他收藏了很多比利时超现实主义者勒内·马格里特的画。在1970年代，我也非常沉迷于超现实主义，特别是马格里特。这在某种程度上解释了这些歌曲的古怪本质。

我总是觉得我在这首歌上做得还不够。《古埃及的精神》可以迷人且神秘，我却不知怎么地走到了相反的一面。"You're my baby / And I love you / You can take a pound of love / And cook it in the stew"（你是我的宝贝 / 我爱你 / 你可以用一磅的爱 / 做成炖菜）。也有非常抒情的时刻——"Spirits of ancient Egypt / Shadows of ancient Rome/…Echoes of sunken Spain"（古埃及的精神 / 古罗马的阴影 /……沉没的西班牙的回响）——所有伟大史诗的传奇，但是和那些时刻相比，你得到的只是一首情歌。这是平凡投向不平凡的一球。一方面，你有古埃及的精神，但突然间又有了凯迪拉克，以及某人用一磅爱来做菜，然后还有杰罗尼莫[1]。他在埃及做什么？或者在罗马？或者在西班牙？一辆凯迪拉克如何穿越爱尔兰海？这是一个超现实的画面。我一直相信，如果你把词语糅在一起，它们就会获得某种意义，你不需要想得太多，也许最好还是把它们扔出去，看看会发生什么。

我一直对埃及历史略知一二："噢，金字塔，那很不错。"但是，在成长过程中，我从来没对它产生过真正的兴趣。我们在纳什维尔附近租了一个农场，为期六周，用来工作，不过也用来骑马以及和家人一起度过乡村夏日时光。琳达和我与切特·阿特金斯夫妇交上了朋友，他们邀请我们在附近晚餐。非常不错。他拿着他的吉他，我拿着我的。我弹了几首我的歌。他让我弹《昨天》。（他启发了我去录制那首我爸爸写的歌，最后我们录制时，切特也在其中演奏了，不过那是另一个故事了。）

总之，晚餐后他突然对我说："你对埃及神话感兴趣吗？"这很突然，完全不合逻辑，

1　杰罗尼莫（Geronimo，1829—1909），印第安人阿帕切部落的首领。

左图：和琳达在一起。纳什维尔，1974 年。

右图：和切特·阿特金斯夫妇在一起。纳什维尔，1974 年。

但我不会轻易陷入慌张，所以我说："嗯，算是吧。"然后他就开始谈论这个。

　　接着，他给了我这本彼得·托普金斯（Peter Tompkins）写的书，《大金字塔的秘密》（*Secrets of the Great Pyramid*），非常引人入迷。其中有一些了不起的理论，包括埃及人比我们想象中知道得更多，以及金字塔底部周围的测量值以某种方式与地球的周长有关。他们是怎么知道地球的周长的？你不可能用卷尺来测量，但是他们算出来了。所以我津津有味地读了这本书，而我珍惜它更是因为，它是切特·阿特金斯的签名藏书。

～～

You're my baby, and I love you
You can take a pound of love
And cook it in the stew....

When you've finished doing that
I know what you'll want to do

Cos you're my baby and I love you

～～

~~Your~~ I'm your baby
   do you love me?
I can drive a cadillac
across the Irish sea
— but when I've finished doing tha
I know where I'll want to be
I'm your baby, do you love me

～～

15. SPIRITS OF ANCIENT EGYPT.

Spirits of ancient Egypt
Shadows of ancient Rome
Spirits of ancient Egypt
hung on the telly
hung on the telly
hung on the telephone .....

You're my baby
I know you know
You could sell an elevator
To Geronimo
And when you're finished doing that
I know where you'll want to go
'You're my baby
I know you know.
Spirits of Ancient Egypt
Echoes of sunken Spain
Spirits of ancient Egypt
Hung on the phone – a – hung on the
phone a – hung on the phone
....again .....

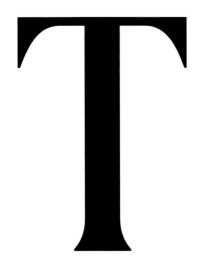

T

Teddy Boy

泰迪男孩

作　者　WRITER	保罗·麦卡特尼　Paul McCartney	
艺术家　ARTIST	保罗·麦卡特尼　Paul McCartney	
录　音　RECORDED	伦敦家中，及伦敦摩根录音棚　At home, London and Morgan Studios, London	
发　行　RELEASED	《麦卡特尼》，1970 年　*McCartney*, 1970	

This is the story of a boy named Ted
If his mother said
Ted, be good, he would

She told him tales about his soldier dad
But it made her sad
Then she'd cry, oh my

Ted used to tell her he'd be twice as good
And he knew he could
'Cause in his head, he said

Momma, don't worry now
Teddy Boy's here
Taking good care of you
Momma, don't worry your
Teddy Boy's here
Teddy's gonna see you through

Then came the day she found herself a man
Teddy turned and ran
Far away, okay

He couldn't stand to see his mother in love
With another man
He didn't know, oh no

He found a place where he could settle down
And from time to time
In his head, he said

Momma, don't worry now
Teddy Boy's here
Taking good care of you
Momma, don't worry your
Teddy Boy's here
Teddy's gonna see you through

She said, Teddy, don't worry now
Mummy is here
Taking good care of you
Teddy, don't worry your
Mummy is here
Mummy's gonna see you through

This is the story of a boy named Ted
If his mother said
Ted, be good, he would

TEL. MOUNTWOOD 3391

THE MIKE ROBBINS AGENCY
(ENTERTAINMENTS)

171 MOUNT ROAD,
HIGHER BEBINGTON,
WIRRAL, CHESHIRE.　　　　D. M. ROBBINS

我有一个亲戚，泰德，是我的表姐贝蒂·丹赫尔（Betty Danher）的儿子，贝蒂在音乐上对我有巨大的影响。她喜欢唱歌，并向我介绍了像《我有趣的情人节》（My Funny Valentine）和《直到有你》这样的歌曲，后来我和披头士一起演出过这些歌。她嫁给了一个名叫迈克·罗宾斯（Mike Robbins）的人，他们让孩子们在音乐的熏陶中长大。

泰德是他们的第一个孩子，这就是我称他为"泰迪男孩"的部分原因。这是一种充满感情的称呼，我只比他大十岁。不过在我年轻时，泰迪男孩是称呼那些小痞子的，那些穿着天鹅绒领长礼服外套、紧身裤和绒面厚底鞋的家伙。他们的鞋子被称作"甲壳虫碾压机"或者"妓院爬行者"。泰迪男孩们在英国很出名，他们在街角闲逛，等着惹点小麻烦。

所以，泰德是这首歌的起点，不过跟以往一样，它有自己的线索，并上演自己的戏码。关于"tales about his soldier dad"（他当兵的爸爸的故事）纯粹是想象。"Teddy boy's here / Teddy's gonna see you through"（泰迪男孩在这里 / 泰迪会帮助你）这句歌词是我想象泰迪尝试表示对妈妈的支持时，会对她说的话。

将这部心理戏剧与两个来源联系在一起并不过分。一个是我现在仍然能感觉到的我失去母亲时的糟糕感受。泰迪是我的一个分身，试图在安慰我母亲的同时，也在安慰我。另一个是《泰迪男孩》写于 1968 年我们所度过的那段古怪的创作时期。实际上，披头士在 1969 年早期为《顺其自然》的电影录制了几次这首歌。它们大多是原声版本，加上一点乔治·哈里森的电吉他，但是我们大家之间有一点分歧，直到 1970 年，我将它收入我的第一张个人专辑《麦卡特尼》，这首歌才正式发行。

泰德后来成了一名成功的艺人，就像他的爸爸一样。整个家庭都踏入了娱乐业。

(10) Momma Miss America. instrumental.

(11) Teddy Boy

This is the story of a boy named Ted
If his mother said, Ted be good, he would,
She told him tales about his soldier dad,
but it made her sad, and she'd cry, oh my!
Ted used to tell her he'd be twice as good,
and he knew he could, 'cos in his head,
he said
CHORUS ~~Teddy~~ Momma don't worry your Teddy Boy's
here,
Taking good care of you
momma don't worry now Teddy is here,
Teddy's gonna see you through.

Then came the day she found herself
a man, Teddy turned and ran, far
away — O.K.
He couldn't stand to see his mother in love
with another man, he didn't know
oh no!

696

(11) <u>Teddy Boy</u> continued.
He found a place where he could
settle down, and from time to time,
in his head, he said ......
<u>CHORUS</u> Momma don't worry ...

.... and she said.
Teddy don't worry, your mummy
is here, taking good care of you ....
Teddy don't worry now mummy is
here, mummy's gonna see you through.

— This is the story of a boy
named Ted, if his mother said,
Ted be good, he would ......
(12) Singalong Junk
instrumental.

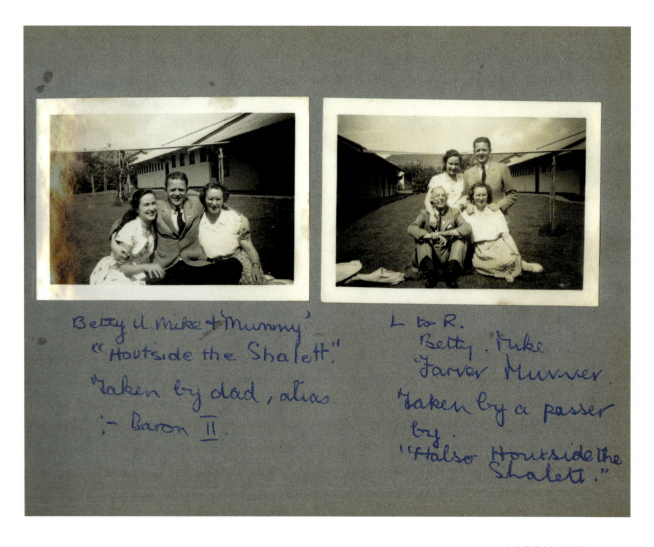

Betty u. Mike + Mummy,
" Houtside the Shalett."
Taken by dad, alias
:- Baron II.

L to R.
Betty. Mike
Farver Murmer
Taken by a passer
by.
" Halso Houtside the
Shalett."

来自保罗童年剪贴簿的照片。

不过在我年轻时，泰迪男孩是称呼那些小痞子的，
那些穿着天鹅绒领长礼服外套、紧身裤和绒面厚底鞋的家伙。

TEDDY BOY.

This is the story of a boy named Ted,
 if his mother said, "Ted, be good!" he would

B She told him tales about his soldier dad
 but it made her sad, and she'd cry, oh my!

—

Ted used to tell her he'd be twice as good
and he knew he could, 'cos in his head,
he said.

DT Mommy don't worry, your Teddy boy's here
Taking good care of you,
Mommy don't worry your Teddy boy's here
Teddy's going to see you through.

Then came the day she found herself a man
Teddy turned and ran far away, oh hey. **OK.**
He couldn't stand to see his mother in love
with another man he didn't know oh oh! **No**
He found a place where he could settle down
+ from time to time, in his head, he said..
Mommy don't worry, your Teddy Boy's here..
etc...

And she said — Teddy don't worry...etc..
& he said — Mommy don't worry. End.

699

Tell Me Who He Is

告诉我他是谁

未录制歌曲。歌词发现于一本笔记本上
表明这首歌写于 1950 年代末或 1960 年代初

Unrecorded song. The lyrics were found in a notebook suggesting
the song was written in the late 1950s or early 1960s.

Tell me who he is
Tell me that you're mine not his
He says he loves you more than I do
Tell me who he is

Tell him where to go
Tell him that I love you so
He couldn't love you more than I do
Tell me who he is

我几乎想不起来有这首歌。也许是在 1960 年代初。也许是从我带着一份歌词动机去找约翰开始的。好像只有一组特定的主题。爱情是其中之一，欲望、分手、报复。那涵盖了很多领域！所以我安于接受这样的想法，一个不忠的女孩，或者假设她不忠。这是非常肥沃的土壤。

下一步你知道，你要进入一个小故事。我总是喜欢这么做。我记得乔治·哈里森问过我："你是怎么做的？"他只会写（或者至少他说他只会写）自己的个人经验——他身上发生了什么，他感觉糟透了，但随后事情开始变好，然后他会写《太阳出来了》（Here Comes the Sun）或者《某些事情》（Something）。

对我来说，一切都和虚构有关。并不是说我不写自传体的歌，而是说以狄更斯的方式来创作也很棒。狄更斯会从一个女孩的角度来写，一个贫穷的女孩。他也许会回忆起他的童年，回忆起他在监狱里的爸爸，回忆起他看见的人们。每件事都有自传的成分，但仅仅是自传并不总是那么精彩。你在做那些，但你只是把"历史"的角色拉进你的歌曲里，并和他们一起表演——给他们一顶可笑的帽子，一顶红色的帽子。红色的？我能找到更好的词吗？

我们刚搬到伦敦时，生活方式中最棒的一点是我们的录音时间。你一般在十点进棚集合；你在十点半开始，工作三个小时；下午一点半时，你有一个小时的休息时间；然后你从两点半工作到五点半，就是那样。在这两个三小时时间段，我们预期要录两首歌。但是这种安排最好的方面是，你一天的工作到五点半就结束了。

那意味着你晚上可以去剧院。你可以去皇家宫廷剧团，可以去老维克的国家剧院，可以去伦敦西区。很多很棒的东西。所以，举个例子，录音结束后，我会和科林·布莱克利（Colin Blakely）一起去看《朱诺和孔雀》，他是一个很棒的演员。那会儿会有那种每周节目清单，譬如《暂停周刊》（Time Out）那样的杂志，你会翻找一番，挑选你想去看的所有东西。你不仅有时间去剧院，你去看的那些东西也会对你的作品产生影响。如果刚刚去国家剧院看了他们制作的《朱诺和孔雀》，第二天当我写歌或者录歌时，那就在我的脑海里。我会想努力达到那种标准。

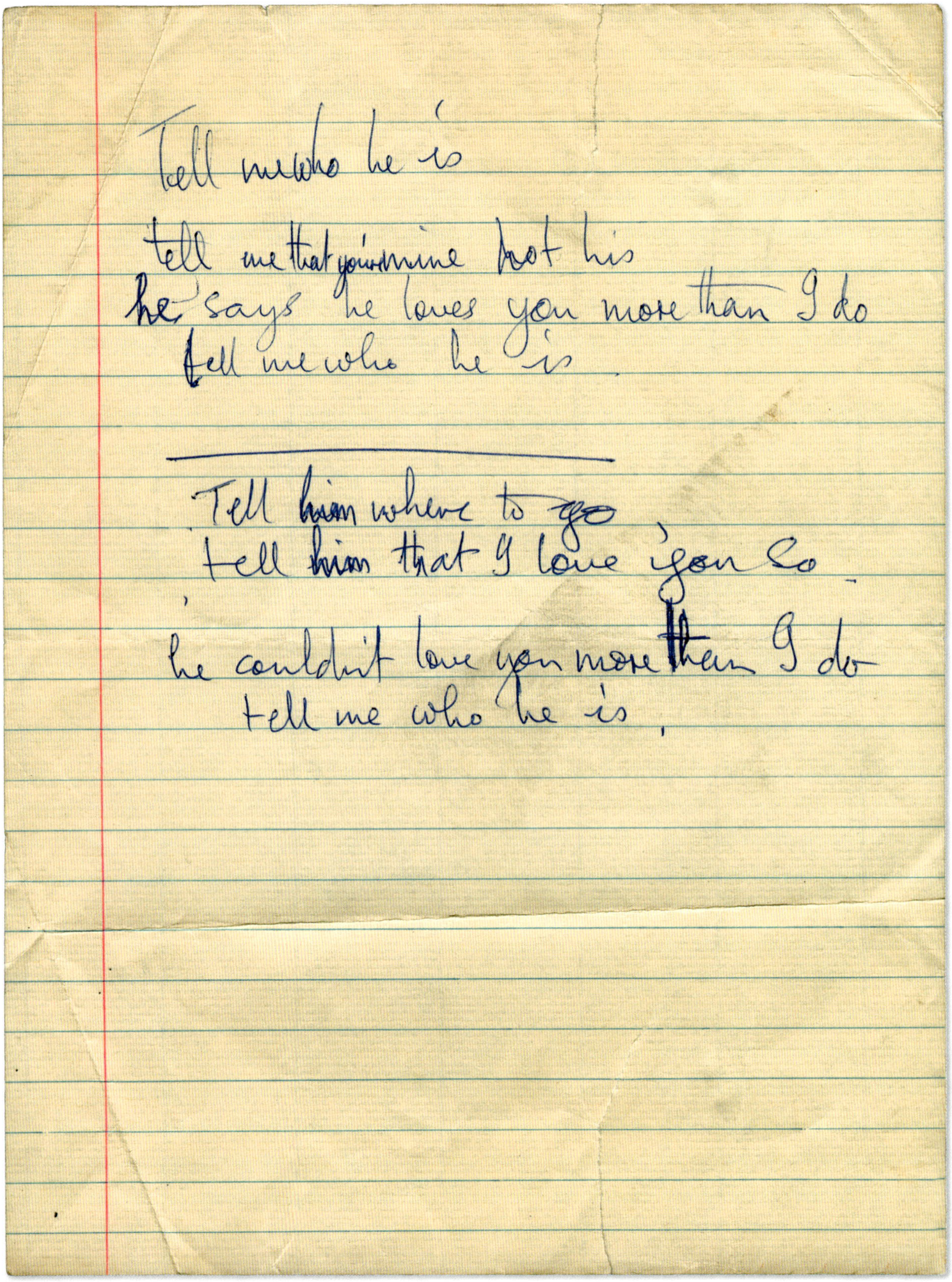

Tell me who he is

tell me that you're mine not his
he says he loves you more than I do
tell me who he is

Tell him where to go
tell him that I love you so

he couldn't love you more than I do
tell me who he is,

披头士乐队早期的明信片，和约翰·列侬、乔治·哈里森、斯图尔特·萨克利夫，以及皮特·贝斯特在一起。汉堡英德拉俱乐部，1960 年。

Temporary Secretary

临时秘书

作　者　WRITER　　保罗·麦卡特尼　Paul McCartney

艺术家　ARTIST　　保罗·麦卡特尼　Paul McCartney

录　音　RECORDED　萨塞克斯郡低闸农场　Lower Gate Farm, Sussex

发　行　RELEASED　《麦卡特尼 II》，1980 年　*McCartney II*, 1980

　　　　　　　　　单曲，1980 年　Single, 1980

Mister Marks, can you find for me
Someone strong and sweet fitting on my knee
She can keep her job if she gets it wrong
Ah but Mister Marks, I won't need her long

All I need is help for a little while
We can take dictation and learn to smile
And a temporary secretary
Is what I need for to do the job

I need a
Temporary secretary
Temporary secrétaire
Temporary secretary
Temporary secretary

Mister Marks could you send her quick
'Cause my regular has been getting sick

I need a
Temporary secretary
Temporary secretary

Mister Marks, I can pay her well
If she comes along and can stay a spell
I will promise now that I'll treat her right
And will rarely keep her til late at night

I need a

She can be a belly dancer
I don't need a true romancer
She can be a diplomat
But I don't need a girl like that
She can be a neurosurgeon
If she's doin' nothin' urgent
What I need's a temporary
Temporary secretary

I need a
I need a
Temporary secretary
Temporary secrétaire
Temporary secretary
Temporary secretary
Temporary secretary
Temporary secrétaire

Now Mister Marks, when I send her back
Will you please make sure she stays on the right track

Well, I know how hard it is for young girls these days
In the face of everything to stay on the right track

Temporary secretary
　(I need a)
Temporary secrétaire
Temporary secretary
Temporary secrétaire
　(I need a)
Temporary secretary
Temporary secretary
Temporary secretary

魔音琴（Mellotron）是披头士在 1960 年代中期录《永远的草莓田》时使用的一种磁带采样回放键盘。我记得在阿比路，有人向我们介绍了这种巨大的、灰色的魔音琴，尽管它是全新的，却像是来自战争期间的东西。百代公司是一个非常好的机构，非常聪明。他们为自己的艺人制作磁带，直到今天那仍然是最好的磁带，它不会掉磁粉。他们的运营很高效。

简言之，他们把这台魔音琴搬到二号录音棚的中间供我们使用，而我们的表现是，"哦嗬。"我们都在试用它。"哇，太奇妙了！"那很有趣，看看我们是否能在歌曲里用到它。我们总是在寻找新的声音和元素。

然后穆格合成器出现了，它有这个房间那么大。罗伯特·穆格到百代公司来亲自演示它，大约是在 1968 或是 1969 年。一位非常和善的炼金术发明家带着几百万个旋钮和设备站在房间中央。他向我们演示了如何演奏，而我最后在《麦克斯韦的银锤》里用上了它。我们喜欢它的那种未来主义的声音，现在仍是。几年前我为 Skype 做了一个项目，创造世界上的第一个音频表情符号——他们称之为"爱表情"，因为他们是为情人节推出的。我创作了一些非常短的音乐片段，大约有五六秒长，来展现不同的情绪。这是一次很有意思的挑战，有一些我从未做过的事情。然后 Skype 加上了一些动画，人们在视频聊天时互相转发。我希望它们有一些未来主义的声音，而穆格是起点。

那个时候，我总是用任何东西来做实验，看看我们是否可以用任何一件新的乐器来做点什么。所以，大约在 1960 年代后期，这些合成器出现时，我们就乱搞一气，看看每一个不同的控制按钮会引向什么，去创造你在别的地方得不到的声音。然后，终

上图：《麦卡特尼 II》录音期间。萨塞克斯郡低闸农场，1979 年。

于，音序器带来了电子音乐变革，开始了一种全新的音乐风格。这些音序器非常吸引人，因为它们允许你去创造一个永无止境的音符序列。所以我会一直摆弄它们，直到我找到一些感兴趣的东西，然后在它的基础上构建一首歌曲。

多年之后，1970 年代末的时候，我在萨塞克斯郡的农场里建了一个小房间，里面放上我会演奏的乐器和一些东西，而我发现了这个音序器，我想："这个东西不错。"那成为一个基础，一个声音的温床，然后它启发了我写这首歌。

如今，不是有很多人知道或记得阿尔弗雷德·马克斯（Alfred Marks）是谁，但在过去，伦敦附近有一个服务机构叫作阿尔弗雷德·马克斯办事处——当然，不要和过去的喜剧演员阿尔弗雷德·马克斯弄混了。这个办事处会在报纸和各种目录上刊登广告。而我想："好吧，我会用上马克斯先生这个名字。"

人们经常说："哦，你们工作很努力"。而我说："我们不工作，我们玩耍。"当事情变得令人厌烦时，我会尽量铭记这个想法。"天啊，我们工作太努力了；不，我们玩得太努力了。"需要一位秘书这主意，虽然只是一位临时秘书，会让我忍不住发笑。所以我把它用到了歌中。

几年前，我们再次开始表演这首歌，因为布莱顿的一位 DJ 挖掘了它。那个 DJ 弄得很好，我想知道我是否也能做到。我和我们的键盘手维克斯·维金斯（Wix Wickens）进行了尝试，他为这首歌做了编程，以便在巡演中现场演奏。

在今天 MeToo 运动的环境下，还能否写这样的一首歌？我很怀疑，我也不想写。但这是一个不同的时代，自那时起，世界取得了进步。今天，在你要求秘书或助手干到半夜之前，你要三思。不过，好的方面是，这首歌没有明显的性暗示，只是口头玩笑。任何关于主人公让秘书在深夜做其他事情的推断，都只会出现在听众的脑海中。

在今天 MeToo 运动的环境下，还能否写这样的一首歌？
我很怀疑，我也想写。
但这是一个不同的时代，自那时起，世界取得了进步。

ARTIST			TAPE BOX No. (2)	
TITLE (7) TEMPORARY SECRETARY.			JOB No.	
1	SEQUENCER.			
2	B/D			
3	SNARE . DRY.			
4	ECHO SNARE (O/D)			
5	SYNTH (Secretary Bits.,)			
6	BASS.			
7	BASS SYNTH (Secretary Bits)			
8	VOICE (Harmony CHORUS.)			
9	VOICE (Chorus)			
10	VOICE (Lead Chorus.)			
11	ACOUSTIC Gtr.			
12	OVATION Elec. ..			
13	TOMS			
14	VOICE Lead			
15	VOICE Lead D/T.			
16	BANJO .			
17				
18				
19				
20				
21				
22				
23				
24				
REMARKS				

Ref. No. 12527

707

ARE YOU BRIGHT, HARDWORKING, INTELLIGENT AND AMBITIOUS, WITH A KEEN INTEREST IN CONTEMPORARY MUSIC, A FRIENDLY PERSONALITY AND A SMART APPEARANCE?

Then what are you doing reading this?

If you are bright then you'll probably have realised that this is an advertisement for Paul McCartney's new single 'Temporary Secretary'.

Only available as a limited edition 12" record, the B–Side is the 10½ minute, previously unavailable "Secret Friend".

No previous experience necessary.

Apply in person at your local record store.

人们经常说："哦，你们工作很努力。"
而我说："我们不工作，我们玩耍。"
当事情变得令人厌烦时，我会尽量铭记这个想法。
"天啊，我们工作太努力了；不，我们玩得太努力了。"

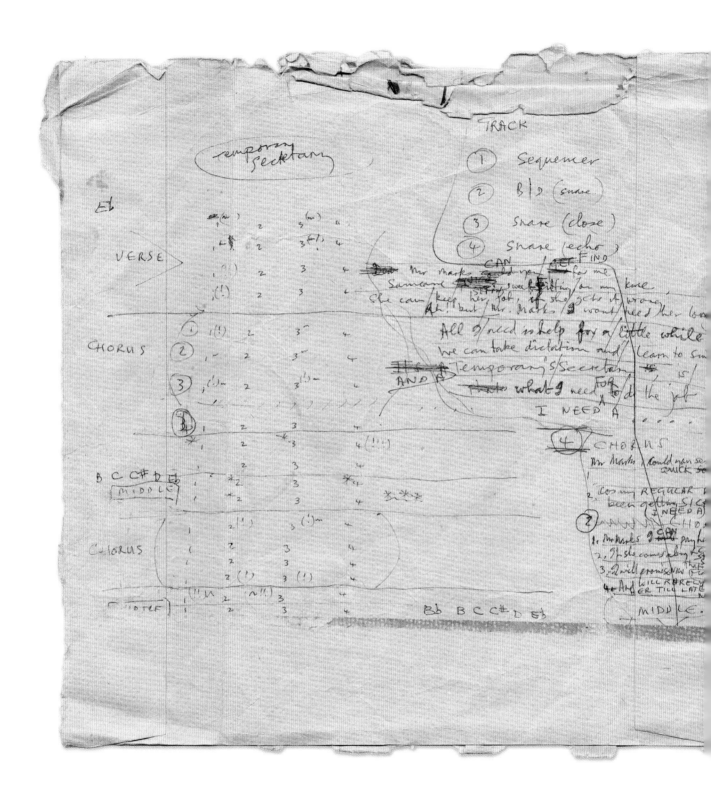

710

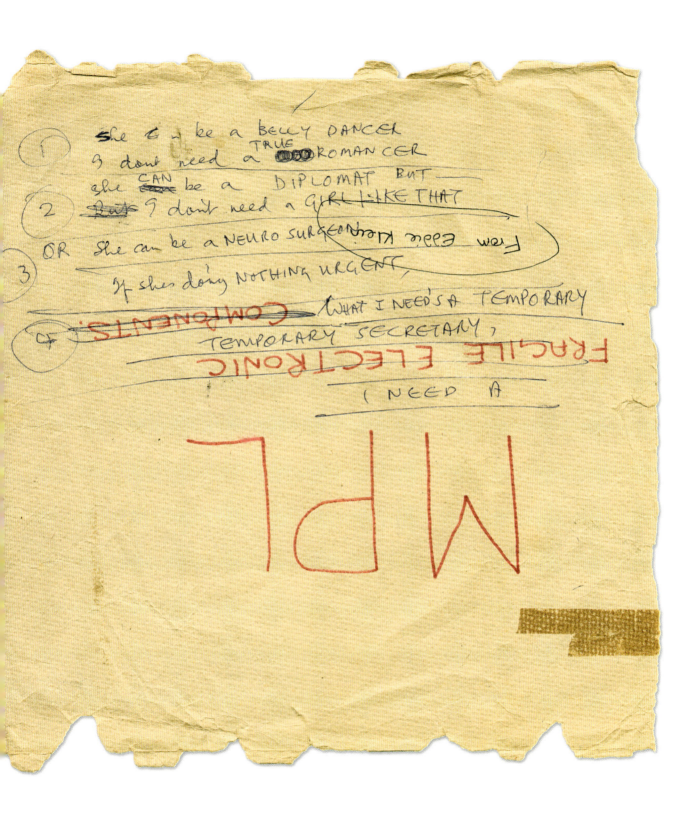

《临时秘书》的歌词和录音笔记。

Things We Said Today
我们今天说的话

作 者	WRITERS	保罗·麦卡特尼和约翰·列侬　Paul McCartney and John Lennon
艺术家	ARTIST	披头士乐队　The Beatles
录 音	RECORDED	伦敦阿比路录音棚　Abbey Road Studios, London
发 行	RELEASED	《辛劳一日的夜》英国 B 面单曲，1964 年　B-side of 'A Hard Day's Night' UK single, 1964
		《辛劳一日的夜》，1964 年　*A Hard Day's Night*, 1964

You say you will love me
If I have to go
You'll be thinking of me
Somehow I will know

Someday when I'm lonely
Wishing you weren't so far away
Then I will remember
Things we said today

You say you'll be mine, girl
Til the end of time
These days, such a kind girl
Seems so hard to find

Someday when we're dreaming
Deep in love, not a lot to say
Then we will remember
Things we said today

Me, I'm just the lucky kind
Love to hear you say that love is love
And though we may be blind
Love is here to stay and that's enough

To make you mine, girl
Be the only one
Love me all the time, girl
We'll go on and on

Someday when we're dreaming
Deep in love, not a lot to say
Then we will remember
Things we said today

Me, I'm just the lucky kind
Love to hear you say that love is love
And though we may be blind
Love is here to stay and that's enough

To make you mine, girl
Be the only one
Love me all the time, girl
We'll go on and on

Someday when we're dreaming
Deep in love, not a lot to say
Then we will remember
Things we said today

《我们今天说的话》是在维京群岛度假时，在一艘游艇上写的，当时我和简·阿舍，以及林戈和他当时的妻子莫琳一起。我们是披头士，所以负担得起游艇度假！一切都很好，除了我被严重晒伤。有一种东西是像我们这样的工人阶级所不知道的，那就是防晒霜。我的阿姨过去常用醋和油。

无论这艘游艇多么让人愉快，我仍然喜欢回到我的小屋里。某个没人可以打扰我的地方。我可以把世界挡在外面，我会坐着随便弹一会儿琴，看看会出来什么东西。

那个时候，我有了一把非常好的 Epiphone 吉他。当我们还是孩子时，我们会幻想我们的偶像用的吉他：吉普森、格雷奇、芬达。但是这些乐器都很贵，我们不得不降低期望。我的期望降得更多；当我大概十八岁时，我买了这把糟糕的小东西，一把罗塞蒂牌实心 7 型吉他——基本上就是一块木板加上一根琴颈，根本不是一件好乐器。不过它是红色的，看起来很闪亮。我是从利物浦的弗兰克·海希乐器店里买的。

我是分期付款买的，尽管我爸爸非常反对分期付款的计划，也许是因为他遭受过损失，或者他知道很多人遭受过损失。1960 年，我带着这把罗塞蒂实心 7 型吉他去了汉堡，这把琴一两个月后就摔碎了。那就是为什么我开始弹钢琴，那就是为什么我比乐队里的其他人演奏钢琴更多一些。但是后来，当我们有了一点钱时，我给自己买了一把 Epiphone 木吉他，所以，到了 1964 年，我有了一把漂亮的好吉他。

在游艇上的特别日子里，我从一个 A 小和弦开始。A 小和弦到 E 小和弦再到 A 小和弦，这让我有一种类似民谣音乐的感觉，异想天开的世界。然后在中间，"Me, I'm just the lucky kind"（我，我只是那种幸运的人）这段，进行到大和弦，并且带来了希望感。关于写歌，我一直热爱并且仍然热爱的是，在两三个小时之后，我可以有一个向所有人展示的新生儿。我想向全世界展示它，而全世界在那个时刻是几个在游艇上的人。

当然，我不得不记住它，因为我没有把它写下来。我没有把音乐写下来——因为我不会。所以一切都在我的头脑里。我一直好奇，为什么对我来说很容易就能记住这些东西。当我用上小磁带录音机或者一些录音设备的时候，我发现记住这些歌曲很难，因为我不会强迫自己去记住它们。回望过去，我还是喜欢当时那样的条件。几年后，当我试图解释为什么我不会读谱或写谱时，将之归结于我的凯尔特传统，游吟诗人的传统。我的父辈训练自己依赖记忆。

YACHT HAPPY DAYS
Yacht Haven
St. Thomas, U. S. Virgin Islands

Dear Dad and Mike,

I've been meaning to write but you know how it is.

Well, as you will have noticed the press got us, but apart from that one incident we've been left alone.

We are, of course, having a great time the boat is nice, and weather etc... is luvverly.

We've been doing quite a bit of snorkelling and I've seen one ~~or~~ or two barracudas (they're the ones that sometimes get you — mind you, the ones I saw were about 1½ feet long.

P.T.O.

右图：保罗的罗塞蒂牌实心 7 型吉他付款收据。利物浦弗兰克·海希乐器店，1960 年。

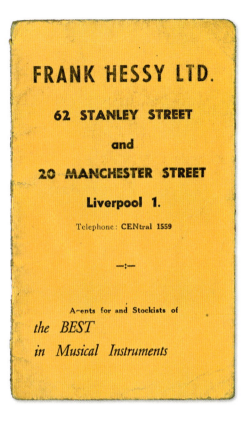

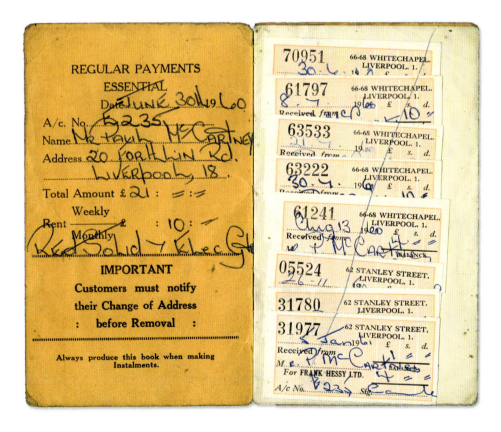

Ticket to Ride

离开的车票

作 者 WRITERS 保罗·麦卡特尼和约翰·列侬 Paul McCartney and John Lennon

艺术家 ARTIST 披头士乐队 The Beatles

录 音 RECORDED 伦敦阿比路录音棚 Abbey Road Studios, London

发 行 RELEASED 单曲，1965 年 Single, 1965

《救命！》，1965 年 Help!, 1965

I think I'm gonna be sad
I think it's today, yeah
The girl that's driving me mad
Is going away

She's got a ticket to ride
She's got a ticket to ride
She's got a ticket to ride
And she don't care

She said that living with me
Is bringing her down, yeah
For she would never be free
When I was around

She's got a ticket to ride
She's got a ticket to ride
She's got a ticket to ride
But she don't care

I don't know why she's ridin' so high
She oughta think twice
She oughta do right by me
Before she gets to sayin' goodbye
She oughta think twice
She oughta do right by me

I think I'm gonna be sad
I think it's today, yeah
The girl that's driving me mad
Is going away, yeah

She's got a ticket to ride
She's got a ticket to ride
She's got a ticket to ride
But she don't care

I don't know why she's ridin' so high
She oughta think twice
She oughta do right by me
Before she gets to sayin' goodbye
She oughta think twice
She oughta do right by me

She said that living with me
Is bringing her down, yeah
For she would never be free
When I was around

She's got a ticket to ride
She's got a ticket to ride
She's got a ticket to ride
But she don't care
My baby don't care
My baby don't care

　　约翰和我曾经搭便车旅行，乔治和我也一起做过几次。这是度假的一种方式。也许我们的父母会预定度假，但是我们不知道该怎么度假。所以我们想出去，就我们两人，带着吉他。约翰年长一点，但我是决定我们要去什么地方的那个人。他带着从他叔叔那里拿的一百英镑，他叔叔是爱丁堡的一位牙医，这些钱是给他的二十一岁生日礼物，我们决定搭便车取道巴黎去往西班牙。我们特意从桥的另一边出发，因为那里是所有长途货车出发的地方。我们会戴上小圆顶礼帽来引起司机们的注意！

　　搭上免费的车后，我们就坐在一起；我们会一起体验当货车司机的感觉。我们了解了在跨海渡轮上是什么感觉，了解了试着在巴黎闲逛时是什么样的。我们会在城市里走上好几英里，坐在盎格鲁街附近的酒吧里，参观蒙马特，看《风流牧羊女娱乐场》[1]。我们感觉自己就像是得到充分报酬的存在主义者，能够从我们一周之内学到的东西里写出一部小说，所以我们再也没去西班牙。我们在一起待了那么久，以至于如果你提出一个问题，我们两个会给出同一个答案。

上图，在巴黎，1961 年。　　　　1　《风流牧羊女娱乐场》（*Folies Bergère*），法国电影，上映于 1956 年。

这么说有点粗鲁，但可以说，整体上我的生活比较优越，而约翰并不是。和我相比，他的生活更艰难，他不得不建造一个更硬的外壳。他是一个非常愤世嫉俗的家伙，不过，就像他们所说的，他有一颗金子般的心。他内心非常柔软，但他的保护层很坚硬。所以那对我们双方都是好事，就好像"异性相吸"。我能让他安静下来，而他会点燃我。我们可以看到彼此需要完善的部分。

开始创作摇滚乐的时候，我们也在同一个层面。你不会想着去写，"她说和我一起的生活很烦（upsetting）。"这就不是摇滚乐，这太过普通平常了。因此，你得写"She said that living with me is *bringing her down*"（她说和我一起的生活让她沮丧）。

约翰和我一直喜欢文字游戏。所以，这句"She's got a ticket to ride"（她有一张离开的车票）当然指的是乘汽车或者火车，但是——如果你真的想知道——它也指怀特岛莱德镇，我的表姐贝蒂和她丈夫迈克在那里经营一家酒吧。那就是他们的工作，经营酒吧。他最后成了巴特林一家度假酒店的娱乐经理。贝蒂和迈克都是娱乐行业的人，拜访他们充满了乐趣，所以约翰和我搭车去了莱德。而当我们写这首歌时，夹杂着这次旅行的回忆。现在回想起来非常温馨，约翰和我挤在一张小单人床上，头对着脚，而贝蒂和迈克进来给我们盖好被子。

上图：约翰·列侬。巴黎卢浮宫，1961 年。

右图：巴黎日记和披头士的乐队标志草图，1961 年。

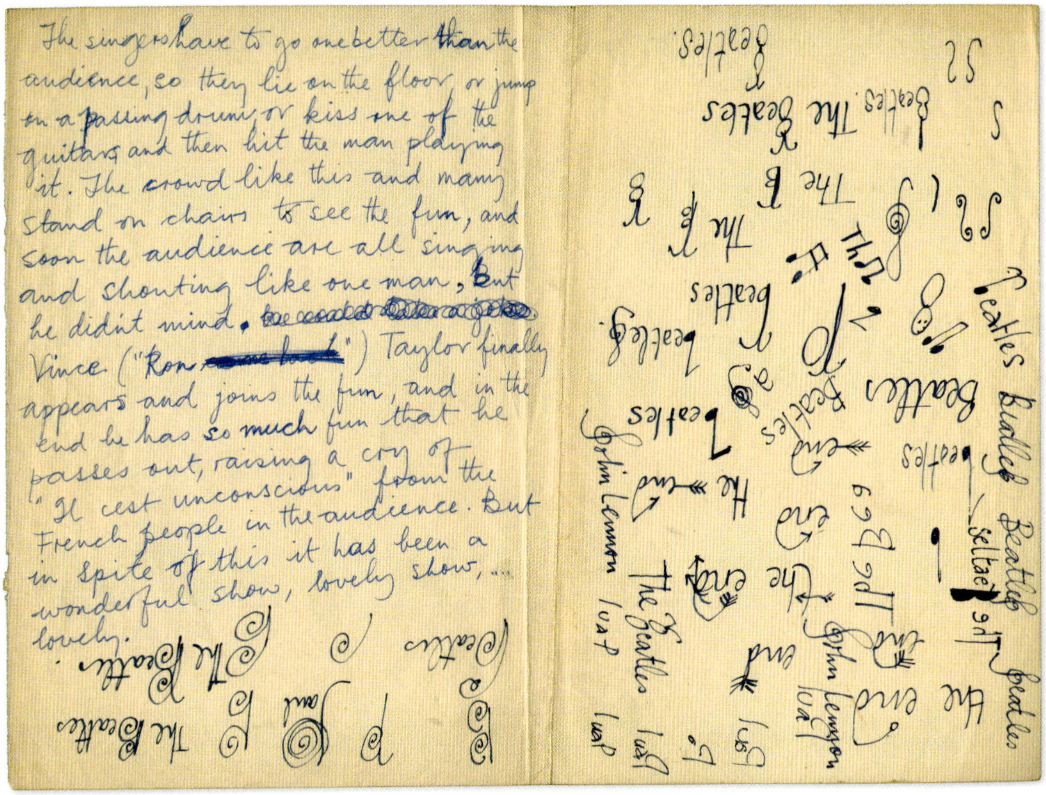

25

The singers have to go one better than the audience, so they lie on the floor, or jump on a passing drum, or kiss one of the guitars and then hit the man playing it. The crowd like this and many stand on chairs to see the fun, and soon the audience are all singing and shouting like one man, But he didn't mind. Vince ("Ron ~~come back~~") Taylor finally appears and joins the fun, and in the end he has so much fun that he passes out, raising a cry of "Il cest unconscious" from the French people in the audience. But in spite of this it has been a wonderful show, lovely show, ... lovely.

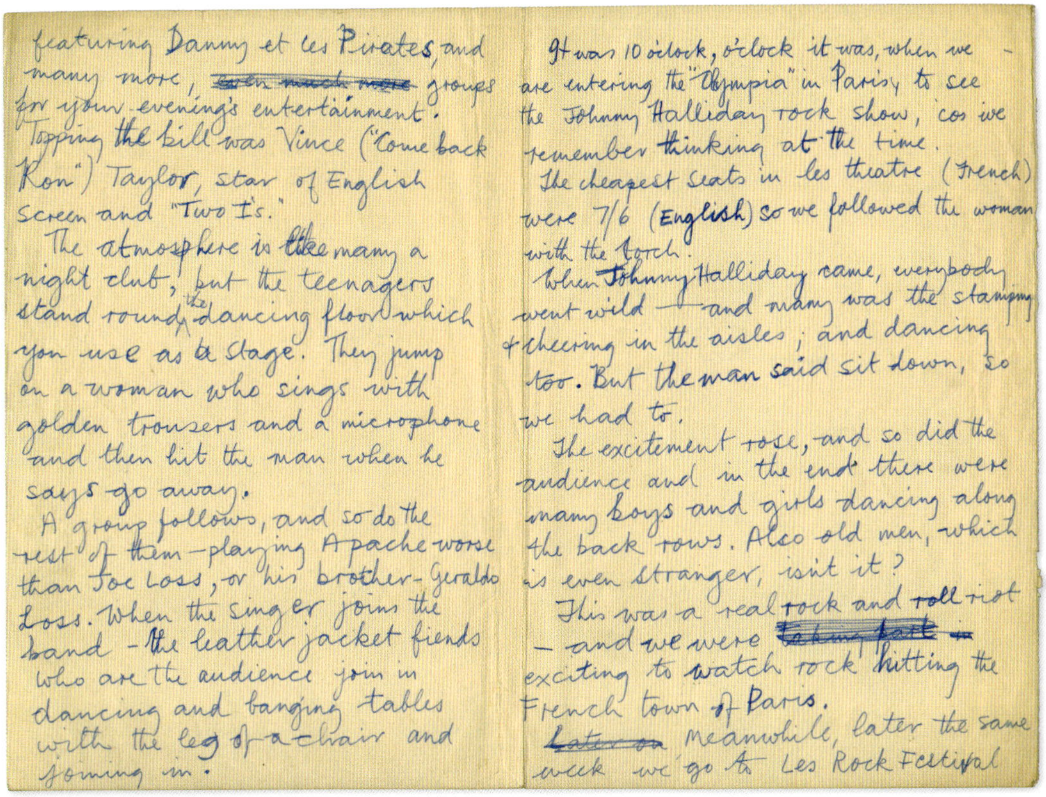

featuring Danny et les Pirates, and many more, ~~even much more~~ groups for your evening's entertainment. Topping the bill was Vince ("Come back Ron") Taylor, star of English screen and "Two I's."

The atmosphere is like many a night club, but the teenagers stand round the dancing floor which you use as a stage. They jump on a woman who sings with golden trousers and a microphone and then hit the man when he says go away.

A group follows, and so do the rest of them—playing Apache worse than Joe Loss, or his brother-Geraldo Loss. When the singer joins the band — the leather jacket fiends who are the audience join in dancing and banging tables with the leg of a chair and joining in.

It was 10 o'clock, o'clock it was, when we are entering the "Olympia" in Paris, to see the Johnny Halliday rock show, 'cos we remember thinking at the time.

The cheapest seats in les theatre (French) were 7/6 (English) so we followed the woman with the torch.

When Johnny Halliday came, everybody went wild — and many was the stamping & cheering in the aisles; and dancing too. But the man said sit down, so we had to.

The excitement rose, and so did the audience and in the end there were many boys and girls dancing along the back rows. Also old men, which is even stranger, isn't it?

This was a real rock and roll riot — and we were ~~taking part~~ exciting to watch rock hitting the French town of Paris.

~~Later on~~ Meanwhile, later the same week we go to Les Rock Festival

Too Many People
太多的人

作 者 WRITER	保罗 · 麦卡特尼　Paul McCartney
艺术家 ARTIST	保罗和琳达 · 麦卡特尼　Paul and Linda McCartney
录 音 RECORDED	纽约 CBS 录音棚　CBS Studios, New York
发 行 RELEASED	《拉姆》，1971 年　*RAM*, 1971
	《阿尔伯特叔叔》/《海军上将哈尔西》B 面单曲，1971 年　B-side of 'Uncle Albert/Admiral Halsey' single, 1971

Too many people going underground
Too many reaching for a piece of cake
Too many people pulled and pushed around
Too many waiting for that lucky break

That was your first mistake
You took your lucky break and broke it in two
Now what can be done for you
You broke it in two

Too many people sharing party lines
Too many people never sleep in late
Too many people paying parking fines
Too many hungry people losing weight

That was your first mistake
You took your lucky break and broke it in two
Now what can be done for you
You broke it in two

Too many people preaching practices
Don't let them tell you what you want to be
Too many people holding back
This is crazy and baby, it's not like me

That was your last mistake
I find my love awake and waiting to be
Now what can be done for you
She's waiting for me

这首歌大约是在披头士解散一年后创作的，当时约翰在用他的歌攻击我，其中的一两首相当冷酷。除了在我脸上来上一拳，我不知道他还希望得到什么。整个事情让我很生气。

我决定也将矛头指向他，但我真的写不出太多恶语，所以我的反击相当含蓄。这相当于 1970 年代的"挑衅歌曲"（diss track）。像这种指责某人行为的歌曲现在很常见，但在那时候，那完全是一种新的"风格"。太多的人"preaching practices"（宣扬实践）这个想法，直指约翰告诉所有人他们应该做什么这种行为——比如说，他告诉我应该和艾伦·克莱因一起去做生意。我已经受够了别人告诉我该做什么，所以我写了这首歌。"You took your lucky break and broke it in two"（你遇到了好运却将它打破）的意思是："你成功了，祝你好运。"不过这非常温和，我真的没有说出任何野蛮的话，这实际上是一首相当乐观的歌；它听上去真的不尖刻。如果你不知道那段历史，我不知道你能否猜到这首歌歌词背后的愤怒。

这一切都有点古怪，也有点令人厌恶，我想说的基本上是："让我们保持理性。披头士还有很多美好之处，将我们割裂的实际上是商业上的东西，那真的有点可悲，所以让我们试着平静下来，让我们给和平一次机会。"

第一段主歌和副歌充满了我能集合起来的所有愤怒，第二句歌词"Too many reaching for a piece of cake"（太多的人想分一块蛋糕），我记得我把它唱成了"滚蛋蛋糕"（Piss off cake），你仔细听还能听出来。又一次，我想到了约翰，但是我的心已经不在其中。我说的是："太多的人认同党派政策。太多的人争抢一块蛋糕、一块饼。"至于"sleep in late"（晚睡），这个说法是否准确，约翰和洋子睡得晚不晚，我不知道（尽管当我开车去韦布里奇去和他一起写歌时，约翰经常起得很晚）。这些通通指涉那些觉得他们的真理是唯一的真理的人，这当然是约翰所说的。

问题在于，许多他们认为是真理的事情都是废话。战争结束了？好吧，并没有。但是我了解你要说的：如果你希望，战争就会结束。所以，如果足够多的人希望战争结束，它就会结束。我不确定那是不是真的，不过这是个了不起的观点，一个很好的想法或说法。我已经接受了洋子待在录音棚里，裹着毯子坐在我的音箱前，我尽了很大的努力才接受这一点。但是当我们解散的时候，每个人都在互相扭打，约翰变得让人厌恶。我真的不知道为什么。也许因为我们成长于利物浦，在那里，人们认同"先下手为强"。

简而言之，我们在 1969 年开了一个会，而约翰出现时说他见了这个叫艾伦·克莱因的家伙，艾伦向洋子承诺给她在锡拉丘兹做一个展览，然后，约翰告诉我们他要离开乐队。基本上事情就是这么发生的。那是三对一，因为其他两个人也跟着约翰，所以看起来好像艾伦·克莱因将拥有整个披头士帝国。我不太赞同这个想法。

实际上，约翰把艾伦·克莱因和洋子都带到录音间里，在写歌时让他们提一些歌词上的建议。在他的歌曲《你如何入睡？》中，"The only thing you done was yesterday"[1]

1　"你所做的事情只是昨天"，出自《你如何入睡？》（How Do You Sleep?）。

这句歌词据说就来自艾伦·克莱因的建议，而约翰说："嗨，不错。放进去吧。"我仿佛能看见他们这么做的时候放声大笑，而我必须努力让自己别把这太当回事儿，但是在我的内心深处，我在想："等一下，我做过的只是'昨天'？我想这是一个有趣的双关语，但是我做过的一切包括《昨天》《顺其自然》《漫长而曲折的路》《埃莉诺·里格比》《麦当娜夫人》……去你的，约翰。"

我必须为作为披头士一部分的自己而战，事实上，也为了作为披头士一部分的他们而战，多年以后他们才意识到这一点，还几乎为此感谢我。今天的人们明白这一点，但是那时候，其他人感觉他们是受害者，被我的行为伤害了。艾伦·克莱因已经和滚石乐队开创了历史。我只是觉得："哎哟，不，这个家伙名声不好。"而老好人约翰说："哦，如果他真的像人们说得那么坏，他就不可能是个完全的坏人。"约翰有这种扭曲的想法，有时候还挺有趣。但当有人要夺走约翰、乔治、林戈和我努力工作才得来的一切时，那就说不上有趣了。

所以，我作为一个理智的人站起来说："这不对。"克莱因想要百分之二十，而我说："告诉他，如果你一定要跟他一起的话，他可以得到百分之十。""噢，不，不，不，"他们反馈说，"不，他想要百分之二十。"在我看来，他们完全昏了头，压根不打算做任何理智的事情。1970 年代初发生了很多互相伤害的事情——他们感觉受到了伤害，我也感觉受到了伤害——但约翰还是约翰，他是那个创作伤人歌曲的人。这是他的灵感包。

我必须为作为披头士一部分的自己而战，
事实上，也为了作为披头士一部分的他们而战，
多年以后他们才意识到这一点，还几乎为此感谢我。
今天的人们明白这一点，
但是那时候，其他人感觉他们是受害者，被我的行为伤害了。

TOO MANY PEOPLE

Too many people going underground

Too many reaching for a piece of cake

...ed and

Too many people pulling pushed around

Too many waiting for that lucky break

That was your first mistake

You took your lucky break and broke it in two

Now what can be done for you

You broke it in two

That was your first mistake

You took your lucky break and broke it in two

Now what can be done for you

You broke it in two

Too may people sharing party lines

in

Too many people never sleeping late   sleep in

Too many people paying parking fines

Too many hungry people losing weight

Too many people preaching practices

Don't let them tell you what you want to be

Too many people holding back -this is crazy

And, baby, it's not like me.

That was your last mistake

I find my love awake and waiting to be

Now what can be done for you

She's waiting for me.

6137
12

724

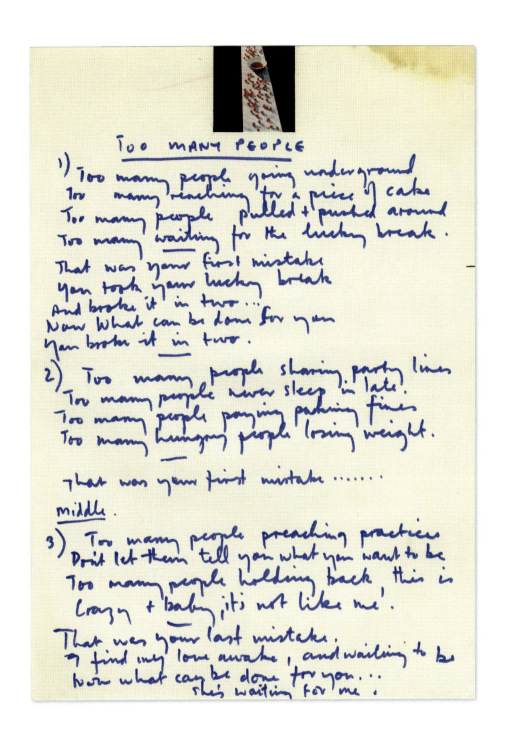

TOO MANY PEOPLE

1) Too many people going underground
Too many reaching for a piece of cake
Too many people pulled + pushed around
Too many waiting for the lucky break.
That was your first mistake
You took your lucky break
And broke it in two...
Now What can be done for you
You broke it in two.

2) Too many people sharing party lines
Too many people never sleep in late.
Too many people paying parking fines
Too many hungry people losing weight.

That was your first mistake.......

middle.

3) Too many people preaching practices
Don't let them tell you what you want to be
Too many people holding back, this is
crazy + baby, it's not like me'.
That was your last mistake.
To find my love awake, and waiting to be
born what can be done for you...
she's waiting for me.

我决定也将矛头指向他，但我真的写不出太多恶语，
所以我的反击相当含蓄。
这相当于 1970 年代的"挑衅歌曲"。

Too Much Rain

太多的雨

作　者　WRITER　　保罗·麦卡特尼　Paul McCartney
艺术家　ARTIST　　保罗·麦卡特尼　Paul McCartney
录　音　RECORDED　伦敦 AIR 录音棚　AIR Studios, London
发　行　RELEASED　《在后院的混乱和创造》，2005 年　*Chaos and Creation in the Backyard*, 2005

Laugh when your eyes are burning
Smile when your heart is filled with pain
Sigh as you brush away your sorrow
Make a vow
That it's not going to happen again
It's not right, in one life
Too much rain

You know the wheels keep turning
Why do the tears run down your face?
We used to hide away our feelings
But for now
Tell yourself it won't happen again
It's not right, in one life
Too much rain

It's too much for anyone
Too hard for anyone
Who wants a happy and peaceful life
You've got to learn to laugh

Smile when you're spinning round and round
Sigh as you think about tomorrow
Make a vow
That you're going to be happy again
It's all right, in your life
No more rain

It's too much for anyone
Too hard for anyone
Who wants a happy and peaceful life
You've got to learn to laugh

作为一个成长于 1950 年代利物浦的男孩，当然要隐藏自己的感受。男孩们几乎从来不会对彼此说"我爱你"。我们只是忙于表现自己的男子气概，却不知道这有时会让你显得鲁莽。直到后来，我们成熟后才意识到，我们这样做是因为想成为强硬的利物浦小伙子。我觉得很多人仍旧在隐藏他们的感受，但是我很幸运地摆脱了这种心态。也许并未全然摆脱。

这首歌的起源是查理·卓别林。不仅因为他是伟大的喜剧演员，他也非常善于编写歌曲。他为他的电影《摩登时代》写了《微笑》这首歌，这也是我一直喜欢的歌曲。那个尽管你的心碎了，但是还在微笑的概念。我们得到这种朴素的鼓励：当你摔倒时，你还可以站起来。"Make a vow / That you're going to be happy again"（立下誓言 / 你会再一次快乐起来）。我有时将这个概念称为"克服之歌"。

这首歌里有一个基础意象。我们把雨和不好的事情联系在一起，把阳光和好事情联系在一起。不过并非仅囿于此，我在歌里用过一两次"Meet you in the fallin' rain"[1]，或者"that was a glorious day with the rain"[2]，或者"it was great to stand out in the rain and be in love"[3]之类的歌词。但是一般来说，雨是坏消息，所以一个人的生命中有太多的雨是不好的。

我们大多数人都能接受生命中总会有阴雨，因为通常我们只会遇到一点雨。但是一些人遭遇了太多的阴雨——比如逃亡的难民，或者某些国家那些一无所有、因为饥饿而死去的人。一部分人需要面对这么多事情，而我们其余的人有那么多值得感恩的事情，这很不公平。

所以，虽然我也许本来会成长为那种利物浦硬汉，但这些年来，我学会了试着放开自己，去理解那么多人的内心和生活中有太多的雨，太多的痛苦。我愿意相信我的一些歌曲也能做到这一点，让人们感受到他们不了解的东西——有人曾经告诉我他们有过那样的体验。许多歌曲对我产生了同样的影响。生活的重负真的有时"too much for anyone"（对任何人都太沉重），不过那就是我们创作歌曲的原因——去试着把雨停下，或者至少，为你撑一小会儿雨伞。

1　"在雨中遇见你"，出自《那会很有意义》（That Would Be Something）。
2　"那是下着雨的美好一天"，出处不明。
3　"站在雨中陷入情网是多么美好"，出处不明。

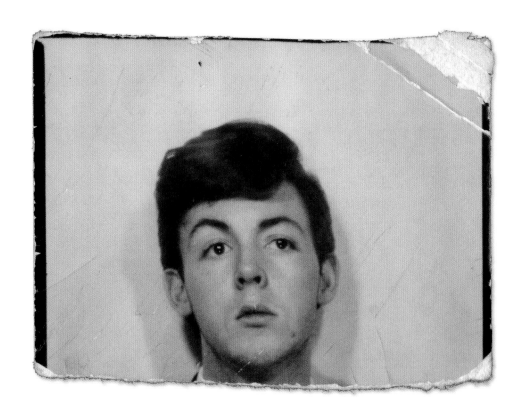

男孩们几乎从来不会对彼此说"我爱你"。
我们只是忙于表现自己的男子气概，
却不知道这有时会让你显得鲁莽。
直到后来，我们成熟后才意识到，
我们这样做是因为想成为强硬的利物浦小伙子。

Tug of War

拔河比赛

作　者　WRITER	保罗·麦卡特尼　Paul McCartney	
艺术家　ARTIST	保罗·麦卡特尼　Paul McCartney	
录　音　RECORDED	萨塞克斯郡公园之门录音棚、蒙特塞拉特岛 AIR 录音棚　Park Gate Studios, Sussex and AIR Montserrat	
发　行　RELEASED	《拔河比赛》，1982 年　*Tug of War*, 1982	
	单曲，1982 年　Single, 1982	

It's a tug of war
What with one thing and another
It's a tug of war
We expected more
But with one thing and another
We were trying to outdo each other
In a tug of war

In another world
In another world we could stand on top of the
　　mountain
With our flag unfurled
In a time to come
In a time to come we will be dancing to the beat
Played on a different drum

It's a tug of war
Though I know I mustn't grumble
It's a tug of war
But I can't let go
If I do you'll take a tumble
And the whole thing is going to crumble
It's a tug of war

Pushing and pushing
Pulling and pulling
Pushing and pulling

In years to come they may discover
What the air we breathe and life we lead
Are all about
But it won't be soon enough
Soon enough for me
No it won't be soon enough
Soon enough for me

In another world we could stand on top of the
　　mountain
With our flag unfurled
In a time to come we will be dancing to the beat
Played on a different drum
We will be dancing to the beat
Played on a different drum
We will be dancing to the beat
Played on a different drum

It's a tug of war
What with one thing and another
It's a tug of war
We expected more
But with one thing and another
We were trying to outscore each other
In a tug of war

Pushing and pushing
Pulling and pulling
Pushing and pulling

在我的成长过程中，拔河比赛是一项非常流行的活动。实际上，它曾经是奥运会的比赛项目，1908 年，一支利物浦警察队在奥运会上赢得了奖牌。在一根大绳子的两端，有两支橄榄球运动员体型的队伍，他们一直拉扯，直到一支队伍将另一支拉过一个标志牌而获胜。这看起来就像是一个很好的隐喻。

还是孩子时，你觉得事情都很简单直接，但是当你长大、经历更多后，你意识到这是善与恶之间永恒的战争。我以为每个人都有很好的家人，但并非人人如此；我以为阳光会永远照射，但它不会；我以为生活总是很美好，但很可惜，它不是。所以因为各种原因，这是一场拔河比赛。你要为了其他人尽己所能，因为如果你不这样，他们也许会摔倒。

这首歌是在 1980 年 12 月约翰去世之前写的，但是当专辑在 1982 年发行时，人们认定这首歌是关于他的，关于我们试图超越对方，因为 "We were trying to outscore each other / In a tug of war"（我们试图超越对方 / 在一场拔河比赛中）。人们常常为某样东西赋予意义以便叙事，当然，它们不一定有效。不过我不在意。歌曲发行后就属于听众了。他们可以对它做任何想做的事情，而我一般不会在旁边说："呃，不是，不是这个意思。"

当然，我能明白人们为何如此诠释它，因为约翰和我确实在试图超越对方 —— 那是我们竞争的本性 —— 并且我们都非常坦诚地承认这一点。但同样重要的是意识到我们的作品在很多方面获益于这样的拔河比赛。有人告诉我约翰如何在听到《即将来临》

上图：斯特拉在运动会上。
萨塞克斯郡，1984 年。

731

左图:《拔河比赛》录音期间。
伦敦 AIR 录音棚,1981 年。

右图: 与录音师埃迪·克莱因
在一起。萨塞克斯郡猪山磨坊,
1985 年。

734 页: 为《拔河比赛》音乐录
影带做的笔记, 1982 年。

后受到激发,去录音棚录制了《双重幻想》[1],我一直很喜欢这个故事,《漂亮的男孩(亲爱的男孩)》〔Beautiful Boy (Darling Boy)〕真的是我的最爱。所以,确实,如果他写了一首好歌,我感觉我必须要写一首更好的,和其他事情一样,这是灵感的一种构成。

你尊敬的人做出好东西确实是一种驱策。在 20 世纪初,毕加索和布拉克相互鼓励。艺术家的历史上总是有这样的拔河比赛式的合作 —— 比如莎士比亚和马洛,或者凡·高和高更。艺术家们彼此启发是一种更积极的思考方式。你不需要告诉任何人,但是你自己心里会想:"好吧,我可以做这个,而且我可以做得更好。"

也许这种阴和阳,以及从两个方面观察事物是双子座的特征。我从来不在意占星术,不过我确实知道传统的双子座分成两半。推和拉,我的性格就是这样。显然,我们是典型的好奇、聪明、适应能力强,并且善于交际。这让我突然想到双子座的人会思考事物的两面性。我已经注意到,这种张力经常出现在我的歌里,比如《乌木与象牙》,或者《你好,再见》——"You say yes, I say no / You say stop and I say go, go, go"[2]。

我想用音效来开始《拔河比赛》,来帮助设置一个场景。然后,机缘巧合,我听说一个国家室内拔河比赛就在附近举行。我让我的录音师埃迪去录下那些声音,他总是有一种瞬间的幽默感,在歌曲开头你听到的咕噜声——那种声音拼贴——是真正的拔河比赛中的声音。于是,这首歌奇妙地从字面含义转入了隐喻的领域。

---

1 《双重幻想》(*Double Fantasy*),约翰·列侬和小野样子的最后一张专辑,1980 年发行。
2 "你说是的,我说不 / 你说停下,我说继续,继续,继续"。出自《你好,再见》(Hello, Goodbye)。

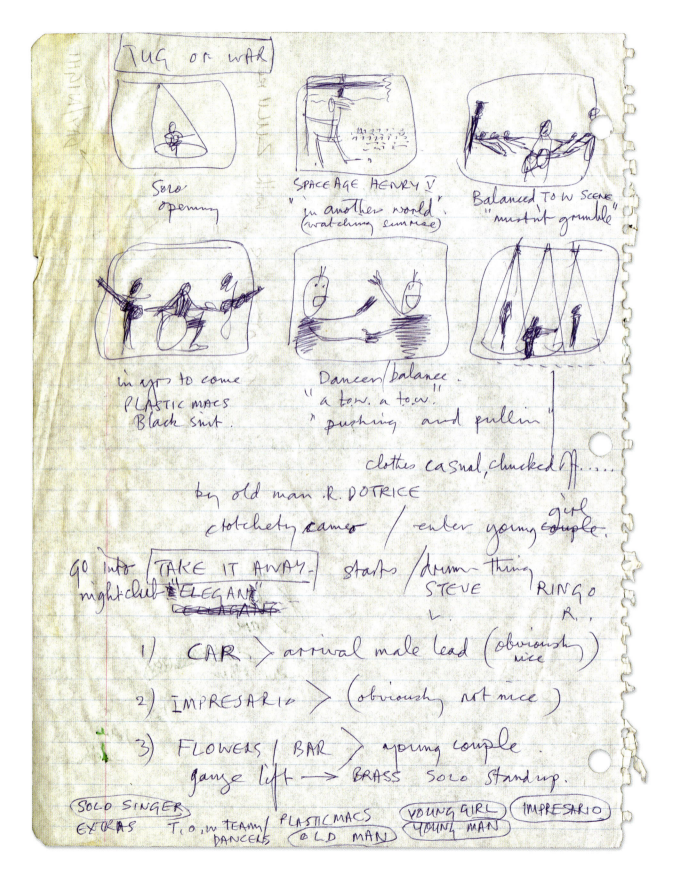

TUG OF WAR

SOLO
opening

SPACE AGE HENRY V
"in another world"
(watching sunrise)

Balanced TOW SCENE
"mustn't grumble"

in yrs to come
PLASTIC MACS
Black suit.

Dancers/balance.
"a tow. a tow."
"pushing and pullin"

clothes casual, chucked off.....

by old man .R. DOTRICE

crotchety cameo / enter young girl couple.

GO into TAKE IT AWAY. starts /drum thing
nightclub "ELEGANT" STEVE   RINGO
ELEGANT L.   R.

1) CAR > arrival male lead (obviously nice)

2) IMPRESARIO > (obviously not nice)

3) FLOWERS / BAR > young couple
gauze left ⟶ BRASS SOLO standup.

SOLO SINGER
EXTRAS   T.O. in TEAM/ PLASTIC MACS   YOUNG GIRL   IMPRESARIO
          DANCERS OLD MAN   YOUNG MAN

TUG OF WAR.

1. It's a tug of war
what with one thing and another
its a tug of war
we expected more
but with one thing and another
we were trying to afde each other
IN It's a tug of war

___

In another world —
In another world we could stand on top of the mountain
with our flag unfurled —
In a time to come.
In a time to come we will be dancing to the beat
played on a different drum [STOP] · STOP · [STOP]

- - - -

2. It's a tug of war
Though But I know I musn't grumble
It's a tug of war
But and I can't let go
If I do you'll take a tumble
and the whole thing is going to crumble
It's a tug of war
___ (pulling and pushing) C, B, A (F)
DAYLIGHT.
In years to come they may discover
what the air we breathe & the life we lead
are all about.
but it won't be soon enough — soon enough for me
(REPEAT) soon enough for me
SOLO (another world) ___ DANCING BEAT 3 TIMES. different drum STOP STOP

3. It's a tug of war
.... we were trying to outscore each other IN ·
PULLING & pushing C, B, A (CHORD C END.

Two of Us

我们两个

作 者 WRITERS	保罗·麦卡特尼和约翰·列侬	Paul McCartney and John Lennon
艺术家 ARTIST	披头士乐队	The Beatles
录 音 RECORDED	伦敦苹果录音棚	Apple Studio, London
发 行 RELEASED	《顺其自然》，1970 年	*Let It Be*, 1970

Two of us riding nowhere
Spending someone's hard-earned pay
You and me Sunday driving
Not arriving on our way back home

We're on our way home
We're on our way home
We're going home

Two of us sending postcards
Writing letters on my wall
You and me burning matches
Lifting latches on our way back home

We're on our way home
We're on our way home
We're going home

You and I have memories
Longer than the road
That stretches out ahead

Two of us wearing raincoats
Standing solo in the sun
You and me chasing paper
Getting nowhere on our way back home

We're on our way home
We're on our way home
We're going home

琳达和我以前喜欢开车出门，"Two of us riding nowhere"（我们两个开车瞎逛）。我们随便往哪个方向走，任何一个伦敦之外的地方，只要能找到一片森林，或者乡村田野，或者有山的地方。我们还是孩子时，都是大自然爱好者，我们都会走进森林去寻找一条小溪。琳达住在纽约州韦斯特切斯特县时就是这么做的，她在某座花园的后面发现了一条小溪。我住在利物浦的政府住宅区，不过我也找到了自己的小溪，作为一个男孩，我会为小溪筑堤，最后又在一日将尽时把它砸破。琳达会在石头下寻找沙罗曼蛇。我们有很多童年故事可以和彼此分享。

琳达最棒的地方是，我们开车出门时，如果我说："天哪，我觉得我迷路了。"她会简单地回答："太好了！"她喜欢迷路。她指出，总会在某处发现"通向伦敦"的标识，到时我们跟着标识走就是了——相当有道理。

有一天，我们开车去乡村，发现了一片看起来非常适合散步的小森林。我停好车。有一张我坐在阿斯顿·马丁里的照片，我坐在驾驶座上，车门开着，我的脚在外面，我拿着我的吉他。那时我正在写《我们两个》。

有这样一句歌词，"Spending someone's hard-earned pay"（花着某人辛苦挣来的钱）。我不知道它出自何处，有什么意义。我不一定想要什么意义；我并不总是为意义叫好，有时候就是感觉对了。我有一次和艾伦·金斯堡聊起诗歌和歌曲，艾伦讲述了他和鲍勃·迪伦的一次谈话，当时他试图纠正迪伦歌词上的一些语法错误，而迪伦说："这是一首歌，这不是诗。"我确实明白他的意思。有时候，有些语句唱起来会很好听。就"Spending someone's hard-earned pay"这句来说，显然不该用"weekly pay packet"（每周的薪水）。你会被那些词语绊住。

关于"We're on our way home"（我们在回家的路上），它的字面意义是回到伦敦，但更多是在指涉试着和曾经的自己取得联系。不过，"sending postcards"（寄明信片）是非常字面意义上的。无论琳达和我什么时候出门，我们会买许多明信片寄给我们所有的朋友。约翰也是一个喜欢寄明信片的人，所以你会从他那里收到一些很好的东西。

然后还有"You and me burning matches"（你和我燃烧火柴）。我记得有一段时间，在很久以前，我们会点燃火柴闹着玩。我弟弟和我在小时候是纵火狂，我爸爸担心我们会把房子烧了，所以他让我们点燃一整包火柴，直到我们完全厌倦为止。

迷路时，在阿斯顿·马丁里创作
《我们两个》。英国某处，1968 年。

APPLE CORPS LIMITED
3 SAVILE ROW LONDON W1
TELEPHONE 01-734 8232
CABLES APCORE LONDON W1

TWO OF US (on our way home.)

① Two of us riding nowhere
Spending someone's hard earned pay
You and me sunday driving
Not arriving on our way back home

CHORUS
We're on our way home
.   ...   we're going home.

② Two of us sending postcards,
writing letters on my wall
You and me burning matches
Lifting latches on our way home.

CHORUS.

MIDDLE   You and I have memories
Longer than the road
That stretches out ahead.

③ Two of us wearing raincoats
Standing solo in the sun
You and me chasing paper, getting nowhere,
On our way home

CHORUS and OUT.. A Quarrymen Original.

DIRECTORS N ASPINALL D O'DELL H PINSKER

739

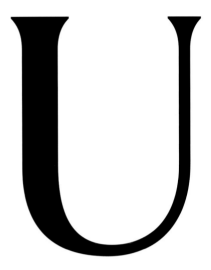

Uncle Albert/Admiral Halsey

阿尔伯特叔叔 / 海军上将哈尔西

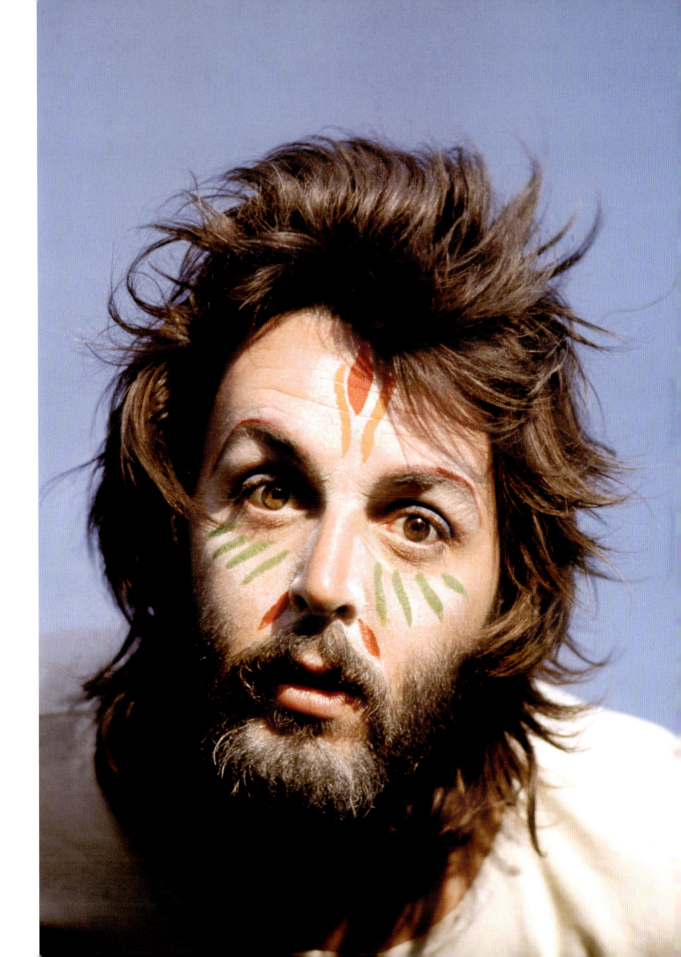

Uncle Albert/Admiral Halsey

阿尔伯特叔叔 / 海军上将哈尔西

作　者	WRITERS	保罗·麦卡特尼和琳达·麦卡特尼　Paul McCartney and Linda McCartney
艺术家	ARTIST	保罗和琳达·麦卡特尼　Paul and Linda McCartney
录　音	RECORDED	纽约 CBS 录音棚　CBS Studios, New York
发　行	RELEASED	《拉姆》，1971 年　RAM, 1971
		单曲，1971 年　Single, 1971

We're so sorry, Uncle Albert
We're so sorry if we caused you any pain
We're so sorry, Uncle Albert
But there's no one left at home
And I believe I'm gonna rain

We're so sorry, but we haven't heard a thing all day
We're so sorry, Uncle Albert
But if anything should happen
We'll be sure to give a ring

We're so sorry, Uncle Albert
But we haven't done a bloody thing all day
We're so sorry, Uncle Albert
But the kettle's on the boil
And we're so easily called away

Hands across the water
Heads across the sky
Hands across the water
Heads across the sky

Admiral Halsey notified me
He had to have a berth or he couldn't get to sea
I had another look and I had a cup of tea
And a butter pie
A butter pie?
The butter wouldn't melt
So I put it in the pie, alright?

Hands across the water
Heads across the sky
Hands across the water
Heads across the sky

Live a little, be a gypsy, get around
Get your feet up off the ground
Live a little, get around
Live a little, be a gypsy, get around
Get your feet up off the ground
Live a little, get around

Hands across the water
Heads across the sky
Hands across the water
Heads across the sky

阿尔伯特叔叔和我爸爸一起在棉花商行工作。爸爸是销售员，阿尔伯特叔叔职位稍微高一点。他当然更有钱一些，住在伯肯黑德，那是利物浦的豪华地段。

我们的家庭聚会非常友好、幽默。或许会有些背后闲话，但我从来没有看到过。请注意，无论什么时候，他们聚在一起都会喝醉。很多叔叔被称作"醉酒艺术家"，意思是喝了一点。而哈里叔叔会喝得酩酊大醉，阿尔伯特叔叔也会。阿尔伯特叔叔会站在桌子上，说着酒话，并且背诵《圣经》，他想让每个人都保持正直。

我很确定这首歌反映了我离开利物浦时对家庭的一种新的乡愁。我不再能经常见到家里人。我们也许会在新年夜聚会上回来，但总的来说，我远离了这一切。这种生活就这样淡去。在所有的披头士成员中，我是唯一会回去的人，其他人很少回去。

在这个舞台上，我想象阿尔伯特叔叔是一个小品中的角色，然后，我进入这个人物——一个傲慢自大的时髦家伙，而不是一个来自利物浦的小孩。口音的变化就足够了。"Hands across the water / Heads across the sky"（双手划过水流 / 头脑穿越天空）指的是作为美国人的琳达和作为英国人的我。

海军上将小威廉·哈尔西（Admiral William Halsey Jr.）在历史上是个重要人物，他在1944年被任命为美国第三舰队司令。我其实不太知道他为什么会出现在这首歌里。我肯定在某个地方读到过他的故事。这首歌出现在我们的专辑《拉姆》里，几个月后又作为单曲发行了。这首歌成为我在后披头士时代的第一首美国冠军单曲。我想我也许也受到了1970年的摩托车电影《无名小卒勇斗大英雄》(*Little Fauss and Big Halsy*）的影响。

上图：保罗与琳达。苏格兰，1971年。

743

哈尔西由罗伯特·雷德福（Robert Redford）扮演，主题曲由卡尔·帕金斯创作、约翰尼·卡什演唱。《阿尔伯特叔叔》里包含了许多和海军上将哈尔西相关的双关语，像 berth/birth（"铺位"/"出生"），以及 sea/see（"大海"/"看见"）："He had to have a berth or he couldn't get to sea"（他必须有个铺位否则不能出海）。

至于"butter pie"（黄油派），它把我们引向琳达。我们已经是素食主义者，而现在不得不想着如何去做圣诞节火鸡。我们用意大利通心粉和奶酪做了一个尝试：让它冷却成固体，然后切开，把它作为我们的通心粉火鸡。我们做的都是类似这样的事情。

我们这一代人做事情和父辈有很大的不同。比如说，我的家人在聚会时喝醉了胡说，而我们在探索其他娱乐领域——他们会觉得这些很奇怪。我们的生活方式非常自由、轻松，非常嬉皮。我在歌中以"吉卜赛"喻指。我们用幽默感来反叛。琳达和我想要我们的个人自由。

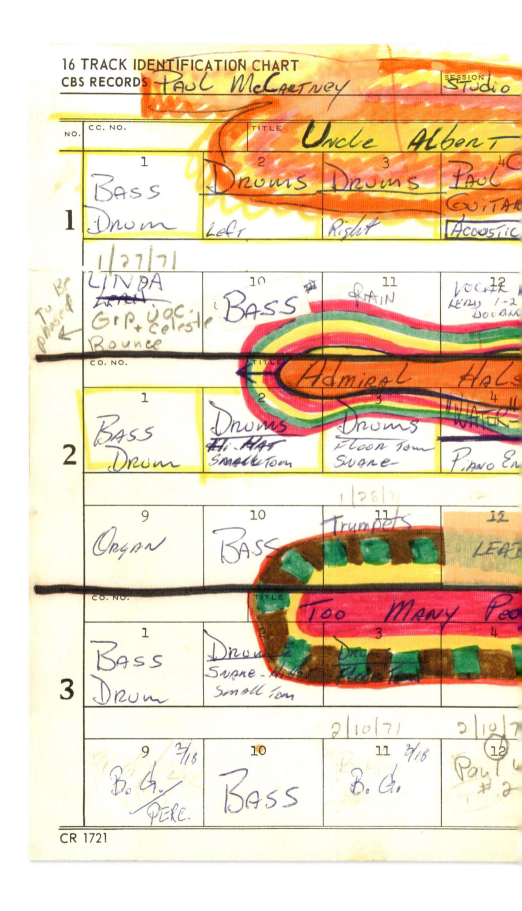

《拉姆》录音时的音轨表，
1970 年。

JOB NO. 216 827 **PRODUCER** McCartney **ENGINEER** TG/TB **DATE** 11/6/70

5 Amp	6 Amp	7 (Use)	8
Hugh Guitar O.D. Double	Hugh Guitar	Paul Guitar Acoustic	Rough Vocal RAIN
1/27/71	1/27/71	1/27/71	

Use →

violins	violas Harp	Basses + cellos	Fr. Horn Bowe

5	6	7	8
Hugh Amp	Hugh Acoustic	Piano	LEAD
1/28/71		1/28/71	

13	14		16
Bone	WHISTLE OOH-END	Fr. Horns	Cue T.B.E.

Guits 1/26/70 Solos

	6	7	8
	Hugh Acoustic	Paul Acoustic	Rough Vocal
	0/10/71	0/10/71	

13	14	15	16 Hugh
P.L. Voc DBL	Paul Voc tripled	Guitar Double	Guitar O.D. Bongos + Shaker

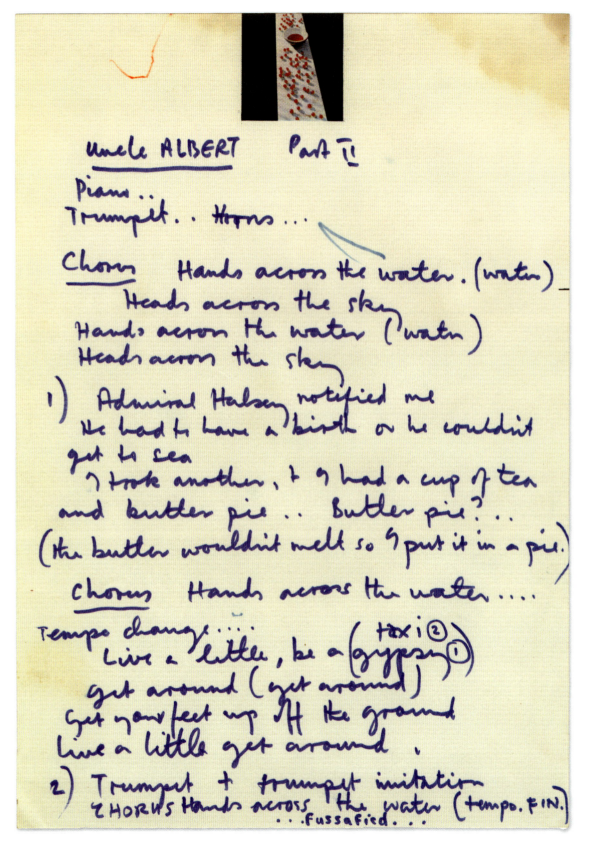

Uncle ALBERT   Part II

Piano ..
Trumpet .. Horns ...

Chorus   Hands across the water. (water)
        Heads across the sky
Hands across the water ('water)
Heads across the sky

1) Admiral Halsey notified me
He had to have a birth or he couldn't
get to sea
    I took another, & I had a cup of tea
and butter pie .. Butter pie? ..
(the butter wouldn't melt so I put it in a pie.)

    Chorus   Hands across the water ....

Tempo change ....
        Live a little, be a (gypsy) ① (taxi ②)
    get around (get around)
Get your feet up off the ground
live a little get around .

2) Trumpet + trumpet imitation
   CHORUS Hands across the water (tempo. FIN.)
        ...Fussafied...

748

Admiral ~~Halsey~~ notified me
~~I hadn't~~ He had ~~to have!~~
~~He couldn't go~~ a birth (berth)
or ~~+ to~~ he couldn't get to see (sea)
took
I ~~had~~ another look, + I had a cup of tea
and
~~on~~ butter pie (butter pie?)
(the butter wouldn't melt so I put ~~tea~~ ~~it~~ in ~~the~~ a pie)
— trumpets.

① Hands across the water
Heads across the ~~Sea~~ sky

② Hands across the table
Heads across the ~~Sea~~

a fussafied person fussafied me,
~~I had to be doing on account of my tender~~
drink
~~I would have liked bonbon, I had to have tea,~~
I'm fussafied —— (fussafied?)

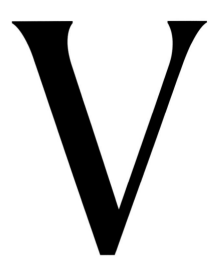

Venus and Mars/Rock Show/Venus and Mars - Reprise   752
金星和火星 / 摇滚演出 / 金星和火星——重现

Venus and Mars/Rock Show/Venus and Mars – Reprise

金星和火星 / 摇滚演出 / 金星和火星 —— 重现

作　者	WRITERS	保罗·麦卡特尼和琳达·麦卡特尼　Paul McCartney and Linda McCartney
艺术家	ARTIST	羽翼乐队　Wings
录　音	RECORDED	新奥尔良海圣录音棚　Sea-Saint Recording Studio, New Orleans
发　行	RELEASED	《金星和火星》，1975 年　*Venus and Mars*, 1975
		《金星和火星》/《摇滚演出》单曲，1975 年　'Venus and Mars' / 'Rock Show' single, 1975

VENUS AND MARS

Sitting in the stand of the sports arena
Waiting for the show to begin
Red lights, green lights, strawberry wine
A good friend of mine follows the stars
Venus and Mars are alright tonight

ROCK SHOW

What's that man holding in his hand?
He looks a lot like a guy I knew way back when
It's silly willy with the Philly band
Could be, oo-ee
Tell me, what's that man movin' cross the stage?
It looks a lot like the one used by Jimmy Page
It's like a relic from a different age
Could be, oo-ee

If there's a ROCK SHOW
At the Concertgebouw
They've got long hair
At the Madison Square
You've got Rock and Roll
At the Hollywood Bowl
We'll be there
Oh yeah

The lights go down
They're back in town, okay
Behind the stacks
You glimpse an axe
The tension mounts
You score an ounce, olé
Temperatures rise as
You see the whites of their eyes

If there's a ROCK SHOW
At the Concertgebouw
You've got long hair
At the Madison Square
They've got Rock and Roll
At the Hollywood Bowl
We'll be there
Oh yeah

In my green metal suit
I'm preparing to shoot up the city
And the ring at the end of my nose
Makes me look rather pretty
It's a pity there's nobody here
To witness the end
Save for my dear old friend and confidante
Mademoiselle Kitty

What's that man movin' to and fro?
That decibel meter doesn't seem to be reading low
But they was louder at the Rainbow
Could be, oo-ee

If there's a ROCK SHOW
At the Concertgebouw
They've got long hair
At the Madison Square
You've got Rock and Roll
At the Hollywood Bowl
We'll be there
Oh yeah

Who's that there? Oh, it's you, babe
Come on now, we're going down to the rock show
Remember last week when I promised I was gonna
*   buy a good seat at the rock show?*
Well I bought it
Come on now get your dress on, place your wig on
*   straight*
We can't be late, come on, we've got a date
We're goin' down to the rock show

VENUS AND MARS – REPRISE
Standing in the hall
Of the great Cathedral
Waiting for the transport to come
Starship 21ZNA9

A good friend of mine
Studies the stars
Venus and Mars
Are alright tonight

Come away on a strange vacation
Holiday hardly begun
Run into a good friend of mine
Sold me her sign
Reach for the stars
Venus and Mars
Are alright tonight

有时候你会写一首歌作为演唱会的开场曲，因为你会想："我要拿什么东西开场？"《魔幻之旅》不错，它向观众发出邀请——"Roll up, roll up for the mystery tour"[1]。我们在邀请观众加入。我们最近会用《辛劳一日的夜》开场，因为这首歌有那种大爆发的和弦。有一些歌在这种场合很有效，因为它们很受欢迎，我真的好像知道我将会在现场演这些歌曲。有时候我会在心里尝试这些。

我有几次故意这么做，《金星和火星》一定是那些歌曲中的一首——"Sitting in the stand of the sports arena / Waiting for the show to begin"（坐在体育场看台 / 等待演出开始）。一个情绪化的简短开场，并且很坚定，编曲有一点点歌剧化。但是我不太喜欢这首歌的其余部分，尤其是它转入《摇滚演出》段落后。最近我会迅速停下来，转唱另一首歌，比如《喷气机》。

当你写了类似《魔幻之旅》这样的东西——"快来呀，快来"——你就是个嘉年华拉客的人，为演出的开场定个调。《摇滚演出》是一首关于乐队世界的歌，歌词描绘了演唱会和音乐节的事情。我们演出的大部分场地是体育场——温布利球场、麦迪逊广场花园——不过我们也在荷兰的阿姆斯特丹音乐厅和好莱坞碗演过。我在想那句歌词"What's that man movin' to and fro"（那个男人来回移动的是什么）。我们过去会用分贝计。现在人们似乎不太在意音量过大，不过在 1970 年代，人们很在意。当地政府会派一个人过来，他会站在你前面，如果你的计量表超过指标，他会告诉你。尽管如此，巡演路上还是会有一种浪漫感。不仅是乐队的成员，也包括我们这些从小就想加入乐队的人，都被那个世界所吸引。而我觉得那也许是人们喜欢这首歌的原因之一。

这首歌写于 1974 年，在那个时候——以及某种程度上在今天——许多去参加演唱会的人也有一些另类思维。比如他们会想知道你的星座，然后把星座特征与你联系起来。我从来不喜欢这些。就我来说，金星和火星只是两个随机的星球。但是当我们发行这张唱片时，我意识到，它们同时也是角色——既是人，也是星球。

那时羽翼乐队的成员总想演《摇滚演出》，而我有点不情愿："哦不，不要斧头和吉米·佩奇[2]以及呆头鹅。我不确定我想演所有这些。"说实话，这首歌让我有点尴尬。我在描写一场摇滚演出，但实际上涉及此事，我的称呼是"摇滚乐演出"。同理，"你在一支摇滚乐团里吗？""不，我在一支摇滚乐队里。"我不会把吉他叫作"斧头"。"嗨，哥们儿，你的斧头怎么样？"我们曾经经常用的词是"胡扯"（gas），"这是胡扯，哥们儿。"在利物浦我们经常说"设备"（gear），这个词意味着某个好东西。你捡起这些俚语，在某个特定时间使用它们，然后往前走到下一个。但它们并不总是越老越好。

所以，我真的把这些星球、"星际"，以及现场演出的想法——所有这些当时的词语——全都扔进了这一首歌里。因为尴尬，我不经常演这首歌。但是我也遇见过喜欢这首歌的人，所以我学会了闭口不谈。

右上：汉弗莱·欧炫（Humphrey Ocean）绘，舞台铅笔草图。"羽翼乐队穿越美国"巡演，1976 年。

右下：汉弗莱·欧炫绘，旧金山牛宫蜡笔草图。"羽翼乐队穿越美国"巡演，1976 年。

1　"快来呀，快来加入神秘的旅行"，出自《魔幻之旅》（Magical Mystery Tour）。
2　吉米·佩奇（Jimmy Page，1944—），齐柏林飞艇乐队吉他手。

1.   # VENUS AND MARS.

Sitting in the stand of the sports arena
Waiting for the show to begin
 Red lights green lights
Strawberry wine,.
A good friend of mine
Follows the stars —
 Venus and Mars
are alright ~~tonight~~

ROCK SHOW.

Whats that man holding in his hand?
He looks a lot like a guy I knew way back when
Its silly willy with the Philly band
    Could be ,.... Oo- ee.....

Whats that man wheeling cross the stage
It look a lot like the one used by Jimmy Page
Looks like a relic from a different age
        Could be,.... Oo — ee.....
    If theres a   ROCK SHOW
      at the Concertgebow ——

There'll be long hair
at the Madison Square,
They got rock and roll
at the Hollywood Bowl.......

Well be there....

Oh yeah ...

———————

The lights go down
They're back in town O.K.
Behind the stacks
You glimpse an axe
The tension mounts
You score an ounce, ole!

    Temperatures rise as
you see the whites of their eyes...

———————

In my green metal suit
I'm preparing to shoot up the city
And the ring at the end of my nose
Makes me look rather pretty.
    It's a pity, there's nobody here
To witness the end......
Save for my dear old friend and confidante
        Mademoiselle KITTY.

Whats that man movin to and fro
His decibel meter doesn't seem to be reading Low
But they was louder at the Rainbow
Could be — oo ee.....

    If theres a ROCK SHOW
at the Concertgebow
They've got long HAIR
At the Madison Square
You got ROCK AND ROLL
at the Hollywood Bowl
    We'll be there...

    Oh yeah....

Repeat ROCK SHOW

        Chorus

        Chorus

        Chorus

Dead on your feet
You don't go far
If you keep on sticking your hand
In the Medicine Jar.

Dead on your feet
You don't go far
If you keep on sticking your hand
In the medecine jar.

What can I do?
I can't let go
You say time will heal
But very slow

Standing in the hall
Of the great cathedral
Waiting for the transport to come

Starship 21ZNA9.

A good friend of mine
Studies the stars,
Venus and Mars
are alright tonight

———————

Come away on a strange vacation
Holiday hardly begun
Run into a good friend of mine
Sold me her sign
Reach for the stars
Venus and Mars
are alright tonight

左图和上图:"羽翼乐队穿越美国"巡演。费城及丹佛,1976 年。

右图:使用西巴克罗姆印相法印刷的《金星和火星》封面照片,1975 年。

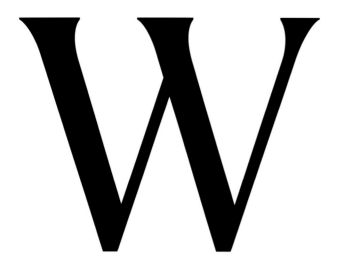

W

Warm and Beautiful

温暖而美丽

作 者 WRITERS	保罗·麦卡特尼和琳达·麦卡特尼　Paul McCartney and Linda McCartney
艺术家 ARTIST	羽翼乐队　Wings
录 音 RECORDED	伦敦阿比路录音棚　Abbey Road Studios, London
发 行 RELEASED	《以音速》，1976 年　*At the Speed of Sound*, 1976

A love so warm and beautiful
Stands when time itself is falling
A love so warm and beautiful
Never fades away

Love, faith and hope are beautiful
When your world is touched by sadness
To each his own is wonderful
Love will never die

Sunlight's morning glory
Tells the story of our love
Moonlight on the water
Brings me inspiration ever after

A love so warm and beautiful
Stands when time itself is falling
A love so warm and beautiful
Never fades away
Never fades away

这是我最喜欢的歌曲之一。这是一首加入了管乐组的歌谣，不过我总是感觉它有种维多利亚风格。它非常真诚。"A love so warm and beautiful / Stands when time itself is falling"（一份如此温暖而美丽的爱 / 任时光流逝依然屹立）。比起普通的"它会持续到永远"，我喜欢这种描述。写这首歌时，我的感觉很好，现在聆听它，我仍然感觉很好。"Love, faith and hope are beautiful"（爱、信任和希望是美丽的）。

我觉得管乐独奏非常可爱，这让我想起了我小时候经常见到的铜管乐队，那时经常有铜管乐队出现在公园或者大街上。我爸爸演奏小号，正如我经常提起的，他有一支自己的小乐队——吉姆·麦克爵士乐队。他为我买的第一件乐器是小号，并且教会了我 C 调的音阶；当你在钢琴上弹奏时，那就变成了降 B 调。一切都很复杂。那就是为什么我们甚至懒得去学音乐。我意识到我希望把小号换成吉他，于是我去征求他的同意，而他说："可以，好吧。"

《温暖而美丽》是在披头士乐队解散几年后写的，这时候我们知道了悲伤。我了解了在内心里寻找帮助，在一首歌里寻求安慰的感觉。我喜欢这样的想法，用一种通用的方式写一首歌，来驱散悲伤。你描写关于这个世界上你知道的最美妙的事情，你试着去写，让它能被轻松传唱，并被正在经历悲伤的人们所接受——那些悲伤时时刻刻不可避免地围绕着我们。

从更个人化的角度来说，这首歌的灵感来源是琳达。琳达和悲伤并没有关系，除了她后来生病之外。从那种意义说，我觉得这首歌是一个古怪的预言。我们的关系很好，不过像所有关系一样，它并不完美。我们有时候会相互反对，并且对彼此生气，但那就是家庭的运作方式。她是一个很有趣的人，诙谐且机智。她对生活有很了不起的看法，当然，她也非常艺术化。悲伤真的和她完全扯不上边。她是一位积极的女士。

将近二十年后，在她的纪念音乐会上，我用一支弦乐四重奏重新编排了这首歌。

上图：保罗与黑堤磨坊铜管乐团（Black Dyke Mills Band）。布拉德福德，1968 年 6 月 30 日。

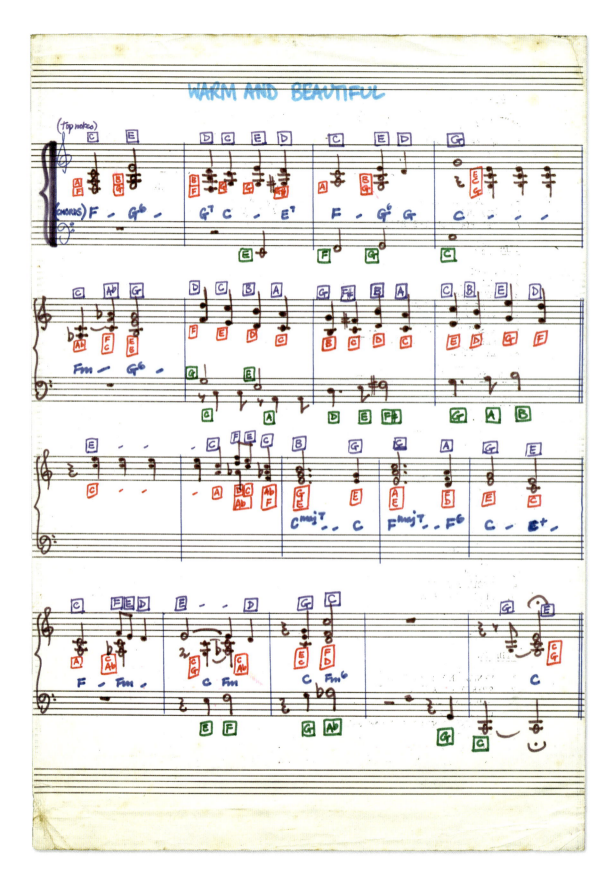

左图：《温暖而美丽》手写乐谱，
1976 年。

上图：乔·英格利希、丹尼·莱恩
和保罗，《以音速》录音期间。
伦敦阿比路录音棚，1976 年。

她对生活有很了不起的看法，当然，她也非常艺术化。
悲伤真的和她完全扯不上边。她是一位积极的女士。

Waterfalls

瀑 布

作　者	WRITER	保罗·麦卡特尼　Paul McCartney
艺术家	ARTIST	保罗·麦卡特尼　Paul McCartney
录　音	RECORDED	萨塞克斯郡低闸农场、苏格兰拉那坎精神录音棚　Lower Gate Farm, Sussex and Spirit of Ranachan Studio, Scotland
发　行	RELEASED	《麦卡特尼 II》，1980 年　*McCartney II*, 1980
		单曲，1980 年　Single, 1980

Don't go jumping waterfalls
Please keep to the lake
People who jump waterfalls
Sometimes can make mistakes

And I need love
Yeah I need love
Like a second needs an hour
Like a raindrop needs a shower
Yeah I need love
Every minute of the day
And it wouldn't be the same
If you ever should decide to go away

And I need love
Yeah I need love
Like a castle needs a tower
Like a garden needs a flower
Yeah I need love
Every minute of the day
And it wouldn't be the same
If you ever should decide to go away

Don't go chasing polar bears
In the great unknown
Some big friendly polar bear
Might want to take you home

And I need love
Yeah I need love
Like a second needs an hour
Like a raindrop needs a shower
Yeah I need love
Every minute of the day
And it wouldn't be the same
If you ever should decide to go away

Don't run after motorcars
Please stay on the side
Someone's glossy motorcar
Might take you for a ride

And I need love
Yeah I need love
Like a castle needs a tower
Like a garden needs a flower
Yeah I need love
Said I need love
Like a raindrop needs a shower
Like a second needs an hour
Every minute of the day
And it wouldn't be the same
If you ever should decide to go away

Don't go jumping waterfalls
Please keep to the lake

"不要上其他人的车。不要和陌生人说话。"写这首歌的时候，琳达和我作为父母，花了大量时间来唠叨这一类父母总是对孩子们唠叨的建议。

这首歌的主角听起来很像是我对我的孩子们说话，建议他们注意安全，不要陷入任何困境中。你希望他们健康地长大，进行自己的冒险，但你不希望他们做危险的事情，因为你不想失去他们。写这首歌时希瑟大约十七岁，那正是作为父母一个有趣的时间段；玛丽大约十岁，还不算青少年，但是正处在一个节点，想要更独立；斯特拉和詹姆斯还要更小一些，大约八岁和两岁，基本上教什么就做什么。不过另一方面，就像我的大多数歌曲一样，它向着它喜欢的方向漫游，变得更像一首情歌。

我觉得我最喜欢这部分："Don't go chasing polar bears / In the great unknown / Some big friendly polar bear / Might want to take you home"（不要去追逐北极熊 / 在广阔的未知之地 / 或许巨大友好的北极熊 / 会试图带你回家）。

我想瀑布这个动机源于我们一家在美国度假期间。这首歌我在羽翼乐队时就开始写了，不过最终出现在我的个人专辑《麦卡特尼 II》里。实际上，这是那张专辑录音过程中唯一一没有经过编曲的歌。我没把它放进羽翼乐队的专辑里，是因为我不太满意歌词；它们只是喷涌而出，而我觉得或许应该做一些修改。不过后来，我渐渐喜欢上了它们原本的样子。于是我精简了一些，让歌词更简单，这首歌成了我那时候最喜欢的歌之一。这首歌的曾经名为"我需要爱"，不过那对我来说太普通了。

还有另外一个版本，一首完全不同的歌，对某些人来说那是一首金曲。我记得自己曾经犹豫，"他们是否听过我的版本？"我觉得副歌段的歌词几乎完全相同，但随后

上图：和斯特拉、琳达、詹姆斯、玛丽及希瑟一起。巴巴多斯，1981 年。

我觉得："很好。这首歌中一定有些好的地方。"要么就那样，要么就"起诉那些浑蛋"。不过就像我一直说到的，歌曲创作者总是从这里偷一点，从那里偷一点。

有个洛杉矶人曾经宣称所有的披头士歌曲都是他写的，我们的回应是："显而易见，它们不是！"但对于那个谎称要提出诉讼的人，这是值得的，因为每个人都会知道他。他会说，"我写了披头士的歌。"人们也许会相信他，也许不会，但他们确实听见他说了这些。《麦卡特尼 II》发行于 1980 年，我们都知道那一年的 12 月所发生的事情，从那时起，披头士拥有了太多狂热歌迷。这首歌很明显是在约翰被枪杀之前写的，而名声是把双刃剑，一些奇怪的人都冒了出来。不过在这首歌的开头，焦虑的父母的建议是具有普遍性的——所有父母的担心。

发表《麦卡特尼 II》时，我说这张专辑有点偶然性。我有点厌倦了和一支乐队一起录音，把每件事做得井井有条。我只是希望好玩和实验一些，所以我从阿比路录音棚借了一些录音设备出来，计划是一两周，不过我玩得很开心，六周后才把设备还回去。我就像被锁在自己实验室里的疯狂教授一样自己捣鼓，意外地完成了十八首歌。我放给一些人听，有人说："把这个去掉，把那个去掉。这就是你的新唱片。"我不是特别确定，只是觉得这会是那种在汽车里放给朋友们听的开心的新音乐。所以，这样自发地录制唱片的缺点是，像《瀑布》这样的歌曲没有得到它应得的编曲。在合成器出现的初期，你会愚蠢地觉得合成器弦乐的音色总是听起来很好，其实并不是。

"不要上其他人的车。不要和陌生人说话。"
写这首歌的时候，琳达和我作为父母，
花了大量时间来唠叨这一类父母总是对孩子们唠叨的建议。

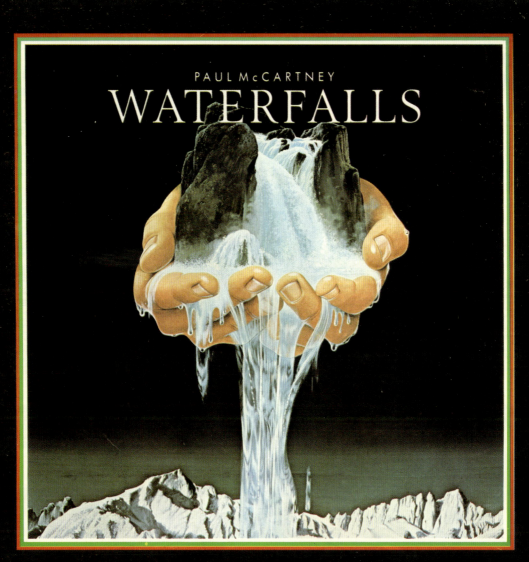

PAUL McCARTNEY
WATERFALLS

Don't go jumping waterfalls
Please keep to the lake
People who jump waterfalls
Sometimes can make mistakes

And I need love, yeah I need love
Like a second needs an hour
Like a raindrop needs a shower
Yeah I need love every minute of the day
And it wouldn't be the same
If you ever should decide to go away

And I need love, yeah I need love
Like a castle needs a tower
Like a garden needs a flower
Yeah I need love every minute of the day
And it wouldn't be the same
If you ever should decide to go away

Don't go chasing polar bears
In the great unknown
Some big friendly polar bear
Might want to take you home

And I need love, yeah I need love
Like a second needs an hour
Like a raindrop needs a shower
Yeah I need love every minute of the day
And it wouldn't be the same
If you ever should decide to go away

Don't run after motor cars
Please stay on the side
Someone's glossy motor car
Might take you for a ride

And I need love, yeah I need love
Like a castle needs a tower
Like a garden needs a flower
Yeah I need love, said I need love
Like a raindrop needs a shower
Like a second needs an hour
Every minute of the day
And it wouldn't be the same
If you ever should decide to go away

Don't go jumping waterfalls
Please keep to the lake

THE NEW SINGLE FROM HIS CURRENT ALBUM McCARTNEY II
SINGLE R6037 · ALBUM PCTC 258

Marketed by EMI Records (UK), 20 Manchester Square, London W1A 1ES. Sales and Distribution Centre, 1-3 Uxbridge Road, Hayes, Middlesex.

① Dont go jumping waterfalls
Please ~~KEEP~~ to the lakes
People who jump waterfalls
Sometimes can make mistakes

CHORUS and I need love
yes — I need ~~love~~ love
like a second needs an ~~———~~ HOUR ~~to~~
Ⓐ like a raindrop ~~needs~~ a shower
I need love every ~~minute~~ of the day if you ever should
~~day~~ ~~and~~ ~~night~~ ~~wouldn't be the same~~ decide to
go away.

② ②Dont go ~~————~~ CHASing polar bears
SOLO On the great unknown
Some big friendly polar bear
Might want to take you home
— and I need love

③ ~~————~~ VERSE
— I need love

④ Dont run after motor cars
Please stay on the side
Someones ~~LOSE~~ motor car
might take you for a ride.

—

I need love
End... Dont go (chasing,)
(jumping.)

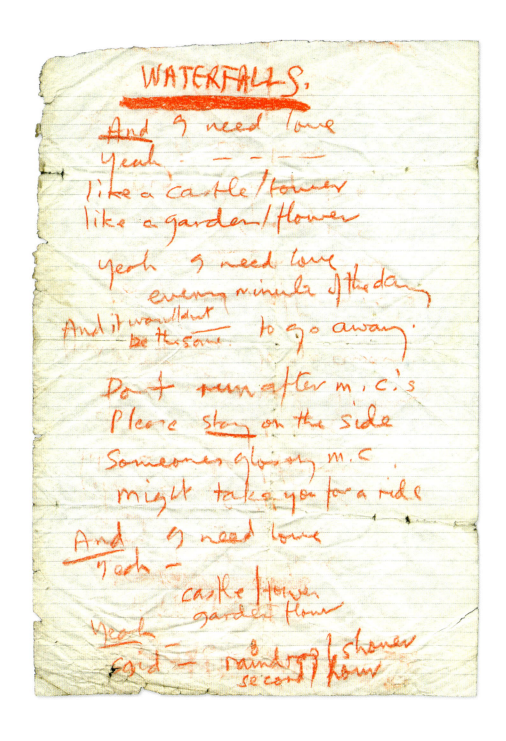

这首歌的主角听起来很像是我对我的孩子们说话，建议他们注意安全，不要陷入任何困境中。

We All Stand Together
我们都站在一起

作　者 WRITER	保罗·麦卡特尼　Paul McCartney
艺术家 ARTIST	保罗·麦卡特尼和青蛙合唱团　Paul McCartney and The Frog Chorus
录　音 RECORDED	伦敦 AIR 录音棚　AIR Studios, London
发　行 RELEASED	单曲，1984 年　Single, 1984

Win or lose, sink or swim
One thing is certain we'll never give in
Side by side, hand in hand
We all stand together

Play the game, fight the fight
But what's the point on a beautiful night?
Arm in arm, hand in hand
We all stand together

La–
Keeping us warm in the night
La la la la
Walk in the light
You'll get it right

Win or lose, sink or swim
One thing is certain we'll never give in
Arm in arm, hand in hand
We all stand together

We all stand together

曾经，我也是个孩子，我也喜欢宝贝熊鲁伯特，那是《每日快报》(*Daily Express*)上的连环漫画角色。他是一个小小的泰迪熊，穿着圆滚滚的老派英国服装，有一条带着黑条格子的黄色小围巾。

我主要是通过连环漫画了解鲁伯特的，不过每年他们会出版一本年度特刊，这就是我的圣诞礼物。鲁伯特的故事总让我心生宽慰。我爸爸抽烟斗，并且总是待在花园里；鲁伯特的爸爸也抽烟斗，并且也总是待在花园里。我认为他们要比我们更矫揉造作一些，但我不会因此反对他们。不管是什么，鲁伯特都能搞定。他有一种了不起的战后态度——"我们可以做这个"的态度。

我当时正在翻阅其中一本年度特刊，我记得我看着衬页，也就是翻开特刊时的第一页，这是一张彩色的双开页纸（不像特刊里的其他内容，那些都是重印的黑白报纸专栏，配着小图片，每幅下面都有押韵的对句）。我脑中几乎有了音乐，描述一个青蛙小提琴手和一些唱歌的青蛙组成的唱诗班。我有了一个想法，我想以鲁伯特为主角拍一部电影，还为此构思了一些歌，但我没有意识到这是一项多么艰巨的任务。我记得，披头士乐队还在一起时，我告诉约翰："我真的想做一部鲁伯特电影。"而他说："不错。

那就去做吧。"那是很棒的鼓励，但你需要的不仅仅是"那就去做吧"。

结果证明我贪多嚼不烂，不过这是一次很好的学习体验。有各种各样的事情牵涉其中，比如从报纸那边获取版权，所有事情都变得太困难。所以我决定和一个朋友，杰夫·邓巴[1]一起做一部短片，他是一位我倾慕的动画师。我们基本上就是从衬页上的这幅图片中获得了这首歌以及乐器的灵感。

我在《我们都站在一起》中唱主音，不过我也在青蛙合唱团中唱多声部的和声，因为我喜欢模仿，而且在动画制作中，找到一个演员并教给他们你想要的东西非常困难。我们面试了伦敦无数适龄的孩子。他们蜂拥而至，我们给了他们一些对白，奇怪的是，他们几乎全都在念，"乌伯特，乌伯特，乌伯特"。而我不停地说："不，是鲁伯特。'你好，我叫鲁伯特。'"最后杰夫说："你应该自己来。"所以最后我也成了鲁伯特的配音。

与国王歌手合唱团[2]及圣保罗天主教堂的唱诗班一起录音很值得纪念。录音监制是乔治·马丁，自1973年的《你死我活》之后，我就没和他合作过，所以这是一个我不想错过的录音。当乔治·马丁这样的人参与进来时，他就会负责，而你会成为旁观者，所以如果他问："保罗，你觉得怎么样？"他可能会重视我的意见，但我无须对结果负责。国王歌手合唱团唱青蛙部分的和声，所以他们必须唱得很准确。而作为国王歌手合唱团，他们做到了。

这是一次非常愉快的录音，而且获得了巨大的成功，歌曲在英国排行榜上升到第三名。几年后我，听说有一位非常优秀的英国女喜剧演员结婚时，她和丈夫选择了这首歌作为婚礼音乐："Win or lose, sink or swim / One thing is certain, we'll never give in / Side by side, hand in hand / We all stand together"（赢或输，成或败 / 可以肯定的是我们绝不屈服 / 肩并肩，手拉手 / 我们都站在一起）。真高兴她喜欢这首歌，并把它用在婚礼上。

有一个较长版本的视频，里面有青蛙，鲁伯特一开始和他妈妈在家里，然后出门去见大象爱德华·特伦克（Edward Trunk）和比尔·獾（Bill Badger）。琼·惠特菲尔德[3]扮演妈妈。人们在《美妙绝伦》（Absolutely Fabulous）和1980年代的情景喜剧《特里和琼》（Terry and June）中认识了她，她很可爱。而我和琼·惠特菲尔德一起表演。想象一下！

这首歌是在1980年录制的，因为剪辑鲁伯特的电影花了一些时间。不过《我们都站在一起》是我想花精力的歌。它保持了针对年轻听众的音乐审美传统，就像《黄色潜水艇》。我写这首歌的时候，斯特拉和詹姆斯还很小，我或许把他们想象成了这首歌的听众。这是一首关于鼓励，以及不放弃的歌曲。歌词很有集体感，而且振奋人心，我可以想象孩子们在学校操场上带着青春的果断一起合唱这首歌。

左上：琼·惠特菲尔德在录制《鲁伯特和青蛙之歌》期间。伦敦AIR录音棚，1982年。

左下：录制《鲁伯特和青蛙之歌》，照片右侧为罗伊·金尼尔（Roy Kinnear）及导演杰夫·邓巴。伦敦AIR录音棚，1982年。

1　杰夫·邓巴（Geoff Dunbar，1944—），英国导演。

2　国王歌手合唱团（The King's Singers），成立于1966年，是由六个男生组成的美声歌唱团体，名字取自于英国剑桥大学"国王学院"。

3　琼·惠特菲尔德（June Whitfield，1925—2018），英国女演员。

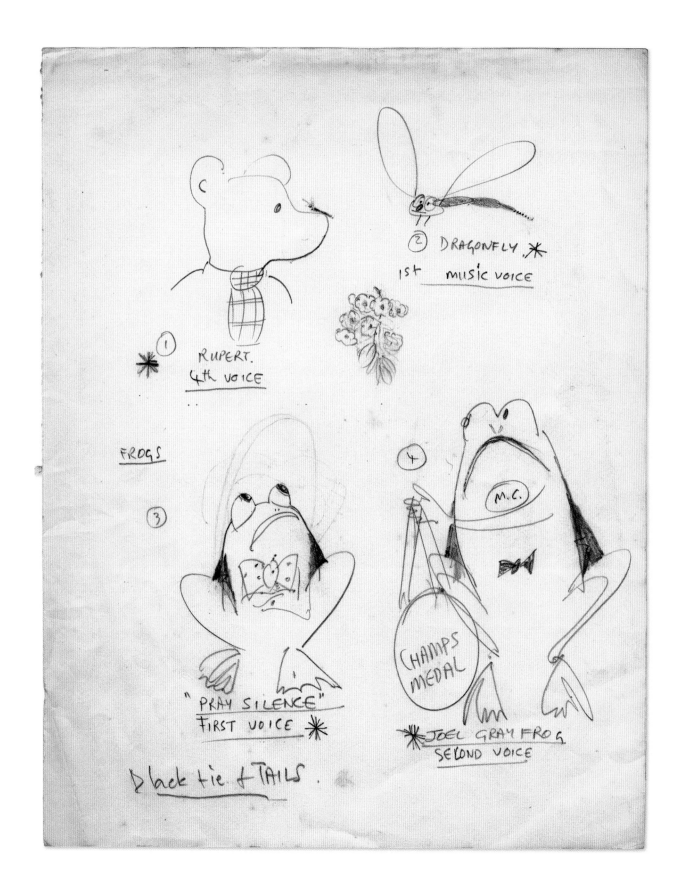

② DRAGONFLY. ✱

1st music voice

① ✱ RUPERT.
4th voice

FROGS

③ "PRAY SILENCE"
FIRST VOICE ✱

④ M.C.

CHAMPS MEDAL

✱ JOEL GRAY FROG.
SECOND VOICE

black tie ∮ TAILS.

A B C D E F G H I J K L M N O P Q R S T U V W X Y Z

.... PULL TOGETHER .

(1) INTRO   win or lose

sink or swim

one thing is certain

we'll never give in

side by side

hand in hand

we all (stand) together

intro ...(pull)

(2) Play the game

fight the fight

But what's the point on a beautiful night

arm in arm

hand in hand

we all stand together .

(3) love .... keeping us warm in the night

lalala. love .... walk in the light

SLOW   you'll get it right ! .....

(4) SOLO — cats — owl — sh.....

Rupert "they're very good . "

aren't they ?.

(5) love ... keeping us warm in the night

lalala love ...walk in the light .. you'll get it right .

REPEAT. (1) → pause on STAND TOGETHER ?

all stand — DIVE . BALLET music

宝贝熊鲁伯特的插画师阿尔弗雷德·贝索尔（Alfred Bestall）、乔治·马丁与保罗。伦敦 AIR 录音棚，1982 年。

我主要是通过连环漫画了解鲁伯特的，
不过每年他们会出版一本年度特刊，这就是我的圣诞礼物。
鲁伯特的故事总让我心生宽慰。
我爸爸抽烟斗，并且总是待在花园里；
鲁伯特的爸爸也抽烟斗，并且也总是待在花园里。

We Can Work It Out

我们可以解决

作 者 WRITERS	保罗·麦卡特尼和约翰·列侬	Paul McCartney and John Lennon
艺术家 ARTIST	披头士乐队	The Beatles
录 音 RECORDED	伦敦阿比路录音棚	Abbey Road Studios, London
发 行 RELEASED	《我们可以解决》/《短途旅行者》双 A 面单曲，1965 年	'We Can Work It Out' / 'Day Tripper' double A-side single, 1965

Try to see it my way
Do I have to keep on talking til I can't go on?
While you see it your way
Run a risk of knowing that our love may soon be gone
We can work it out
We can work it out

Think of what you're saying
You can get it wrong and still you think that it's alright
Think of what I'm saying
We can work it out and get it straight or say goodnight
We can work it out
We can work it out

Life is very short and there's no time
For fussing and fighting, my friend
I have always thought that it's a crime
So I will ask you once again

Try to see it my way
Only time will tell if I am right or I am wrong
While you see it your way
There's a chance that we might fall apart before too long
We can work it out
We can work it out

那是在 1965 年，我和简·阿舍之间的事情进行得并不顺利。人们都有过小吵小闹，那时候你会想："天哪，我希望他们理解我的出发点"或者"我希望他们可以明白"。他们显然不明白，他们觉得我是白痴或者暴君或者其他什么。这只是普通的情侣间的事情，她想要这样，我想要那样，我想说服她，或者她要说服我。大多数时候我们相处得很好，但偶尔，我们中的一方会受到伤害。

时间告诉我，数百万人都经历过这些小小的争吵，然后意识到情侣间的这种争吵有多么常见，但这首特别的歌不是这样的，它的意思是："试着从我的角度来看问题。"当你是词曲创作者时，在歌曲中表达自己的观点是好事，而披头士的歌将会被几百万人听到，你可以在歌曲中传播一个好的信息："我们可以解决"。如果你想用一句话来说，那就是，"让我们不要吵了"。如果你想用两句话来说："让我们不要吵了 / 听我说"。很明显，这很自私，但这首歌就是这样。

我开始写这首歌，是在一次争吵后试图摆脱糟糕的情绪。那次争吵在我的脑海里很鲜活。你没法在两个星期之后写出这样的歌，你必须立刻就写。写歌是一种表达想法的好方式，允许你说一些你也许不会对其他人说的话。

我写了第一段的主歌，然后在约翰家里，我和他写了桥段。当我们带着它进录音棚时，乔治·哈里森建议我们试试华尔兹的模式，用停顿的三连音，结果让这首歌有了一种巨大的摩擦和断裂感。

但断裂感是真实的，我们确实"fall apart before too long"（不久后会分崩离析）。悲伤的是，我和简真的分开了，那意味着她母亲也会离开我的生活。玛格丽特·阿舍是真正的母亲型的人，我失去我的母亲后，她填补了那个位置。现在，我又一次失去了母亲。

上图：披头士乐队。《谢谢你的幸运星》。伦敦，1964 年。

WE CAN WORK IT OUT.

① Try to see it my way
do I have to keep on talking till I can't go on.
While you see it your way
you run the risk of knowing that our love may soon be gone.
we can work it out - etc.

② Think of what you're saying
You can get it wrong and still you think that it's alright
think of what I'm saying,
we can work it out & get it straight or say goodnight

we can work it out

We Got Married

我们结婚了

作 者 WRITER	保罗·麦卡特尼	Paul McCartney
艺术家 ARTIST	保罗·麦卡特尼	Paul McCartney
录 音 RECORDED	萨塞克斯郡猪山磨坊	Hog Hill Mill, Sussex
发 行 RELEASED	《泥土中的花朵》，1989 年	Flowers in the Dirt, 1989

Going fast
Coming soon
We made love in the afternoon
Found a flat
After that
We got married

Working hard
For the dream
Scoring goals for the other team
Times were bad
We were glad
We got married

Like the way you open up your hearts to each other
When you find a meeting of the minds
It's just as well love was all we ever wanted
It was all we ever had

Further on
In the game
Waiting up til the children came
Place your bets
No regrets
We got married
We got married
We got married

Nowadays
Every night
Flashes by at the speed of light
Living life
Loving wife
We got married

I love the things that happen when we start to discover
Who we are and what we're living for
Just because love was all we ever wanted
It was all we ever had

It's not just a loving machine
It doesn't work out
If you don't work at it

　　1969 年 3 月，琳达和我在马里波恩市政大厅登记结婚。我想我可以写点"和法官在大厅里，我们签署文件"之类的东西，只用一些字面的记忆和简单的描述。但这首歌写在我们结婚许多年后，我开始用更普遍的视角思考，想象每个男人和每个女人的结合。它其实是任何婚姻的故事，不一定关于我 —— 尽管其中很多细节或许是我的。

　　"Going fast / Coming soon / We made love in the afternoon / Found a flat / After that / We got married"（进展迅速 / 很快到来 / 我们在午后做爱 / 找到公寓 / 在此之后 / 我们结婚了）。那听起来确实像是一场奉子成婚的婚姻。约翰是我们乐队里第一个结婚的人，那确实是奉子成婚。那时候，这种事比现在更令人尴尬。现在，人们甚至懒得结婚，人们找不到必须结婚的理由。但是约翰在伦敦找到一间公寓，他和他的第一任妻子辛西娅结婚了。我相当确定，我在这里也参考了一点他们的故事。

　　"Working hard / For the dream / Scoring goals for the other team"（努力工作 / 为了梦想 / 为另一个队加分）。我觉得，无论多么努力，你不可能把一切都做好，所以尽管你为了梦想而努力工作，但结果可能是在为另一个队加分。那也被称为"乌龙球"。这句歌词或许会让人想起披头士的解散 —— 我们所有人都犯了错误。"It's just as well love was all we ever wanted / It was all we ever had"（爱也正是我们所渴望的 / 它是我们拥有的一切）。我最喜欢这句歌词，它有种非常忧伤的感觉，有一点像阿尔伯特·金的那句 "If it wasn't for bad luck / You know, I wouldn't have no luck at all"[1]。

　　有些东西仿佛从天而降，这是写歌的魔力之一。我并未对这首歌进行太多构思，但它就那样出现了，当它甜美地落下时，你感到非常幸运，宛若天赐。你经常会听到

1　"如果不是因为运气不好 / 你知道，我根本不会不走运"，出自美国布鲁斯音乐大师阿尔伯特·金（Albert King）的《生于坏兆头》（Born Under A Bad Sign）。

作曲家说："我就是突然想到了。"坐下来分析并不是我写歌的方式，但是你确实学会了如何让韵律、节奏和韵脚出现在你面前。我觉得《我们结婚了》是这样的一首歌，就是那种，就像他们所说的——"就是突然想到了"，当那样的事情发生时，你总会感觉非常幸运。你想："啊，我会喜欢唱它的。"

歌曲的前面，我们谈到了另一个队；后来，我们谈到"Further on / In the game"（更近一步 / 在游戏里）。我觉得这是典型的年轻父母："Waiting up til the children came"（等待着孩子们的到来）——等你有了孩子，接下来[1]就是等待你的孩子安全到家。你可以理解成某一个意思，或兼而有之。

如果像我这样写了这么多歌曲，你就会学会很多小花招。称它们为小花招也许有点轻视它们，我们可以漂亮地称它们为"技巧"，不过当你动手操作时，它们还是花招。你大概不会把它们写下来，并且想："这些是我的花招。"但它们就储存在你的头脑里，当你写歌时，会用上你最喜欢的那一个。我的一个花招是两句短歌词后面接一句长歌词：

进展迅速 / 很快到来 / 我们在午后做爱

我相信，它与我读过的许多东西都有呼应和类似之处，甚至是像这样的童谣：

大雨，大雨 / 快走开 / 其他日子再来吧[2]

1　原句为"next thing you know"，既指字面意义的"接下来发生的事情是"，也有"事情发生得令人措手不及"之意。
2　原句为"Rain, rain / Go away / Come again another day"，出自英文童谣《大雨快走开》（Rain rain go away）。

Going fast coming soon
we made love in the afternoon
found a flat   after that   (2nd time
                                           Simple as that!)
we got married .

                                             N.B.
                             (backing sounds)
                            "a" "oo" etc...
                            "uh"...

working hard —   for the dream
Scoring goals for the other team
(Thing!)   we were
(were) it was bad   ~~bubbbbbba~~ glad
we got married .

Like the way you ●●● open up your hearts,
—WHEN to each other
          YOU FIND
●●●●●● "A meeting of the minds,

Early days, later on, children came to us one by one
Now we may & bless the day
are got married — — —....) ..

789

When I'm Sixty-Four

当我六十四岁时

作 者 WRITERS　　保罗·麦卡特尼和约翰·列侬　Paul McCartney and John Lennon

艺术家 ARTIST　　披头士乐队　The Beatles

录 音 RECORDED　　伦敦阿比路录音棚　Abbey Road Studios, London

发 行 RELEASED　　《佩珀军士孤独之心俱乐部乐队》，1967 年　*Sgt. Pepper's Lonely Hearts Club Band*, 1967

When I get older, losing my hair
Many years from now
Will you still be sending me a valentine
Birthday greetings, bottle of wine?
If I'd been out til quarter to three
Would you lock the door?
Will you still need me, will you still feed me
When I'm sixty-four?

You'll be older too
And if you say the word
I could stay with you

I could be handy, mending a fuse
When your lights have gone
You can knit a sweater by the fireside
Sunday mornings, go for a ride
Doing the garden, digging the weeds
Who could ask for more?
Will you still need me, will you still feed me
When I'm sixty-four?

Every summer we can rent a cottage
In the Isle of Wight
If it's not too dear
We shall scrimp and save
Grandchildren on your knee
Vera, Chuck and Dave

Send me a postcard, drop me a line
Stating point of view
Indicate precisely what you mean to say
Yours sincerely, wasting away
Give me your answer, fill in a form
Mine for evermore
Will you still need me, will you still feed me
When I'm sixty-four?

说到"mending a fuse"（修保险丝），我是那种会做手工活的人。这当然和约翰不一样，他甚至不知道怎么换插头。在 1950 年代，大多数人都会换插头！而保险丝总是被烧断。

《当我六十四岁时》的旋律在我十六岁的时候就已经写出来了。它是我的派对歌曲片段之一，当我们在为披头士准备歌曲时，我觉得在其中加上歌词应该非常不错。旋律本身有种杂耍剧院歌曲的感觉。我突然想到的是，六十四岁也许比六十五岁更有趣。恰好是临近退休的年纪。我总是试着给事情做些改变，而不是——就这首歌而言——写一首直截了当的杂耍剧院歌曲。

现在，我震撼于那时歌曲相对复杂的风格，也许部分原因是我当时读了太多书。一个影响因素是路易斯·麦克尼斯[1] 的诗《风笛音乐》（Bagpipe Music）中的幽默感：

> 约翰·麦克唐纳发现了一具尸体，把它藏在沙发下，
> 等待着它的复活并用扑克牌敲打它，
> 卖掉它的眼睛换来纪念品，卖掉它的血换来威士忌，
> 保留它的骨头当作哑铃以备在他五十岁时使用。

麦克尼斯很擅长描写日常生活。我觉得他会认可"You can knit a sweater by the fireside / Sunday mornings, go for a ride"（你可以在炉边织毛衣 / 星期天的早上，开车去逛）。退休的人会做的所有舒服的事情。接下来我写的是"Doing the garden, digging the weeds"（修剪花园，去掉杂草）。"Digging the weeds"是"抽点大麻"的另一种说法。我们总是喜欢悄悄塞进这样一些小玩笑，因为我们知道我们的朋友们会明白。

观察一下的话，你会发现这首歌的押韵方式是 ABCC 式（hair / now / valentine / wine）。更惯常的做法是 ABAB 式。在那段时期的很多歌曲里，我都在抵制传统的主歌结构。这也给了这首相当简单的歌曲一种特别的活力。

麦克尼斯的另一个能力是管理一组角色。关于孙辈"Vera, Chuck and Dave"（薇拉、查克和戴夫）一句，"查克"在英国不是一个很大众的名字，不过在电视里有很多叫"查克"的人，譬如 1958 到 1963 年间播放的电视剧《火枪手》（The Rifleman）里的查克·康纳斯[2]。从本质上说，这是一个有趣的名字，部分是因为"chuck"有时候意味着呕吐；还有查克·贝里，你说"查克·贝里"时，听起来并不逗乐；这和语境有关。

接下来是"Send me a postcard, drop me a line / Stating point of view"（给我寄明信片，给我写一句话 / 说说你的观点）。我一直觉得英国广播公司从《当我六十四岁时》里拿了这个词，观点，作为他们以观众来信为基础的电视节目的名字。有些英国广播公司的人甚至就是这么对我说的。不过这个节目开始于 1961 年，所以也许情况正相反。

1　路易斯·麦克尼斯（Louis MacNeice，1907—1963），爱尔兰诗人。此处所引诗歌原句为："John MacDonald found a corpse, put it under the sofa, / Waited till it came to life and hit it with a poker, / Sold its eyes for souvenirs, sold its blood for whisky, / Kept its bones for dumb-bells to use when he was fifty."

2　查克·康纳斯（Chuck Connors，1921—1992），美国演员、作家、职业篮球运动员和棒球运动员。

When I get older losing my hair,
many years from now
Will you still be sending me a Valentine
Birthday greetings bottle of wine,
If I'd been out till quarter to three
Would you lock the door
Will you still need me, will you still feed me,
when I'm sixty four.

Middles.
- - - - - - - -
You'll be older too,
And if you say the word, I could stay with you

I could be handy, mending a fuse
When your lights have gone,
You can knit a sweater by the fireside
Sunday mornings go for a ride
Doing the garden, digging the weeds
Who could ask for more,
Will you still need me, etc . . . . .

Mid. Every summer we can rent a cottage,
in the Isle of Wight, it its not too dear.
We shall scrimp and save
. . . Grandchildren on your knee
Vera, Chuck and Dave
. . . .
Send me a postcard, drop me a ~~line,~~ line,
Stating point of view
Indicate precisely what you mean to ~~say~~ say
~~Yours ~~~~waiting for you~~
~~Yours sincerely~~ wasting away
~~give~~ me your answer fill in a form
mine for ever more . . .
etc . . .

我曾经在一个老朋友家遇见一位弹钢琴的女士。她说："麦卡特尼先生，我希望你不介意，不过我把'当我六十四岁时'改成了'当我八十四岁时'，有时甚至是'当我九十四岁时'。"那些人觉得六十四岁还相当年轻。我在二十四岁左右写下了《当我六十四岁时》，所以那个时候看起来，六十四岁已经相当老了。现在，这个年纪看起来还是精力充沛。

《我们的世界》[1]电视直播特别节目的新闻发布会。伦敦阿比路录音棚，1967 年 6 月 25 日。

1 《我们的世界》（*Our World*），1967 年的全球性的电视直播节目，首次在全球同步播出。

When Winter Comes
在冬天到来时

作　者　WRITER　　　保罗·麦卡特尼　Paul McCartney
艺术家　ARTIST　　　保罗·麦卡特尼　Paul McCartney
录　音　RECORDED　　萨塞克斯郡猪山磨坊　Hog Hill Mill, Sussex
发　行　RELEASED　　《麦卡特尼 III》，2020 年　*McCartney III*, 2020

Must fix the fence by the acre plot
Two young foxes have been nosing around
The lambs and the chickens won't feel safe
　　until it's done

I must dig a drain by the carrot patch
The whole crop spoils if it gets too damp
And where will we be with an empty store
When winter comes

When winter comes
And food is scarce
We'll warn our toes
To stay indoors
When summer's gone
We'll fly away
And find the sun
When winter comes

I must find the time to plant some trees
In the meadow where the river flows
In time to come they'll make good shade
　　for some poor soul

When winter comes
And food is scarce
We'll warn our toes
To stay indoors
When summer's gone
We're gonna fly away
And find the sun
When winter comes

Must fix the fence by the acre plot
Two young foxes have been nosing around
And the lambs and the chickens won't feel safe
　　until it's done

When winter comes
And food is scarce
We'll warn our toes
To stay indoors
When summer's gone
We're gonna fly away
And find the sun
When winter comes

And find the sun
When winter comes

上图：在农场里。苏格兰，
1973 年。

　　在披头士的事情变得让人沮丧之后，琳达和我决定离开伦敦，去我们在苏格兰的农场生活。因为乐队的解散，那段时期相当艰难，不过，这也让我有机会从另一面审视自己。

　　首先，以及最重要的是，我们自己做了一切。那时一家子是琳达、希瑟、还是婴儿的玛丽，以及我。我们要吃东西，就开着一辆小路虎去镇上，买回来自己烧。没有人帮助我们，除了一个牧羊人，因为这是一个牧羊场。这是一段让我成为男人的体验。如果需要挂一张画，我来挂；如果农场里有什么活儿，我去干；如果需要一张新桌子，我会做一张。

　　《在冬天到来时》是一系列活动的记忆，那些活动充实了我，每一个都构成一幅美好的场景。我会修理栅栏、挖水渠、照顾鸡、莫名地种了一个菜园，这都是我学习的事情。你要把栅栏架好，否则狐狸就会叼走小鸡。你要挖一条水渠，因为如果蔬菜地太潮湿，什么也长不出来。所有这些新的体验都进入那段时期写的歌里，比如《乡村之心》（Heart of the Country）。

　　我在利物浦长大，并且跟着披头士一起上路，一圈又一圈地周游世界，而现在，我在一个偏远之地的农场里，那真是美妙极了。这个小农舍没有浴室，但是有一个钢制的大盆，他们在里面清洗挤奶设备，所以我们就往里面注水，大约两个小时后会注满。这不算快，但是充满乐趣。我们要拿起毛巾就跑——因为浴室在隔壁的谷仓里，而冬天真冷。我们会跑进门、跳进浴缸，这并不容易。但是我们还年轻，并且充满活力，而孩子们太小了，还不懂得抱怨。我们会跳进大盆里享受奇妙的日式洗浴。曾经，在我的生活里，这是我永远不会做的事情，而这是令人惊讶的解放。我做了如今很多年

在农场里。苏格兰，1973 年。

轻人梦寐以求的事情——著名的"间隔年"[1]。我感觉很多人想要那样的自由，逃离激烈的竞争。

"I must find the time to plant some trees"（我一定要找时间去种一些树）。事实上，我正是这么做的，尽管我的树种得很糟糕。不过我们正在学习这些新技巧，很好玩，现在我是这方面的能手。我只是掀起一块草皮，把树苗的根埋在下面，然后把草皮扔回去。苏格兰的天气可以很恶劣，而这是一个山地农场，所以说起来真的没有多少树。在小山顶上我们住的地方，唯一可以生存的是道格拉斯冷杉树，或者挪威云杉之类的。我写这首歌的时候，大约在 1990 年代初，这些我在苏格兰种下的小树苗已经长成了巨人——三十英尺高的巨人。

我在 2019 年重新发现了这首歌，当时我在为《火焰派》的档案发行听过去的样带。它感觉很特别，所以我把它挑出来，在我的录音工作室为这首歌制作了一个视频短片，当时正是 2020 年，英国因为新冠病毒的流行而进行第一次封锁的时候。事实上，它最终启发了后来的《麦卡特尼 III》专辑。

1　间隔年（gap year），指欧美青年在升学或毕业之后、工作之前，进行一次长期的旅行，让学生在步入社会前体验与自己生活的社会环境不同的生活方式。

WHEN WINTER COMES

① must fix the fence by the acre plot
   Two young foxes have been nosing around
The lambs and the chicken won't feel safe
   Until its done.

② must dig a drain by the carrot patch
   The whole crop spoils if it gets too damp,
   And where will we be with an empty store
   When winter comes

CH. When winter comes
    and food is scarce
will warm our toes
To stay indoors
when summer's gone
will fly away
And find the sun
When winter comes

③ I must find the time to plant some trees
In the meadow where the river flows
In time to come they'll make good shade
for some poor soul

When winter comes ...
         etc. ...
         Repeat ① ... + CH

在农场里。
苏格兰，1969—1973 年。

Why Don't We Do It in the Road?

我们为什么不能在路上做？

作　者	WRITERS	保罗·麦卡特尼和约翰·列侬　Paul McCartney and John Lennon
艺术家	ARTIST	披头士乐队　The Beatles
录　音	RECORDED	伦敦阿比路录音棚　Abbey Road Studios, London
发　行	RELEASED	《披头士》，1968 年　*The Beatles*, 1968

Why don't we do it in the road?
Why don't we do it in the road?
No one will be watching us
Why don't we do it in the road?

Why don't we do it in the road?
Why don't we do it in the road?
No one will be watching us
Why don't we do it in the road?

Why don't we do it in the road?
Why don't we do it in the road?
No one will be watching us
Why don't we do it in the road?

我们在二号录音棚做混音，那基本上是披头士在阿比路的专用工作室，我已经厌倦了干坐在那儿。每个人都回家了，但我们仍在那里，十点、十一点、午夜。除了一个保安，或者某个看门的人，已经没有人在那里了。所以我和林戈偷偷溜进三号棚，只有他和我。我想以一句咒语为基础，在此之上做一首"打发时间"的歌曲。

"咒语"这个词并非完全和主题无关，那一年的早些时候，我和玛哈里希·玛赫西·优济在印度时，我就有了这首歌的动机。在瑞诗凯诗，我恰好看见两只猴子在丛林里交配，这看起来那么自然，世界上最自然的事情，而我被这个想法吸引。它们完全自由自在，无拘无束。

当琳达和我有了我们的第一个孩子玛丽时，我去了家庭计划协会（Family Planning Association），试着做一个尽职尽责的父亲，多了解一些我们要经历的事情。不是因为我不知道生活的真相，而是我在分享以及请教："我们有孩子了。你有什么信息要告诉我们吗？"他们给了我一本叫《从受孕到出生》（*From Conception to Birth*）的小册子。那是令人兴奋的体验。那时候我才发现，普通的一次射精包含了超过四千万个精子。还有精子寻找卵子、制造新有机体的决心。胎儿在发育早期就有生殖器是事实吗？我简直惊呆了。

当然，这些细节比这首歌来得晚，不过这本小册子解释了一切。它解释了我对穿着夏装的女孩的痴迷，以及我为何忍不住去看她们；我为何会有那种原始的冲动，想让一切铺陈在眼前。现在我明白，这种新生物的最初动力之一是自我复制。

所以，这首歌的感觉相比我的大部分歌曲有点直言不讳——更直率地面对你，不过那是因为它所表达的原始冲动。而那也是摇滚乐的力量之一。它可以是原始的、自然的、粗犷的。它非常简单，甚至粗糙，但它和我们内心深处的某些东西有关，甚至可能更广泛地涉及神经系统。

上图：猴子。瑞诗凯诗，1968 年。

右图：《披头士》录音期间，混音
台前的保罗和林戈。伦敦阿比路
录音棚，1968 年。

With a Little Help from My Friends

在我朋友们的一点帮助下

作 者 WRITERS	保罗·麦卡特尼和约翰·列侬	Paul McCartney and John Lennon
艺术家 ARTIST	披头士乐队	The Beatles
录 音 RECORDED	伦敦阿比路录音棚	Abbey Road Studios, London
发 行 RELEASED	《佩珀军士孤独之心俱乐部乐队》，1967 年	*Sgt. Pepper's Lonely Hearts Club Band*, 1967

What would you think if I sang out of tune?
Would you stand up and walk out on me?
Lend me your ears and I'll sing you a song
And I'll try not to sing out of key

Oh I get by with a little help from my friends
I get high with a little help from my friends
I'm gonna try with a little help from my friends

What do I do when my love is away?
Does it worry you to be alone?
How do I feel by the end of the day?
Are you sad because you're on your own?

No, I get by with a little help from my friends
Get high with a little help from my friends
I'm gonna try with a little help from my friends

Do you need anybody?
I need somebody to love
Could it be anybody?
I want somebody to love

Would you believe in a love at first sight?
Yes I'm certain that it happens all the time
What do you see when you turn out the light?
I can't tell you but I know it's mine

Oh I get by with a little help from my friends
Get high with a little help from my friends
I'm gonna try with a little help from my friends

Do you need anybody?
I just need someone to love
Could it be anybody?
I want somebody to love

Oh I get by with a little help from my friends
I'm gonna try with a little help from my friends
Oh I get high with a little help from my friends
Yes I get by with a little help from my friends
With a little help from my friends

对林戈开点小玩笑其实特别有意思。"如果我唱歌走调了，你会怎么办？"实际上，约翰和我写的这首歌，音域对林戈来说没有任何问题，他有一种和我们不同的演唱风格。这首歌是我们专门为他量身定做的，我想这也是他在《佩珀军士》中极为出彩的原因之一。

《在我朋友们的一点帮助下》的演唱风格与《佩珀军士》专辑的整体风格非常一致——一种现场表演的风格，而这首歌是由"比利·希尔斯"演唱的。对那些记忆足够好的人来说，比利·希尔斯是 1966 年我在一次交通事故中被"去世"时，据说在披头士乐队中取代我的人。那是一个不停流传的疯狂谣言。现在，比利·希尔斯现身了，就在这里，乔装成林戈·斯塔尔！所以，这首歌是林戈在这部轻歌剧中的角色的开场白。

"Lend me your ears"（听听我吧）——好吧，你知道这是从哪里来的。1964 年 4 月是莎士比亚的四百周年诞辰，那一年，电视上在放《尤利乌斯·恺撒》[1]。这一切在我们的记忆里还很鲜活。

约翰和我在这首歌里塞进了一两个我们的私人小玩笑："I get high with a little help from my friends"（在我朋友们的一点帮助下我会兴奋）。一般来说，我们兴奋时不会写歌。只有一首歌是在那种状况下创作的。那首歌叫《词语》（The Word），不过我不觉得那首歌有多好，我甚至不确定那是我们在迷幻状态下写的，我们也许是在写完后进入了迷幻状态。

乔·科克尔[2]在一年后翻唱这首歌时，把它带到了无人能想象的境地。我曾经认识的一个人，丹尼·科德尔（Denny Cordell）听到了那首歌——他是我在那些午夜派对上认识的朋友，大家经常坐在一起放唱片。他给我打电话说："我和乔·科克尔一起弄了一首你和林戈的歌，我觉得真的非常好。我可以放给你听吗？"我说："好啊，当然。"于是他就过来了，我想是在萨维尔街 3 号的苹果公司录音棚。结果，哇，我的意思是我知道他要翻唱这首歌，但我不知道他会做这种把歌曲降速的激进编曲，因为我们的版本是非常兴高采烈的。后来，当时的美国副总统斯皮罗·阿格纽（Spiro Agnew）宣称这首歌鼓励吸毒，试图禁止这首歌，它因此在美国成了一首颠覆性的歌曲。约翰·贝鲁西对乔·科克尔的扮演令它更加出名。他闹剧式地演绎这首歌，然后摔倒了。[3]非常滑稽。

在这首歌里，我最喜欢的歌词是，"What do you see when you turn out the light?"（当你关上灯你看见了什么？）我想象着当你躺在床上，钻进被窝，关上灯时的样子。其实说的是你的生殖器，就是这样。每个人都这么做：在灯光熄灭后抚摸自己。但是我不能说："当你关上灯你看见了什么？你的生殖器。"这不是在仔细端详。

1　《尤利乌斯·恺撒》（Julius Caesar），莎士比亚的戏剧作品。
2　乔·科克尔（Joe Cocker，1944—2014），英国摇滚乐及爵士乐歌手。
3　指约翰·贝鲁西（John Belushi）1976 年在《周六夜现场》上模仿乔·科克尔，调侃了科克尔对披头士《在我朋友们的一点帮助下》的翻唱。

《佩珀军士孤独之心俱乐部乐队》
新闻发布会上的保罗、林戈与约
翰。伦敦，1967 年 5 月 19 日。

A LITTLE HELP FROM MY FRIENDS (BAD FINGER BOOGIE)

What would you think if I sang out of tune
Would you throw ~~a tomato at me~~ Stand up and walk out on me
lend me your ears and I'll sing you a song,
& I'll try not to ~~p~~ SING out of key
¹Oh I'll get by with a little help from my friends
        high - - - - - - -
    try . . . .

What do I do when my love is away
(does it worry you to be alone)
How do I feel by the end of the day
(are you sad because you're on your own)
²No, I get by with a little help from my friends
(etc. - - - - - - - .

Do you need anybody
+ I just need somebody to love
could it be anybody
+ Yes, I just want somebody to love

+ Would you believe in a love at first sight,
Yes I'm certain that it happens ~~every~~ ALL THE ~~day~~ TIME,
+ What do you see when you turn out the light,
I can't tell you but I know it's mine,
    Oh I get by - - - . . . . . -
+

+ Do you need anybody
+ I just need somebody to love,
could it be anybody — — etc. -
Oh I get by with a little help from my friends

End -

乔 · 科克尔在一年后翻唱这首歌时，把它带到了无人能想象的境地。

Women and Wives

女人和妻子

作　者	WRITER	保罗·麦卡特尼　Paul McCartney
艺术家	ARTIST	保罗·麦卡特尼　Paul McCartney
录　音	RECORDED	萨塞克斯郡猪山磨坊　Hog Hill Mill, Sussex
发　行	RELEASED	《麦卡特尼 III》，2020 年　*McCartney III*, 2020

Hear me, women and wives
Hear me, husband and lovers
What we do with our lives
Seems to matter to others
Some of them may follow
Roads that we run down
Chasing tomorrow

Many choices to make
Many chains to unravel
Every path that we take
Makes it harder to travel
Laughter turned to sorrow
Doesn't get me down
Chasing tomorrow

When tomorrow comes around
You'll be looking at the future
So keep your feet upon the ground
And get ready to run

Now hear me, mothers and men
Hear me, sisters and brothers
Teach your children and then
They can pass it to others
Some of them may borrow
Tales you handed down
Chasing tomorrow

Hear me, women and wives
Hear me, husband and lovers
What we do with our lives
Seems to matter to others
Some of them may follow
Roads that we run down
Chasing tomorrow
Get ready to run

Chasing tomorrow
Get ready to run

赫迪·莱德贝特（Huddie Ledbetter），或者铅肚皮，绝对是我的偶像之一。我读过一本关于他生活的书，特别有意思，书里有许多图片。我在钢琴上随便弹着，那本书就放在钢琴上，我看着它，寻找灵感。我还记得他的风格，他们总说他的男中音太大声，所以你不得不调低唱片机的音量。

我开始用一种更强硬的嗓音、带点布鲁斯的方式来唱，然后这首歌就出现了："Hear me, women and wives / Hear me, husband and lovers / What we do with our lives / Seems to matter to others"（听我说，女人和妻子 / 听我说，丈夫和爱人 / 我们要怎样生活 / 似乎对别人很重要）。这是那种"好好教育你的孩子们"一类的想法，就像 CSNY[1] 那首歌里唱的一样。这首歌的创作过程很轻松，我对它也很满意。

我把这首歌带到录音棚里时，试着在脑海里留住铅肚皮带来的灵感。这是一首非常简单的小曲，我在录制时也尽量保持那种简单。我弹的是原来比尔·布莱克在猫王专辑里用过的那把低音提琴，它的音色很美。我弹得不太好，所以低音线非常简单，大多数时候是空弦音。我很喜欢弹这把琴，只要不是在一家爵士俱乐部里弹上一整晚就行——毕竟，为此，我得先练习一下。

我很幸运，关于这首歌有着很美好的回忆。我写它时大约是 2020 年的春天，我的女儿玛丽走进房间，她说，"噢，我喜欢这个"，然后开始唱她自己的版本。如果有人说"噢，我喜欢这个"，那是一种很大的激励。你在乐器店可买不到这个。

上图：女儿玛丽拍摄的照片。
萨塞克斯郡猪山磨坊，2020 年。

1　指 Crosby, Stills, Nash & Young，美国摇滚乐队，简称 CSNY，此处所指歌曲为"Teach Your Children"。

我弹的是原来比尔·布莱克在猫王专辑里用过的那把
低音提琴，它的音色很美。
我弹得不太好，所以低音线非常简单，大多数时候是空弦音。

WOMEN and WIVES

1. Hear me women and wives
Hear me husbands and lovers
What we do with our lives
Seems to matter to others
Some of them may follow
Roads that we run down
— Chasing tomorrow

2. Many choices to make
Many chains to unravel
Every path that we take
Makes it harder to travel
Laughter turned to sorrow
Doesn't get me down
Chasing tomorrow

MID ———————— When tomorrow comes around
" You'll be looking at the future
— Keep your feet upon the ground
you And get ready to run

3. Hear me mothers and men
Hear me sisters and brothers
Teach your children and then
They can pass it to others
Some of them may borrow
Tales you handed down
— Chasing tomorrow —— (SOLO)
Repeat 1. Get ready to run
Chasing tomorrow — get ready to run.

Hear me (daughters) (women) and wives
Hear me husbands and lovers
What we do with our lives
Seems to matter to others.
Some of them (will) (may) follow
Roads that we run down
... CHASING (making) tomorrow ...

Many choices to make
(Heavy) (Many) chains to unravel
Every path that (I) (WE YOU) take
(MAKES IT) (getting) harder to travel
Laughter turns to sorrow
Doesn't get me down
... CHASING (making) tomorrow ...

(Can) (could) you tell me
When tomorrow comes around
That you set a (cool) (good) example
To the children (listening) (will be) listening to you
(you can) (willing) help them
Keep their feet upon the ground
& you simply love them more
Than you ever loved before.
Hear me mothers and men
Hear me brothers and sisters

The World Tonight
今晚的世界

作　者	WRITER	保罗·麦卡特尼	Paul McCartney
艺术家	ARTIST	保罗·麦卡特尼	Paul McCartney
录　音	RECORDED	萨塞克斯郡猪山磨坊	Hog Hill Mill, Sussex
发　行	RELEASED	《火焰派》，1997 年	Flaming Pie, 1997
		单曲，1997 年	Single, 1997

I saw you sitting at the centre of a circle
Everybody, everybody wanted
Something from you
I saw you sitting there

I saw you swaying to the rhythm of the music
Caught you playing, caught you praying to the
Voice inside you
I saw you swaying there

I don't care what you want to be
I go back so far I'm in front of me
It doesn't matter what they say
They're giving the game away

I can see the world tonight
Look into the future
See it in a different light
I can see the world tonight

I heard you listening to a secret conversation
You were crying, you were trying not to
Let them hear you
I heard you listening in

No never mind what they want to do
You've got a right to your point of view
It doesn't matter what they say
They're giving the game away

I can see the world tonight
Look into the future
See it in a different light
I can see the world tonight

I can see the world tonight

I saw you hiding from a flock of paparazzi
You were hoping, you were hoping that the
Ground would swallow you
I saw you hiding there

I don't care what you want to be
I go back so far I'm in front of me
It doesn't matter what they say
They're giving the game away

I can see the world tonight
Look into the future
See it in a different light
I can see the world tonight

一首关于一个人坐在圆圈中心，每个人都想从他那里得到一些东西的歌曲？那几乎说的就是我。作为年轻的披头士，当我们成名，亲戚朋友开始在电视上看到我们时，他们对我们说的第一件事是："哦，你变了。"而我们回答："我们没变。是你对我们的看法变了。我们仍然是同样的四个人，周游世界，开怀大笑，不过你对我们的看法不一样了。"

那只是开始，之后会慢慢出现一些要求。都是些简单的小事情，比如帮忙解决医疗问题，或者帮着买个房子，你知道——"我没有定金"，或者"我需要一笔临时贷款"，或者随便什么。起初你会帮忙，因为事情并不太麻烦，而且他们人都很好，他们是家人和朋友。出身于我那样的家庭，我知道没有人是富裕的，所以能帮助他们很不错，特别是医疗方面的事情。我总是说，有钱的最大好处之一是，如果有人因为疾病或医疗状况陷入困境，你可以送他们去看一位好医生，他们不用等上六个月才能做手术。

这是相当令人欣慰的。但是随着时间推移，其他事情出现了，比如："借我点钱。我会在年底前还给你。"你放贷款，不要利息，没问题，但当到了年底时，你就处在一个非常尴尬的境地，不得不说："呃，那笔钱怎么说？你有什么想法吗？"换句话说就是："付钱，你这个笨蛋！"但事情常常变得很糟糕。过去我很天真地陷入其中，然后，我长大了。

我记得我爸爸跟我说过，如果他赢了足球彩票，那有点像是国家彩票——那时候奖金大约是七万五千英镑，应该相当于现在的一百万——他会把一千英镑分给他的亲戚，就这些。显然，他在这方面的事情上更成熟，更有经验。然后我突然发现："啊，我明白了。原来他是这个意思。"于是，我渐渐意识到，我不需要帮助所有人。这一直延续到今天。

上图："新世界"巡演圣地亚哥站的媒体摄影师，1993 年。

"I saw you hiding from a flock of paparazzi"（我看见你在躲避一群狗仔队）。那真的是我们生活中的一部分，于是我把它安在这个人身上，不管他是谁。"You were hoping that the / Ground would swallow you"（你在希望 / 地面会吞没你）——那就是总结。你就是希望地面可以吞没你，或者吞没他们。我喜欢使用普通的句子，并把它们放在某种听上去不普通的语境里。我想很多有创造力的人都是这么做的。

有狗仔队跟着，真的很不愉快。当我最初和披头士一起出名时，我把媒体看作可爱的无赖。我们认识其中的很多人，他们也承认自己是无赖。他们过去很可爱，至少其中一些人很可爱，所以我觉得这是我能做出的最好的诠释。我有许多记者朋友，那没问题，但后来发生了什么我们早先就提起过：当时的摄影师会偷拍简和我的照片。这是一种侵犯，就好像他们在捉迷藏中抓到了你——只不过我并不是在玩捉迷藏游戏。这真的改变了你的整个生活方式，因为你知道任何角落里都可能有一个长焦镜头。

时至今日仍是这样，但是现在我在其中生活，而且我也已经习惯。就在上个星期，我们去海边散步时，我对南希说："他们来了。"很确定，有两个家伙，趴在汽车引擎上。我尽量让自己不为此烦恼，但这事总会很让人生气。你会在你认为很自由的地方成为自己，你觉得这是属于你自己的时刻。在过去，我会对他们说："天哪，你没意识到自己做的是一份多么糟糕的工作吗？你就像学校里打小报告的人。"我仍然不喜欢他们，并且修正了他们是可爱的无赖的观点。现在，他们代表了一个我不想了解的世界。

这首歌里有一句是我写过的歌词中的最爱之一："I go back so far I'm in front of me"（我往回走了很远才站在我的面前）。这是那种你说不出它的含义，但确实了解它的意思的句子。虽然我不知道我是怎么写出来的！

你就是希望地面可以吞没你，或者吞没他们。
我喜欢使用普通的句子，
并把它们放在某种听上去不普通的语境里。
我想很多有创造力的人都是这么做的。

Saw you Sitting.

(1) I saw you sitting
(~~at~~) ~~At~~ The centre of a circle
Everybody .... everybody
wanted something from you
I saw you sitting.

(2) I saw you swaying
To the rythm of the music
caught you playing
caught you praying
(with) To the voice inside you
I saw you ~~swaying~~ (there).

(BR) I don't care how it used to be
I go back so ~~far~~, its in front of me
I don't ~~caring~~ what ~~people say~~
As long as the music goes then hey hey
~~people~~   (you're gonna)

(CH) I can see the future
I can feel the world tonight
love can make me happy
~~its gives me an appetite~~
LIVING IN THE MOONLIGHT.

(3) I heard you ~~talking~~ WHISPER , , ,
to a group of ~~people~~
They were hanging
They were hanging
on your every syllable,
I Heard a whisper

(BR) Never mind what they think of you
you be anything ~~it~~ you wanna do
~~let them~~ have it all their own
as long as the music goes then hey hey

I CAN SEE THE WORLD TONIGHT.

1. I saw you sitting at the centre of a circle
Everybody everybody
wanted something from you
(I saw you sitting there).

2. Saw you swaying
To the rhythm of the music
Caught you playing
Caught you praying
To the voice inside you.
Saw you swaying, there.

[BR] I don't care what you wanna be
I go back so far, I'm in front of me
It doesn't matter what They say,
They're ~~Don't~~ giving the game away.

(CH.) I can see the world tonight
look into the future
~~See~~ it in a different light
I can see the world tonight

3. I heard you ~~listening to a secret conversation~~
listening to a secret conversation,
You were crying
you were trying
Not to let Them hear you
I heard you listening in.

[BR] Never mind, what They want to do
You've got a right, to your point of view
It doesn't matter what they say
They're ~~it~~ giving the game away

The World You're Coming Into

你到来的这个世界

作　者	WRITERS	保罗·麦卡特尼和卡尔·戴维斯　Paul McCartney and Carl Davis
艺术家	ARTIST	利物浦皇家爱乐乐团　Royal Liverpool Philharmonic Orchestra
录　音	RECORDED	利物浦天主教堂　Liverpool Cathedral
发　行	RELEASED	单曲，1991 年　Single, 1991
		《保罗·麦卡特尼的利物浦清唱剧》，1991 年　*Paul McCartney's Liverpool Oratorio*, 1991

MARY DEE
The world you're coming into
Is no easy place to enter
Every day is haunted
By the echoes of the past
Funny thoughts and wild, wild dreams
Will find their way into your mind

The clouds that hang above us
May be full of rain and thunder
But in time they slide away
To find the sun still there
Lazy days and wild, wild flowers
Will bring some joy into your heart
And I will always love you
I'll welcome you into this world

MARY DEE AND BOY SOLO
You're mine and I will love you

　　这首歌基本上是一首咏叹调，出自《利物浦清唱剧》，但是随着时间推移，它对于我有了更多的意义。我很少以古典音乐的形式创作，《利物浦清唱剧》是我的第一次。真正令我感动的是，我成长的城市的爱乐乐团在如此重要的时刻——它们的一百五十周年纪念日——向我发出邀约，邀请我加入这场庆典。这首歌以女高音独唱开始，在录音里是由卡纳娃女爵唱的。她对着她的宝宝唱歌："The world you're coming into / Is no easy place to enter"（你到来的这个世界 / 不是容易进入的地方）。就生理上来说，无论对她自己还是宝宝，光是出生时身体受到的冲击就足以令人窒息。我们中的任何一个人能在出生中幸存，都是个谜。这是一次痛苦的经历。

　　更别说还有生活的挫折，我们遭遇的一切。就像我们大多数人很快意识到的那样，就像我们在当前的历史中一次又一次发现的那样，这个世界不是容易进入的地方。"Every day is haunted / By the echoes of the past / Funny thoughts and wild, wild dreams / Will find their way into your mind"（每一天都被往昔的 / 回音所困扰 / 有趣的思想和狂野的，狂野的梦 / 会找到进入你头脑的方法）。

　　你会听到她对腹中胎儿的一些教诲。"The clouds that hang above us / May be full of rain and thunder / But in time they slide away / To find the sun still there / Lazy days and wild, wild flowers / Will bring some joy into your heart"（我们头顶上的云 / 也许充满雨和闪电 / 但当它们飘走时 / 发现太阳仍在那里 / 慵懒的时光和狂野的，狂野的花朵 / 将为你的心灵带来快乐）。然后是"And I will always love you / I'll welcome you into this world"（我将永远爱你 / 欢迎你来到这个世界）。她的孩子和她合唱了最后一部分，母子的优美二重唱。

　　这首歌某种程度上让我想起了母校利物浦学院男子高中的拉丁文格言：*Non nobis solum, sed toti mundo nati*——并非只为我们自己，而是为了我们出生于此的整个世界。这首歌关于母子间的关系，但那个孩子长大后不得不离开母亲，进入世界。那才是这句格言真正派上用场的地方。我仍在向我父母学习，比如我爸爸说的"现在就做"。学校的格言也出现在《利物浦清唱剧》里的其他地方，开场"战争"部分的"Non nobis solum"一句中。

　　前几天，正在思考这篇文章时，我突然想到，在某种程度上，这首歌是对我母亲玛丽的一种庆贺，她是一位助产士。也许这就是我对这首歌越来越感兴趣的原因。

上图：妈妈玛丽和同事。

and the child...

ACROSS TOWN

The working MEN (all male)
concerned more about the rights
and wrongs of adultery.
MR. DINGLE advises HIM
to relax, and go for a drink, where
they can forget their troubles.
SHE ... has a child inside

⑦ CRISES. She comes through
the traffic ... is home and
sings a song to her unborn child
as she sits in the bedroom.
He lurches home through traffic
. and enquires where his dinner
is SHE regrets the passing of
childhood HE too ...

824

THEY each have their (J)
own private worries and
an argument develops...
It is irrational but effective.
<u>SHE</u> reminds him she doesn't
need this....she needs love
he isn't sure if she ever loved him.
CLIMAX.
As she leaves she breaks the news
that he is about to become a father.

SHE runs into street ...
Dark, wind, rain umbrellas
car headlights and is knocked
down by a car. Slow motion
scene of her being taken to hospital

The <u>nurse</u> sings to her
as she sleeps, and assures
her she will look after her but
says she is not sure if the
baby is in danger.. sleep.

825

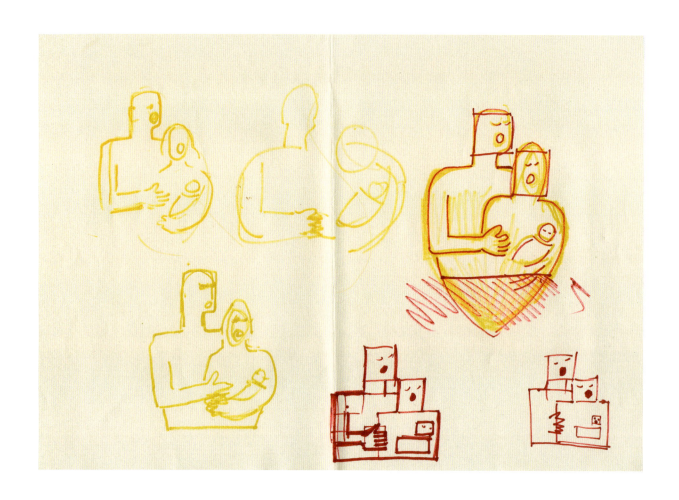

上图:《利物浦清唱剧》专辑封套
的设计草图,1991 年。

左图:保罗与卡尔·戴维斯。
萨塞克斯郡,1990 年。

右图：卡纳娃女爵，利物浦天主
教堂，1991 年。

下图：《利物浦清唱剧》的场景
设计草图，1991 年。

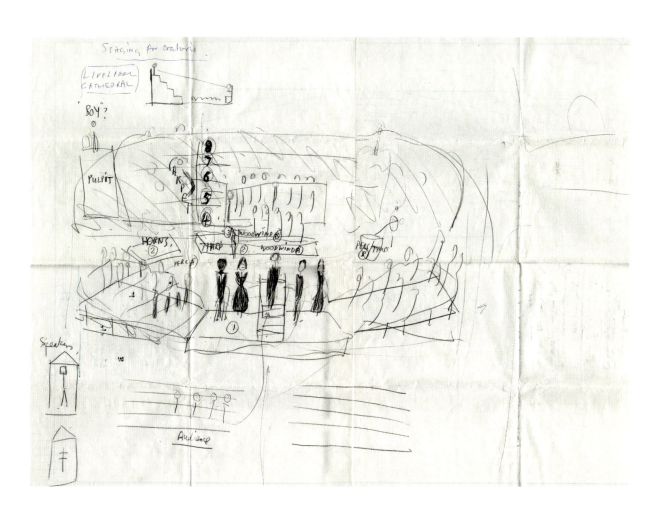

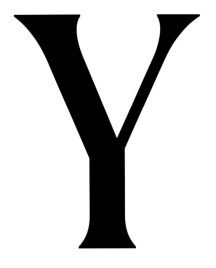

Yellow Submarine

黄色潜水艇

作 者 WRITERS	保罗·麦卡特尼和约翰·列侬	Paul McCartney and John Lennon
艺术家 ARTIST	披头士乐队	The Beatles
录 音 RECORDED	伦敦阿比路录音棚	Abbey Road Studios, London
发 行 RELEASED	《埃莉诺·里格比》/《黄色潜水艇》双 A 面单曲，1966 年	'Eleanor Rigby' / 'Yellow Submarine' double A-side single, 1966
	《左轮手枪》，1966 年	Revolver, 1966

In the town where I was born
Lived a man who sailed to sea
And he told us of his life
In the land of submarines

So we sailed on to the sun
Til we found the sea of green
And we lived beneath the waves
In our yellow submarine

We all live in a yellow submarine
Yellow submarine, yellow submarine
We all live in a yellow submarine
Yellow submarine, yellow submarine

And our friends are all aboard
Many more of them live next door
And the band begins to play

We all live in a yellow submarine
Yellow submarine, yellow submarine
We all live in a yellow submarine
Yellow submarine, yellow submarine

As we live a life of ease
Every one of us has all we need
Sky of blue and sea of green
In our yellow submarine

We all live in a yellow submarine
Yellow submarine, yellow submarine
We all live in a yellow submarine
Yellow submarine, yellow submarine

所有那些关于一个人出海的作品，那些歌谣、《帕特里克·斯彭斯爵士》[1]、《古舟子咏》[2]，更别提刘易斯·卡罗尔了：

> "时候不早了，"海象说，
> "说到这么多：
> 鞋子、船只、密封蜡，
> 卷心菜和国王，
> 为什么大海会滚烫——
> 以及猪是否有翅膀。"[3]

胡说八道的传统是我中学六年级在英国文学课上跟我的老师艾伦·杜邦德学到的。他在剑桥上学时的老师是 F. R. 利维斯，后者也许是当时最有名的英国文学评论家。我知道这些年来我一直在谈论艾伦·杜邦德，但是老实说，我不能夸大他对我的影响。我不太愿意用这种陈词滥调，但他确实启发了我的灵感。

《黄色潜水艇》的很大一部分潜台词是，即便在那个时候，披头士也还是生活在我们自己的密封舱里，我们有自己的小气候，我们自己控制的环境。杜邦德会向我介绍像"潜台词"这样的词。

另一个不能夸大的因素是，当时以水下世界为特色的电视节目令人难以置信地受欢迎。有奥地利的潜水员汉斯（Hans）和洛特·哈斯（Lotte Hass）。洛特曾经是海报模特。劳埃德·布里奇斯（Lloyd Bridges）出演的连续剧《海上巡航》（*Sea Hunt*）那时候也在播，还有《海豚的故事》（*Flipper*），关于一只海豚的电视节目，在 1964 年至 1967 年之间播出。

那个水下世界相当神奇。我觉得它带来的可能性碰巧与我们战后的经历不谋而合。当我们在利物浦还是孩子时——"In the town where I was born"（在我出生的城市里）——生活环绕着炸弹、定量配给和废墟。我爸爸是个消防员，谈起燃烧弹就是家常便饭。我们的娱乐活动通常是自制的，年纪大的人唱的歌曲就是你的娱乐。你学会了用很少的东西来度日。所以，当你得到更多东西时，就好像从黑白世界进入彩色世界。

对披头士乐队来说——尽管那个时候我们并不知道——表达我们走出黑白世界的喜悦实际上促成了新的彩色世界的爆发。这很难相信，但是我们在其中扮演了积极的角色。我们帮着把"Sky of blue and sea of green"（蓝色的天空和绿色的海洋）变得如此生机勃勃。

1　《帕特里克·斯彭斯爵士》（Sir Patrick Spens），流传于中世纪的英文歌谣，创作者不详。
2　《古舟子咏》（*The Rime of The Ancient Mariner*），英国诗人柯勒律治创作的歌谣体长诗，又译《老水手之歌》。
3　《爱丽丝镜中奇遇记》中的寓言诗《海象和木匠》，此处所引诗歌原句为："'The time has come,' the Walrus said, / 'To talk of many things: / Of shoes - and ships - and sealing-wax - / Of cabbages - and kings - / And why the sea is boiling hot - / And whether pigs have wings.'"

《黄色潜水艇》的很大一部分潜台词是，
即便在那个时候，披头士也还是生活在我们自己的密封舱里，
我们有自己的小气候，我们自己控制的环境。
杜邦德会向我介绍像"潜台词"这样的词。

左图:《黄色潜水艇》中的原始
赛璐璐作品,1968 年。

上图: 与林戈·斯塔尔、乔治·哈
里森一起参加《黄色潜水艇》新
闻发布会。伦敦,1968 年 7 月
8 日。

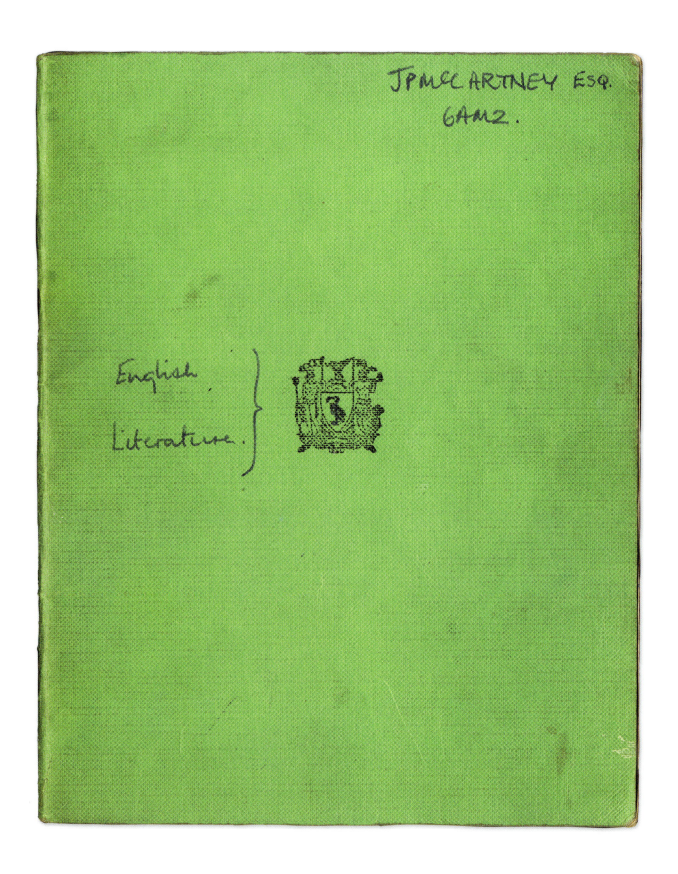

a rather grand effect and possibly to explain more clearly, to other scholars, the position Eve was in. Besides the classical references being used to achieve a feeling of greatness, they are used earlier in the book to give an impression of vast distances. In his search for Adam and Eve, Satan travels the length of the world. To show the extent of this paradise, Milton mentioned such distant-sounding names as..." Pontus, the pool Maeotis, the river Ob, Orontes, Darien, the Ganges, and the Indus."

Milton's ability to delve into the minds of his characters and give a clear representation of what he sees there, gives an indication of an imaginative mind. Satan's first impression of Eve is one of a deep infatuation for her, so much so that " her heavenly form angelic ... her graceful innocence, her every air of gesture or least action, overawed his malice" and left him feeling "stupidly good, of enmity disarmed, of guile, of hate, of envy, of revenge."

Milton often allows his imagination to run away with him, and he inserts opinions, which are obviously his own, into the minds of his characters. Adam says that " nothing lovelier can be found in woman than to study household good, and good works in her husband to promote."

In spite of this insertion of his own opinions, he makes his

[marginal annotations in red:] What about imagination? · What's a near-sounding word like? · ??? · Sed out properly

上图：保罗的英国文学课本中的约翰·弥尔顿《失乐园》散文节选，上面有艾伦·杜邦德的批注。

ABOVE: (TOP TO BOTTOM) Nichols, Me, Gill, Hooper.

Yesterday

昨 天

作 者	WRITERS	保罗·麦卡特尼和约翰·列侬　Paul McCartney and John Lennon
艺术家	ARTIST	披头士乐队　The Beatles
录 音	RECORDED	伦敦阿比路录音　Abbey Road Studios, London
发 行	RELEASED	《救命！》，1965 年　*Help!*, 1965
		美国单曲，1965 年　US single, 1965
		《昨天……和今天》，1966 年　*"Yesterday"… and Today*, 1966

Yesterday
All my troubles seemed so far away
Now it looks as though they're here to stay
Oh, I believe in yesterday

Suddenly
I'm not half the man I used to be
There's a shadow hanging over me
Oh yesterday came suddenly

Why she had to go I don't know, she wouldn't say
I said something wrong, now I long for yesterday

Yesterday
Love was such an easy game to play
Now I need a place to hide away
Oh I believe in yesterday

Why she had to go I don't know, she wouldn't say
I said something wrong, now I long for yesterday

Yesterday
Love was such an easy game to play
Now I need a place to hide away
Oh I believe in yesterday

　　阿舍家的房子就在温波尔街。楼顶有一个非常小的房间，带着一面小窗户。一间阁楼，很适合艺术家。那里没有多余的空间放我的唱片——其中许多唱片是在英国发售之前，从美国寄给我的。它们不得不被放在外面的楼梯平台上。但是不知怎么的，阁楼里有一架钢琴——一架锯短的小钢琴，就放在我的床边。我在梦中听到了这段旋律，醒来后，我想："我喜欢这首曲子。这是什么？是弗雷德·阿斯泰尔，还是科尔·波特？这是什么？"

　　我从床上起身，钢琴就在那里，就在旁边。我想我应该试着弄清楚这首曲子是如何发展的，我觉得这是我早些年听过又忘记的某首旧曲子。我只有这段旋律，现在又有了一些和弦。为了巩固记忆，我用一些假歌词把它凝实在脑海中："炒蛋，哦我的宝贝，我多么爱你的大腿，炒蛋"。我不经常用假歌词，这种情况很少见。

　　就这样，我有了这么一首曲子，我想那天早晨我在外面见的第一个人是约翰。我问："这首歌是什么？"他说："我不知道。我从未听过。"我从乔治·马丁和我的朋友歌手阿尔玛·科根（Alma Cogan）那里听到了同样的回答，科根对流行歌曲有着相当全面的了解。几个星期过去了，显然没有人知道这首歌，它并未在这世间降生，只存在于我的脑海里。于是我认领它，并花了一些功夫，添加些东西完善它。这就像是在街上捡到了十英镑钞票。

　　这首宛若天降的歌出现不久后，我们开始拍摄电影《救命！》——不过那个时候它名为《八只手臂拥抱你》（*Eight Arms to Hold You*），而我们不太喜欢这个名字。《一夜狂欢》在前一年取得了巨大成功，我们面临着做出后续作品的压力，但一直没有好剧本。我想我们已经拒绝了太多版本，因而当我们对其中一版点头时，也只是大概浏览过，并没有认真对待。这种经历让我们很欣赏某些演员，他们会说："我很想工作，亲爱的，

上图：从温波尔街的阁楼看出去的风景。伦敦，1964 年。

《救命！》拍摄片场的林戈·斯塔尔、保罗及乔治·哈里森。巴哈马，1965 年。

但是我找不到好剧本。"

　　我们最终同意的剧本中有一段关于找回林戈的戒指的情节。这一切都有点乱七八糟，我们不是真的很有兴趣。我们也不太擅长背台词，有时甚至是在去拍摄现场的路上，我们才在车里第一次读对台词。说实话，我们已经开始摆脱那个把我们类型化的"拖把头"漫画形象了。不过，这部电影有一点值得称道。如果我们提议："我们可以去一个好地方拍这段吗？"他们就会同意。从一个拍摄地点跳到下一个未必对这部电影有所帮助，但挺好玩。我们会说："我从来没去过加勒比，可以把那地方写进故事吗？"于是他们就这么做了。"你以前滑过雪吗？""没有！""没问题，让我们也把那个加进电影里！"

　　所有这一切发生在《昨天》的孵化期，一有机会，我就会要求在附近搞来一架钢琴，以便继续创作。我想桥段就是在片场写的。而我干这事的频繁程度，让影片的导演理查德·莱斯特一听到这首歌就开始烦躁。有一天他咆哮道："如果我再听到那个，我就把他妈的钢琴搬走！"他问起这首歌叫什么名字时，我回答："炒蛋。"我想这对解决问题没什么帮助。

音乐部分很顺利，但是歌词仍然只有这一句，"炒蛋，哦我的宝贝，我多么爱你的大腿，炒蛋"。所以，在电影拍摄的间歇期，简和我去葡萄牙度了一个短假，我们降落在里斯本并借了一辆车。三个小时左右——时速大约一百八十英里——开到了法罗群岛附近的阿尔布费拉。我们计划住在布鲁斯·韦尔奇（Bruce Welch）家。他是克里夫·理查德与阴影乐队[1]的成员，一个非常慷慨的哥们儿，他在那里等我们，介绍一下他借给我们的这间公寓的情况。去阿尔布费拉的路上，我坐在车后座什么也没做。天很热，沙尘飞扬，我半睡半醒。在这样的状态下，我喜欢做的事情之一就是思考。"'炒蛋，呸，呸……'那会怎么样？"我开始考量一些选项。我想保持这个旋律，所以，我要在此基础上填上符合音节的词。"炒蛋"——"哒-哒"，你可以写"昨天"和"突然"。[2]我还记得我想："人们喜欢悲伤的歌。"就连我自己也喜欢悲伤的歌。到达阿尔布费拉时，我已经完成了歌词。

当我们回到家后，我给乐队听了这首歌。虽然在音乐会上，我们有时会四个人一起演奏它，但是录音时，林戈说："我觉得它用不着鼓。"乔治加了一句："好吧，我也觉得我没办法编进去更多吉他。"然后约翰说："我没什么想法。我觉得你应该自己一个人做这首歌。这真的是一首个人的歌曲。"这在当时真的是一件大事，因为我们之前从来没有这么录过，以前一直是乐队一起录音。

犹豫了一阵子后，我决定试试，而乔治·马丁想在这首歌里加入弦乐四重奏——他当时做我们的制作人已经好几年了，他还不到四十岁，却备受我们信任和尊敬。我对弦乐四重奏的主意有点担心，觉得这听上去太古典了，但他像慈父一般循循善诱："让我们试试看，如果你不喜欢，我们可以把它去掉。"于是我去了他家，我们喝了几杯茶，规划出弦乐听上去应该是什么样。乔治觉得巴赫是个好参考；而我想加进一些巴赫不会用的音符，试图让这首歌更现代一些，于是我们加入了降七音，那通常被称作"蓝调音"（blue note）。所以这首歌的编曲比较特别。

也是在这阵子，我们意识到这首歌在 F 调上会更好听。但我是用 G 调写的。你会习惯用某些和弦创作，而如果你试着在吉他上用不同的调弹奏，就不得不重新学习这首歌，因为那会让这首歌听起来改头换面。如果你想要更高的调，可以用一个叫作变调夹的东西；但如果你想要更低的调，就不那么容易了——你没有空间。所以，我们所做的是把吉他整个重新调音。这意味着当你弹 G 音符时，实际上听起来是 F 音。这种调音法现在已经相当普遍了，不过那时候，把全部六根弦都重新调音还是一个新花招，这意味着，我可以用我写歌时的方式来弹奏我们认为更好听的调式。

关于《昨天》，另一件有意思的事情是，它差点被录成一首电子前卫风格的歌曲。我们尝试录制这首歌时，我对迪莉娅·德比希尔[3]的作品非常着迷。她是电子音乐先锋，在英国广播公司无线电工作室工作，她更广为人知的作品是为《神秘博士》创作的主

<hr />

1　克里夫·理查德与阴影乐队（Cliff Richard & The Shadows），英国摇滚乐队，1950 年代末成立于利物浦。
2　此处原文为三音节节奏的"Scrambled eggs"，替代同样三音节节奏的"yes-ter-day"和"sud-den-ly"。译为中文后为双音节。
3　迪莉娅·德比希尔（Delia Derbyshire，1937—2001），英国前卫电子音乐家。

YESTERDAY.

Yesterday, all my troubles seemed so far away,
now it looks as though they're here to stay,
oh I believe in yesterday.

Suddenly, I'm not half the man I used to be
There's a shadow hanging over me
Yesterday came suddenly.

middle &.
Why she had to go, I don't know
she wouldn't say,
I said something wrong. now I long
for yesterday......

Yesterday, love was such an easy game to
play
Now I need a place to hide away
oh I believe in yesterday.

题音乐。乔治·马丁几年前和无线电工作室一起完成了一些作品，还曾化名阴极射线（Ray Cathode）发行了他们的第一首商业歌曲，叫作《实时节拍》（Time Beat）。我去见了迪莉娅，她带我去了她在花园里的一间小屋，有点像实验室。我们聊起她的创作方式，但最后，我们还是选择了乔治的编曲。

《救命！》专辑发行时，莱斯特正在度假，于是我给他寄了一张唱片，附言："我希望你喜欢'炒蛋'！"接下来，这首歌获得了令人难以置信的成功。唱片公司想把它作为单曲发行。我们不允许他们在英国这么干，因为我们是一支摇滚乐队，但我们没插手他们发行美国单曲的事儿，反正我们不在那儿生活。一些了不起的人也翻唱了它，马文·盖伊[1]的版本是我特别喜爱的翻唱之一。玛格丽特·阿舍还将这首歌当作她在市政厅音乐学院（Guildhall School of Music & Drama）给学生出的测试题。

当有人告诉我类似《昨天》是有史以来最流行的歌曲这样的事情时，我仍然会觉得有点奇怪。据说，《滚石》杂志把它选为 20 世纪最佳歌曲。对于这首神秘降世的歌曲，这一切似乎隆重至极。

一些人觉得很难相信我写《昨天》的时候才二十二岁。每次唱到"I'm not half the man I used to be"（我不再是从前的我）这句歌词时，我会想起写这首歌的八年前，我母亲已经去世。有一种说法是，这是一首关于"失去母亲"的歌，对此，我总是回答："不，我并不觉得。"但是，你知道，我越想——"Why she had to go I don't know, she wouldn't say"（我不知道她为什么必须离开，她没有说）——就越觉得那也许是创作背景的一部分，是这首歌背后的无意识。奇怪的是，我们的母亲死于癌症这件事根本没人讨论。我们几乎不知道癌症是什么，但是在这首歌中显现出一种体验，一种你几乎无法描述的甜蜜与痛苦并存的体验，对此，我并不感到惊讶。

就在前不久，有人问我，当我变老时，我是否和我的歌曲之间有了不同的关系。录好的唱片不会改变，但我们会慢慢变老，而随着年纪的增长，你和一首歌的关系也在变化。写《昨天》时，我刚刚从利物浦搬到伦敦，开始观察整个新世界在我面前展开的可能性。但是，那时候，我所有的昨天也只是短短的一段时期。随着时间的流逝，现在这首歌似乎更有意义——是的，更令人感伤。我必须承认，那是我真正热爱的关于写歌与演奏音乐的一个方面。

1　马文·盖伊（Marvin Gaye，1939—1984），美国灵魂乐歌手。

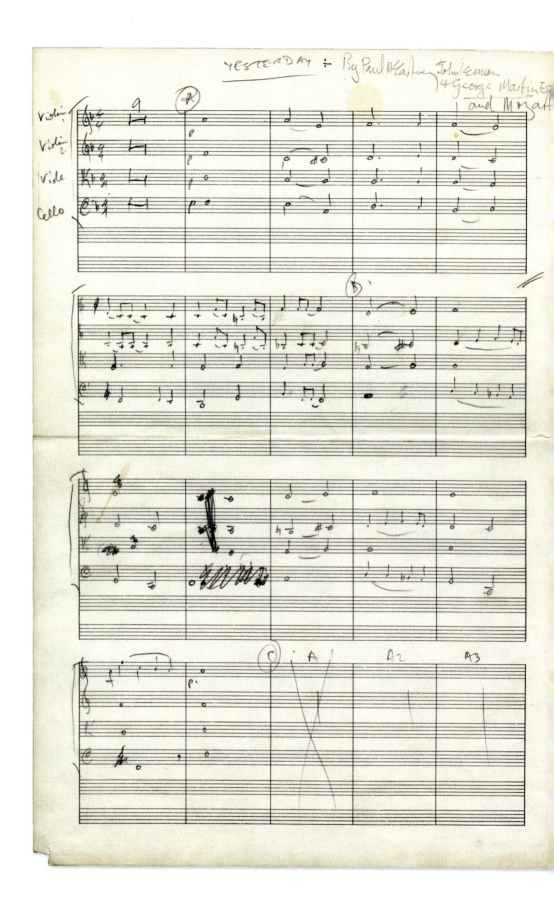

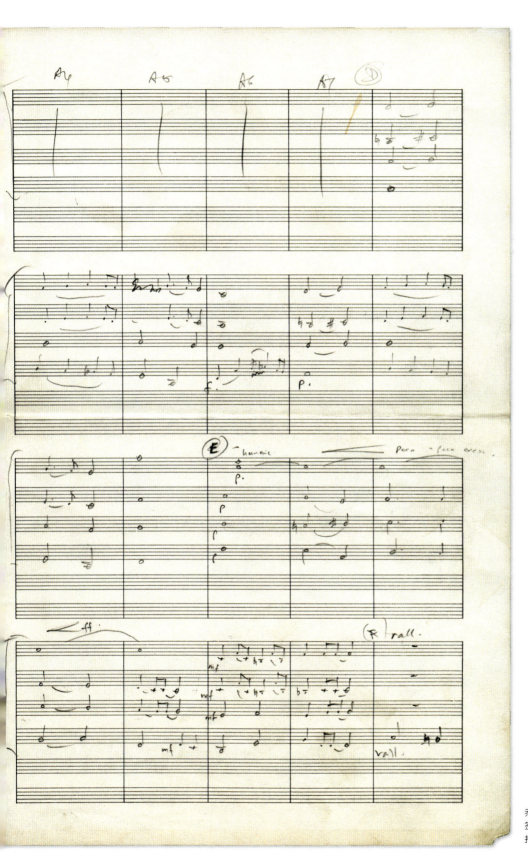

乔治·马丁为《昨天》手写的曲谱，签名为保罗、约翰·列侬，以及"莫扎特"，1965 年。

左图：理查德·莱斯特。伦敦，
1989 年。

右图：拍摄《救命！》期间。
奥地利阿尔卑斯山，1965 年。

我干这事的频繁程度，
让影片的导演理查德·莱斯特一听到这首歌就开始烦躁。
有一天他咆哮道：
"如果我再听到那个，我就把他妈的钢琴搬走！"

You Never Give Me Your Money

你从来不给我你的钱

作　者　WRITERS　　保罗·麦卡特尼和约翰·列侬　Paul McCartney and John Lennon

艺术家　ARTIST　　披头士乐队　The Beatles

录　音　RECORDED　伦敦奥林匹克之声录音棚、伦敦阿比路录音棚　Olympic Sound Studios, London and Abbey Road Studios, London

发　行　RELEASED　《阿比路》，1969 年　*Abbey Road*, 1969

You never give me your money
You only give me your funny paper
And in the middle of negotiations
You break down

I never give you my number
I only give you my situation
And in the middle of investigation
I break down

Out of college, money spent
See no future, pay no rent
All the money's gone
Nowhere to go

Any jobber got the sack
Monday morning turning back
Yellow lorry slow
Nowhere to go

But oh, that magic feeling
Nowhere to go
Oh that magic feeling
Nowhere to go, nowhere to go

One sweet dream
Pick up the bags and get in the limousine
Soon we'll be away from here
Step on the gas and wipe that tear away
One sweet dream
Came true today

One, two, three, four, five, six, seven
All good children go to heaven

所有披头士的事情都变得过于沉重，而"沉重"在那个时候对我有着特别的含义。它意味着比压抑更过分。它意味着不得不去参加会议，和其他的披头士、会计，以及艾伦这家伙一起坐在会议室里。他是一个纽约奸商，来到伦敦，和滚石乐队聊了聊，让他们相信他是合适的操盘手。他也说服了山姆·库克[1]，让对方相信他是适合人选。我觉得很可疑，但其他人不觉得，所以我们为此吵了一架，而我被否决了。我试图成为理性先生和明智先生，但一切都失控了。

那是 1969 年初，披头士已经开始解体。约翰说他要离开，但艾伦·克莱因要求我们守口如瓶，因为他正忙于和国会唱片公司谈判。几个月来，我们不得不保持沉默。我们生活在一个谎言中，我们知道约翰已经离开乐队。

艾伦·克莱因和迪克·詹姆斯都出现在这首歌的背景中，他们卖掉了我们在北方之歌[2]的版权，却没有给我们机会去买下这家公司。对于所有那些想搞垮我们，或者仍旧试图搞垮我们的人，有趣的是，我们在这首歌里直接摊牌了。我们知道他们在做什么，而他们一定也明白我们知晓了一切这个事实。我们说得再直白不过了。

说起来，我们从小就有零花钱。周末时长辈会给你一些钱，生活就是这样。我们多少依旧活在这种模式中。当我们第一次有了些真金白银，和会计聊天时，他们问我们要用这些钱做什么，我们回答存到银行。那个时代，你仍然可以通过储蓄存款的利息来赚钱。但是他们说："不，不，不。你不应该那么做。你应该用它来投资。"

我不想这么做，因为我认为投资风险太大。我们知道钱会生钱，但我们并没有真正理解这种事。所以，关于"来路不明的钱"的想法大多时候还只停留在我们的脑海里。契约被写在可笑的文件上。歌曲背后隐藏着"契约是两人间的联系"的概念。而关于"And in the middle of negotiations / You break down"（然后在谈判过程中 / 你崩溃了）这句歌词："negotiation"既是商业谈判，也是爱情谈判；"breakdown"既是谈判破裂，也可以是精神崩溃。

问题是，到了这个阶段，一切都需要谈判，而沟通不畅是当时的常态。我们不再一起写歌了。每个人都自己带点这个、带点那个到音乐里。我们都知道，作为披头士的这一人生阶段正在走向终结。我们正在准备一张专辑，心知这也许是我们最后的狂欢。尽管《顺其自然》发行得比较晚，《阿比路》确实才是我们在录音棚里录制的最后一张专辑。

然而，这也有好处。我和琳达结婚了，我们的关系让我从沉闷的内讧和财务事务中得到了喘息。"One sweet dream / Pick up the bags and get in the limousine"（一个甜蜜的梦 / 收拾行李跳上豪华轿车）这一句指的就是琳达和我仍然可以在周末消失在乡村里。那拯救了我。

---

1   山姆·库克（Sam Cooke，1931—1964），美国灵魂乐 / 流行乐歌手。
2   北方之歌（Northern Songs），披头士乐队的歌曲版权所属公司。

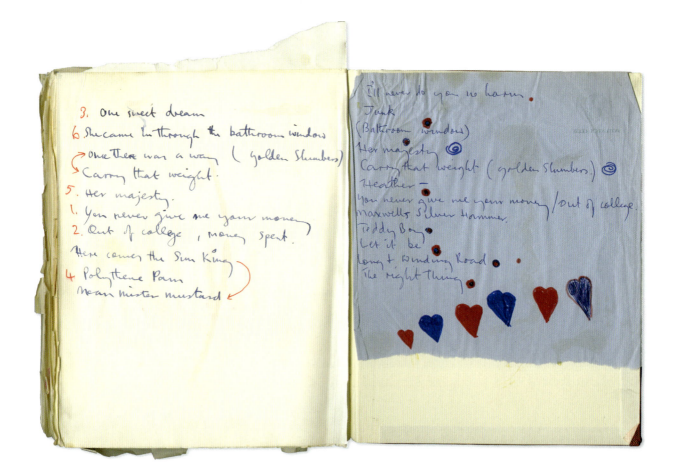

问题是，到了这个阶段，一切都需要谈判，
而沟通不畅是当时的常态。
我们不再一起写歌了。
每个人都自己带点这个、带点那个到音乐里。
我们都知道，作为披头士的这一人生阶段正在走向终结。

上左：琳达与保罗。莫琳·斯塔基拍摄，伦敦苹果唱片公司办公室，1969 年。

上右：和约翰·伊斯曼、约翰·列侬、小野洋子、艾伦·克莱因、莫琳·斯塔基、林戈·斯塔尔及彼得·霍华德在一起。伦敦苹果唱片公司办公室，1969 年。

You Tell Me

你跟我说说

作　者 WRITER	保罗·麦卡特尼	Paul McCartney
艺术家 ARTIST	保罗·麦卡特尼	Paul McCartney
录　音 RECORDED	伦敦阿比路录音棚、萨塞克斯郡猪山磨坊	Abbey Road Studios, London and Hog Hill Mill, Sussex
发　行 RELEASED	《记忆将满》，2007 年	Memory Almost Full, 2007

When was that summer when the skies were blue?
The bright red cardinal flew down from his tree
You tell me

When was that summer when it never rained?
The air was buzzing with the sweet old honeybee
Let's see
You tell me

Were we there, was it real?
Is it truly how I feel?
Maybe
You tell me

Were we there, is it true?
Was I really there with you?
Let's see
You tell me

When was that summer of a dozen words?
The butterflies and hummingbirds flew free
Let's see
You tell me
Let's see
You tell me

莫里斯·舍瓦利耶的专辑《琪琪》（GIGI）中有一首老歌，叫作《我记得很清楚》（I Remember It Well），是这样的："我们在九点相见，我们在八点相见，我准点到达，不，你迟到了／啊，是的，我记得很清楚"[1]。我喜欢这个。一个很棒的小故事。歌曲里的男人记得不太清，但是女人记得，《你跟我说说》有点像。

这只是记忆。我经常想："哦天哪，我真的见过猫王。我真的去过他家，那一刻真的发生了。"就这些。就是发生了。有时候我会掐一把我自己，想着："我真的和猫王坐在同一个沙发上，聊着这些东西吗？"我希望对它再有三倍清晰的记忆，我希望回到过去："Were we there, was it real? / Is it truly how I feel? / Maybe / You tell me"（我们在那里吗，是真的吗？／那真的是我感受到的吗？／也许吧／你跟我说说）。

这首歌出自专辑《记忆将满》。发行后不久，有人向我指出，专辑名的字母重新组合后恰好是"献给我的灵魂伴侣 LLM"[2]——琳达的中间名字是露易丝（Louise）。这只是巧合，但我喜欢这种玄妙。专辑的名字实际上源自我手机上的一则提示，说手机里的东西太多了。不过我想："我们的记忆在这些年里几乎总是满的，有太多的事情发生。"我觉得这是用一种诗意的方式来总结现代生活。

由于琳达的父亲在汉普顿有个住所，我开始和她一起去那里。那是四十多年前的事——也许是五十多年前。我想我就是在那儿写下了这首歌，在 21 世纪初的某个时候，也许关于"红衣主教"[3]的歌词同样出自那里，我在那儿看到了它们。"When was that summer of a dozen words?"（那个话语不多的夏天是什么时候？）当一切顺利时，没有人会说话。你可以只是和某人一起坐着看书读报，你几乎不说话，因为不需要；如此放松而舒适。"When was that summer when it never rained?"（那个永不下雨的夏天是什么时候？）我喜欢的是，我甚至无须尝试回忆那是哪一年。

我记得在 1960 年代听过一个故事，当时所有人都在关注印度和印度神秘主义，故事说的是某个人去拜访一位朋友，他走进房间找了个角落坐下，他们不说话。他们是那么好的朋友，除非确实有什么事情要说，否则他们不用交谈。无须"你觉得昨天的球赛怎么样"之类的寒暄，他们就在彼此身边，不需要说任何东西。当他们说话时，交谈必定有意义。我喜欢那个房间里平和的画面。

我尊敬的两位音乐人，大卫·吉尔摩和保罗·维勒[4]分别给我发信息说，"哇，我喜欢那首"，说这首歌是他们最喜欢的我的歌曲之一。你收到的大部分反馈一般来自评论家，所以能得到听众，尤其是真正的音乐家的反馈非常棒，这说明歌曲令他们深受触动，甚至令他们愿意费心给你写信。不过如今，人们用手机发消息；现在没有多少人愿意坐下来，用漂亮的老式巴西尔登邦德牌文具对消息做一些扩展。

我自己也不这么写信了，但我必须承认，我确实喜欢手写。我在学校里学习的时候就很喜欢，而且我的手写体挺像样。我怀念旧文具，我热爱写信的礼仪。乔治·马

1　原句为 "We met at nine, we met at eight, I was on time, no, you were late / Ah, yes, I remember it well"。
2　"Memory Almost Full" 的字母可重新组合为 "For my soulmate LLM"。
3　"红衣主教"（red cardinal）为北美红雀的别名，它是世界上最美丽耀眼的鸟类之一，又名红衣凤头鸟。
4　保罗·维勒（Paul Weller，1958— ），英国朋克乐队 The Jam 的主唱。

左图：和保罗·维勒在一起。
伦敦 AIR 录音棚，1982 年。

右上：上学时的地理散文，
1956 年。

右下：麦卡特尼家和伊斯曼家的
家庭照。东汉普顿，1975 年。

丁总是写信感谢我送他的生日礼物。我们一起完成了《当我六十四岁时》，所以我一直送一瓶红酒当作他的生日礼物，而他会手写一段优美的文字回复。这总是让人高兴。实际上，大多数信我还留着。乔治的遗孀，朱迪·马丁夫人（Lady Judy Martin），有同样的感觉。这是我在成长过程中学会的处事方式，也是某个特定阶层的处事方式。我街头的工薪阶级朋友们似乎很少写信，但我的家庭有写信的习惯，我后来交的一些朋友大多住在像汉普斯特这样的地方，他们会在上午检查信箱，并且回信。他们有那种小信封剪，他们也相当会遣词造句："亲爱的亨利，收到你的来信真让人惊喜。我昨天正想着你……"我喜欢那种礼仪。

你知道，明信片就相当于工人阶级的信件。你过去经常写明信片，而且试图写得有趣。那就是"The air was buzzing with the sweet old honeybee"（甜美的老蜜蜂在空气中嗡鸣）这类句子的用武之地。现在我们有了照片墙（Instagram），而明信片就是那个时代的照片墙。

PERU:

Mainly mestizo & indian. Boundaries indeterminate. Until 1940's boundaries in dispute. Home of the Incas. An Andean country, including part of Pacific coast + pt. of Amazon Basin. ∴ varied features + climate.

Coastal Region. mostly no coast range.
From 3°s to 18°s lat. Hot desert climate. mechanism is same as N. Chile (Cold offshore current etc.....) Condensation - fog; the "garua". Sufficient moisture for some drought resisting plants. Series of sea-birdinhabited islands - guano (droppings) for fertilizer. Deposits depleted by ruthless collectors. In 1919 the president of ~~Chile~~ Peru reorganised trade. Limited diggings etc... Important crops—

YOU TELL ME.

~~3 rin~~

① When was that Summer ~~when~~ the skies were ~~blue~~,
the Bright red cardinal flew down ~~from the (a)~~ HIS FROM THE tree
~~(lets see)~~ — you tell me .
~~see~~

② When was that Summer when it never rained
The air was ~~buzzing~~ (BUZZING) with the sweet old honey bee
~~lets see~~ — you tell me .
lets see

m
i   ~~where we~~ There, was it real
D   is it ~~true, the~~ (TRULY), (HOW) I feel,
    ~~lets see~~ — you tell me . / chord / repeat line.
       maybe

③ When was that Summer when the air was still
~~ocean breeze~~
A fragrant ~~perfume~~ filtered from the ~~sea~~.
SOLO ~~lets see maybe~~ — you tell me

m
i   were we There, is it true
D   was I really there with you
    lets see — you tell me .

When was ~~that~~ Summer of the blazing heat
The air was buzzing with the sweet old honey bee
maybe ~~lets see~~ — you tell me . (REPEAT)?

④ When was that summer of a dozen words
The butterflies & humming birds ~~flew~~ (FLEW) free
lets see — you tell me
        (REPEAT) END.

856

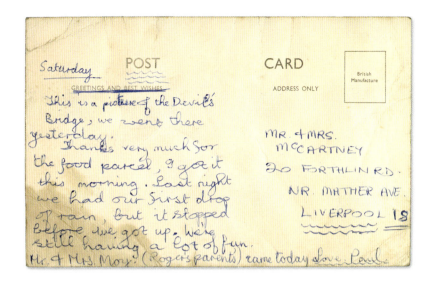

1950 年代的家庭明信片。

Your Mother Should Know

你妈妈应该知道

作　者	WRITERS	保罗·麦卡特尼和约翰·列侬　Paul McCartney and John Lennon
艺术家	ARTIST	披头士乐队　The Beatles
录　音	RECORDED	伦敦查佩尔录音棚、伦敦阿比路录音棚　Chappell Recording Studios, London and Abbey Road Studios, London
发　行	RELEASED	《魔幻之旅》，1967 年　*Magical Mystery Tour*, 1967

Let's all get up and dance to a song
That was a hit before your mother was born
Though she was born a long, long time ago
Your mother should know
Your mother should know
Sing it again

Let's all get up and dance to a song
That was a hit before your mother was born
Though she was born a long, long time ago
Your mother should know
Your mother should know

Lift up your hearts and sing me a song
That was a hit before your mother was born
Though she was born a long, long time ago
Your mother should know
Your mother should know

Sing it again
Da, da, da, da, da, da, da, da, da
Da, da, da, da, da, da, da, da, da, da, da
Though she was born a long, long time ago
Your mother should know
Your mother should know

在我大约二十四五岁的时候，我的金阿姨到伦敦来拜访我。原因之一是要跟我聊聊抽大麻的罪过。她的绰号是"控制"，她是被一家人派来当使者的。我猜有些话传到了家里人那儿，说"我们的保罗"在伦敦变得有点狂野，所以需要有人去看看他。总之，她到卡文迪什大街来拜访我，我已经在那儿住了一段时间。当你的阿姨来看你时，你会做一些小时候做的事情。所以，我就坐在那里，弹弹钢琴，喝了点酒，玩纸牌，好好聊了会儿天。气氛很温暖，这首歌就出自那种家庭的感觉。

萦绕在这首歌背后的是著名的警句"母亲什么都知道"，很多我们的歌迷已经开始觉得父母只是一帮老糊涂，什么都不知道。然而实际上，一些父母或许相当激烈地认为披头士乐队很危险。这并没有给我们带来太大困扰，因为我们知道我们不是这样的，相反，我们的大部分作品都非常乐观，而且充满善意。

《你妈妈应该知道》绝对属于相当友善的那一类。歌曲的构思很简单，真的，可以轻易转换成我们父母时代流行的某种拉格泰姆[1]歌曲。那时候没有人这么觉得，但我们确实是父母那一代音乐的忠实歌迷。我们承认受到了许多歌曲令人难忘的旋律和结构的影响。正是结构——主歌，副歌，主歌，副歌，桥段，主歌，副歌——让这些歌曲得以流传。

现在，在俱乐部、餐厅或者健身房里听到持续四五分钟的单调的砰砰声时，我就会和人们开玩笑。我总是想象一个像科尔·波特那样经典的词曲创作者——经常使用主歌—副歌—桥段结构的创作者——回来听这些"音乐"的样子。他很可能只会将之视为用来给真正的音乐伴奏的节拍。

这或许有点冒险，我听上去像是那些视披头士为垃圾，声称我们的作品不会长久的人。我记得曾听我爸爸说起，祖父抱怨他的音乐，芝加哥爵士乐——杰里·罗尔·莫顿[2]和路易斯·阿姆斯特朗——是"罐头"音乐。

而这首歌是对旧日流行的回首，我猜"金曲"这个词会产生共鸣。毕竟，我们的工作是为披头士乐队创作金曲。事实上，我今天仍在做同样的事。我看不出试图写出金曲有什么问题。你可以从两个角度看待"金曲"这个词——要么是粗俗的商业主义，要么是试图触动人们。我们知道，把一首"before your mother was born"（你妈妈出生之前）的歌造就成金曲的东西，也恰恰会造就现在和未来的金曲。我说"恰恰"，但实际上这是一种把我们所有人黏合在一起的无形品质，正是它令我们成为一个世界性的听众群体。

1　拉格泰姆（ragtime），流行于1920年代的美国黑人音乐风格，后来演化成爵士乐。
2　杰里·罗尔·莫顿（Jelly Roll Morton，1890—1941），美国爵士音乐家。

下图：和金阿姨及表妹凯丝（Cath）
在一起。利物浦，1967 年。

右图：和约翰·列侬在《魔幻之旅》
的拍摄现场。肯特郡西莫灵英国皇
家空军基地，1967 年。

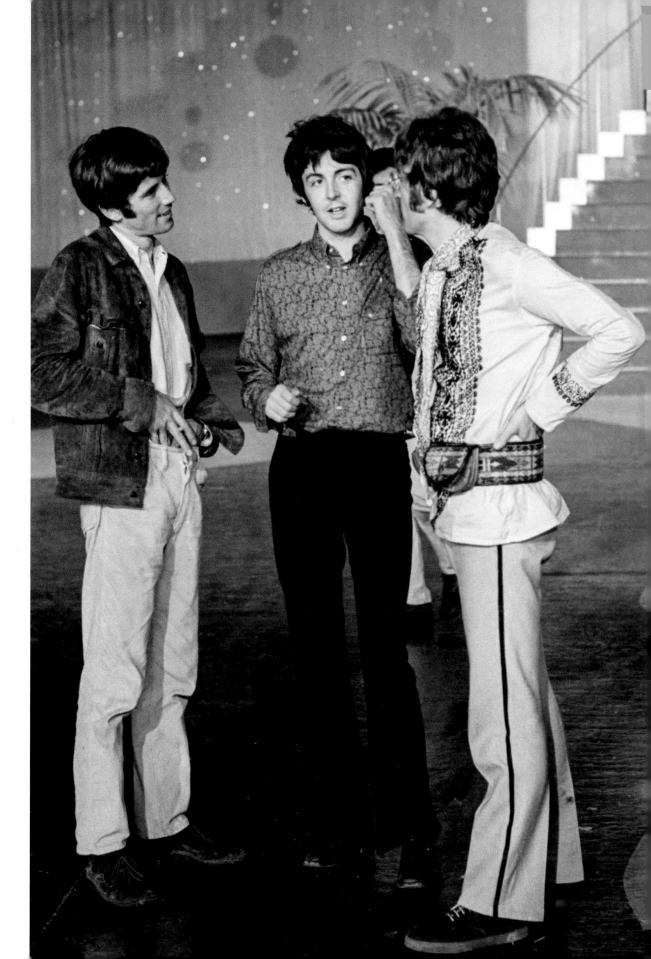

致 谢

特别感谢南希、我的孩子们和我亲爱的家人，以及约翰·伊斯曼、李·伊斯曼、罗伯特·威尔和斯图尔特·普罗菲特（Stuart Proffitt）。

MPL 传媒

阿莱克斯·帕克（Alex Parker）

奥伊夫·科贝特（Aoife Corbett）

本·汉弗莱斯（Ben Humphreys）

伊西·宾厄姆（Issy Bingham）

马克·莱维（Mark Levy）

南希·杰弗里斯（Nancy Jeffries）

陆南松（Nansong Lue）

帕特里夏·奥赫恩（Patricia O'Hearn）

理查德·米勒（Richard Miller）

萨拉·布朗（Sarah Brown）

史蒂夫·伊瑟尔（Steve Ithell）

以及伦敦 MPL 的所有工作人员

诺顿旗下利弗莱特出版公司

LIVERIGHT/W.W. NORTON

安娜·奥勒（Anna Oler）

科迪莉亚·卡尔弗特（Cordelia Calvert）

堂·里夫金（Don Rifkin）

德雷克·麦克菲利（Drake McFeely）

伊丽莎白·科尔（Elisabeth Kerr）

伊丽莎白·克莱门森（Elizabeth Clementson）

加布里埃尔·卡恰克（Gabriel Kachuck）

海利·布雷肯（Haley Bracken）

乔·洛普斯（Joe Lops）

朱莉娅·里德海德（Julia Reidhead）

尼克·科利（Nick Curley）

彼得·米勒（Peter Miller）

丽贝卡·霍米斯基（Rebecca Homiski）

斯蒂芬妮·希尔伯特（Stephanie Hiebert）

史蒂夫·阿塔多（Steve Attardo）

史蒂文·佩斯（Steven Pace）

威廉·鲁辛（William Rusin）

企鹅旗下艾伦莱恩出版社

ALLEN LANE/PENGUIN PRESS

艾丽丝·斯金纳（Alice Skinner）

伊莎贝尔·布莱克（Isabel Blake）

吉姆·斯托达特（Jim Stoddart）

凯蒂·班亚德（Katy Banyard）

莉兹·帕森斯（Liz Parsons）

丽贝卡·李（Rebecca Lee）

萨姆·沃尔特斯（Sam Voulters）

诗亭（Thi Dinh）

设计师

特里伯诺（Triboro）

译后记

　　2021 年的 5 月底，我收到编辑陈雅君的信息，询问我是否有时间和兴趣翻译保罗·麦卡特尼的歌词集。当时的我正在山西的某座山上，准确地说，是在某座山的半山腰上，抽烟、晒太阳、听风的声音，并且用石块笨拙地搭一座属于自己的坛城。这次联系或多或少地把我拉回到了现实世界中，当然，我有兴趣，而比有兴趣更重要的是，我有的是时间。我环顾四周的山群，意识到自己终究要回到本来的世界里，过自己该过的生活，做自己该做的事情。于是接下来的很长一段时间，我就这样以文字的方式进入了麦卡特尼的人生中，听他平静地说起自己每一首歌词背后的创作故事，以及创作瞬间的所思所想，当然还有他和父母家人之间，和爱人之间，以及和乐队成员之间的爱恨情仇。而现在，就有了中文版的《保罗·麦卡特尼：歌抒人生》，也终于，到了该写译后记的时候了。

　　（一）
　　先说说披头士乐队吧。但是我突然意识到，我其实完全不知道该如何向不了解这支乐队的人介绍这支乐队，究竟该从哪里说起呢？或者也许，在我的潜意识里想的是，披头士乐队还需要介绍吗？应该没有人会不知道这支乐队吧。话说回来，就算我愿意，我恐怕也没有能力找到更新鲜的词语来描述这支乐队。也许应该简单地说，就是直到现在，全世界的流行音乐产业仍然在持续不断地从这支乐队的身上吸取养分和灵感，从音乐、歌词、创作技巧，到录音室技术运用、乐队运作方式，再到乐队成员们各自参与社会生活各个领域的方式，是这四个人，约翰·列侬、保罗·麦卡特尼、乔治·哈里森和林戈·斯塔尔，用他们的努力和才华，引领着三分钟长度的传统流行歌曲产业进入当代艺术的殿堂，彻底改变了流行音乐的样貌。

披头士乐队身上发生的一切现在都已经变成了传奇。他们在利物浦略显戏剧化的相遇相识，在汉堡经历的疯狂演出，第一首单曲出人意料的突然爆发，随之而来横扫美国的巡演，"披头士狂热"这个新名词成为一种现象，被英国女王授勋，成为摇摆伦敦的精神领袖，告别舞台后在录音室里的声音探索，带领花童一代进入迷幻之旅，屋顶天台上的最后演出，以及伴随着 1960 年代一起落幕的，令所有人惊愕和伤心的分手，这所有的一切无不透露着时代的气息，也许更应该说，他们就是时代，没有披头士乐队，那个时代将无法成立。

不过说起来有点尴尬，我最初听披头士乐队的时候，却完全无法进入他们的音乐，我甚至认为这支乐队是被人为地抬高到某个位置上的，只是因为他们悦耳的旋律迎合了大众的审美。对那个时候的我来说，他们不够锋利，不够暴烈，不够强硬，不够冷漠，也不够黑暗，说起来，他们似乎在哪方面都达不到我的审美需求——想想看，我当时正经历着青春期最艰难和糟糕的某个阶段，根本做不到心平气和地和任何事物相处。直到有一次大病之时，我大概有两个星期的时间，整天听《白色专辑》《魔幻之旅》和《阿比路》这三张专辑，这才算是彻底感受到了披头士的音乐中所包含的能量。这种能量可以归结为某种类似宗教的体验——卸下你的重负，让我们带你去一个地方，在那里一切都很美好，而一切也都是虚幻。他们透过磁带录音机的喇叭向我召唤。我后来回想起来，感觉似乎是某种天意使然，一切皆有时，恰好是让我在身体最糟糕的时刻，体会到这支乐队的伟大之处，不得不说，这算得上是一种最好的治疗手段。

我周围有很多热爱披头士乐队的朋友，每个人热爱他们的理由都不尽相同。有意思的是，我注意到好像每个人都有一个排名，那是关于这四位成员在乐队中的地位的排名。不幸的是，林戈似乎永远是排在第四位的那个人（我猜就算是在全世界的歌迷范围内排起来，他也几乎都是排在第四位的那个）。而前三位，根据排名者的性格和审美差异，略有不同，我自己的排名是：约翰、乔治、保罗和林戈。但是，在翻译完这本书之后，我觉得我有必要修改一下自己的看法了。现在我的排名是：约翰、保罗、乔治和林戈。是的，现在我对麦卡特尼有了更多的敬意，我不再把他看作仅仅是长着一张娃娃脸，只会写些优美旋律讨歌迷（尤其是女歌迷）欢心的甜心先生了。我意识到，是麦卡特尼作为领头人，将披头士乐队带入了艺术的领域，让其他三位成员创造性地接受了声音艺术，使得传统流行歌曲成为能够容纳古怪声音的音乐戏剧。而更出乎我的意料的是，由于乐队的词曲署名一直都是列侬-麦卡特尼，我没想到有许多像诗歌一样优美的歌词，那些让我在大病期间得到过无数次安慰的歌词，其实是由麦卡特尼创作的。

披头士乐队解体之后，四位成员的个人音乐生涯，我了解最多的是约翰·列侬，也确实没有太多关心过其他三位成员后来的发展，这也许和大多数歌迷一样吧。在翻译这本书的同时，我才意识到，麦卡特尼的人生传奇，不仅仅在于他是披头士成员之一，也必然要包含他的个人音乐生涯，以及他和妻子琳达组建的羽翼乐队。麦卡特尼从利物浦的工人阶级成长为音乐家，被万众崇拜，最终成为对几代人持续产生影响的偶像；而在披头士乐队解散之后，他如何度过一段艰难的时光，然后开始组建自己的乐队，以一种不同于披头士乐队的运作方式继续自己的音乐生涯，并且到达另一个顶峰。在这本书里，这些过程通过一首一首的歌曲被描述出来，让人恍惚间觉得一切进行得顺滑而且有逻辑，一位音乐家的职业生涯似乎本来就应该是这样。但是我们也无法忽略，麦卡特尼在幽默而轻松地回顾自己的人生时，在不经意间透露出的无数次的挫败感、焦虑、孤独和疲惫，当然还有艰难时刻，这才是真实的人生。这一次，麦卡特尼终于放下了对媒体的戒备，像一位真正的老人一样坦诚回顾自己的一生，而不再用永远的娃娃脸和迷人的微笑来伪装自己。

（二）

再说说歌词创作。在某一期《滚石》音乐杂志上，有一篇关于回顾平克·弗洛伊德乐队的深度报道，其中的一个段落给我留下了非常深的印象。鼓手尼克·梅森在被问到他们的歌曲创作时说，"歌词在我们的歌曲创作中一点也不重要，我们是音乐家，我们乐队没人在乎歌词"，记者描述坐在一旁紧盯着梅森的主唱罗杰·沃特斯的心理活动——他一脸怒气的样子就像是在说，蠢货，那是你们不在乎，不要把我扯进来。我对这段文字所呈现出来的画面记忆深刻，以至于到现在都似乎亲身经历了那个采访的现场。这大概也是因为我对罗杰·沃特斯的情绪感同身受，而且我几乎可以肯定，几乎每一位词曲作者，一定也会说出同样的话。

平克·弗洛伊德乐队，成立于1966年，那时候离披头士乐队的分崩离析还剩下不到三年的时间。他们既是披头士乐队的追随者，也是披头士乐队的挑战者。平克·弗洛伊德乐队的第一位主唱，希德·巴瑞特，他的大部分歌词灵感来源于刘易斯·卡罗尔的小说《爱丽丝梦游仙境》及其续篇《爱丽丝镜中奇遇记》，这部小说同样也是披头士乐队音乐灵感的重要来源之一。你几乎可以把这看作两支乐队的交接点，两支伟大的乐队在传承时的偶尔交集。而在另一方面，作为挑战者的平克·弗洛伊德乐队快速地转向了合成器和电子设备，并创造出某种仿佛来自外太空的奇幻声音；几乎在同一时期，离开了披头士乐队的麦卡特尼却回到自己的苏格兰农场，过起了田园隐居生活，从创作到生活方式都回归到大自然的根源。

说回到歌词，我想每一位歌词创作者都会在某个时刻被问到某首歌词的含义、背后的故事、写作的方式等等这些问题；不过我猜大多数词作者都不会正面回答这个问题，他们或者完全回避，或者含糊其词，或者编造出另一个匪夷所思的传奇。因为在很多时候，歌迷群体，以及大部分乐评人，对于发掘某首歌词背后的故事表现出超乎寻常的狂热，甚至远远超过了歌词本身所呈现出的含义。以至于像鲍勃·迪伦这样的创作者甚至不得不宣称他的歌词毫无意义，不过这也无法阻挡大众和乐评人对迪伦的过度解读。披头士乐队当然也逃脱不了类似的困扰，这种闹剧的最高峰当数查尔斯·曼森宣称在《手忙脚乱》这首歌里听到了天启四骑士的声音，并以此为依据杀害无辜的人。所幸的是，麦卡特尼在晚年时，在他的编辑劝说之下有了这个想法，用他的歌词来描述他的生活，并用他的生活来解释这些歌词，歌词和生活相互交织，相互映照，然后就有了这本《歌抒人生》。在我看来，这绝对是用第一视角去解读流行乐历史上最流行的一些歌曲的最佳范例。

以我个人的经验而言，并不是每一位创作者都愿意把自己的生活写成歌词，录进唱片，并成为公众谈资的一部分。和诗歌一样，歌词写作中也包含了大量的非个人化写作，即使歌词中出现大量的"我"，那也只是创作者用某种自我代入的方式来描写他人的故事。这种旁观者的角度更像是来自早期布鲁斯音乐的传统，比如说这种，"我早上醒来我的宝贝离开了我，她和一个男人去了加利福尼亚，我听着火车的汽笛在我的耳边响起，可是我怎么追也追不上她"，再比如这样的，"我杀死了我的宝贝因为她背叛了我，我开枪时她的男朋友就躺在身旁"。所有这些布鲁斯歌手，都是在用他人的伤痛来缓解自我的伤痛，就好像当我们了解了别人悲惨的生活和遭遇时，我们的共情能力让我们巧妙地消解了自己的悲惨境遇。列侬和麦卡特尼早期的很多歌词都承袭了这个传统，在那个时代，谁不是这样呢？虽然列侬和麦卡特尼诉说的不过是类似心爱的姑娘离他而去这样的事情，不过这已经足以引起青春期少男少女的共鸣了。直到鲍勃·迪伦的出现，流行音乐的歌词创作才发生了改变，就像乐评人所说的，"猫王给了摇滚乐身体，而迪伦给了摇滚乐一个灵魂"。列侬和麦卡特尼当然不会错过迎接这个有趣的灵魂的到来，于是披头士的歌词也在慢慢地从非个人化的方式，过渡到了基于个人体验的写作，以及诗歌化——这本书里也提到，麦卡特尼创作的最具代表性的诗歌化歌词是《埃莉诺·里格比》。

而我经常被问到的一个问题，是歌词和诗歌的区别在哪里，或者说，连接这两者之间的边界在哪里。这真的是一个宏大的命题，要阐述这个命题恐怕需要另一篇论文。我通常只能以我个人的经验来作答。简单地说，大部分歌词需要有相对严格的格律和韵脚，要遵循某种限制，并且要和乐器演奏的音律相伴；而当代诗歌，尤其是自由体诗歌，并不需要特别遵守某种韵脚和格律的限制。然后通常我接下来就会被问到，你的歌词里有多少部分是直接或者间接地来自你的诗歌？我想这个提问的重点其实是，该如何打通歌词和诗歌之间的界限？我不知道这个问题的准确答案是什么，我猜无数词作者都会有这方面的期望和努力。而这本书也许在某种意义上可以解答这个问题，麦卡特尼的歌词以及他对歌词的解读方式带给我的启发就是，也许歌词和诗歌从来就没有边界，也许诗意并不是单独存在于某一首，或者某几首歌词中，诗意其实一直存在，贯穿于词作者全部创作中，也贯穿于个体生活的点点滴滴之中。

（三）

最后，聊一下关于翻译。这是我翻译的第二本书。说起来实在是有点惭愧，我自认并不是一个优秀的翻译者，甚至在某些时候，我的翻译也许连合格都谈不上。不过，我年轻时的阅读背景几乎都来自翻译作品，这些作品总是让我忘记了其实写作者原本使用的是另一种语言，而不是用汉语在写作。后来我才渐渐意识到，每一部作品后面都有一位优秀翻译者的名字，像裘小龙、绿原、袁可嘉、吕六同、林少华、孙仲旭，以及我的好友董楠（她翻译了很多我喜爱的乐队传记作品），还有很多很多我叫不出名字的翻译者。这些人让我感受到，作为语言和思想的中间人，翻译是一件特别美好的事情，很辛苦，但是很美好。所以我非常感谢雅众文化和编辑陈雅君，让我有可能在这样一个艰难的时世中，在整个世界面临病毒和封锁的时间里，有机会参与到这份美好之中。而现在，在设计师山川（他也是全世界无数的麦卡特尼死忠粉之一）的辛勤工作之后，这本书终于呈现出它该有的样子，希望作为读者的你也能享受到这份美好。

杨海崧

北京

2023 年 5 月

版权声明

Page 471 (top) Donald Duck © Disney

Page 832 © Subafilms Ltd.

Pages 842–843 'Yesterday' arranged by George Martin, courtesy of George Martin / Airborn Productions Ltd.